Single- and Multiple-Chip
Microcomputer
Interfacing

Single- and Multiple-Chip Microcomputer Interfacing

G.J. Lipovski
University of Texas

Prentice-Hall, Inc.
Englewood Cliffs, New Jersey 07632

Library of Congress Catalog Number: 87-60656

Editorial/production supervision: Barbara Marttine Webber
Cover design: Karen Stevens
Manufacturing buyer: S. Gordon Osbourne

Printed in the United States of America

10 9 8 7 6 5 4 3 2 1

ISBN 0-13-810557-X 025 {PRENTICE-HALL ED.}

ISBN 0-13-810573-1 025 {MOTOROLA ED.}

Prentice-Hall International (UK) Limited, *London*
Prentice-Hall of Australia Pty. Limited, *Sydney*
Prentice-Hall Canada Inc., *Toronto*
Prentice-Hall Hispanoamericana, S.A., *Mexico*
Prentice-Hall of India Private Limited, *New Delhi*
Prentice-Hall of Japan, Inc., *Tokyo*
Prentice-Hall of Southeast Asia Pte. Ltd., *Singapore*
Editora Prentice-Hall do Brasil, Ltda., *Rio de Janeiro*

Dedicated to my mother

Mary Lipovski

Contents

Single- and Multiple-Chip Microcomputer Interfacing

List of Figures

List of Tables

Preface

By 1980, the microcomputer had changed so many aspects of engineering that the cliche "microcomputer revolution" echoed from almost every other magazine article and learned paper in the field. It is a great tool. This book's predecessor, *Microcomputer Interfacing: Principles and Practices*, was written at that time to establish some design theory for this dynamic field. Since then, two significant changes have prompted the development of a successor to that book: the evolution of powerful single-chip microcomputers and the IEEE Computer Society Curriculum Committee recommendation for a course on microcomputer interfacing and communication. The development of powerful single-chip microcomputers introduces a new design choice: to use either a microprocessor in a personal computer with some 64K bytes of memory and an operating system, or a less costly single-chip microcomputer with much less overhead. This decision is largely based on the designer's understanding of the capabilities and limitations of the single-chip microcomputer. The development of a standard curriculum for a course lends stability to this once chaotic field. This book aims to teach the principles and practices of microcomputer systems design in general, and interfacing in particular, and to foster an understanding of single-chip microcomputers within the guidelines of the IEEE Computer Society Curriculum Committee recommendations.

This book's predecessor evolved from a set of notes for a senior level course in microcomputer design. The course – which is still taught – focuses on the combined hardware-software design of microcomputer systems. It emphasizes principles of design because theory is as necessary for a solid foundation in design as theory is in any engineering discipline. However, it also emphasizes the practices – the details of how to get a system to work – because microcomputer system design requires "hands-on" experience. There is a remarkable difference between a student who merely reads about microcomputers and a student who has worked with one – clear evidence that theory has to be taught with practice. Practical experience is desirable in almost any engineering course. This is not always possible. But microcomputer systems are inexpensive enough that the school or the student can afford this "hands-on" opportunity; and the joy of seeing the principles work is so attractive that the student often can't get enough of the material to be satiated. The development of very powerful, inexpensive single-chip microcomputers furthers this opportunity. So the course, this book's predecessor, and this book, all emphasize both the principles and practices of microcomputer design.

The principles and practices of microcomputer design have to cover both hardware and software. A purely hardware approach might appeal to a seasoned digital system designer or an electrical engineering student, but it leads to poor choices that either do not take full advantage of software's tremendous power or that force unnecessary constraints and therefore higher costs on its development. However, a purely software approach misses the opportunity to understand how and why things happen, and how to take advantage of the hardware. The IEEE Computer Society Curriculum Committee recommends a combined hardware-software approach.

A combined hardware-software approach does require more background. The course this book is based on is the second of a two-course sequence. The first course teaches basic assembler language programming. It is really just a standard computer science course on assembler language programming, but it is taught with an assembler language of a microcomputer. The textbook, *Fundamentals of Microcomputer Programming*, Wagner and Lipovski, MacMillan, Inc., 1984, was developed for that course. The second course builds on that background and also presumes some background in logic design, as would be obtained in a standard introductory course on that topic. This book, however, has three chapters that survey these topics. These chapters can be skimmed as a review of the required background material or carefully studied as a condensed tutorial if the reader has not had the earlier courses or their equivalents. Because they are intended as review or intensive tutorial material, to prepare the readers for the book's main subject, these three chapters are comparatively compressed and terse.

We make the practices discussed in this book concrete through detailed discussion of the Motorola M6800 family of microcomputers and the 6811 microprocessor instruction set. However, these products are used as a means to the end of teaching principles and practices in general, rather than to promote the use of specific Motorola products. Applications notes and catalogues are available from Motorola to that end. Specific, detailed discussion encourages and aids the reader in learning through "hands-on" experience and vitally contributes to his enthusiasm for and understanding of the principles. The 6800 family is used primarily because the MC68HC11A8 is believed to be the most easily taught single-chip microcomputer. Its instruction set is as complete as that of any other comparable machine, supporting enough addressing modes and index registers to teach the intelligent use of data structures, and it is symmetrical and comparatively free of quirks and warts that detract from the subject under discussion. Nevertheless, we stress that detailed comparisons between the M6811 and other well-designed microcomputers clearly show that others may be better than the M6811 for different applications. However, a comparative study of different microcomputers and applications is beyond the scope of this book.

The first three chapters quickly survey the background needed for the remainder of the book. Chapter 1, which covers computer architecture and the instruction set of the M6811, is intended to be as a survey for a reader that is acquainted with some other assembly language – either that of another microcomputer or of a large machine. Chapter 2 covers some software techniques, including subroutine parameter and local variable conventions, that are very useful in microcomputers. Chapter 3 covers basic computer organization, but confines itself to those aspects of the topic that are particularly germane to microcomputers. For example, basic computer organization traditionally covers floating point arithmetic, but this chapter doesn't; and this chapter dwells on tristate busses, a topic not often covered in computer organization.

The rest of the book covers three basic themes: input-output (I/O) hardware and software, analog signals, and communications. Parallel I/O ports are covered in chapter 4, interrupts and alternatives in chapter 5, analog components in chapters 6 and 7, communications devices in chapter 8 and magnetic storage and CRT display devices in chapter 9. The simple parallel I/O port and the synchronous serial I/O port – especially attractive in interfacing slow devices because it economizes on pins – are displayed in chapter 4. Hardware and software aspects are studied side by side. The reader need no longer be intimidated by the basic interface. Chapter 5 discusses interrupts and their alternatives. Hardware/software tradeoffs are analyzed, and different techniques are exemplified. Chapter 6 surveys the traditional (voltage) analog components that are commonly used in microcomputer I/O systems. Sufficient information is provided that the reader can understand the uses of, the limitations of and the advantages of analog components, and can springboard from this chapter to other texts, magazine articles, or discussions with colleagues to a fuller understanding of analog design. Chapter 7 introduces the counter/timer as an interface to frequency-analog signals. Techniques to generate signals with a frequency or to measure a signal with a frequency that is analog to some quantity are discussed. Moreover, the hardware-software alternatives to using this most interesting integrated circuit are discussed and evaluated. Chapter 8 describes communications devices. The Universal Asynchronous Receiver Transmitter and its cousins are thoroughly studied, and other communications techniques are described. Finally, chapter 9 introduces the magnetic storage device and the CRT display device.

This book is designed to accompany a laboratory. A laboratory manual is available for the students, and an instructor's manual gives solutions to all the problems in this text and to the laboratory experiments. The laboratory can be implemented with chips wired by means of proto-boards, as shown on the cover of this book, and a dumb terminal. It can be better implemented with a Macintosh in place of the dumb terminal, and a program DEBUG11 is provided by means of Motorola's free-ware bulletin board, which includes a text editor, assembler and terminal program, and facilitates the efficient finding and correction of programming errors in about a minute. An assembler, editor and terminal program on the IBM-PC can be used instead, and the assembler is available from Motorola. Rather than proto-boards, the M68HC11EVM and M68HC11EVB boards may be used with all the experiments. These alternatives make it easy for a school that has a laboratory with existing equipment to develop a course using the 6811.

Some remarks on this book's style are offered. On the one hand, terms are formally introduced and used as carefully as possible. This is really necessary to make some sense out of a subject as broad and rich as microcomputer system design. There is no room for muddy terminology or the use of undefined jargon. Even though the terminology used in trade journals and manufacturers' applications notes is inconsistent and often contradictory, the terminology used in a text must be clear and consistent. On the other hand, a book full of definitions is too hard to read. The first version of the course notes that lead to this book tended to be ponderous. Moreover, students are more tuned to television colloquialism today, and are turned off by "third person boring" that is often the style of today's learned textbooks. So we condescend to "first person conversational", and we enjoy it. The "we" in this book stands not only for the author but also his colleagues and his teachers, as well as his students who have taught him a great deal – who have collectively inspired and developed the principles and practices discussed in the book. But we admit to occasionally exploring *Webster's Collegiate* for just the right word because we enjoy the challenge and even allowing a pun or two where it does not interfere with the presentation of the material. We can't deny it: microcomputer design is fun, and we have fun talking about it. Please forgive us if it shows in this book's style.

Acknowledgments

The author would like to express his deepest gratitude to everyone who contributed to the development of this book. In addition to a number of faculty members, students, and colleagues in industry who helped in no small part, special thanks are due to Bob Pinteric at Motorola, who coordinated the development of the accompanying lab and solution manual, and Peter Song at the University of Texas, who developed the accompanying lab and solution manual. While this text was prepared and run off using a Macintosh and LaserWriter, running WriteNow, I express my deep gratitude to my secretary, Sue Yensan, who proofread the book and found many typos, and who entered in almost all of the copy editor's alterations. The cooperation of Motorola as a corporation in financially supporting Peter and in supplying development boards and chips, and the kind assistance of Motorola staff - such as the Santa Claus of parts supply, Chet Freda, and exceptional reviewers Naji Naufel and Jim Sibersroth - made this book's development a real pleasure. While Motorola contributed to this book's development, they gave me complete freedom to say what I believed, and occasionally I have criticized the hand that fed me. However, I am pleased to observe that I had very few criticisms of the Motorola 6811, which is an incredibly powerful component and a vehicle for teaching a considerable range of concepts.

About the Author

G. Jack Lipovski has taught electrical engineering and computer science at the University of Texas since 1976. He is a computer architect internationally recognized for his design of the pioneering data-base computer, CASSM, and the parallel computer, TRAC. His expertise in microcomputers is also internationally recognized by his being a past director of Euromicro and an editor of IEEE Micro. Dr. Lipovski has published more than 70 papers, largely in the proceedings of the annual symposium on computer architecture, the IEEE transactions on computers and the national computer conference. He has authored two books and edited three. He has served as chairman of the IEEE Computer Society Technical Committee on Computer Architecture, member of the Computer Society Governing Board, and chairman of the Special Interest Group on Computer Architecture of the Association for Computer Machinery. He received his Ph.D. degree from the University of Illinois, 1969, and has taught at the University of Florida. He has consulted for Harris Semiconductor, designing a microcomputer, and for the Microelectronics and Computer Corporation, studying parallel computers. His current interests include parallel computing, data-base computer architectures, artificial intelligence computer architectures, and microcomputers.

Single- and Multiple-Chip
Microcomputer
Interfacing

1

Microcomputer Architecture

Microcomputers, microprocessors, and the subject of microprocessing are at once quite familiar and a bit fuzzy to most engineers and computer scientists. When we teach a course on microcomputer interfacing, we start by asking this simple question, "What is a microcomputer?", and we find a wide range of answers. The designer must also be familiar with the instruction set of the microcomputer which he or she is interfacing to an input/output (I/O) system. Clearly, we have to understand these concepts quite well beforehand to be able to discuss and design those interfaces. This chapter contains essential material on microcomputers and microprocessors needed as a basis for understanding the discussion of interfacing in the rest of the book.

We recognize that the designer must know a lot about basic computer architecture and organization. But the goal of this book is to impart enough knowledge so the reader, on completing it should be ready to design good hardware and software for microcomputer interfaces. We have to trade material devoted to basics for material needed to design interface systems. There is so much to cover and so little space, that we will simply offer a summary of the main ideas. If you have had this material in other courses or absorbed it from your work or from reading those fine trade journals and hobby magazines devoted to microcomputers, this chapter should bring it all together. Some of you can pick up the material just by reading this condensed version. Others should get an idea of the amount of background needed to read the rest of the book. (See the bibliography at the end of this chapter for recommended additional reading.)

For this chapter, we assume the reader is fairly familiar with some kind of assembler language on a large or small computer or is able to pick it up quickly. In the chapter, he or she should learn about the software view of microcomputers in general and the MC68HC11 single-chip microcomputer in particular.

1-1 An Introduction to the Microcomputer

Just what is a microcomputer and a microprocessor, and what is the meaning of microprogramming – which is often confused with microcomputers? This section will

Portions of section 1-1 were adapted with permission from "Digital Computer Architecture,", pp 298-327 by G. J. Lipovski, and "Microcomputers,", pp. 397-480 by G. J. Lipovski and T.K. Agerwala, in the *Encyclopedia of Computer Science and Technology,* 1978, Belzer et. al., courtesy of Marcel Dekker, Inc.

survey these concepts and other commonly misunderstood terms in digital systems design. It describes the architecture of digital computers and gives a definition of architecture. Unfortunately, the study of computers is rather heavy with concepts and, therefore, with terminology. But it is rather light on theorems and formulas. We will offer a lot of concepts and their definitions to help clarify later discussions; but we've got a typical "chicken-and-egg" problem when we try to define these ideas without using terms we haven't defined. This section simply opts to get the flavor of a few important concepts, so using some terms that will be properly defined later shouldn't matter. It can be reread when undefined terms are explained, to get a solid foundation in microcomputing. (Also note that all *italicized* words are in the index, which serves as a glossary to help you find terms that are defined later.)

Because the microcomputer is pretty much like other computers except it is smaller and less expensive, these concepts apply to large computers as well as microcomputers. The concept of the computer is presented first, and the idea of an instruction is scrutinized next. The special characteristics of microcomputers will be delineated last.

1-1.1 Computer Architecture

Actually, the first and perhaps the best paper in computer architecture, "Preliminary discussion of the logical design of an electronic computing instrument," by A. W. Burks, H. H. Goldstein, and J. von Neumann, was written 15 years before the term was coined. We find it fascinating to compare the design therein with all computers produced to date. It is a tribute to von Neumann's genius that this design, originally intended to solve nonlinear differential equations, has been successfully used in business data processing, information handling, and industrial control, as well as in numeric problems. His design is so well defined that most computers – from large computers to micro computers – are based on it, and they are called *von Neumann computers* .

In the early 1960s a group of computer designers at IBM – including Fred Brooks – coined the term "architecture" to describe the "blueprint" of the IBM 360 family of computers, from which several computers with different costs and speeds (for example, the IBM 360/50) would be designed. The *architecture* of a computer is its instruction set and the input/output (I/O) connection capabilities. Computers with the same architecture can execute the same programs and have the same I/O devices connected to them. Designing a collection of computers with the same "blueprint" has been successfully copied by several manufacturers. Motorola has used this idea in developing the computers discussed in this book; computers built from the MC6800, MC6802, and MC6808 have the same architecture. This strict definition of the term "computer architecture" applies to this fundamental level of design.

However, the term "computer architecture" has become very popular and is also used to describe the computer system in general, including the implementation techniques and organization discussed next. In fact, it is difficult to get two computer architects to agree on a precise definition of computer architecture. While we are frustrated by such vagueness, it is probably due to the rapid evolution of this dynamic and exciting discipline.

The *organization* of a digital system like a computer is usually shown by a block diagram which shows the registers, busses, and data operators in the computer. For example, the MC6800 and MC6802 have the same architecture because they have the same instruction set and can use the same I/O devices, but since they are internally a little different, they have different organizations. Incidentally, the organization of a computer is also called its *implementation* . Finally, the *realization* of the computer is its actual hardware interconnection and construction. For example, the MC6800 and the MC68A00 have the same block diagrams and instruction sets, but the latter may be made with faster transistors, which enable it to run twice as fast as the former. (Actually, the MC6800, MC68A00, and MC68B00 are made the same way at the same time. They are then tested. Those with the fastest transistors are sold as MC68B00, the next fastest as MC68A00, and the slowest as MC6800.) Therefore, the MC68A00 has a different realization than the MC6800. It is entirely reasonable for a company to change the realization of one of its computers by replacing the hardware in a block of its block diagram with a newer type of hardware. The implementation or organization remains the same while the realization is different. (In this book, when we want to discuss an actual realization, we will name the component by its full part number, like MC6800 or MC68A00. But we are usually interested in the architecture or the organization only. In these cases, we will refer to a component as the 6800 – architecture, with no leading letters – or the M6800 – organization, with a leading M. This should help clear up any ambiguity, while also being a natural, easy-to-read shorthand.

As better technology becomes available, and as experience with an architecture reveals its weaknesses, a new architecture may be crafted that includes most of the old instruction set and some new instructions. Programs written for the old computer should also run, with little or no change, on the new one, and more efficient programs can perhaps be written using the new features of the new architectures. Such new architecture is *upward compatible* from the old one if this property is preserved. In this book, we will focus on the 6811 architecture, which is upward compatible from the 6801 and its parent, the 6800.

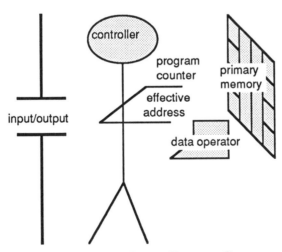

Figure 1-1. Analogy to the von Neumann Computer

The architecture of von Neumann computers is disarmingly simple, and the following analogy shows just how simple. (For an illustration of the following terms, see figure 1-1.) Imagine a person in front of a mailbox, with an adding machine and window to the outside world. The mailbox, with numbered boxes or slots, is analogous to the *primary memory;* the adding machine, to the *data operator* (arithmetic-logic unit); the person, to the *controller;* and the window, to *input/output* (I/O). The person's hands *access* the memory. The primary memory is called a *random access memory* (RAM) because the person is free to access words in any order (at random) without having to wait any longer for a word because it is in a different location. Each slot in the mailbox has a paper which has a string of, say, 8 1s and 0's (*bits*) on it. A string of 8 bits is a *byte*. A string of bits – whether or not it is a byte - in a slot of the memory box is called a *word* .

With the left hand the person takes out a word from slot or box *n*, reads it as an instruction, and replaces it. Bringing a word from the mailbox (primary memory) to the person (controller) is called *fetching* . The hand that fetches a word from box *n* is analogous to the *program counter*. It is ready to take the word from the next box, box *n* + 1, when the next instruction is to be fetched.

An instruction in the 6811 is a *binary code* like 01001100. Consistent with the notation used by Motorola, binary codes are denoted in this book by a % sign, followed by 1s or 0's. (Decimal numbers, by comparison, will not use any special symbols.) Since all those 1s and 0's are hard to remember, a convenient format is often used, called *hexadecimal notation* . In this notation, a $ is written (to designate that the number is in hexadecimal notation, rather than decimal or binary), and the bits, in groups of 4 are represented as if they were "binary coded" digits 0 to 9 or letters A, B, C, D, E, F to represent values 10, 11, 12, 13, 14, and 15, respectively. For example, %0100 is the binary code for 4, and %1100 is the binary code for 12, which, in hexadecimal notation, is represented as $C. The binary code 01001100, mentioned previously, is represented as $4C in hexadecimal notation. Whether the binary code or the simplified hexadecimal code is used, instructions written this way are called *machine-coded* instructions because that is the actual code fetched from the primary memory of the machine, or computer. However, this is too cumbersome. So a *mnemonic* (which means a memory aid) is used to represent the instruction. The instruction $4C in the 6811 or 6800 actually increments (adds 1 to) accumulator A, so it is written as

INCA

(The 6811 accumulators and other registers are described in section 1-2. 1.)

An *assembler* is a program that converts mnemonics into machine code so the programmer can write in convenient mnemonics and the output machine code is ready to be put in primary memory to be fetched as an instruction. The mnemonics are therefore called *assembler language* instructions.

While a lot of interface software is written in assembler language and most examples in this book are discussed using this language, a portion of the software to interface I/O devices is often so short that it can be written in machine code. Moreover, quick fixes to programs are often written in machine code. Finally, an engineer should want to know exactly how an instruction is stored and how it is understood. Therefore, in this chapter we will show the machine code for some assembler language instructions that are important and that you might have some difficulty picking up on your own.

Many instructions in the 6811 are entirely described by 1 8-bit word. However, some instructions require 16 or 24 bits or more to fully specify them. They are stored in words in consecutive primary memory locations (box numbers) so that when an instruction like that is fetched, each of the words can be fetched one after another.

Now that we have some ideas about instructions, we resume the analogy to illustrate some things an instruction might do. For example, an instruction may direct the controller to take a word from a box, *m* , in the mailbox, with the right hand, copy it into the adding machine, thus destroying the old word, and put the word back in the box. This is an example of an instruction called the *load* instruction. In the 6811 an instruction to load accumulator A with the word at location 256 in decimal, or $100 in hexadecimal, is fetched as three words:

$$\$B6$$
$$\$01$$
$$\$00$$

where the second word is the most significant byte, and the third is the least significant byte, of the address and is represented by mnemonics as

LDAA $100

in assembler language. The main operation – bringing a word from the mailbox (primary memory) to the adding machine (data operator) – is called *recalling* data. The right hand is used to get the word; it is analogous to the *effective address.*

As with instructions, assembler language uses a shorthand to represent locations in memory. A *symbolic address,* which is actually some address in memory, is a name that means something to the programmer. For example, location $100 might be called ALPHA. Then the assembler language instruction above can be written as follows:

LDAA ALPHA

(We will be using the symbolic address ALPHA in most of our examples in this chapter, and it will represent location $100. Other symbolic addresses and other locations can be substituted, of course. The way a symbolic address is written as a label, and the way the assembler assigns locations to them, will be discussed when we consider data structures in the next chapter.) It is important to remember that a symbolic address is just a representation of a number, which usually happens to be the numerical address of the word in primary memory to which the symbolic address refers. As a number, it can be added to other numbers, doubled, and so on. In particular, the instruction

LDAA ALPHA+1

will load the word at location $101 (ALHPA + 1 is $100 + 1) into the accumulator.

Generally, after such an instruction has been executed, the left hand (program counter) is in position to fetch the next instruction in box $n + 1$. For example, the next instruction may give the controller directions to copy the number in the adding machine into a box in the mailbox, causing the word in that box to be destroyed. This is an example of a *store* instruction. In the 6800 or 6811, the instruction to store accumulator A into location $100 can be written like this:

STAA ALPHA

The main operation in this store instruction – putting a word from the adding machine (data operator) into a box in the mailbox (primary memory) – is called *memorizing* data. The right hand (*effective address*) is used to put the word into the box.

Before going on, we point out a feature of the von Neumann computer that is easy to overlook, but is at once von Neumann's greatest contribution to computer architecture and yet a major problem in computing. Because instructions *and* data are stored in the primary memory, there is no way to distinguish one from the other except by which hand (program counter or effective address) is used to get the data. We can conveniently use memory not needed to store instructions – if few are to be stored – to store more data, and vice versa. It is possible to modify an instruction as if it were data, just before it is fetched, although a good computer scientist would shudder at the thought. However, through an error (*bug*) in the program, it is possible to start fetching data words as if they were instructions, which produces strange results fast.

A *program sequence* is a sequence of instructions fetched from consecutive locations one after another. To increment the word at location $100, we can load it into the accumulator using the LDAA instruction, increment it there using the INCA instruction, and then put it back using the STAA instruction. (A better way will be shown later, but we do it in three instructions here to illustrate a point.) This program sequence is written in consecutive lines as follows:

LDAA ALPHA
INCA
STAA ALPHA

Unless something is done to change the left hand (program counter), a sequence of words in contiguous boxes will be fetched and executed as instructions. For example, a sequence of load and store instructions can be fetched and executed to copy a collection of words from one place in the mailbox into another place.

However, when the controller reads the instruction, it may direct the left hand to move to a new location (load a new number in the program counter). Such an instruction is called a *jump* . A similar instruction is used to execute a program called a *subroutine*, which is located in a different part of memory, and then return to the instruction right below this instruction. Such an instruction – a *jump to subroutine* – not only changes the program counter like a jump, but also saves the old value of the program counter so that when the subroutine is finished, the old value of the program counter is restored (to return to the routine right after the jump to subroutine instruction). The last instruction of the subroutine – a *return from subroutine* instruction – causes the program counter to be restored. Subroutines are especially useful in small computers so common operations that are not instructions can be made into subroutines, because instructions in a small computer are rather primitive. Moreover, a jump instruction may direct the person in the analogy to jump, for instance, only if the number in the adder is positive. If that number is not positive, the next instruction is fetched and executed because the left hand is not moved. This is a *conditional jump*. Jumps and conditional jumps permit some instructions to be fetched and executed over and over again. In this way, one can write a program, consisting of a few hundred instruction words, which can move and change thousands of data words. Jumps and conditional jumps are essential for repeatedly executing the same program sequences. The computer's forte is its ability to "massage" large quantities of data under the control of a program stored in memory.

The *(hardware or I/O) interrupt* is an architectural feature that is very important to I/O interfacing. Basically, it is evoked when an I/O device needs service, either to move some more data into or out of the device, or to detect an error condition. *Handling* an interrupt stops the program that is running, causes another program to be executed to service the interrupt, and then resumes the main program exactly where it left off. The program that services the interrupt (called an *interrupt handler or device handler*) is very much like a subroutine, and an interrupt can be thought of as an I/O device tricking the computer into executing a subroutine. However, an interrupt service program should not disturb the current program in any way. The interrupted program should get the same result no matter when the interrupt occurs. One of the problems in satisfying this requirement is that the interrupt service routine may call up subroutines also used by the program that was running. If the subroutine is currently being executed, data from the program that was running could get mixed up with data used in the interrupt service routine, producing errors. If this is avoided, then the subroutine is said to be *reentrant* because it can be entered again, even when it is entered and not finished. Reentrancy is important in designing software for interfaces. Related to it is *recursion* – a property whereby a subroutine can call itself as many times as it wants. While recursion is a nice abstract property and useful in working with some data structures discussed in chapter 2, it is not generally useful in interfacing; however, recursive subroutines are usually reentrant, and that is important.

Most modern computers have condition code bits which are set by some instruction and tested by a conditional branch instruction. The register containing these bit values also contains bits that control interrrupts. The condition code register, accumulators, program counter, and other registers in the controller and data operator are collectively called the *machine state* and are saved and restored whenever an interrupt occurs.

To facilitate the memory functions, the effective address can be computed in a number of ways, called *addressing modes*. The 6811 addressing modes will be explained in section 1-2.1.

1-1.2 The Instruction

In this section the concept of an instruction is described from different points of view.

The instruction is discussed first with respect to the cycle of fetching, decoding, and sequencing of microinstructions. Then the instruction is discussed in relation to hardware-software trade-offs. Some concepts used in choosing the best instruction set are also discussed.

The controller fetches a word or a couple of words from primary memory and sends commands to all the modules to execute the instruction. An instruction, then, is essentially a complex command carried out under the direction of a single word or a couple of words fetched as an inseparable group from memory.

The bits in the instruction are broken into several fields. These fields may be the bit code for the instruction or for options in the instruction, or for an address in primary memory or an address for some registers in the data operator. For example, the instruction LDAA ALPHA may look like the bit pattern 10110110000000100000000 when it is completely fetched into the controller. The leftmost bit and the fifth to eighth bits from the left – 1,0110 – tell the computer that this is a load instruction. Each instruction must have a different code word, like 1,0110, so the controller knows exactly which instruction to execute just by looking at the instruction word. The second bit from the left may identify the register that is to be loaded: 0 indicates that accumulator A is to be loaded. Bits 3 and 4 from the left, 11, indicate the address mode to access the word to be loaded. Finally, the last 16 bits may be a binary number address: 0000000100000000 indicates that the word to be loaded is to come from word number $100 (ALPHA). Generally, options, registers, addressing modes, and primary memory addresses differ for different instructions. It is necessary to decode the instruction code word, 1,0110, in this example, before it can be known that the second bit from the left, 0, is a register address, the third and fourth bits are address mode designators, and so on.

The instruction is executed by the controller as a sequence of small steps, called *microinstructions* . As opposed to instructions, which are stored in primary memory, microinstructions are usually stored in a small fast memory called *control memory*. A microinstruction is a collection of data transfer *orders* that are simultaneously executed; the *data transfers* that result from these orders are movements of, and operations on, words of data as these words are moved about the machine. While the control memory that stores the microinstructions is normally written at the factory, never to be rewritten by the user (read-only memory – ROM), in some computers it can be rewritten by the user. Writing programs for the control memory is called *microprogramming.* It is the translation of an instruction's required behavior into the control of data transfers that carry out the instruction.

The entire execution of an instruction is called the *fetch-execute cycle* and is composed of a sequence of microinstructions. Access to primary memory being rather slow, the microinstructions are grouped into *memory cycles,* which are fixed times when the memory fetches an instruction, memorizes or recalls a data word, or is idle. A *memory clock* beats out time signals, one clock pulse per memory cycle. The fetch-execute cycle is thus a sequence of memory cycles. The first cycle is the *fetch* cycle when the instruction code is fetched. If the instruction is *n* bytes long, the first *n* memory cycles are usually fetch cycles. In some computers, the next memory cycle is a *decode* cycle when the instruction code is analyzed to determine what to do next. The 6800 and 6811 don't need a separate cycle for this. The next cycle may be for *address calculations.* Data may be read from memory in one or more *recall* cycles. Then the instruction's main function is done in the *execute* cycle. Finally, the data may be memorized in the last cycle, the *memorize* cycle. This sequence is repeated indefinitely as each instruction is fetched and executed.

I/O devices may request an interrupt in any memory cycle. However, the data operator usually has bits and pieces of information scattered around and is not prepared to stop the current instruction. Therefore, interrupts are always recognized at the end of the current instruction, when all the data are organized into accumulators and other registers (the machine state) that can be safely saved and restored. The time from when an I/O device requests an interrupt until data that it wants moved is moved, or the error condition is reported or fixed is called the *latency time*. Fast I/O devices require low latency interrupt service. The lowest latency that can be guaranteed is limited to the duration of the longest instruction (and the time to save the machine state) because the I/O device could request an interrupt at the beginning of such an instruction's execution.

It is conceivable to design an instruction to execute a very complicated operation in just 1 instruction. Also, certain operations can be performed on execution of some address modes in an instruction that uses the address rather than additional instructions. It is also generally possible to fetch and execute a sequence of simple instructions to carry out the same net operation. The program sequence we discussed earlier can actually be done by a single instruction in the 6811:

INC ALPHA

It recalls word $100, increments it, and memorizes the result in location $100 without changing the accumulator. If a useful operation is not performed in a single instruction like INC ALPHA, but in a sequence of simpler instructions like the program sequence already described, such a sequence is either a macroinstruction or a subroutine.

It is *macro* if, every time in a program that the operation is required, the complete sequence of instructions is written. It is a subroutine if the instruction sequence is written just once, and a jump to the beginning of this sequence is written each time the operation is required. In many ways macroinstructions and subroutines are similar techniques to get an operation done by executing a sequence of instructions. Perhaps one of the central issues in computer architecture design is this: What should be created as instructions or included as addressing modes, and what should be left out, to be carried out by macros or subroutines? On one extreme, it has been proven that a computer with just one instruction can do anything any existing computer can. It may take a long time to carry out an operation, and the program may be ridiculously long and complicated, but it can be done. On the other extreme, most programmers might find complex machine instructions that enable one to execute a high level (for example, FORTRAN) language statement desirable. Such complex instructions create undesirable side effects, however, such as long latency time for handling interrupts. However, the issue is overall efficiency. Instructions, which enable selected operations to be performed by a computer to be translated into programs, are selected on the basis of which can be executed most quickly (speed) and which enable the programs to be stored in the smallest room possible (the inverse of program density) without sacrificing low latency. (The related issue of storing data as efficiently as possible is discussed in the next chapter.) The currently popular RISC (Reduced Instruction Set Computer) computer architecture philosophy exploits this concept.

The choice of instructions is complicated by the range of requirements in two ways. Some applications need a computer to optimize speed while others need their computer to optimize program density. For instance, if a computer is used like a desk calculator and the time to do an operation is only 0.1 sec, there may be no advantage to doubling the speed because the user will not be able to take advantage of it, while there may be considerable advantage to doubling the program density because the cost of memory may be halved and the cost of the machine may drop substantially. But, for another instance, if a computer is used in a computing center with plenty of memory, doubling the speed may permit twice as many jobs to be done, so that the computer center income is doubled, while doubling the program density is not significant because there is plenty of memory available. Moreover, the different applications computers are put to require different proportions of speed and density.

No known computer is best suited to every application. Therefore, there is a wide variety of computers with different features, and there is a problem picking the computer that best suits the operations it will be used for. Generally, to choose the right computer from among many, a collection of simple well-defined programs pertaining to the computer's expected use, called *benchmarks*, are available. Some benchmarks are: multiply two unsigned 16-bit numbers, move some words from one location in memory to another, and search for a word in a sequence of words. Programs are written for each computer to effect these benchmarks, and the speed and program density are recorded for each computer. A weighted sum of these values is used to derive a figure of merit for each machine. If storage density is studied, the weights are proportional to the number of times the benchmark (or programs similar to the benchmark) is expected to be stored in memory, and the figure of merit is called the *static efficiency*. If speed is studied, the weights are proportional to the number of times the benchmark (or similar routines) is expected to be executed, and the figure of merit is called the *dynamic efficiency*. These figures of merit, together with computer rental or purchase cost, available software, reputation for serviceability, and other factors, are used to select the machine.

In this chapter and throughout the subject of software interface design, the issue of efficiency continually appears in the selection instructions for "good" programs. The 6811 has a very satisfactory instruction set, with several alternatives for many important operations. Readers are strongly encouraged to develop the skill of using the most efficient techniques. They should try to select instructions that execute the program the fastest, if dynamic efficiency is prized, or that can be stored in the least number of bytes, if static efficiency is desired.

1-1.3 Microcomputers

One can regard microcomputers as similar to the computers already discussed, but which are created with inexpensive technology. Small computers have been classified according to the number of bits in a word, the number of words in memory, and the combined price of the data operator, controller, and memory. The original classification of micro-, mini-, and midicomputers by Bell in 1970 is outdated, so we offer a classification for today. We first offer an informal definition of these terms in table 1-1.

Table 1-1. Classification of Computers

Class	# Memory Words	Cost ($)	#Bits/Word
Single-Chip Microcomputer	8000	2 - 5	8
Personal Computer	512K	100 - 2000	8 to 32
Minicomputer	2M	10,000	32 to 64
Large (Mainframe) Computer	>2M	1,000,000	~64

Rapid technological improvements have blurred the distinction between these classes and dropped their costs. We offer a more precise delineation than that in table 1-1. An *integrated circuit die*, or *chip*, is a thin sheet of silicon, about 0.04 by 0.04 inches, on which transistors and other components are constructed, to make part of a system. (See figure 1-2a.) It is an *LSI* or large-scale integrated circuit chip if it has about 1000 transistors. Such a die is usually put in a ceramic or plastic container, called a *dual in-line package*, about 0.3 by 0.8 inches. (See figure 1-2b.) The chip can also be put in a *surface mount carrier*, as shown in figure 1-2c. These are much more compact than dual in-line packages, but are hard to service. It is now possible to put the controller and data operator on a single LSI integrated circuit or a small number of LSI integrated circuits. Such a combination of data operator and controller is called a *microprocessor*. If a memory and I/O module are added, the result is called a *microcomputer*. The integrated circuits are normally put on a *printed circuit card* like the one diagramed in figure 1-2d, and several cards may be mounted like pages in a book on a *motherboard* (shown on figure 1-2e) that acts like a book's binder to connect the boards together. If the entire microcomputer (except the power supply and some of the hardware used for I/O) is put in a single chip, we have a *single-chip microcomputer*.

Single-chip microcomputers are characterized by very low cost and by the absence of software programs available to use on them. For example, single-chip microcomputers cost around $2 in 1985. More powerful single-board microcomputers often used in personal computers cost from $100 to $1000. The heart of a microcomputer, the microprocessor, is only about $10. Actually, a *personal computer*, whether small or large, is any computer used by one person at a time. However, single-board microcomputers are quite adequate for the text editing and game playing needs of one person, so personal computers are essentially single-board computers. These moderately priced systems use operating systems and high level languages, discussed in chapter 2, to make it easier and cheaper to write software for a typical interfacing application. However, there are single- and multiple-board computers using microprocessors, which are intended for industrial control rather than personal computing. The 6811 is a particularly useful example for this book because it can function as a stand-alone single-chip microcomputer and as a microprocessor in a multiple-chip microcomputer, such as a personal computer or a multiple-board computer, as we discuss at the end of this chapter. It is thus suitable for illustrating the concepts of interfacing to both types of systems.

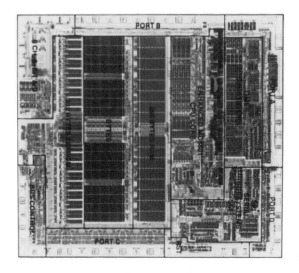

a) Chip

b) Dual In-Line Package

c) Surface Mount Carrier

d) Printed Circuit Card

e) System with a Mother Board

Figure 1-2. Microprocessor, Microcomputer, and System
(Photos © 1987 by Motorola Inc., used with permission.)

Minicomputers are characterized by the abundance of software (such as loaders, debuggers, assemblers, and compilers) available for them and the ability to run several users' programs "simultaneously" using time-sharing. The distinction between minicomputers and personal computer microcomputers is blurred because some architectures are available either as minicomputers (PDP-11/45) or as microprocessors (PDP-11/LSI). The distinction is further blurred by the availability of 32-bit microprocessors, such as the 68020, and the capability of putting up to 1 gigabyte of memory on a microcomputer. Moreover, more software is becoming available for microcomputers. Nevertheless, the terms microcomputer and minicomputer are commonly used to describe small computers.

Ironically, this superstar of the '70s, the microcomputer, was born of a broken marriage. At the dawn of the decade, we were already putting pretty complicated calculators on LSI chips. So why not a computer? Fairchild and Intel made the PPS-25 and 4004, which were almost computers, but were not von Neumann architectures. Datapoint Corporation, a leading and innovative terminal manufacturer and one of the larger users of semiconductor memories, talked both Intel and Texas Instruments into building a microcomputer they had designed. Neither Intel nor Texas Instruments were excited about such an ambitious task, but Datapoint threatened to stop buying memories from them, so they went ahead. The resulting devices were disappointing – both too expensive and an order of magnitude too slow. As a recession developed, Texas Instruments dropped the project, but did get the patent on the microcomputer. Datapoint decided they wouldn't buy it after all, because it didn't meet specs. For some time, Datapoint was unwilling to use microcomputers. Once burned, twice cautious. It is ironic that two of the three parents of the microcomputer disowned the infant. Intel was a new company and could not afford to drop the project altogether. So they marketed it as the 8008, and it sold. It is also ironic that Texas Instruments has the patent on the Intel 8008. The 8008 was incredibly clumsy to program and took so many additional support integrated circuits that it was about as large as a computer of the same power that didn't use microprocessors. Some claim it set back computer architecture at least ten years. But it was successfully manufactured and sold. It was in its way a triumph of integrated circuit technology because it proved a microcomputer was a viable product by creating a market where none had existed, and because the 8080, which was designed to be upward compatible to the 8008, is one of the most popular microcomputers in the world (in fact it is the microcomputer copied behind the iron curtain).

We will study the 6811 in this book. However, the 8080 discussed above, the Zilog Z80 and the MOS Technology 6502 microprocessors are at least as popular. Beside these 8-bit-word microprocessors, 16-bit-word microprocessors like the Intel 8086, the Zilog Z8000 and the Motorola 68000 are used when more powerful software requiring more memory would be needed than would fit in a 6811. We chose to discuss 8-bit microprocessors in this book because we encourage the reader to build and test some of the circuits we describe, and 8-bit-wide memories and processors are less expensive (especially if you connect power up backwards and pop the ICs) and the same concepts can be discussed as with 16-bit microcomputers. We chose the 6811 because it has an instruction set with enough features to illustrate good software practices. One implementation, the MC68HC11A8, has electrically erasable programmable read-only memory, which we discuss in chapter 3, and this novel component makes the 6811 architecture easy to experiment with. The BUFFALO monitor in read-only memory in that implementation is also quite good. A single-chip microcomputer can be used for a large variety of experiments. Nevertheless, other microcomputers have demonstrably better static and dynamic efficiency for certain benchmarks. Even if they have comparable (or even inferior) performance, they may be chosen because they cost less, have a better reputation for service and documentation, or are available, while the "best" chip does not meet these goals. The reader is also encouraged to study other microcomputers and to be prepared to use them if warranted by the application.

The microcomputer has unleashed a revolution in computer engineering. As the cost of microcomputers approaches ten dollars, computers become mere components. They are appearing as components in automobiles, kitchen appliances, toys, instruments, process controllers, communication systems, and computer systems. They should replace larger computers in process controllers much as fractional horsepower motors replaced the large motor and belt shaft. They are "fractional horsepower" computers. This aspect of microcomputers will be our main concern through the rest of the book, since we will focus on how they can be interfaced to appliances and controllers. However, there is another aspect we will hardly have time to study, which will become equally important: their use in conventional computer systems. We are only beginning to appreciate their significance in computer systems. Consider the following (slightly overstated) conjectures:

1. The problem of software portability – getting a program moved from one computer to another – will be solved! Just buy a software package for $30,000, then that software can be written for a microcomputer, and the firm that wrote the software will give you *a free* microcomputer.
2. The solution of large problems will depend only on the patience of programmers. They could spend a lot of money solving these problems on a large computer. Instead, they buy cheap microcomputers, load a program one night, and return a week later to get the answer. Then they could even throw away the microcomputers and the cost of solving the problem could still be less than on a large computer.
3. Future computers will be aggregates of microcomputers. A "mess o' micros" will be more economical than a larger processor.

Microcomputers continue to spark startling innovations; however, the features of microcomputers, minicomputers, and large computers are generally very similar. In the following subsections the main features of the 6811, a von Neumann architecture, are examined in greater detail.

1-2 The 6811 Instruction Set

A typical machine has six types of instructions and several addressing modes. Each type of instruction and addressing mode is described soon in general terms. The types and modes indicate what an instruction set might look like. They also give concrete details about how the 6811 works, which help you understand the examples in this book.

This section talks about the instruction set. It does not fully define the 6811's instruction set because you could get lost in details. The handy *Programming Reference Guide, MC68HC11A8* available from Motorola (document MC68HC11A8 RG/AD), should be used to fully specify the 6811 instruction set. The only way to really learn an instruction set is to write a lot of programs. It can't be learned just by reading a book (even one as fine as this!). Nevertheless, some insight can be offered in a book like this by discussing some useful aspects of the instruction set.

1-2.1 6811 Addressing Modes

The instructions discussed in section 1-1 have taken a word from memory where the address of the word is given directly in the instruction. This mode of addressing, called *direct addressing,* is widely used on large computers. By the most commonly accepted definition, direct addressing must be able to effectively address any word in primary memory. The number of bits needed to directly address n words of memory is $\log_2 n$. For a standard-sized 65,536-word memory, 16 bits are required to address each word. If the width of each word is 8 bits, an instruction may require 24 bits for the instruction code bit pattern and the address. This hurts static efficiency, because a lot more bits are needed than with other modes introduced in this section. It also hurts dynamic efficiency, because a lot of time is needed to pick up all those words. Then more efficient addressing modes are used to access most often needed words faster and to get to any word in memory by some means, without using as many bits as are needed to directly address each word of memory. This problem leads to the addressing modes that are especially important in small computers. In the remainder of this section, we discuss addressing modes to show what might be generally expected in a computer, and also what is available on the 6811. (See table 1-2.) The notation used in Motorola's literature differs from that used in other manufacturers' literature and in textbooks. Although both are given in this table, because we're using the 6811 to teach general principles, we'll use the general terminology, rather than Motorola's, throughout the book.

Table 1-2. Addressing Modes for the 6811

Mode (General)	Mode (Motorola)	Example	Use
Implied	Inherent	SWI	Improve efficiency
Register	Register	INCA	Improve efficiency
Immediate	Immediate	LDAA #1 2	Initialize registers, provide constant operands
Page 0	Direct	LDAA ALPHA	Store global data (address 0 - $ff)
Direct	Extended	LDAA ALPHA	Access any word in memory
Index	Index	LDAA 5,X	Address arrays
		LDAA 3,Y	"
Page Relative	Relative	BRA ALPHA	Provide position independence

What everyone else calls direct addressing Motorola calls "extended addressing," which you should know only if you want to read their literature. Motorola uses the term "direct addressing" for a short form of addressing that uses an 8-bit address, which we will call page 0 addressing. Their terminology would be correct for a primary memory of only 256 words. Then direct addressing would just need to address a small memory, and addressing more memory would be called extended addressing. It seems the designers of the original 6800 assumed most systems would only require such a small (primary) memory. But as we now know, garbage accumulates to fill the container, so if we build a bigger container, it will soon be filled. Thus, we should also use the term direct addressing when we use a 16-bit displacement as the effective address.

In the following discussion of addressing modes, the instruction bits used as an address, or added to get the effective address, are called the *displacement*. Also, in the following discussion an address is calculated the same way – in jump instructions – for the program counter, as for the effective address, in such instructions as LDAA or STAA. Some people get confused about the addressing modes used in jump instructions because they think that JMP ALPHA should take a word from location ALPHA to put it into the program counter using direct addressing in the same way as in the instruction LDAA ALPHA. No. JMP ALPHA loads the address of ALPHA into the program counter. The simple analogy we used earlier makes it clear that the program counter is, like the effective address, a "hand" to address memory and is treated the same way by the addressing modes.

Some techniques improve addressing efficiency by avoiding the calculation of an address to memory. *Implied addressing* is a technique whereby the instruction always deals with the same register or a fixed word in memory so that no bits are required within the instruction to specify it. An example is a kind of jump to subroutine instruction called the software interrupt (SWI; this instruction will be further explained in 1-2.2; it is also called TRAP or SVC). When the SWI is executed, the old value of the program counter is saved in a specific place (to be described later) and the new program counter value is gotten from two other specific places (memory location $FFF6,$FFF7). The instruction itself does not contain the usual bits indicating the address of the next instruction: the address is implied. Motorola and others also call this mode "inherent. "

A similar mode uses registers as the source and destination of data for instructions. This is called *register addressing*. The 6811 has accumulators that can be so used, called *accumulator A, accumulator B,* and *accumulator D*. Accumulator D is a 16-bit accumulator for 2-word data operations and is actually the same as the two 8-bit accumulators A and B joined together. That is, if accumulator A has $3B and accumulator B has $A5, then accumulator D has $3BA5, and vice versa. In some instructions, such as INC, one can increment a word in memory using direct addressing, as in INC ALPHA, or one can increment a register, such as INCA. Thus, register addressing can be used instead of memory addressing to get data for instructions. This mode substantially improves both static and dynamic efficiency because fewer bits are needed to specify the register than a memory word and a register can be accessed without taking up a memory cycle.

Another nonaddressing technique is called *immediate addressing*. Herein, part of the instruction is the actual data, not the address of data. In a sense, the displacement is the data itself. For example, a type of load instruction,

LDAA #$10

puts the number $10 into the accumulator. Using Motorola's notation, an immediate address is denoted by the # symbol. The LDAA instruction, with addressing mode bits for immediate addressing, is $86, so this instruction is stored in machine code like this:

$86
$10

The number $10 is actually the second word (displacement) of the 2-word instruction. This form of addressing has also been called literal addressing.

Page addressing is closely related to direct addressing. (Two variations of page addressing appear in the 6811, and will be discussed later.) If 8 bits can be used to give the address inside the instruction, then 2^8 or 256 contiguous words can be directly addressed with these bits. The 256 contiguous words in this example are called a *page* .

Generally, for a subroutine, some data are needed only by that subroutine (*local data*), and there are some data that must be shared with other subroutines (*global data*). Global data should be stored on page 0, where it can be accessed by *page 0 addressing* (which Motorola calls "direct addressing"). The displacement, an 8-bit number, is considered the low byte and is padded with 0's in the high byte to form a 16-bit address. Page 0 addressing is used to get the global data more efficiently because a shorter (2-byte) instruction, rather than a longer direct addressed (3-byte) instruction is used.

Page relative addressing calculates the effective address by adding an 8-bit 2's complement displacement to the program counter to get the address for a jump instruction (a *branch*) because one often jumps to a location which is fairly close to (on the same page as) where the jump is stored. The displacement is added to the program counter when it actually points to the beginning of the next instruction. This addressing mode only works if the jump address is within -128 to +127 locations of the next instruction's address after the branch instruction. For example, the place we want to branch to may contain the instruction code for LDAA ALPHA. To identify that we want to jump or branch to that place, we put a label to the left of the instruction code so that the label begins in the leftmost column, flush against the left margin. Unlabeled instructions must begin, then, with a space so the assembler will not mistake an instruction mnemonic for a label. If the preceding instruction is at locations $200, $201, and $203, it is written as follows:

L LDAA ALPHA

and the label L will be the symbolic address of the instruction, which may be used in jump or branch statements. For example, a branch to location $200 (L) is denoted like this:

BRA L

If L is at location $200 and the instruction is at location $1F0, then the program counter is at location $1F2 when the address is calculated, and the BRA instruction (whose instruction code is $20) will be assembled and stored in memory as

$20
$0E

Note that the assembler language instruction uses the symbolic address L rather than the difference between the addresses, as in BRA L-$F2, and the assembler automatically determines the difference between the current program counter address and the effective address and puts this difference into the second word (displacement) of the instruction.

If we move the program intact from one place in memory to another (the branch instruction and the place it jumps to move together), their relative address remains unchanged. You may use page relative addressing instead of the direct addressing used in a jump instruction. But the instruction and the data may be more than -128 or +127 locations apart. Therefore, branch instructions can only be used in place of jump instructions for short programs in the 6811. If a program does not use direct addressing in jump statements it has a characteristic called *position independence*. This means a program can be loaded anywhere in memory, and it will run without change, thus simplifying program and subroutine loading. This also means that a read-only memory can be loaded with the program and will work wherever it is addressed. The latter feature permits programs written in read-only memories to be usable in a larger range of installations, because the addresses need not conflict with those used by other programs, so these programs can be sold in larger quantities and will therefore be less costly.

Although page 0 and page relative addressing permit one to access global data and program segments that are branched near to that which is branched from, one cannot access much of it. For example, if a page is 256 words, then a 20 x 20-word global array cannot be stored entirely on page 0. This is solved by *index addressing* whereby a small array (3 x 16) of fast registers in the controller module, called *index registers*, is used to obtain the address. In a load instruction using index addressing, some bits choose the (16-bit) index register, to which some part of the instruction (8 bits) is added to get the address of the word that is recalled. Rather than a 3-byte instruction, a 2-byte instruction is used to get the data. The word in the index register is unchanged by this operation. Note that the index register can be loaded with the address of any word in memory, so any word can be recalled by means of index addressing. Moreover, without changing the index register contents, any word above the one the index register points to can be recalled by using different values for the displacement (8 bits) added (as an unsigned number) to the index register. This makes index addressing quite versatile for handling arrays. However, in very small machines there are no bits available in the instruction for adding to the index registers. The address is exactly the contents of the index register. This special, simple form of index addressing is called *pointer addressing* and the index registers are called *pointer registers*. While pointer addressing can be used to recall any word in memory, it is more difficult to use than index addressing because the register must be reloaded each time to recall or memorize a word at a different location. Pointer addressing is only used in the 6811 with a stack pointer, to be discussed shortly.

In the 6811, 3 index/pointer 16-bit registers are used, called X,Y, and S. The S register is a special *stack pointer*. It has special meaning and in our experience must be treated with respect. One can use the X and Y registers in 2- and 3-word instructions using index addressing in which the last 8 bits are an unsigned displacement.

Index addressing is denoted by putting the displacement followed by a , and the index register name, as in this:

LDAA ALPHA,X

If index register X has the value 5, then this instruction puts the word at location $105 into accumulator A. An instruction using the Y index register rather than X is generally stored in machine code form just as the same instruction would be using the X register, except the first byte of the operating code is $18, called a *prebyte* , and the second and third bytes of the instruction using Y are the same as the first and second bytes of the instruction using X. Thus, the X register should be used to get to the most often stored data, since the Y register requires longer (and slower) instructions.

A part of memory, called the *stack buffer*, is set aside for a *stack* . In a single-chip microcomputer, the stack is in the random access memory along with the data. The stack pointer, S, initially contains the largest address of any word in the stack buffer. The instruction DES decrements the stack pointer, INS increments the stack pointer, and TSX transfers the stack pointer to X (actually it adds 1 to the value of S and puts the sum in X). *Pushing* a word that is in accummulator A onto this stack is essentially equivalent to this program segment:

DES
TSX
STAA 0,X

and *pulling* (or popping) a word from this stack into accummulator A is roughly equivalent to this program segment:

TSX
LDAA 0,X
INS

Special instructions, described soon, also push or pull words from this stack.

The stack fills out, starting at high addresses and building toward lower addresses, in the stack buffer. If it builds into addresses lower than the stack buffer, a *stack overflow* error occurs, and if it is pulled too many times, a *stack underflow* occurs. If no such errors occur, then the last word pushed onto the stack is the first word pulled from it, a property that sometimes labels a stack a LIFO (last in, first out) stack. Stack overflow or underflow often causes data stored outside of the stack buffer to be modified. This bug is hard to find.

The jump to subroutine instruction pushes the 2-byte return address onto the stack, least significant byte first (which then appears at the higher address) and supplies a new value for the program counter using addressing modes available for the instruction, as in words from the stack, putting them in the program counter. If nobody changes the stack pointer S, or if the net number of pushes equals the net number of pulls (the stack is *balanced*) between the jump to subroutine and the corresponding return from subroutine, then the last instruction causes the calling routine to resume exactly where it left off when it called the subroutine. This method of handling return addresses allows easy *nesting of subroutines*, whereby the main program jumps to a subroutine, say A, and subroutine A in turn jumps to subroutine B. When the main program jumps to subroutine A, it pushes the main program's return address onto the stack. When A jumps to subroutine B, it pushes A's return address onto the stack, on top of (in lower memory words than) the other return address. When B is completed, the address it pulls from the stack is the return address to subroutine A. And when A is completed, the address it pulls from the stack is the return address to the main program. Hardware interrupts and the SWI instructions save return addresses as well as the contents of all the accumulators and index registers (the machine state), by pushing them onto the stack, and a *return from interrupt* instruction pulls them from the stack in reverse order.

The stack in the 6811 is a good place to store local data. It can also be used to supply arguments for a subroutine and return results from it, as discussed later. To save local data, one can push it on the stack and pull it from the stack as in the program segments just mentioned. A reasonable number of words can be stored this way. Moreover, if the subroutine is reentered (see section 1-1.1 near the end), the local data for the subroutine's first execution are saved on the stack as new local data are pushed on top of them and the new data are used by the subroutine's second execution. When the first execution is resumed, it uses the old data. Keeping all local data on the stack this way ensures reentrancy. (This will be discussed in the next chapter.) Note that the subroutine must pull as many words from the stack as it pushed, before the return from subroutine instruction is executed, or some data will be pulled by that instruction into the program counter, which is a particulary troublesome program bug.

The stack pointer S must be treated with respect. It should be initialized to point to the high address end of the stack buffer as soon as possible, right after power is turned on, and should not be changed except by incrementing or decrementing it to effectively push or pull words from it. Some programmers like to re-use data already pulled from the stack, using an instruction sequence like TSX DEX LDAA 0,X. This is not safe. If an interrupt occurs, or if subroutines store return addresses or local variables on the stack, such words above the stack pointer will be written over. Words above the stack pointer must be considered garbage and may not be read after they are pulled. Some programmers like to set S to address good data, to read the data by pulling them. Woe to those programmers. The stack pointer will generally overwrite good data with return addresses each time a subroutine is called or an interrupt (either hardware or SWI) is serviced. Moreover, because the tools used to analyze a faulty program (such as breakpoints and trace steps) use interrupts to store return addresses and registers these tools may be useless for diagnosing faults in a program that mishandles the S register.

1-2.2 6811 Instructions

We now focus generally on the instruction set of a von Neumann computer, and in particular on the instructions in the 6811. The instructions are grouped together in this section to see the available alternatives. The lowly but important move instruction is discussed first. The arithmetic and the logical instructions are covered next. Edit instructions such as shifts, control instructions such as jump, and, finally, I/O instructions are covered in the remainder of this section.

The simplest is a *move* instruction, such as load and store. This instruction moves a word to or from a register, in the controller or data operator, from or to memory. Typically, a third of program instructions are moves. If an architecture has good move instructions, it will have good efficiency for many benchmarks. (Table 1-3 lists the 6811's move instructions.)

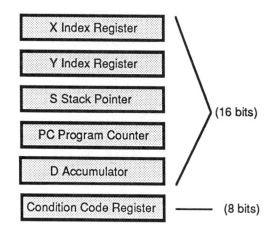

a. The Machine State

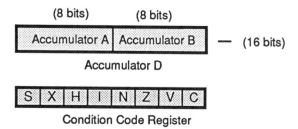

b. Breakdown of D and CC Registers

Figure 1-3. Registers in the 6811

We have discussed the LDAA and STAA instructions, which are in this class. New instructions, PSHA, PULA (and so on), XGDY, and TST are 6811 move instructions, as is CLR, which is an alternative to one of these. Since move instructions move data between controller and data operator registers and memory, we wish to display all these registers first. (See figure 1-3.) The condition code register bits control interrupts and save the results of operations. (See figure 1-3b.) When a result is obtained, the *zero* bit Z is usually set to 1 if the result was 0; to the *negative* bit N if the result was negative; to the *carry* bit C if an add operation produced a carry; and to an *overflow* bit V if an add operation produces an invalid result considered in the 2's complement number system because of overflow. These bits can be tested by a later conditional jump instruction. A *half-carry* bit H is used in decimal arithmetic. Also, 2 *interrupt inhibit* bits (also called an *interrupt mask* bit) I and X are kept in the condition code; when they are set, interrupts are not permitted. Finally, a *stop disable* bit S is used to prevent the execution of the STOP instruction, discussed later. Condition codes are used to generalize the conditional jump capability of the computer and to control interrupts.

The load and store instructions can load or store any of the 8-bit registers A or B or the 16-bit registers X, Y, S, or D. The instructions with * may use addressing modes immediate, direct page, direct, and indexed to access a memory word (except a store instruction may not use immediate addressing). The instruction LDX ALPHA puts the words at locations $100 and $101 into the X index register, and so on. Note that an index register can be used in an addressing mode calculation even when that register itself is being changed by the instruction, because in the fetch-execute cycle, the addresses are calculated before the data from memory is recalled and loaded into the register. In particular, the instruction

LDX 0,X

is both legal and very useful. If X has the value $100 before the instruction is executed, the instruction gets 2 words from location $100 and $101, then puts them into the index register. Note that the richness of the addressing modes contributes greatly to the efficiency of the lowly but important move instructions.

Table 1-3. 6811 Move Instructions

LDAA *	STAA **	TAB	PSHA	CLRA
LDAB *	STAB **	TBA	PULA	CLRB
LDD *	STD **	TAP	PSHB	CLR ***
LDX *	STX **	TPA	PULB	TST A
LDY *	STY **	TSX	PSHX	TST B
LDS *	STS **	TXS	PULX	TST ***
		TSY	PSHY	
		TYS	PULY	

*Memory may be accessed by direct page (8-bit) or
by direct (16-bit), indexed, or immediate addresses.
**Memory may be accessed by direct page (8-bit) or
by direct (16-bit) or indexed addresses.
*** Memory may be accessed using direct (16-bit) or indexed
addresses.

Transfer and exchange instructions permit movement of data among registers of similar width. TAB moves the contents of accumulator A to accumulator B without changing A. Similarly TBA moves B to A, TAP moves A to the condition code register, and TPA moves the condition code register to A. TSX moves S to X, TXS moves X to S, TSY moves S to Y, and TYS moves Y to S, with the following correction. Due to an anomaly inherited from the 6800, S points to the first available word in the stack buffer which is not being used in the stack and which is one location lower than the stack's top word. To make addressing easier, so LDAA 0,X accesses the top word on the stack, TSX increments the stack pointer value as it moves it into X without changing S (and TSY increments the value as it moves it into Y). Conversely, TXS decrements the value of the X register as it moves it into S without changing X (and TYS decrements Y as it moves it into S). The XGDX instruction can exchange the 2 bytes in X with those in D and the XGDY instruction can exchange the 2 bytes in Y with those in D.

The PSHA instruction is capable of pushing the byte in accumulator A onto the stack, and the PULA instruction is capable of pulling a byte from the stack into accumulator A; similarly PSHB and PULB work on accumulator B, PSHX and PULX work on X, and PSHY and PULY work on Y.

Table 1-4. 6811 Arithmetic Instructions

```
ADDA *, ADDB *      INCA, INCB,INC **       ADDD *
ADCA *, ADCB *      DECA, DECB,DEC **       SUBD *
ABA                 NEGA, NEGB,NEG **       CPD *,CPX *,CPY *
SUBA *, SUBB *      ASLA, ASLB,ASL **       INX,INY,INS
SBCA *, SBCB *      ASRA, ASRB,ASR **       DEX,DEY,DES
SBA                 LSRA, LSRB,LSR **       FDIV, IDIV
CMPA *, CMPB *      LSLA,LSLB,LSL**         ASLD,LSRD,LSLD
CBA
                 (Special: DAA   MUL   ABX,ABY)
```

* Memory may be accessed using immediate,
direct page (8-bit), direct (16-bit), or indexed addressing.
** Memory may be accessed using direct (16-bit) or indexed addressing.

The load and store instructions change two of the condition codes which can be used in conditional branch instructions. The N bit is set if the moved word is negative and is cleared if it is positive. The Z bit is set if the moved word is 0 and cleared otherwise. The other move instructions previously discussed do not change the codes. If you want to set the condition codes as in a load instruction, but you are not interested in moving the word to an accumulator, then the TSTA or TSTB instruction can be used. It is like half a load instruction because it sets the condition codes like a LDA instruction but does not change A. Similarly, an instruction TST ALPHA will set the condition codes like LDAA ALPHA but will not change A. The instructions with ** in table 1-3 may use direct or indexed addressing to access words in memory. Finally, because a load instruction with an immediate operand is used to initialize registers, since most initial values are 0, a separate instruction CLR is provided. It may be used rather than LDAA #0 to improve efficiency. However, CLR changes the V and C condition codes, while LDAA #0 doesn't, so the longer LDAA #0 instruction is sometimes used to avoid altering these bits.

The *arithmetic* instructions add, subtract, multiply, or divide the value of the accumulator with the value of a word taken from memory. The 6811 has arithmetic instructions to be used with 8-bit registers and some arithmetic instructions to be used with 16-bit registers. The 8-bit arithmetic instructions are discussed first, then the 16-bit instructions. Table 1-4 lists these arithmetic instructions.

The basic 8-bit ADD instruction can add any word from memory into either accumulator A or accumulator B. This instruction may use addressing modes immediate, page 0, direct and indexed to access a memory word. The instruction is straightforward except for the setting of condition codes. The same instruction is used for unsigned adds as for 2's complement adds; only the testing of the codes differs. For example:

ADDA ALPHA

will add the contents of accumulator A to word $100 of memory and put the result into accumulator A. Usually, the result is 1 bit wider than the operands, and the extra leftmost bit is put into the carry flip-flop. For unsigned numbers, the carry is often considered an overflow indicator; if the carry is 1, the result in the accumulator is incorrect because when the word is put back into the (8-bit-wide) memory, the ninth bit in the carry won't fit, and so the result in memory will also be incorrect. Also, the carry is used to implement multiple precision arithmetic, which is very important in a microcomputer, and will be discussed shortly. The N and Z condition codes are set, just as in the load and store instructions, to reflect that the result of the addition is negative or zero. A half-carry bit, used in decimal arithmetic (discussed shortly), is set in this instruction and the overflow bit V is set to 1 if the result is erroneous as a 2's complement number. A 2's complement overflow will occur if the two numbers being added have the same sign and the result has a different sign. Have you ever added two positive numbers and got a negative number? That's an overflow. Or if you add two negative numbers and get a positive number, that too is an overflow. But if you add two numbers of different signs, an overflow cannot occur. In using these condition codes in branch instructions, we must be careful to test the carry bit, not the overflow bit, after an unsigned binary add, since the carry bit is set if an unsigned overflow occurs; and we must remember to test the overflow bit V after a 2's complement add, because it is set if the result is erroneous as a 2's complement number.

The *add with carry* instruction ADC is used to effect multiple precision arithmetic. It adds a number from memory into the accumulator and sets the condition codes, as in the ADD instruction, and also adds in the old carry flip-flop value in the least significant bit position. To add the 16-bit number at ALHPA (most significant byte at $100 and least significant byte at $101) to a 16-bit number at BETA (where BETA is the symbolic address for location $102, with the most significant byte at $102 and least significant byte at $103), we can execute this program segment:

```
LDAA   ALPHA+1    GET LEAST SIGNIFICANT BYTE OF FIRST WORD
ADDA   BETA+1     ADD TO LEAST SIGNIFICANT BYTE OF SECOND
STAA   BETA+1     PUT BACK IN THE SECOND WORD
LDAA   ALPHA      GET MOST SIGNIFICANT BYTE OF FIRST WORD
ADCA   BETA       ADD TO MOST SIGNIFICANT BYTE OF SECOND
STAA   BETA       PUT BACK IN SECOND WORD
```

(Note that for longer programs we put comments on the right hand side of each instruction. Readers should develop this habit so their programs can be easily understood later.) In this program segment, the ADD instruction generates a carry, stored in the C condition code bit. The STAA and LDAA instructions do not change this bit. The ADCA instruction adds the number at BETA to accumulator A, adds the carry bit in the least significant position, and then produces a new carry to put into the C bit, which is the carry from this add operation. Note that the ADDA instruction might set the carry bit, just as if an unsigned overflow had occurred, and might also set the Z, V, and N bits, but these results are not important and should be ignored. These condition codes are changed again by the ADCA instruction, and they indicate the true sign and overflow bits, which should be tested by conditional branch instructions.

The 6811, like most microcomputers, has a similar set of subtract instructions. The instruction

SUBA ALPHA

subtracts the word from location $100 from accumulator A and sets the condition codes as follows. N, Z, and V are set to indicate a negative result, 0 result, or 2's complement overflow, as in the ADD instruction. The carry flip-flop is actually the borrow indicator; it is set if subtraction requires a borrow from the next higher byte or if an unsigned underflow error exists because the result, a negative number, can't be represented as an unsigned number. The *subtract with carry* SBC instruction is used exactly like the ADC instruction to implement multiple precision subtraction.

Subtraction is often used to compare two numbers, sometimes just to see if they are equal. The results are tested in conditional branch instructions. However, if we are comparing a given number against several numbers to avoid reloading the given number, it can be left in an accumulator, and a *compare* instruction, such as CMPA, can be used. CMPA is just like the subtract instruction, but it does not change the accumulator, so the number in it can be compared to others in later instructions. The condition codes are changed and can be tested by conditional branch instructions. Note, however, that there is no compare with carry instruction to be used with multiple precision comparison; the SBC instruction is used for this.

Because we often add or subtract just the constant 1, or negate a 2's complement number, special short instructions are provided to improve efficiency. The instructions INC, DEC, and NEG can increment, decrement, or negate either the accumulator or any word in memory. An unusual quirk of the INC and DEC instructions: they do not change the carry bit like the add instructions. This makes them useful to count out executions of a "DO LOOP" that has an add operation inside it, so that the carry from one add instruction execution will not be destroyed by the INC or DEC instructions, thus allowing it to be used in the next add instruction execution in the loop. In any event, the carry is really not needed, since it is set after an INC exactly when the Z bit is set, and after a DEC instruction when the number being decremented was 0 just before the instruction was executed. INC and DEC may increment or decrement a word in memory: Those instructions with ** in table 1-4 may use direct or indexed addressing to access words in memory. Also, adding a number to itself and doubling it is an arithmetic left shift ASL, and dividing a 2's complement number by 2 and halving it is an arithmetic right shift ASR. Similarly, LSR divides an unsigned number by 2. The condition codes for ASL are set just as if you did add the number to itself, and the ASR and LSR instructions set N and Z as in the move instructions, and shift the low-order bit that is shifted out of the word into the C bit. These edit instructions are also arithmetic instructions and can be applied to either accumulator or to any word in memory.

The 6811 has several 16-bit arithmetic instructions. ADDD will add 2 words from memory (as if recalled by the LDD instruction) to the D accumulator; SUBD and CPD will likewise subtract and compare a 16-bit number from memory to the D accumulator. Similar to CPD are CPX and CPY, where X or Y is used instead of D. INS, INX, INY increment S, X, and Y, and DES, DEX, and DEY decrement S, X, and Y. There are also the ASLD instruction (also called LSLD) that shifts accumulator D left 1 bit, effecting a multiply by 2 of a 2's complement or unsigned number; LSRD that effects a divide by 2 of an unsigned number; and ASRD that effects a divide by 2 of a 2's complement number. These instructions are very useful for 16-bit arithmetic, but the 8-bit arithmetic instructions can implement multiple precision arithmetic to handle 24-bit, 32-bit, or 40-bit numbers.

Special instructions act on the accumulators only. They enable us to multiply 2 unsigned 8-bit numbers, to add numbers using the binary coded decimal number representation (BCD), to divide a 16-bit number by a 16-bit number, and to add B to X or Y. To multiply 2 8-bit unsigned numbers, put them in accumulators A and B, and execute the MUL instruction. The 16-bit result will be put in accumulator D. To execute arithmetic on binary coded decimal numbers, with two BCD numbers in the left 4 bits and right 4 bits of a word, add them with the ADDA instruction or the ADCA instruction, followed immediately by the DAA (decimal adjust accumulator A) instruction. DAA uses the carry and half-carry to correct the number so the sum is the BCD sum of the two numbers being added. Note, however, that accumulator A is an implied address for DAA, and the half-carry is only changed by the ADD and ADC instructions, so the DAA instruction only works after the ADDA and ADCA instructions. The instruction FDIV divides accumulator D by index register X considered as a fraction, leaving the quotient in X and the remainder in D. The instruction IDIV divides accumulator D by index register X considered as an integer, leaving the quotient in X and the remainder in D. These powerful instructions are not used often. In writing this book we used IDIV in one program in a problem at the end of a chapter, and we did not use FDIV. Finally, ABX adds the contents of B, as an unsigned number, to X, and ABY adds B to Y.

A third group of instructions is the *logic* group. (See table 1-5.) The instruction:

ANDA ALPHA

will logically "and," bit by bit, the word at $100 in memory to the accumulator A. We can "and" into either accumulator A or accumulator B. For example, if the word at location $100 were 01101010 and at accumulator A were 11110000, then after such an instruction is executed the result in accumulator A would be 01100000. A "bit test" instruction BIT "ands" an accumulator with a word recalled from memory but only sets the condition codes and does not change the accumulator. It may be used, like the CMP instructions, to compare a word – without destroying it – to many words recalled from memory to check if some of their bits are all 0. The "and" instruction AND, the "or" instruction ORA, the "bit test" instruction BIT, and the "exclusive or" instruction EOR can work with either accumulator or with any word in memory. The complement instruction COM will complement each bit in the accumulator or any word in memory. Instructions with ** in table 1-5 may use direct or indexed addressing to access words in memory.

Bit-oriented instructions permit the setting of individual bits (BSET) and the clearing of those bits (BCLR). The instruction BSET ALPHA 4 will set bit 2 in word ALPHA, and BCLR ALPHA 4 will clear it. Instructions with *** in table 1-5 may use only page 0 or indexed addressing to access the memory word being tested, and, after a space, we put a field to indicate the pattern of bits to be ORed, or complemented and ANDed, into the word at the effective address. Note that more than 1 bit can be set or cleared in one instruction. These powerful instructions are severely limited by the absence of a direct addressing mode. In writing this book, we were disappointed because we wanted to use them for I/O but found little use for them there.

Table 1-5.   6811 Logic Instructions.

EORA *, EORB *	COMA, COMB, COM **
ORAA *, ORAB *	SEC, SEI, SEV
ANDA *, ANDB *	CLC, CLI, CLV
BITA *, BITB *	BSET ***, BCLR ***

* Memory may be accessed using direct page (8-bit)
direct (16-bit), or indexed addressing.
** Memory may be accessed using direct (16-bit) or indexed addressing.
*** A word in memory is specified using direct page (8-bit) or indexed addressing, and
(after a space) a pattern of bits is specified.

The condition codes are often set or cleared. The interrupt mask bit I may be set to prevent interrupts and cleared to allow them. The carry bit is sometimes used at the end of a subroutine to signal a special condition to the routine it returns to and is sometimes cleared before the instructions ADC or SBC, so it is often set or cleared. Therefore, special logic instructions, CLC, CLI, and CLV clear C, I, or V, and SEC, SEI, and SEV set C, I, or V, respectively.

The next class of instructions – the *edit* instructions – rearrange the data bits without changing their meaning. The edit instructions in the 6811, shown in table 1-6, can be used to shift or rotate either accumulator or a word in memory that is selected by any of the addressing modes. Most microcomputers have similar shift instructions. A right logical shift LSRA will shift the bits in the accumulator right one position, filling a 0 bit into the leftmost bit and putting the old rightmost bit into the C condition code register. Similarly, a logical left shift LSLA will shift the bits in the accumulator left one position, filling a 0 bit into the rightmost bit and putting the old leftmost bit into the C condition code register. A machine generally has several left and right shifts. The 6811 also has arithmetic shifts corresponding to doubling and halving a 2's complement number, as discussed in the arithmetic instruction group. However, although there are different mnemonics for each, the LSLA and ASLA instructions do the same thing and have the same machine code. The rotate instructions ROLA and RORA circularly shift the 9 bits in accumulator A and the carry bit C 1 bit to the left or the right, respectively. They are very useful for multiple word shifts. For example, to shift the 16-bit word in accumulator D (accumulators A and B) 1 bit right, filling with a 0, we can execute this program sequence:

LSRA
RORB

The RORB instruction rotates the bit shifted out of accumulator A, which is held in the C condition code bit, into accumulator B. Of course, this technique is more useful when more than 2 bytes must be shifted. Memory words can be shifted without putting them in the accumulator first. Instructions with ** in table 1-6 may use direct or indexed addressing to access words in memory. Since an 8-bit word is inadequate, multiple precision shifting is common in microcomputers, and the RORA and ROLA instructions are very important. Also for this reason, microcomputers do not have the multiple shift instructions like LSRA 5, which would shift accumulator A right 5 bits in one instruction. Such an instruction would require saving 5 bits in the condition code registers to implement multiple precision shifts. That is generally too messy to use. Rather, a loop is set up, so inside the loop, 1 bit is shifted throughout the multiple precision word, and the loop is executed as many times as the number of bits to be shifted. However, the 6811 has instructions ASLD, LSLD, and LSRD to shift the 16-bit accumulator D the way ASL, LSL, and LSR shift 8-bit accumulators. Some computers have more complex edit instructions than the shifts discussed here, such as instructions to format strings of output characters for printing.

Table 1-6. 6811 Edit Instructions

ASLA,ASLB,ASL **	LSLA, LSLB, LSL **	ROLA, ROLB, ROL **
ASRA, ASRB, ASR **	LSRA, LSRB, LSR **	RORA, RORB, ROR **
	LSLD,ASLD,LSRD	

** Memory may be accessed using direct (16-bit) addressing
or indexed addressing.

Another instruction group is the *control* group of instructions that affect the program counter. (See table 1-7.) These instructions are essential in any computer and are especially important in microcomputers because the cost of memory is high compared to the processor's. Next to move instructions, conditional branches are most common, so their performance has a strong impact on a computer's performance. Also, microcomputers with an instruction set missing such operations as floating point arithmetic, multiple word shifts, and high-level language (FORTRAN) operations, implement these "instructions" as subroutines rather than macros, to save memory space. The machine code produced by a FORTRAN compiler in particular is full of very little but subroutine calls. Unconditional jumps and no-operations are considered first, then the conditional branches and finally the subroutine calls are scrutinized.

The left column of table 1-7 shows unconditional jumps. As noted earlier, the JMP instruction can use direct (16-bit) or indexed addressing mode, but the effective address is put in the program counter. BRA is preferred because it is shorter and uses relative addressing, which may be preferred for position independent code and thus allows the program to execute properly anywhere in memory. The *no-operation* instructions do absolutely nothing. Why have them, you ask? Programs providing signals to the "outside world" – known as real time programs – may need time to execute a program segment for timing the length of a pulse. No-operation instructions provide delays for that purpose. NOP delays two memory cycles and branch never BRN delays three. Also, when we test a program, these instructions can be placed to save room for other instructions we will later insert. An interesting instruction unconditionally skips over 1 or 2 words which might be executed as instructions if a jump is made directly to them. The CPX instruction using immediate addressing does this, except it will change the condition codes (usually no problem). Therefore, that instruction can be called SKIP2. An example of its use is given shortly.

Table 1-7. 6811 Control Instructions

Unconditional	Conditional Simple	Conditional 2's Complement	Conditional Unsigned	Bit Conditional	Subroutine & Interrupt
JMP *	BEQ ****	BGT ****	BHI ****	BRSET *****	JSR *
BRA ****	BNE ****	BGE ****	BHS ****	BRCLR *****	BSR ****
BRN ****	BMI ****	BEQ ****	BEQ ****		RTS
NOP	BPL ****	BLE ****	BLS ****		RTI
SKIP2	BCS ****	BLT ****	BLO ****		SWI
	BCC ****				STOP
	BVS ****				WAI
	BVC ****				

* Direct or indexed addressing may be used.
**** Relative addressing specifies which address to branch to.
***** A word in memory is specified using direct page (8-bit) or indexed addressing, (after a space) a pattern of bits is specified, and (after a space) a relative address is put.

The 6811 has only conditional branch instructions, rather than conditional jumps or conditional subroutine calls and conditional subroutine returns (as does the 8080). The conditional branch tests one or more condition codes, then branches to another location specified by the displacement if the condition is true, using relative addressing.

A set of simple branches can test any one of the condition codes, branching if the bit is set or clear. For example, BCC L will branch to location L if the carry bit is clear, while BCS L will branch there if the carry bit is set. Other sets test combinations of condition codes (the Z, N, and V bits) that indicate 2's complement inequalities. The last set tests combinations of the Z and C bits that indicate unsigned number inequalities. Column 2 of table 1-7 tests each condition code separately. The BMI and BPL instructions check the sign bit and should be used after LDAA, STAA, and TST (or equivalent) to check the sign of a 2's complement number that was moved. The BCC and BCS instructions test the carry bit, which indicates an overflow after adding unsigned numbers or the bit shifted out after a shift instruction. The BVS and BVC instruction set tests the V condition code, set if an overflow occurs on adding 2's complement numbers. The Z bit is also tested easily, but since we often compare two numbers to set the Z bit if the two numbers are equal, the instruction is called BEQ and the complementary instruction is BNE. These last two instructions are also used in the 2's complement and unsigned number branches discussed next.

The branches listed in the middle column of table 1-7 are used after a compare (or subtract) instruction to sense the inequalities of the two numbers being compared as 2's complement numbers. The following program sequence shows an example of the "branch on greater than" instruction, as well as the SKIP2 instruction:

```
     CMPA    ALPHA COMPARE ACCUMULATOR A TO ALPHA
     BGT     L        BRANCH TO L IF ACCUMULATOR A > ALPHA
     LDAB    #$10     OTHERWISE PUT $10 IN B
     SKIP2            AND EXECUTE CPX #, TO SKIP NEXT 2 WORDS
L    LDAB    #$20     IF BRANCHED, PUT $20 IN B
```

If the 2's complement number in accumulator A is greater than the number at location ALPHA, then the branch is taken, putting $20 in accumulator B and going onward. If the 2's complement number in accumulator A is less than or equal to the number in location ALPHA, the branch instruction is a no-operation (like BRN) and the next instruction is executed, which puts $10 into accumulator B. The next instruction, shown here as SKIP2, is actually the CPX immediate instruction (generated by an FCB $8C directive: see chapter 2), which effectively skips over the instruction LDAB #$20 by picking up both words as if they were the CPX instruction's immediate operand. After this instruction is executed, the program following this portion is executed exactly as if the branch had been taken and LDAB #$20 had been executed.

The fourth column shows an equivalent set of branches that sense inequalities between unsigned numbers. The program segment just presented could, by putting the instruction BHI in place of BGT, compare the unsigned numbers in accumulator A against the number at location ALPHA, putting $20 in accumulator B if the register was higher than the word, otherwise putting $10 in accumulator B. These instructions test combinations of the C and Z bits and should only be used after a compare or subtract instruction to sense the inequalities of unsigned numbers. To test 2's complement numbers after a compare, use the branches in the middle column of table 1-7; and to test the sign of numbers after a load, store, or test, use the BPL or BMI instructions.

As a memory aid in using these conditional branch instructions, remember that signed numbers are greater than or less than and unsigned numbers are higher than or lower than (SGUH). Also, when comparing any register with a word from memory a branch like BGT branches if the register *is (greater than) the memory word* .

Analogous to the logic instructions BCLR and BSET are conditional branch instructions BRCLR (branch if clear) and BRSET (branch if set). BRCLR ALPHA 4 L branches to location L if bit 2 of location ALPHA is clear; BRSET ALPHA 4 L branches to L if it is set. Instructions with ***** in table 1-7 may use only page 0 or indexed addressing to access the memory word being tested, as well as a field to indicate the bit to be tested and, if the test is passed, a field to indicate where to go. This instruction may test several bits at once but is hampered by the lack of a 16-bit addressing mode.

Conditional branches are used in *DO-loops*. A DO-loop repeats a given program segment a given number, say n, times. Suppose you want to move 128 words from one memory area to another, and that index register X points to the lowest address of the area the words are moved from, while Y points to the lowest address of the area the words are moved to.

```
       LDAA   #128        ACCUMULATOR A IS USED AS A COUNTER
  L    LDAB   0,X         GET A WORD FROM FIRST AREA
       INX                MOVE POINTER TO NEXT WORD
       STAB   0,Y         PUT THE WORD IN THE SECOND AREA
       INY                MOVE POINTER TO NEXT WORD
       DECA               COUNT DOWN
       BNE    L           LOOP 128 TIMES
```

Note that the first execution of the loop moves the lowest addressed word from the first to the second area and increments both pointer registers. The DECA instruction will change accumulator A from $80 to $7F. Since the result is not 0, the BNE instruction will effect a branch to location L, which repeats the loop. Note that the loop is executed $80 times if $80 is put into the accumulator used as a counter. Instructions like LDAA #$80 are *loop initialization* program segments, and instructions like DECA and BNE L are *loop control* program segments. The pair of initialization and control instructions in the preceding example are used often, because an accumulator is useful as a counter. Alternatively, an index register, because it is a 16-bit register, can be used as can a word in memory, if the accumulators are in heavy use. Further, the loop control can use a compare instruction, like CPX, to test whether the index register stops looping when the register points to a final address.

When writing machine code, many programmers have difficulty with relative branch instructions that branch backwards. We recommend using 16's complement arithmetic to determine the negative branch instruction displacement. The 16's complement is to hexadecimal numbers as the 2's complement is to binary numbers. To illustrate this technique, the preceding program is next listed in machine code. The program begins at location $200, and the addresses of each word are shown on the left with the value shown on the right in each line. All numbers are in hexadecimal.

```
200 86
201 80
202 E6
203 00
204 08
205 18
206 E7
207 00
208 18
209 08
20A 4A
20B 26
20C xx
```

The displacement used in the branch instruction, the last instruction in the program – shown as xx –. It can be determined as follows. When the branch is executed, the program counter has the value $20D, and we want to jump back to location $202. The difference, $20D - $202, is $0B, so the displacement should be -$0B. A safe way to calculate the displacement is to convert to binary, negate, then convert to hexadecimal. $0B is 00001011, so the 2's complement negative is 11110101. In hexadecimal, this is $F5. That is not hard to see, but binary arithmetic gets rather tedious. A faster way takes the *16's complement* of the hexadecimal number. Just subtract each digit from $F (15), digit by digit, then add 1 to the whole thing. -$0B is then ($F-0),($F-B) + 1 or $F4 + 1, which is $F5. That's pretty easy, isn't it!

Another important use of conditional branches is the *decision tree*. We may need a rather complex set of tests to determine what to do next. For example, if we want to go to location L1 when index register X is less than $300 and accumulator A is negative, to L2 when X is less than $300 and A is positive, to L3 when X is $300, to L4 when X is greater than $300 and accumulator B is 3, to L5 when X is greater than $300 and B is 6, and to L6 when X is greater than $300 and B is neither 3 nor 6, use the following:

```
L0    CPX   #$300        CHECK X AGAINST $300
      BEQ   L3           IF EQUAL, GO TO L3
      BMI   T1           IF LESS, TEST A
      CMPB  #3           IT IS POSITIVE; IF B IS 3
      BEQ   L4           GO TO L4
      CMPB  #6           SEE IF IT IS 6
      BEQ   L5           IF SO, GO TO L5
      BRA   L6           OTHERWISE GO TO L6
T1    TSTA               X IS NEGATIVE; TEST A
      BMI   L1           IF A NEGATIVE, GO TO L1
      BRA   L2           OTHERWISE, A IS MORE, GO TO L2
```

To show the flow of control, *flow charts* are often used. A diamond shows a two-way or a three-way branch on an arithmetic comparison. Rectangles show program segments. Lines into the top of a diamond or rectangle show which program segments can precede this one, and lines on the bottom of a rectangle show program segments that follow this segment. If a segment is on another page, its label can be shown in a circle. (See figure 1-4.)

Flow charts are especially important when complex decision trees are used to analyze data. Because they are also useful in all programs, some believe one must write a flow chart before beginning any part of the program. We believe one should do so when writing more than about a hundred lines of code. In many programs used in interfacing, however, comments on each assembler line of code are more useful than flow charts to document the program well. We will use comments in this book more than flow charts, because most segments we write are rather short. Nevertheless, we encourage the reader to write flow charts for longer programs and for short programs that implement complex decision trees.

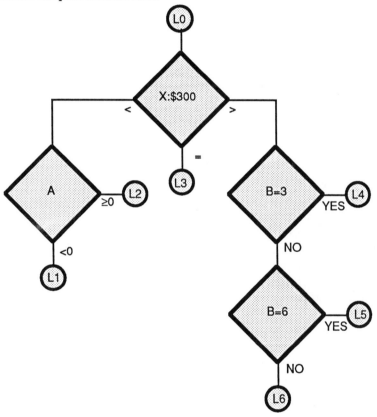

Figure 1-4. Flow Chart

The rightmost column of table 1-7 shows subroutine jumps and similar instructions. Use the JSR with (8-bit) direct page or (16-bit) direct or index addressing, or BSR with relative addressing, which allows position independent code. These instructions not only reload the program counter, they also save on the stack its former value, which points to the instruction right below the JSR or BSR and to which one returns at the end of a subroutine using an RTS instruction.

The PULX or PULY instruction can pull the return address into X or Y, making it easy to use the index register to get the data the return address points to. We will use this to pass arguments into subroutines. JMP 0,X is used to return to the calling program from the subroutine.

The *software interrupt* instruction (SWI) is a 1-word "jump to subroutine. " This instruction is actually equivalent to the following program segment:

```
        BSR   PSHPC          SAVE PROGRAM COUNTER
PSHPC   PSHY                 SAVE REGISTERS, Y FIRST (ON BOTTOM)
        PSHX                 THEN X
        PSHB                 THEN D
        PSHA
        TPA                  THEN THE CONDITION CODE REGISTER
        PSHA
        TSX
        LDD   7,X            GET OLD PC SAVED BY PSHS
        ADDD  #L+2-PSHPC     GET RETURN ADDRESS (POS. INDEPENDENT)
        STD   7,X            PUT IN PLACE OF PC SAVED BY PSHS
        LDX   $FFF6
L       JMP   0,X
```

The SWI instruction is very useful for testing programs as a *breakpoint* . A breakpoint is used to stop a program that is being tested so one can execute a *monitor* program that examines or changes the contents of registers or memory words. Being 1 word long, it can be inserted in place of any instruction. Suppose we tried to use a JSR instruction to jump to the monitor, so we could replace a single-length instruction like INCA, and we also jumped to the instruction just below it from somewhere else. Since the instruction just below must be replaced by the second word of the JMP instruction, and since it also was jumped to from somewhere else, it would jump into the middle of the JMP instruction and do some damage. This is a difficult problem to resolve, especially since a breakpoint is often used in a program that doesn't work right in the first place. So a SWI instruction can be used without fear that some jump instruction might jump into the second word, which might happen with a longer instruction. This instruction saves all the registers automatically, thus making it easy to analyze them by examining the top 9 words on the stack. However, this marvelous trick does not work if the program is in read-only memory, because an instruction in ROM can't be replaced by the SWI instruction.

The SWI instruction is also useful as a convenient subroutine call to execute I/O operations and other complex "instructions," like floating point add. Such a subroutine can be modified and moved as long as the words in locations $FFF6 and $FFF7 point to the subroutine's beginning, because the routines that call this subroutine do not have to be modified when the subroutine is changed and moved. As we find on the 6811, a single SWI instruction can be used both for breakpoints and special subroutine calls.

The STOP instruction will stop the computer until either a reset signal or interrupts are received. The instruction WAI is used to synchronize the 6811 to interrupts and to wait for them. It is useful here to compare I/O interrupts with the SWI instruction. Like SWI, they save the state of the machine, then jump indirectly through various pairs of locations in high memory. The condition code bits X and I govern these interrupts. (SWI, WAI, and I/O interrupts in the 6811 will be further discussed in chapter 5.)

After completion of a routine entered by any SWI or hardware interrupt, the last instruction executed is return from interrupt (RTI). It pulls the top 9 words from the stack, replacing them in the registers the interrupt took them from. RTS should never be used after such a routine. This is a common error, in our opinion, and should always be checked when interrupts and SWIs don't seem to work.

The next class of instructions is the I/O group for which a wide variety of approaches is used. Generally, there are word-sized registers in the I/O devices and control logic in the registers. There are instructions to transfer a word from the accumulator to the register in the I/O device; to transfer a word from the register to the accumulator; and to start, stop, and test the device's control logic. In the 6811 architecture, there are no special I/O instructions; rather, I/O registers appear as words in primary memory (*memory mapped* I/O). The LDAA instruction serves to input a word from an input register, and STAA serves to output a word. Moreover, instructions like INC ALPHA will, if ALPHA is the location of a (readable) output register, modify that register in place so the word is not brought into the accumulator to modify it. CLR, ASR (which happens to be a test and set instruction needed to coordinate multiple processors), and DEC can operate directly on (readable) output registers in a memory mapped I/O architecture. Indirect addressing can be used by programs in read-only memory so they can work with I/O registers even if they are at different locations. The indirect address can be in read-write memory and can be changed to the address of the I/O device. That way, a program in a read-only memory can be used in systems with different I/O configurations. Thus, the production of less expensive read-only memory software becomes feasible. This aspect of the architecture is of central importance to this book and will be dealt with extensively.

1-3 Organization of the M68HC11

In this section, we describe the programmer's view of the MC68HC11's hardware – a particular implementation of the 6811 architecture – considering its general implementation and its particular input/output hardware. Because we will present hardware descriptions in a style similar to the block diagrams programmers commonly see, we will also call our descriptions *block diagrams*. After then discussing the MC68HC11 memory and I/O organization, we introduce the memory map, which explains the location of memory and I/O devices so programmers can write instructions to access them.

1-3.1 Notation for Block Diagrams

A *block diagram* is used to describe hardware organization from the programmer's point of view (see section 1-1.1). It is especially useful for showing how IC's work so a programmer can focus on the main ideas without being distracted by details unrelated to the software. In this memory-mapped I/O architecture, a register is a location in memory that can be read or written as if it were a word in memory. A block diagram shows modules and registers as rectangles, with the most important inputs and outputs shown around the perimeter. Also, the effects of software instructions can be shown nicely on a block diagram; for instance, if the LDX $4000 instruction reads a 16-bit word from a certain register or module, this can be shown, as in figure 1-5. The LDX instruction could be replaced by LDY, LDD, or any instruction that can read 16 bits of data in 2 consecutive bytes. The instruction and the arrow away from the module show it can be read (a readable register). If an instruction like STX $4000 appears there and an arrow is shown into the module, it can be written (a writable register). And if both are shown (LDX/STX and a double arrow), the register is read-write. If an instruction like LDAA appears by the line to a register, an 8-bit word can be read, and if STAA appears there, then an 8-bit word can be written in the register. Finally, a range of addresses can be shown as in LDA/STA $8000/$8003; this means the module can read-write for addresses $8000, $8001, $8002, $8003.

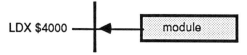

Figure 1-5.   Block Diagram Showing the Effect of an Instruction

1-3.2 M68HC11A8 I/O and Memory Organizaton

As chapter 3 will clarify, most microcomputers are, as von Neumann computers, organized around memory and a bus between memory and the controller and data operator. This can be explained by a block diagram like figure 1-6, without showing instructions and addresses as in figure 1-5. The controller sends an address to memory on an address bus and a command to read or write. If the command is to write, the data to be written is sent on the data bus. If the command is to read – as when the processor fetches an op code – the controller waits for memory to supply a word on the data bus and then uses it; and if the command is to read – as when the processor recalls a data word – the data operator puts the word from the bus into some register in it. Memory mapped I/O uses a "trick": it looks like memory so the processor writes in it or reads from it just as if it reads or writes memory words.

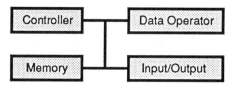

Figure 1-6.   Organization of a von Neumann Computer

The MC68HC11A8 can operate in the single-chip mode or the expanded bus mode. In the *single-chip mode*, the MC68HC11A8 can be the only chip in a system, for it is self-sufficient. The processor, memory, controller, and I/O are all in the chip. (See figure 1-7.) The controller and data operator execute the 6811 instruction set discussed earlier. The memory consists of 256 words of RAM, 8K words of ROM, and 512 words of *EEPROM (electrically erasable programmable read-only memory)*. EEPROM memory can be read like a ROM, but can also be erased and programmed by special instructions, as described in chapter 3. The I/O devices include 5 parallel I/O registers described in chapter 4, a serial peripheral interface (SPI) described in chapter 4, a serial communication interface (SCI) described in chapter 7, a timer described in chapter 8, and an A/D converter described in chapter 6.

MC68HC11A8

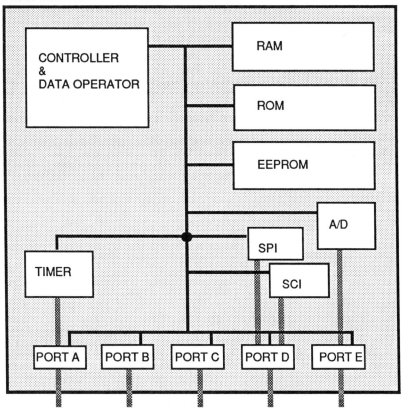

Figure 1-7. Single-Chip Mode of the MC68HC11A8

The expanded bus mode of the MC68HC11A8 removes two of the parallel ports, using their pins to send the address and data busses to other chips. RAM, ROM, and PROM (programmable read-only memory) can be added to this expanded bus. (See figure 1-8.)

MC68HC11A8

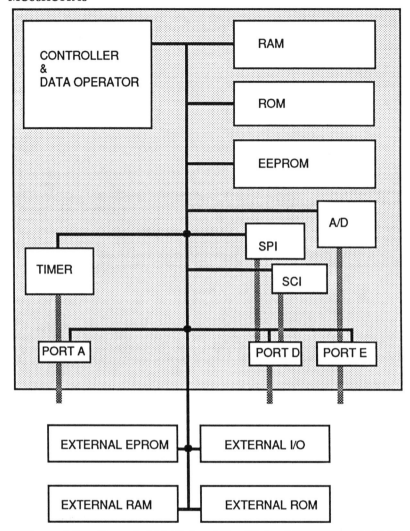

Figure 1-8. Expanded Multiplexed Bus Mode of the MC68HC11A8

A significant advantage of the MC68HC11A8 processor is that it can be used in either the single-chip or the expanded multiplexed bus mode. The former mode is obviously useful when the resources within the MC68HC11A8 are enough for the application – that is, when there is enough memory and I/O devices for the application. The latter mode is required when more memory is needed, when a program is in an EPROM and has to be used with the MC68HC11A8, or when more or different I/O devices are needed than are in the MC68HC11A8. We are excited about using it to teach interfacing, because it can show single-chip computer interfacing concepts, as well as those of conventional multiple-chip system interfacing (in personal computers).

1-3.3 The Memory Map of the MC68HC11A8.

A *memory map* is a description of the memory showing what range of addresses is used to access each part of memory or each I/O device. Figure 1-9 uses a block diagram to present a memory map for the MC68HC11. The single-chip mode is shown; the expanded multiplexed bus mode is missing the PORT B and PORT C I/O devices, but has additional memory or I/O devices in the map any place the MC68HC11A8 memory and I/O are absent.

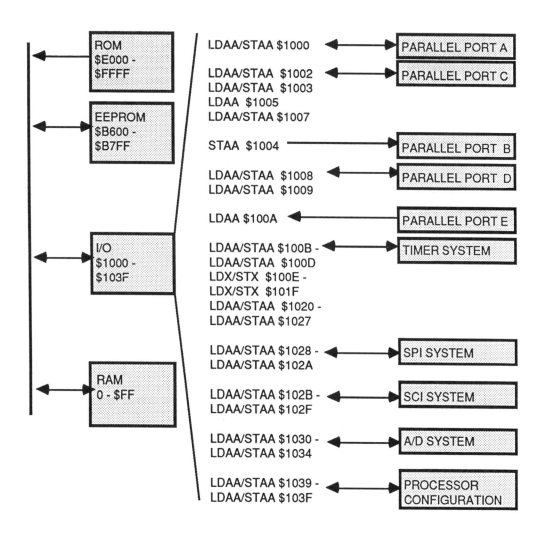

Figure 1-9. Memory Map of the MC68HC11A8

Actually, the RAM and I/O may be put anywhere in memory (on a 4K boundary), but we will use them in the locations shown in figure 1-9 throughout this text. RAM is at lowest address to take advantage of page 0 addressing, and I/O is at $1000 to $103F. The ROM at $E000 has a program – a monitor – described in chapter 2. Your program may be put in RAM or in EEPROM, which is at $B600. If you're using a chip with the BUFFALO monitor, it uses the top bytes of RAM for its data, so you can use the remaining low bytes of RAM for your program or data.

1-4 Conclusions

In this chapter, we have surveyed the background in architecture needed for microcomputer interfacing. The first section covered bare essentials about von Neumann computers, instructions and what they do, and microcomputers. You will find this background helpful as you begin to learn precisely what happens in an interface.

The middle section covered addressing modes and instructions that you may expect in any microcomputer, discussing those in the 6811 in more detail. The general comments there should help if you want to learn about another machine. And the 6811 comments should help you read the examples and do some of the experiments suggested in the book. Some elementary programming techniques, such as decision trees and DO-loops, were also presented. While you probably know these techniques, it is essential to ensure that all readers have the necessary basic information for understanding what follows.

The final section described some of the hardware used in interfacing, as seen from the programmer's perspective. You need to know this to write interfacing programs, described in more detail later.

If you found any section difficult, we can recommend additional readings. There are plenty of fine books on computer architecture. You may have one already. We encourage you to reread it to reinforce the ideas that it presents, rather than read several new ones superficially. But if you haven't read one yet, we recommend *Introduction to Computer Organization and Data Structures,* by H. Stone, McGraw Hill Inc, 1972 or any of Stone's later books, because he covers architecture and data structures together. The following articles I've written may also be useful: "Digital Computer Architecture" in volume 7, and – with further information on microcomputers, including a comparison of different microcomputers – "Microcomputers" in volume 10, of the *Encyclopedia of Computer Science and Technology* , Belzer and others, editors, Marcell Dekker Inc. This 20-volume encyclopedia, incidentally, has many excellent articles, some of which are splendid tutorials covering about every topic in computer science. Further information on the 6811 is limited at the time of writing, although several books have been announced that promise to cover it. The *MC68HC11A8 Advance Information HCMOS Single-Chip Microcomputer,* Motorola Inc., 1985 (request document MC68HC11 ADI 1207) covers M68HC11 organization and MC68HC11A8 realization. Sections 1 and 2 give the MC68HC11A8's basic organization and realization, and section 10 gives the instruction set and addressing modes of the 6811 architecture. We have not attempted to duplicate the diagrams and discussions in that book because you will probably refer to it while reading this book; we also present an alternative view of the subject, so you can use either or both views. The *MC68HC11 HCMOS Programmer's Reference Manual*, Motorola Inc., 1985 (request document MC68HC11 PM/AD) is an accurate reference manual on the execution of each 6811 instruction, and *Programming Reference Guide, MC68HC11A8*, available from Motorola (request document MC68HC11A8 RG/AD), is a handy summary.

Because we are using the 6811 architecture and MC68HC11A8 realization solely as tools for teaching interfacing principles, we do not attempt to show you every feature of the MC68HC11A8. Consult the *MC68HC11A8 Advance Information HCMOS Single-Chip Microcomputer* for information about all the alternative uses of this chip.

Note:

All examples and problems in this book
refer to the MC68HC11A8, P suffix
48-pin Dual-in-line Package
running the BUFFALO monitor, with
256 bytes of memory at 0 - $FF
I/O registers at $1000 - $103F
and 512 words of EEPROM at $B600 -B7FF

Problems

Problems 1 to 3 in this chapter and many problems in later chapters are paragraph correction problems. We use the following guidelines for all these problems.

The <u>paragraph correction</u> problems have been found useful in helping students understand concepts and definitions. The paragraph has some correct and some erroneous sentences. Your task is to rewrite the paragraph so the whole paragraph is correct without any sentences that do not fit into the paragraph's theme. However, if a sentence is correct, you should not change it, and you cannot use the word "not" or its equivalent to correct the sentence. Consider the first sentence in problem 1. "The architecture is the block diagram of a computer." This is incorrect. It can be made correct by changing "architecture" to "organization," or by changing "block diagram" to either "programmer's view" or "instruction set and I/O connection capabilities." Any of these corrections would be acceptable. The second sentence is correct, however, and should not be rewritten. Try to complete the problems without referring to the chapter, then check your answers by looking up the definitions. If you get a couple of sentences wrong, you're doing fine. But if you have more trouble, you should reread the sections the problem covers.

1. * The architecture is the block diagram of a computer. Von Neumann invented the architecture used on microcomputers. In it, the controller is analogous to the adding machine. We "recall" words from primary memory into the controller, using the program counter (left hand). Symbolic addresses are used in assembler languages to represent locations in this memory. A macro is a program in another part of memory that is called by a program, so that when the macro is done, the calling program resumes execution at an instruction below the jump to macro. An (I/O) interrupt is like a subroutine that is requested by an I/O device. The latency time is the time needed to completely execute an interrupt. To optimize the speed of execution, choose a computer with good static efficiency. A microcomputer is a controller and data operator on a single LSI chip, or a few LSI chips. A chip is called an LSI chip if it has about a hundred transistors.

2. * Addressing modes are especially important because they affect the efficiency of the most common class of instructions, the arithmetic class. Direct addressing has the operand in a part of the instruction called the displacement, and the displacement would be 8 bits long for an instruction using it to load an 8-bit accumulator. Indirect addressing allows programs to be position independendent. The 6811 has direct page addressing which is a "quick-and-dirty" index addressing mode. Index addressing is especially useful for jumping to nearby locations. If we want to move data around in memory during execution of a program, indirect addressing is the only mechanism that can efficiently access single words as well as arrays.

3. * The 6811 has 96 bits of register storage, where the D accumulator is really the same as the X index register. The X register serves as an additional stack pointer, and instructions to push or pull can use X. Add with carry is used in multiple precision arithmetic. It can add into accumulator D. The 6811 has an instruction to divide one unsigned number into another unsigned number. The DAA instruction can be used after an INCA instruction to increment a decimal number in accumulator A. BGT, BLT, BGE, and BLE can be used after comparing 2's complement numbers. The SWI instruction is particularly useful as a subroutine call to a fast, short subroutine, because it is a fast instruction.

4. Identify which applications would be concerned about storage density and which about speed. Give reasons for your decisions.
    a. Pinball machine game
    b. Microwave oven control
    c. Home security monitor
    d. Fast Fourier transform (FFT) module for a large computer
    e. Satellite communications controller

5. Write the (hexadecimal) code for a BRA L instruction, where the instruction code is at locations $12A and $12B and
    a. L is location $12F
    b. L is location $190
    c. L is location $12A
    d. L is location $120
    e. L is location $103

6. Write the op code for the following instructions, assuming the first byte of the op code is at $208A and L is at $2095, X is $1000 and Y is $8000, and explain in words what happens when it is executed (including the effects on the condition codes):
    a. BSET $52 $12
    b. BCLR $34,X 5
    c. BSET 3,Y $7F
    d. BRCLR $EE 6 L
    e. BRSET 3,Y 8 L

7. Suppose a memory is filled except for the program that follows, like this: the word at address $WXYZ is $YZ (for example, location $2538 has value $38). Assuming that an address in X never points to the program, what will the value of X be after each instruction is executed in this program:

            LDX #$1
            LDX 0,X
            LDX 4,X

8. Suppose the condition code register is clear and the ADDA APLHA instruction is executed. Give the value in the condition code register if

a. Accumulator A is $77, ALPHA is $77
b. Accumulator A is $C8, ALPHA is $77
c. Accumulator A is $8C, ALPHA is $C8
d. Repeat c for SUBA ALPHA

9. Explain under what conditions the H, N, Z, V, and C bits in the condition code register are set. Also explain the difference between overflow and carry.

10. If the accumulator A contains the value $59 and ALPHA contains the value $6C, what will be the value of the condition code register after the following instructions. (Assume the condition code register is clear before each instruction.)
   a. ADDA ALPHA
   b. SUBA ALPHA
   c. TSTA
   d. COMA
   e. BITA ALPHA
   f. EORA ALPHA

11. Repeat problem 10 assuming that the accumulator A contains the value $C9, ALPHA contains the value $59, and the condition code register is set to the value $FF before each instruction.

12. Explain, in terms of condition code bits, when the branch is taken for the following conditional branch instructions:
   a. BEQ
   b. BGT
   c. BHI
   d. BHS
   e. BLE
   f. BPL

13. How many times does the following loop get repeated when the instruction CND is
   a. BNE
   b. BPL
   c. BLT

```
              LDAA          #200
LOOP          statement list
              DECA
              CND           LOOP
```

Show calculations or explain your answers.

14. What is the value of accumulator B after the following program ends, when the instruction COND is

a. BEQ
b. BMI
c. BGT
d. BVS

```
        LDAA        #200
                    CLRB
        LOOP        DECA
                    COND        EXIT
                    INCB
                    BRA         LOOP
        EXIT        SWI
```

Show calculations or explain answers.

15. Convert the following high-level programming language construct into 6811 assembly language instructions, assuming that the variable A is already assigned to the accumulator A. As long as the expression in the while statement is true, the statements inside curly brackets are repeated.

$$A = 10;$$
$$while (A > 3)$$
$$\{ statements;$$
$$A = A -1; \}$$

16. Repeat problem 15 with the following high-level programming language construct:

$$A = 10;$$
$$do$$
$$\{ statements;$$
$$A = A - 1; \}$$
$$while (A > 3)$$

17. Give the 6811 instruction sequences that perform the same operation as the following non-existent 6811 instructions. State whether the condition codes are set properly or not.
a. XGXY
b. NEGD
c. ASRD

18. BETA initially contains the value $9C. What is the value of BETA after the following instructions:
a. BCLR BETA $15
b. BSET BETA $38

19. BETA initially contains the value $9C. Will a branch occur after these instructions:
a. BRCLR BETA $64 HERE
b. BRSET BETA $64 HERE
c. BRCLR BETA $61 HERE
d. BRSET BETA $84 HERE.

20. What are the hexadecimal values of registers D and X after the FDIV instruction if they contain these values:
   a. $4000, $8000, respectively
   b. 0. 5, 0. 75

21. Repeat problem 20 with IDIV instruction and
   a. D = $0064, X = $0002
   b. D = $0064, X = $0003

22. What are the values of registers A and B after the MUL instruction if they contain these values:
   a. $80, $80, respectively
   b. $8C, $45

23. Show the decision tree and write the program for the following tests:
   a. Go to location L1 if accumulator A is less than 7 and index register X is less than $8257, L2 if A is less than 7 and X is greater than or equal to $8257, L3 if A is equal to 7, L4 if A is greater than 7 and Y is greater than $C027, L5 if A is greater than 7 and Y is less than $C027, L6 if A is greater than 7 and Y is equal to $C027.
   b. Go to location L1 if index register X is less than $9214 and accumulator B is greater than accumulator A, L2 if A is greater than B and X is less than $9214, L3 if X is less than $9214 and A is equal to B and Y is less than or equal to $FF27, L4 if A is equal to B and Y is equal to $FF27 and X is less than $9214, L5 is X is greater than or equal to $9214 and A is greater than or equal to 0, L6 if X is greater than or equal to $9214 and A is negative.

24. Given two unsigned numbers in accumulators A and B, write a routine that will put the greater number in accumulator A and the lesser in B.

25. Given five 1-byte numbers stored in locations $10 to $14, write a routine that will put the greatest number in accumulator A, assuming that the numbers are in 2's complement representation.

26. Given five 1-byte unsigned numbers stored in locations $10 to $14, write a routine that will add the numbers and store the sum in location $15. What error conditions could occur?

27. Five 2-byte 2's complement numbers are consecutively stored in locations from $10 and on, with high byte first. That is, $10 contains the high byte of first number, $11 the low byte of first number, $12 the high byte of second number, and so forth. Write a routine that will add the numbers and store the sum in locations $20 and $21. What error conditions are possible?

28. A 5-byte unsigned number is stored in locations $10 to $14, with the most significant byte first (in lower memory). A second 5-byte number is stored in locations

$20 to $24 in similar fashion. Write a routine that will add the two numbers and put the result in locations $20 to $24. The routine should set the carry and/or overflow bits correctly upon exit.

29. Give a sequence of 6811 instructions that would be position independent and perform the same operations as each of these:
   a. LDX TABLE
   b. BRA LOOP where branching range may require 16 bit relative offset.
   c. LDAA A,X where the byte in A is used as the 2's complement offset from X

30. Write a routine that will branch to ALPHA if the bits in location CC are as follows:
   a. Bit 3 XOR bit 1 = 0
   b. Bit 2 + bit 0 = 0
   c. Bit 2 + (bit 3 XOR bit 1) = 1

2

Programming Microprocessors

Each reader has unique programming skills and backgrounds. In our experience, the "average" student of microcomputer interfacing usually has problems with the four programming techniques studied in this chapter. The first, and most important, technique is the handling of data structures. The first subsection provides a brief, microcomputer-oriented discussion of data structures. The second technique, addressed next, is the writing of structured and modular programs and the use of high-level languages and documentation. The third technique, which deals with the problem of how to handle subroutines is discussed next. The fourth technique, discussed last – multiple precision arithmetic – is especially important in a short word-width computer, yet is not well known. But, clearly, we must understand these concepts quite well so we can discuss and design those interfaces. This chapter is intended to cover programming techniques needed in the discussion of interfacing in the rest of the book.

Other interface design books devote as much as half the book to the topics covered in this chapter. The topics covered are very important. The interface designer must know a lot about basic programming. As the industry matures, the problems of matching voltage levels and timing requirements, discussed in the next chapter, are being solved by better-designed chips, but the chips are getting larger and thus there is an increasing demand on interface designers to write more software to control them. There is, as in chapter 1, so much to cover and so little space, that we will offer a summary of the main ideas. If you have covered this material in other courses or absorbed it from experience this chapter should bring it all together. You may pick up the material just by reading this condensed version. Others should get an idea of the amount of background needed to read the rest of the book. (See the bibliography in section 2.5 for additional reading.)

For this chapter, we assume the reader has programmed in assembler language on a large or small computer or can pick it up quickly. From the chapter, he or she should learn the general fundamentals of microcomputing software and the programming practices specifically applicable to the MC68HC11A8 microprocessor. The reader should also become capable of writing programs with around a hundred lines of code and debugging them with little difficulty. The reader should become familiar with the basic ideas of arithmetic, data structures, and subroutine handling, and should be well prepared to understand the interfacing programs discussed in the remainder of the book.

2-1 Data Structures

Data structures are at least as important as programming techniques, for if the program is one-half of the software, the data and its structure are the other half. When we discussed storage density as an architecture characteristic, we discussed only the amount of memory needed to store the program. We are also concerned about data storage and its impact on static and dynamic efficiency, as well as the size of memory needed to store the data. Prudent selection of the data structures a progam uses can shorten or speed up the program. These considerations about data structures are critical in microcomputers.

A data structure is one among three views of data. The *information structure* is the view of data the end user sees. For instance, end user may think of his of her data as a table, like table 2-1 in this book. The programmer sees the same data as the *data structure* : strongly related to the way the data are accessed but independent of details such as size of words and position of bits. It is rather like a painter's template, which can be filled in with different colors. So the data structure may be an array of characters that spell out the words in table 2-1. The *storage structure* is the way the information is actually stored in memory, right down to the bit positions. So the table may appear as an array of 8-bit words in the machine structure.

The data structure concept has been found a bit hard for some very practical engineers to accept. Its usefulness lies in its ability to provide a level of abstraction allowing us to make some overall observations of how we store things, which can be applied to similar storage techniques. For instance, if we can develop a concept of how to access an array, we can use similar ideas to access arrays of 8-bit or 24-bit words, even though the programs could be quite different. But here we must stress that a data structure is simply a kind of template that tells us how data are stored and is also a menu of possible ways the data can be written or read. Two data structures are different if they have different templates that describe their general structure or if the menus of possible access techniques are different.

To prepare for the discussion of data structures, we'll study assembler directives next. Then we'll present a class of data structures based on indexing and, finally, a class based on sequential position.

2-1.1 Assembler Directives

To discuss examples of storage structures, we introduce the notion of *assembler directives*. These appear just like instructions in an assembler language program, but they tell the assembler to do something other than create the machine code for an instruction. (See table 2-1 for a list of directives.) Most of the directives we need are used to allocate space for data storage. However, two, used in later examples, that do not allocate data are briefly discussed here with the other assembler directives.

The NAM statement and the END statement are assembler language directives used to begin and end a program to be processed by an assembler. (They can be omitted, but they should be put in.) The program then appears as follows:

```
NAM  PROG1
.... (your program)
END
```

Table 2-1. Assembler Directives for the 6811

Directive	Meaning
NAM N	Declares that the name of this program is N
END	Terminates the program
ORG N	Sets the origin to location N, so succeeding code is written, starting at location N
L RMB N	Allocates N words and designates L as the label of the first word of the area being allocated.
L EQU N	Declares label L to have value N
L FCB N1,N2	Forms (generates) one byte per argument, assigns label L to the first byte
L FDB N1,N2	Forms (generates) two bytes per argument, assigns label L to the first byte of the first argument
L FCC 'ABC'	Forms (generates) ASCII coded characters for each character between single quotes, assigns label L to the first character.

The program name to the right of the NAM directive is printed on the program listing at the top of each page. Rather than numbering programs, we use this method when referring to a program in another section of this book.

Some other assembler directives allocate storage in one way or another. To *allocate* means to find room for a variable or program in memory. The place an assembler puts data is the value of a *location counter*. The *origin* statement is used to set the value of the location counter, thus telling the assembler where to put the next word it generates after the ORG. For example, the sequence

$$\text{ORG} \quad \$100$$
$$\text{LDAA} \quad \text{ALPHA}$$

will put the instruction code word for LDAA at location $100 (when the program is loaded in memory) and each succeeding word in consecutive locations following that, by incrementing the location counter as each byte is generated. By using the ORG directive to insert words further down in memory than they should be without the ORG directive, an area of memory can be left aside to store data.

A second directive – *reserve memory bytes* RMB – can be used to allocate an area of memory. As an example,

$$\text{L RMB} \quad \$100$$

allocates $100 words for some data and lets you refer to it (actually the first byte in it) using the label L. The value to the right of the RMB mnemonic (which may be an algebraic expression) is added to the location counter. The assembler will skip over the $100 words to put its next word $100 words further down (at higher addresses) than it would have. The words in this area can be accessed by using the label for the RMB directive with an offset. For instance, to load the first word from this area into accumulator A, use LDAA L; to load the second word, use LDAA L+1; and so on. Incidentally, the number of words can be 0 in an RMB directive; this can be used to put a label on a line without putting an instruction on it. Some examples could use such an RMB 0 rather than the NOP they did use.

A third way to allocate words of memory for data is to use the *equate* directive EQU. A directive like

ALPHA   EQU $100

can be put anywhere in the program. This will tell the assembler that wherever ALPHA appears in the program, the number $100 is to be substituted. EQU directives are useful ways to tell the assembler where variables are located and are especially useful to label I/O registers in memory and locations in other programs to jump or branch to.

The ORG, RMB, and EQU directives tell the assembler where areas of data are to be put but do not fill those areas with initial values. The directives that follow will not only provide room for variables but will also *initialize* the words with constants when the program is loaded.

The *form constant byte* directive FCB will put a byte in memory for each operand of the directive. The value of an operand is put into memory when the location counter specifies the address and the location counter is incremented for each operand. FCB 10 will put $0A in a word in memory. The directive

L FCB 1,2,3

will initialize three words in memory to be

01
02
03

and will tell the assembler that L is the symbolic address of the first word, whose initial value is $01. The location counter is incremented three times. *Form double byte* FDB will initialize 2 consecutive words for each argument. The value of each operand is put in 2 consecutive words and the location counter is incremented by 2 for each operand. For example, the directive

L FDB 1,2,3

will initialize 6 consecutive words in memory, as follows:

00
01
00
02
00
03

Section 2-1 Data Structures

and will tell the assembler that L is the address of the first word in this area, whose value is $00. The location counter is incremented six times. The FDB directive is especially useful in putting addresses in memory, so they can be used in indirect addressing or can be picked up into an index register. If ALPHA is $100 because an EQU directive set it to that value or because it is a label of an instruction or directive like FCB which begins at location $100, then the directive

FDB ALPHA

will generate the following 2 bytes in memory

01
00

Table 2-2. ASCII Codes

	00	10	20	30	40	50	60	70
0			spc	0	@	P	`	p
1			!	1	A	Q	a	q
2			"	2	B	R	b	r
3			#	3	C	S	c	s
4	eot		$	4	D	T	d	t
5			%	5	E	U	e	u
6			&	6	F	V	f	v
7			'	7	G	W	g	w
8	bsp		(	8	H	X	h	x
9			)	9	I	Y	i	y
A	lf		*	:	J	Z	j	z
B			+	;	K	[	k	{
C	ff		,	<	L	\	l		
D	cr		-	=	M	]	m	}
E			.	>	N	^	n	~
F			/	?	O	_	o	del

Finally, *form constant characters* FCC will generate the code words for the letters in the argument of the instruction using the *ASCII code*, shown in table 2-2, which encodes each character as an 8-bit byte. The special characters are *eot* end of text, *bsp* backspace, *lf* line feed, *ff* form feed (begin on new page), *cr* carriage return, *spc* space, and *del* delete. The argument can be expressed in different ways, but in this book, all letters to be coded and stored will be enclosed in double quotes. For each character, its ASCII value is put in the memory word specified by the location counter and the location counter is incremented. The assembler directive

L FCC "ABC"

will generate the following pattern in hexadecimal in memory:

41
42
43

and let the assembler know that the label L refers to the address of the first letter that is stored as the word $41.

Data structures divide into three main categories: indexable, sequential, and linked. Indexable and sequential, discussed here, are more important. Linked structures are very powerful, but are not easy to discuss in abstract terms. They will be sketched in a concrete example in chapter 4.

2-1.2 Indexable Data Structures

Indexable structures include vectors, lists, arrays, and tables. A *vector* is a sequence of elements, where each element is associated with an index i that can be used to access it. To make address calculations easy, the first element is usually associated with the index 0, and each successive element with the next integer (*zero-origin indexing*), but you can change the index origin of the vector to 1 if you are willing to slightly modify the routines. Also, the elements in a vector are considered numbers of the same *precision* (number of bits or bytes needed to store an element). We will normally consider 1-byte precision vectors, although we soon show an example of how the ideas can be extended to n-byte precision vectors.

To illustrate a vector, suppose that the vector V has elements 31, 17, and 10. This can be defined in assembler language by the directive

V FCB 31,17,10

and we can refer to the first element as V(0), which happens to be 31. However, the same sequence of values could be called the vector U and could be defined in double precision as

U FDB 31,17,10

and the first element, now called U(0), is the first 2 words. To put the ith element of the first vector V into accumulator B, assuming that the integer i is in accumulator B, use the program segment

```
LDX    #V
ABX
LDAA   0,X
```

but to put the ith element of the second vector U into accumulator D, use

```
LDX    #U
ASLB
ABX
LDD    0,X
```

The ASLB instruction doubles the index to get the address of the first word to be put in accumulator B in the LDD instruction because each element takes 2 words.

A *list* is like a vector, being accessed by means of an index, but the elements of a list can be any combination of different precision words, characters, code words, and so on. For example, the list L can have three elements: the double precision number 5, the three characters ABC, and the single precision number 7. This list can be implemented in assembler language as follows:

```
L       FDB     5
        FCC     'ABC'
        FCB     7
```

and would be stored in machine code as follows:

```
                00
                05
                41
                42
                43
                07
```

Indexing can be used to get elements from a list, but since the elements can be different sizes, we can't use a simple computation on i to get the ith element. To get L(2), which is the single precision number 7, for example, we could execute the instruction LDAA L+5.

A *linked list* structure is a list in which some elements are addresses of (the first word in) other lists. A linked list structure is flexible and powerful and is widely used in advanced software. It can be useful in some interface applications and is concretely discussed in section 4-2.3 to show how simple it really is.

An *array* is a vector whose elements are vectors of the same length. We normally think of an array as a two-dimensional pattern, as in

```
        1       2       3
        4       5       6
        7       8       9
       10      11      12
```

If we consider the rows of the array as the elements of a vector that consists of rows, the data structure is called a *row major order* array. This can be implemented in assembler language as follows:

```
A1      FCB     1,2,3
        FCB     4,5,6
        FCB     7,8,9
        FCB     10,11,12
```

and row 0 is the vector 1,2,3. Alternatively, if the array is considered a vector of column vectors, the structure is a *column major order* array. Here, column 0 is the vector 1,4,7,10, and the array can be described in assembler language as

```
A2    FCB   1,4,7,10
      FCB   2,5,8,11
      FCB   3,6,9,12
```

Depending on which order is used, an element from the ith row and jth column can be extracted from an array by a polynomial evaluation. For example, in a row major order array where each row has n 1-word elements, the address of the (i,j)th element is

$$\text{address} = (i \times n) + j + \text{address of } A1(0,0)$$

Note that the MUL instruction can be used in the 6811 to compute array addresses. For instance, if n is 3, and i and j are in accumulators A and B respectively, the following routine will put $A1(i,j)$ into accumulator A

```
PSHB          SAVE FOR AFTER MULTIPLY
LDAB #3       PUT n INTO ACCUMULATOR B
MUL           MULTIPLY i IN ACCUMULATOR A BY n
TSX           GET TO TEMPORARY HOLDING SPOT FOR j
ADDB 0,X
ADCA #0       PROPAGATE CARRY
ADDD #A1      ADD ADDRESS OF A1(0,0) INTO X
XGDX          POINT X TO A1(i,j)
LDA   0,X     GET A(I,J) INTO ACCUMULATOR A
INS           BALANCE THE STACK
```

Note, however, that sometimes multiplication can be more easily done by shifting left and possibly adding the original to the shifted numbers. For example, multiplication of the value of accumulator B by 4 is more efficiently done by two executions of the instruction ASLB (or LSLD for 16-bit addresses). Finally, column major order arrays can be handled in like manner, essentially by exchanging i and j in the above examples.

Row major order arrays are just as useful as column major order arrays. However, if one often picks up consecutive words along the same row, then row major order is preferable, since these can be picked up by incrementing an index register rather than adding a constant to it, such as in the INX instruction. In general, the reader should be prepared in using arrays, to choose the representation of arrays that allows the greatest use of incrementing, rather than developing an unthinking preference for either row major order or column major order.

A *table* is to an array as a list is to a vector. It is a vector of identically structured lists (rows). Tables often store characters, where either a single character or a collection of n consecutive characters are considered elements of the lists in the table. Index addressing and the INX instruction are useful for accessing tables, especially if the tables are stored in row major order. If the index register points to the first word of any row, then the displacement can be used to access words in any desired column. Also, index addressing with INX can be used to select consecutive words from a row of the table.

2-1.3 Sequential Data Structures

The other important class of data structures is sequential structures, which are accessed by relative position. Rather than having an index i to get to any element of the structure, only the "next" element to the last one accessed may be accessed in a sequential structure. Strings, stacks, queues, and deques are sequential structures important in microcomputers.

A *string* is a sequence of elements such that after the ith element has been accessed, only the $(i+1)$st element can be accessed – or in some cases the $(i-1)$th or both – can be accessed. In particular, a string of ASCII-coded characters is a *character string* and is used to store text, such as the sequence of characters put into an assembler which embodies the program that is to be assembled. Strings are nicely handled by index addressing and the INX or DEX instructions.

Strings are so simple that they are hardly worth discussing, but they are so omnipresent that we must discuss them. In particular, we note the ways to identify the length of a string. They are:

1. Give the length of the string as a binary number. Put this number in a counter, say accumulator B, and use an instruction like DECB to count down as each character is read from the string.

2. Give the address of the end of the string. Suppose the string pointer is in X. Use an instruction like CPX to compare X to the end of the string.

3. Put a special character after the end of the string. Often the ASCII code for a carriage return ($0D) a line feed ($0A) or an END-OF-TEXT ($04) is put there. When the character is loaded, say into accumulator A, use CMPA #$0D or the equivalent to detect the end of the string.

4. Since ASCII codes are 7 bits long, set the sign bit of the last character to 1, the sign bits of the other characters being 0. As the character is loaded, say by a LDAA 0,X instruction, the end can be detected by a BMI instruction. You need to remove the sign bit by an ANDA #$7F instruction before using the ASCII character.

The characters you type on a terminal are usually stored in memory in a character string. You can use a typed word as a command to execute a routine, with unique words for executing each routine. The following routine, which begins at address SRCH, shows how a character string is stored and how it can be compared against another string, so it can jump to a routine if the two strings are equal. One string, presumably the one typed in the terminal, is stored in memory, and the address of the first character in the string is stored in the 2 words at ALPHA. The string that it is compared against (START) is stored at BETA, which is 5 characters long. The following routine will jump to STRT if the two strings are equal, otherwise it will go on to execute the next instruction after the label NOGD. (We also illustrate some of the assembler directives here that we have just discussed, such as NAM, END, and RMB 0.)

```
        NAM   SEARCH
        ORG   $100      PUT DATA AFTER LOCATION $100
ALPHA   RMB   2         RESERVE FOR ADDRESS OF INPUT STRING
BETA    FCC   'START'   CHARACTER STRING COMPARED AGAINST
        ORG   $200      PUT PROGRAM AFTER LOCATION $200
SRCH    LDX   ALPHA     GET ADDRESS OF STRING TYPED IN
        LDY   #BETA     GET ADDRESS OF STRING TO BE COMPARED
        LDAA  #5        SET LOOP FOR 5 EXECUTIONS
LOOP    LDAB  0,X       GET LETTER TYPED IN, MOVE POINTER
        CMPB  0,Y       COMPARE TO EQUIVALENT LETTER, MOVE PTR
        BNE   NOGD      STRINGS NOT EQUAL
        INX             MOVE  POINTERS
        INY
        DECA            COUNT DOWN
        BNE   LOOP      UNTIL 5 CHARACTERS COMPARED
        JMP   STRT      IF ALL 5 CHECK, THIS IS THE STRING, GO TO STRT
NOGD    RMB   0         IF SOME CHARACTER DIFFERS, CONTINUE HERE
        END
```

Inside the loop, we compare, one character at a time, the input string against the string START. If we detect any difference, we exit to label NOGD because the user did not type the string START. But if all five characters match up - the user did type the word START - the program jumps to the routine at STRT, presumably to start something.

Besides character strings, bit strings are important in microcomputers. In particular, a very nice coding scheme called the *Huffmann code* can pack characters into a bit stream and achieve about a 75% reduction in storage space when compared to storing the characters directly in an ASCII character string. It can be used to store characters more compactly and can also be used to transmit them through a communications link more efficiently. As a bonus, the encoded characters are very hard to decode without a code description, so you get a more secure communications link using a Huffmann code.

The code is rather like Morse code, in that frequently used characters are coded as short strings of bits, just as the often-used letter "e" is a single dot in Morse code. To insure that code words are unique and to suggest a decoding strategy, the code is defined by a tree having two branches at each branching point (*binary tree*), as shown in figure 2-1. The letters at each end (leaf) are represented by the pattern of 1s and 0's along the branches from the left end (root) to the leaf. Thus, the character string MISSISSIPPI can be represented by the bit string 111100010001011011010. Note that the ASCII string would take 88 bits of memory while the Huffmann string would take 21 bits. When you decode the bit string, start at the root and use each successive bit of the bit string to guide you up (if 0) or down (if 1) the next branch until you get to a leaf. Then copy the letter and start over at the root of the tree with the next bit of the bit string. The bit string has equal probabilities of 1s and 0's, so techniques used to decipher the code based on probabilities won't work. It is particularly hard to break a Huffmann code.

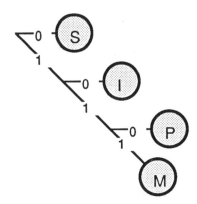

Figure 2-1. A Huffmann Coding Tree

Now that we have shown how nice the Huffmann code is, we must admit a few problems with it. To efficiently store some text, the text must be statistically analyzed to determine which letters are most frequent, to assign these the shortest codes. Note that S is most common, so we gave it a short code word. There is a procedure for generating the best Huffmann code, which is presented in many information theory books, but you have to get the statistics of each letter's occurrences to get that code. Nevertheless, though less than perfect, one can use a fixed code that is based on other statistics if the statistics are reasonably similar. Finally, although the code is almost unbreakable without the decoding tree, if any bit in the bit string is erroneous, your decoding routine can get completely lost. This may be a risk you decide to avoid because the code has to be sent through a communications link that is pretty error-free.

A *deque* is a generalized data structure that includes two special cases: the stack and the queue. A deque (pronounced deck) is a sequence of elements with two ends we call the top and the bottom. You can only access the top or bottom elements on the deque. You can *push an element on top* by placing it on top of the top element, which makes it the new top element, or you can *push an element on the bottom* making it the new bottom element. Or you can *pull (or pop) the top element* deleting the top element from the deque, making the next to top element the top element and putting the old top element somewhere else, or *pull (or pop) the bottom element* in like manner.

Deques are theoretically infinite, so you can push as many elements as you want on either the top or bottom: but practical deques have a maximum capacity. If this capacity is exceeded, we have an *overflow* error. Also, if you pull more elements than you push an *underflow error* exists. A deque is implemented in assembler language by allocating an area of N words of memory as a *buffer* for it, as with an assembler directive

DEQUE RMB $10

The buffer is an area of memory set aside for use as the deque expands, and cannot be used by any other data or program code. The programmer allocates as much room for the buffer as appears necessary for the worst case (largest) expansion of the deque.

Two pointers are used to read or write on the top or bottom, and a counter is used to detect overflow or underflow. Though the pointers are usually stored in memory, for simplicity we will assume that index register X points to the top of the deque and index register Y points to the bottom, and accumulator A contains the number of words in the deque. The deque is implemented by the use of index addressing and the DEX instruction to push words on the top, and index addressing and INX to pull words from the top. Similarly, index addressing and the INX instruction can be used to push words on the bottom, and index addressing and the DEX instruction can be used to pull words from the bottom. As words are pulled from top or bottom, more space is made available to push words on either the top or bottom. To take advantage of this, we think of the buffer as a ring or loop of words, so that the next word below the bottom of the buffer is the word on the top of the buffer. That way, as words are pulled from the top the memory locations can become available to store words pushed on the bottom as well as words pushed on the top, and vice versa. Then to initialize it, we can execute the following program segment:

```
        CLRA              SET COUNT TO 0
        LDX    #DEQUE     INITIALIZE TOP POINTER
        LDY    #DEQUE     INITIALIZE BOTTOM POINTER
```

To push a 1-word element from accumulator B on the top (lower address), execute:

```
        CPX    #DEQUE       SEE IF POINTER IS ON TOP OF BUFFER
        BNE    L1           IF SO
        LDX    #DEQUE+$11   PUT IT ON THE BOTTOM
L1      INCA                FIND NUMBER OF WORDS IN DEQUE
        CMPA   #$10         COMPARE WITH MAXIMUM NUMBER
        BLS    L2
        JMP    ERROR        IF TOO HIGH, THEN JUMP TO ERROR ROUTINE
L2      DEX
        STAB 0,X            PUT WORD ON TOP OF DEQUE, MOVE POINTER
```

And to pull a 1-word element into accumulator B from the top, use this routine

```
        DECA                DECREASE SIZE OF DEQUE
        BPL    L3
        JMP    ERROR        IF NEGATIVE, SIGNAL UNDERFLOW ERROR
L3      LDAB   0,X          GET DATA
        INX                 MOVE POINTER
        CPX    #DEQUE+$10   IF AT BOTTOM OF THE BUFFER
        BNE    L4           THEN REPLACE
        LDX    #DEQUE       AT TOP OF BUFFER
L4      RMB    0
```

Similar routines are used to push and pull the bottom word from the deque.

Note that you cannot really associate the ith word from either end of a deque with a particular location in memory. In fact, in a pure sense, you can only access the deque's top and bottom words and cannot read or write any other word in the deque. In practice, we sometimes access the ith element from the deque's top or bottom by using a displacement with the pointers that point to the top and bottom words – but this is not a pure deque. We call it an *indexable deque* to give it some name.

A *stack* is a deque in which you can push or pull on only one end. We have discussed the stack accessed by the stack pointer S, which permits the machine to push or pull words from the top of the stack to save registers for subroutine calls, as well as SWI and hardware interrupts. Now we consider the stack as a special case of a deque. (Actually, the stack in the 6811 can be made a special case of indexable deque using the TSX instruction with index addressing.) It is an example of a stack that pushes or pulls elements from the top only. Another equally good stack can be created that pushes or pulls elements only from the bottom of the deque. In fact, if you want two different stacks in your memory, have one that pushes and pulls from the top and another that pushes and pulls from the bottom. Then both stacks can share the same buffer, as one starts at the top of this buffer (lowest address) and builds downward, while the other starts at the bottom (highest address) and builds upward. A stack overflow exists when the top pointer of the stack that builds upward is equal to the bottom pointer of the stack that builds downward. Note that if one stack is shorter, then the other stack can grow longer before an overflow exists, and vice versa. You only have to allocate enough words in the buffer for the maximum number of words that will be in both at the same time.

Programs to push or pull on the two stacks are simpler than the general program that operates on the general deque, because the pointers do not roll around the top or bottom of the buffer. The 6811 PSHA, PULA, and similar instructions push or pull from one stack, while the other increments and decrements using INY and DEY with Y index addressing; for instance, the operation to push accumulator A is implemented as STAA 0,Y INY, and to pull accumulator A, as DEY LDAA 0,Y. Note that Y points 1 word below the deque's bottom. This extra stack will shortly be used in the discussion of multiple precision arithmetic functions.

The final structure that is important in microcomputer systems is the *queue*. This is a deque in which we can push data on one end and pull data from the other end. In some senses, it is like a shift register, but it can expand if more words are pushed than are pulled (up to the size of the buffer). In fact, it has been called an elastic shift register. Queues are used to store data temporarily, such that the data can be used in the same order in which they were stored.

Other data structures – such as multidimensional arrays, PL/I structures, trees, partially ordered sets, and banyan graphs – are important in general programming. You are invited to pursue the study of data structures to improve your programming skills. However, this section has covered the data structures we have found most useful in microcomputer interface software.

2-2 Writing Clear Programs

The MC68HC11, with 8K words of ROM, is large enough to consider the advantages of writing clear programs over the expense of writing short programs. The Motorola 6805 has so little memory – 2K words of ROM – that static efficiency is paramount, and the programs are so short that readability is less important to a good programmer, who can comprehend them even if they are unclearly written. When a program is larger than 16K, readability is significant – even for a good programmer – because it may have to be written by several programmers who read each other's code, and may have to be maintained long after the original programmers have gone. The MC68HC11 is right in the middle. Sometimes, when a large program must fit into the 8K ROM and static efficiency is critical, a clear programming style may be sacrificed, but it should be used when there is room, even if memory will be wasted. Moreover, good style can even be used when static efficiency must be optimized and some nonstandard trick will shorten the program code.

A significant technique for writing clear programs is good documentation, such as comments and flow charts. Of course, these do not take up memory in the machine code, so they can be used when static efficiency must be optimized. Another technique is the use of consistent programming styles that constrain the programmer, thereby reducing the chance of errors and increasing the reader's ease of understanding. Also, a major idea in clear programming methodology is modular top-down design.

2-2.1 Documentation

Documentation consists of comments and flow charts that describe the program. We will make some obvious statements about comments, introduce the use of high-level languages to provide comments, and correlate high-level languages with flow charts.

Some rather obvious things can be said about writing comments. After each instruction is written in assembler language, a comment can be written in the remainder of the line. You should use this opportunity to explain what you are doing. However, you may be tempted to rewrite the instruction, as in

LDAA ALPHA LOAD ACCUMULATOR A WITH ALPHA

This, of course, doesn't make sense. The comment should explain the strategy you are using, rather than repeat what you are doing. If several instructions in a program segment perform one function, you can write the English sentence that describes what is going on, with part of the sentence on each line, as in

```
LDAA   ALPHA    IF ALPHA IS NOT THE SAME
CMPA   BETA     AS BETA, THEN GO
BNE    L1       TO TEST THE NEXT ENTRY
```

It is also better to use meaningful self-documenting labels than labels like ALPHA and L1. Then comments may not be needed to explain the code's logic. For example, if ALPHA in the preceding program is the current "priority," BETA is the last "priority," and L1 is a program segment that tests the next entry, we can use labels (abbreviated to six letters, or whatever the assembler permits) as in

```
LDAA   CURPTY
CMPA   LSTPTY
BNE    TSTNXT
```

so the code is self-documenting. In much of this book, we must combine bit values into a control word for an I/O device. The use of equates can assist in documentation by providing self-documenting labels that add up (or OR up) the bit values. For example, if a control register of some I/O device is such that bit 7 (the sign bit) enables interrupts, bit 4 starts the I/O device, and bit 0 (least significant bit) makes it run at half speed, we can define labels at the beginning of a program

```
ENINT   EQU   %10000000
START   EQU   %00010000
HLFSP   EQU   %00000001
```

so that later in the program we can write a self-documenting program segment

```
LDAA      #ENINT+START+HLFSP
STAA      CNTRL
```

A line beginning in an asterisk (*) is considered a comment. Several such lines can be used to insert remarks in a program. It is particularly useful to put them in front of a subroutine to explain how it is used, so the reader does not have to scrutinize the entire subroutine to determine this. More will be said about this after subroutines are discussed.

Since we have been saddled with the English language – perhaps the most imprecise of all languages, although expressive and beautiful – documentation in English is subject to misinterpretation. An alternative is to use a high-level programming language in comments in assembler language programs to explain what is going on. Among well-known high-level languages, C is closest to assembler language. We will use C in this book. For those who understand C, the assembler language program will be precisely explained by the C program in the comments.

A slightly different mode of programming is to write the original program in a high-level language like C, get the compiler to generate assembler language (in ASCII), then modify that assembler program and assemble it into machine code. Experience has shown that the average programmer can write something like 10 lines of (debugged and documented) code per day, whether the language is assembler or higher level. But a line of high-level language code produces about 6 to 20 useful lines of assembler language code, so if the program is originally written in a high-level language and later translated into assembler language, we might become six to twenty times more efficient. However, assembler language code produced by a high-level language is significantly less statically and dynamically efficient than the best code produced by writing in assembler language. Thus, after a high-level language program is written, it is usually converted first to assembler language, where it is tidied up, after which the assembler language program is assembled into machine code. As a bonus, the original high-level language can be used to provide comments to the assembler language program.

There is a cross-compiler on UNIX V to compile C programs for the 6811, so after one writes a C program for the 6811, one gets the assembler language code that is developed. Moreover, the Motorola 6809 microprocessor, which is quite similar to the

6811, has a number of C compilers, especially for the OS9 operating system on it. Thus, one can write a C program for the 6809, get the 6809 assembler language code that is developed, and translate this by hand or with the help of a program into 6811 assembler language code, which can then be cleaned up and assembled.

To use the C language as a documentation tool, or to write the original program in C and translate it to assembler language, we introduce C language rudiments. We will explain the basic form of a C procedure, the simple and the special numeric operators, conditional expression operators, conditional and loop statements, functions, and "pigeon C" useful in documentation. However, we do not intend to give all the rules of C that you need to write good programs.

A C program consists of one or more procedures, the first of which is called main, and the others "subroutines." All the procedures, including main, are written as follows:

> *declaration of global variable;*
> *declaration of global variable;*
>
>   .
>
> *procedure_name(parameter_1,Parameter_2,...)*
> *declaration of parameter_1;*
> *declaration of parameter_2;*
>
>   .
>
> *{*
>   *declaration of local variable;*
>   *declaration of local variable;*
>
>   .
>
>   *statement;*
>   *statement;*
>
>   .
>
> *}*

Each *declaration of a parameter or a variable* and each statement ends in a semicolon (;), and two or more of these can be put on the same line. Carriage returns and spaces (except in names and numbers) are not significant in C programs and can be used to improve readability. The periods (.) in the example do not appear in C programs, but are meant here to denote that one or more declaration or statement may appear. Parameters and variables used in the 6811 are usually 8-bit (*char*) or 16-bit (*int*) types. More than one variable can be put in a declaration; the variables are separated by commas (,). A vector having *n* elements is denoted by the name and square brackets around the number of elements *n*, and the elements are numbered 0 to *n*-1. For example, the declaration *int a,b[10];* shows two variables, a scalar variable *a* and a vector *b* with ten elements. Variables declared outside the procedure are global, and those declared within a procedure are local. *Statements* may be algebraic expressions that generate assembler language instructions to execute the procedure's activities. A *statement* may be replaced by *{statement; statement; ...}*. (This will be useful in conditional and loop statements discussed soon.) Operators used in statements include the usual ones for addition, subtraction, multiplication, and division, and a number of very useful operators that convert efficiently to assembler language instructions or program segments. Table 2-3 shows the conventional operators that we will use in the C programs in this text. Although they are not all necessary, we will use a lot of parentheses in our C programs so we will not have to learn the precedence rules of C grammar.

Table 2-3. Conventional C Operators Used in Expressions

=	make the left side equal to the expression on its right
+	add
-	subtract
*	multiply
/	divide
%	modulus (remainder after division)
&	logical bit-by-bit AND
|	logical bit-by-bit OR
~	logical bit-by-bit negation

The following example of a simple C program using these declarations and statements assigns 2 to a, 3 to b, and then puts the $a+b$ th element of the ten-element vector c into d.

```
main()
{
 int a,b,c[10],d;
 a = 2; b = 3;
 d = c[a+b];
}
```

Some very powerful special operators are available in C. Table 2-4 shows the ones we use in this book. For each operator, an example is given together with its equivalent result using the simple operators of table 2-3.The assignment operator = returns the value it assigns so that value can be used in an expression to the left of the assignment operation: the example shows 0 is assigned to c, and that value (0) is assigned to b, and then that value is assigned to a. The increment operator ++ can be used without an assignment operator, as shown on the next line, or in an expression in which it increments its operand after the former operand value is returned to be used in the expression. For example, $a[i++]$ will use the old value of i as an index to get $a[i]$, then it will increment i. Similarly, the decrement operator -- can be used in expressions. If the ++ or -- appear in front of the variable, then the value returned by the expression is the updated value; $a[++i]$ will first increment i, then use the incremented value as an index into a. The next two rows show the use of the + and = operators used together to represent adding to a variable, and - and = together to represent subtracting from a variable. The last two rows of table 2-4 show shift left and shift right operations and their equivalents in terms of multiplication or division by powers of 2.

Table 2-4. Special C Operators **Table 2-5.** Conditional Expression Operators

operator	example	equivalent to:
=	a=b=c=0;	a=0;b=0;c=0;
++	a++;	a=a+1;
--	a-;	a=a-1;
+=	a+=2;	a=a+2;
-=	a-=2;	a=a-2;
<<	a<<3	a*8
>>	a>>3	a8

&&	AND
||	OR
!	NOT
>	Greater Than
<	Less Than
>=	Greater than or Equal
<=	Less Than or Equal
==	Equal to
!=	Not Equal To

A statement can be conditional, or it can involve looping to execute a sequence of statements which are written within it many times. We will discuss these control flow statements by giving the flow charts for them. (See figure 2-2 for conditional statements, 2-3 for case statements, and 2-4 for loop statements. We will refer to these figures throughout the remainder of this book whenever a program we write fits one of these simple standard forms.)

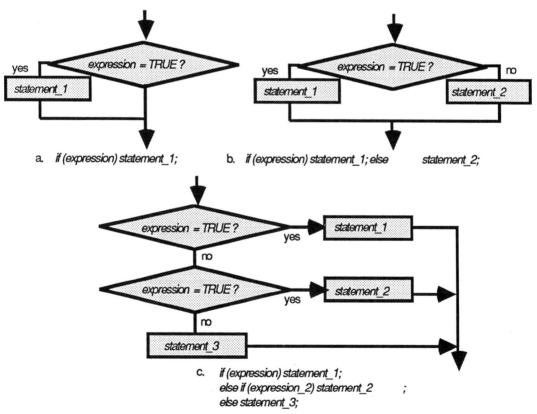

a. *if (expression) statement_1;*

b. *if (expression) statement_1; else   statement_2;*

c. *if (expression) statement_1;*
    else if (expression_2) statement_2   ;
    else statement_3;

Figure 2-2. Conditional Statements

Simple conditional expressions of the form *if then* (shown in figure 2-2a) full conditionals of the form *if then else* (shown in Figure 2-2b) and extended conditionals of the form *if then else if then else if then ... else* use conditional expression operators (shown in table 2-5). (In the last conditional expression, the *else if* part can be repeated as many times as needed, and the last part of the expression is an *else*.) Variables are compared using *relational operators* (> and <), and these are combined using *logical operators* (&&). For example, *(a>5)&&(b<7)* is true if *a* > 5 and *b* < 7.

Consider a conditional expression like *if(alpha>0) beta=10; else if(gamma ==0) delta++; else if((epsilon!=0)&&(zeta==1)) beta=beta<<3; else beta=0;* where each variable is *char*. We use this example because it contains many operators just discussed. This can be coded in assembler language as

```
         TST     APLHA   if (alpha>0)
         BLE     L1
         LDAA    #10      eta = 10;
         STAA    BETA
         BRA     L4
L1       TST     GAMMA   else if( gamma ==0)
         BNE     L2
         INC     DELTA    delta++;
         BRA     L4
L2       TST     EPSILN   else if((epsilon != 0)
         BEQ     L3
         LDAA    ZETA     &&(zeta==1))
         CMPA    #1
         BNE     L3
         ASL     BETA     beta=beta<<3;
         ASL     BETA
         ASL     BETA
         BRA     L4
L3       CLR     BETA     else beta=0;
L4       RMB     0
```

Note that the program comments are simple, concise, and accurate – a tribute to the value of C as a documentation language.

A useful alternative to the conditional statement is the *case* statement. (See figure 2-3.) An expression giving a numerical value is compared to each of several possible comparison values, then the matching comparison value determines which statement will be executed next. The case statement (such as the simple one in figure 2-3a) jumps into the statements just where the variable matches the comparison value and executes all the statements below it. The *break* statement can be used (as shown in figure 2-3b) to exit the whole case statement after a statement in it is executed, in lieu of executing the remaining statements in it.

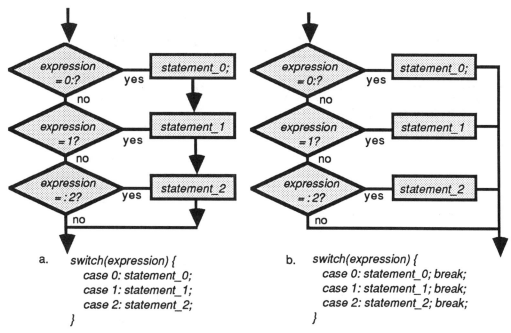

a. switch(expression) {
        case 0: statement_0;
        case 1: statement_1;
        case 2: statement_2;
    }

b. switch(expression) {
        case 0: statement_0; break;
        case 1: statement_1; break;
        case 2: statement_2; break;
    }

Figure 2-3. Case Statements.

Consider an expression like *switch(letter){ case 'g': i=1; break; case 'r': i=2; break; case 's': i=3;break;}*. This can be coded in assembler language as

```
LDAA  LETTER          switch(letter) {
      CMPA #'g         case 'g':
      BNE   L1
      LDAA #1          i=1;
      BRA   L3         break;
L1    CMPA #'r         case 'r':
      BNE   L2
      LDAA #2          i=2;
      BRA   L3         break;
L2    CMPA #'s         case 's':
      BNE   L4
      LDAA #3          i=3;
L3    STAA I           NOTE THAT I IS STORED HERE FOR EACH CASE
L4    RMB  0           }
```

Note again the simplicity of the C comments. However, we observe a "trick" that improves static efficiency in the second to the last line: the code that stores the value assigned to variable *i* is put in one place rather than in each case, as suggested by the C program statement. You should explain such an optimization result with a comment.

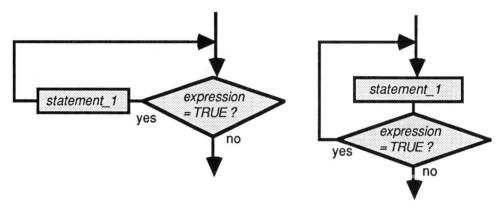

a. *while(expression) statement;*   b. *do statement while (expression);*

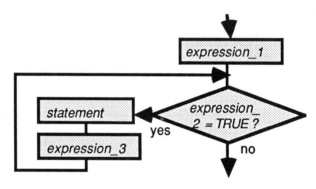

c. *for(expression_1;expression_2;expression_3)statement;*

Figure 2-4. Loop Statements

Loop statements can be used to repeat a statement until a condition is met. A statement within the loop statement will be executed repeatedly. The *while* statement of figure 2-4a tests the condition before the loop is executed and is useful if, for example, a loop may have to be done 0 times; the *do while* statement tests the condition after the loop is executed at least once, but it tests the result of the loop's activities. The expressions in both these loop statements are exactly like the expressions of the conditional statements, using operators as shown in table 2-5. The very powerful *for* statement (shown in figure 2-4c) has three expressions separated by semicolons (;). The first expression is used to initialize variables used in the loop; the second is a test for completion in the same style as the while statement; and the third is used to update the variables each time after the loop is executed. Any of the expressions in the *for* statement may be omitted. The *break* statement will cause the *for, while,* or *do while* loop to terminate just as in the *case* statement, and is used in a conditional statement. For instance, *for(;;) {i++; if(i==30) break;}* executes the statement *{i++; if(i==30) break;}* indefinitely, but the loop is terminated when *i* is 30. For example, the statement *for(i=0;i<10;i++) alpha[i]=0;* will clear the (first 10) elements of the array *alpha*. It can be coded in assembler language as follows:

```
        LDX    #0        for(i=0;
L1      CPX    #10               i<10;
        BHI    L2
        CLR    ALPHA,X          alpha[i]=0;
        INX                            i++)
        BRA    L1
L2      RMB    0
```

Note the indenting of the comments so the *for* statement can be seen as a whole, because the last expression of the *for* statement is done after the statement within the *for* statement. This program segment is only useful if the array *alpha* is on page 0, and is not particularly statically efficient. A more efficient assembler language program is

```
*for(i=9;i ! = 0; ) alpha[i--]=0;
        LDX    #ALPHA+9
        LDAB   #9
L1      CLR    0,X
        DEX
        DECB
        BNE    L1
```

If the C statement only suggests the assembler language statements as a group, it can be put on one comment line rather than splitting it between lines.

An important feature of C is its ability to describe variables and addresses of variables. If *a* is a variable, then *&a* is the address of *a*. If *a* is a variable that contains an address of another variable *b*, then **a* is the contents of the word pointed to by *a*, which is the contents of *b*. (Note that *a*b* is *a* times *b* but **b* is the contents of the word pointed to by *b*.) Whenever you see *&*, read it as "address of" and whenever you see ***, read it as "contents of word pointed to by."

ASCII codes of characters and strings are enclosed by quotes; for example,*'a'* is the ASCII code of the single letter *a*, and *"ALPHA"* is the ASCII code of the character string consisting of the code of *'A'* followed by the code of *'L'*, and so on.

A procedure may be called by another procedure. However, to get the result of a procedure out of it, we need to use a technique that is introduced in a later section. A procedure may be used as a function. The value returned by the function is put in a *return statement*. For instance, the function *power* can be written

```
    power(i,j)
    int i,j;
    {
      int k,n;
      n=1;
      for(k=0;k<j;k++) n=n*i;
      return(n);
    }
```

This function can be called by a statement *a=power(b,2)*.

The final feature of C we need is the comment: anything enclosed by /* and */ . This is useful, in writing "*pigeon C*" programs, to specify an operation. For example, we can write a specification for a program that, when getting a key command from a keyboard, and executes a "go" operation if the key is *'g'*, a reverse operation if *'r'*, and a stop operation if *'s'*:

```
main()
{
  char keycode;
  /* get a key into keycode */
  switch (keycode) {
    case 'g': /* go */; break;
    case 'r': /* reverse */; break;
    case 's': /* stop */; break;
  }
}
```

The flow chart for this program is shown in figure 2-3b. A "pigeon C" program can also call procedures that are themselves not written yet, but are clearly understood.

When an assembler language program is written, a flow chart should be given (unless it is trivial), and the equivalent C program should be shown. Other comments should be added to explain special requirements or "tricky" operations. In particular, subroutines should be extensively commented, as we discuss later. This section provides enough information about C so you can use it to document assembler language programs.

2-2.2 Programming Style

We conform our programming techniques to some style to make the program easier to read, debug, and maintain. Although this constraint generally produces less efficient code, the use of a consistent style is recommended, especially in longer programs where there is enough memory, but not where static efficiency is paramount. One programming style – discussed first – is to rigidly enforce reentrancy and use some conventions to make this rather automatic. The second programming style we discuss – structured programming – uses only simple conditional and loop operations and avoids GOTO statements. After this we discuss top-down and bottom-up programming. The final style we describe is the rigid enforcement of position independence, a style easier to enforce in more powerful architectures like the Motorola 6809 and 68000 but which can be enforced with some loss of efficiency in the 6811.

Program segments may have multiple entry points and multiple exit points. (See figure 2-5.) Such a program segment occurs anywhere in a program, usually a part written on consecutive lines. An *entry point* is any instruction that may be executed after an instruction not in the program segment, and an *exit point* is any instruction that may be followed by an instruction not in the program segment. A program segment may or may not be a subroutine; when it is, the discussion here also applies to the next section on subroutines.

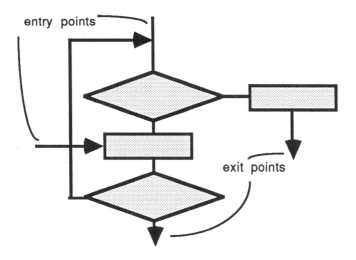

entry points

exit points

Figure 2-5. A Program Segment

The main problem in writing good programs is the handling of variables. Variables used in programs are local or global. *Local variables* are temporary variables used only by one program segment. *Global variables* are variables shared by two or more program segments. For example, several program segments may be written to handle a floppy disc, and global variables may be used to keep track of the floppy disc's status, so all program segments can access those variables. Only variables shared by several routines, which are to be located independent of the order of calling subroutines, are global variables.

In the 6811, local variables should be stored on the stack, for reasons which will be given at the end of this discussion. In the 6811, if global variables are short, they should be stored on the direct page, or if they would use too much of the direct page, their address could be stored on the direct page to be loaded into an index register efficiently. However, the ability to use index addressing on the stack in the 6811 encourages the use, whenever possible, of dynamic local variables rather than global variables.

A convention that greatly aids a program's clarity is this:
1. Determine what a program segment will be. Usually it is a subroutine.
2. Determine what variables in the program segment are local. These are temporary variables used in the program segment and not anywhere else.
3. On *each* entry point to the program segment, allocate *all* the local variables at once and in the same way on each entry point; and on *each* exit point, deallocate *all* the local variables in the same way, as shown next. Do *not* push or pull anything on the stack in the rest of the program segment (only nesting is permitted, as discussed later).

To allocate local variables on the stack, we move the stack pointer towards lower memory. We can make room for *n* variables at once by the sequence:

```
        TSX
        XGDX
        SUBD #n
        XGDX
        TXS
```

Of course, for less than 7 bytes of local storage, use as many DES instructions as needed. In that case, use TSX at the end to make X point to the top of the stack, for reasons that appear shortly. We can deallocate *n* local variables by the instruction sequence

```
        TSX
        XGDX
        ADDD #n
        XGDX
        TXS
```

Of course, for less than 7 bytes of local storage, use as many INS instructions as needed.

If the allocation just described is done on each entry point, then X points to the top of the stack, and index addressing using X can access the local variables. Index register Y is available for handling data structures. If both index registers are needed, X can be easily restored to its position by TSX after its use for some other operation. In the preceding discussion, index register Y can be exchanged with X if that improves efficiency. For example, consider a procedure with some local variables

> *sub()*
> *{*
> *char j,k,l,m;*
> *j=k+l+m;*
> *}*

It is coded as:

```
SUB     DES             ALLOCATE
        DES             ALL FOUR
        DES             LOCAL
        DES             VARIABLES
        TSX             SET X
        LDAA  1,X       GET K
        ADDA  2,X       ADD L
        ADDA  3,X       ADD M
        STAA  0,X       PUT IN J
        INS             DEALLOCATE
        INS             ALL FOUR
        INS             LOCAL
        INS             VARIABLES
        RTS
```

Note that the declaration of variables in C directly corresponds to the allocation of variables in assembler language. Use equates to make the code more readable and to avoid bugs:

```
J       EQU   0
K       EQU   1
L       EQU   2
M       EQU   3
SUB     DES             ALLOCATE
        DES             ALL FOUR
        DES             LOCAL
        DES             VARIABLES
        TSX             SET X
        LDAA  K,X       GET K
        ADDA  L,X       ADD L
        ADDA  M,X       ADD M
        STAA  J,X       PUT IN J
        INS             DEALLOCATE
        INS             ALL FOUR
        INS             LOCAL
        INS             VARIABLES
        RTS
```

In the program segment, the local variables can each be *accessed using the same offset* from the X pointer (which points to the top of the stack) to get the local variables on the stack every time the variable is used, and S may be transferred to X any time X has to be restored, because we do not push or pull on the stack. Equates can be used to make this quite readable.

Normally, local variables are undefined when the program segment begins execution, and may have to be *initialized* before they have known values. That is, values may have to be put in the memory locations allocated for the variables. This is especially true of reentrant subroutines, and forgetting to initialize them is a common and insidious bug. Note that PSHA and similar instructions can simultaneously allocate and initialize the local variables for better efficiency.

Variables have to be deallocated at the end of the program segment. Note that deallocation can be done by PULA and similar instructions if the local variable is needed, such as when it is the return value of a function. Deallocation makes the physical memory available for another program segment so the same memory gets used over and over again. Memory is thus optimally used: the amount a program needs is just the sum of the number of local variables of the worst case nesting of program segments (including subroutines), where the worst case is a point in running the program where the largest number of local variables are stacked up.

In some block-structured languages like ALGOL and PASCAL the program blocks are written so the inner, lower-level blocks can access local variables of outer blocks, using the dynamic (run-time) calling sequence. This can also be done in assembler language programs. Within inner program segments, you can access local variables (called *dynamic local variables*) of outer program segments, if you know where they are located. You can locate them by knowing how many additional bytes have been allocated on the stack since the outer segment allocated the variable you access in the inner segment and adding this number to the offset you used, thus getting the variable in the outer program segment. Figure 2-6 shows the main idea. The local variable of an outer segment is accessed in an inner segment by using an offset equal to the offset used in the outer segment plus the number of bytes that have been allocated since the outer segment. (We assume the inner segment is not a subroutine, so there is no return address on the stack.) Of course, equates can be used to clarify the program. For instance, if the variable is ALPHA in the outer segment, we write APLHA EQU 0, and the first access to ALPHA in the outer segment can be written STAA ALPHA,X. The directive SGALCT EQU 2 can be put at the beginning of the inner segment, and the second access to ALPHA in the outer segment can be written LDAA ALPHA+SGALCT,X. After the inner segment is over, the third access to ALPHA in the outer segment is written LDAA ALPHA,X.

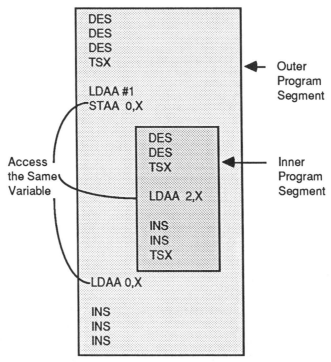

Figure 2-6. Nested Program Segments

One can use inner segments to pass arguments to subroutines using the stack. One can also use the stack as a very temporary variable, although this use is almost trivial. For example, the best way to transfer X to D is the sequence

```
PSHX
PULA
PULB
```

One can identify the allocation, initialization, and deallocation of this program segment, which is an inner program segment of a larger one, but it is rather trivial because no local variables are accessed in it, so we won't bother to make a big issue of it.

In the 6811, the use of the stack to store local variables is usually recommended. (With 8K words of ROM, there is usually enough room for extra instructions.) This technique optimally uses the scarce 256 words of RAM. Also, the programs become reentrant, so they can – as all such programs can – be used in interrupt handlers. You may never know when a routine may have to be used in a handler, so if it is already reentrant, you won't need to rewrite it. For example, we once wrote a text editor in which all the code was in some interrupt handler or another and the code in the main program did nothing. Also, you may use a routine that is not reentrant in a handler and find out that the resulting program works most of the time but fails sometime for no apparent reason – because an interrupt happened to occur while a non-reentrant program segment, being used by the handler, was being executed.

We now turn our attention to another programming style that can be used in microcomputers to improve the code's clarity. An element of *structured programming* is the use of single entry point, single exit point program segments. This style makes the program much more readable because, to get into a program segment, there are no circuitous routes which are hard to debug and test. The use of C for specification and documentation can force the use of this style. The conditional and loop statements described in the last section are single entry point, single exit point program segments and they are sufficient for almost all programs. The *while* loop technique is especially attractive because it tests the termination condition before the loop is done even once, so programs can be written that accommodate all possibilities, including doing the loop no times. And the *for* loop is essentially a beefed-up *while* loop. You can use just these constructs. That means avoiding the use of GOTO statements. Several years ago, Professor Edsger Dijkstra made the then controversial remark, "GOTOs Considered Harmful!" Now, most good programmers agree with him. The only significant exception is the reporting of errors. We sometimes GOTO an error reporting or correcting routine if an error is detected – an abnormal exit point for the program segment. We heard a story (from Harold Stone) that Professor Goto in Japan has a sign on his desk that says "Dijkstras Considered Harmful!" (Professor Goto denies this.) Errors can alternatively be reported by a convention such as using the carry bit to indicate the error status: you exit the segment with carry clear if no errors are found and exit with carry set if an error is found. Thus, all segments can have single exit points.

Top-down design is a program-writing methodology that has produced programs more quickly than adhoc and haphazard writing. The idea is to write a main program that calls subroutines (or just program segments) without yet writing the subroutines (or segments). A subroutine is used if a part of the program is called many times, and a program segment – not a subroutine – is used if a part of the program is used only once. The main program is executed to check that the subroutines and segments are called up in the proper order under all conditions. Then the subroutines (or segments) are written in lower level subroutines (or segments) which are then tested. This is continued until the lowest level subroutines (or segments) are written and tested. This methodology requires the use of superior documentation to describe the subroutine and program segments so they can be fully tested before they are actually written. "Pigeon C" is a very useful tool for that purpose. Also, the inputs and outputs of subroutines have to be carefully specified. This will be discussed at the end of the next section.

The inverse of top-down design is bottom-up design, in which the lowest level subroutines or program segments are written first and then fully debugged. These are built up, bottom to top, to form the main program. To test the subroutine, you write a short program to call the subroutine, expecting to discard this program when the next higher level program is written. Bottom-up design is especially useful in interface design. The lowest level subroutine which actually interfaces to the hardware is usually the trickiest to debug. This methodology lets you debug that part of the program with less interference from other parts. Bottom-up design is like solving an algebra problem with three separate equations in three separate unknowns, each equation being in one unknown. Whereas, putting all the software and hardware together before testing any part of it is like simultaneously solving three equations in three unknowns. As the first algebraic problem is much easier, the use of bottom-up design is also a much easier way to debug interfacing software. In a senior level interfacing course at the University of Texas, students who tried to get everything working at once spent 30 hours a week in lab, while those who used bottom-up design spent less than 10 hours a week on the same experiments.

Combinations of top-down and bottom-up design can be used. Top-down design works well with parts of the program that do not involve interfacing to hardware, and bottom-up design works better with parts that do involve interfacing.

Position independence can be enforced in the 6811, although that is not always desirable. The BSR, BRA, and conditional branch instructions provide for position independence for short programs. The long jumps, however, can be position independent using the following code in place of a jump such as JMP L2:

```
          BSR    L1
    L1    PULA
          PULB
          ADDD   #L2-L1
          PSHB
          PSHA
          RTS
```

Note that BSR is used as a kind of push PC, and RTS as a kind of pull PC instruction. The ADDD instruction adds the position independent displacement to the program counter. A similar segment may be used for jumps to subroutines. This kind of routine should only be used if the labels L1 and L2 are moved together as the program is moved around, such as when they are both in the same external ROM in an extended multiplexed bus mode MC68HC11. This provides the capability to write ROM that can be used in different systems, although they may appear in different places in each system's memory map. Because the same ROM can be used in more systems, its design cost is spread out over more users, and thus its cost is less. A ROM similar to the Motorola 6839, which is used in 6809 systems to provide floating point subroutines, could be made for the 6811; such a ROM should use position independent code.

In this section, we discussed some programming styles useful in larger programs on the 6811. These styles do not produce the most statically and dynamically efficient code, so they may not be useful if efficiency is required. However, the use of local variables on the stack to enforce reentrancy and conserve RAM memory is often desirable; the use of structured programming – especially single entry, single exit program segments – and the use of top-down and bottom-up design are often desirable; and the enforcement of position independence is occasionally necessary.

2-3   Subroutines and Arguments

One area, often inadequately understood, of great importance in microcomputer interfacing software is the way subroutines are called, and the way arguments are passed into them and results are passed from them. Since the instruction set of a typical microcomputer is rather limited, the kinds of functions usually needed in most applications are implemented as subroutines. In fact, the code generated by some high-level language compilers consists usually almost exclusively of subroutine calls, as we noted earlier. These techniques for programming subroutines are discussed in this section.

   The passing of arguments has two aspects. A conceptual or strategic aspect is associated with how you want the argument treated, and an implementation or tactical aspect is associated with how you actually do it. The conceptual aspect is often covered in computer science courses. It is especially important in high-level languages, because when you program in these languages you really don't care how the arguments are actually handled, provided they are handled in a conceptually consistent manner. Even in assembler language, the conceptual aspect is important because you want to know what you are doing in a strategic sense. We cover this first. The implementation aspect, discussed next, is also important to assembler language programmers because they must be concerned with how the arguments are passed. We then discuss the calling and returning mechanisms to show alternatives to the BSR and RTS instructions. Finally, we discuss the subroutine documentation and give a concise blueprint for writing subroutines with style.

2-3.1 Passing Parameters (Conceptual Level)

Conceptually, *arguments* or *parameters* are data passed from or to the calling routine to or from a subroutine, like the x in $sin(x)$. In an implementation, the parameter has either some register in the machine state or some storage location, with a symbolic address associated with that location inside the subroutine, such as y. It is called the *formal parameter*. The calling routine has a register or memory location with its symbolic address, available for the parameter that is usually different each place the subroutine is called. The register or memory location with its symbolic address in the calling routine is called the *actual parameter*. For example, at one place in the program we put *sin(alpha)*, in another, *sin(beta)*, and in another, *sin(gamma)*. *alpha*, *beta*, and *gamma* are actual parameters in these examples.

   At the conceptual level, arguments are called by value and result, reference, or name. In *call by value and result*, the formal parameters inside the subroutine are usually registers. The values of the actual parameters from the calling routine are really transferred from their memory locations in the calling routine to the registers in the subroutine before the subroutine begins to execute its operation. The values of formal parameters in the registers are moved to their actual parameters after the subroutine is finished. However, any mechanism whereby the actual values (rather than their addresses) are passed to the subroutine or actual results (rather than their addresses) are returned from the subroutine are called by value and result. In general, only parameters passed from the calling routine to the subroutine are moved before the subroutine begins execution, and only the results of the subroutine are copied into the calling routine's actual parameters after the end of a subroutine's execution, but the same formal parameter (register) can be used for input and output.

In *call by reference*, the data remains in the calling routine and is not actually moved to another location, but the address of the data is given to the subroutine and the subroutine uses this address to get the data whenever it needs to. Large vectors, lists, arrays, and other data structures can be more effectively called by reference so they don't have to be copied into and out of the subroutine's local variables. Conceptually, arguments passed in call by reference are evaluated just before the subroutine is called and are not reevaluated as the subroutine is executed. If an argument is called by reference, you should normally use it only for input, or only for output, and not both, since input arguments are supposed to behave as if they were evaluated just before the subroutine call, and are supposed to stay that way throughout the subroutine.

The last mechanism, *call by name,* allows complex actual arguments to be passed to a subroutine. These actual parameters are effectively (if not actually) inserted into every occurrence of the corresponding formal parameters inside the subroutine and are reevaluated each time they are met as the subroutine is executed. Call by name is useful when you want to refer to an argument by its address but you change it in the subroutine, so it has different values at different times in the subroutine. Call by name is also useful when actual parameters are subroutines, for example, as arguments to another subroutine. If you wrote a subroutine called *plot* to plot a graph, you could pass an argument that would be the address of a subroutine like *sin* – as in *plot(&sin)* – and *sin* would be reevaluated each time the *plot* routine was ready to plot a new point on the graph. If you used call by reference, the argument *sin* would be evaluated just once, just before the subroutine was entered, so your plot would be a straight line. Finally, conceptually, call by name is used to handle error conditions. One argument – the address of a subroutine to go to if an error is detected – is only executed if the error occurs and so is a call by name argument.

In C, the & and * operators are used to indicate call by name. Otherwise, (scalar) parameters are passed in call by value, and the result of a function is passed in call by result. Parameters inside the parentheses can only be passed into the procedure and not out of it. Suppose a procedure is used to evaluate the power of a number instead of a function, as was used earlier. We can use call by name to get the result of the operation out of the procedure. The procedure is written

```
power(i,j,n)
int i,j,*n;
{
  int k;
  n=1;
  for(k=0;k<j;k++) n=n*i;
}
```

and the calling routine calls up such a procedure with *power(i,3,&r)*. In the procedure, the result is put in the last parameter. As parameters inside the parentheses are only put into the procedure, we pass the address of the result into the procedure (hence the & in front of the actual parameter *r*). Inside the procedure, when we declare the third formal parameter, we use * to say that the word *n* points to is an integer. The C compiler generates the correct code for using the address to get the value out of the procedure. Using call by name, C can pass the address of a parameter into the procedure, so data can be returned from the procedure using that address.

2-3.2 Passing Parameters (Implementation Level)

We now consider implementation details of the 6811's subroutine call arguments. The passing of arguments is implemented by means of registers, global variables, a stack, an argument list, or a table. In discussing these techniques, we'll be concerned with 6811 features useful in carrying them out.

In the 6811, the X,Y, and D (or A and B) registers can serve to hold arguments or results. While the index registers naturally lend themselves to passing addresses – in call by reference or call by name – these can be transferred to or exchanged with the D register using XGDX or XGDY instructions, so they can also be used to pass parameters by value. Also, the carry bit in the condition code register can be used to pass a 1-bit result that can be used in instructions like BCC and BCS. If a subroutine does not have many arguments, this is usually the best way, being easy to understand and use, to pass them. Its main disadvantage is that it is not completely general. Most high-level languages need a completely general technique because compilers are usually not smart enough to pass parameters some ways to some subroutines and other ways to other subroutines. Therefore, if you want to use a subroutine that was written to be called by a high-level language routine or you want to write a subroutine that can be called by a high-level language routine, you may have to pass the arguments in one of the ways described next.

In an example of passing arguments by registers, assume all variables are of type *char* and the calling routine is *m=power(h,3);*. The subroutine is described in C as

```
power(i,j)
char i,j;
{
  char n;
  n=1;
  for( ;j>0 ;j--) n=n*i;
  return(n);
}
```

This is coded in assembler – first the calling routine, then the subroutine – as follows

```
        LDAA H
        LDAB #3
        BSR   POWER          m=power(h,3);
        STAB M
```

```
POWER   PSHA            power(i,
        PSHB            j) char i,j;
        TSY
        LDAB #1         char n; n=1
L1      DEC  0,Y        for( ; j<0;j--)
        BMI  L2
        LDAA 1,Y        n=n *i;
        MUL
        BRA  L1
L2      INS             BALANCE THE STACK
        INS
        RTS             return(n);
```

An argument can be put in a global variable, and then the subroutine can find the argument there. Results can be passed in the other direction through global variables. This is like supplying arguments through FORTRAN COMMON. It is too easy to forget to supply one of the critical arguments, and it is easy to use the same location inadvertently to supply an argument to a subroutine that calls another, and for that subroutine to supply an argument to the subroutine that it calls. Also, arguments for one subroutine can accidentally get mixed up with arguments in another subroutine. To diagram such a situation, we use *coat hanger diagrams*. (See figure 2-7.) Each horizontal row represents the execution of a routine or subroutine, and the calling and returning points are shown as breaks in the line. If we use a global variable like ARG1 in the first subroutine after another subroutine (perhaps several levels down) that also uses the variable ARG1 is called, then the first subroutine will have the wrong value in ARG1 when it uses ARG1. Finally, such a technique is not reentrant. Global variables have to be used to pass arguments in very small computers like the 6805. There is no way to get to the stack or the return address to use the techniques described next. However, if either of these paths is available in the architecture, global variables should be avoided. We recommend against passing arguments in global variables.

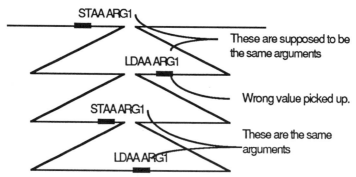

Figure 2-7. Coat Hanger Diagram Showing a Bug Using Global Variables

The stack provides a completely general mechanism for passing arguments. Suppose the argument X for the subroutine SIN(X) is in accumulator A. To call the subroutine SIN, execute the following program segment:

```
PSHA
BSR SIN
```

Inside the subroutine, we can get the value of the argument, but the obvious way will not work. Do *not* execute the instruction

```
PULA
```

This will pull the high byte of the return address into A, rather than the argument you want. However, because the argument is the third word from the top of the stack, it can be picked up as follows:

```
TSX
LDAA 2,X
```

When the subroutine is finished, the RTS instruction is used to pull the 2-word return address from the stack. But we are not through. The argument is still on top of the stack. If the calling routine is itself a subroutine, when it executes its RTS instruction, it will pull the argument from the stack into the program counter and jump to some dangerous place. After the subroutine has returned to the calling routine, the calling routine must remove the argument (balance the stack). To delete it, you could use a PULA instruction, or, if the argument is no longer needed, an INS instruction. You should recognize this as the special nested program segment case discussed in the last section, whereby the subroutine is (dynamically) executed within the small program segment that puts the arguments on the stack for the subroutine, using the same rules to find variables on the stack for subroutines as were used in inner and outer program segments. You can also think of this as providing "holes on the stack" through which to pass the arguments.

Any number of arguments can be pushed onto the stack this way, and can, if the instruction TSX is used at the beginning of the subroutine, be accessed inside the subroutine using index addressing with the X register. Values can be passed in the manner described, as can addresses be passed for call by reference, or subroutine addresses for call by name. As an example of the latter, the *plot* subroutine may need an argument which is the subroutine of the function to be plotted, such as the SIN routine. To pass the address of the *sin* subroutine, we can execute this routine:

```
LDX    #SIN
PSHX
BSR    PLOT
```

(The preceding example is not position independent, but can be made so.) Inside the *plot* subroutine, to call the *sin* subroutine, the instruction

```
TSX
LDX    2,X
JSR    0,X
```

can be used. Note that after the *plot* subroutine returns to the calling routine, the argument must be deleted from the stack so two INS instructions can be used.

Results can also be returned on the stack, but again the obvious way doesn't work. If, inside the subroutine, you push a result on the stack, then return and expect to pull it from the stack, the return instruction RTS will pull the result before you can, which will effect a jump to some unknown place. Rather, a "hole" for the result is inserted on the stack before the subroutine is called; the result can be put in the hole with a technique that is the reverse of the one used to pass arguments to the subroutine. Again, this is just a special case of the inner and outer program segment access mechanism described in the last section. The calling routine can be written

```
DES
BSR    SIN
PULA
```

And the subroutine can put the result in the "hole" by executing the instructions

```
TSX
STAA 2,X
```

Note that any number of results can be passed this way. Before the subroutine is called, a "hole" must be created for each result, and, to balance the stack after the subroutine has returned to the calling routine, each result must be pulled from the stack (or deleted). Thus, the stack is a completely general technique for passing arguments and results.

If a second stack is used, not the one used to save the return address, then arguments can be pushed on that stack by the calling routine and pulled by the subroutine, without fear of messing up the return addresses or having them in the way. This technique is especially useful for arithmetic routines and will be used in section 2-4.

The next technique for passing arguments is the *argument list*. It is almost as general as the stack technique, and is the most commonly used for high-level language subroutines. A high-level language subroutine call, like the FORTRAN statement

```
CALL SUB (A,B,C)
```

is most efficiently implemented (using call by reference) in assembler language as the following code:

```
BSR    SUB
FDB    A,B,C
```

Note that the microprocessor, when it executes the BSR instruction, saves what it thinks is the return address, which is actually the address of the word below the BSR instruction. That turns out to be fortuitous. It helps us get to the argument list, which is the list of addresses created by the FDB directive. To put the value of the word at address C into accumulator B inside the subroutine, execute the following program segment:

```
TSX
LDX   0,X    GET THE ADDRESS OF THE ARGUMENT LIST IN X
LDX   4,X    GET THE THIRD ARGUMENT INTO X
LDAB  0,X    GET THE VALUE OF C INTO ACCUMULATOR B
```

Note that once one of the index registers, like X, points to the argument list, any argument can easily be obtained by repeated use of index addressing. If C is the address of an array, that address can be put into an index register so index addressing can be used to access words in that array, as follows:

```
TSX
LDX   0,X    GET ADDRESS OF ARGUMENT LIST
LDX   4,X    GET ADDRESS OF ARRAY INTO X
```

Similarly, values can be passed and arguments can be called by name, through the argument list. Note that simple execution of RTS will not work, because the first argument will be executed as an instruction. Rather, if the argument list is 6 words long, we can execute the following program segment rather than the RTS:

```
PULX
JMP   6,X
```

What makes this technique only *almost* completely general is that, especially in microcomputers, the program may be stored in read-only memory so it doesn't have to be loaded each time power is turned on. This means that the argument list, in read-only memory, cannot be changed. So if arguments are to be called by value, they cannot be placed in the argument list unless they are the same each time the subroutine is called from that place. That condition sometimes occurs, and we'll discuss an example with the SWI "subroutine" call shortly. Although not completely general, it is faster than the stack approach because the calling routine does not have to set up and delete the arguments. It can also be used by subroutines called by high-level language programs. Moreover, it can pass the relative address of a local variable on the stack, as long as this address is added to the stack pointer value when it is used, thus giving a reentrant capability to the calling program that is absent if the address is a global address.

A final technique is to pass, using an index register, the address of a list or table into the subroutine. The contents of the list can be essentially the same as the argument list just described, but since the list need not be in ROM, its elements can be modified and replaced with the results before the subroutine is called. The code to do this is essentially the same as for in-line argument lists, except the address of the table must be loaded into the index register before the call is made to the subroutine, and the subroutine need not extract the return address from the stack, nor need it branch around the argument list. Passing the address of a list is often used in subroutines that handle disks, because the same list can be used as an argument for different disk handling subroutines that access the same disk and different lists can be passed through those subroutines to handle different disks. This technique is often used in operating systems for "low-level access" to disks and other similar complex I/O devices.

2-3.3 Calling and Returning Mechanisms

Subroutines are called by the JSR and BSR instructions and use the RTS instruction to return to the main program. In addition, you can use the PULX JMP 0,X instructions rather than RTS to get around argument lists, as just described. However, the SWI and RTI pair can be used to advantage in some cases.

The SWI is an alternative to the usual BSR subroutine call. The 6811's SWI instruction can be attractive because it saves all the registers. And, as we have discussed, you may want an argument list to follow the SWI instruction, where one of the arguments (the first) is a call by value argument that tells you exactly which routine to execute. The "subroutine call" is written this way:

```
        SWI
        FCB     0
```

Inside the SWI "subroutine," the (only) argument can be obtained by using the saved PC, which are the seventh and eighth words from the top of the stack. To put this argument into accumulator B, execute the following as the first instructions in the "subroutine":

```
L       TSX
        LDX     7,X
        LDAB    0,X
```

(The address L is put into locations $FFF6 and $FFF7, so that SWI will cause a "jump" to that instruction.) This argument can be used to jump to a number of routines by jumping through a *transfer vector* – a vector of addresses of starting locations of the different routines, such as:

```
TVEC FDB L0,L1,L2,L3,L4
```

To jump to the *i*th routine, where *i* is in accumulator B, double B and add it to the address of the vector, then jump indirectly, as in

```
        ASLB
        LDX     #TVEC
        ABX
        LDX     0,X
        JMP     0,X
```

(The preceding transfer vector and routine are not position independent, but it is not too hard to make them so.) Note that if the argument after the SWI instruction were the number 2, we would jump to L2, and so on. This particular argument is likely to be the same actual argument, whenever the subroutine is called from the same place in memory, so it is an example of a call by value that can be stored in a read-only memory argument list. Note that more arguments can be passed in an argument list to an SWI. Finally, note that the RTI instruction will return to execute the arguments as instructions. To avoid that, modify the return address before the RTI so it skips over as many words as there are arguments. For instance, to skip over one argument, execute this routine to exit from the SWI:

```
        TSX
        INC    8,X
        BNE    L
        INC    7,X
   L    RTI
```

The SWI is especially useful for I/O software that you might write to interface your hardware. Suppose a bug in the I/O software is discovered after a lot of code has been written that uses it. Fixing that bug may change the sizes and entry points for many of the I/O subroutines. If the SWI "subroutine" technique is used with the transfer vector, only the transfer vector has to be modified, and the other software will still use the same argument. If a BSR subroutine were used, every address in an I/O subroutine call would have to be changed throughout all the programs. SWI "subroutines" are therefore often used for I/O. However, the key aspect of the SWI mechanism is indirect addressing. If you have a transfer vector, like TVEC in the preceding example, in a fixed place in memory, the instruction LDX TVEC+6 JSR 0,X would jump to a (JSR type) subroutine at location L3. If you rewrote those subroutines, you would only need to rewrite the transfer vector, and all the programs calling the subroutines would remain the same. This technique is especially useful when programs are also on different read-only memories. If all subroutine calls to subroutines on a read-only memory JSR indirectly through a transfer vector at the beginning of that read-only memory, then if that read-only memory is changed, the transfer vector can also be changed, and no other read-only memories need changing to adjust the addresses of the subroutine calls to this read-only memory.

2-3.4 A Blueprint for Writing Subroutines

We now offer a "blueprint" for calling and writing a subroutine, and a useful example of a subroutine. The following considerations should be given before anything is written:

1. What are the local and global variables, and what are the arguments and the results? How are the arguments and results to be passed: by value and result, by reference, or by name? Will they be passed in registers on the stack pointed to by S (or another stack), or through an argument list or an external list?
2. Will we use BSR or JSR calls, or should we use SWI calls?

When you write the subroutine call, the following sequence of code should appear (although sections that do not pertain may be omitted).

1. Push any arguments to be passed on the stack, and make "holes" for any results to be passed back on the stack. Set up the address of an external list, if it is used.
2. Jump to the subroutine.
3. Write the argument list, if it is used. Use FDB directives for addresses and 2-

word operands, FCB for 1-word operands, and FCC for character strings. These may be mixed in any order.

4. Pull any values returned on the stack and delete any values passed into the subroutine from the stack.

Inside the subroutine, the following sequences might be expected:

1. Make room on the stack for local variables. Initialize those local variables that may be read before data are written in them. Note that local variables can be simultaneously allocated and initialized by the PSH instructions.

2. Your routine can be put next.

        a. If argument lists are used, set up an index register, such as Y, to point to the beginning of the list, as in TSY LDY 0,Y or by PULY, which pulls Y from the stack. The index register can be used for other operations, but must be reloaded with the argument list's address each time an argument is needed. If it is set up, a call by value 1-word argument can be put into accumulator A by the instruction LDAA n,Y, and a call by reference or name argument by LDX n,Y LDAA 0,X, where n is the argument's position in the list.

        b. If a stack is used, arguments called by value on the stack can be picked up by TSX LDAA n,X, and call by reference or name by TSX LDX 0,X LDAA n,X, where n is the argument's position on the stack. (Remember: the return address is -usually- on the stack.)

        Temporary variables can be pushed and pulled using PSH and PUL instructions, if they are pulled in the reverse order to which they are pushed, provided that the nested program segment rules are followed.

3. When you are ready to leave a subroutine, delete all local variables from the stack first. Use the return (RTS, PULX JMP n,X or RTI) that corresponds to the call. If an argument list is used, remember to move the program counter over the argument list before returning (several techniques for this have been shown.) If you should use the RTS or RTI to exit a subroutine but instead you use a BRA or JMP to jump to an error routine and do not return, remember to balance the stack by deleting the return address and other registers also saved on the stack.

2-3.5 Subroutine Documentation

We will introduce the need for clear documentation with a real example (adapted from a 6800 program to a 6811 program) that also conveys a very important additional concept, so we kill two birds with one stone. (Another reason for using a rather complex example will be given at the end of this discussion.)

    This routine *hashes* a character string into an address. That is, it converts any string of characters you may type on a terminal into a number from 0 to 19, and that number is used as an address. The important hash routine property is that when you pass the same character string to it, you always get the same number to use as an address. The actual computations done inside the routine are not really important as long as they are done the same way each time. Generally, the input characters are mixed together like restaurant "hash," hence the term. The routine is usually developed experimentally, though, to separate the character strings into different addresses as evenly as possible. Hashing is used to search for a character string to get information about it. Hashing helps narrow down the search by starting at a place indicated by the address provided by the routine, close to where the string starts. In particular, the hashing routine described soon is the actual routine that Motorola uses in its MDOS software to search a disc's directory. (In fact, if you know some of the terminology used with discs, this hash routine determines which sector of the directory the string is (probably) on. That sector is read, and the string is compared to all those strings on the sector. When a matching string is found, the track and sector number that begins the file is read from words after it.)

This subroutine needs a character string. If it is variable length (the Motorola routine fixes the length to ten), we won't want to pass the string by value but by reference. We can provide the address of the first character of the string. To account for the variable length, we can supply the length as a call by value parameter. The result is a small number, so it can be returned in a register. The parameters can be passed in an argument list to enhance storage efficiency. The length, which will go into an accumulator, and the address, which will go into an index register, can be picked up by a LDAA 0,Y instruction. To do this, the length is the first argument. The calling routine to hash a ten-character string at location ALPHA will then be written

```
BSR   HASH
FCB   10
FDB   ALPHA
```

The hash subroutine is shown next. Of importance to this discussion on subroutines, the first two lines pick up the arguments, and the last line returns past the argument list. The result is left in accumulator B.

```
HASH    PULY        GET RETURN ADDR., POINTS TO THE ARGUMENT
        LDAA 0,Y    GET STRING COUNT TO A
        LDX 1,Y     GET STRING ADDRESS TO X
        INY         MOVE RETURN ADDRESS PAST ARGUMENT LIST
        INY
        INY
        PSHY        PUT RETURN ADDRESS BACK ON THE STACK
        PSHA        SAVE COUNT STACK
        PSHX        SAVE STRING POINTER ON THE STACK
        CLRB        CLEAR THE PLACE TO COMPUTE THE RESULT
        TSY         Y BECOMES TOP-OF-STACK POINTER
LOOP    PSHB        SAVE RESULT AND CONDITION CODES ON STACK
        TPA
        PSHA        SAVE CONDITION CODE
        LDX  0,Y    GET STRING POINTER
        LDAB 0,X    GET A CHARACTER
        INX         MOVE POINTER
```

```
            STX   0,Y    PUT IT BACK ON THE STACK
            SUBB  #$25   MAKE CHARACTER UNIQUE
            BPL   NOCLR  IF NEGATIVE
            CLRB         MAKE IT ZERO
NOCLR       PULA         RESTORE CONDITION CODES
            TAP
            TSX
            ADCB  2,X    ADD TO MODIFIED CHARACTER
            INS
            ROLB         DOUBLE, FOLD CARRY BACK
            DEC   2,Y    DECREMENT COUNT
            BNE   LOOP   UNTIL COUNT BECOMES ZERO, LOOP
            RORB         UNDO LAST ROLB
            LDAA  #$11   MULTIPLY BY 11
            MUL
            ANDB  #$1F   CLEAR HIGH THREE BITS
            CMPB  #19    IS IT WITHIN THE DESIRED RANGE?
            BLS   EXIT   IF SO, RESULT IS IN B
            SUBB  #20    PULL IT WITHIN RANGE
            CMPB  #9     IF NOW LOWER THAN 9
            BHI   EXIT   THEN DOUBLE IT
            ASLB         AND THEN
            BITB  #2     EXTEND THE
            BEQ   EXIT   LOWEST BIT
            ORAB  #1
EXIT        INS          DELETE COUNTER ON STACK
            INS          DELETE POINTER ON STACK
            INS
            RTS          UPDATED RETURN ADDRESS IS ON STACK
```

You might wonder, when reading this subroutine, about some characteristics that affect the way you use it. These should be supplied as comments. Comments can be put on a full line in assembler language by beginning the line with a "*". Comments for a subroutine should (really, must) have the following information:

1. A brief description of the subroutine's meaning that should enable readers to determine if this is the one they are looking for.
2. A list of all arguments, what they mean, and whether they are called by value and result, reference, or name.
3. A good clear example of a subroutine call, identifying which arguments are passed on the stack, through the argument list, or in registers, and identifying whether BSR or SWI calls are to be used.
4. A list of all other registers, global memory words, and temporary storage locations that are changed or destroyed by the subroutine.
5. A description of any error conditions and how they are reported, and any abnormal exits from the subroutine that may be taken to handle errors.

Finally, all subroutines, unless they would be worse with these features, should be position independent and reentrant. You should note in the comments at the beginning of the subroutine when either feature is lacking.

We cannot stress enough the need for good opening comments. With them, it is easy to know if, for example, the Y register is untouched by the subroutine, or how to supply an argument and where the result is to be found. Without them, the subroutine program has to be studied thoroughly each time it is used. That's usually too much trouble, as you can appreciate by the preceding example. Try to glean this critical information from the subroutine without the use of comments. (We deliberately chose this hash routine to make that point, because it is rather messy inside.)

The following is a good example of opening comments for the preceding subroutine:

```
***********************************************************
*
* HASH  CONVERTS N LETTER CHARACTER STRING AT ADDRESS
*     ADDR INTO A NUMBER FROM 0-19
*
* CALLING SEQUENCE:
*
* BSR HASH
* FCB  N CALL BY VALVE
* FDB ADDR CALL BY REFERENCE
*
* DESTROYS CC,A,X,AND Y
* RETURNS HASHED ADDRESS IN B
```

We have examined different strategies for calling subroutines and passing arguments, and different techniques for implementing those strategies. We should now be prepared to write subroutines for interface software.

2-4 Arithmetic Operations

A microcomputer provides some challenging problems in implementing arithmetic operations. An 8-bit word is really very short. Even a 16-bit number is often too small. Consider business data processing, for example. If we keep track of money in binary to the penny, an 8-bit unsigned number can keep track of only $2.55, and a 16-bit unsigned number, only $655.35. That's not enough for most applications. In 1946, von Neumann told us in his great paper that begot the computer, that scientific computers need at least 40 bits. IBM chose a 32-bit word for its 360/370 and has learned from experience that almost all scientific computations require double precision arithmetic (64 bits) because you do need about 40 bits for scientific computation. A 16-bit word is just fine for address calculations and for feedback control systems but is inadequate for just about everything else. So even if the 6811 has 16-bit arithmetic instructions, we have to study, as we do in this section, the effective handling of multiple precision arithmetic.

Another problem may be storage density. Rather than having one subroutine for 16-bit addition, another for 24-bit addition, and so on, we may want to have only one subroutine that can handle any precision. In fact, with a little effort, we can implement arithmetic functions that are capable of adding numbers of different precision and of expanding the precision of a number when overflow occurs. With this power, there is less need for floating point arithmetic; however, the resulting routines will be slower than routines optimized for fixed precision. Such fixed precision routines can be fairly easily written, though, if the variable precision routines are understood.

About the only way we know that handles variable precision numbers efficiently is keeping them on a stack (*operand stack*). This stack contains, as elements, numbers of arbitrary size. Conceptually, you can push a number on the stack or pull a number from it, and you push or pull a whole number regardless of how big it is. We will now discuss how any algebraic formula can be converted into a program of subroutine calls that perform the arithmetic on this stack.

A *dyadic* operation is an operation, like addition, that requires two operands. Any dyadic operation works this way: pull one number from the stack to be used as the first (left) operand, and pull another number from the stack to be used as the second (right) operand; perform the dyadic operation; push the result back on the stack. A *monadic* operation, such as negate, requires one operand. All monadic operations work this way: pull a number from the stack, operate on it, and push the result on the stack; finally, a *push* operation like PUSH ALPHA copies a number stored at location ALPHA, pushing it on top of the stack.

Consider a simple algebraic formula, such as

$$(A + B) / (C - D)$$

In the following program this formula can be evaluated with dyadic operations implemented as the subroutines ADD, SUB, and DIV and as the subroutine PUSH that uses a call by reference argument in an argument list to determine what to push:

```
BSR   PUSH
FDB   A
BSR   PUSH
FDB   B
BSR   ADD
BSR   PUSH
FCB   C
BSR   PUSH
FCB   D
BSR   SUB
BSR   DIV
```

(You should pencil a stack to convince yourself that the result of the addition is saved conveniently on the stack as the subtraction is set up and the results of both are available when the divide subroutine needs them.)

The first problem in dealing with arithmetic operations is to find out how to write the program of subroutine calls to implement any arbitrary algebraic formula; and the second problem is to find a way to implement the subroutines that perform the operations. These problems, as we show, can be solved. To write the subroutines in correct order, the expression having its operators in the middle (infix expression) must be converted to one having its operators at the end of the operands (suffix expression). For example, A + B is written A B + . This expression directly represents the subroutine calls PUSH A, PUSH B, and ADD, which are the correct calls to implement the addition operation. (Incidentally, suffix expressions are popularly called Polish or Reverse Polish Notation, because they were invented by the Polish logician Jan Lucasiewicz.

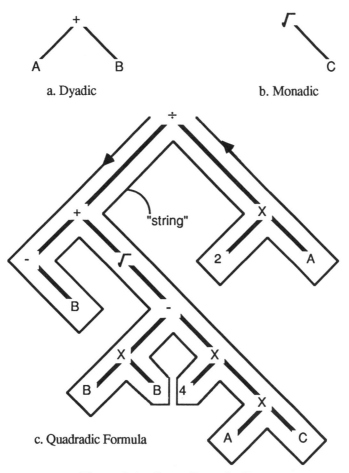

a. Dyadic   b. Monadic

c. Quadradic Formula

Figure 2-8. Some Formula Trees

One can write the expression in suffix form and then write the subroutine calls, but there is a shorter way using *formula trees*. Figure 2-8a shows the formula tree for a typical dyadic operation, such as addition, and figure 2-8b shows the formula tree for a typical monadic operation such as finding a square root. If an argument is evaluated by another formula, that other formula is replaced by its own formula tree (to reduce the need for extra symbols and subroutines). A complex expression, such as the solution to the quadradic formula, is written as follows (the formula tree is shown in figure 2-8c):

$$\frac{-B + \sqrt{((B \times B) - (4 \times (A \times C)))}}{2 \times A}$$

To write the subroutine calls, wrap a "string" tightly around the tree. (See figure 2-8c.) Follow the string from left top, around the tree to right top, and copy a subroutine call the *last* time you meet a symbol (as you pass it on its right) – a PUSH A when you meet a symbol A, a MULT when you meet an x, and so on. These are the subroutine calls produced by the dyadic operation formula tree. The monadic operation formula tree produces the subroutine calls PUSH C and SQRT. The quadradic formula tree produces these subroutine calls for a 6811 program:

BSR	PUSH
FDB	B
BSR	PUSH
FDB	B
BSR	MULT
BSR	PUSH
FDB	FOUR
BSR	PUSH
FDB	A
BSR	PUSH
FDB	C
BSR	MULT
BSR	MULT
BSR	SUBT
BSR	SQRT
BSR	PUSH
FDB	B
BSR	SUBT
BSR	PUSH
FDB	TWO
BSR	PUSH
FDB	A
BSR	MULT
BSR	DIV

(The symbolic addresses A,B, and C are for the variables in the quadradic formula, and the symbolic addresses FOUR and TWO are for the constants 4 and 2.) Conversion to a formula tree is fairly simple. In fact, if you get used to formula trees, they are easier to write and check than conventional infix expressions. Also, conversion from a formula tree to the program is mechanical and simple. (Note that this technique can help you use calculators that use "Reverse Polish Notation.")

We now consider the technique used to implement a variable length number stack on the 6811. To avoid having return addresses in the way, a stack different from that pointed to by the S register is used, and the operand stack uses the Y index register, building from low addresses to high addresses in the same buffer space as is used by the stack pointed to by the S register. (See figure 2-9.) Y points to the word below (at the next larger address than) the bottom word on the operand stack. The bottom number, call it A, is, say, 3 words long – call them A2,A1, and A0, where A0 is the least significant word of the number. The bottom number is stored in consecutive locations, with A2 at the lowest address, then A1 next, then A0, and then 3 – the length of the number – at the highest address, which is on the bottom of the operand stack. (See figure 2-9.) Likewise, another number, call it B, is stored, with its most significant word at lowest address and length at highest address, right above A on the operand stack.

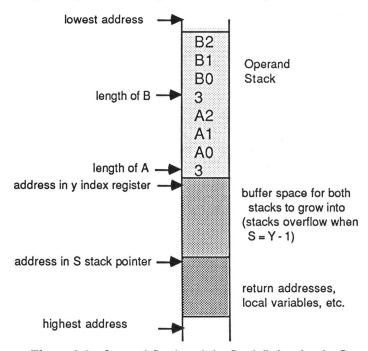

Figure 2-9. Operand Stack and the Stack Pointed to by S

Consider adding the bottom two numbers on the operand stack, assuming they are the same size. Conceptually, you should pull the whole bottom number from this operand stack, pull the next number, then add the numbers and push the whole result on the operand stack. Actually, you can work 1 word at a time. Add A0 to B0, put the result where B0 was before, then add A1 and B1 with the carry and put the result where B1 used to be, and so on. Note that decrementing the Y index register before using it can be used to pick up the words A0, A1, and A2, and that a second index register X can similarly access the second operand B0, B1, and B2 and put the results back in their place. (Decrementing an index register before using it is equivalent to autodecrement addressing on such machines as the 6809.) The following subroutine ADD does just that.

```
*************************************************************
*
* ADD  ADDS THE BOTTOM TWO NUMBERS ON THE OPERAND STACK
*
* CALLING SEQUENCE
*
* JSR ADD
*
* DESTROYS A,B,X
*
ADD     DEY           MOVE TO GET LENGTH OF TOP
        LDAB 0,Y      GET LENGTH OF BOTTOM NUM. ON OP. STACK
        PSHY          SET UP X TO SECOND NUMBER ON STACK
        PULX          BY FIRST PUTTING IT AT TOP OF TOP ARGUMENT
        NEGB          NEGATE SO ABX SUBTRACTS
        ABX           MOVE PAST THE BODY OF THE TOP ARGUMENT
        DEX           MOVE PAST THE LENGTH OF THE BOTTOM ARG.
        CLC           CLEAR CARRY
LOOP    DEX           MOVE POINTER TO SECOND NUMBER
        DEY           MOVE POINTER TO TOP NUMBER
        LDAA 0,Y      GET A WORD OF THE SECOND NUMBER
        ADCA 0,X      ADD TO CORRESPONDING WORD OF NEXT NUMBER
        STAA 0,X      PUT THE NUMBER BACK
        INCB          INCREMENT COUNTER (WAS MADE NEGATIVE)
        BNE  LOOP     ADD ALL WORDS
        RTS           RETURN FROM SUBROUTINE
```

Other dyadic functions can be performed in the same way. Note that, with subtraction, the preceding formula was, to correctly implement formulas derived as the bottom number must be subtracted from the next to bottom number because A - C becomes PUSH A, PUSH C, SUBTRACT. Multiplication and division are quite a bit harder and will be discussed near the end of this section.

Monadic functions are best implemented using another index register such as X because the Y pointer must be left where it was. Consider the left shift function, which doubles a number shown in the following subroutine:

```
*************************************************************
*
* LFTSFT LEFT SHIFT (DOUBLE) THE BOTTOM NUMBER
*    ON THE OPERAND STACK
*
* CALLING SEQUENCE
*
* BSR LFTSFT
*
* DESTROYS A,X
```

```
*
LFTSFT    PSHY              COPY POINTER TO INDEX REGISTER X
          PULX
          DEX
          LDAA 0,X          GET LENGTH
          CLC               CLEAR CARRY
LOOP      DEX               MOVE POINTER
          ROL  0,X          ROTATE A WORD
          DECA              OVER ENTIRE LENGTH OF NUMBER
          BNE    LOOP  IN DO-LOOP
          RTS
```

Note that in a shift right subroutine, you must start shifting the high order word first and increment the index register.

Generally, the stack can have numbers of different lengths because the length is stored with the number. When two numbers to be added just might have different lengths, we can check their lengths and expand the smaller one using a routine like the one we used to move 128 words in memory. Also, after an overflow is detected, the result can be expanded in like manner.

Numbers stored elsewhere in memory than on the operand stack may or may not have their length stored with them. When you push such numbers onto the operand stack, push most significant word first, as in the routine shown next. On calling this subroutine, X points to the most significant word of the number in memory to be pushed, and accumulator A has the number of words in the number to be pushed.

```
************************************************************
* PUSH  PUSHES A NUMBER FROM LOCATION L OF LENGTH N
*    ONTO THE OPERAND STACK
* CALLING SEQUENCE
* LDAA #N
* LDX #L
* JSR PUSH
*
* DESTROYS A,B,X
*
PUSH      PSHA              SAVE TO PUT ON BOTTOM OF WORD
LOOP      LDAB 0,X          GET WORD FROM NUMBER BEING PUSHED
          INX
          STAB 0,Y          ONTO THE STACK
          INY               MOVE POINTER
          DECA              COUNT NUMBER OF WORDS BEING MOVED
          BNE    LOOP  LOOP UNTIL DONE
          PULA              RECOVER LENGTH
          STAA 0,Y          PUSH LENGTH LAST
          INY               MOVE POINTER
          RTS
```

Because pulling a number from the stack to be written elsewhere in memory is the opposite of pushing a number, remember to pull the least significant byte first and write it at the highest address in the memory location reserved for the number.

Multiplication and division require a little more effort. The problem with multiplication is if you multiply an n bit number by an m bit number you get an n x m bit number. If the number sizes are variable, you must allocate a variable amount of room for the extra bits produced by multiplication. The best solution to the problem is to treat multiplication as a triadic operation, such as A + (B x C), where A and C are numbers of the same precision. If you want to perform standard dyadic multiplication, make A 0, but push this 0 (of the same length as C) on the stack first. However, you can just as easily execute a simultaneous multiply and add, which would leave room, where A and B are stored on the stack, for the final product. Also, the formula trees can be adapted to this triadic operation. The multiply operator has three branches below it for the A, B, and C in the preceding expression. The string technique works just fine to convert an arbitrary expression into subroutine calls, even if triadic multiplication operations are used. Finally, division can be a problem because integer divide produces two results: the quotient and the remainder. But the formula tree (now a more general graph called a Hasse diagram) and the string technique can be adapted to this too.

Finally, conversion from one number system to another can be done on the operand stack. The other stack, pointed to by S, is used to temporarily save the whole number on the bottom of the operand stack. One word at a time is pulled from the other stack, and the converted number is formed on the operand stack according to the conversion rule. In many cases, the best way of converting from number system A to number system B is not to use the remainder method suggested in most elementary textbooks, but to write the definition of the number system A, such as the decimal number system

$$N = (((N2 \times 10) + N1) \times 10) + N0$$

and perform the arithmetic in the number system B on the stack. It works beautifully.

The use of a variable precision operand stack allows simple and efficient arithmetic in the 6811. We recommend that you use it when you need to. Moreover, knowing how to use it will help you write fixed precision routines that you may need if speed is a major concern.

2-5 Conclusions

In this chapter, we have surveyed the architecture and software background needed for microcomputer interfacing. The first section covered bare essentials about the von Neumann computer, the instruction and what it does, and the microcomputer – a useful background for understanding the details of what happens in an interface.

The middle section covered the addressing modes and instructions that you may expect in any microcomputer and discussed those in the 6811 in more detail. The general comments in these sections should help you if you want to learn about another machine. The specific comments on the 6811 should help you read the examples and do some of the experiments suggested in the book. Some elementary programming techniques, such as decision trees and DO-loops, were also presented. While you probably know these techniques, it is necessary to ensure that all readers have this basic information.

The final section presented some slightly more complex software techniques, such as the description and handling of data structures, subroutine calling and argument passing techniques, and multiple precision arithmetic techniques. These are the most common valuable techniques in interfacing microcomputers, often, in our opinion, inadequately covered in prior courses or in working experience.

If you found any section difficult, we can recommend additional readings. There are plenty of fine books on computer architecture. You may have one already. We encourage you to reread it to reinforce the ideas that it presents rather than to read several new ones superficially. But if you haven't read one yet, we recommend *Introduction to Computer Organization and Data Structures,* by H. Stone, McGraw Hill Inc., 1972 or any of Stone's later books, because he covers architecture and data structures together. You can reinforce the information gained from this chapter by reading any of the fine books on assembler language programming, such as *Introduction to Microprocessors: Software, Hardware, Programming,* by L. Leventhal, Prentice-Hall Inc., 1978. Other fine books are available on these topics, and more are appearing daily. We might suggest contacting a local college or university instructor who teaches architecture, microprocessors, or assembler language programming for the most recent books on these topics.

Problems

Problems 1 and 2 are paragraph correction problems (see guidelines at the end of chapter 1). Problems 3 to 28 and many problems in later chapters are programming problems. We recommend the following guidelines for these problems: Unless otherwise stated, answer all programming problems in assembler language, using a format that would be accepted without errors by the Motorola AS11 6811 cross-assembler (or, for the 6800, by the Motorola RASM assembler). In all programs you write as answers to questions, each line of code must have comments which tell the reader what you are doing; but do not just rewrite the instructions in slightly different words. Subroutines must follow the style recommended in section 2-3.4. Unless otherwise noted, you should try to write position independent, reentrant programs with the greatest static efficiency.

1.* The information structure is the way the programmer sees the data, and is dependent on such details as the size of words and positions of bits. The data structure is the way the information is actually stored in memory, right down to the bit positions. The assembler directive L RMB $100 will assign the value $100 to the label L, and the directive L FDB BETA, where BETA is $34, will initialize 1 word in memory to be $34, whose address is assigned to the label L.

2.* A queue is a sequence of elements with two ends, in which an element can be pushed or pulled from both the top and bottom. A stack is a special case of queue, where an element can only be pushed from one end and pulled from the other. An important element in structured programming is the use of single entry and single exit point in a program segment. A calling routine passes the address of the arguments, called formal parameters, to the subroutine. In call by value and result, the data are not actually moved to another location, but the address of the data is given to the subroutine. Large vectors, lists, and arrays can be more effectively called by reference.

3. A 40-bit unsigned number, least significant byte at location N and each next more significant byte at the next higher location, is to be added to another 40-bit unsigned number, which has least significant byte at M and each next more significant byte at the next higher address. Write a. the shortest program to add the number at N to the number at M, result to M, and b. the fastest program to add the number at N to the number at M, result to M. Neither program need check for overflow.

4. Write a program which will add two single-precision vectors

$$C(I) = A(I) + B(I) \text{ for } I = 0 \text{ to } n\text{-}1$$

where A(0) is at address AR, B(0) is at address BR, C(0) is at address CR, each successive element is at the next higher address, and the number n is in accumulator B, $n < 256$.

5. Write a program to subtract an unsigned decimal number at N from an unsigned decimal number at M. Each number has 10 digits, stored 2 digits per byte, and the numbers are oriented as in problem 3. Jump to ERROR if the result is negative.

6. Write a program to convert a 10-digit decimal at location N and the next four locations, oriented as in problem 3, into an ASCII character string beginning with the first character at location M representing the most significant digit, the next character representing the next most significant digit, and so on, in the next 9 words. Suppress leading 0's by replacing them with blanks.

7. Write a flow chart and program that will check each of the 5 words at location FLAG and the next four locations and branch to location L0 if FLAG + 0 is negative, L1 if FLAG + 1 is negative, and, in general, Ln if FLAG + n is negative. If 2 words are negative, 1 word at FLAG + i and 1 word at FLAG + j, and $i < j$, then the program will only branch to Li. (This is called a polling sequence.)

8. Write a program and its flow chart to write an n-checkerboard pattern in an area of memory and then check to see that it is still there after it is completely written. An n-checkerboard pattern is 2 to the nth words of 0's, followed by two to the nth words of $FF, followed by 2 to the nth words of 0's, . . . repeated throughout the memory area. Assume that before the program begins, index register X contains the lowest address in this area, Y contains the highest address, and accumulator A contains the number n, $n <$ 8. (This pattern is used to check dynamic memories for pattern sensitivity errors.)

9. Write a 6811 assembly language reentrant SWI "subroutine" to compare the value of register A (high byte) and B (low byte) against index register X, setting the condition codes exactly as in the 6811 instruction CPX.

10. Write a 6811 assembly language reentrant SWI "subroutine" to replace the 6811 instruction PSHX, not using that instruction.

11. Suppose A is a zero-origin 5 by 7 array of triple precision numbers, stored in row major order. Write an assembler language subroutine to put $A[i,j]$ into location N, $N+1$, and $N+2$, where, on calling this subroutine, the address of A is in X, the address of N is in Y, and i and j are in accumulators A and B. Your subroutine should jump to location ERROR if the indexes are outside the array's range.

12. Suppose a table starting at location TBL has ten rows, and each row has a five-letter ASCII character string followed by a 16-bit address, in row major order. Write a routine to jump to the address in the row if the five characters are the same as the five characters at location INSTR and the next four words.

13. Suppose a string of 11 ASCII characters, consisting of only the letters S, I, P and M, is stored at location STRNG, as if generated by

STRNG FCC 'MISSISSIPPI'

Write a subroutine to convert this (or any other such string) to Huffmann code, as defined by the coding tree in figure 2-1, storing the code as a bit string, first bit as most significant bit at location CODE, as allocated in

CODE RMB 20

Then write a subroutine that decodes such a code at location CODE, using the coding tree in figure 2-1, putting the ASCII string back as it was at location STRNG.

14. Write two subroutines, one to push and one to pull a word from the bottom of a deque, assuming that the word is to be taken from or put into accumulator A and the Y pointer points to the word below (at the next higher address than) the bottom word on the deque.

15. Write a subroutine that will calculate the sum of first N positive integers, namely 1, 2, . . . N. The subroutine is to be called with the calling sequence shown below, and the result is to be passed out in place of the value N in the stack.

```
                    LDAA #N
                    PSHA
                    BSR SUM
```

16. Write the subroutine described in problem 15, but with the following calling sequence:

```
                    BSR SUM
                    FCB N
```

The result should be returned in accumulator A, and the subroutine should return to its proper place by skipping over the actual parameter N.

17. Write a subroutine that will multiply $L1$-byte unsigned integer N with one-byte unsigned integer M and store the result in locations starting at P. The value of $L1$ is in accumulator B, and M is in A. The number N is oriented as in problem 3. The calling sequence is

```
            LDAA #M
            LDAB #L1
            BSR MULT
            FDB N,P     N and P are the address of the multiplicand and result.
```

18. Write a subroutine equivalent to the FORTRAN statement:

$$IF(A)\ 1,2,3$$

It will jump to FORTRAN line 1 if A is negative, to line 2 if A is 0, and to line 3 if A is positive. (Note, you must balance the stack by removing the return address.) It will be called in assembler language, passing A in call by value by putting it in accumulator A, and using call by name labels for FORTRAN lines 1, 2, and 3:

```
            LBSR    IF
            FDB     L1,L2,L3
```

19. Write position independent, reentrant programs that will
   a. Jump to the subroutine at location L2 through this transfer vector
   b. Jump to Li, where i is in accumulator B, and to ERROR if i is out of range
   c. Exit from the routine at Li to the routine at Li+1 so all routines are done in order and so that L0 is done after L3; you will jump to this routine each time you finish routine Li (Note: see the program segment at the end of section 2-2.2.)
Use a position independent transfer vector:

L FDB L0-L,L1-L,L2-L,L3-L

20. Write a subroutine that pushes a block onto the stack pointed to by S, so that the words on the stack are in the same order in memory as they were in the block. The block is defined as the list BLOCK

```
        BLOCK   FDB   0
                FCB   4
                FCC 'ABC'
```

21. Write a formula tree and subroutine call program that will evaluate the following:

   a. SIN (X) = X - (X**3/3!) + (X**5/5!) - (X**7/7!) + (X**9/9!)
   b. A x X**3 + B x X**2 + C x X + D
   c. A x X + B x Y + C x Z

The subroutines should use the push, dyadic multiply, add, and subtract routines only, and the formula tree and the program should be written so that the maximum number of numbers on the stack at any time is kept to a minimum. Assume that all numbers are signed binary integers (part a will have to be scaled by multiplying all coefficients by 9!) of equal length n, and that n is in location LEN. Store all coefficients so you won't have to compute them.

22. Write a subroutine to:
a) subtract the bottom number on the operand stack from the next bottom number.
b) negate the bottom number on the stack.
c) convert the bottom number on the operand stack from binary to binary-coded decimal.
Assume no overflows or unequal length numbers. Assume the stack grows downward.

3

Bus Hardware and Signals

Understanding the data and address busses is critical, because they are at the heart of interfacing design. This chapter will discuss what a bus is, how data are put onto it, and how data from it is used. The chapter progresses logically, with the first section covering basic concepts in digital hardware, the next section using those concepts to describe the control signals on the bus, and the final section discussing the important issue of timing in the microprocessor bus.

The first section of this chapter is a condensed version of background material on computer organization and realization (as opposed to architecture and software discussed in earlier chapters) needed in the remainder of the book. They lead to the study of bus timing and control – very important to the design of interfaces. How important can be shown in the following experience. Microcomputer manufacturers have applications engineers who write notes on how to use the chips the companies manufacture and who answer those knotty questions that systems designers can't handle. The author had an opportunity to sit down with Charlie Melear, one of the very fine applications engineers in the Microcomponents Applications Engineering group at Motorola's plant. Charlie told me that the two most common problems designers have are 1. improper control signals for the bus, whereby several bus drivers are given commands to drive the bus at the same time, and 2. failure to meet timing specifications for address and data busses, problems which will be covered in the chapter's last sections. These problems come up so often that studying them in depth can save a lot of frustration in interface design.

This chapter introduces a lot of terminology to provide background for later sections and enable you to read data sheets provided by the manufacturers. The terminology is as close as possible to that used in industry: logic diagram conventions conform to those used in *Electronics* magazine and to the Texas Instruments *The TTL Data Book*, and microprocessor notation conforms to that used in Motorola data sheets. However, some minor deviations have been introduced where constructs appear so often in this book that further notation is useful.

This chapter should provide enough background in computer organization for the remaining sections. After reading the chapter, you should be able to read a logic diagram or the data sheets describing microcomputers or their associated integrated circuits, and should have a fundamental knowledge of the signals and their timing on a typical microcomputer bus. This chapter should provide adequate hardware background for later chapters. However, if you find it difficult, additional reading is recommended. As in the last two chapters, a bibliography will be offered at the end of this chapter.

3-1 Digital Hardware

The basic notions and building blocks of digital hardware are presented in this section. While you have probably taken a course on digital hardware design that most likely emphasized minimization of logic gates, microcomputer interfacing requires an emphasis on busses. Therefore, this section focuses on the digital hardware that can be seen on a typical microcomputer bus. The first subsection provides clear definitions of terms used to describe signals and modules connected to a bus. The second subsection considers the kinds of modules you might see there.

3-1.1 Modules and Signals

Before the bus is explained, we need to discuss a few hardware concepts, such as the module and the signal. Since we are dealing in abstractions, we do not use concrete examples with units like electrons and fields.

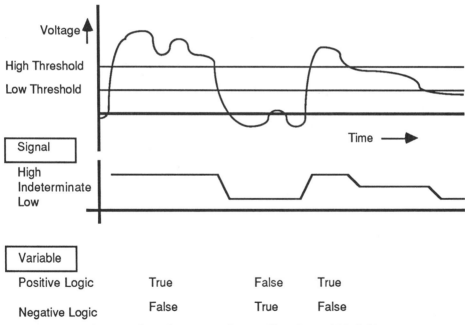

Figure 3-1. Voltage Waveforms, Signals, and Variables

One concept is the binary *signal*. (See figure 3-1.) Although a signal is a voltage or a current, we think of it only as a *high* signal, if the voltage or current is above a predefined threshold, or as a *low* signal, if it is below another threshold. We will use the symbols H for high and L for low. A signal is *determinate* when we can know for sure whether it is high or low. Related to this concept, a *variable* is the information a signal carries, and has values *true* (T) and *false* (F). For example, a wire can carry a signal, L, and, being a variable called "ENABLE," it can have a value T to indicate that something is indeed enabled. We use the expression "to *assert a variable*" to mean to make it true, "to *negate a variable*" to make it false, and "to *complement a variable*" to make it true if it was false or make it false if it was true. Two possible relations exist between signals and variables. In *positive logic*, a high signal represents a true variable and a low signal, a false variable. In *negative logic*, a high signal represents a false variable and a low, a true variable. Signals, which can be viewed on an oscilloscope or a logic analyzer, are preferred when someone, especially a technician, deals with actual hardware. Variables have a more conceptual significance and seem to be preferred by designers, especially in the early stages of design, and by programmers, especially when writing I/O software. Simply put, "true" and "false" are the 1 and 0 of the programmer, the Architect, and the system designer, and "high" and "low" are the 1 and 0 of the technician and IC manufacturer. While nothing is wrong with using 1 and 0 where the meaning is clear, we use the words true and false when talking about software or system design and the words high and low when discussing the hardware realization, to be clear.

Two types of variables and their corresponding signals are important in hardware. A *memory variable* is capable of being made true or false and of retaining this value, but a *link variable* is true or false as a result of functions of other variables. A link variable is always some function of other variables (as the output of some gate). At a high level of abstraction, these variables operate in different dimensions; memory variables are used to convey information through time (at the same point in space), while link variables convey information through space (at the same point in time). Some transformations on hardware, like converting from a parallel to a serial adder, are nicely explained by this abstract view. For instance, one can convert a parallel adder into a serial adder by converting a link variable that passes the carry into a memory variable that saves the carry. Also, in a simulation program, we differentiate between the types because memory variables have to be initialized and link variables don't.

A *synchronous* signal can be viewed as associated with a periodic variable (for example, a square wave) called a *clock*. The signal or variable is indeterminate except when the clock is asserted. Or, alternatively, the value of the signal is irrelevant except when the clock is asserted. Depending on the context, the signal is determinate either precisely when the clock changes from false to true or as long as the clock is true. The context depends on what picks up the signal and will be discussed when we study the flip-flop. This is so in the real world because of delays through circuitry, noise, and transmission line ringing. In our abstraction of the signal, we simply ignore the signal except when this clock is asserted, and we design the system so the clock is asserted only when we can guarantee the signal is determinate under worst case conditions. Though there are asynchronous signals where there is no associated clock and the signals are supposed to be determinate at all times, most microprocessor signals are synchronous; so in further discussions, we will assume all signals are synchronous. Then two signals are *equivalent* if they have the same (H or L) value whenever the clock is asserted.

The other basic idea is that of the *module*, which is a block of hardware with identifiable input, output, and memory variables. The input variables are the *input ports* and output variables are the *output ports*. Often, we are only interested in the behavior. Modules are *behaviorally equivalent* if, for equivalent values of the initial memory variables and equivalent sequence of values of input variables, they deliver equivalent sequence of values of output variables. Thus, we are not concerned about how they are constructed internally, nor what the precise voltages are, nor the signals when the clock is not asserted, but only the signals when the clock is asserted.

In section 1-1.3, we introduced the idea of an integrated circuit (IC) to define the term microprocessor. Now we discuss more about it. An integrated circuit is a module that is generally contained in a *dual in-line package*. This is a long rectangular plastic or ceramic package with pins along both the long edges (hence the term dual in-line). The pins are the input and output ports. Viewed from the top, one of the short edges has an indent or mark. The pins are numbered counterclockwise from this mark, starting with pin 1. Gates are defined in the next section, but will be used here to describe degrees of complexity of integrated circuits. A *small scale integrated circuit*, or SSI, has about 10 gates on one chip, a *medium scale integrated circuit* (MSI) has about 100, a *large scale integrated circuit* (LSI) has about 1,000, and a *very large scale integrated circuit* (VLSI) has more than 10,000. SSI and MSI circuits are commonly used to build up address decoders and some I/O modules in a microcomputer, LSI and VLSI are commonly used to implement 8- and 16-bit word microprocessors, 64K-bit and 128K-bit memory chips, and some complex I/O chips.

A *family* of integrated circuits is a collection of different types made with the same technology and having the same electrical characteristics, so they can be easily connected with others in the same family. Chips from different families can be interconnected, but this might require some careful study and design. The *low-power Schottky* or LS family, and the *complementary metal oxide semiconductor* or CMOS family, are often used with microprocessors. The LS family is used where higher speed is required, and the CMOS family, where lower power or higher immunity to noise is desired. The HCMOS family is a high-speed CMOS family particularly useful in MC68HC11 designs because it is fast enough for address decoding but requires very little power and can tolerate large variations in the power supply.

A block diagram was introduced at the beginning of section 1-3. In block diagrams, names represent variables rather than signals, and functions like AND or OR represent functions on variables rather than signals. An AND function, for example, is one in which the output is T if all the inputs are T. Such conventions ignore details needed to build the module, so the module's behavior can be simply explained.

Logic diagrams describe the realization of hardware to the level of detail needed to build it. In logic diagrams, modules are generally shown as rectangles, with input and output ports shown along the perimeter. Logic functions are generally defined for signals rather than variables (for example, an AND function is one whose output is H if its inputs are all H). It is common, and in fact desirable, to use many copies of the same module. The original module, here called the *type*, has a name, the *type name*. Especially when referring to one module copy among several, we give each copy a distinct *copy name*. The type name or copy name may be put in a logic diagram when the meaning is clear, or both may be put in the rectangle or over the left upper corner. Analogous to subroutines, inputs and outputs of the type name are *formal parameter names*, and inputs and outputs of the copy name are *actual parameter names*. Integrated circuits in particular are shown this way: formal parameters are shown inside a box representing the integrated circuit, and pin numbers and actual parameters are shown outside the rectangle for each connection that has to be made. Pins that don't have to be connected are not shown as connections to the module. (Figure 3-3 provides some examples of these conventions.)

Connections supplying power (positive supply voltage and ground) are usually not shown. They might be identified in a footnote, if necessary. In general, in LSI and VLSI N channel MOS chips such as microprocessors and input/output chips discussed in these notes, Vss is the ground pin (0 volts) and Vcc or Vdd is usually +5 volts. You might remember this by a quotation improperly attributed to Churchill: "*ground the SS* ." For SSI and MSI chips, the pin with the largest pin number is generally connected to +5 volts while the pin kitty-corner from it is connected to ground. One should keep power and ground lines straight and wide to reduce inductance that causes ringing, and put a capacitor (.1 microfarad disc) between power and ground to isolate the ICs from each other. When one chip changes its power supply current, these *bypass capacitors* serve to prevent voltage fluctuations from affecting the voltage supplied to other chips, which might look like signals to them. Normally, such a capacitor is needed for four SSI chips or one LSI chip, but if the power and ground lines appear to have noise, more capacitors should be put between power and ground.

In connections to inner modules, negative logic us usually shown by a small bubble where the connection touches the rectangle. In inputs and outputs to the whole system described by the logic diagram, negative logic is shown by a bar over the variable's name. Ideally, if a link is in negative logic, all its connections to modules should have bubbles. However, since changing logic polarity effects an inversion of the variable, designers sometimes steal a free inverter this way; so if bubbles do not match at both ends, remember that the signal is unchanged, but the variable is inverted, as it goes through the link.

A logic diagram should convey all the information needed to build a module, allowing only the exceptions we just discussed to reduce the clutter. Examples of logic diagrams appear throughout these notes. An explanation of Figures 3-2 and 3-3, which must wait until the next section, should clarify these conventions.

3-1.2 Drivers, Registers, and Memories

This section describes the bus in terms of the D flip-flop and the bus driver. These devices serve to take data from the bus and to put data onto it. The memory – a collection of registers – is also introduced.

A *gate* is an elementary module with a single output, where the value of the output is a Boolean logic function of the values of the inputs. The output of a gate is generally a link variable. For example, a three-input NOR gate output is true if none of its inputs are true, otherwise it is false. The output is always determined in terms of its inputs. A *buffer* is a gate that has a more powerful output amplifier and is often used to supply the power needed to put signals onto a bus, discussed soon. And in these cases, the gate may be very simple, so that it has just one input, and the output is the complement of the input (inverting) or the same signal as the input (non-inverting).

Your typical gate has an output stage which may be connected to up to f other inputs of gates of the same family (f is called the *fan-out*) and to no other output of a gate. If two outputs are connected to the same link, they may try to put opposite signals on the link, which will certainly be confusing to inputs on the link, and may even damage the output stages. However, a *bus (or buss)* is a link to which more than two gate outputs are connected. The gates must have specially designed output amplifiers so that all but one output on a bus may be disabled. The gates are called *bus drivers*. An upper limit to the number of outputs that can be connected to a bus is called the *fan-in*.

An *open collector gate* or open collector driver output can be connected to a *wire-OR* bus, (the bus must have a *pull-up resistor* connected between it and the positive supply voltage). If any output should attempt to put out a low signal, the signal on the bus will be low. Only when all outputs attempt to put out a high signal will the output be high. Generally, the gate is a two-input AND gate, inputs in positive logic and output in negative logic. Data, on one input, are put onto the bus whenever the other input is true. The other input acts as a positive logic *enable*. When the enable is asserted, we say the driver is *enabled*. Since this bus is normally used in the negative logic relationship, the value on the bus is the OR of the outputs. That is so common that the bus is called a wire-OR bus.

A *tristate gate* or tristate driver has an additional input, a *tristate enable*. When the tristate enable is asserted (the driver is enabled), the output amplifier forces the output signal high or low as directed by the gate logic. When the enable is not asserted, the output amplifier lets the output float. Two or more outputs of tristate gates may be connected to a *tristate bus*. The circuitry must be designed to insure that no two gates are enabled at the same time, lest the problem with connecting outputs of ordinary gates arises. If no gates are enabled, the bus signal floats – it is subject to stray static and electromagnetic fields. In other words, it acts like an antenna.

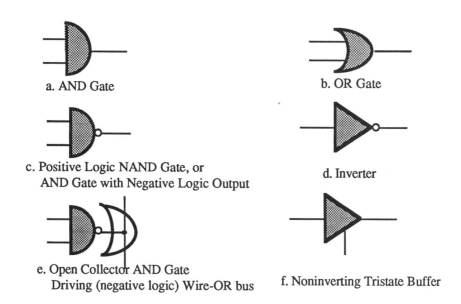

a. AND Gate

b. OR Gate

c. Positive Logic NAND Gate, or
   AND Gate with Negative Logic Output

d. Inverter

e. Open Collector AND Gate
   Driving (negative logic) Wire-OR bus

f. Noninverting Tristate Buffer

Figure 3-2. Some Common Gates

Gates are usually shown in logic diagrams as D-shaped symbols, the output on the round edge and inputs on the flat edge. (See figure 3-2 for the positive logic AND, NAND, and other gates.) Even though they are not shown using the aforementioned convention for modules, if they are in integrated circuits, the pin numbers are often shown next to all inputs and outputs.

Dynamic logic gates are implemented by passing charges (collections of electrons or holes) through switches; the charges have to be replenished, or they will discharge. Most gates use currents rather than charges and are not dynamic. Dynamic logic must be pulsed at a rate between a minimum and a maximum time, or it will not work; but dynamic logic gates are more compact than normal (static) logic gates.

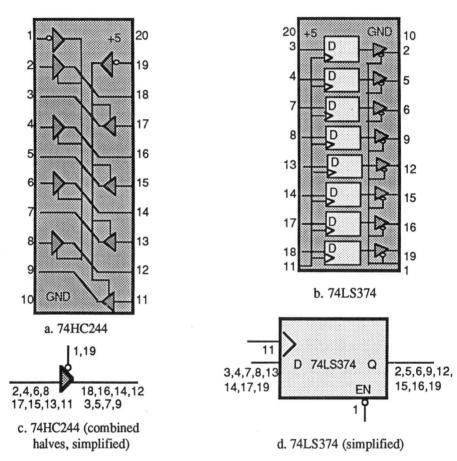

a. 74HC244

b. 74LS374

c. 74HC244 (combined halves, simplified)

d. 74LS374 (simplified)

Figure 3-3. Logic Diagrams for a Popular Driver and Register

Gates are usually put into integrated circuits so that the total number of pins is 14 or 16, counting two pins for positive supply voltage and ground. This yields, for instance, the quad two-input NAND gate, the 7400, which contains four two-input positive logic NAND gates. The 74HC00 is an HCMOS part with the pin configuration of the older 7400 TTL part. The 7404 has six inverters in a chip; it is called a hex inverter, so it is a good treat for Halloween (to invert hexes). A typical microprocessor uses an 8-bit-wide data bus, where eight identical and separate bus wires carry 1 bit of data on each wire. This has, in an IC, engendered octal bus drivers, with eight inverting or non-inverting bus drivers that share common enables. The 74HC244 and 74HC240 are popular octal non-inverting and inverting tristate bus driver integrated circuits. Figure 3-3a shows a logic diagram of the 74HC244, in which, to clearly show pin connections, the pins are placed along the perimeter of the module exactly as they appear on the dual in-line package. A positive 5-volt supply wire is connected to pin 20, and a ground wire, to pin 10. If the signals on both pins 1 and 19 are low, the eight separate tristate gates will be enabled. For instance, the signal input to pin 2 will be amplified and output on pin 18. If pins 1 and 19 are high, the tristate amplifiers are not enabled, and the outputs on pins 18,16,...,9 are allowed to float. This kind of diagram is valuable in catalogues to most clearly show the inputs and outputs of gates in integrated circuits.

To save effort in drawing logic diagrams, if a number n of identical wires connect to identical modules, a single line is drawn with a slash through it and the number n next to the slash. If pin connections are to be shown, a list of n pin numbers is written. Corresponding pins in the list at one end are connected to corresponding pins in the list at the other end. Commonly, however, the diagram is clear without showing the list of pin numbers. Also, if a single wire is connected to several pins, it is diagrammed as a single line, and the list of pins is written by the line. Figure 3-3c, shows how the 74HC244 just discussed might be more clearly shown connecting to a bus in a logic diagram. Note the eight tristate drivers, their input and output links shown by one line and gate symbol. The number 8 by the slash indicates the figure should be replicated 8 times. The NOR gate output, a single link, connects to the enables of all 8 bus drivers.

A *D flip-flop*, also called a (1-bit) latch, is an elementary module with *data input* D, *clock* C, and *output* Q. Q is always a memory variable having the value of the bit of data stored in the flip-flop. When the clock C is asserted (we say the flip-flop is *clocked*), the value of D is copied into the flip-flop memory. The clock input is rather confusing because it is really just a WRITE ENABLE. It sounds as though it must be the same as the microcomputer system clock. It may be connected to such a clock, but usually it is connected to something else, such as an output of a controller, which is discussed in section 3-2.1. It is, however, the clock that is associated with the synchronous variable on the D input of that flip-flop, since the variable has to be determinate whenever this clock is asserted. As long as C is asserted, Q is made equal to D. As long as C is false, Q remains what it was. Note that, when C is false, Q is the value of D at the moment when C changed from true to false. However, when C is asserted, the flip-flop behaves like a wire from D to Q, and Q changes as D changes. D flip-flops are used to hold data sent to them on the D inputs, so the data, even though long since gone from the D input, will still be available on the Q output.

A *D edge-triggered flip-flop* is an elementary module like the D flip-flop, except that the data stored in it and available on the Q output are made equal to the D input only when the clock C changes from false to true. The clock causes the data to change (the flip-flop is clocked) in this very short time. A *D master slave flip-flop* (also called a dual-rank flip-flop) is a pair of D flip-flops where the D input to the second is internally connected to the Q output of the first, and the clock of the second is the complement of the clock of the first. Though constructed differently, a D master slave flip-flop behaves the same as the D edge-triggered flip-flop. These two flip-flops have the following property: data on their Q output are always the former value of data in them at the time that new data are put into them. It is possible, therefore, to use the signal output from an edge-triggered flip-flop to feed data into the same or another edge-triggered flip-flop using the same clock, even while loading new data. This should not be attempted with D flip-flops, because the output will be changing as it is being used to determine the value to be stored in the flip-flops that use the data. When a synchronous signal is input to a D edge-triggered flip-flop, the clock input to the flip-flop is associated with the signal, and the signal only has to be determinate when the clock changes from false to true.

In either type of flip-flop or in more complex devices that use flip-flops, the data have to be determinate (a stable high or a stable low signal) over a range of time when the data are being stored. For an edge-triggered or dual-rank flip-flop, the *setup time* is the time during which the data must be determinate before the clock edge. The *hold time* is the time after the clock edge during which the data must be determinate. For a latch, the setup time is the minimum time at the end of the period when the clock is true in which the data must be determinate; and the hold time is the minimum time just after that when the data must still be determinate. These times are usually specified for worst case possibilities. If you satisfy the setup and hold times, the device can be expected to work as long as it is kept at a temperature and supplied with power voltages that are within specified limits. If you don't, it may work some of the time, but will probably fail, according to Murphy's Law, at the worst possible time.

In most integrated circuit D flip-flops or D edge-triggered flip-flops, the output Q is available along with its complement, which can be thought of as the output Q in negative logic. They often have inputs, set, which if asserted will assert Q, and reset, which if asserted will make Q false. Set and reset are often in negative logic; when not used, they should be connected to a false value, or high signal. Other flip-flops such as set-reset flip-flops and JK edge-triggered flip-flops are commonly used in digital equipment, but we won't need them in the following discussions.

A *one-shot* is rather similar to the flip-flop. It has an input TRIG and an output Q, and has a resistor and capacitor connected to it. The output Q is normally false. When the input TRIG changes from false to true, the output becomes true and remains true for a period of time T which is fixed by the values of a resistor and a capacitor.

The use of 8-bit-wide data busses has engendered ICs that have four or eight flip-flops with common clock inputs and common clear inputs. If simple D flip-flops are used, the module is called a *latch*, and if edge-triggered flip-flops are used, it is a *register*. Also, modules for binary number counting (*counters*) or shifting data in one direction (*shift registers*) may typically contain four or eight edge-triggered flip-flops. Note that, even though a module may have additional capabilities, it may still be used without these capabilities. A counter or a shift register is sometimes used as a simple register. More interestingly, a latch can be used as a non-inverting gate or using the complemented Q output, as an inverter. This is done by tying the clock to true. The 74HC163 is a popular 4-bit binary counter, the 74HC164 and 74HC165 are common 8-bit shift registers, and the 74HC373 and 74HC374 are popular octal latches and registers, with built-in tristate drivers. The 74HC374 will be particularly useful in the following discussion of practical busses, since it contains a register to capture data from the bus, as well as a tristate driver to put data onto the bus.

The following conventions are used to describe flip-flops in logic diagrams. The clock and D inputs are shown on the left of a square, the set on the top, the clear on the bottom, and the Q on the right. The letter D is put by the D input, but the other inputs need no letters. The clock of an edge-triggered flip-flop is denoted by a triangle just inside the jointure of that input. This triangle and the bubble outside the square describe the clocking. If neither appears the flip-flop is a D flip-flop that inputs data from D when the clock is high; if a bubble appears, it is a D flip-flop that inputs data when the clock is low; if a triangle appears, it is an edge-triggered D flip-flop that inputs data when the clock changes from low to high; and if both appear, it is an edge-triggered D flip-flop that inputs data when the clock input changes from high to low. This notation is quite useful because a lot of design errors are due to clocking flip-flops when the data is not ready to be input. If a signal is input to several flip-flops, they should all be clocked at the same time, when the signal will be determinate.

The logic diagram of the 74HC374 is shown in figure 3-3b as it might appear in a catalogue. Note that the common clock for all the edge-triggered D flip-flops on pin 11 makes them store data on their own D inputs when it rises from low to high. Note that, when the signal on pin 1 is low, the tristate drivers are all enabled, so the data in the flip-flops is output through them. Using this integrated circuit in a logic diagram, we might compact it using the bus conventions, as shown in figure 3-3d.

An *(i,j) random access memory* (RAM) is a module with i rows and j columns of D flip-flops, and an address port, an input port, and an output port. A row of the memory is available simultaneously and is usually referred to as a *word,* and the number j is called the *word width*. There is considerable ambiguity here, because a computer may think of its memory as having a word width, but the memory module itself may have a different word width, and it may be built from RAM integrated circuits having yet a different word width. So the word and the word width should be used in a manner that avoids this ambiguity. The output port outputs data read from a row of the flip-flops to a bus and usually has bus drivers built into it. Sometimes the input and output ports are combined. The address port is used to input the row number of the row to be read or written. A *memory cycle* is a time when the memory can write j bits from the input port into a row selected by the address port data, read j bits from a row selected by the address port data to the output port, or do nothing. If the memory reads data, the drivers on the output port are enabled. There are two common ways to indicate which of the three possible operations to do in a memory cycle. In one, two variables called *chip enable* (CE) and *read/not write* (R/W) indicate the possibilities; a do nothing cycle is executed if CE is false, a read if CE and R/W are both asserted, and a write if CE is asserted but R/W is not. In the other, two variables, called *read enable* (RE) and *write enable* (WE), are used; when neither is asserted, nothing is done, when RE is asserted, a read is executed, and if WE is asserted, a write is executed. Normally, CE, RE, and WE are in negative logic. The *memory cycle time* is the time needed to complete a read or a write operation and be ready to execute another read or write. The *memory access time* is the time from the beginning of a memory cycle until the data read from a memory are determinate on the output, or the time when data to be written must be determinate on the input of the memory. A popular fast (20-nanosecond access time) (4,4) RAM is the 74LS670. It has four input ports and four separate output ports; by having two different address ports it is actually able to simultaneously read a word selected by the read address port and to write a word selected by the write address port. A larger, slower (500-

nanosecond cycle time) (2048,8) RAM is the 6116. It has an 11-bit address, eight input/output ports, and CE and W variables that permit it to read or write any word in a memory cycle. A diagram of this chip appears in figure 3-13a, when we consider an example that uses it in section 3-3.2.

Several cousins to the RAM are used in microcomputers, especially to store fixed data and programs. A *read-only memory* (ROM) is a rather large memory that can be read but can never be written into. The pattern stored in the memory is determined by a mask used in the final stages of manufacturing the chip. This mask is rather expensive; so ROMs are mass-produced using standard patterns and thus are not at all expensive. A *programmable read-only memory* (PROM) is a ROM that can be written into (*programmed*) by the designer by burning fuses inside it for each bit; a fuse is blown if an F is stored, and not blown if a T is stored. PROMs can be programmed by the designer, but he or she cannot unblow a fuse. An *erasable programmable read-only memory* (EPROM) is a PROM that, instead of fuses, uses static charges on a buried conductor in a dielectric insulation layer. A charge on the conductor cuts off the current below it, so it acts like a blown fuse. The charges are programmed similarly to a PROM's, but they can be removed by exposing the insulator to ionizing ultraviolet light. The *electronically erasable programmble memory* (EEPROM) is like an EPROM that can be erased by an electrical pulse rather than an ultraviolet light. It is not quite a RAM, however, as it takes ~10 msec. to erase and write. These devices – ROMs, PROMs, EPROMs, and EEPROMs – are often used to store fixed data and programs.

Recently, the programmable array logic (PAL) chip has become readily available and is ideally suited to implementing microcomputer address decoders and other "glue" logic. (See figure 3-4.) A PAL is basically a collection of gates whose inputs are connected by fuses like the PROM just mentioned. The second line from the top of figure 3-4 represents a 32-input AND gate that feeds the tristate enable of a 7-input NOR gate, which in turn feeds pin 19. Each crossing line in this row represents a fuse, which, if left unblown, connects the column to this gate as an input; otherwise the column is disconnected, and a T is put into the AND gate. Each triangle-shaped gate with two outputs generates a signal and its complement, and feeds two of the columns. The second line from the top can have any input from pins 2 to 9 or their complement, or the outputs on pins 12 to 19 or their complement, as inputs to the AND gate. For each possible input, the fuses are blown to select the input or its complement, or to ignore it. Thus, the designer can choose any AND of the 16 input-output variables or their complements as the signal controlling the tristate gate. Similarly, the next seven lines each feed an input to the NOR gate, so the output on pin 19 may be a Boolean "sum-of-products" of up to seven "products," each of which may be the AND of any input-output or its complement. This group of eight rows is basically replicated for each NOR gate. The middle four groups feed registers clocked by pin 1, and their outputs are put on pins 14 to 17 by tristate drivers enabled by pin 11. The registers can store a state of a sequential machine, which will be discussed further in chapter 4. PALs such as the PAL16L8 have no registers and are suited to implementing address decoders and other collections of gates needed in a microcomputer system. There is now a rather large family of PALS, having from zero to eight registers and one to eight inverted or noninverted outputs in a 20-pin DIP, and there also are 24-pin DIP PALs. These can be programmed to realize just about any simple function, such as an address decoder.

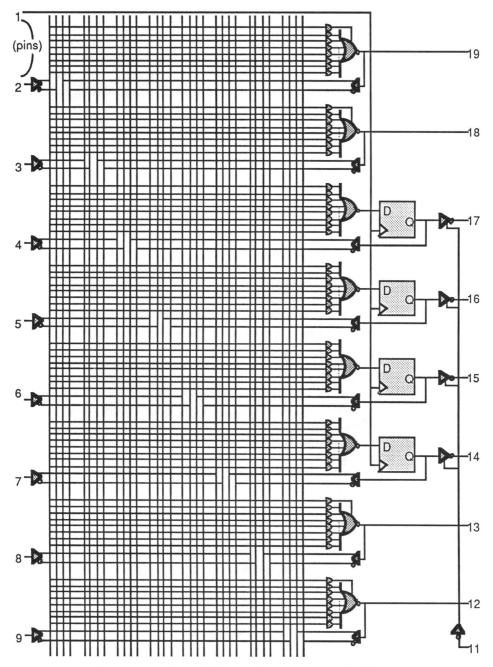

Figure 3-4. 16R4 PAL Used in Microcomputer Designs

3-2 Control Signals and their Sequences in a Microprocessor

One of the main problems designers face is how to control bus drivers so two of them will never try to drive the same bus at the same time. To approach this problem, the designer must be acquainted with control signals and the sequences of control signals generated by a microprocessor. This section is devoted to aspects of microprogramming and microcomputer instruction execution necessary for the comprehension and explanation of control signals on the microcomputer bus. The first subsection covers the basics of microprogramming, laying the groundwork for the next subsection. That subsection discusses the way the MC68HC11 actually executes an instruction such as LDAA #5. With this discussion, you should understand the sequencing of control signals, which is at the heart of the aforementioned problem.

3-2.1 Data Transfers and Microprograms

We now look at the control of a bus by examining the data transfer and the microprogram. *Microprogramming,* explained in this subsection, is the discipline of writing microprograms to convert instructions read by the computer to the actions that carry out those instructions. It will be used in the next subsection to discuss the timing of signals on the MC68HC11 address and data busses. Because microprogramming is an extensive subject that can barely be covered in a whole course, this subsection covers only those aspects important in designing microcomputer-based systems. One part of a microprogram deals with the control of the machine, and the other deals with the sequence of control, much the way jump instructions control a program. We will eschew the study of the sequence and concentrate on how the microprogram controls the computer. At this level of detail, one can best explain bus data transfer concepts.

The concept of the data transfer focuses our attention on the data as they move from module to module. This is an orthogonal view of the sequential machine that concentrates on a module as different data are moved into it. For simplicity, we will discuss data transfers on a single bus; and for concreteness, we will describe a bus using the integrated circuits just discussed.

Consider a bus, to which the outputs of several drivers and the D inputs to several registers are attached. The operation of moving data through this bus by enabling exactly one of the drivers and clocking one or more of the registers, is a *data transfer*. A data transfer here takes place in a time called a *microcycle*. The driver selected to send out the data is enabled throughout almost all of the microcycle, and the clocks of the registers selected to receive the data are asserted so that they copy the data near the end of the microcycle, while the enable is still asserted. Suppose A and B are registers. The data transfer describes the actual movement of data. We denote a data transfer thus:

$$A \leftarrow B$$

meaning that in this microcycle, the value that was in B at its beginning is copied into register A.

We offer to clear up some common misconceptions about data transfers. Some worry about clocking two registers at the same time – that this might drain the signal on the bus, perhaps making it too weak to recognize. Actually, a register uses the same amount of signal output from a driver, whether or not it is clocked. It is only important that the number of inputs physically connected to the bus be less than the fan-out of the bus drivers. Usually, tristate gate enables and latch clocks are in the negative logic relation. That is, when off, they are high, and when on, they are low. The reason for this convention is that TTL decoders, which usually generate these control signals, are easier to build and faster if their outputs are in negative logic. If they are asserted (low) throughout the microcycle or at least during as much of the microcycle as possible, the driver will put data on the bus throughout the cycle and the data will be clocked into the latch throughout the cycle. The value actually stored there will be that value input at the very end, when its clock input rises from low to high, as the signal changes from true to false. (The register clocks also use negative logic to be interchangeable with latches, but a little gremlin inverts the variable because the register is actually clocked by the beginning of the next cycle. But the explanation is only of interest as a good question for a Master's degree exam. Practically speaking, we make sure that the edge that clocks data into the register occurs at the end of the microcycle.)

The enables on the tristate gates and the clocks on the registers are called *control variables* and are generated by a *controller*. The assignment of value(s) to control variable(s) is a *micro-order*. The driver enable variables should have the following property: that exactly one of them is asserted, while the others are false. A collection of variables in which only one variable is asserted is called *singular*. For instance, if the variables A, B, and C are singular, they can have the values TFF, FTF, or FFT. The values TTF or TTT are not permitted (and in a strict sense of the term, FFF is not permitted). The driver enable variables must be singular, and, although they don't have to be, the register clock variables are often singular. It is possible to more compactly store and transmit a collection of n singular variables by *encoding* them in binary; that is, each variable is assigned a number from 0 to n-1, and the binary number of the asserted variable is stored and transmitted. The binary number is called a *code* for the driver or clock that it enables. This way, for instance, three wires can be used in lieu of eight wires. However, ultimately, the code has to be *decoded* so that the singular variables are individually available to enable each driver or clock each register. A related idea is that of *recoded* control variables. Suppose a module, such as an integrated circuit, has its control variables encoded so that, for instance, eight sources inside the module can put data onto a bus and only three wires, or pins, are needed to actually send the code into the module to select the source. If the system will only need three of these sources of data, then really only two wires are needed to uniquely identify the source. The n sources are assigned numbers 0 to n-1, and the binary numbers are stored and sent. A *recoder* then converts these into the codes actually used by the device. Encoding and recoding can be used to advantage to reduce the cost of the controller, but their operation can add some time to the microcycle, slowing down the processor. This may be unacceptable in some cases.

The controller can be built using one-shots, shift registers, and a mess of gates, or it can be designed around a memory. Because the latter is much easier to describe and becoming more popular, we discuss it here. First, the relatively simple *horizontal microprogram* technique is discussed. A *control memory* C stores a *microprogram*. One row, say row *i*, is read out during a microcycle. Each column, say column *j*, directly feeds an enable or clock control variable. The bit in row *i*, column *j*, is true if the *j*th enable or clock is to be asserted whenever the *i*th row is read out. Although it is not essential, a counter can provide addresses to sequentially read each row out of the memory, row *i*+1 right after row *i*. The microprogram is written for the memory, and the memory is filled with the desired values, so that when it is read out, the data transfers will be executed as desired.

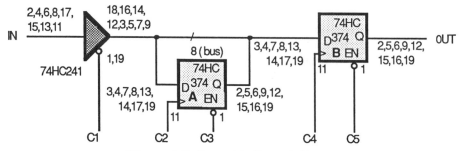

Figure 3-5. Bus with Control Signals

We now give a concrete example of the data transfer and the horizontal microprogram. Consider a simplified bus (see figure 3-5). Suppose, in one microcycle, we wish to transfer the variable IN to the register A (shown in boldface), and, in the next microcycle, to transfer the contents of A into B. (The data in B are always output in link OUT.) This is denoted by the transfers written in two successive lines:

$$A \leftarrow IN$$
$$B \leftarrow A$$

To transfer this data, the following micro-orders are given. In the first microcycle, C1 and C2 are asserted. This puts the data IN onto the bus and then copies this data into register A. In the second microcycle, C3 and C4 are asserted. Consider a slight variation of this microprogram. In one microcycle, the data IN are to be sent to both registers A and B. This is denoted

$$A \leftarrow IN; B \leftarrow IN$$

and the two data transfers on the same line are assumed to take place simultaneously in the same microcycle. Now, to put IN on the bus, C1 is asserted, and both C2 and C4 are simultaneously asserted. By this means, the data are copied simultaneously into both registers.

Some remarks about timing are now noted. When asserted, C1 and C3 should be held low (since they are in negative logic) for the whole duration of the step. When the edge-trigger clocks C2 and C4 are to be asserted, the rising edge of the signal on pin 11 should arrive towards the end of the step, while C1 or C3 are still asserted. Normally, these clock variables are ANDed with a square wave, so they are never asserted during the first half of the microcycle; there will thus always be a rising edge at the end of the microcycle even if the variable is asserted in two successive microcycles. This rising edge also has to occur when the data is determinate, to satisfy the setup and hold times of all the flip-flops that are loading it. The step's duration must be longer than the delay time for a signal to travel from any output to any input, including the setup and hold times of the flip-flops loading it. This delay time essentially determines the fastest clock that can be used with the system.

To continue our example, horizontal microprograms will be shown for the aforementioned data transfers. Suppose C1, C2, C3, and C4 are output from the respective columns of control memory, and the transfer A ← IN is ordered whenever row 5 is read, and the transfer B ← A is ordered whenever row 6 is read. Then the control memory will have the following words in rows 5 and 6, respectively:

$$TTFF$$
$$FFTT$$

Note that if stored in negative logic, the control memory will have in rows 5 and 6:

$$LLHH$$
$$HHLL$$

We distinguish between the signal and the variable here because, if we were to use 1 and 0 when we write the microprogram on paper, we would write line 5 as 1100, but when we store it in the control memory, we write the same line as 0011. For the second microprogram, if it is executed when row 8 is read, row 8 will be

$$TTFT$$

or, if the memory stores variables in negative logic,

$$LLHL$$

These concepts are now extended. Suppose a collection of control variables, coming from columns m to n of the control memory, are singular. (That is, at most, one of the control variables is ever asserted at any given time.) Then we can compress them into fewer variables and columns by encoding them. A decoder module will be needed to decode the codes to obtain the singular control variables needed for the drivers and registers; the codes are then stored in the compressed columns in lieu of the singular control signals themselves. Moreover, if recoders are used on the outputs of some columns to further compact the number of columns, the recoded codes are then stored therein. This compaction process can be carried to an extreme, so that only one code is stored on each row of the control memory, and all control variables are derived from it by a collection of decoders and recoders. Such a microprogram is called *vertical* as opposed to horizontal. Note that in a horizontal microprogram, all control variables have their own columns in the control memory, and no decoding or recoding is used. Most microprograms have some decoding and recoding and are thus somewhere between vertical and horizontal microprograms.

We extend our example to show how vertical microprogramming is implemented. Noting that the gate enables C1 and C3 in the previous example must be singulary because only one data word can be put on the bus in a microcycle, we can encode them so that the code T orders C1 asserted, and the code F orders C3 asserted. Then if the memory stored this code, followed by the clocks C2 and C4, the first microprogram would be stored thus:

TTF
FFT

In general, if n control variables are singulary, they can be encoded into $\log_2 n$ bits to save quite a bit of microprogram storage space. Note that if the clocks were also encoded, another column could be deleted, but the second microprogram would not work because no code would permit both clocks to be enabled simultaneously. A further example is offered to show the concept of recoding. Suppose a microprogram memory has the following rows:

TFTTFT
TTFTTT
FFFFFF
FFTFFT

in which the leftmost two columns and the rightmost two columns have only the patterns TF...FT, TT...TT, FF...FF and FF...FT and never have any other patterns. Since there are only four patterns, they could be replaced by two ($\log_2 4$) columns and a recoder would be used to recover the original codes. The recoder can be implemented with gates or a small ROM or an equivalent device called a programmable logic array. Suppose we implement the recoder with a ROM having the following pattern:

FFFF
TTTT
TFFT
FFFT

and the original microprogram is then rewritten so that, say, the first two columns generate an address into this ROM, making the ROM generate the control signals from its columns 1 to 4 that were generated from columns 1, 2, 5, and 6 of the original microprogram. Then the new microprogram would look like this:

TFTT
FTFT
FFFF
TTTF

Using recoding, it is possible to generate the hundreds of control signals needed to run a computer from microprograms with word widths of a few 10s of bits.

3-2.2 The Fetch-Execute Cycle

Our attention will soon focus on the microprocessor's data and address busses. To feel comfortable with the signals we see, we first look inside the microprocessor to see how it executes a typical instruction.

Recall from Section 1-1.2 that an instruction is executed in a period called a fetch-execute cycle, which is composed of several memory cycles. The first memory cycle is called the fetch cycle, and is used to fetch the first word of the instruction (or the first few words, if the instruction takes several words) from memory. The next memory cycles decode and execute the instruction. A memory cycle, the basic time unit of the primary memory connected to the microprocessor, may correspond to one or several microcycles, which are the basic time units for data transfers inside the microprocessor.

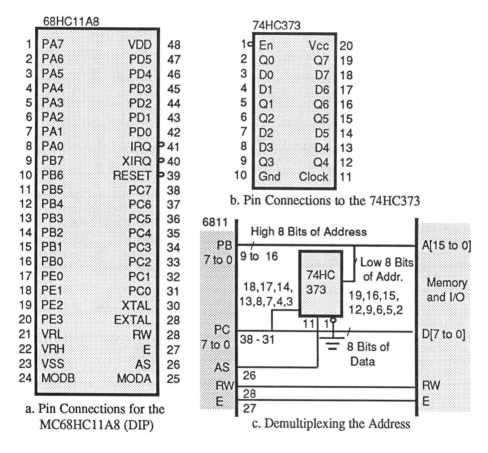

Figure 3-6. Connections to the MC68HC11 for the Expanded Multiplexed Bus Mode

The MC68HC11 uses a multiplexed data bus in the expanded multiplexed, as opposed to the single-chip, mode (see section 1-3.2). We use the expanded multiplexed mode in following discussion because we wish to examine the address and data busses using a logic analyzer, and because these busses must be examined outside the chip. The single-chip mode is identical to the multiplexed mode except that the busses are internal to the chip, so they can't be examined, and they are not time-multiplexed. The reason for the use of multiplexing will become clear when we examine the timing of the signals in a later section. Figure 3-6a shows the pin connections of the MC68HC11 (48-pin dual in-line plastic package) and figure 3-6b shows the pin connections of an 74HC373 used to recover the low 8 bits of the address from the data bus. This chip is essentially identical to the 74HC374 shown in figure 3-3b, except that the chip is a latch with a positive clock rather than a register with a rising edge clock. The MC68HC11 pins used for ports B and C in the single-chip mode are used for the address and data busses in the external multiplexed mode. Port B provides the high 8 bits of the address at all times. Pin 9 on the MC68HC11 provides address bit 15, pin 8, bit 14, and so on. Port C provides the low 8 bits of the address during a part of the memory cycle when the address strobe AS is high, and provides the 8 data bus bits at another time. Figure 3-6c shows the circuit needed to recover the low bits of the address from the multiplexed data bus. The MC68HC11 pin 38, which contains bit 7 of the data or address, is connected to pin 18 of the 74HC373, which is the data input for the flip-flop whose output is on pin 19, which provides address bit 7; and the MC68HC11 pin 37, which is address/data bit 6, is put into pin 17 of the 74HC373, which outputs address bit 6 on pin 16; and so on. The clock input of the 74HC373 is connected to address strobe AS, pin 26 of the MC68HC11, and the enable pin on the 74HC373 is connected to ground to enable the chips's outputs. (See figure 3-14b for a complete logic diagram of this circuit.)

We now examine the memory cycles to execute the instruction

LDAA #5

in a microprocessor like the MC68HC11. The instruction takes 2 words of memory, say from rows 100 and 101. The operation code (opcode) $86 indicating this is an LDAA instruction is in row 100, and the immediate operand 5 is in row 101.

In the previous section, we studied one bus, using popular driver and register integrated circuits. However, although to study the microprocessor, we would have to know about unconventional circuits used inside a large integrated circuit, we can and will use drivers and registers that are behaviorally equivalent to those studied previously. We will ignore the control lines and show only the address and data busses for clarity. (See figure 3-7.) The following discussion is actually how, within these limitations, the MC68HC11 executes the LDAA#5 instruction. We will concentrate on the behavior of an expanded multiplexed bus implementation, since that will permit us to talk about what we observe with a logic analyzer and what we have to interface to, but the same ideas apply inside the chip to the single-chip mode.

In the microprocessor, a 16-bit internal address bus that sends an address to internal memory also connects through tristate bus drivers to the external 16-bit address bus that sends addresses to external memory. The 8-bit data bus inside the microprocessor sends data to or from internal memory; or it sends data through tristate drivers to or takes data through a buffer register from the external 8-bit data bus connected to the external memory. A read/write control signal R/W is asserted when the external memory is requested to read and is false when it should write. Address and data bus signals are multiplexed and demultiplexed to get them out of the microcomputer chip, but this transformation is not important to the following discussion and is ignored.

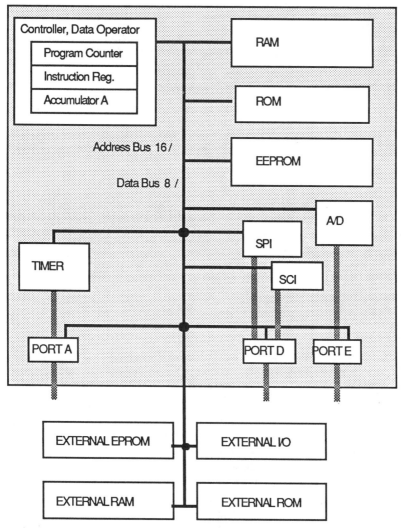

Figure 3-7. MC68HC11 Microprocessor (Expanded Multiplexed Bus)

Several 16-bit registers, including the program counter (PC), can put data onto the internal address bus, and a 16-bit incrementer is able to input data from this bus, increment the data, and feed them to the PC. Several 8-bit registers, including accumulator A (ACCA), can put data on the internal data bus. An adder adds data on the internal data bus to data selected from one of several registers, including ACCA, and inputs the result to one of these registers. Data on the external data bus can be put on the internal data bus, and this in turn can be put into several registers, including ACCA and the instruction register (I).

In describing the data transfers, we must use more notation. PC ← PC + 1 means that the register PC is loaded with the old value of PC (there at the beginning of the microcycle) plus 1. That is, it is incremented. A+B is the binary number sum of the contents of registers A and B. M[PC;] is the row of memory M whose address is the binary number PC. In the first memory cycle of any instruction, the instruction must be fetched into the I register using the address supplied by the PC register, and the PC register must be incremented as follows:

$$PC \leftarrow PC + 1; I \leftarrow M[PC;]$$

After the instruction is fetched into I, the controller in the microprocessor begins to decode the instruction, to issue micro-orders to carry it out. Here each instruction is different. For the LDAA #5 instruction, the second memory cycle will require us to get the immediate operand (the number 5) into ACCA. The operand is recalled using the program counter, since it is stored as the second word of the instruction. The program counter has to be incremented so that it is ready to fetch the next instruction. The following data transfer notation,

$$PC \leftarrow PC + 1; ACCA \leftarrow M[PC;]$$

means that next instruction has been fetched and decoded in the next cycle. And in the following memory cycle, it will be executed.

These data transfers take place in the following way. The fetch cycle always enables the PC register's bus drivers to put the PC register's contents (100) onto the internal address bus to internal memory; this is then put onto the external address bus to send the instruction's address to external memory. Only one of the two memories will respond by reading back a word. Meanwhile, the PC register clock is asserted, so it copies the output of the incrementer at the end of the cycle. The PC now has 101. By asserting the R/W control line, the internal or external memory is ordered to read the word at the address 100. This word, the opcode for the LDAA instruction, is sent by means of the data bus to be clocked into the I register at the end of the cycle. In the second memory cycle, the PC sends address 101 to memory and is incremented, just as in the first cycle. It now becomes 102. Again, memory is ordered to read the word at the address (101) onto the data bus. By this time, the opcode has been decoded as an LDAA, so the data are clocked into the ACCA register at the end of the cycle.

When we look at the microprocessor, we see only the activity on the external address bus and the external data bus, and the R/W control. We can sometimes infer the activity inside the integrated circuit microprocessor from these signals, but usually it does not matter whether we know what is going on. We see that in the first memory cycle, the fetch cycle, the contents of the program counter are output on the address bus, and the instruction appears on the data bus; and in the second memory cycle, the program counter plus one appears on the address bus, as the immediate operand appears on the data bus; and the R/W signal is high in both cycles. What we see is what we need to interface to a memory or an I/O device. We need not know that the instruction actually takes three cycles from beginning to end. Nor do we need to know which internal registers are used to hold the data from one cycle to the next. But there is an advantage to being aware of such internal activity: some unusual signals that appear on the busses from time to time will make sense.

We can see the external address, the external data bus signals, and the R/W signal, on a *logic analyzer*. This flexible instrument is capable of storing and displaying a sequence of digital signals. A pattern is set up in the logic analyzer, and when this pattern is found on the busses, the data are stored in the logic analyzer for each consecutive clock cycle until the memory in the logic analyzer is full. Then the display can be used to examine the memory to see what happened.

The 6811 has a rich instruction set and a lot of addressing modes. This makes it a challenge to describe the behavior on the busses for each instruction. But it is often necessary to know what is happening on them because we need to coordinate them with some other operations; or, if we need to find out why the system is not working, this is the only thing we can look at using a logic analyzer. Figure 3-8 presents a breakdown of all the 6811 instructions and the sequences that honor the interrupts (SWI instruction). Figure 3-8 can be used to determine what is happening on the address and data busses and the R/W line during each memory cycle in the execution of each instruction, to establish the timing for I/O operations, to interpret the signals on a logic analyzer, or just to find out exactly how long an instruction takes to be executed.

The memory cycles are denoted by letters, whose interpretation is given in table 3-1. They tell you which register in the MC68HC11 supplies the address, but they do not tell you whether the register is incremented in that memory cycle. Since the registers are usually fairly far apart, you can use this rough information to read the logic analyzer. Figure 3-8 is organized to help you read the output of a logic analyzer.

The left top of figure 3-8 shows an optional F shown in parenthesis. This means a cycle is used to fetch a prebyte, if there is one. There is a prebyte of \$CD for the instructions CPD n,Y CPX n,y, LDX n,Y, and STX n,Y. There is a prebyte of \$1A for CPY n,X, LDY n,X, STY n,x, and all the CPD instructions except CPD n,Y. There is a prebyte of \$18 for all instructions that have a Y in their mnemonic or that use Y index addressing except the ones noted above. In any of these instructions, an initial fetch is needed to fetch the prebyte.

Figure 3-8 can be used to find the sequence for an instruction. The top row shows that the instruction ABA is executed by the sequence FF. That is, this instruction takes two cycles, and the program counter gives the address both times. (The second fetch of this 1-byte instruction fetches the first byte of the next instruction, which is ignored; it will be fetched again later.) ASLA and ASLB, denoted by ASLr in figure 3-8, have the same sequence as ABA. Line 3 has a special TEST instruction used for checking the part at the factory; it is FFFF*, where * means repeat indefinitely. Line 6 shows that the instruction LDD d, using direct addressing, has the sequence FFFDD; 3 bytes are fetched and then the 2-byte piece of data is read using the effective address. On line 8, the instruction JSR d has a sequence FFFDSS. Three bytes are fetched with the program counter, then the piece of data at that address is read (it is the first byte of the instruction in the subroutine to be jumped to, and is ignored; it will be fetched again later), and then the stack pointer is used to write the return address. Line 10 shows that the instruction TST d has the sequence FFFDNN; the last two cycles are where the location \$FFFF is read and the piece of data read is ignored. The 6811 is doing something inside the controller and data operator, and tells memory to read \$FFFF so it will do something harmless during these cycles. The S* in the WAI sequence, about two-thirds of the way down the figure, means repeatedly read the last byte stacked an arbitrary number of times (while the interrupt is being waited for); and H means a high byte is read – to get the

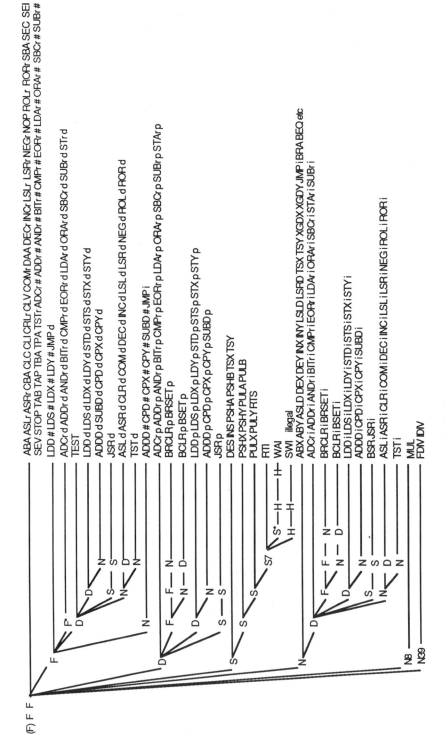

Figure 3-8. MC68HC11 Memory Cycle Sequences

124

address of the interrupt handler. The S7 in the sequence for RTI means seven stack operations, and N8 in the second to bottom line means eight null cycles are used.

Figure 3-8 can be used to read the output of a logic analyzer. There is a signal on a pin on the MC68HC11 that indicates a new instruction is being read. If it is a prebyte, as recently described, then it accounts for the fetch shown in parentheses. Then follow the tree to decode the pattern. For instance, if the pattern is FFFDDN, then the instruction is ADDD d CPDd CPX d or CPY d, and the prebyte and opcode will help you determine more exactly what it is.

Table 3-1. Symbols Used in Figure 3-8

F	Fetch an Opcode: PC used
D	Recall or Memorize Data: Effective Address Used
S	Read or Write on Stack: Stack Pointer Used
H	Read High Memory -Locations of Interrupt Handlers
N	Null - Read Location $FFFF and Ignore Data
#	Immediate Address
p	Page 0 (8-bit) Address
d	Direct (16-bit) Address
i	Index Address with 8-bit Offset
r	Register: A or B
*	0 or More Occurrences of the Previous Symbol
8	8 Occurrences of the Previous Symbol

The real value of figure 3-8 is in interpreting a pattern read from the logic analyzer. The D symbol corresponds to the memory cycles in which data are read from or written to memory. The address bus shows the effective address that was computed by the instruction, and the data bus shows the piece of data that was read or written. This is what you need to find the bugs in a program. With a little practice, you should be able to determine what each instruction is doing on the address and data busses in each of its memory cycles. But it will become even more clear when you use a logic analyzer, as you will when we study the timing of I/O operations in section 4-2.1 and the sequence that honors an interrupt in section 5-2.2.

3-3 Interfacing to the Bus

One of the most common problems faced by interface designers is the problem of bus timing and the generation of control signals to the bus. These will be considered in this section. The first subsection considers the analysis of timing information needed to connect a microprocessor to another device. The second subsection shows a simple example of a complete interfacing design to connect a memory to a microcomputer. The third subsection considers the connection of boards to motherboards, the timing of signals through them, and the consideration of control signals that are used to drive this expanded bus.

3-3.1 Address and Data Bus Timing

To connect memory or I/O registers to the microprocessor, the actual timing requirements of the address bus and data bus have to be satisfied. If one uses modules from the same family, such as integrated circuits designed to be compatible with the Motorola MC6811, the timing requirements are usually automatically satisfied. However, when mixing modules from different families or when putting heavy demands on the modules' capabilities, one may have to analyze the timing requirements carefully. Therefore, we discuss them here.

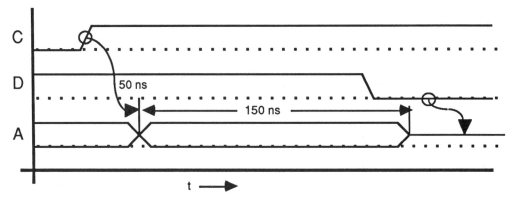

Figure 3-9. Some Timing Relationships

Timing diagrams are used to show the requirements. A timing diagram is like an oscilloscope trace of the signals, such as is shown in figure 3-9. For collections of variables, like the 16 address lines shown by the trace labeled A, two parallel lines indicate that any particular address line may be high or low, but will remain there for the time interval where the lines are parallel. A crossing line indicates that any particular line can change at that time. A line in the middle of the high and low line levels indicates the output is floating because no drivers are enabled, or the output may be changing as it tries to reach a stable value. A line in the middle means the signal is indeterminate; it is not necessarily at half the voltage. (Motorola also uses a cross-hatch pattern like a row of X's to indicate that the signal is invalid but not tristated, while a line in the middle means the output is in the tristate open circuit mode on the device being discussed. That distinction is not made in this book, because both cases mean that the bus signal is indeterminate and cannot be used.) Causal relationships, such as a control variable C causing the address lines to change, are shown by arrows from cause to effect. The cause is usually an edge if the change is made by clocking a register, or a level if the effect is a result of enabling a driver. On the left side of figure 3-9, we indicate that a rising edge of C causes the address lines A to change. Note the circle around the edge showing the cause is the edge. On the right side, we indicate that a low level of signal D causes the address lines to float. Timing is usually shown to scale, as on an oscilloscope, but delays from cause to effect are shown by writing the time by the arrow, and requirements are indicated the way dimensions are shown on a blue print. On the left, the addresses change 50 nanoseconds after C rises, and, in the middle, we indicate the address should be stable for more than 150 nanoseconds.

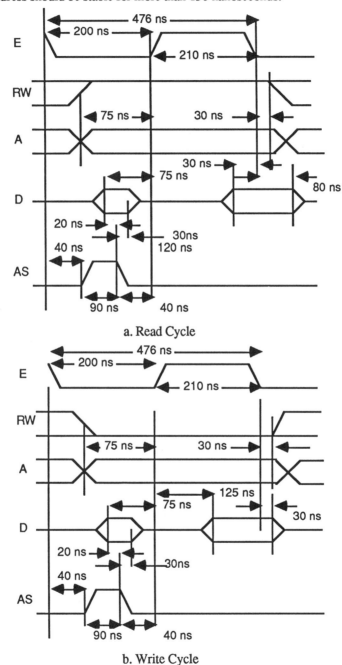

a. Read Cycle

b. Write Cycle

Figure 3-10. Timing Relationships for the MC68HC11

Whether the microprocessor is putting the data into the I register or the DBI register, memory signals are the same. The signals for writing data are similar. We'll look at an example to show the principles of bus transfers, using approximate numbers for timing. (See figure 3-10 for approximate timing relationships of the MC6811.) The timings represent worst case numbers and don't necessarily add up; for instance, the E clock is low for at least 200 nanoseconds and high for at least 210 nanoseconds (adding up to 410 nanoseconds) but the cycle time may be no shorter than 476 nanoseconds. Other microprocessors have similar timing relationships.

The clock used in memory (called the *E clock* or the *enable*) is shown in figure 3-10 as trace E; it can have a little faster than a 1/2 microsecond square wave (the period may be 476 nanoseconds). A memory cycle begins and ends when E falls from high to low. The AS *Address Strobe* is like the E clock but is used to clock the low-order bits of the address from the multiplexed data bus, as shown in figure 3-6. This 90-nanosecond pulse occurs 40 nanoseconds after E falls. The address bus is indeterminate until 75 nanoseconds before E rises. This delay is due to the propagation of control signals to gate drivers and the propagation of the address through the internal AB bus to the external A bus. The address's low 8 bits are on the multiplexed address and data bus for 20 nanoseconds before and 30 nanoseconds after the address strobe falls. In a read cycle, the read/write signal, shown in trace R/W, remains high throughout the cycle, and the microprocessor expects valid data on the data bus for 30 nanoseconds before and 80 nanoseconds after the falling edge of E. These times are the setup and hold times of the I and DBI registers inside the MC6811. If any data line changes in this interval, the microprocessor may input either an L or H on that line. The memory is responsible for providing valid and constant signals during this interval during the setup and hold time. In a write cycle, the R/W signal is guaranteed low at the time the address becomes stable and can rise 30 nanoseconds after the beginning of the next cycle. Due to delays in the path of the control signal and the delay through the bus driver between the DB bus and D bus (see figure 3-7), the data to be written are put on the D bus and are guaranteed determinate 125 nanoseconds after the rising edge of E and remaining stable for 30 nanoseconds after E falls. These signals are available to use to control the memory. We note, however, that R/W does not have a rising edge whose timing can be depended upon. R/W is *not a timing signal.* You cannot depend on it to satisfy setup and hold times. Similarly, address signals are not precisely aligned with the memory cycle. Such timing signals are often required and can be obtained by ORing the R/W with the inverted E clock or ANDing E with address signals (see figure 4-16 in section 4-1.2).

The use of E and AS in the MC6811 can simplify your interface logic. The address and R/W signals are determinate from the falling edge of AS until the falling edge of E, and the data are determinate when E is high.

In analyzing timing requirements, one compares the timing of two parts, such as the microprocessor and some memory to be connected. The object is to verify whether data will be available at the receiver when needed. One should be aware that a part may not meet all of its specifications. Some manufacturers just test a few parts from each batch, while others (such as Motorola) test each part for most specifications. A design in which some requirements are not satisfied may still work because some parts may surpass their specifications. In fact, if you are willing to take the time or pay the expense, you can *screen the parts* to find out which ones meet your tighter specifications. However, if the system fails because the design does not meet its parts' specifications, we blame the designer. If the design meets specifications but the system fails, we blame the part manufacturer or the part.

A typical memory has timing requirements that must be compatible with those of the microprocessor. In discussing these, we will give the approximate requirements of the very popular 6116, a 2K-byte, 1-byte-wide random access memory. The same memory is manufactured by different companies and even by the same company, with different timing requirements. Such variations are designated by letters or numbers added to the name 6116, such as in 6116-A, 6116-15, or MCM65116-20 (the letters MCM and the extra digit 5 have to do with how Motorola numbers memory chips; the 20 refers to the cycle time of 200 nanoseconds – see figure 3-11). We discuss this one.

The memory has a chip enable CE, read/write W, output enable G, an 11-bit address A, and 8 data pins D7 to D0. (See figure 3-11a.) The timing requirements are especially simple if G is connected to ground.

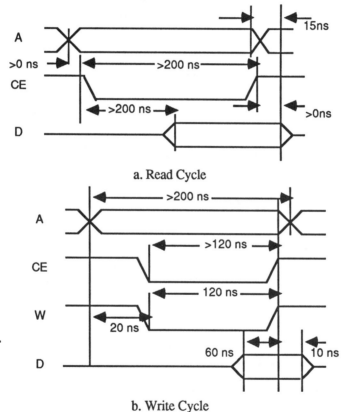

a. Read Cycle

b. Write Cycle

Figure 3-11. Timing Requirements of the Motorola MCM65116-20

In a read cycle, timing is based on the CE signal. The cycle begins when the address bus signal becomes stable. CE must fall after the address is stable and must be low for 200 nanoseconds. Data are available on the data bus pins from the byte addressed by A, 200 nanoseconds after CE falls and may go away as soon as CE rises or 15 nanoseconds after A changes.

In a write cycle, timing is based on the W signal. To prevent writing in the wrong word, the W signal should not fall until A has been stable for 20 nanoseconds and should be low for at least 120 nanoseconds, and the chip enable CE should be low for 120 nanoseconds while R/W is low. The data input on the data pins should be stable 60 nanoseconds before and 10 nanoseconds after the rising edge of W. These are the 6116's setup and hold times. If these requirements are met, the data input on the data bus pins will be stored in the bit at the address given by A. (Some 6116 chips require a rising edge on W to perform a write, and the 68HC11 leaves R/W low throughout the writing cycles of an instruction like STD and PSHX, so the high byte may not be written.)

We will now show why a multiplexed address and data bus are used. Note from figure 3-11 that data on the data pins of a memory like the 6116 are only provided at the end of a memory cycle in a read and are only needed at the end of the memory cycle in a write. The signals on the data bus in the first part of each memory cycle may be anything, for they are ignored. There is a shortage of pins on any integrated circuit, as we will observe again and again in this text. Therefore, to save pins, the address can be sent out of the MC68HC11 on the data pins.

To analyze the requirements to see if this 6116 is compatible with the MC68HC11, the requirements are compared for the read and write cycles. It turns out that the write cycle is satisfied, so we examine it first. The read cycle is not satisfied, as we see later.

For the write cycle, the requirements center on the 6116 W signal. The recently discussed OR gate could be used to modify R/W to fit with a 6116 memory so it occurs at a predictable place, when addresses are valid. The timing diagram for the 6116 should line up so that its W corresponds to the negative of E for the MC68HC11. We have to show that the address is valid to the 6116 when it is needed and that the data to the 6116 are steady when the 6116 writes them. Figure 3-12b shows that these requirements are satisfied. We verify that W derived from the MC68HC11 E clock is low for at least the 200 nanoseconds the 6116 requires, as shown by the heavy line (note it is low for the last 210 nanoseconds of the cycle), and that the address is determinate before W falls (note that it is determinate 75 nanoseconds before the MC68HC11 E rises). The address needed by the 6116 must last until its CE signal rises (because the MC68HC11 address is stable until at least 30 nanoseconds after the MC68HC11 E signal falls). This is shown by the gray areas of the address traces. The data must be determinate for 60 nanoseconds before the 6116 CE signal rises (they are stable for at least 125 nanoseconds before the MC68HC11 E clock rises) and stable for 10 nanoseconds after that rising edge (they are stable for 30 nanoseconds after the MC68HC11 E clock falls). This is shown by the gray areas of the data traces.

For the read cycle, the timing diagrams are referenced so the MC68HC11 E signal can be inverted to provide the 6116 enable CE, as shown by the heavy line in figure 3-12a. We verify that the CE signal is long enough, as we did in the write cycle analysis. We verify that the address from the MC68HC11 is stable while the 6116 needs it, as we did with the write cycle. It is satisfied, as shown by the gray areas of the address traces. Now we determine if the data get back to the MC68HC11 in good shape. We slide the 6116 timing diagrams so the time the MC68HC11 E clock rises is matched to the time the 6116 CE signal is to fall. To verify that the 6116 memory puts out stable data exactly when the MC68HC11 processor must receive stable data, we check to ensure that the gray area shown in the MC68HC11 data input signal falls entirely within the time the 6116 CE signal is to fall. To verify that the 6116 memory puts out stable data exactly when the MC68HC11 processor must receive stable data, we check to ensure that the gray area shown in the MC68HC11 data input signal falls entirely within the time the 6116 memory output is stable. It does not satisfy the setup (the data are stable only 10 nanoseconds before the falling edge of the MC68HC11 E clock, while they should be stable 30 nanoseconds) and hold times (the data need to be stable 80 nanoseconds after the falling edge of the MC68HC11 E clock, but are stable 0 nanoseconds) for the MC68HC11, so this memory chip cannot be used.

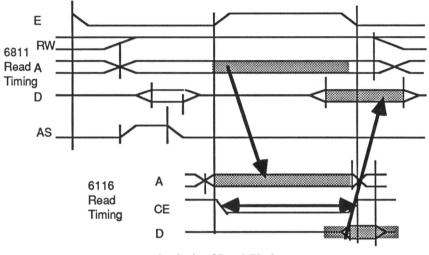

a. Analysis of Read Timing

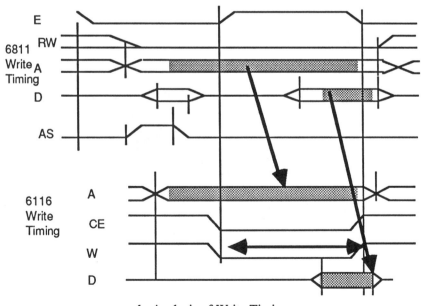

b. Analysis of Write Timing

Figure 3-12. Analysis of Memory Timing

Of the several possible solutions the following are the most practical: slow down the processor; use a faster memory; or modify the CE signal with some extra hardware. To achieve the first solution, you can slow down the MC68HC11's clock to lengthen the cycle so stable data will reach the MC68HC11 earlier in its cycle. To achieve the second, use a faster version of the 6116. For instance, the MCM65116-12 has access times of 120 nanoseconds, and the output of the memory could be allowed to stay on the data bus (because it has capacitance and thus holds the voltage on it for a short time) if no other device tries to drive it, so all requirements would be met. We could therefore use the MCM65116-12 rather than the MCM65116-20 to build a memory for the MC68HC11. To achieve the third solution, the 6116 CE signal could be generated by ORing the negative logic output of the address decoder with the complement of the E clock signal or else ANDing E into the address decoder input. Using some extra hardware, we could generate a CE that falls when AS falls, and rises when E falls. This would also satisfy the timing, but would be more work than the other two solutions.

We have observed that an analysis of timing requirements can help us select the parts needed to build a system. And, surprisingly, a 200-nanosecond cycle memory does not necessarily have timing characteristics that make it compatible to work with a 1/2 microsecond cycle microcomputer. We reiterate, though, that parts not meeting specifications on paper may work some of the time. However, it is best when a designer satisfies the requirements; then, if the system does not work, he or she can blame the parts supplier rather than personally take the blame.

3-3.2 The Design of a (2024,8) Memory for an MC68HC11

The design of a memory for a microprocessor illustrates some of the previous section's principles and introduces the decoder. The same principles are used in interfacing I/O registers, discussed in the next chapter, and these may be the object of many design travails.

The (n,8) memory such as the 6116 is very common because it is easy to make a (m,8) memory for an 8-bit processor. The memory we design for the MC68HC11 will appear at addresses $4000 to $47FF (hexadecimal). (See figure 3-13.) Since 2048 words need 11 bits of address, the low-order 11 bits from the address outputs of the MC68HC11 and 74HC373 are directly connected to the corresponding address pins of the 6116. The inverted R/W output of the MC68HC11 is ANDed with the E clock to obtain the 6116 W, and each of the data pins of the 6116 is connected to one of the MC68HC11's data bus pins.

The chip enable CE remains as the only signal to consider. It can come from an address decoder that will output a true (low) value whenever an address between $4000 and $47FF is put on the address bus. Analyzing all 2048 of these addresses, we can verify that the low-order 11 bits of the addresses can be T or F, but the high-order 5 bits must be FTFFF for all these addresses and no other addresses than these have such values. (The low-order 11 bits are decoded within the memory chip to select the byte to be read or written.) However, as noted in the analysis of timing, the E clock must be factored in to shape the 6116 CE signal. Thus, another input to the decoder ANDs the E clock into the 6116 CE signal. As the address bus is in positive logic, a 6-input positive logic AND gate with negative logic output will output a T (L) if each high-order address bit (except bit 14) is inverted, and each is input to the gate. (The simplified logic diagram is shown in figure 3-13b and the detailed logic diagram in figure 3-13c.)

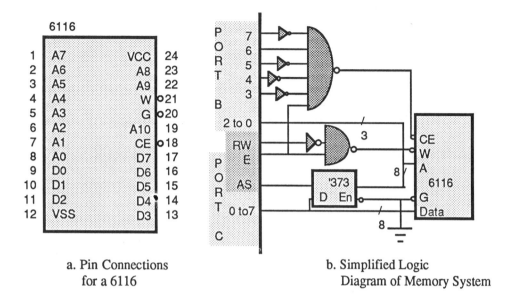

a. Pin Connections
for a 6116

b. Simplified Logic
Diagram of Memory System

Figure 3-13. An MCM6116 Memory System

Although the principle is the same, the implementation of address decoders in a typical microcomputer is usually simplified. These simplifications are now discussed.

If one required 4096 words of memory, one could connect two memory modules of the kind just discussed to the MC68HC11 as follows. The W and 11 low-order address lines are connected to all 6116 memories, the data bus pins from each memory module are connected to an MC68HC11 data bus pin, and the CE lines for each memory are connected to different decoders. If the first module should hold words $4000 to $47FF, the aforementioned decoder is used for it; if the other module holds words $4800 to $4FFF, its decoder would be almost identical – the only difference would be that address bit 11 would not be inverted on input to this AND gate. Up to 32 such memory modules could be connected to an MC68HC11 this way, to build a complete memory for it. However, most microcomputers only have as much memory as they will need and this may be around 8000 words.

Especially when many modules are used, a decoder integrated circuit is used to decode the high order bits of the address. The 74154 is a popular decoder that can select up to 16 modules; it has 16 different circuits like the AND gate in figure 3-13 to select each module. However, the tendency to use a chip just because it is there should be avoided. Most memory modules use the individual gate inside each module rather than a decoder integrated circuit outside the module to enable the memory. This reduces the number of pin connections between modules, and pin connections are much more costly than gates in current technology.

When a small number of modules is used, *incompletely specified decoding* may greatly simplify the hardware. Consider the system in figure 3-13 again. If address bit 11 is disconnected and its input to the decoder gate tied high, this memory would respond to addresses $4000 to $4FFF, and the first word in the memory would respond to addresses $4000 and $4800. If the program uses words $4000 and $4800, they will in fact be the same words. Similarly, $4001 and $4801 would be the same words. But if, say, the words from $4800 to $4FFF are never used in the program, then a simpler decoder without bit 11 would be adequate. It is possible to extend this technique to delete further decoder inputs. If only one memory module is used with the MC68HC11, then all inputs could be eliminated using this technique, and CE could be tied to the inverse of the MC68HC11 E clock. Then the same word in the module would be selected if the address were 0, $0800, $1000, $1800, $2000, and so on. Incompletely specified decoding can eliminate much of the hardware used to decode addresses in a microcomputer. But it should only be used when the program can be trusted to avoid using duplicate addresses. The technique is especially useful for small microcomputers dedicated to execute a fixed program which has no software bugs that might use duplicate addresses. It is not as useful for microcomputers used for software development.

Table 3-2. Address Assignments for a Microcomputer

Address line	15	14	13	12	11	10	9	8	7	6	5	4	3	2	1	0
memory mod 1	F	F	F	F	F	F	X	X	X	X	X	X	X	X	X	X
memory mod 2	T	T	T	T	T	T	X	X	X	X	X	X	X	X	X	X
register 1	T	F	F	F	F	F	F	F	F	F	F	F	F	F	F	T
register 2	T	F	F	F	F	F	F	F	F	F	F	F	F	F	T	F

We consider an example of an incompletely specified decoder. As we will see in the next chapter, input/output registers are implemented as if they were memory modules like the one just designed, but they have just one word in them. Suppose you use two memory modules, with addresses 0 to $03FF in the first and $FC00 to $FFFF in the second, and that two 1-word memory modules (I/O registers) at addresses $8001 and $8002 can be addressed. The permissible values of address variables are shown in table 3-2 (X is a "don't care").

Inspection of the permissible addresses indicates that memory module 1 is selected exactly when address 15 is false, and memory module 2 is selected exactly when address 14 is true. The registers are selected exactly when the two memory modules are not selected, and address lines 0 and 1 distinguish the two registers apart. Assuming positive logic address signals from the MC68HC11 and negative logic enables on all modules (the most common case), then the enable for the first memory module is address line 15, and for the second is the inverted address line 14; the register enables are simple logic functions of address lines 15, 14, 1, and 0. The entire decoder can be built from a single 7410 integrated circuit.

Returning to the design of the memory for the 6811, we can use incompletely specified decoding to simplify the logic of figure 3-13b, so the address decoder and the circuit producing the W signal can be implemented in one chip. The 74HC139 is a dual 1-of-4 decoder. It contains an assortment of 3-input NAND gates with inverters on several of the inputs. We assume the (2048,8) memory is the only device to be attached to the MC68HC11, and the MC68HC11 is configured as shown in figure 1-9. The 6-input NAND gate shown in figure 3-13b can be reduced to a 3-input NAND gate, which can be implemented in the 74HC139, by examining the address map of the MC68HC11. Note that inverted address bit A15 and address bit A14 and the E clock must be NANDed to get the memory chip enable for the following reasons. An inverted A15 is needed to prevent the memory from being enabled when ROM at $E000-$FFFF is accessed. A14 must be used to prevent enabling the memory when RAM at 0-$FF or I/O at $1000-$103F is accessed. As noted earlier, E must be used because the address is not stable during a good part of the first half of the memory cycle. The other address bits A13 to A11 are not needed to distinguish the memory from other devices in the memory map, so they can be eliminated from the decoder.

The 3-input NAND gate can be implemented in one of the gates in one half of the 74HC139. The other half of the 74HC139 can implement the circuit deriving the W pin of the memory chip. Although only two inputs are needed, the gates in the 74HC139 are 3-input NAND gates. The extra input could be tied high or low so it doesn't interfere. However, there is a minor point that involves the reset operation of the MC68HC11A8 which can use the extra input. When the MC68HC11A8 is reset, it sometimes writes randomly in memory. To prevent this, we can put the inverted reset signal into the NAND gate. The simplified final circuit is shown in figure 3-14a.

A complete logic diagram for the circuit is shown in figure 3-14b. A picture of this system appears on the front cover of this book. Entirely powered by a battery, this circuit is safe for experimenters. The MC68HC11A8 takes only 20 milliamperes, so the battery will last a long time. The MAX232 chip provides the necessary voltages and level conversion to connect a terminal or a personal computer such as a Macintosh to this circuit. See chapter 7 for additional details on communication systems and the use of this chip. The right half of this figure can be used as a single-chip microcomputer, but MODA (pin 25) needs to be grounded for single-chip operation.

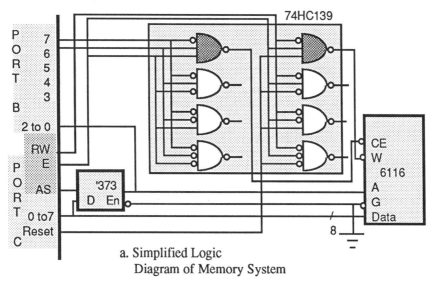

a. Simplified Logic
Diagram of Memory System

Figure 3-14. Practical Memory System

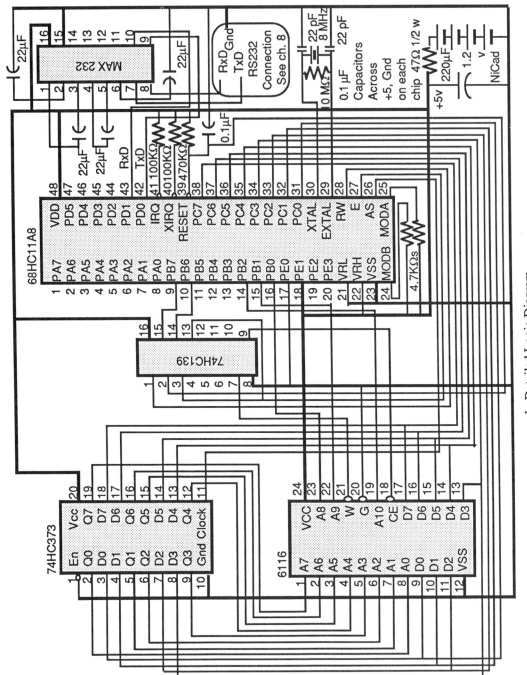

b. Detailed Logic Diagram
Figure 3-14. (continued)

136

3-3.3 Backplanes for Multiboard Computer Systems

A microprocessor has sufficient capability to drive one regular TTL gate, about four gates of the LS family, or around ten CMOS or HCMOS gates or other LSI MOS chips designed to be connected to the microprocessor. When a larger number of gates are connected or more than one regular TTL gate is to connect to a microprocessor line, buffers are usually used to raise the drive capability of that line. Especially when the system is built on several different printed circuit cards, buffers are used to send data between the cards.

Four problems commonly appear in the design of expanded busses. The first is the interconnection pattern of the bus drivers: without sufficient planning, there is a tendency to design straggly busses. The second problem is the satisfaction of timing requirements. The third is the prevention of enabling more than one bus driver at any time. And the fourth is the suppression of noise.

It is too easy to let the design of a system sort of grow, so that the signals are improperly distributed. Signals like the clock and R/W that is ORed with the complement of the E clock, have edges used as references to capture data on the busses. These edges usually should arrive at every point in the system at precisely – or as close as possible to – the same time. The difference in time between the arrivals of a signal at different points in the system is called the *skew*. If an output can be connected to f inputs, a tree structure with fan-out f is the best way to distribute a signal; the source of the signal drives f buffers, each of these drives f buffers, and so on. All modules using the signals should be at the leaves of the tree, with the same number of buffers between them and the source. Although buffers, even of the same type, can have significantly different delays, this practice reduces the skew to a minimum – however, even this minimum skew may still represent a significant problem.

Although the address bus is less time critical, the 16 address lines are usually distributed using a tree structure, with a pair of octal buffers like the 74HC244 at each branch of the tree. The data bus is not so easy to form, because it carries signals bidirectionally, from microprocessor to memory and from memory to microprocessor. A way to implement this type of bus in a tree is to use a pair of buffers like the 74HC244, connected back-to-back so the inputs of one connect to the outputs of the other. Alternatively, a 74HC245 contains a pair of drivers equivalent to two 74HC241s in the beforementioned configuration. Only one of the two drivers can be enabled at any time, and if several such buffers connect to a node of the tree, only one of the drivers feeding the node may be enabled. To determine which drivers to enable, we use some logic that considers the data's source, which must be either at the root or a leaf of the tree. At most, one source may be selected at any time. If a source on a leaf sends data, all rootward-going drivers between the leaf and the root are enabled, and, in all other branches of the tree, the leafward drivers are enabled. The signal will reach all the nodes on the tree in the shortest possible time. In a trivial bus using only one pair of drivers, the microprocessor is at the root, and all the devices are connected at the other end of the branch, at the only leaf. The R/W signal is the only one needed, because, when asserted, data flow rootward, and when not, data flow leafward. While the trivial case is by far the most common, the general case is also very simple.

When busses are expanded using drivers in this way, we must be aware of the delays through these buffers when we check the timing requirements of memories and other devices. Generally, the longest delay for any signal through the expanded bus must be added to the delays for signals using the bus in the analysis of the timing requirements. Also, the edges of the clock and R/W ORed with the complement of the clock signals may have to be delayed by the same amount as the signal to cancel the skew caused when the signal is sent through such expanded busses.

The analysis technique of section 3-3.1 using sliding timing diagrams can be modified to handle expanded busses, but a more general technique uses *interval arithmetic*. In many cases, delays can only be specified as a minimum value and a maximum value, which is an *interval* <min, max>. An arithmetic system has been defined for operating on intervals. For example, if one interval <min1,max1> is added to another interval <min2,max2>, the sum is a new interval <min1 + min2, max1 + max2>. For instance, the sum of <1,5> and <3,4> is <4,9>. The negative of an interval <min,max> is <-max,-min>. For instance, the negative of <-2,5> is <-5,2>.

So, delays can be specified as intervals, and can be added or subtracted using interval arithmetic. Using this tool, skews can be accounted for so we can be assured that, when an edge of a timing signal arrives, the setup and hold times are satisfied.

Consider an example of skewing calculations. Suppose that the data bus from an MC6811 is driven through one 74HC245 and the R/W signal is ORed with the complement of E through one 74HC32, to an MCM65116-20 random access memory chip. Will this satisfy the timing requirements, or will an MCM65116-12 be needed, as in the earlier analysis of timing requirements? The problem is to determine the time interval that the data from the MC6811must be stable so it is stable at the inputs of the 6116 throughout that chip's setup and hold times. Intuitively, we know that the MC6811 must supply stable data for a time (T6811) longer than the setup and hold time interval of the 6116 (T6116), to which the delay time through the 74HC32 (T7432) is added and from which the delay time through the 74HC245 (T74245) has been subtracted.

A formula can be checked out intuitively as if all intervals were just ordinary numbers. The minimum interval during which the MC6811 must provide stable data is

$$T6811 = T7432 + T6116 - T74245$$

The intervals are defined so 0 is the time that an ideal R/W signal rising edge would appear at that point. The setup and hold times for a device are <-setup, hold> and the delays are <min delay, max delay>. If the 74HC245 has a delay between 9 and 18 nanoseconds (the interval <9,18>), and the 74HC32 has a delay between 6 and 11 nanoseconds (the interval <6,11>), and the 6116 needs a setup and hold time of <-60,10> nanoseconds, the source of the data must make the data stable for a minimum interval of

$$\begin{aligned}
T6811 &= T7432 + T6116 - T74245 \\
&= <6,11> + <-60,10> - <9,18> \\
&= <6,11> + <-60,10> + <-18,-9> \\
&= <-72,12>
\end{aligned}$$

So the data on the output of the MC6811 must be stable 72 nanoseconds before and 12 seconds after the rising edge of the complemented E signal at the input to the 74HC32. This is not satisfied by the MC6811, so the Intel 6116-1 must be used again.

The interval arithmetic method is very general and useful in the analysis of skewing and in worst case analysis in general. Operations for multiplication, division, and complex functions such as SINE and so on can be defined precisely for intervals, and the execution of these operations is mechanical and clean. However, one must be careful to intuitively check the formula to make sure that the interval's upper and lower bounds really represent the worst cases. Finally, interval arithmetic tends to be pessimistic if two variables appear in two parts of a formula and should cancel. For instance, if the interval A is <1,2>, then, using the rules of interval arithmetic, A - A is evaluated as <-1,1> rather than <0,0>. The formula should be written so that each variable appears just once, if possible, or, if not possible, the answer should be regarded as worse than the real worst case.

The bus that interconnects printed circuit boards is often implemented on a board called a *motherboard* or *backplane*, into which the other boards are plugged. This bus can be a standard type so that boards made by different manufacturers can be plugged into it. The *S-100* bus − so named because it has 100 pins − is a standard type extensively used for Intel 8080 computer systems, which can also be used with other systems like the M6811. Though developed by manufacturers that service the hobby market, this bus is now a standard for small quantity industrial systems design because there is a large range of "off-the-shelf" printed circuit boards that can be plugged into it. In fact, the S-100 bus is an IEEE standard.

Often, different boards, designed independently of each other, are plugged into the motherboard or backplane, giving rise to the troublesome problem of bus driver control. Unfortunately, it is easy to design the logic that controls the drivers so that a driver from one board is driving the backplane bus exactly when another driver wants to drive the same bus. Although this problem can occur on any bus, it is especially troublesome on the backplane bus because the boards it interconnects are often designed at different times. The solution is good documentation. Each board should be documented to show exactly when it drives signals onto the backplane bus, as a function of the addresses on the address bus or other control signals (such as direct memory access acknowledge signals, discussed in chapter 5).When a new board is designed, it should be checked to see if it can ever conflict with an existing board. Also, when no explanation can be found for erroneous behavior on the bus, check all boards again to see if two drivers are driving the bus at the same time.

A technique Terry Ritter of Motorola recommends is to design all tristate bus drivers to implement *break-before make* control, using the terminology that describes relay contacts. All tristate bus drivers should be disabled for the first quarter of every memory cycle, when the E clock is low. That way, tristate drivers will not drive the bus in different directions while the address and R/W signals are indeterminate.

Many motherboards, especially those for the S-100 bus, use *active terminations*. To reduce the electrical noise and ringing on the signals, each line is *terminated* by connecting it through a (2000-ohm) resistor to a voltage that is half the positive supply voltage. The resistor absorbs the energy that causes the noise. Half the supply voltage is chosen so, whether the driver drives the bus high or low, about the same amount of power is absorbed by the terminator, and thus if several bus lines are terminated together, those that are high will supply current needed by others that are low. This voltage is easily established by an audio amplifier integrated circuit, such as an LM384, because it automatically sets its output to half the supply voltage. Alternatively, if the board is well designed, noise may not be a problem, and active terminations may not be needed.

In this subsection, some of the most common problems in interface design have been discussed. Remember to keep the expanded bus as much like a symmetrical tree as possible. When confirming the timing requirements, use interval arithmetic. Check the logic that determines which drivers are enabled under which conditions, and keep accurate records of these conditions. Finally, use a noise-free motherboard, or supply active terminations on it to suppress noise. By following this advice, you can avoid many of the most common interface design problems.

3-4 Conclusions

The study of microcomputer data and address busses is critical because scanty knowledge in these areas leads to serious interface problems. Before getting on these busses, data inside the microprocessor are unobservable and useless for interfacing. But when data are on the bus, they are quite important in the design of interface circuitry. This chapter has discussed what address, data, and control signals look like on a typical microcomputer bus, supporting that discussion with descriptions of some mechanisms and components that generate those signals. You should now be able to read the data sheets and block or logic diagrams that describe the microprocessor and other modules connected to the bus. You should also be able to analyze the timing requirements on a bus. And, finally, you should have sufficient hardware background to understand the discussions of interface modules in the coming chapters.

If you found any difficulty with the discussion on hardware modules and signals, a number of fine books are available on logic design. We recommend *Fundamentals of Logic Design*, second edition, by C. H. Roth, West Publishing Co., 1979 because it is organized as a self-paced course. However, there are so many good texts in different writing styles, that you may find another more suitable. Computer organization is also covered in a number of fine texts, such as *Fundamentals of Microcomputer Architecture,* by K. L. Doty, Matrix Publishers, Inc. or *Computer Hardware and Organization*, by M. E. Sloan, Science Research Associates, Inc. Further details on the MC68HC11 can be obtained from the *MC68HC11A8 HCMOS Single-Chip Microcomputer, (ADI 1207)* Motorola, 1985; section 11 gives the timing specifications of the microcomputer. As noted earlier, we have not attempted to duplicate the diagrams and discussions in that book because we assume you will refer to it while reading this book; also, we present an alternative view of the subject so you can use either or both views. The final section in this chapter, however, has not been widely discussed in texts available before now. But several books on interfacing are currently being introduced, and this central problem should be discussed in any good book on interfacing.

Problems

Problems 1 to 4 are paragraph correction problems. See the guidelines at the end of chapter 1.

1.* A negative logic signal has a low signal representing a true variable. To negate a variable is to make it low. A synchronous variable is one that repeats itself periodically, like a clock. A family of integrated circuits is a collection of integrated circuits that have the same architecture. A block diagram describes the realization of some hardware, to show exactly how to build it. In a block diagram, logic functions are in terms of true and false variables. The Vss pin is normally connected to +5 volts on an LSI chip. We normally put bypass capacitors, .001-microfarad capacitors across power and ground, about every 4 SSI chips.

2.* A buffer is a gate whose output can be connected to the outputs of other buffers. Open collector drivers can be connected on a bus, called a wire-OR bus, which ORs the outputs in positive logic. When a tristate bus driver is disabled, its outputs are pulled to 0 volts by the driver. A flip-flop is a module that copies the variable on the D input when the CLOCK input is high, and leaves the last value in it at other times. The setup time for a D edge-triggered flip-flop is the time the data must be stable before the edge occurs that clocks the data into the flip-flop. The word width of a microcomputer is the number of bits put into the accumulator during a LDA instruction. The memory cycle time is the time from when the address is stable until data can be read from or written into the word addressed. Read-only memories are used to store changing data in a typical microprocessor. A programmable array logic (PAL) chip is similar to a PROM, having fuses that are blown to program the device, and it is suitable for "glue" logic and address decoders.

3.* Microprogramming is the programming of microcomputers. A data transfer is the movement of data, such as from a register through a driver onto a bus, then into another register. A data transfer occurs over a memory cycle. It is caused by asserting control variables that come from the controller. A group of singulary control variables can be encoded in binary to make the controller faster. In vertical microprograms, each control variable appears as the output from a column of the control memory. In designing interfaces for microcomputers, you have to use these control variables from the controller inside the microprocessor to enable the drivers and clock the registers in the interface hardware.

4.* The ADDA immediate instruction begins, as all instructions begin, by recalling the first byte of the instruction code word. The program counter is incremented first, then used as the address to read a word from memory. The second byte of the instruction is then fetched to get the immediate address, which is brought in and added to the accumulator in the same memory cycle. This instruction takes just two memory cycles.

5. The output signals of a gate are defined for each input signal by table 3-3. What is the usual name for the logic function when inputs and outputs are considered variables if:

Table 3-3. Outputs of a Gate

A	B	C
L	L	L
L	H	L
H	L	L
H	H	H

a. A, B, and C are positive logic variables

b. A and B are positive logic and C is negative logic

c. A and B are negative logic and C is positive logic

d. A, B, and C are negative logic variables

6. Using the bus in figure 3-5, write a horizontal microprogram in successive microcycles to successively 1. put input IN into register B, 2. put input IN into register A, 3. put register A into register B. In the implementation, assume the first column on the left feeds C1, the next feeds C2, the next feeds C3, and the right column feeds C4 (C5 is connected to TRUE). Show the segment of control memory that can be executed sequentially to cause these transfers: a. using block diagram conventions (T,F), and b. using logic diagram conventions (H,L).

7. Figure 3-15a shows a simple bus. Specify which control signals are asserted – and whether asserted means to make them high or low – to cause each of the following transfers: a. C ← IN3, b. D ← IC, c. C ← IN4, d. D ← IN4, e. C ← IN3; D ← IN3.

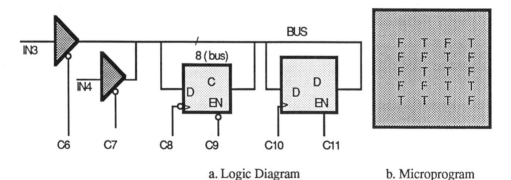

a. Logic Diagram   b. Microprogram

Figure 3-15. Bus for Problems 3-7 to 3-9

8. A microprogram that uses encoded control bits has been written for the system in figure 3-15a. The control memory has four columns and five rows as shown in figure 3-15b. The leftmost two columns determine which data are transferred onto the bus; C6 is asserted if these bits are FF, C7 if FT, C9 if TF, and C11 if TT. The 3rd column is C8 and the 4th, C10. Write the data transfers (e.g. C ← IN3) that occur as each row is read.

9. Suppose that the bus in the middle of figure 3-5 is connected to the bus of figure 3-15a, and IN3 of 3-14a is connected to OUT of figure 3-5. Write a microprogram to exchange the words in registers C and D that are in figure 3-15a. Show a. the data transfers, and b. the block diagram (T,F) control memory, assuming the columns, from left to right, supply the control variables from C1 to C11, respectively.

10. Describe the data transfers that would execute the instruction ADDA #5 using registers in figure 3-7.

11. The output displayed by a logic analyzer is as follows: each next lower row corresponds to the next consecutive memory cycle; column 1 gives the R/W signal (R for read and W for write) during the memory cycle; and columns 2 and 3 give the values (in hexadecimal) for the address and data busses during the memory cycle. Show the output displayed by such a logic analyzer for each of the following instructions: (assume ALPHA is $100, X is $102, Y is $304, S is $400, and PC is $506.

    a. ADDD ALPHA (16-bit direct)
    b. ORAA 1,X
    c. PULX
    d. ASL 3,Y

12. The 2114 is a (1024,4) random access memory chip that is as easy to use as the MCM65116-20 shown in figure 3-11 but is obviously smaller. The MCM21L14-20, the MCL21L14-25, the MCM21L14-30, and the MCM21L14-45 are realizations of the 2114, the first listed being the fastest and most expensive and the successive ones being slower and cheaper.

Parameter	xx-20	xx-25	xx-45	xx-30
Read Access	<,200>	<,250>	<,450>	<,300>
CE - DO Delay	<, 70>	<, 85>	<,120>	<,100>
Read Hold	< 50,>	< 50,>	< 50,>	< 50,>
Write Length	<120,>	<135,>	<200,>	<150,>
Write Set-up	<120,>	<135,>	<200,>	<150,>

a. Table of Values for xx = MCM21L14   All times are intervals <min,max>

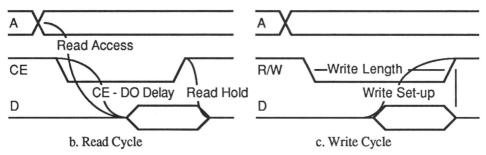

b. Read Cycle   c. Write Cycle

Figure 3-16. Timing Characteristics of Several 2114s

Figure 3-16a gives the timing characteristics of the realizations. For definitions of the read timing characteristics, see figure 3-16b, and for write timing characteristics, see figure 3-16c. The read access time is the delay from when the address is stable until the output data are determinate; the CE - DO delay is the time from when CE is low until data are determinate; the read hold is the time the data remain determinate after CE becomes high or the address changes, whichever is earlier; the write length is the time R/W has to be low; and the write setup is the time the data must be stable before R/W rises in a write cycle. The time from when the address is stable before RW can be asserted low, the time the address must remain stable after RW is negated high, and the hold time that the data must remain stable after R/W rises are all 0 in all realizations of the 2114. The other times are specified as intervals <min, max> in figure 3-16a.

Assuming the 2114 is connected directly to an MC68HC11A8, with a. an 8.4-MHz crystal (f=1/476 ns described in figure 3-10), and b. a 3.58-MHz crystal (assume all timing expands proportionately to the crystal frequency), choose the cheapest memory that satisfies all the timing requirements. What is the maximum delay on the data bus that could be permitted without violating a timing requirement, and how much time is allowed for decoding the address to get the CE signal, assuming the address gets to the decoder when it gets to the memory?

13. Repeat problem 12 for a 4.2-MHz crystal using the data in the *MC68HC11A8 HCMOS Single-chip Microcomputer* (Document ADI1207, table 11.7).

Problems 14 to 20 and many of the problems in later chapters are hardware design problems. We recommend the following guidelines for these problems:

Hardware designs should minimize cost, which means using a minimal number of chips (where actual chips are specified), and, when the number of chips is the same, a minimal number of gates, and then a minimal number of pin connections, unless otherwise noted. When logic diagrams are requested, use bubbles to represent negative logic and gates representing high and low signals, and show pin numbers where applicable. A logic diagram should describe a circuit in enough detail that one could use it to build a circuit from. Assume the address and data base are positive logic and decoder IC outputs and enables are negative logic, unless otherwise indicated in the problem or data sheets for the ICs. When block diagrams are presented, show variables and gates representing true and false values, and show the maximum detail you can, unless otherwise stated. (Note that a box with SYSTEM written inside it is a block diagram for any problem, but is not a good answer; give the maximum amount of detail in your answer that is possible with the information provided in the question.)

14. Draw a logic diagram of a (1024,8) memory using 2114 chips and 74HC04, 74HC30, and 74HC32 gates so that words in the range $2C00 to $2FFF are read and written in this memory. Show all pin connections between these chips and the 6811 so the logic diagram is detailed enough to build the memory. The pin connections to the 6811 are shown in figure 3-6; the pin connections to the SSI chips are shown in any HCMOS or LSTTL data book (pins for both families are generally identical); and those of the 18-pin 2114 are as follows: chip select CS (negative logic) – pin 8, R/W – pin 10, 10 address bits – pins 1 to 7 and 15, 16, and 17, four data pins used for both input and output of data – pins 11 to 14, +5 volts – pin 18, and ground – pin 9. (Note that the address pins are interchangeable, and the data pins are interchangeable because the memory will work correctly if you switch an address pin for another address pin or a data pin for another data pin.)

15. Using just one 74HC10, show a logic diagram that can implement the decoder for the memories and registers selected in table 3-2. For this realization, answer the following:

   a. what memories or registers will be written into by the instruction STA $9002,
   b. what memories or registers are stored into by STA $FFFF,
   c. what memories or registers are written into by the instruction STAA $80FF,
   d. what memories or registers are written into by the instruction STA $4000, and
   e. what five different addresses, other than $8001, access register 1?

16. Show a block diagram for a minimum cost decoder that will select memory module 1 for addresses in the range $0000 to $1FFF, memory module 2 for addresses in the range $F000 to $FFFF, register 1 for address $4000, and register 2 for address $8000.

17. A Z80 microprocessor has negative logic RD and WR control variables instead of the R/W signal and E clock of the 6811. When RD is asserted low, the Z80 has put a stable address on the address bus and wants memory to read the word at this address, and when WR is asserted low, the Z80 has put stable data on the data bus and a stable address on the address bus, and wants memory to write the data at the address it gave. Show the logic diagram of a decoder (but do not show ICs or pin numbers), using n-input AND gates and inverters, to select a MCM65116 memory whenever an address is presented in the range $5800 to $5FFF, and show logic to provide the R/W signal for the MCM65116 chips. Note that when neither RD nor WR are asserted low, CE should be negated high.

18. Give the logic diagram for a printed circuit card (4096,8) memory that can plug into a backplane bus. The memory, using MCM65116s, will respond when the address is in the range $4000 to $4FFF, as in figure 3-13. However, it connects to a 16-bit positive logic address bus, an 8-bit positive logic data bus, and R/W, which is high if data are being read, on the backplane, rather than the 6811, as in figure 3-13. Use the high-order bits of the address in the decoder to detect the address, as in figure 3-13. But feed the low-order address bits and the R/W signal to the memories through 74HC14 inverters on the board; this distributes the address over the 8-pin load and feeds the data from the backplane to the MCM65116's D0 - D7 pins, then from these pins to the data bus on the backplane, through a bidirectional bus amplifier − a 74HC245. You must carefully design the control for the bus drivers. The 74HC245 should drive the backplane bus only when a word is read from $4000 to $4FFF and at no other time. Otherwise, reduce your logic to a minimum.

19. Give the logic diagram for a circuit to control bus drivers for the backplane bus. A printed circuit card has some LSI chip on it (it doesn't matter yet which one) whose eight data pins connect to inputs of an 74HC245, called driver A, whose outputs connect to the backplane data bus; this backplane data bus connects to inputs of another 74HC245, called driver B, whose eight outputs connect to the eight data pins on the LSI chip. The control circuit enables driver A, so data from the LSI chip can be put on the backplane bus, by asserting EA low; it also enables driver B, so data on the backplane can be sent

to the LSI chip, by asserting EB low. The control circuit has input R/W, which is high if memory is being read and low if it is being written; negative logic CE, which is asserted low if the LSI chip is being written into or read from, and a positive logic DACK. (DACK is direct memory access acknowledge. In direct memory access, as will be discussed in chapter 4, the LSI chip behaves like the microprocessor by supplying data to be written in memory or by picking up data read from memory.) Design the control circuit so that data from the LSI chip is put on the backplane only when R/W is high and CE is true, or when DACK is true and R/W is low, and so that data from the backplane is sent to the LSI chip at least when R/W is low and CE is true, or when R/W is high and DACK is true. Otherwise, reduce your logic to a minimum.

20. Assume that an R/W signal is generated by a 74HC32 for MCM65116-20 memories and the data from the microprocessor passes through more than one 74HC245 bidirectional bus driver to the data pins on the MCM65116.

a. Write an expression to determine the minimum interval T6811 that the MC68HC11A8 has to maintain stable data if the R/W signal passes through a series of n 74HC32s and the data pass through a series of m 74HC245s to get to the MCM65116-20s, in terms of the setup and hold times T6116 for the MCM65116, the delay times T7432 for the 74HC32, and the delay T74245 for the 74HC245.

b. Using the delays T7432 and T74245 and the MCM65116-20's setup and hold time T6116 as <6,11>, <9,18>, and <-180,0>, for each n (number of 74HC32s) determine the maximum number m (of 74HC245s) that can be permitted to connect the MC68HC11A8 to the MCM65116-20.

4

Parallel and Serial Input-Output

The first three chapters were compact surveys of material you really need to know to study interface design. That is why they were a little heavy with concepts and definitions. In the remainder of the book, we will have more expanded discussions and more opportunities to study interesting examples and work challenging problems. The material in these chapters is not intended to replace the data sheets provided by the manufacturers, nor do we intend to simply summarize them. If the reader wants the best description of any chip discussed at length in the book, data sheets supplied by Motorola should be consulted. The topics are organized around concepts rather than around integrated circuits because we consider these more important in the long run. In the following chapters, we will concentrate on the principles and practices of designing interfaces with I/O LSI chips in general, and, in particular, with Motorola chips compatible with the MC68HC11A8.

Although this chapter is not the longest, it is the most important chapter in this book. The simple parallel and serial I/O devices are studied, both from a hardware and software viewpoint. These are the most common I/O devices and are key building blocks of all the other I/O devices. So they are exceedingly important to the design of interfaces.

The first section considers some principles of parallel I/O architecture, looking at I/O devices from the programmer's point of view. You have to consider the architectural alternatives before you design either the hardware or the software. This section also shows how to build the simplest parallel I/O devices. The second section introduces some very simple software used with parallel I/O devices. While the software is simple, the memory cycle timing, which is often very important and which we will study carefully, is a little more intricate. Also, microcomputers are often used to replace the digital logic and relays in obsolete industrial controllers. The software for such controllers is also studied in this section. The third section introduces the LSI parallel I/O chips and the I/O devices that are available in the single-chip mode of the M6811. Some general observations are made, then the M6821 and single-chip mode I/O devices are introduced. Indirect I/O is then discussed. Serial I/O devices, considered next, are particularly easy to connect to a computer like the M6811 because a small number of wires are needed, and are useful when the relatively slow operation of the serial I/O device is acceptable. These devices are called *synchronous* because a clock is used.

Asynchronous serial devices are discussed in chapter 8, where communications systems are described. Finally, an application of the M6821 to build a simple tester for integrated circuits is considered.

Upon finishing this chapter, the reader should be able to design hardware and write software for simple parallel and serial input and output devices. An input device using a bus driver, an output device using a register, a shift-register-based serial I/O device, a device using an M6821, or one employing the ports on a MC68HC11A8 chip should be easy to design and build. Programs of around 100 lines to input data to a buffer, output data from a buffer, or control something using programmed or interpretive techniques should be easy to write and debug. Moreover, the reader will be prepared to study the devices introduced in later chapters, which use the parallel and serial I/O device as a major building block.

4-1 Input-Output Architecture and Simple I/O Devices

We first consider the parallel I/O device's architecture - another way of saying we'll look at such a device from the programmer's viewpoint. One aspect, introduced in the first subsection, is whether I/O devices appear as words in primary memory, to be accessed by LDAA and STAA instructions, or as words in an architecturally different memory, to be accessed by different instructions. Another aspect is whether the device can be read from or written in or both. The "write-only memory" is usually only a topic for a computer scientist's joke collection, but it is a real possibility in an I/O device. To understand why you might use such a thing, the hardware design and its cost must be studied. So we introduce I/O device hardware design, which will also be useful in the next section, which introduces the software used with these devices.

4-1.1 Isolated and Memory Mapped I/O

There are two major ways in a microcomputer to access I/O, relative to the address space in primary memory. Using the first, *isolated I/O*, the devices are read from by means of *input instructions,* such as IN 5. This kind of instruction would input a word from I/O device 5 into an accumulator. Similarly, *output instructions* like OUT 3 would output a word from an accumulator to the third I/O device. Using the second, *memory-mapped I/O*, the device is considered a word in memory, at some location, such as $4000. A standard load instruction like LDAA $4000 is then an input instruction, and a store instruction like STAA $4000 is an output instruction. There is no need for a separate input or output instruction. Some machines like the 6811 have no separate I/O instructions and exclusively use memory-mapped I/O; other machines have I/O instructions and can use either isolated I/O or memory mapped I/O.

As we discussed in the last chapter, memory-mapped I/O uses the data and address busses just as memory uses them. The microprocessor thinks it is reading or writing data in memory, but the I/O devices are designed to supply the data read or capture the data written at specific memory locations. As in the memory design in section 3-3.2, the basic hardware is enabled or clocked by an address decoder that decodes the address on the A bus. The decoder can either be completely specified, built with decoder integrated circuits, or incompletely specified. Generally, though, it must enable or clock the device when a specific memory address is sent out and must not clock it when any other address used by the program is sent out. Isolated I/O is really quite similar in hardware to memory mapped I/O. To save pins, the device address is sent from the microprocessor on the same bus as the memory address, but some (variable) control signal is asserted when the address is an I/O address and not a memory address. So the memory address decoders must be built to enable or clock the memory only when this variable is false, and the I/O address decoders must be built to enable the device only when this variable is true.

Each technique has some advantages. Isolated I/O instructions, such as are used in the INTEL 8080, use a 1-byte opcode and a 1-byte device address, while almost all memory mapped I/O instructions have a tendency to be 3 bytes long or tie up an index register to use 2-byte instructions. This extra length can be a serious problem if a program for a dedicated application uses a lot of I/O operations and must fit into the smallest possible size memory to save cost, and tying up an index register may require saving and restoring it. However, the 6811 has direct page addressing and index addressing, which can be used to improve the static efficiency of I/O routines. The device address decoder is simpler, since it need consider only 8, rather than 16, address bits and some control signals. More important, isolated I/O is not as susceptible to software errors as is memory-mapped I/O. In the latter case, especially if the microcomputer has a stack in memory, an error in a loop that has an instruction to push data onto the stack can fill memory with garbage in no time. In our personal experience, this happens all too often. If output registers send signals to turn on motors, say in a tape drive, putting garbage in them could produce interesting effects (spill tape, stretch and change density of tape). Memory-mapped I/O is sometimes awkward when large memories, like the 65536, 8 memories, occupy the addresses needed for memory-mapped I/O registers. You have to design the address decoder so the memory does not put data on the bus when the input device is read.

Nevertheless, memory-mapped I/O is gaining in popularity because most microcomputers have instructions that operate directly in memory, such as INC $4000, ROL $4000, or the BSET, BRCLR instructions. Indexed addressing can be used with memory-mapped I/O if the program is in read-only memory. The index register can be loaded from a RAM location, the contents of which are different in different systems. The program can be mass-produced for use in many systems, to take advantage of the low cost of read-only memories, yet the different systems could have I/O devices at different addresses. The address loaded into the index register, in read-write memory, can be modified, while the program, in read-only memory, can be left alone. The use of these instructions operating directly on (readable) output registers in memory-mapped I/O is very powerful; their use can also shorten programs that would otherwise need to bring the word into the accumulator, operate on it, then output it; and the use of index addressing makes programs in read-only memory efficient and economically attractive.

We do have to worry about accidentally writing over the output registers when we use memory-mapped I/O. Memory-mapped I/O can be protected, however, by a *lock*.

The lock is an output register which is itself not locked, so the program can change it. The lock's output is ANDed with address and other control signals to get the enable or clock signals for all other I/O registers. If the lock is F, no I/O devices can be read or written. Before reading an I/O device, the program has to store T in the lock, then store F in the lock after all I/O operations are complete. The Radio Shack Color Computer uses a "Multipack Extension" module that uses a lock. In dedicated microcomputers that execute fully debugged programs, a lock is not needed, but in software development systems, a lock can drastically reduce the ill effects of memory-mapped I/O, while allowing most of its advantages.

4-1.2 Basic Input and Output Devices

Architecturally, a (1-word) parallel I/O device has an address in memory (or device number, if isolated I/O is used) and a capability for reading and writing. Concerning the address, we consider whether we should use completely or incompletely specified addressing (explained in section 3-3.2, when we studied the design of a memory), and we consider where the device will be addressed by the program in memory. The latter may depend on the location of other memories and devices. For example, if two devices are addressed in consecutive locations, the STD instruction can load them from the accumulators efficiently. Concerning the read and write capabilities of the device, we will devote the rest of the subsection to this subject.

The basic input device is capable of sampling a signal when the microcomputer executes an input instruction (or an equivalent instruction in memory-mapped I/O) and of reading the sample into the accumulator (or operating on it as if it were a memory word). Since most microcomputers use tristate bus drivers, the device must put the sample of data onto the data bus exactly when the microprocessor executes a read command with this device's address.

A typical input device is shown in figure 4-1a as set up for memory mapped I/O to input 8-bit data SRC whenever an LDAA $4000 instruction, or its equivalent, is executed. The decoder is completely specified to fully decode all 16 address bits for the address $4000 and to check that R/W and E are high. Whereas a 17-input AND gate would be nice, the largest AND gate has 13 inputs. But to save inverters, negative logic input positive logic output AND gates (positive logic NOR gates) are useful. A gate in the 74HC4078 is well suited to check that eight inputs are low. Three of these can check the 15 address bits that must be low. Feeding these into an eight-input positive logic input negative logic output AND gate, together with address bit 14, E and R/W – which must be high – completes the decoder. A 74HC30 positive logic eight-input NAND gate can be used. The actual input device, an octal bus driver like the 74HC244, is enabled with the output from the decoder.

To prevent the device from driving the multiplexed data bus when the low byte of the address is on it, an input device must be designed so it never drives the bus in the first quarter of the memory cycle, as address and control lines are indeterminate then. A signal variable that is true from when the address strobe AS falls until the E clock falls, is high for the last three quarters of the cycle, when the aforementioned signals are determinate. The output of a circuit that produces such a signal, or the E clock itself (for a shorter time when the address and R/W are determinate), can be used in the decoder of an input device to prevent the generation of noise spikes. This insures that the drivers "break before make" in old-fashioned relay terminology.

Sometimes a single-bit input is required. It can be grouped with seven other single inputs and treated as a word input. Instructions like BSET, BRCLR can be used to handle bits individually. Alternatively, a single tristate driver can be enabled to put the data on one of the data lines. A 74HC125 has four independent tristate drivers suitable for this application. The other data lines will be floating when this input is read, and should be ignored by the program. Usually, the sign position is used for single inputs like this because it can be sensed in a branch on sign instruction, like the BPL and BMI instructions of the 6811.

If a number of single inputs should be used, where each is to be a single bit in a word for convenience in software, a collection of them can be implemented in a *selector* or *multiplexor* that has a tristate output. An *n* input by one output selector is an n position switch that can, by means of an address, select one of *n* inputs to be output. Coupled with a tristate driver in the same integrated circuit, this makes an ideal 1-bit-wide input device for n inputs. A 74HC251 is a 1-of-8 selector with tristate output. For instance, the 3 least significant address bits are used as an address by the multiplexor to choose one of eight inputs; the remaining 13 bits and R/W are examined by a decoder for the correct address, to enable the driver in the selector. The bits will appear as the sign bit of 8 words in consecutive address locations in memory having the same high order 13 bits.

The output device usually has to hold output data for an indefinite time – until the program changes it. The basic output device is therefore a latch or register which is capable of clocking data from the data bus whenever the microcomputer executes an output instruction (or an equivalent instruction in memory-mapped I/O). The D bus is connected to the D input of the register or latch, and the clock is connected to an address decoder so that the register is clocked when the microprocessor executes a write command at the address selected for this device.

Figure 4-1b shows a typical memory-mapped output device that will hold and output an 8-bit word of data written at memory location $4FFF, as in the STAA $4FFF instruction. The data are constantly available as the signal DST to some external hardware because the tristate enable E is asserted low. For example, each bit could be used to control a single traffic light, to turn it on if true and off if false. Two eight-input positive logic input negative logic output gates (74HC30s) check for the presence of highs required in the positive logic address bits 14 and 11 to 0, as well as clock E, and, using 74HC04 inverters, lows on bits 13 and 12. These outputs and address bit 15 and R/W (which must be low) feed a tree network of 74HC32 negative logic input and output AND gates. This develops the clock for a register with positive (rising edge-triggered) clock input, such as the 74HC374.

We emphasize the need to put the E clock signal into the decoder, so that it asserts its output (low) only when the E clock is high. The MC68HC11A8 guarantees that the data on the data bus are determinate then. The clock of a latch should only be asserted then. Also, the edge that clocks data into a register must occur at the end of a memory cycle. The R/W signal (which may not even be needed in the decoder if the address is never used for a recall or fetch memory cycle) rises at the beginning of the next memory cycle when the data are indeterminate. If you do not use the E clock signal in your decoder, you may be outputting garbage whenever you write in the device. (Decoders to LSI I/O devices, however, may not have this E input or they may fail to satisfy setup and hold times. The E signal is put on a pin of the LSI chip and ANDed with the chip select signals from the decoder inside the LSI chip.)

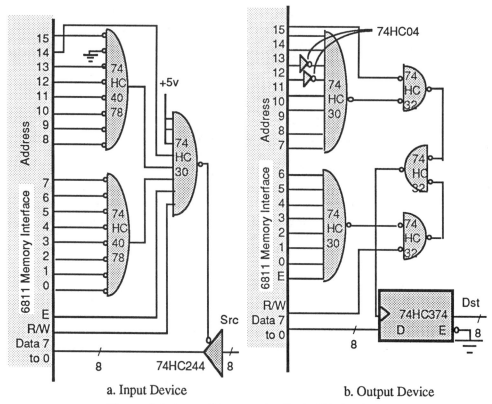

a. Input Device   b. Output Device

Figure 4-1. Logic Diagrams for Basic I/O Devices

If a single-bit output is required, a flip-flop having 1 bit of the D bus connected to its D input can be used, of course. If this output will take data from some input bit that is in the sign position, it, too, should be connected to the most significant bit of the data bus, to avoid having to shift bits as they are moved.

If a number of single-bit outputs should be implemented, up to 8 can be put in an *addressable latch* like the 74LS259, which has eight D flip-flops internally connected to a decoder. The chip has a single D, an address, an enable input, and Q outputs from each of the flip-flops. The D input to the chip is connected to all D inputs of the flip-flops and exactly one of them is clocked, as selected by an address, when the chip is enabled. The chip is used like the selector. The address bus's 3 least significant bits are connected to the chip's three address pins, the data bus's most significant bit is connected to the D input, and the other 13 address lines and R/W are connected to a decoder to supply the enable signal to the addressable latch.

We have discussed the basic input and output devices as separate modules. The basic input device, which the program cannot write in, is a "read-only memory." In effect, some external system writes data into it, which the microprocessor can only read. Similarly, the basic output device is write-only. The microcomputer can only write, but not read, data in it. It is a "write-only memory" as far as the program is concerned and is read by the outside world.

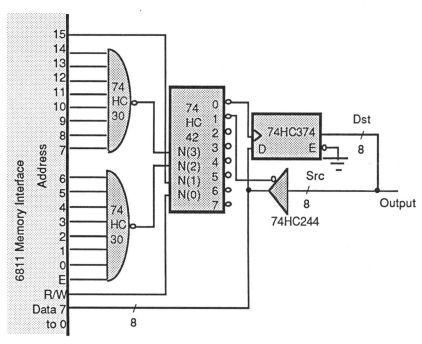

Figure 4-2. Logic Diagram of a Readable Output Register

An output device can be combined with an input device at the same address that inputs the data stored in the output register. This *readable output device* is more costly than the basic output device, which is read-only, but is more flexible. Figure 4-2 shows a readable output device that can be read from or written in at location $7FFF. It is actually a basic output device whose output is available to the outside world and which is connected to a basic input device at the same memory address so it can be read. The decoder is constructed so that the basic output device is clocked when location $7FFF is written into, and the input device is enabled when location $7FFF is read from. The 74HC30s check to ensure that the clock E is high and that addresses 14 to 0 are high. These gates assert their outputs low when the address is correct. The rest of the decoding is done by a 74HC42, a standard "1-of-10" decoder used in a non-standard way. The input to the 74HC42 is a 4-bit number N, with the N*th* output asserted low, and the other outputs high. The 2 high bits of N are the outputs of the 74HC30s, and the 2 low bits are address bit 15 and R/W. Output 0 is asserted low when N is LLLL, which occurs only when the device is being written into. Output 1 of the decoder is asserted low when N is LLLH, which occurs only when the device is being read. So we connect output 0 to the output register's clock and output 1 to the enable of the tristate gate that forms the input device. A decoder integrated circuit is useful in building address decoders in place of gates if it replaces a number of gates, thus reducing the number of packages used; but an address decoder does not have to use a decoder chip, and decoder chips can be used just for the few gates that happen to be in them.

Note that the decoder must sense R/W low and E high for it to assert the output latch clock or for it to generate a clock edge for an output register, ensuring that the output device will be clocked only when a word is being sent from the microprocessor and is valid on the data bus. The decoder, which can drive the bus as long as the address is stable, should only enable the input bus driver if R/W is high. To avoid having two drivers driving the data bus, however, it should be disabled when the address and R/W are indeterminate; it may also be built to enable the input driver only when E is high.

A readable output register then behaves like a 1-word read-write memory. Such an output register is very useful in memory-mapped I/O because it is essential for the operation of memory-to-memory instructions like INC $4000, ROL $4000, or the BSET and BCLR instructions. Such instructions will not work if the output device is the basic kind shown in figure 4-1b because they first read and then write the word in the register. An output register with read capability is useful when several programs written by different people at different times use the same register. One program can check, by reading the register, to see if another wrote something in it. This kind of output register is useful in software development systems because it can be examined when the program is being debugged. However, the basic output register without read capability is often quite adequate. The word written there can also be stored in RAM whenever it is written, if it must be known by some other program. Keeping two copies of the word, one in the output register and the other in a RAM word, is usually less costly than building the extra hardware to make the output register readable.

In two successive instructions, a copy of the data may be stored in a simple output register and then stored in a RAM location. However, it is possible to design the address decoder so that when a word is written into the output register, it is simultaneously written in a RAM word. For instance, if the RAM is located at 0 to $7FF, and the output device is at $7FF, then an instruction STAA $7FF will write the data into both the highest word in the RAM and the output device. Of course, if location $7FF is read, the RAM will supply the already written data to the output device. (Note: these data are not necessarily what are on the output lines as they are in a true readable output device.) We call this word in RAM a *shadow* of the output register, and the device is a *shadowed output device*. Such a device is cheaper than a readable output device but acts like it.

It is possible to wire some inputs of an input device to some output bits of an output device appearing at the same address, and to some external signals, so that when this input device is read, it reads the part of the output register to which it is connected. Those bits read from the output register are readable, so the device is a *partially readable output device*. For example, if bits 6 to 0 of an input device are connected to bits 6 to 0 of an output device that appears at the same address, but bit 7 of the input device is connected to an external signal, it is possible to read bits 6 to 0 and rewrite them, as is done by the INC ALPHA instruction, but to input bit 7 from the outside world, which can be sensed in an instruction like BMI after the INC ALPHA instruction (see problem

15). Partially readable output devices are quite often used as control registers to send commands to external hardware and to read the status of that hardware together with the commands that have been sent earlier. We will see them in many I/O devices.

We note that two completely different input and output devices can use the same address. If the 74HC244's input in figure 4-2 were connected to some signals other than the output of the 74HC374, figure 4-2 would then show both a basic input device and a separate basic output device at the same address. When this location is read, the input device is enabled, and when this location is written, the output device is clocked. It is often cheaper to use the same memory address for two completely different devices like this because they can share their address decoder hardware.

Finally, we introduce a technique widely used to pulse devices – an *address trigger* – is a mechanism whereby the address decoder itself provides a pulse that does something. Generating the particular address in the execution of an instruction will cause the address decoder to output a pulse that can be used to trigger a one-shot, clear or set a flip-flop, or be output from the computer. Figure 4-3 shows an example of a trigger on the address $7FFF. Figure 4-3a shows, with a dashed line, an address trigger in a block diagram. This address trigger is shown triggering a one-shot; the one-shot is not part of the address trigger. Note that the instruction LDAA $7FFF does not load data from the one-shot, nor does STAA $7FFF store anything from the accumulator into it. These instructions could simultaneously load or store data in another register even while the address triggers the one-shot in a manner similar to the shadow output device, or they might load garbage into the accumulator or store the accumulator into a nonexistent storage word (which does nothing). Also, any instruction that reads the location could be used instead of LDAA (for instance, LDAB) or any that writes could be used instead of STAA. Note that some instructions that operate on memory (for example, INC $7FFF) first read and then write in the location, so they can produce two pulses. Figure 4-3b shows how this is implemented in hardware. If an instruction like LDAA $7FFF or STAA $7FFF is executed, the decoder will pulse causing the one-shot to "fire."

The addresses are indeterminate during the first quarter of a memory cycle, so an address like $7FFF might be temporarily generated at that time even though the instruction does not use this address. An invalid address can accidentally trigger some action if an address trigger is used. Therefore, it is necessary to AND the E clock into the address decoder, so its output will always be false during the first half of the cycle. In these cases, E must be true for the address decoder to assert its output. The E clock in the M6811 can be used to indicate a valid memory address, but the address is valid just a bit longer than that. An M6811 VMA (valid memory address) signal that is longer than the E clock pulse can be generated by a JK flip-flop and an OR gate, becoming true when AS falls (because the high signal on the J input sets the flip-flop when AS falls) and becoming false when E falls (because the high signal on the K input clears the flip-flop when E falls). The popular timer chip, the LM555 discussed in chapter 6, requires a longer trigger to be reliably fired than will be available from the E clock of a 2-MHz MC68HC11A8, so a VMA signal can be generated to trigger it reliably. (Note this signal in the decoder in figure 4-3b; there is a minor timing problem with this circuit – see problem 6 at the end of this chapter.)

A point about software should be emphasized. It is easy for a program error, especially one that pushed data onto the stack, to generate addresses that can trigger devices via an address trigger. Recall that an I/O lock can be used to prevent such addresses from being decoded.

Finally, some variations of an address trigger are the *read address trigger*, which produces a pulse only when a memory read operation generates the address, and a *write address trigger*, which generates a pulse only when the address is recognized in a memory write operation. Obviously, to build a read address trigger decoder, put the R/W signal into the AND gate, as in figure 4-3b, and to build a write address trigger decoder, put the inverted R/W signal into the decoder.

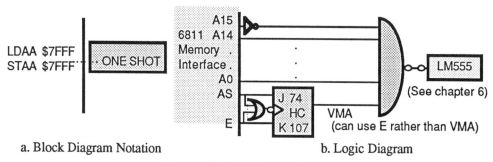

a. Block Diagram Notation   b. Logic Diagram

Figure 4-3. Address Trigger

This section discussed the architecture of parallel I/O devices. If you design an I/O device, you must consider these issues, and even if you use an LSI I/O chip, you must be aware of these issues that were considered by the chip's designers. The architecture is generally specified first, so the hardware and software can be developed simultaneously from that specification. In computers that have isolated I/O, we can use isolated I/O or memory-mapped I/O. We use completely specified I/O in development systems that could be used to debug erroneous programs because, even with a logic analyzer, an error using an illegal address is particularly hard to pin down. We use incompletely specified addressing in small systems that execute fixed (error free) programs to save some logic in the decoder. A 1-word I/O device can be a simple input, a simple output, a readable output, or a partially readable output device. In general, you should use the simplest output device, unless a more complex one is required. Most output devices we've seen are simple, and most that you design will be simple.

This section also showed how a simple input or output device, a readable output device, a shadowed output device, or an address trigger can be realized in hardware, by way of explaining the rationale for the architectural alternatives. We will use these devices in the next section to show how the software uses them.

4-2 Input-Output Software

Software for input and output devices can be very simple or quite complex. In this section, we look at some of the simpler software. The software to use a single input and a single output device to simulate (replace) a wire will be considered first, since it provides an opportunity to microscopically examine what is happening in input and output instructions. We next discuss input to and output from a buffer. Programmed control of external mechanical and electrical systems is discussed next. We will discuss the control of a traffic light and introduce the idea of a delay loop used for timing. Then, in a more involved example, we'll discuss a table-driven traffic light controller. Finally, we'll discuss a linked-list interpreter, which can implement a sequential machine.

4-2.1 I/O Transfers and Buffered Input and Output

We'll now discuss three simple things we do with I/O devices: moving data through a computer under the control of a computer, gathering data that is collected at an input, and supplying a stream of data to an output.

Timing of these operations is often critical. We will consider the timing of I/O operations in terms of memory cycles, using the technique introduced in section 3-2.2. The logic analyzer can be used to examine the address and data bus on a memory cycle basis to see what actually happens – to confirm the timing. This makes a very good experiment, which we recommend to really give you the feel of instruction execution.

Suppose that a 1-word input device is implemented to input data SRC in location $4000 and a word output device outputs data to DST in location $4FFF. (See figure 4-1.) The following program will simulate a (bundle of) wire from SRC to DST:

```
L   LDAA  $4000   4  F,F,F,D
    STAA  $4FFF   4  F,F,F,D
    BRA   L       3  F,F,N
```

Table 4-1. Logic Analyzer Output for a Simulated Wire

R	0100	B6	LDAA OP CODE
R	0101	40	HIGH ADDRESS
R	0102	00	LOW ADDRESS
R	4000	34	READ INPUT
R	0103	B7	STAA OP CODE
R	0104	4F	HIGH ADDRESS
R	0105	FF	LOW ADDRESS
W	4FFF	34	WRITE OUTPUT
R	0106	20	BRA OP CODE
R	0107	F8	DISPLACEMENT
R	FFFF	58	NULL CYCLE

The timing of these instructions, shown in the comment field, can be determined using the technique discussed in 3-2.2. The symbols F, N, and D are those defined in table 3-1 to represent fetch, null, and recall or memorize cycles. The LDAA instruction, for example, consists of the following memory cycles: Fetch, Fetch, Fetch, Recall. In fact, if you looked at a logic analyzer, and L were location $100, location $FFFF had value $58, and the input device read the value $34, then the picture on the display giving the R/W signal (values R for read and W for write), address, and data (in hexadecimal) for one loop execution would look as it does in table 4-1.

The LDAA instruction takes four memory cycles, and data are read from $4000 in the fourth cycle. The STAA instruction takes four memory cycles, and data are written into $4FFF in the last cycle. Finally, the BRA instruction takes three cycles. The entire loop takes 11 cycles. If a cycle takes one-half a microsecond, data at the input are sampled every 5 1/2 microseconds and then are output after a delay of 2 microseconds. Thus, it is not a perfect wire. But it is reasonably close.

The reader is not encouraged to build a microcomputer with these registers just to replace a wire. This example shows that data are in fact sampled and delayed by a microcomputer. It also shows that input and output can be very simple. However, a simple pair of I/O devices like this could be used to monitor the data being moved through it, then check and modify it. Or it could have several input and output devices and could route data from one input to another output device under software control. This is the basic function of many microcomputers used in communications systems. Once a microcomputer is in the path of a signal, its intelligence can be used to advantage.

A second application of input software is the sampling of inputs and storage of the samples in memory, to get a "movie" of what happened. An *input buffer* is an area of memory set aside to store the incoming words. It is like a stack buffer discussed in section 1-2.1. Normally the first word read from the input port is put at the top (least address) word in the buffer, and successive words are put in successively higher locations. The following program will collect $100 words from the input SRC (figure 4-1a) into a buffer located between $200 and $2FF:

```
        NAM     INBUF
        LDX     #$200   INITIALIZE POINTER
    L   LDAA    $4000   GET A WORD FROM THE INPUT DEVICE
        STAA    0,X     PUT IN BUFFER, MOVE POINTER
        INX
        CPX     #$300   ALL WORDS IN?
        BNE     L       NO, LOOP FOR ANOTHER WORD
        END
```

This basic routine can collect $100 successive samples from the input device. It could be used to collect data as in a "movie," or, if the input were connected to a paper tape reader and the paper tape reader could be pulled so that a pattern of holes appeared each time the recall cycle of the LDAA instruction was executed, the patterns could be copied into memory. This is the basis of secondary memory I/O devices and communications devices like UARTs. A similar program can feed consecutive words from a buffer to an output device. But one of the problems often faced is timing. How fast can data be read? How fast will data be output? The timing study for the "wire" program can be used to answer these questions. The input to buffer program takes 18 memory cycles to complete the loop. If the E clock is 2 MHz, data is sampled every 9 microseconds. (A faster program is possible – see problem 7.)

4-2.2 Programmed Logic Control

Microcomputers are often used for *logic-timer* control. In this application, some mechanical or electrical equipment is controlled through simple logic involving inputs and memory variables, and by means of delay loops. (Numeric control, which uses A/D and D/A converters, is discussed in chapter 6.) A traffic light controller is a simple example, in which light patterns are flashed on for a few seconds before the next light pattern is flashed on. Using LEDs instead of traffic lights, this controller can be used in a simple and illuminating laboratory experiment. Moreover, techniques used in this example extend to a broad class of controllers based on logic, timing, and little else.

In the following example, a *light pattern* is a collection of output variables that turns certain lights on and others off. (See figure 4-4.) Each bit of the output register LIGHTS turns on a pair of lights (through a power amplifier, discussed in chapter 6) if the bit is T. For example, if the north and south lights are paralleled, and the east and west lights are similarly paralleled, six variables are needed; if they are the rightmost 6 bits of a word, then TFFFFF would turn on the red light, FTFFFF would turn on the yellow light, and FFTFFF would turn on the green light in the north and south lanes. FFFTFF, FFFFTF, and FFFFFT would similarly control the east and west lane lights. Then TFFFFT would turn on the red north and south and green east and west lights. We will assume that the basic output register at location $4FFF (called LIGHTS in the program) is connected so its right 6 bits control the lights as just described. It is constructed as in figure 4-1b. Also, for further reference, TIME will be a binary number whose value is the number of quarter-seconds that a light pattern is to remain on. For example, the pair LIGHT = TFFFFT and TIME = 5 will put the red north and south and green east and west lights on for one-and-a-quarter seconds. Finally, a *sequence* will be several pairs of light patterns and associated times that describe how the traffic lights are controlled. In this example, the sequence is a *cycle*, a sequence that repeats itself forever. The input, in this example, will be a binary number N read from a basic input register that appears to be at location $4000.

This approach is to *program* the sequences by means of immediate operands. See the following program, for example:

```
        LDAA  #%00100001    TURN ON RED N-S  AND GREEN E-W
        STAA  LIGHTS        PUT INTO OUTPUT REGISTER LIGHTS
        LDAA  #10           SET OUTER LOOP COUNTER
L1 LDX  #41667              SET INNER LOOP TO DELAY 1/4 SEC
L2 DEX                      DECREMENT  INDEX  REGISTER X
        BNE   L2            LOOP  FOR  A  QUARTER  SECOND
        DECA                DO  THE INNER LOOP  10  TIMES
        BNE   L1
```

In this technique, as the program is executed, it supplies immediate operands (as in line 1) to the output register (as in line 2) and immediate operands (as in line 3) to control the duration of the light pattern. A loop, such as lines 5 and 6, or a pair of nested loops, such as lines 4 to 8, is called a *delay loop*. It is used to match the time of the external action with the time needed to complete the instruction. Delay loops are extensively used in I/O interface programs. The delay loops use index register X to count out a quarter-second delay (in the inner loop in lines 5,6). Index register X or Y can be used as counters. Since the loop takes exactly six memory cycles and a memory cycle is one-half-microsecond in our examples, the loop should be cycled (250,000/6) = 41,666.666 times. The fourth line sets up the index register to be decremented that number of times in the inner loop. An outer loop is executed a number of times specified by the number in accumulator A in line 3. Since each inner loop takes .25 seconds, the total delay will be about 2.5 seconds. Another segment of the program much like this one could be written to output another pattern for another time period. The entire sequence could be programmed by writing segments like this one for each pattern.

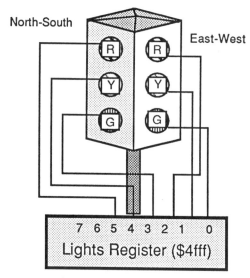

Figure 4-4. Traffic Light

We observe that the program has some undesirable features. The inner loop may take .25 seconds, but the setup instructions make the delay a few microseconds longer. While the average motorist won't be too upset about this error, if several traffic lights along a street have different programs in them, these minuscule errors could accumulate so that in a month or two the lights may be so far out of sequence as to stop the flow of traffic at every light. With a little effort, though, the delays can be trimmed so each program segment is precisely timed. Writing such a program takes a fair amount of effort, but timing can be adjusted so errors do not accumulate, and traffic can flow smoothly without needless stopping at each light. However, the memory cycle must also be adjusted to be precisely 1 microsecond in this example, since the timing is predicated on an accurate delay for each memory cycle. This can be achieved using a crystal-controlled oscillator to provide the microcomputer clock, but the controllers will have to be resynchronized every few months because even a crystal has limited accuracy. Noting that the problem is the relative error between controllers, an easier solution would use some global clock to keep all the controllers synchronized. Though slow and not precisely accurate, the 60-Hz power line provides a universal clock to keep them in synchronization. The inner loop would wait for the rising edge of the power line signal, and the outer loop would count in 60*ths* of a second, for instance.

4-2.3 Table and Linked List Interpreters

A better way than programming a control sequence using immediate operands is described in the following paragraphs. This method makes it easier to write and modify the control sequences, and to store them in a small microcomputer memory. These advantages are so great that the technique introduced in this section is usually recommended for most applications.

An *interpreter* is a program that reads values from a data structure such as a table, a bit or character string, list, or a linked list structure to control something, like drill presses or traffic lights, or to execute high-level languages like BASIC, APL, or LISP. You might like to scan section 2-1 to review data structures before looking at interpreters. Table and linked-list interpreters are particularly useful in interface applications. The table interpreter is described first, then the linked-list interpreter is introduced by modifying the table interpreter.

A light pattern cycle can be stored in a table. The table has two columns – one to store the pattern and the other to store the time – with one row for each pair. Consecutive rows are read from the table to the output register and to the delay loop. For example, a cycle could be described by table 4-2.

Table 4-2. Traffic Light Sequence

LIGHT	TIME
TFFFFT	10
TFFFTF	4
FFTTFF	14
FTFTFF	4

Tables are stored like arrays in a computer. Recall from section 2-1.2 that arrays can be stored in row major order or column major order. We store the preceding table in row major order because the rows are accessed as a whole using index addressing and the INX instruction. The table can be stored in the MC68HC11A8 this way:

```
FCB     %100001
FCB     10
FCB     %100010
FCB     4
FCB     %001100
FCB     14
FCB     %010100
FCB     4
```

If the first word is at location 100, then the first row of the table is stored in location 100 and 101, with location 100 containing 00100001 and location 101 containing 00001010. The next rows are stored below this one in the same way.

In a table interpreter for this table, shown soon, the first line sets the index register to point to the first word in the table. The next two lines read the light pattern from the entry in the first column into the output register. The delay time is next read, then the delay loop is entered. Index register X is set up to count 41,666 inner loop cycles, as before, and the delay time read from the table is used to count out the number of times this loop is executed by the outer loop. Index register Y has already been incremented twice by INY instructions and is now pointing to the next row in the table, and the preceding program is essentially repeated. This way, consecutive rows are read out to control the consecutive light patterns. However, after the last row is read out, the index register must be repositioned to point to the first row, to cycle the patterns. This is done, in the last three lines, by comparing the index register with the address of the word just beyond the end of the table and branching to line 1 to reload the index register when it reaches that point.

```
          NAM   TRAF
L         LDY   #TBL     POINT TO FIRST ROW
L0        LDAA  0,Y      GET LIGHT PATTERN, MOVE POINTER
          INY
          STAA  LIGHTS   OUTPUT PATTERN
          LDAA  0,Y      GET DELAY (IN 1/4 SECS)
          INY
L1        LDX   #41666   SET UP LOOP FOR 1/4 SECOND
L2        DEX            DECREMENT INDEX REGISTER X
          BNE   L2       DELAY 1/4 SECONDS
          DECA
          BNE   L1       EXECUTE INNER LOOP "DELAY" TIMES
          CPY   #TBL+8   AT END OF TABLE?
          BNE   L0       NO, GO TO NEXT ROW
          BRA   L        YES, REINITIALIZE
          END
```

Linked-list interpreters strongly resemble sequential machines. We have learned that most engineers have little difficulty thinking about sequential machines, and that they can easily learn about linked-list interpreters by the way sequential machines are modeled by a linked list interpreter. (Conversely, programmers find it easier to learn about sequential machines through their familiarity with linked-list structures and interpreters from this example.) Linked-list interpreters or sequential machines are powerful techniques used in sophisticated control systems, such as robot control. You should enjoy studying them, as you dream about building your own robot.

A *Mealy sequential machine* is a common model for (small) digital systems. While the model, described soon, is intuitive, if you want more information, consult almost any book on logic design, such as *Fundamentals of Logic Design,* by C. H.

Roth, West Publishing Co., Chapter 14. The machine is conceptually simple and easy to implement in a microcomputer using a linked-list interpreter. Briefly, a Mealy sequential machine is a set S of internal states, a set I of input states, and a set O of output states. At any moment, the machine is in a *present* internal state and has an input state sent to it. As a function of this pair, it provides an output state and a *next* internal state. The next internal state becomes the present internal state in the next moment.

The Mealy sequential machine can be shown in graph or table form. (See figures 4-5a and 4-5b for these forms for the following example.) In this example, the machine has internal states S = {A,B,C}, input states I = {a,b}, and output states O = {0,1}. The graph shows internal states as nodes, and, for each input state, an arc from a node goes to the next internal state. Over the arc, the pair, input state/output state, is written. In the table, each row describes an internal state and each column, an input state. In the table, the pair, next internal state/output state, is shown for each internal state and output state. In this example, if the machine were in state A and received input a, it would output 0 and go to state B; if it received input b, it would output 1 and go back to state A.

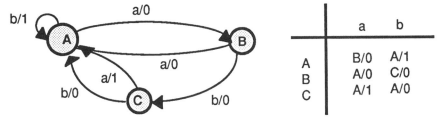

	a	b
A	B/0	A/1
B	A/0	C/0
C	A/1	A/0

a. Graph Representation

b. Table Representation

Figure 4-5. Mealy Sequential Machine

Consider a simple example of a sequential machine operation. If the machine starts in internal state A and the input a arrives, it goes to state B and outputs a 0. In fact, if it starts in state A and receives the sequence abbaba of input states, it will go through the internal state sequence BCABCA, and it will generate the output state sequence 000001.

The table representation can be stored in a microcomputer in standard row major order. The following directives show how this can be done in the 6811:

A	FDB	B	NEXT STATE FOR PRESENT STATE A, INPUT a
	FCB	0	OUTPUT FOR PRESENT STATE A, INPUT a
	FDB	A	NEXT STATE FOR PRESENT STATE A, INPUT b
	FCB	1	OUTPUT FOR PRESENT STATE A, INPUT b
B	FDB	A	NEXT STATE FOR PRESENT STATE B, INPUT a
	FCB	0	OUTPUT FOR PRESENT STATE B, INPUT a
	FDB	C	NEXT STATE FOR PRESENT STATE B, INPUT b
	FCB	0	OUTPUT FOR PRESENT STATE B, INPUT b
C	FDB	A	NEXT STATE FOR PRESENT STATE C, INPUT a
	FCB	1	OUTPUT FOR PRESENT STATE C, INPUT a
	FDB	A	NEXT STATE FOR PRESENT STATE C, INPUT b
	FCB	0	OUTPUT FOR PRESENT STATE C, INPUT b

If this table is stored, beginning at location $0100, then the row for state A will start at $0100, for B at $0106 and for C at $010C. The first 3 words, at locations $0100 to $0102, would be

FFFFFFFT
FFFFFTTF
FFFFFFFF

The interpreter for this table (or linked-list structure) would read an input, presumably from an input register SRC at location $4000, and send the output to an output register DST at location $4FFF, as before. The input state 'a' is the value $00, when read from the input register, and 'b' is $01. The internal state is associated with the row being read, and this is determined by the index register X. If the initial internal state is A, then the program implements this by initializing X to the address of the row associated with state A. The table is stored as just shown and is interpreted by the following program:

```
        LDX    #A     POINT TO INITIAL STATE A
L1      LDAA   SRC    READ INPUT STATE
        BEQ    L2     IF INPUT IS "b"
        INX           MOVE OVER 3 WORDS
        INX
        INX
L2      LDAA   2,X    READ OUTPUT STATE
        STAA   DST    INTO OUTPUT REGISTER
        LDX    0,X    PUT ADDRESS OF NEXT STATE IN X
        BRA    L1     REPEAT FOREVER
```

The first line initializes index register X to start the machine in state A. The input state is read and examined. If it is 'a' (value 0), the third word of the table is output, and the first and second words give the address of the row associated with the next state. Line 3 branches to line 7 to read the output state, and line 8 outputs it. Line 9 gets the address associated with the next state, so that when line 1 is reentered the same operation is repeated for that state. However, if the input is 'b' (1), the INX instructions add 3 to index register X so lines 7 to 9 pick up the output and next states from the sixth, fourth, and fifth words of the table, respectively.

We introduced the linked-list structure by comparing it to a row of the table. The structure is accessed (read from or written in) by a program, an interpreter. The key idea is that the next row to be interpreted is not the next lower row, but a row specified by reading one of the table's columns. For example, after interpreting the row for state A, if a 'b' is entered, the row for A is interpreted again because the address read from words 5 and 6 of the table is this same row's address. This view of a list is intuitively simple. More formally, a *linked list structure* is a collection of *blocks* having the same *template*. A block is a list like the row of the table and the template is like the column heading. Each block is composed of *fields* that conform to the template. Fields can be 1 bit to 10s of bits wide. They may or may not correspond directly to memory words (bytes), but if they do, they are easier to use. In our example, the block (row) is composed of 4 fields: the first is a 16-bit field containing a next address, the second is an 8-bit output field, and the third and fourth fields are like the first and second. Addresses generally point to the block's first word, as in our example, and are loaded into the index register to access data in the block. Fields are accessed by using the offset in indexed addressing. Another block is selected by reloading the index register to point to that block's first word. Rather than describe blocks as rows of a table, we graphically show them, with arcs coming from address fields to the blocks they point to, as in figure 4-6. Note the simple and direct relationship between figure 4-6 and figure 4-5a. This intuitive relationship can be used to describe any linked-list structure, and, without much effort, the graph can be translated into the equivalent table and stored in the microprocessor memory.

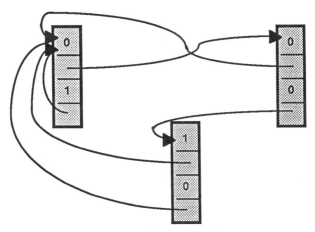

Figure 4-6. A Linked-List Structure

Linked-list structures are especially useful in the control of sophisticated machines, robots, and so on. You can model some of the operations as a sequential machine first, then convert the sequential machine to a linked-list structure and write an interpreter for the table. You can also define the operations solely in terms of a linked list and its interpretive rules. Some of our hardware colleagues seem to prefer the sequential machine approach, but our software friends insist that the linked-list structure is much more intuitive. You may use whichever you prefer.

The interpreters are useful for logic-timer control. A table is a good way to represent a straight sequence of operations, such as the control for a drill press that drills holes in a plate at points specified by rows in the table. A linked-list interpreter is more flexible and can be used for sequences that change depending on inputs. Interpreters are useful in these ways for driving I/O devices. Their use, though, extends throughout computer applications, from data base management through operating systems, compilers, and artificial intelligence.

4-3 Programmable Parallel Input-Output Devices

Microcomputers often use LSI chips called *Programmable Parallel Input-Output Devices* that are capable of being both inputs and outputs, selected under software control. The programming of the selection is – how shall we put it? – different. In the first subsection, we will offer you some reasons for having to program these devices in such an illogical manner and introduce the programming ritual used to select these devices' mode of operation. The M6821 is such a programmable chip that is in the same family as the M6811. We will introduce it in the second subsection to show how rituals are written. The parallel I/O registers that are internal to the M6811 and therefore usable in the single-chip mode, are discussed in the last section. Although they are easier to use than an external M6821, we discuss them after the M6821 because their features can be understood as special cases of the M6821 technique.

4-3.1 Problems with LSI I/O and the Ritual

The first microcomputers were rather disappointing, especially in their I/O. Although the computer's central processing unit was put on a large-scale integrated circuit, the I/O section was implemented with tens of small- and medium-scale integrated circuits. These early microcomputers were not much smaller in physical size than minicomputers because so much circuitry was needed for I/O, and they were quite a bit slower than minicomputers. Motivated by the need for more compact I/O, integrated manufacturers began to develop large-scale integrated circuits for I/O.

The first general class of I/O devices that were converted to large-scale integrated circuit chips were the 8-bit-wide parallel I/O devices which we are now discussing. Serial I/O devices and counters were converted later, and these will be the subject of considerable scrutiny in the following chapters. These chips have some quirks that appear at first to be design errors but really are consequences of some unusual characteristics of large-scale integrated circuitry. To reassure the reader, we will review the rationale for these annoying characteristics.

The two key problems for large scale integrated circuit applications are volume production and pins. The cost of designing such a chip is around a million dollars, but the chip has to sell for around ten dollars. Therefore, they can only be designed if they can be sold in hundreds of thousands. So they are often designed for use in several similar applications, to encompass a sufficient market to pay for the design. For example, the 74HC374 can be used as an output register, of course, and by connecting its outputs to the data bus, it can function as an input register. So one chip can work as either an input or output device. Possibly twice as many chips will be sold if they can be used in both applications, as will be sold if they can only be used in one. To further extend the use of a chip, some pins can be added that determine how it functions. These *parameter pins* are normally connected to positive supply or ground, so a T or F can be constantly input to select a function. The INTEL 8212 is an excellent example of a chip with parameter pins; a mode pin MD is strapped to low to make the chip serve as an input device and to high to make it an output device. The CMOS 4034 is a readable output register that can serve as a shift register using a shift control pin. The Universal

Asynchronous Receiver Transmitter (UART), discussed in chapter 8, is an example of parameterization taken to an extreme. The pins used for parameterization are not cheap. They cannot be used for data input and output. More pins require a larger chip that takes more area on a printed circuit board. Not only is the larger chip more expensive, but the area on the printed circuit board is also costly, as some boards around one square foot can cost a few hundred dollars just for the bare board.

An alternative to the use of parameter pins is to literally put these connections inside the chip itself, with the parameters to be stored in a *control register*. This register looks rather like the data register in an I/O chip, in that an output instruction can load it with data. However, the values stored in it are used to set parameters that determine how the chip will function. For example, 1 bit in a control register may determine if the chip is to function as an input register or an output register. This technique solves both the volume production and the pin problem; it permits the same chip to be used in various similar applications, but it does not require a large number of pins to select the specific function the chip performs.

A less important and similar problem is that some LSI chips have too many registers and not enough pins. The address used to select the register is sometimes provided in part by bits that, to avoid using other pins, are stored in other registers inside the chip. The effect of this is that several registers appear at the same location – to be read by an instruction like LDAA $8000, for instance – but the register that is actually read depends on some bits in another register, and you have to store an appropriate word in that other register to be able to read the register you want.

Moreover, it seems every solution creates some new problem. The control register has to be *initialized* to set the parameters when the microcomputer is powered on. This must be done before the device is actually used and can be done just before it is used or right after power is turned on. Initializing the control register *configures* the device. The initialization routine is rather like an obscure *ritual* that is hard to explain and understand but is relatively easy to do. The programmer has to determine exactly which bits in the control word have to be set to make the chip perform its specific function, and the correct sequence in which to set these bits. While the initialization ritual is most efficiently done before the device is used, this technique is especially prone to software bugs that do such things as write garbage all over memory, including memory-mapped control registers. Input registers become output registers, interrupts are mysteriously generated, and other marvelous happenings follow. Using some bits of a control register to select a register from a collection of registers is like a magician's hat trick – now you see it, now you don't. When analyzing an erroneous program, it is difficult to know if a program error has changed one of the hidden registers. You have to check them too. The hat trick is one feature of LSI I/O chips that makes life difficult for programmers. Of course, if you can't trust the program, the best thing to do is put a lock on the I/O device decoder to minimize all these calamities.

Improved semiconductor technology permitted the implementation of single-chip microcomputers like the MC68HC11A8. The I/O devices could be put on the same chip as the processor, thus reducing the need for tricky solutions to avoid pins, since the connections to I/O devices inside the microcomputer chip need no pins. However, the need for standardization mentioned above has created another problem: because the microcomputer chip must have a set of I/O devices that is the same for a large number of users, you seem to get either too many devices, and thus you do not use all of them, or else you need a device that is not on the chip. In the latter case, the solution is to have an expansion mode like the MC68HC11A8 expanded multiplexed bus mode, which permits the addition of I/O devices and memory to a single-chip microcomputer. The I/O devices on the single-chip microcomputer will be discussed in the third subsection of this section.

4-3.2 The M6821 Input-Output Registers

The M6821 is a large-scale integrated circuit designed for parallel I/O that incorporates a control register to increase its flexibility. This chip is also called a *peripheral interface adapter* or PIA. We rather use the part name M6821 than the name PIA. The use of names like PIA remind us of alchemy - oil of vitriol, eye of bat, and so on - at least, they smack more of advertising than engineering. We simply don't like them. Besides, Motorola produces two different chips, the M6820 and the M6821, both called PIA. More chips like the PIA will probably be produced, and they may be named PIA, if that is Motorola's wish. So we prefer to use part names like M6821 in this book. But you can use either, and you should know both.

The chip has two almost identical I/O devices in it; each device has a data register that can be either an input register or an output register, or part input and part output register using a technique we discuss below. Each device has eight pins, *peripheral data* pins, to accept data from the outside world when the device is an input register or to supply data to the outside world when it is an output device. Each device has hardware to generate interrupts. Its I/O circuitry is discussed now. The interrupt circuitry will be discussed in chapter 5, after the appropriate concepts have been introduced. The M6821 is fully described in a Motorola data sheet.

Each device in the M6821 has three 8-bit registers, *data, direction,* and *control.* (See figure 4-7a.) The direction register determines, on a bit by bit basis, whether a data register bit is treated as an input bit or an output bit. In the most common case, the direction bits are all T or all F, which makes the whole data register either an 8-bit output register or an 8-bit input register, respectively. Both the devices in the 6821 are capable of being input, readable output, or partially readable output registers. These three registers in one device are accessed as just 2 words of memory using a "hat trick." A bit in the control register acts as a seventeenth address bit to select either the data or direction register. For example, these 2 words might be $8000 and $8001. If the program reads or writes in $8001, it always reads or writes data in the control register. If the program reads or writes in location $8000, it accesses the direction register if bit 2 of the control register is F, or it accesses the data register if that bit is T. The pin connections for the M6821 are shown in figure 4-7b for reference later in this chapter.

Suppose the device at $8000 and $8001 is to be an input device. The following ritual will be put in the reset routine to select this mode:

```
CLR    $8001
LDD    #$0004
STD    $8000
```

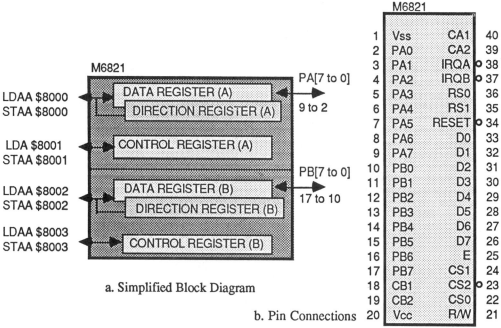

Figure 4-7. The M6821

a. Simplified Block Diagram

b. Pin Connections

The first instruction clears bit 2 in the control word so that when location $8000 is accessed, the direction register will be read from or written in. The next instruction puts 0 into the high-order and 4 into the low-order bytes of the index register. The last instruction stores these 2 bytes in locations $8000 and $8001 respectively. Observe carefully that the high-order byte is first stored by the STD instruction at location $8000, so it is stored in the direction register, thus making the device an input register. The low-order byte is then stored. It puts a T in control bit 2, so that any following instructions that access location $8000 will see an input device. Thereafter, the program can read the data on the peripheral data pins whenever it executes an LDAA $8000 instruction or its equivalent. However, an instruction like STAA $8000 will do nothing, since this device is configured to be an input device. There is no need to reinitialize the device each time it is read, as it will remain an input device until the control and direction registers are altered.

If the device is to be configured as a readable output, the following ritual is performed before the device is ever used:

```
CLR   $8001
LDD   #$FF04
STD   $8000
```

The first instruction clears bit 2 in the control register so the STD instruction can put all Ts in the direction register to make the device an output device. The STD instruction also sets bit 2 so thereafter location $8000 is an output register. The instruction STAA $8000 will store in the data register a word, whose value will be available on the peripheral data pins to the outside world. The output register is also readable. An instuction LDAA $8000 will read the word in the output register that was last stored there and is being output on the peripheral data pins. Also, an instruction like INC $8000 will read the current value, add 1, and store the new value in the output register. Again, it is not necessary to execute the initialization ritual each time data are to be read or written in the data register; once the direction and control register are set up as above, the data register is treated as a readable output register.

Since each bit in the data register is selected for input or output by the corresponding bit in the direction register, it is possible to make the same device an input for some bits and an output for others (a partially readable output device). For example, if 2 output bits are needed and 6 input bits are needed, the following ritual will make the 2 low-order bits outputs and the others inputs:

```
CLR    $8001
LDD    #$0304
STD    $8000
```

If an STAA $8000 instruction is executed, the 2 low-order bits are stored in the output register, the other bits being discarded in the input bit positions. An LDAA $8000 will read the 2 low-order bits last stored there and the other 6 bits from the corresponding peripheral data pins that input data from the outside world.

A *reset* pin is provided on most I/O chips, and this is connected to a similar pin on the MC68HC11A8. When power is first turned on, or when this (negative logic) signal is asserted low (by a panic button reset switch), the MC68HC11A8 is restarted in a manner discussed in chapter 5. In this restart program, we can often guarantee that all registers in all I/O chips are cleared, so it is unnecessary to execute a full initialization ritual. In particular, the M6821's direction registers (and the other registers) are cleared, so the device is (almost) configured as an input device. This is the safe way to configure an I/O device so two outputs won't be connected to the same line, one driving it high while the other pulls it low. If the device is initially automatically configured as an input device until the programmer configures it, at least the gate outputs won't be stressed or destroyed. But it is necessary to change the M6821's control register so bit 2 is T, or you will actually read the direction register when you think you are reading the input data register. After reset, to configure an M6821 as an input device at location $8000, execute the instruction

```
LDAA    #$4
STAA    $8001
```

This is one of the most common errors in using the M6821, assuming it is configured as an input device when power is applied or the machine is reset. So remember: you must change the control register before you can use the data register as an input. Otherwise, you will be reading the direction register.

Many object to this technique of loading two control registers at the same time, observing that it is hard to read and thus is bad programming practice. However, the reason we call such program segments "rituals" is that they do not conform to standard programming practices and rules. The key to using this technique successfully is to avoid making a mistake in the generation of the control word that is put in the immediate operand, which is quite tricky to determine. So, we don't object to such tricks as using a 16-bit register to load two control registers in an initialization ritual. The other 16-bit registers, X or Y, can be used in place of D if D has something in it. (However, some I/O chips are not capable of loading two registers in consecutive memory cycles due to poor design, so you may have to load them one at a time using STAA instructions.)

As noted in section 2-2.1, equate directives should be used to generate the constants used in rituals, so the code will be self-documenting or at least as clear as possible. For example, the previous program segment can be written as follows. At the beginning we write

```
DATOUT EQU   4
PORTAC EQU   $8001
```

and in the program we can put

```
LDAA   #DATOUT
STAA   PORTAC
```

The M6821 chip has two almost identical devices called the A and B devices. The B device behaves as we just discussed; the A device has outputs like open collector outputs with pull-up resistors inside the chip, so that, when a bit is configured as an output bit and is read by an LDAA $8000 instruction, the data that is read is, in fact, the positive logic AND of the bit stored in the output register and the outputs of any gates driving this bus line. Usually, the A and B devices occupy four consecutive words in memory; for example the A data/direction register is at location $8000, the A control register is at $8001, the B data/direction register is at $8002 and the B control is at $8003. However, it is possible and often desirable to connect the address pins to the chip in a different manner. It is possible to put A and B data/direction registers at $8000 and $8001, respectively, and A and B control at $8002 and $8003, respectively. Then the data registers can be read or written using the LDD $8000 and STD $8000 instructions as if they were 16-bit data registers.

4-3.3 M6811 Single-Chip Parallel Input-Output Registers

The M6811 has five parallel I/O ports, named A through E. These are all available in the single-chip mode, although they share some pins with other I/O devices and cannot be used as parallel I/O devices when their pins are used for some other I/O function. Ports B and C are not available in the expanded multiplexed bus mode, but a special I/O chip, the M68HC24, can be used to replace the missing registers in this mode so it functions exactly like the single-chip mode.

This subsection covers the simple parallel I/O organization of these five registers. The next chapter will consider the optional interrupt and handshake modes that can be used with these registers, and chapters on analog, counter, and communications devices will consider the conflicts between their use and the use of other I/O devices, also discussed in these chapters.

The memory locations of all the I/O devices as a group can be moved to any 4K boundary (0, $1000, $2000, ..., $F000) as discussed in Chapter 5. In the following examples, we will use index addressing, assuming that X points to the lowest addressed register in the I/O group, which is the parallel A port register. Direct (16-bit) addressing may be used with instructions like LDAA, INC, and ROL, but not with the very useful BRSET group. Direct page (8-bit) addressing may be used if the registers are moved to page 0, with instructions like LDAA and the BRSET group, but not with instructions like ROL and INC. Since all the memory instructions can use index addressing, we use index addressing with index register X (although Y can obviously be used too) in the following discussion.

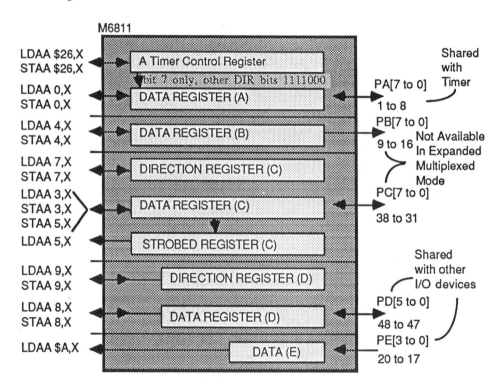

Figure 4-8. Simplified Block Diagram of MC68HC11A8 Parallel I/O Registers

The parallel I/O ports in the M6811 can be understood by comparing them to an M6821 parallel port. Ports C and D behave like an M6821 parallel port, except that the direction register is at a different location rather than at the same location as the data register, so there is no need to change a control bit to perform a "hat trick," and port D and its control register are missing the high 2 bits (they read as Fs). An extra input for port C is available for a handshake mode, discussed in chapter 5. Port E is an input register, permanently configured as if the direction bits were all Fs. In the dual in-line package discussed in this book, the high-order 4 bits are missing, but in another implementation, all 8 bits are available for input. Port B is a readable output register, like an M6821 port with direction bits permanently configured all Ts. Port A has a programmable direction bit for bit 7, but the other bits are permanently configured like an M6821 with direction register x1111000, so the low 3 bits are inputs, and the next 4 bits are readable outputs. The direction bit for port A bit 7 is bit 7 of a timer control register in which other bits are used to control timer functions.

The reasons for these variations from the M6821 model are due to pin limitations and the pins' other uses. The D port's high-order 2 bits are needed for synchronization signals, discussed in Chapter 5, so they are not available as port D data bits, and the 48-pin dual in-line package has only enough pins for port E's low-order 4 bits. Because port E is also used for A/D converter inputs sensitive to leakage currents which would be hard to control if an output register shared the same pins, port E is only an input register. Since port B is used in the expanded multiplexed mode to output the low byte of the address, it is permanently configured as a readable output register. Port A pins (except bit 7) are used for different input and output functions for the timer, so they are permanently configured as either input or readable output bits, depending on how they are used in the timer. Port A pin 7 can be configured as input or output. Only port B, which is used in the expanded multiplexed mode as the bidirectional multiplexed data bus, and port D, are general purpose parallel I/O ports.

These various ports can be chosen for an application depending on their special features. In the expanded multiplexed mode, the pins for ports B and C are used for the address and multiplexed address-data busses and are not available for parallel I/O, but these ports can be made available by connecting an external M6824 chip to the data bus in that mode. In the single-chip mode or expanded multiplexed mode with an M6824, port B is preferred for parallel output, port E is preferred for 4-bit parallel input, and ports C and D are preferred for parallel I/O operations that use LDAA and STAA instructions or their equivalents. Port A may be useful for parallel I/O operations for a device that just happens to need 3 or 4 input bits and 4 or 5 output bits. The BSET and BCLR instructions are generally useful on any output register bit, and the BRCLR and BRSET instructions are generally useful on any input register bit. However, the use of some of the pins for other I/O functions may alter the availability of the parallel ports.

Initialization rituals for these I/O devices can be designed by analogy to the initialization ritual for the M6821. Since ports A (except bit 7), B, and E are permanently configured, they do not need an initialization ritual. Bit 7 of port A is often configured as an input by a BCLR $26,X $80 instruction and as an output by a BSET $26,X $80 instruction, to avoid altering other bits in that location that are used to control the timer. The ritual used for the M6821 can be modified to initialize ports C and D. For example, to configure port D as a 6-bit output register, use an initialization ritual such as

```
LDAA #$3F
STAA  9,X
```

Then data can be written into port D by an instruction

$$STAA \; 8,X$$

The parallel I/O ports that are on the MC68HC11A8 chip itself are already "wired up," so they are easiest of all the parallel I/O devices to use. They make the single-chip mode of the MC68HC11A8 so very useful. We now consider examples of their use.

4-4 Indirect Input-Output

We now come to a somewhat surprising technique that is particularly suited to the MC68HC11A8 single-chip computer. Up to now, the I/O device has been attached to the address and data busses. We shall call this *direct I/O*. Alternatively, the address, data, and control pins of an I/O device can be connected to a parallel I/O device's I/O port pins, such as ports B and C of an MC68HC11A8 operating in single-chip mode. Explicit bit setting and clearing instructions can raise and lower the control signals for the I/O chip.

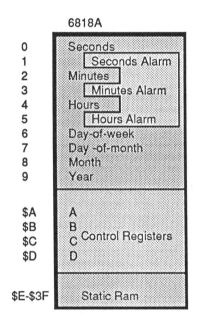

Figure 4-9. 6818A Time-of-Day Chip

We call this *indirect I/O*. Although indirect I/O is slow, and therefore cannot be used in some applications, it is very easy to debug and is a good way to experiment with an LSI I/O chip. We will give an example of the use of indirect I/O, using an MC6818A time-of-day clock chip, and then discuss the limitations and advantages of this technique.

We want to keep track of the time of day, so we choose the MC6818A or MC146818A time-of-day clock chip to do this even when the microcomputer is turned off. Figure 4-9 shows the memory organization of the MC6818A. The current time is in locations 0 to 9, except for locations 1, 3, and 5, which hold an alarm time that can be compared to the current time to generate an interrupt. Control registers at locations $A to $E allow different options. The remainder of the memory (locations $F to $3F) is CMOS low-power RAM. After an initialization ritual, which puts $80 into control register B and $F into control register A, the time may be loaded into locations 0 to 9, and then $8 is put into control register B to start the timekeeping. These locations 0 to 9 can be read after that to get the current time of day.

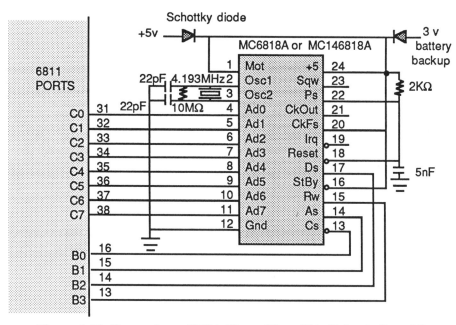

Figure 4-10. Connecting a 6818A Time-of-Day Chip Using Indirect I/O

This chip can be connected directly to the time-multiplexed address and data bus of the MC68HC11A8. However, we may wish to use the MC68HC11A8 in single-chip mode. The MC6818A can be connected to ports B and C, as shown in figure 4-10. Control signals (address strobe AS, data strobe DS, read-write RW, and chip select CS) are set high or low to write a word D into address A. They are initially high, except for DS which is low. We first raise AS high, put address A to port C, make CS and RW low, drop AS low, make DS high, put D to port C, drop DS low, and raise CS high. The procedure to read data from a memory location in the MC6818A is essentially the same, except that RW remains high and data D are read from port C.

We next examine a program to write the time of day, initially stored in MC68HC11A8 memory at locations YR to SE. The ports and port bits are defined first for readability, then the MC68HC11A8 memory locations are allocated. The main program is then given. The key subroutine that sends data to the chip is then shown. We are primarily interested in the subroutine. The input parameters are the data MC6818A passed in ACCA and the MC6818A address passed in ACCB. The main program merely calls up this subroutine to transfer 1 byte at a time from the 6811 memory to the MC6818A memory. The subroutine sets and clears bits in port B which in turn raise and lower the control lines to the MC6818A, as recently described.

```
PORTB EQU   4        CONTROL - INDEX FROM $1000
RW    EQU   8            WRITE LINE
DS    EQU   4            DATA STROBE
AS    EQU   2            ADDRESS STROBE
CS    EQU   1            CHIP SELECT
PORTC EQU   3        DATA I/O - INDEX FROM $1000
DIRC  EQU   7        DIRECTION - INDEX FROM $1000
*
YR    RMB   1
MO    RMB   1
DM    RMB   1
DW    RMB   1
HR    RMB   1
MN    RMB   1
SE    RMB   1
*
      LDX   #$1000     SET UP FOR BSET ETC.
      CLR   DIRC,X     INITIAL BUS DIRECTION IS IN
      LDAA  #RW+CS     INIT. R/W AND CHIP SELECT HIGH
      STAA  PORTB,X    AND DATA STB., ADDRESS STB. LOW
*
      LDD   #$800B     CONTROL SET TO LOAD
      BSR   OUTA
      LDD   #$F0A
      BSR   OUTA
      LDAA  YR
      LDAB  #9
      BSR   OUTA
      LDAA  MO
      LDAB  #8
      BSR   OUTA
      LDAA  DM
      LDAB  #7
      BSR   OUTA
      LDAA  DW
      LDAB  #6
      BSR   OUTA
      LDAA  HR
```

```
          LDAB  #4
          BSR   OUTA
          LDAA  MN
          LDAB  #2
          BSR   OUTA
          LDAA  SE
          CLRB
          BSR   OUTA
          LDD   #$80B            CLEAR CONTROL, ENABLE RUN
          BSR   OUTA
          SWI
   OUTA   BSET  DIRC,X $FF       MAKE PORT C OUTPUT
          BSET  PORTB,X AS       ASSERT ADDRESS STROBE
          STAB  PORTC,X          REGISTER ADDRESS TO PORT C
          BCLR  PORTB,X CS+RW    ASSERT CHIP SELECT, R/W LOW
          BCLR  PORTB,X AS       NEGATE ADDRESS STROBE
          BSET  PORTB,X DS       ASSERT DATA STROBE
          STAA  PORTC,X          DATA TO PORT C
          BCLR  PORTB,X DS       NEGATE DATA STROBE
          BSET  PORTB,X CS+RW    NEG. CH. SEL. HIGH FOR READ MD.
          CLR   DIRC,X           MAKE PORT B INPUT AGAIN
          RTS
```

The example shows how a rather complex and powerful chip like the MC6818A can be connected to a single-chip MC68HC11A8 computer. Observe that the subroutine rather tediously, but methodically, manipulates the MC68181A's control signals. A STAA instruction in direct I/O is simply replaced by a subroutine in indirect I/O that does the same thing. While the program shows how the MC6818A memory can be written into, similar routines can read that memory. (See problem 16 at the end of this chapter.) The main point of this section is the concept of indirect I/O, which we now elaborate on further.

Besides being a good way to connect complex I/O devices to a single-chip computer, indirect I/O is a very good way to experiment with an I/O chip. The main advantage is that the connections to the chip are on the "other side" of an I/O port, rather than directly on the MC68HC11A8's address and data busses. Therefore, if you short two wires together, the MC68HC11A8 still works sufficiently to run the BUFFALO monitor. You have not destroyed the integrity of the microcomputer. You can then pin down the problem by single-stepping the program and watching the signals on the ports with a logic probe. There is no need for a logic analyzer.

We used this technique to experiment with a floppy disk controller chip and a CRT controller chip set in chapter 9. We got these experiments to work in perhaps a quarter of the time it would have taken us using direct I/O. That experience induced us to write a whole section on this technique here in chapter 4. There is a limitation to this approach. Recall from chapter 3 that some chips use "dynamic" logic, which must be run at a minimum as well as a maximum clock speed. The use of indirect I/O may be too slow for the minimum clock speed required by dynamic logic chips. However, if the chip is not dynamic, this indirect I/O technique is very useful for interfacing to complex I/O chips.

4-5 Synchronous Serial Input-Output

Except for the parallel registers implemented inside the MC68HC11A8, parallel registers and their address decoders take a lot of wiring to do a simple job. Just wire up an experiment using them, and you will understand our point. In production designs, they use up valuable pins and board space. Alternatively, a serial signal can be time-multiplexed to send 8 bits of data in eight successive time periods over one wire, rather than sending them in one time period over eight wires. This technique is limited to applications in which the slower transfer of serial data is acceptable, but a great many applications do not require such a fast parallel I/O technique. Serial I/O is similar to indirect I/O covered in the last section, but it can be faster than indirect parallel I/O because special hardware is provided in the MC68HC11A8 and in serial I/O chips that makes this an attractive alternative.

This section considers the serial I/O system that uses a clock signal in addition to the serial data signal; such systems are called synchronous. Chapter 8 considers asynchronous serial communication systems that dispense with the clock signal. Synchronous serial systems are useful for relatively fast (1 megabit per second) communication between a microcomputer and serial I/O chips or between two or more microcomputers on the same printed circuit board, while asynchronous serial systems are better suited to slower (9600 bits per second) longer distance communications. The first subsection examines some simple chips that are especially suited for synchronous serial I/O. We then consider the use of a parallel I/O port and software to communicate to these chips. Finally, we study the serial peripheral interface (SPI) in the MC68HC11A8, a hardware device specially designed for this serial I/O technique.

4-5.1 Serial I/O Chips

Although serial I/O can be implemented with any shift register, such as the 74HC164, 74HC165, 74HC166, and 74HC299, two chips – the 74HC595 parallel output shift register and the 74HC597 parallel input shift register – are of special value. These are discussed in here for use in later examples.

The 74HC589 is a shift register with an input register and a tristate driver on the serial output of the shift register. (See figures 4-11b and 4-11d.) Data on the parallel input pins are transferred to the input register on the rising edge of the register clock RCLK. Those data are transferred to the shift register if the load signal LD is low. When LD is high, data in the shift register are shifted left on the rising edge of the shift clock SCLK and a bit is shifted in from IN, as in the 74HC595, but the data shifted out are available on the OUT pin only if EN is asserted low; otherwise it is tristated open.

The 74HC595 is a shift register with an output register and tristate driver on the parallel outputs. (See figures 4-11a and 4-11c.) For reasons given in section 4-4.3, we consider the shift register to shift left rather than right. A shift occurs on the rising edge of the shift clock SCLK. A bit is shifted in from IN and the bit shifted out is on OUT. On the rising edge of the register clock RCLK, the data in the shift register are transferred into the output register. If the output enable EN is asserted low, the data in the output register are available to the output pins; otherwise they are tristated open.

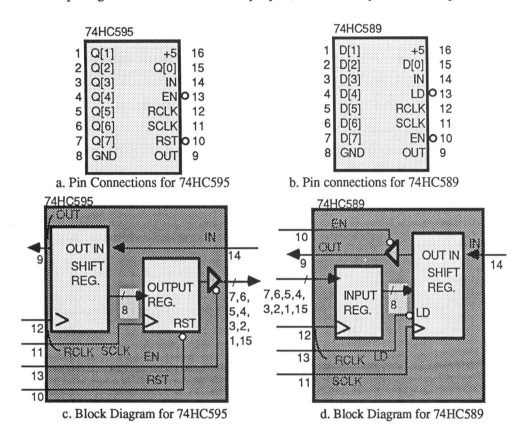

Figure 4-11. Simple Serial Input-Output Ports

These chips can be connected in series or parallel configurations. (See figure 4-12.) The 74HC589 can be connected in a series configuration to make a longer register, as we see in the figure 4-12a 24-bit input port. The outputs OUT of each chip are connected to the inputs IN of the next chip to form a 24-bit shift register. Each chip's RCLK pins are connected to an MC68HC11A8 port pin to clock the input registers together, each chip's LD pins are connected to an MC68HC11A8 port pin to load the shift registers together, and each chip's SCLK pins of each chip are connected to an MC68HC11A8 port pin to clock the shift registers together. The EN pins are connected to ground to enable the tristate drivers. In the software considered in a later subsection, we will load the input registers at one time to get a consistent "snapshot" of the data, then load this into the shift register at one time by making LD low, and then, with LD high, send 24 pulses on SCLK to shift the data into the MC68HC11A8.

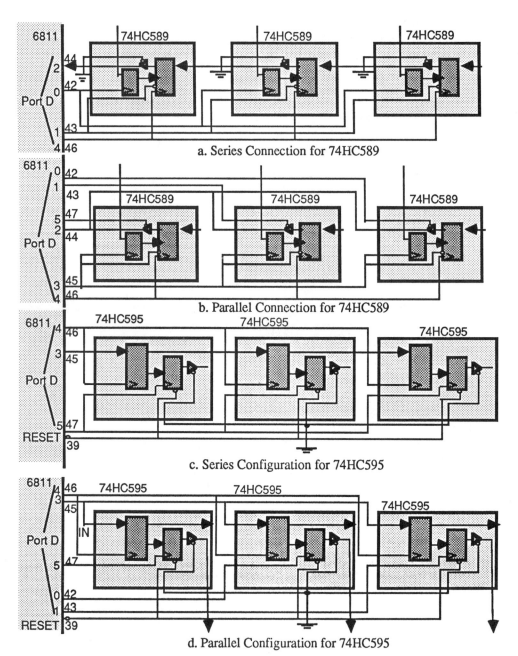

Figure 4-12. Configurations of Simple Serial Input-Output Registers

The 74HC589 can be connected in a parallel configuration to make several separate input ports, as we see in the three 8-bit input ports of figure 4-12b.. The outputs OUT of each chip are connected to a common tristate bus line, and the tristate enables EN of each chip are connected to MC68HC11A8 output pins, but the other pins are connected as in Figure 4-12a. (For the problems at the end of the chapter, LD and RCLK are tied together to save a port bit.) Any of the input ports may be selected by asserting its tristate enable low, the others being negated high. Then a sequence similar to that discussed in the previous paragraph will input the data on that chip, using eight pulses on SCLK. While this configuration requires more output pins on the MC68HC11A8, it permits the software to choose any chip to read its data without first having to read the chips in front of it in a series shift register.

Figures 4-12c and 4-12d show the corresponding series and parallel configurations for the 74HC595. Reset can be connected to the MC68HC11A8 reset pin which resets the system when it is turned on or when the user chooses. The output enable EN is connected to ground to assert it. The series configuration makes a longer shift register. The parallel configuration makes separate ports that can output data by shifting the same data into each port, but only pulsing the RCLK on one of them to transfer the data into the output register.

Variations of these circuits are useful. Series-parallel configurations, rather than simple series or simple parallel configurations, may be suited to some applications. The 74HC595 RCLK signals can come from the logic associated with the data's source, rather than from the microcomputer, to acquire the data when the source determines that data are ready. The 74HC589 output enable EN can be used to connect the output to a parallel data bus, so it can be disabled when other outputs on that bus are enabled. These configurations are shown here just to suggest some obvious ways to connect serial ports.

4-5.2 Control of Serial I/O Chips Using a Parallel Port

Serial I/O chips can be controlled by software, using parallel I/O register bits to control the lines to the chips. We discuss the general principles after we consider this example: the sending of 24 bits of data to a series configured output, as shown in figure 4-12c.

To continue the example used in the previous subsection through to the next subsection, we will use port D in the same way the upcoming serial peripheral interface will be used. The shift register clock is connected to port D bit 3, and the data out are connected to bit 4. The output buffer register clock is connected to bit 5 because, in the next subsection, it is an available bit in port D. The BSET and BCLR instructions are well suited to individually controlling the signals to the 74HC589. Note from figure 4-8 that port D data are at location 8 in the I/O register area. Assuming X points to the I/O registers (if port A is at $1000, X is $1000), the instruction

BSET 8,X $10

will set the 74HC589 inputs IN to T, and

BCLR 8,X $10

will clear these inputs to F. The other lines can be controlled in a similar manner.

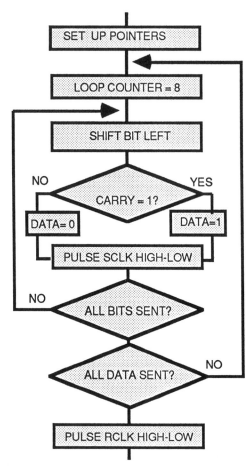

Figure 4-13. Flow Chart for Series Serial Data Output

A program segment to control the 24-bit serial output is based on the flow chart in figure 4-13. The C program for this operation is given as an example of documentation described in 2-2.1:

```
serial_out(buffer) char *buffer;
{
  char *portd, *p;
  int i,j;
  for(p=buffer; p<buffer+3; p++) {
    j = *p;
    for(i=7; i>=0; i--){
        if ((0x100 & (j = j <<1))==0)  *portd = *portd & 0xf7;
        else *portd = *portd | 8;
        *portd += 0x10; *portd -= 0x10; /* pulse shift clock */
    }
  }
    *portd += 0x20; *portd -= 0x20; /* pulse output register clock */
}
```

After setting up the pointers X and Y, an outer loop puts out 1 byte at a time, and then the RCLK line is pulsed to put the data into the output buffer register. The outer loop reads a byte from a buffer and from an inner loop that shifts 1 bit at a time into the D port output, clocking the SCLK after each bit is sent. Note the value of a flow chart, C program, comments, and meaningful labels in making the following program segment readable.

```
PORTD   EQU   8                     PAR. OUTPUT PORT CONTROLLING CHIPS
DATA    EQU   8                     DATA OUT ON D PORT BIT 3
SCLK    EQU   $10                   SHIFT REGISTER ON PORT D BIT 4
RCLK    EQU   $20                   OUTPUT BUFFER REGISTER CLOCK
        LDX   #$1000                PRESUMED ADDRESS OF I/O REGISTERS
        LDY   #BUFFER               BEGIN ADDRESS OF DATA TO BE SENT
OUTLP   LDAA  0,Y                   GET DATA FROM BUFFER
        LDAB  #8                    SET UP LOOP COUNTER FOR 8 DATA BITS
INLP    LSLA                        GET DATA BIT, MOST SIG. BIT FIRST
        BCC   SEND0                 CARRY IS THE BIT TO BE SENT: IF TRUE,
        BSET  PORTD,X DATA    MAKE DATA HIGH
        BRA   RESUM                 SKIP CHANGING BACK
SEND0   BCLR  PORTD,X DATA    ELSE MAKE DATA LOW
RESUM   BSET  PORTD,X SCLK    PULSE CLOCK
        BCLR  PORTD,X SCLK    REMOVE PULSE
        DECB                        COUNT DOWN
        BNE   INLP                  UNTIL ALL BITS TRANSFERRED
        INY                         MOVE POINTER
        CPY   #BUFFER+3             CHECK IF ALL BYTES SENT
        BNE   OUTLP                 IF NOT, SEND MORE
        BSET PORTD,X RCLK      PROVIDE A RISING EDGE TO RCLK
        BCLR PORTD,X RCLK      RECOVER RCLK FOR NEXT OP.
```

Program segments for the other configurations in figure 4-12 are similar to this one. These are proposed in problem 16 at the end of this chapter. The basic concept is that the individual signals needed to control the external chips can be manipulated by setting and clearing bits in parallel I/O registers. As the preceding example shows, this is really very easy to do using BSET and BCLR instructions in the 6811. Input bits can be tested in a similar manner by the BRCLR, BRSET instructions; the BITA and BITB instructions are also useful, as are the LSLA instructions. With all these alternative ways to control and test parallel I/O bits, it is easy to write programs that will interface to serial I/O devices via a parallel I/O register.

4-5.3 The MC68HC11A8 Serial Peripheral Interface

The previous subsection showed how synchronous serial devices can be manipulated in software, using bits in a parallel I/O port on the MC68HC11A8. The MC68HC11A8, however, has a *serial peripheral interface* (SPI), described in this subsection, that can perform these functions in hardware, resulting in simpler software and faster operation. We first describe the hardware and then give some examples of its use.

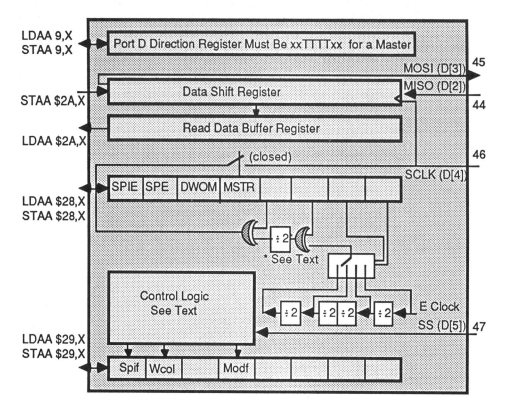

Figure 4-14. The MC68HC11A8 Serial Peripheral Interface

Figure 4-14 shows the organization of the serial peripheral interface. The pertinent registers are the data register (read or written at $2A,X$), a control register (at $28,X$), a status register (at 29), and, since this interface shares pins with the D port, the D direction register (at $9,X$). Although it can be used for multicomputer communication, as described later in this subsection, to use it with the peripheral chips just described, it is made a *master* of the communication system. To prepare this interface for use, the following ritual is performed:

```
LDX   #$1000  PRESUMED: THE I/O REG. ARE AT $1000 TO $103F
LDD   #$1850  CONFIG. THE D PORT FOR OUTPUT IN BITS 4,3
STAA  9,X     AND THE CONTROL REG. FOR MASTER MODE,
STAB  $28,X   WITH CLOCK = 1 MHZ, NOR. LOW, RISING EDGE
```

To use the SPI with serial peripherals, the serial peripheral enable (SPE) bit, bit 6 of the control register, must be set, and the master (MSTR) bit, bit 4 of the control register, must be set. Then bits 5 to 3 of the D port are controlled by the SPI, as described herein. Otherwise they are available as general purpose I/O bits, as described in section 4-3.3. When used as SPI bits, the direction bits of these D port bits must be set (bit 6 may be cleared if this MC68HC11A8 is a slave in a configuration with several 6811s communicating via SPIs). The low-order bits of the control register determine what kind of shift register clock is to be used. For a 2-MHz E clock, if bits 1,0 are FF, then the shift clock is 1 MHz; if they are FT, then the shift clock is 500 KHz; if they are TF, then the shift clock is 125 KHz; if they are TT, then the shift clock is 62500 Hz. These bits control a multiplexer which chooses different clocks from divide-by-2 (counter) stages. The last stage generates exactly 8 pulses after a write address trigger is obtained when the data shift register is stored into. Since the 74HC589 and 74HC595 are capable of operating at 1MHz, the ritual chooses FF for these bits. Control bit 3 determines the level of the shift clock when no data are being shifted: it is equal to that bit. Control bits 2 and 3 determine the edge that is used to clock the data in the shift registers: if they are equal, data are shifted on the rising edge of the shift clock; otherwise data are shifted on the falling edge. This ritual uses FF because the 74HC589 and 74HC595 shift on the rising edge (the level doesn't matter in this ritual). Finally, as used in the following examples, port D bits 5, 1, and 0 are used as outputs to control the 74HC589 and 74HC595 chips (bit 5 is associated with the SPI but is a simple output bit of port D, if the direction bit associated with it is T).

The SPI's basic operation is to exchange data between the SPI's shift register in the MC68HC11A8 and the shift register in the external chip. Writing data out through the SPI is quite simple. Data are written directly into the shift register. Writing data generates an address trigger that starts the control logic to generate the shift clock. Status bit 7, the serial peripheral interface flag (SPIF) bit, is set after the data have been sent out and must be T for data to be read. The other status bits, bits 6 and 4, indicate that errors have occurred if they are set. After data are read into the shift register, they are automatically copied into the read data buffer so the program has time to read the data, even if more data are being shifted in while the program is reading the last byte that had been shifted in. (This is called double buffering). Writing data into the (master) shift register starts the shift clock, so even if you only want to receive data, you write something into the (master) data register to start the clock. Reading the data register clears the status register for the next operation. Data may not be written into the shift register until the SPIF bit is cleared, so even if you only want to write data, you have to read the data register to clear the SPIF bit. Thus the exchange operation, assuming X points to the I/O registers, is:

```
      STAA   $2A,X   PUT DATA OUT, START THE SHIFT CLK
L1    TST    $29,X   WAIT FOR SPIF TO BE TRUE AFTER ALL
      BPL    L1      BITS HAVE BEEN SHIFTED IN/OUT
      LDAA   $2A,X   READ DATA, CLR SPIF FOR NEXT EXCHANGE
```

As an example, consider reading the data input to the 74HC589s in figure 4-12a into 3 bytes pointed to by the Y register. The flow chart for this program segment is shown in figure 4-15. The C program is shown below:

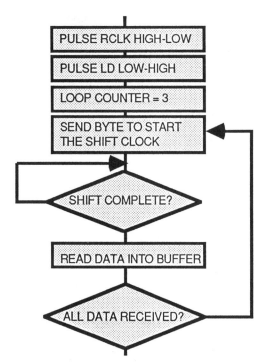

Figure 4-15. Flow chart for Data Input from Series Serial Input Interface

```
spi_out(buffer) char *buffer;
{
    char *portd, *dsr ,*spc *p;
    /* port D, Data Shift Register, Serial Peripheral Control */
    *portd += 1; *portd -= 1; /* pulse Register Clock */
    *portd -= 2; *portd += 2; /* pulse Shift Register Load */
    for(p=buffer; p<buffer+3; p++){
        *dsr = *p; /* write data word to shift register */
        while((*spc & 0x80) == 0) ; /* wait for SPIF to set */
        dummy = *dsr; /* Clear SPIF */
    }
}
```

First, we provide a rising edge to the RCLK pin on these chips to get a simultaneous sample of all inputs into their input buffer registers. Next we assert LD low to copy that data into their shift registers, then return LD high to permit shifting the data. Then we execute the program segment above this point three times, generating 24 clock pulses and putting the received data into 3 consecutive bytes pointed to by the Y register, incrementing Y each time a byte is written. The following program segment will transfer the 3 bytes, assuming the preceding initialization ritual has been executed and that X points to the I/O registers, Y points to the beginning of the buffer where the input data will be stored, and data bits 0 and 1 of the D port are TF:

```
PORTD  EQU   8          PAR.L OUTPUT PORT CONTROLLING CHIPS
RCLK   EQU   0          INPUT BUFFER REGISTER CLOCK IN PORT D
LD     EQU   1          LOAD BUFFER TO SHIFT REGISTER IN PORT D
       BSET  PORTD,X RCLK      PROVIDE RIS. EDGE TO RCLK
       BCLR  PORTD,X RCLK      RECOV. RCLK FOR NXT OP.
       BCLR  PORTD,X LD    ASSERT LD LOW TO LOAD SHIFT REG.
       BSET  PORTD,X LD    NEG. LD HIGH TO PERMIT SHIFTING
       LDB   #3               SET UP LOOP COUNTER
L0     STAA  $2A,X   PUT DATA OUT, START THE SHIFT CLK
L1     TST   $29,X   WAIT FOR SPIF TO BE TRUE AFTER ALL
       BPL   L1      BITS HAVE BEEN SHIFTED IN/OUT
       LDAA  $2A,X   READ DATA, CLR SPIF FOR NEXT EXCHANGE
       STAA  0,Y     PUT DATA INTO BUFFER
       INY           MOVE POINTER
       DECB          COUNT DOWN
       BNE   L0      UNTIL ALL BYTES TRANSFERRED
```

Note that garbage is written out in the instruction with label L0 to start the shift clock; the SPI output pin MOSI is not connected in this configuration and sending data causes no problem. Program segments for the other configurations in figure 4-12 are similar and are left as exercises in problem 17 at the end of the chapter. The program segment for figure 4-12b is a bit tricky and should be verified in an experiment, because the data shifted out must be low to load the input buffer but high for LD to be high so data can be shifted in; yet a rising edge of RCLK, on the same output as LD to save port D bits, is needed to load the data into the input buffer register.

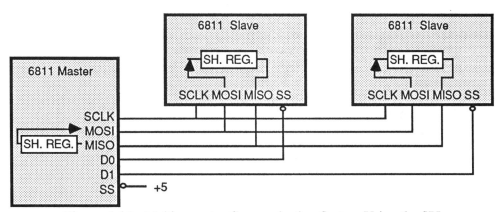

Figure 4-16. Multicomputer Communication System Using the SPI

The SPI interface can be used to communicate among several 6811s. (See figure 4-16.) The SCLK pins are connected together, as are the MOSI (Master Out, Slave In) and MISO (Master In, Slave Out) pins. One MC68HC11A8 is made a master, and all the others are *slaves*. The master has its MSTR bit in the control register set, while the slaves have MSTR clear and port D direction bit 5 clear. The master controls the slaves through a parallel output port like port D by making exactly one slave SS input low. The SS input on the master must be high. Then the SPI exchanges the data of the master SPI shift register with the data in the selected slave SPI shift register using a program like that just shown. The slave can monitor its SPIF bit, status bit 7, to detect when data have been exchanged, using synchronization techniques discussed in the next chapter. It is also possible for several 6811s to cooperate as equals, with any one of them being a master at any time. To detect errors, this requires a protocol, discussed in chapter 8, and the use of the 2 status bits we have not discussed here.

The serial port is a valuable alternative to the parallel port. It requires substantially less hardware. The MC68HC11A8's SPI interface makes it easy to use these devices, but, with a modest amount of software, any parallel I/O register can be used to control them. However, a parallel port is required where speed is needed, since the serial port, especially using software control, is considerably slower than the parallel port.

4-6 An Example: An IC Tester

In this section we consider a design problem to show how parallel I/O devices are built and programmed. Elements of top-down design are exemplified, and the interconnection of the M6821 to an M6811 and the ritual to initialize the device are demonstrated.

We want to be able to test small- and medium-scale ICs at the behavior level. That is, we want to be able to put an IC into a socket, then run a test program that will determine whether the IC provides the correct sequence of outputs for any sequence of inputs; but we are not testing the delays, the input and output electrical characteristics, or the setup, hold, rise, or fall times of signals. We want to be able to test standard 14- and 16- pin ICs in which +5 is applied to pin 14 (16), and pin 7 (8) is grounded. Such ICs comprise about 90% of the ones we use. Such a tester could be used to check ICs bought at bargain mail-order houses.

In principle, there are two design strategies: top-down and bottom-up. In top-down design, you try to understand the problem thoroughly before you even start to think about the solution. This is not easy, because most microcomputer design problems are said to be *nasty*; that means that it is hard to state the problem without stating one of its solutions. In bottom-up design, one has a solution – a component or a system – for which one tries to find a matching "problem." This is like a late-night TV show character, Carnak the Magnificent. Carnak reads the answer to a question written inside an envelope, then he opens the envelope and reads the question. This is bottom-up design. We do it all the time. The answer is microcomputers, now what was the question? Now if you are an applications engineer for Zilog, you are paid to find uses for a chip made by Zilog. But if you are a design engineer, you *must* design in a top-down manner! This philosophy of top-down design is so important that we will preach about it again in chapter 7.

We now approach the design of this IC tester in a top-down manner. We actually need 14 I/O bits to supply signals to all the pins and to examine the outputs for all the pins except power and ground. But the pins are not standard from chip to chip. Pin 1 may be an input in one chip and an output in another chip. The M6821 or a 6811 port such as C or D would be more suitable than the simple parallel or serial I/O device, because a line to the M6821 can be made an input or an output under control of software for different chips. Note that this is not always the case, and a simpler I/O device (using 74HC374, 74HC244, 74HC589, or 74HC595 chips) may be indicated because it may be cheaper and use up less board space. The 6811 C and D ports have just the right number of bidirectional bits (8+6). However, the MC68HC11A8 would not be able to use the SPI nor the asynchronous communications interface, so conflicts with these very useful devices rule out using the bidirectional ports on the 6811. Thus, we are left with the 6821. (We are a bit guilty of bottom-up design here because we chose a problem in such a way that it would point to using the M6821 which we are studying at this time.) To keep up with the 2-MHz MC68HC11A8, we need a "B" version of the 6821, the MC68B21.

To wire the M6821, we must study its pin connections and those of the MC68HC11A8 which must be connected to it. (See figure 4-7b.) We digress for a moment to learn the M6821's interconnection rules, but we will return shortly to the design problem when we know what lines are to be used.

The M6821 has ten pins to connect to the outside world for each device, A and B. Eight pins called PA0 to PA7 and PB0 to PB7 are the parallel I/O pin connections, and four pins called CA1, CA2, CB1, and CB2 are used in the interrupt circuitry discussed in chapter 5. The remaining pins on the M6821 are connected to the memory interface of the MC68HC11A8 in an almost methodical manner. The so-called enable pin E, which is actually a clock, is connected to the E clock or to a signal that is a slightly delayed E clock to account for skew in the data bus. This pin should never be held high or low for a long time on any LSI I/O chip, because many of them use dynamic logic that is clocked by this signal. Although the M6821 does not use dynamic logic, its control is sequenced by shift registers that depend on the E signal to keep going. Never use this signal as part of the addressing mechanism to enable the chip. If you do not periodically clock this pin, signals (which are actually charges on capacitors) will become indeterminate inside an LSI I/O chip. The data bus pins on the M6821 are connected to the data bus to the M6811, of course, and the R/W pin to the R/W line, and RESET to the RESET bus line; IRQA and IRQB are used for interrupt signals and are not connected in this example.

The remaining address pins, CS0, CS1, CS2, and RS0 and RS1 are connected to the address decoder. For any register in the chip to be accessed, CS0, CS1, and CS2 have to be HH and L, respectively. CS2 is often used as the chip enable, since the decoder usually outputs the enable in negative logic. CS0 and CS1 can be used as positive logic enables, in lieu of putting these inputs into the decoder, to simplify the decoder. Finally, the RS1 and RS0 pins are normally connected to address bits 1 and 0. If RS0 is connected to address bit 0 and RS1 to address 1, then, if the chip is selected by addresses $8000 through $8003, the A device data/direction and A device control appear at $8000 and $8001, respectively, and the B device data/direction and control appear at $8002 and $8003. If RS0 is connected to address bit 1 and RS1 is connected to address bit 0, then the A control and B data direction register locations are swapped. This makes the two data registers appear as one 16-bit data register that can be used with LDD $8000 to input a 16-bit word or with STD $8000 to output a 16 bit word.

For our design, we clearly connect PA and PB to the integrated circuit under test in a consistent manner that makes it easy the to understand and program the test sequences. To load and read 16 bits, a STX and LDX instruction would be convenient. Therefore, we will configure the devices so the A data register appears at location $8000 and the B data register appears at location $8001. The A control register will be at location $8002 and the B control register at $8003. To be consistent, then, PA will input or output data to the high number pins and PB to the low number pins. A rugged socket will be used for 16-pin ICs, with power and ground connections permanently wired to pins 16 and 8, and PA6 to PA0 connected to pins 15 to 9 and PB6 to PB0 connected to pins 7 to 1, and a second rugged socket will be used for 14-pin ICs, with power and ground connections permanently wired to pins 14 to 7, and PB5 to PB0 connected to pins 6 to 1, respectively. The user will plug a 16-pin IC into the 16-pin socket and not put anything in the 14-pin socket to test a 16-pin IC, or plug a 14-pin IC into the 14-pin socket and nothing into the 16-pin socket to test it. This configuration makes it possible to input or output data from the 16-bit X index register so that the rightmost bit corresponds to pin 1, the next to pin 2, and so on, to reduce the chances of programming errors, but also makes it impossible to try to connect an output register to power or ground, which may destroy the output circuitry.

We now consider the connections between the M6821 and the M6811. (See figure 4-17a.) It hardly has to be said, but Vss (pin 1) on the M6821 is grounded (remember: ground the SS), pin 20 is connected to +5 volts, and a .1-microfarad capacitor is connected between these two pins, as close as possible to the pins. We repeat this only because we've mysteriously lost a good number of M6821s in the lab and about the only way to burn out the chip is to apply power and ground backwards. As noted above, R/W (pin 21) is connected to R/W on the M6811, E (pin 25) is connected to the 6811 E pin (34), and RESET (pin 34) to the RESET line. The data bus is connected: D0 to D7 (pins 33 to 26) are connected to the data bus. To configure the chip so the data registers can appear in locations $8000 and $8001, we need to connect RS0 (pin 36) to address bit 1 and RS1 (pin 35) to address bit 0. The decoder should recognize any address between $8000 and $8003. This means that gates need be connected so that CS0, CS1, and CS2 are HH and L, respectively, only when the address bus has the following pattern: HLLLLLLLLLLLLLXX (where XX is a "don't care"). We can put address bits 15 and 14 into CS1 and CS2 and design some gates that output an H when bits 13 to 2 are all low to feed CS0, which would be a 12-input positive logic NOR gate. Though there are a large number of good ways to build such a gate from simpler gates, we leave the rest of the design as an exercise.

We now turn to the programming aspect of the design. The general scheme will be as follows. A pattern of T and F values will be put into the direction registers, an F if the corresponding pin is an output from the test IC (and an input to the M6821) and a T if the corresponding pin is an input (output from the M6821). Then a pattern will be put in the data register to set up the inputs to the IC under test wherever inputs are needed. The bits corresponding to the output pins are "don't cares." Then the data will be read from the I/O devices, and the bits corresponding to the test chip's output pins will be examined. They will be compared against the bits that should be there, and these bits will come from the program. The bits corresponding to the input pins on the test chip are "don't cares" here. To reduce the storage requirements, the test IC input bits and the bits compared to the output bits can be stored in the same 16-bit word. Two 16-bit patterns are needed, for the direction register and the combined test chip input pattern/required output pattern. If pin i+1 is an input pin on the test IC, bit i in the direction pattern is T, and bit i in the combined pattern is the value to be put on the test IC's input pin; otherwise, if the pin is an output from the test IC, bit i in the direction pattern is F, and bit i in the combined pattern is the value that should be on the pin if the chip is good. A direction pattern will be set up once, just before the chip is inserted and a sequence of combined patterns will be tested, one at a time, to check out the chip. Ideally, these sequences should be read from a table by a table-driven interpreter. For simplicity in this example, however, we will show a programmed sequence, using immediate operands.

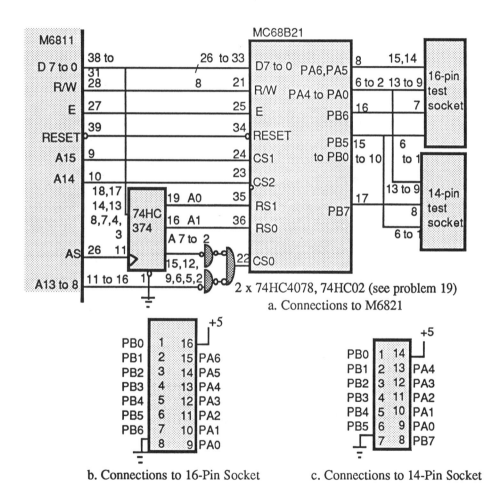

a. Connections to M6821

b. Connections to 16-Pin Socket

c. Connections to 14-Pin Socket

Figure 4-17. A Logic Diagram for a Chip Tester

Tests for different chips will of course, require different programs. A sample program is now discussed, to test the 74HC00 chip. Other combinational logic chips can be tested in an almost identical manner. Chips with memory variables require initialization of these variables and more care in testing. Also, a thorough test of any chip can require a lot of patterns. If a combinational chip has n inputs, then 2^n patterns must be tested. However, a simple test can be used to detect almost all the bad chips. For example, a quad 2 input NAND gate like the 74HC00 contains four independent gates, which can be tested simultaneously. Table 4-3 is the truth table for one of the four gates in the 74HC00. The program for this test is shown below the table and is explained intest following it.

Table 4-3. Truth Table for the 74HC00

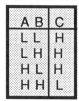

A	B	C
L	L	H
L	H	H
H	L	H
H	H	L

```
           NAM    TST00
           CLRA            CLEAR ACCUMULATOR D
           CLRB            IN ORDER TO CLR THE CONTROL REGISTER
           STD    $8002    IN ORDER TO ACCESS THE DIRECTION
           LDD    #%1111101101011011     REG TO MAKE PINS 3,6,8,11
           STD    $8000    OUTPUTS, PUT IN DIRECTION REGISTER
           LDD    #$0404   CHANGE CONTROL TO ACCESS DATA
           STD    $8002
           LDD    #%0000010010100100     TRY PAT. FOR FIRST ROW
           STD    $8000    OF TRUTH TABLE. PUT TO INPUT PINS
           CPD    $8000    CHECK RETURNED BITS, SHOULD BE 1
           BNE    ERROR IF NOT, BAD CHIP
           LDD    #%0000110110101101     TRY PAT. FOR SECOND ROW
           STD    $8000    JUST AS IN THE PREVIOUS ROW
           CPD    $8000    CHECK RETURNED BITS, SHOULD BE 1
           BNE    ERROR IF NOT, BAD CHIP
           LDD    #%0001011010110110     TRY PAT. FOR THIRD ROW
           STD    $8000    AS WE DID FOR OTHER PATTERNS
           CPD    $8000    CHECK RETURNED BITS, SHOULD BE 1
           BNE    ERROR IF NOT, CHIP IS BAD
           LDD    #%0001101100011011 TRY LAST ROW OF TRUTH
           STD    $8000    TABLE. THIS TIME, OUTPUT SHOULD
           CPD    $8000    BE A 0 FOR EACH GATE.
           BEQ    OK       IF SO, CHIP IS GOOD.
    ERROR ...              REPORT THE CHIP IS BAD
    OK    ...              REPORT THE CHIP IS GOOD
           END
```

We will supply the two inputs, A and B, and check to see if the output is correct. This can be done for each gate simultaneously. The inputs A and B for one gate are on pins 1 and 2, and the output C is on pin 3. These correspond to the rightmost bit positions, bits 0, 1, and 2, respectively, as they are output from the M6821. At the same time, the same pattern is applied to inputs A and B on pins 4 and 5, and the output on pin 6 is checked and applied to inputs on pins 10 and 9, the output is checked on pin 8 and applied to pins 13 and 12, and the output is checked on pin 11. All gates are checked for the correct behavior for the first row of the truth table at one time. The next three rows are checked in like manner. But such a test will not detect a possible short from one of the gates to another inside the chip. Nevertheless, the simpler test will be quite useful for our application.

The chip has outputs on pins 3, 6, 8 and 11, and the other pins are inputs. So XXXTTFTTFXFTTFTT should be put into the direction register. The "don't cares" (X) can be made outputs to simplify the comparison step. This is stored in the direction register in lines 4 and 5 in the program. Lines 8 to 11 test the first truth table entry for each gate simultaneously, where all the inputs are low (and the program variables are false). If the expected pattern is not read back, the program branches to ERROR to report the chip is defective. In like manner, the other three truth table entries are checked in the following rows. If all patterns are read and verified, the program branches to OK to report that the chip tested good.

4-7 Conclusions

The parallel I/O device is the most flexible and common I/O device. When designing a parallel I/O device, the first step is to decide on the architecture of the device. Select the address and I/O capability. The hardware can be implemented using simple TTL MSI chips or an LSI chip like the M6821. This chapter showed how to use the popular 74HC244 and 74HC374 medium-scale integrated circuits to implement these devices. This approach is really very simple and is often desired because it uses less board space and cheaper ICs than the other approach discussed, that of using a large scale parallel I/O chip like the M8621. The M6821 was introduced and shown to be more flexible. This chip is often used in printed circuit card microcomputers that are mass-produced and intended for a wide variety of applications. It can be configured by the appropriate ritual for almost any parallel I/O device. It can also be used to implement two I/O devices on one (large) chip rather than on (two) smaller chips. This can be attractive if the devices are readable outputs, because it takes more (small) chips to build both the input and output parts of the device. If the device is changed from input to output under software control, the programmable parallel output chip, or ports C or D on the 6811, are better. We saw how easy it is to use the 6811 ports. An indirect I/O technique was presented, which is especially useful for experimenting with most LSI I/O chips. A slight variation of this idea using serial I/O was shown to be quite attractive because there is special hardware designed to be used this way. Finally, we saw some details on how to connect the M6821 to the MC68HC11A8 in hardware. This example showed the use of and need for top-down design.

We can use the same approach to designing an IC or an I/O system as we can for studying it, and thus develop an understanding of why it was designed as it was and how it might be used.

We saw some I/O software that moved data through a microcomputer, moved data into a buffer, and implemented a traffic light controller using the simple I/O devices. Because timing is important to these programs, we studied the timing of such program segments.

The interfacing of a microcomputer to almost any I/O system has been shown to be simple and flexible, using parallel I/O devices. In the remaining chapters, these techniques are extended to analog interfacing, counters, communications interfacing and display and magnetic recording chips.

For more concrete information on the 68HC11, please consult the *MC68HC11A8 HCMOS Single-Chip Microcomputer (ADI 1207)*. In particular, section 4 describes parallel I/O and section 6 presents the serial interface. As noted earlier, we have not attempted to duplicate the diagrams and discussions in that book because we assume you will refer to it while reading this book; we also present an alternative view of the subject, so you can use either or both views.

Problems

Problems 1 and 14 are paragraph correction problems. See the problems at the end of chapter 1 for guidelines. Guidelines for software problems are given in the problems for chapter 2 and for hardware problems, in chapter 3.

1*. Memory-mapped I/O is used on the M6811 and is popular on microcomputers that have isolated I/O, because it can use instructions that operate directly on memory and is more reliable in the face of a runaway stack than is isolated I/O. However, if a program error writes over I/O devices, a lock can be used to prevent the calamity. A basic input device is a tristate driver and a decoder; the decoder needs only to look at the address and the R/W line to see if the device is to be read. A basic output device may use a latch or a register, and a decoder. The decoder must check the address and the R/W signal, and that is all it must check to be sure the device is to be written in. A basic output device is a write-only register that cannot be read by the program. Therefore, the program should keep an extra copy of a word in such an output device if it wants to know what is in it. The data can be recorded automatically in memory by using an address trigger. Such output devices are commonly used because they are cheaper than readable output devices. The selection of read-write capabilities is the architectural issue that must be settled early in the design so the hardware and software design can proceed.

2. A group of eight 1-bit input devices is to be addressed at locations $2C30 to $2C37 so they will be read in the sign bit position. Show the logic diagram of such a device, whose decoder is fully specified and whose input is a 74HC251 1-of-8 multiplexor with tristate output.

3. A group of eight 1-bit output devices is to be addressed at locations $73A8 to $73AF so they will write the sign bit of these words. Show the logic diagram of such a device, whose decoder is fully specified and whose output latches are in the 74HC259 addressable latch. (Note: this group of output devices can have the same address as a read-write memory using a shadow, so that when words are written in the memory, the sign bits appear in the outputs of the corresponding latch to be used in the outside world.)

4. An output system having 16 output bits is addressed at location $D3A3. If a number $2n + 1$ is written into this location, the nth 1-bit latch is set, $0 \leq n < 16$ and if a number $2n$ is written into this location, the nth 1-bit latch is cleared. Show a logic diagram of such a system of output latches, whose address decoder is fully specified and whose latches are in two 74HC259 addressable latches. (Note: this type of output is well suited to controlling solenoids and lights, since it is as easy to generate an immediate operand like $2n + 1$ as it is to set an ordinary output register and there is less chance that another output will be accidentally changed when one is changed.)

5. Show the logic diagram of a partially readable output register, which is addressed at location $8023. The 7 least significant bits of the output are readable, but the most significant bit read comes from the outside world. The address decoder is to be

completely specified and should include the 74HC139 dual 1-of-4 decoder. Use a 74HC244 for the input device and a 74HC374 for the output device. Show all chips and pin numbers.

6. The address trigger in figure 4-3 has a timing problem because the OR gate delays the clock on the 74HC107 until after the data on the J and K inputs become low. Consider using an additional OR gate in the same package as the OR gate used to generate the clock (delays of gates in the same package track each other quite well) or using an RC circuit to delay J and K. Draw a circuit a. using the OR gate approach and b. using the RC time constant approach, and determine the value of a series resistor, assuming the JK flip-flop has very large input resistance and a capacitance of 10 pF.

7. Write all possible input buffer programs like INBUF (Section 4-2.1) which are the fastest in execution, and give the rate at which words can be input to the buffer for this set of programs, assuming a 2 MHz E clock. Consider using different addressing modes.

8. A pair of input devices, at locations $6F39 and $6F3A, can be read by the LDD $6F39 instruction. They are connected to a 16-bit serial in parallel out shift register to input into a buffer 1-bit serial data shifted into the shift register.
    a. Show the logic diagram for this pair of devices using 74HC374s and a pair of 8-bit serial in parallel out shift registers that use 74HC164s, using fully specified decoding for the address decoder.
    b. Write a (fastest) program for a 2-MHz MC68HC11A8 to store this data into a buffer, using LDD and STD instructions. How many bits/second can it collect?
    c. Suppose your program starts at location $1AB2, give a picture similar to table 4-1 that would appear on a logic analyzer, showing the R/W bit, and the address and data bus values in hexadecimal, for every memory cycle in one execution of the DO-loop, assuming that $3D is input from device $6F39, and $2C is input from device $6F3A.

9. Suppose a 1-bit input device using a 74HC125 inputs a signal A in the sign bit of location $8000. Measure the time from when A is low until it is high.
    a. Show a logic diagram of the input device using incompletely specified decoding, assuming that the program uses only addresses 0 to $1000, $8000 (for this device), and $F000 to $FFFF.
    b. Write a program to measure this pulse width as accurately as you can, putting the width (binary number in microseconds) in accumulator D, assuming the E clock is 1 MHz and the pulse width is shorter than 65 milliseconds.

10. Design a traffic light controller that uses the power line frequency to time the lights and immediate operands to control the lights. Use an expanded bus MC68HC11A8 DIP implementation.
    a. Show a logic diagram of the I/O system. The input device, at location $4000, inputs a 60-Hertz square wave signal in the sign position of the word, using a 74HC125, and the output device, at location $4000, using a 74HC374, outputs a 6-bit light pattern to control the lights, as in figure 4-4. Use incompletely

specified decoding, assuming the program will use only the addresses 0 to $80, $4000 (for these devices), and $FF00 to $FFFF.

b. Show a program segment that tests the input so as to wait exactly one-half second.

c. Write a program, using immediate operands to control the light patterns and using the program segment in b to time the lights, to sequence the lights as in table 4-2.

11. Write a linked-list interpreter to control the traffic light in figure 4-4 and linked lists to output.

a. The sequence in table 4-2.

b. A late night sequence in which the north-south lanes see a blinking red light, and the other lanes see a blinking yellow light which blinks on for 1 second and off for 1 second.

c. A fire truck emergency sequence in which the north-south lanes see red while the others see green for 20 seconds, then the east-west see yellow for 2 seconds while north-south is still red, then the north-south see green and the others see red for 10 seconds, and then the sequence in table 4-2 is begun with its first line.

12. Consider a vending machine controller. Its input register at location $8000 has value 0 if no coins are put into the machine, 1 if a nickel, 2 if a dime, 3 if a quarter, and 4 if the coin return button is pressed. The output register, at location $8000, will dispense a bottle of pop if the number 1 is output, a nickel if 2 is output, a dime if 3 is output, and a quarter if 4 is output. This vending machine will dispense a bottle of pop if 30 cents have been entered, will return the amount entered if the coin return button is pressed, and otherwise will keep track of the remaining amount of money entered (i.e. it will not return change if >30 cents are put in).

a. Show the logical design of the I/O hardware, assuming incompletely specified decoding if the program uses only addresses 0 to $80, $8000 (for these devices), and $FF00 to $FFFF. Use 74HC195 and 74HC374 chips.

b. Show a graphical sequential machine description of this controller. Internal states S = {0,5,10,15,20,25} will represent the fact that the total accumulated money is 0, 5, 10, 15, 20, and 25 cents. Input states I = {B,N,D,Q,R} will represent that no (blank) inputs are given; that a nickel, a dime, a quarter are given; or that the coin return button has been pressed. Output states O = {b,p,n,d,q} will represent the fact that nothing (blank) is done, or a bottle of pop, a nickel, a dime, or a quarter respectively, is to be returned. Assume the coin return button is pressed repeatedly to return all the coins as the sequential machine steps through its internal states.

c. Show a program to implement this sequential machine by a linked-list interpreter, and show the linked list. Assume the outputs have to be asserted for 0.1 seconds to activate the solenoids, and then the blank (0) output must be written to release the solenoids that dispense the bottles and the money. Assume that you have to guard against responding to an input and then checking it again before it has been removed. (Hint: respond to an input only when it changes from that input back to the blank input.)

13. Show a linked list and a linked-list interpreter that decodes the Huffmann code, using the coding tree given in figure 2-1. This linked list can be interpreted first as a sequential machine. Note that the 0s and 1s of the Huffmann code input are input states, the nodes, except the root node of the tree, are internal states, and the characters M, I, S, and P and the null output N are output states. The sequence of outputs, after the Ns are removed, should be the decoded outputs. The input string is assumed to be infinite, so the program does not stop.

     a. Show the sequential machine graphical representation and table representation.

     b. Assume the input Huffmann-coded string is stored in a buffer after location IN, most significant bit first, and the output characters, without the N (null) outputs, are stored in a buffer after location OUT. Show the linked list and the interpreter for the 6811.

14.* The key problems that lead to the ritual for LSI I/O chips are the need to compress the size of the I/O system, using LSI, the need to produce as many copies of an LSI chip to spread the high design cost, and the need to keep the size of the chip below the size that is economically feasible. The ritual sets up control registers that fashion the LSI I/O device into a particular device you might have built from MSI chips. Selecting the bits to store in the control register is analogous to picking the MSI chips from a catalog for a hardware design. Nevertheless, this creates serious problems for the programmer because it takes a long time to execute this ritual, and the registers hidden by a hat trick are difficult to watch if a programming error changes them.

15. A scanning monitor scans (eight) input lines and jumps to a routine if a line is true (low). Design a scanning monitor that uses a device of an M6821 as a partially readable output register. When you write into location $8000, the low-order 3 bits are output to address a 74HC251 selector to examine one of eight inputs. When you read from location $8000, the low-order 3 bits are the address you sent to the selector, and the most significant bit is the output of the selector.

     a. Show a logic diagram of a partially readable output device, using an M6821 so the A device appears at locations $8000 and $8001, and using incompletely specified decoding, assuming the program uses only the addresses 0 to $3FFF, $8000 and $8001 (for this device), $8002 and $8003 for some other device not in the I/C as the M6821 used for the scanning monitor, and $C000 to $FFFF. Show connections from the PA lines to the selector and all pins tied high or low.

     b. Write a program ritual to initialize this device so the low-order 7 bits are outputs and the most significant bit is an input.

     c. Write a program that continually scans the inputs and jumps to location Li when the ith input is high. Use index addressing loading X from the jump table

     TBL   FDB   L0-TBL,L1-TBL,L2-TBL,L3-TBL,...,L7-TBL

Note: The INC instruction can simultaneously change the input and sense the bit that was input; however, be careful to observe that the device is read before it is written by an INC $8000 instruction. (This routine is used to scan keyboards and is further discussed in chapter 6.)

16. Write a program similar to that in section 4-4 to read the time of day from the 6818A into variables YR to SE. (Disregard a possible timing problem, in which you may be reading the time when it is changing.)

17. Write program segments for software control of serial I/O devices using 6811 port D:

a. For figure 4-12a, by direct analogy to the program in section 4-5.2. Put the 24 bits read into IN (left '589), IN+1 (middle '589) and IN+2 (right '589), D[1] in LSB.

b. For figure 4-12b. Assume accumulator A has the desired device number to be read, device 0 on the left, 1 in the middle, 2 on the right. The returned data should be in accumulator A.

c. For figure 4-12d. Assume accumulator A has the desired device number to be written into, as addressed in problem b, and accumulator B has the data to be written.

For all serial transfers, assume the least significant bit is sent/received first.

18. Write program segments for SPI control of serial I/O devices:

a. For figure 4-12b. Assume accumulator A has the desired device number to be read.

b. For figure 4-12c, by direct analogy to the program segment in section 4-5.3.

c. For figure 4-12d. Assume accumulator A has the desired device number to be written into, as addressed in problem 17b, and accumulator B has the data to be written.

19. Show the logic diagram for a decoder for the MC68B21 pin CS0 in figure 4-17. Show all pins.

20. Write a program, similar to TST00 in section 4-6, to test a 74HC04 hex inverter in the tester in figure 4-17.

21. Write a program, similar to TST00 in section 4-6, to test a 74HC74 dual flip-flop in the tester in figure 4-17.

22. Write a table interpreter to test 14- or 16-pin integrated circuits, using the tester in figure 4-17. The first row will define the inputs and outputs of the device and the remaining rows will define a sequence of tests on the device. The table will have a 16-bit row, bit 0 outputting or testing pin 1, and bit i, pin i+1, and bit 15 will be 0, except for the last row of the table, where it is 1.

a. Write a table in assembler language for a test on the 74HC00.

b. Write a table in assembler language for a test on the 74HC74.

23. Design a hardware breakpoint device. This device monitors the M6811's address bus to compare the address against a breakpoint address. The breakpoint address is written in output registers at locations $8000 and $8001, which are the A and B devices of an

M6821. Use full address decoding. The address (when it is determinate) is compared with these 2 words by open collector exclusive NOR gates (74HC266s) whose outputs are connected in a wire-AND bus. If they are equal, the outputs of the gates will be high, otherwise the outputs will be low. (The output can be used to generate an interrupt, discussed in the next chapter, that stops the program when the address matching the number in the output registers is generated.

a. Show a complete logic diagram of the M6811 and M6821 and a decoder that will implement this system, but do not show the memory which will be attached to the M6811. Show all connections, and show actual 74HC gates and pins for your design.

b. Show a routine to set up the device so the output will be asserted high when the address $4F27 is present and determinate on the address bus.

24. Two microcomputers will send words to each other through a "window." The "window" appears as a programmable, parallel I/O device at location $8000 in the first microprocessor, and at location $4000 in the second. To send a word, the first writes the word in location $8000 so the second can read that word at $4000; or the second writes a word in location $4000 so the first can read it at location $8000. This window is realized with a pair of M6821s, one in each microcomputer, whose PA ports are tied together. The device must be configured as an input device when not in use.

a. Write a program segment to output a word from the first microcomputer.

b. Assuming the first microcomputer has output a word, write a program segment to input that word into accumulator A of the second microcomputer.

25. Two MC68HC11A8 microcomputers will send words to each other through a "window." The "window" appears as a 6821 A device at location $8000 in the first, operating in expanded multiplexed bus mode, and as a port C at location $1005 in the second microprocessor, operating in single-chip mode. To send a word, the first writes the word in location $8000 so the second can read that word at $1005; or the second writes a word in location $1005 so the first can read it at location $8000. The device must be configured as an input device when not in use.

a. Write a program segment to output a word from the first microcomputer.

b. Assuming the first microcomputer has output a word, write a program segment to input that word into accumulator A of the second microcomputer.

26. One MC68HC11A8, operating in single-chip mode (computer A), is to check out a second MC68HC11A8, operating in expanded multiplexed bus mode (computer B). Computer B has a (2048,8) 6116 memory (see figure 3-6) from $4000 to $47FF and a 6821 at location $8000 to $8003. Computer A's port C is connected to the data bus of computer B, and A's port B is the high byte of the address, bits 7 to 3 of port A are address bits 7 to 3, and bits 4 to 0 of port D are address bits 2 to 0, R/W, and E of computer B. The MC68HC11A8 and 74HC373 in computer B are removed from their sockets so they will not interfere, and computer A is used to check out the memory and I/O in computer B.

a. Show a single-logic diagram of the two computers combined. Show all pin connections.

b. Show a program segment for computer A that will write a word $3C into location $4328 in computer B.

c. Show a program segment for computer A that will read the word at location $4328 in computer B into ACCA of computer A.

d. Write a program for computer A that will fill the 6116 memory in computer B with $3C, then read back the data stored there, comparing it to $3C. Go to ERROR if it is not found.

e. Assume the 6821's port A is connected directly to its port B in computer B. Write a program for computer A that will initialize the 6821, and put $3C into port A in computer B and read back the data in port B there, comparing it to $3C. Go to ERROR if it is not found.

5

Interrupts and Alternatives

The computer has to be synchronized with the fast or slow I/O device. The two main areas of concern are the amount of data that will be input or output and the type of error conditions that will arise in the I/O system. Given varying amounts of data and different I/O error conditions, we need to decide the appropriate action to be taken by the microcomputer program. This is studied in this chapter.

One of the most important problems in the design of I/O systems is timing. In section 4-2.1, we saw how data can be put into a buffer from an input device. However, we ignored the problem of synchronizing with the source of the data, so we get a word from the source when it has a word to give us. I/O systems are often quite a bit slower, and are occasionally a bit faster, than the computer. A typewriter may type a fast 30 characters per second, but the computer can send a character to be typed only once every 33,333 memory cycles. So the computer often waits a long time between outputting successive characters to be typed. Behold the mighty computer, able to invert a matrix in a single bound, waiting patiently to complete some tedious I/O operation. On the other hand, some I/O systems, such as disks, are so fast that a microcomputer may not take data from them fast enough. Recall that the time from when an I/O system requests service (such as to output a word) until it gets this service (such as having the word removed) is the latency. If the service is not completed within a maximum latency time, the data may be over-written by new data and thus will be lost before the computer can store it.

Synchronization is the technique used to get the computer to supply data to an output device when the device needs data, or get data from an input device when the device has some data available, or to respond to an error if ever it occurs. Eight techniques are used to match the slow I/O device to the fast microprocessor. Real-time synchronization is conceptually quite simple; in fact we have already written a real-time program in the previous chapter to synchronize to a traffic light. Gadfly synchronization requires a bit more hardware, but has advantages in speed and software simplicity. Two kinds of interrupt synchronization, polled and vectored, are faster and require more hardware. Direct memory access and context switching are faster synchronization mechanisms. Isolated buffer and time-multiplexed memories can be used for very fast I/O devices. These synchronization techniques are discussed in this chapter.

The first section presents some I/O synchronization principles from the viewpoint of the I/O device, for the M6821 and the parallel ports in the M6811. The next section shows, from the microprocessor viewpoint, how to approach synchronization with slower I/O devices, including interrupts used for synchronization in a microcomputer like the MC68HC11A8. Section 5-3 discusses approaches to synchronization with faster I/O devices that require more processors and are more powerful than interrupts, including direct memory access (DMA) using the M6809. The M6844 DMA chip will be introduced to make the concepts more concrete, but we emphasize again that these concepts can be extended to DMA chips made by other manufacturers. The last section considers special interrupt and reset features of the 6811.

This chapter should provide a fundamental understanding of I/O synchronization in general and interrupt handling in particular. By the end of the chapter, the reader should be able to use the parallel I/O ports in the MC68HC11A8 and connect a parallel I/O chip like the M6821, recognize interrupts, write programs to handle interrupts, and, using them, input or output a buffer of data or report or correct an error.

5-1 Synchronization in I/O Devices

We first study the synchronization problem from the I/O device viewpoint. The first subsection introduces some general principles, including the busy/done states, and defines the terminology for the different approaches to synchronizing I/O devices with microcomputers. An example, a paper tape reader system, is introduced and will be used in later sections to illustrate the different approaches. The second subsection introduces the interrupt mechanics of the M6821 integrated circuit. Again, the object of using this chip is to make the discussion more concrete, but the techniques can be used on other processors made by Motorola or other manufacturers. Finally, the synchronization mechanisms used on the M6811 parallel ports are discussed.

5-1.1 Synchronization Principles of I/O Devices

An example of a paper tape reader and punch will be used to illustrate the different approaches to I/O synchronization. Paper tape is used in environments like machine shops, which would be hostile to floppy disks due to dust and fumes. The example will illustrate both the collection of data from a tape in a buffer, with the recognition of and response to error conditions, and the output of data to punch such a tape. An M6821 will be used for reading the tape so data input from the paper tape is read from location $8000, and the associated control register is located at location $8001. Another control register at location $8003 will be used to signal an error condition. A parallel port on the MC68HC11A8 will be used to punch the tape. We need to use more of the control registers in the M6821 and M6811 parallel ports than we used in the previous chapter, and we will consider that in the next subsections when we show concrete examples of interrupt techniques using the M6811.

Data from the data register can be read just as in the previous chapter and will be put into a buffer, as we now discuss. (See Figure 5-1.) The pattern of holes across a one-inch-wide paper tape corresponds to a word of data; in each position, a hole is a true value, and the absence of a hole is a false value. At any time, the values of such a pattern of holes under the paper tape head can be read by an instruction like LDAA $8000. The computer can advance the paper when the next pattern is to be read. Recall from Section 4-2.1 that a buffer is an area of memory reserved for input data. A paper tape reader will have a buffer in which words read from the tape can be written. The first pattern is read, then put into the first word of the buffer, the second pattern is read and put into the second word of the buffer, and so on, until all the patterns have been read and put in the buffer, as we did in the program called INBUF. When this happens, the buffer is said to be *full*, and some program that uses the data in the buffer may be started.

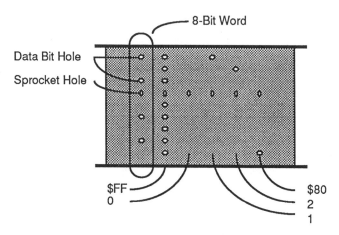

Figure 5-1. Paper Tape

The paper tape reader may have an error condition, such as when the paper tape is to be read (before the buffer is full) but no paper tape is under the reader. Responses to this error condition may be to correct the error, whereby the microcomputer would reload some paper tape into the reader and continue reading it, or just to report the error to someone who is attending the paper tape reader. The error could be reported by typing out a message on a "console typewriter," if one is available, or by turning on a light or sounding an alarm of some kind. In general, whenever one takes data from an input device or puts data into an output device, error conditions can occur, and the hardware and software that interface the microcomputer to the device must be able to correct the error or at least report it so an attendant can correct it.

A paper tape punch will place holes in the paper, representing the data in a buffer, in a manner converse to how the paper tape reader reads them. The paper tape punch could also have an error condition. However, we are focusing on alternative designs, so we will now ignore error checking in this device. A queue, rather than a buffer, can be used to supply the data to be punched. Subsection 5-2.5 will show how a queue can be used for the storage of input or output data.

The various approaches one can use to synchronize a computer with an I/O device so one can take data from it or send data to it use a simple but general model (a Mealy sequential machine) of the device. (See figure 5-2.) In this model, the device has three states: the *idle, busy,* and *done states.* The device is in the idle state when no program is using it. When a program begins to use the device, the program puts it in the busy state. If the device is in the idle state, it is free to be used, and, if in the busy state, it is still busy doing its operation. When the device is through with its operation, it enters the done state. Often, the done state implies the device has some data in an output register that must be read by the program. When the program reads the data, it puts the device into the idle state if it doesn't want to do any more operations, or into the busy state if it wants more operations done. An error condition may also put the device into the done state and should provide some way for the program to distinguish between a successfully completed operation and an error condition. Note that the program puts the device into the busy state or the idle state; this is called, respectively, *starting* or *stopping* the device. The device enters the done state by itself. This is called *completing* the requested action. When the device is in the done state, the program can get the results of an operation and/or check to see if an error has occurred.

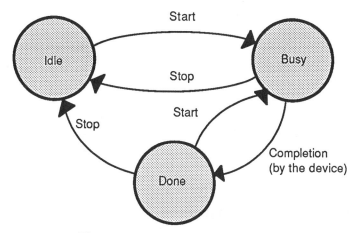

Figure 5-2. State Diagram for I/O Devices

We continue our running example to illustrate the meaning of these states. The idle state indicates the paper tape reader is not in use. The program starts the paper tape reader by putting it into the busy state. In that state, a motor pulls the paper tape until the next pattern is under the read head that reads a word from the tape. When the final pattern is under the tape reader or no paper is left, the reader enters the done state. The computer recognizes that when the reader is in the done state, data from the pattern should be read through the data register at location $8000 and put into the buffer in the next available location, or that an error condition might exist. Once read, if the program intends to read the next pattern because more words are needed to fill the buffer, it puts the reader back into the busy state to restart it. If it doesn't want to read another pattern because the buffer is full, it puts the device into the idle state to stop it. If an error condition is signaled, the device is left in the done state so it won't be used until the error is read and possibly fixed or reported. Note that there is a difference between the idle state and the done state. In the done state, some data in the input register are ready to be read, and the I/O device is requesting the computer to read it, or an error has rendered the device unusable; while in the idle state, nothing is happening, and nothing need be done.

In some I/O systems which do not return values back to the computer, however, the done state is indistinguishable from the idle state, so only two states are required. Consider the punch. The idle state corresponds to when the punch is not in use. The busy state corresponds to when the device has been given a byte to punch but has not yet completed that operation. The done state corresponds to when the holes have been punched, and another byte of data can be sent to the punch. In this case, with no error conditions to examine in the done state, the done and idle states are indistinguishable, and we can consider that the device has just two states: idle and busy.

An address trigger, introduced in section 4-1.2, can be used to start or stop a device. Suppose that two flip-flops code the state of the device so they are FF if the device is IDLE, FT if it is BUSY, and TF if it is DONE. Then to start the device, the first flip-flop must be cleared, and the second must be set. An address trigger can be connected to the clear input of the first flip-flop and to the set input of the second. Any instruction that generates the address can start the device by generating the trigger signal.

5-1.2 The M6821 Interrupt Mechanism

The interrupt mechanism in the M6821 can be used to illustrate various synchronization principles, so we introduce a little more of it here. Recall that control bit 2 is used to determine whether the direction register or the data register can be accessed, if that bit is, respectively, F or T. We now explore the use of the other control bits.

Each of the two devices in the M6821 has a primary interrupt mechanism and another mechanism that can be configured as a secondary interrupt mechanism or an output bit. The control register of either the A or B device governs a primary interrupt request mechanism, as shown in figure 5-3a. The control register is partially readable. Bit 7 of the control register is the read-only output of the D edge-triggered flip-flop IRQA1. Upon reading the control register, the sign bit will be this value. When it is set, we say *IRQA1 recognizes an interrupt.* A pin, CA1, and a control register bit, 1, determine when IRQA1 is set. If bit 1 is false, IRQA1 is set on a high to low transition of the signal on the CA1 pin; if true, IRQA1 is set on a low to high transition of the CA1 pin's signal. Because the IRQA1 bit is read-only, writing in the control register does not change it. However, because an interrupt usually requires reading the data from the data register, IRQA1 is cleared to false when the data register in that device is read. That is, an address trigger is used, so reading the data register also clears the IRQA1 flip-flop. One of the common errors in using the M6821 is to try to clear the IRQA1 flip-flop by writing 0 into the control register. It must be cleared by reading the data register. (Similarly, reading the direction register will not clear IRQA1, so you have to set control bit 2 before you can read the data register to clear IRQA1.) Control register bit 0 is ANDed with IRQA1, the output going in negative logic to the IRQA pin. This output can be sent through a negative logic wire-OR bus to the M6811 microprocessor IRQ pin (or other pins discussed in section 5-3). Alternatively, the IRQA pin can be left disconnected or can even be connected to a light or an alarm if that is useful.

The primary interrupt mechanism is always available for use. A second part of the control logic can be used to implement a secondary interrupt mechanism, or one of three different 1-bit output mechanisms, depending on the values of control bits 5 to 3. (See figures 5-3b to 5-3e.)

If the other part is to be used as a second interrupt, then the user makes control bit 5 false. Then control bits 6, 4, and 3 function for this part exactly as control bits 7, 1, and 0 function for the device interrupt we discussed earlier. (See figure 5-3b.) That is, the IRQA2 flip-flop can always be read as bit 6. It is set if bit 4 is false and the CA2 input has a high to low transition, or if bit 4 is true and CA2 has a low to high transition, and is cleared when the data register is read. Writing in the control register does not change the read-only bit, bit 6, just as it doesn't change bit 7. The value of IRQA2 is ANDed with control bit 3, and ORed into the wire-OR bus through the same IRQA pin used by the IRQA1 flip-flop.

The logic connected to CA2 can use CA2 as an output if control bit 5 is T. Three modes are available. If control bit 4 is also a T, then control bit 3 is output in positive logic on the CA2 pin to give an extra output bit. This mode is simply called the *extra one bit output* mode. (See figure 5-3c.) For example, if control bits 0 and 1 are supposed to be false, and we want to access the data register, then storing $34 in the control register will output a low signal on the CA2 pin, and storing $3C in the control register will output a high on that pin. This extra output bit can be changed by the program, so, for instance, it can control a motor in the I/O system.

If control bits 5 to 3 are T F F, CA2 is essentially the contents of the IRQA1 flip-flop. This mode is called *handshaking* because this is the same principle, called by the same name, as is used in asynchronous communication, which is discussed in chapter 8. The external logic sets IRQA1 via CA1 and can read the value of this flip-flop to control a motor via CA2. For instance, the motor can advance the paper tape in our example, as long as this output is low. When the next pattern is aligned, a signal through the CA1 pin simultaneously requests IRQA1 to recognize an interrupt, and turns the motor off. When the data register is read, IRQA1 is cleared and the motor is started to get the next pattern. If control bits 5 to 3 are T F T, CA2 is normally high and drops for just one memory cycle when the data register is read. This mode is called *pulse* for obvious reasons. (See figure 5-3e.) This is an example showing the address trigger available as an output to control an external part of the I/O system. This can be used to trigger an external one-shot to make a motor move one pattern ahead on the tape. The two devices in an M6821 are almost identical. There are control pins for each; CA1 and CA2, which are the control pins for the A device, correspond to control pins CB1 and CB2 for the B device. Separate interrupt signal outputs IRQA and IRQB are used for each device so they can be wired to different busses discussed later, or one can be connected while the other is not. The logic associated with CA1 and CB1 is identical. The logic associated with CA2 is as discussed above, but the logic associated with CB2 is just a bit different. The logic for the B device is designed to make it more useful for output, while the A device is designed to be more useful for input. CB2 is pulsed with a negative signal when control bits 5 to 3 are T F T, and the data register is written in, rather than read from, as is CA2. (That is, replace read address trigger LDAA $8000 with write address trigger STAA $8000 in figures 5-3d and 5-3e for the B device.) CB2 is not quite the value of the IRQB1 flip-flop in the B device; it becomes high when IRQB1 is set, but it becomes low when the data register is written in, while the IRQB1 register is cleared when the data register is read from. (In the A device, CA2 is the positive logic output of IRQA1.) With these minor differences, which are easy to forget, the two devices in an M6821 are very flexible and can be used for almost any parallel I/O requirement.

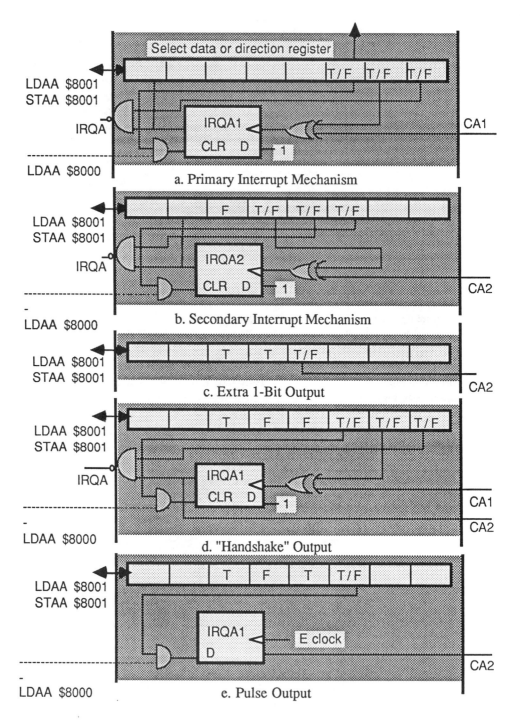

Figure 5-3. M6821 Device A Interrupt/Output Mechanisms

5-1.3 Synchronization Mechanisms for the M6811 Parallel Ports

Ports B and C in the M6811 are able to use synchronization mechanisms like the M6821 when the M6811 is in the single-chip mode, or the M6824 when the M6811 is in the expanded multiplexed bus mode. The STRA and STRB pins act rather like the CA1 and CA2 pins on the M6821, and the parallel I/O control register (PIOC) is like the M6821 control register. However, there is a strobed register (C) that can be used for additional synchronization mechanisms. Figure 5-4 shows the three modes that can be implemented with this hardware in the M6811.

Figure 5-4a shows the simple handshake mode, which is used when bit 4 of the PIOC (HNDS) is F. Both the B and C ports may use handshaking independently of each other. A write to port B causes a pulse to appear on the STRB pin, a write address trigger. This pulse can be used to inform the output circuitry that some new data have arrived. The least significant bit of the PIOC register determines the polarity of this pulse: if it is F, then STRB is normally high and is pulsed low when port B is written into, and if T, then STRB is normally low and pulsed high when the write occurs. The second least significant bit (EGA) governs the edge of the STRA pin that causes the most significant bit of the PIOC register (STAF) to be set and data to be transferred from the C port pins into the strobed C register. If EGA is T, the actions take place on the rising edge of STRA, if F, on the falling edge. The most significant bit of PIOC (STAF) can be tested to see if input has arrived, or if bit 6 of the PIOC is set, then an IRQ interrupt is requested, as we consider in the next section. STAF is cleared by a sequence of two address triggers: reading the control register PIOC, followed by reading the strobed register (C). The program can read the data register (C) to get the current value of the inputs, which does not affect STAF, or the strobed register (C) to get the values that occurred when the selected edge on the STRA pin occurred, and to clear the STAF bit. PIOC bit 5 determines the port C bus driver structure: if T, then port C outputs are open drain for wire-OR logic, like the PA outputs of the M6821; if F, then they are tristate outputs like the PB outputs of the 6821.

When bit 4 of the PIOC (HNDS) is T, then either input handshaking is used; if bit 3 of the PIOC (OIN) is F (figure 5-4b) or if T, output handshaking is used (figure 5-4c). In both cases, the 2 least significant bits and bits 5 to 7 of the PIOC register (INVB, EGA, CWOM, STAI, and STAF) have the same meaning as in the simple handshake mode, but port B is not involved in the handshake, and STRB is essentially the value of STAF. This corresponds to the "handshake" mode of the M6821, shown in figure 5-3d. PLS determines whether the value of STAF is sent to the SRTB pin, or a pulse is sent when STRB is set. In the input handshake mode, figure 5-4b, STAF is cleared by a read from the strobed register (C); in the output handshake mode, figure 5-4c, STAF is cleared by writing to the same address as the strobed C register, but the data are actually written into the data register (C). Also, in the latter mode, if STRA is low, the direction register (C) bits are ignored, and the direction is forced outward. This permits STRA to act on port C like an output enable on the 74HC373 if the direction register (C) is all Fs.

The M6811's versatile handshake modes can be used in most applications. These will be shown in examples in the following section.

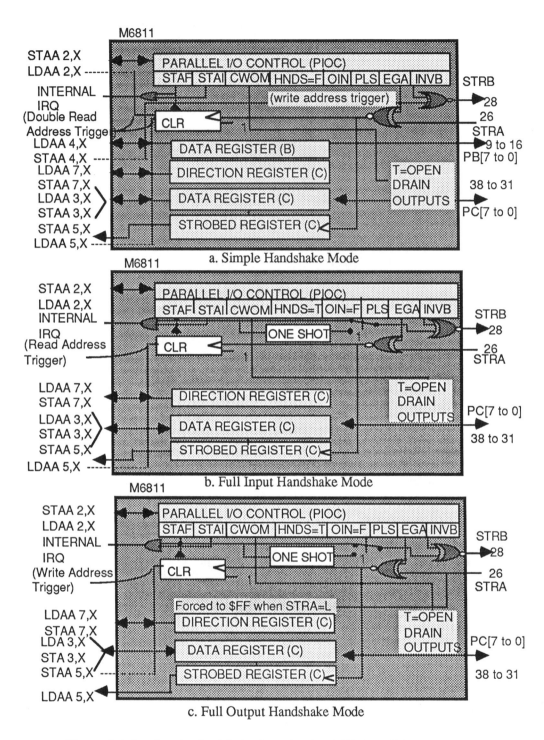

Figure 5-4. Synchronization Mechanisms for the M6811 Parallel Ports

5-2 Slow Synchronization Mechanisms

There are four ways a microcomputer can synchronize with a slower I/O device, as discussed in this section. Two ways, real-time and gadfly synchronization, are simple but less efficient than the other ways, single, and polled and vectored interrupts. Each is studied in a subsection, and the particular features of the MC68HC11A8 are discussed in the last subsection. Four alternatives, which require additional hardware for even faster synchronization, are introduced in the next section.

5-2.1 Real-Time Synchronization

Real-time synchronization uses the timing delays in the program to synchronize with the delays in the I/O system. While this is considered bad programming by almost all computer scientists, it is a practical alternative in some primitive microcomputers that are dedicated to one application, such as the traffic light controller discussed in 4-2.2 or a microcomputer that is dedicated to control a printer. The natural delay in executing useful programs can also be used to provide the required elapsed time. The traffic light controller in section 4-2.2 used delay loops to time out the light pattern that was displayed. The device has IDLE, BUSY, and DONE states, but the computer has no way of reading them in the real-time program technique. Instead, it starts operations and keeps track of the time in which it expects the device to complete the operation. Busy-done states can be recognized, however, by the program segment being executed in synchronization with the device state. The device is started, and the time it takes to complete its busy state is matched by the time a program takes before it assumes the device is in the done state. While an exact match in timing is occasionally needed, usually the microcomputer must wait longer than the I/O device takes to complete its busy state. In fact, the program is usually timed for the longest possible time to complete an I/O operation.

We consider a real-time program for our paper tape reader, as shown soon. Assume that $80 patterns read by the device are stored in consecutive words in a buffer, and the first word of the buffer is called BUFFER. Also, assume that power has just been turned on, and the RESET line has just cleared all the registers in the M6821 that input the pattern at location $8000. Assume that a motor pulls paper through the reader at a constant rate, and the paper tape reader requires exactly the same time to move the paper to read the next pattern as the microcomputer takes to execute the delay loop T times and to execute the other instructions in the outer loop one time. Finally, assume that the program executes its first LDAA $8000 instruction exactly when the first pattern can be read from the tape. In the first four lines, the pointer to store incoming words is set up, the M6821 is configured as an input device, and a counter to keep track of the number of words left to be input is initialized. The main loop reads a word into the buffer, moves the pointer to be ready to read the next word, waits the prescribed time, then repeats if more words are to be read.

The following is a C program for this operation. Its flow chart is shown in figure 5-5.

```
real(buffer) char *buffer;
{
    int i,j; char *device;
    *(device+1) = 4 ;
    for(i=128 i !=0;  i--){
        buffer(i) = *device ;
        for(j=N; j>=0; j--) ;
    }
}
```

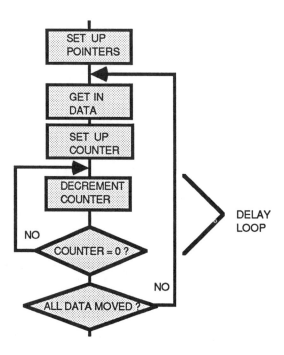

Figure 5-5. Flow Chart for Real-time Input

```
     NAM    REAL
     LDX    #BUFFER  ADDRESS OF FIRST WORD OF BUFFER TO X
     LDAA   #4       CONFIGURE M6821 FOR INPUT
     STAA   $8001    AND DISABLE INTERRUPT
     LDAA   #$80     SET UP TO COUNT INCOMING WORDS
L1   LDAB   $8000    READ A WORD FROM THE INPUT REGISTER
     STAB   0,X      PUT IT INTO THE BUFFER
     INX             MOVE POINTER
     LDAB   #T       SET UP DELAY LOOP
L2   DECB            COUNT OUT WAIT TIME
     BNE    L2       LOOP UNTIL TIME OUT
     DECA   COUNT    NUMBER OF WORDS TO BE READ
     BNE    L1       REPEAT PROGRAM UNTIL ALL WORDS READ
     END
```

Busy-done states can be recognized as the program segments are executed in synchronization with these states. The IDLE state is associated with the first four lines. Since we assume the paper holes are positioned to be read on the first execution of the LDAB instruction, that instruction corresponds to a DONE state, as do the instructions that decrement A and branch to this instruction. The delay loop corresponds to the BUSY state. Although the significance of these states is not quite so important in real-time synchronization, their association to the program segments is useful in comparing this to other synchronization techniques.

We now consider the real-time program to punch a tape in a single-chip MC68HC11A8. Consideration of the ports available leads us to choose port B for parallel output because simple handshaking can be used to signal the external hardware that new data has arrived. The flow chart and C program are sufficiently similar to those just given, that we leave them as an exercise for the reader. Assuming N bytes (N<=256) are to be punched, that the external device motor is started by a negative pulse on the STRB pin of the MC68HC11A8, and that the time to punch a hole and then move the tape is known to take T cycles of the delay loop, the following program will punch the tape:

```
        NAM  RLPNCH
PCR     EQU  2          PARALLEL CONTROL REGISTER
PORTB   EQU  4          PORT B DATA REGISTER
        LDX  #1000      I/O DEVICES PRESUMED AT $1000 TO $103F
        CLR  PCR,X      CLEAR ALL PARALLEL CONTROL REGISTER BITS
        CLRB            LOOP COUNTER
LOOP    LDY  #BUFFER    DATA BUFFER
        ABY             GET LOCATION OF WORD
        LDAA 0,Y        GET DATA
        STAA PORTB,X    PUT OUT WORD
        LDY  #T         WAIT TIME
DLY     DEY             DELAY LOOP
        BNE  DLY
        INCB            MOVE POINTER
        CMPB #N         ALL DONE?
        BNE  LOOP       NO: LOOP
```

Real-time synchronization uses the least amount of hardware of all the approaches to the synchronization problem, but the effort in writing the program may be the highest because of the difficulty of precisely tailoring the program to provide the required time delay. This approach is also sensitive to errors in the speed of the I/O system. If some mechanical components are not oiled, the I/O may be slower than what the program is made to handle. The program is therefore often timed to handle the worst possible situation and is the slowest of the techniques for synchronizing to an I/O system.

5-2.2 Gadfly Synchronization

The device interrupt can be used in *gadfly* synchronization. The technique is named after the great philosopher, Socrates, who was called the "gadfly of Athens" because he kept pestering the local politicians like a pesky little fly until they gave him the answer he wanted (regrettably, they also gave him some poison to drink). Similarly, the program continually bothers one or more devices to determine what they are doing. As in the Socratic method of teaching, it keeps asking the same question until it gets the answer it wants. This bothering is usually implemented in a loop, called a *gadfly loop*, in which the microcomputer continually inputs the device state of one or more I/O systems until it detects the done state or an error condition in one of the systems. In this technique, the IRQA1 flip-flop may be used to indicate the done state. When the I/O system determines the IRQA1 flip-flop is done with its operation, it sets the IRQA1 flip-flop by a signal sent through the M6821's CA1 pin. The program continually tests the value of IRQA1, waiting for it to become true. The program may decide to send it some more data or take some data from it and restart it or leave it idle. Also, the IRQB1 flip-flop can be used to indicate an error. If the I/O system can detect an error, it can send an edge of a signal through an M6821's CB1 pin to set the flip-flop. The program can periodically test the flip-flop used in this way; if it sees one set, it can jump to a program to handle the error condition.

We rework both our examples to show how the gadfly technique works. As in the previous example, BUFFER is the address of the first word in the buffer, which is to be filled with N words. We will assume that CA2 is used as an output to control the motor that pulls the tape forward; the motor advances the tape as long as CA2 is high. (See figure 5-6.) So we want to be able to make CA2 an output. We will assume that CA1 is normally high, but drops low when a pattern is positioned to be read by the paper tape reader. We want the device to change from BUSY to DONE when CA1 falls. The "handshaking mode" of the M6821 would be ideal, because the motor is automatically stopped when the next pattern is ready to be read and is restarted when the data is read from the input register so the next pattern will be positioned to be read. Finally, to detect an error, such as no paper in the reader, we will assume that CB1 is normally high, becoming low when no paper is sensed. We want to jump to a program called ERROR if CB1 falls.

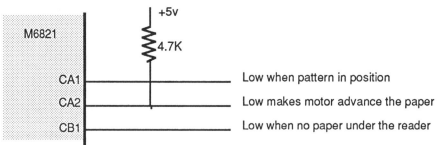

Figure 5-6. Connections to a Paper Tape Reader

The program is similar to that used for the real-time technique, except that the control registers must be initialized and a gadfly loop is used in place of the delay loop.

The gadfly loop is put in front of the instruction that reads the word (the delay loop was put after it) because we want to check that the word is in place before we read it. This is necessary in a gadfly program. We will assume that all registers, including the direction registers, have been cleared by a RESET signal when the machine was turned on. To initialize the control registers, that for device A should configure CA2 for output in the handshake mode and set IRQA1 when the CA1 input signal falls. This means bits 5,4,and 3 should be TFF, and bit 1 should be F. Also, when the program is reading data, bit 2 must be T or the direction register will be read instead. Bits 7 and 6 cannot be written, so they are "don't cares," and since the IRQA output is not connected, bit 0 is also a "don't care." So the control word should be XXTFFTFX. Making "don't care" X's into F's, for convenience, the hexadecimal number $24 should be written into control register A at location $8001. Note that when the machine is turned on, the CA2 is initally a high impedance input, so a pull-up resistor (shown in figure 5-6) makes the signal on CA2 high to prevent the motor from advancing the tape. When $24 is put into the control register, CA2 becomes an output, which is initially low, to advance the tape. Similarly, the other control register, at location $8003, should be loaded with $04 to configure the device for gadfly programming.

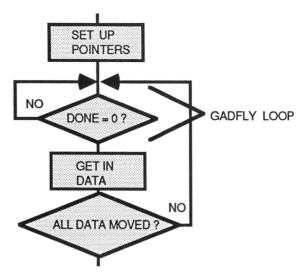

Figure 5-7. Flow Chart for Gadfly Input

The following is a C program for this operation. Its flow chart is in figure 5-7.

```
gadfly(buffer) char *buffer;
{
  int i; char *device;
  *(device+1) = 0x24;
  for(i=127; i>=0; i--){
    while((*(device+1))&0x80==0) ;
    buffer(i) = *device ;
  }
}
```

The gadfly program exhibits the idle, busy, and done states. The idle state is in effect if the A device control bit 5 is false (as it is when power is turned on), since the CA2 line is configured as an input, and is pulled high to prevent the motor from pulling the tape. The busy state is in effect when control bit 7 is false and control bits 5 to 3 are TFF, because the output on CA2 is low and the paper tape is advancing but the CA1 input has not fallen to indicate the device has completed its action. The done state is indicated by control bit 7 true and bits 5 to 3 THH, since this is caused by the completion of the action. Note that a start command is the writing of $24 into the control register, the completion signal is the falling edge of CA1, and the stop command is the clearing of the control register, as in the last step of the program segment. The gadfly synchronization technique monitors the busy-done states of the device to synchronize with it.

```
        NAM   GADFLY
        LDAA  #$24      SET UP CONTROL WORD TO SET IRQA1 ON
        STAA  $8001     FALLING EDGE OF CA1, USE CA2 IN HANDSHAKE
        LDAA  #4        SET UP CONTROL WORD TO SET IRQB1 ON
        STAA  $8003     FALLING EDGE OF CB1
        LDX   #BUFFER   INITIALIZE POINTER TO BUFFER
        LDAA  #$80      GET SIZE OF BUFFER TO COUNT INPUT WORD
L1      LDAB  $8003     CHECK FOR ERROR
        BMI   ERROR     REPORT ERROR IF FOUND
        LDAB  $8001     CHECK FOR DONE STATE
        BPL   L1        LOOP UNTIL IRQA1 IS SET, WHEN NEXT PAT.
        LDAB  $8000     CAN BE READ. THEN READ PATTERN.
        STAB  0,X       PLACE WORD IN BUFFER
        INX             MOVE POINTER
        DECA            COUNT OUT WORDS, TO SEE WHEN BUFFER
        BNE   L1        IS FULL, IF NOT LOOP AGAIN
        CLR   $8001     PUT DEVICE IN IDLE STATE
        .
        .
        .
ERROR   LDAA  $8002     CLEAR IRQB1
        END
```

A few remarks about the LDAA $8002 instruction at location ERROR are in order. An error condition will set the IRQB1 flip-flop, and, testing this, the program will jump to location ERROR. If a message is sent to the attendant, who reloads the paper and restarts the program, the gadfly loop will promptly exit to ERROR again, even though there is paper in the reader. This will frustrate the attendant, because every time the paper is reloaded, there will be an error message. Poor soul. The IRQB1 flip-flop must be cleared somewhere in the program following ERROR, before the gadfly loop is reentered. The only way to clear IRQB1 is to read the associated data register. Hence the instruction LDAA $8002. We are not interested in the data in the data register; they are garbage. We are doing this to generate an address trigger to clear the IRQB1 flip-flop. A final note is offered. Observe that the B device was initialized in lines 3 and 4 of the program, so that control bit 2 is T. Why bother? If this is not done, reading location $8002 in the error-handling routine will read the direction register, which does not clear the IRQB1 flip-flop. This flip-flop is cleared only when the data register is read, and control bit 2 must be T to read the data register.

We now consider a gadfly technique in the paper tape punch example. Consideration of the available ports leads us to choose port C because that port can use the full handshake on output. The direction bits for port C must be set to output because they are capable of bidirectional movement (port B used in RLPNCH is permanently configured as output, so the direction need not be initialized there). As in the previous example, we assume the punch motor is started by a negative pulse on STRB, and now we assume the punch returns a rising edge signal on STRA when the holes have been punched and the punch is ready for another operation. The STAF bit will indicate that the punch is done: it is set by the rising edge signal on STRA and cleared when another word is stored in the output register. We store it at the same address as the strobed data (C) register to generate an address trigger to clear SPIF. Here is the program:

```
            NAM     GADPNH
PCR    EQU     2            PARALLEL CONTROL REGISTER
PORTC  EQU     5            (BUFFERED) PORT C DATA REGISTER
DDRC   EQU     7            DIRECTION FOR PORT C
            LDX     #1000        I/O DEVICES PRESUMED AT $1000 TO $103F
            LDD     #$FF18       SET HNDS AND OIN FOR FULL OUT. HNDSHK
            STAB    PCR,X        IN THE  PARALLEL CONTROL REGISTER BITS
            STAA    DDRC,X       SET ALL BITS IN PORT C TO OUTPUT
            CLRB                 LOOP COUNTER
LOOP   LDY     #BUFFER DATA BUFFER
            ABY                  GET LOCATION OF WORD
            LDAA    0,Y          GET DATA
            STAA    PORTC,X PUT OUT WORD
GDFY   TST     PCR,X        WAIT FOR SPIF TO BECOME SET
            BPL     GDFY         WHEN STRA GETS RISING EDGE
            INCB                 MOVE POINTER
            CMPB    #N           ALL DONE?
            BNE     LOOP         NO: LOOP
```

This discussion provides an opportunity to relate one of the best stories in computer design, which was confessed by a member of the design team at a EUROMICRO conference a couple of years ago. (This is a true story, but for obvious reasons we won't give any names.) Designing a computer, they wanted to make it faster. They had a lot of programs written for the computer. So they ran these programs and kept track of which instruction was executed most often. Make that instruction run faster, they reasoned, then the machine should run faster. They did find an instruction that occurred much more often than the others, and they did manage to change the machine to make this instruction run quite a bit faster without slowing down the other instructions. But in making this change, they didn't get the machine to run any faster! Why? It should run faster! It turned out that the instruction was used in a gadfly loop, and anyway had to wait for completion of I/O operations. So the computer now *waited* faster. The moral of the story: collecting statistics does not neccessarily a better computer make. Another moral: computers spend a lot of time in gadfly loops.

5-2.3 Single Interrupts

In this section, we consider interrupt hardware and software. Interrupt software can be very tricky. Nevertheless, based on what we have learned from the last chapter and the previous sections, we should find interrupt software quite easy to use. At one extreme, some companies actually have a policy never to use interrupts, but instead to use gadfly programs. At the other extreme, some designers insist on using interrupts just because they are readily available in microcomputers and I/O chips like the M6821. We advocate using interrupts when they are neccessary but using simpler techniques whenever possible.

In this subsection, we will consider a microcomputer that has just one interrupt. We will examine the IRQ line and consider the sequence of actions leading to an interrupt. Then we will consider the paper tape reader example. In the next subsections, the multiple interrupt case will be studied, using two techniques called polling and vectored interrupts. These will be simple extensions of the single interrupt case.

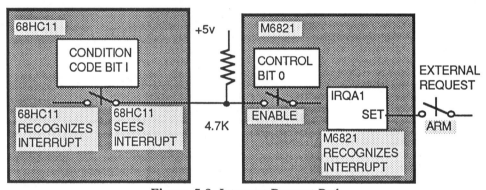

Figure 5-8. Interrupt Request Path

Interrupt techniques can be used to let the I/O system interrupt the processor when it is done, so the processor can be doing useful work until it is interrupted. Also, latency times resulting from interrupts can be less than latency times resulting from a variation of a gadfly approach, whereby the computer executes a subroutine, checks the I/O device, then executes another subroutine, and then checks the devices, and so on – and that can be an important factor for fast I/O devices. Recall the basic idea of an interrupt from chapter 1: that a program P currently being executed can be stopped at any point, then a device handler program D is executed to carry out some task requested by the device and the program P is resumed. The device must have some logic to determine when it needs to have the processor execute the D program, and a wire to the microprocessor to inform it that the device needs service. P must execute the same way whenever and regardless if D is executed. Therefore, D must somehow save all the information that P needs to resume without error. Usually, all the registers used by D must be saved. This may be done automatically by hardware. Moreover, any memory words that might be used by D and P must be saved and restored. When D is finished, it must execute some instruction, like a subroutine call that resumes P exactly where it left off.

The sequence of actions that lead to an interrupt and that service it are outlined below. (See figure 5-8.) Seven steps are executed, in the following sequence:

1. The external hardware determines it needs service either to move some data into it or out of it or to report an error. When this happens, we say an *external interrupt is requested.*

2. The I/O chip like the M6821 receives a signal, such as the rising edge of the CA1 signal. It sets a flip-flop, such as IRQA1, which is an *interrupt request flip-flop*. When this happens, we say the IRQA1 flip-flop recognizes an interrupt (as we noted in section 5-1.2). If the I/O device will recognize an interrupt when an external interrupt is requested, we say the device is *armed;* otherwise it is disarmed.

3. The I/O device asserts a (low) signal on a (wire-OR) bus line, such as IRQ, to the IRQ pin of the M6811. When this happens, we say *IRQA1 requests an interrupt.* When the IRQ pin on the M6811 is low, we say the *microprocessor sees an interrupt request.* If the I/O device asserts the IRQ signal (low) when it recognizes an interrupt, we say the *device is enabled;* otherwise it is disabled.

4. The microprocessor has a condition code flip-flop I, the *interrupt mask* flip-flop. When this bit is true, we say the *microprocessor is masked* (or the *microprocessor is disabled*); otherwise the *microprocessor is enabled.* If this bit is false when the IRQ input is low, we say the *microprocessor recognizes an interrupt.* (The I flip-flop can be controlled by the programmer to disable interrupts from being recognized when the program is unable to cope with them. This flip-flop is also controlled by hardware in the next step.)

5. The microcomputer is generally in the middle of an instruction it cannot stop. Therefore, if a microprocessor recognizes an interrupt, it will *honor an interrupt* at the end of the current instruction. When the M6811 honors an IRQ interrupt, it acts as if an SWI instruction were executed, saving the state of the machine on the stack and jumping indirectly through an address stored in high memory. However, whereas the SWI uses $FFF6 and $FFF7 as an indirect address, the IRQ interrupt uses $FFF2 and $FFF3. Importantly, the interrupt mask bit I is set in the condition code register after the former value of the condition codes is saved on the stack. (Some differences between the various interrupt handlers available for the M6811 are discussed in section 5-4.)

6. Beginning at the address specified by $FFF2 and $FFF3 is a routine called a *handler.* (When we consider multiple sources of interrupts, we will distinguish between the interrupt handler and the device handler, but for now we refer to it as a handler.) The handler is like a subroutine, in particular like an SWI "subroutine." It performs the work requested by the device. It may move a word between the device and a buffer, or it may report or fix up an error. One of a handler's critically important but easy to overlook functions is that it must remove the cause of the interrupt (by clearing the interrupt request flip-flop).

7. When it is completed, the handler executes an RTI instruction, which restores the state of the machine and resumes the program where it left off.

Some points about the interrupt sequence must be stressed. The MC68HC11A8, like most computers, sets an interrupt mask as soon as it honors an interrupt. If it didn't, the first instruction in the handler would be promptly interrupted – an infinite loop that will fill up the stack. Fortunately, the machine automatically sets the mask bit for you so this won't happen. And you do not even have to worry about clearing it, because step 7 just stated restores all the registers, including the condition code and its interrupt mask bit, to the values they had before the interrupt was honored. Since the mask bit was cleared then (or there never would have been an interrupt), it will be clear after the RTI instruction is executed. However, the programmer can clear that bit using a CLI instruction if he or she needs to permit interrupts before the handler is finished. Note that the I/O device is generally still asserting IRQ (low) because it doesn't know what is going on inside the microprocessor. If the RTI is executed or the interrupt mask bit is otherwise cleared, this same device will promptly interrupt the processor again and again, – eventually hanging up the machine. Before the handler executes RTI or clears the mask, it *must* remove the source of the interrupt! (Please excuse our frustration, but this is so simple yet so much of a problem.)

A note is offered about enabling and arming interrupts. A disarmed interrupt is completely ignored. You disarm a device when you know it will externally request an interrupt but you have no intention of honoring it. A disabled interrupt is postponed but not ignored. You disable an interrupt when you are not prepared to honor it right now but will honor it later. Disarming takes place before the interrupt request flip-flop is set, so it completely inhibits that setting. Disabling takes place, in effect, after the interrupt request flip-flop is set, so it is still set if the device or the microcomputer is later enabled. However, the interrupt request flip-flop can be cleared just before the interrupt is enabled. This is sometimes necessary because we do not know the state of that flip-flop when we enable the interrupt, so we must prevent the possibility of getting an interrupt right away before we are expecting it.

In the M6821, the primary interrupt IRQA1 is always armed, although external logic can be used to disarm it. The secondary interrupt IRQA2 is armed when control bit 5 is made false, which causes CA1 to become an input. The primary interrupt is enabled if control bit 0 is true, and the secondary interrupt is enabled when control bit 3 is true and control bit 5 is false. Note that when the gadfly technique is used, you disable the interrupts (either by clearing control bits 0 and 3, or by setting mask bit I in the 6811).

We now consider the paper reader tape example, using a single interrupt for requesting that input data be put in the buffer. The hardware is the same as in earlier examples. The software is in three parts. The initialization routine is shown here:

```
LDX     #$200       INITIALIZE BUFFER
STX     POINT       SAVE IN GLOBAL VARIABLE
LDAA    #$80        SET UP COUNTER
STAA    COUNT       IN GLOBAL VARIABLE
LDX     #EXIT       SET UP RETURN ADDRESS
STX     RETAD       TO GO TO WHEN BUFFER IS FULL
LDD     #$25        SET UP DEVICE TO SET IRQA1 ON
STD     $8001       FALL OF CA1, ENABLE INTERRUPTS
LDAA    $8000       CLEAR IRQA1, IN CASE IT WAS SET
CLI                 CLEAR INTERRUPT MASK BIT
```

This initialization sets up global variables to hold the address where we are putting the data and where we keep track of the number of words yet to be brought in. The return address is set up so that when the buffer is full, we will go there. These are allocated by assembler directives like COUNT RMB 1 and POINT RMB 2 that appear in the program when page 0 is allocated. The M6821 ritual configures it for this application. Note from figure 5-3 that control bit 0 is to be true to enable the interrupt from IRQA1, but bit 1 should be false to set IRQA1 on the falling edge. Of course, bit 2 must be made true, and bit 5 is true, so that the secondary interrupt is disarmed. The direction register is cleared to make all bits inputs. The IRQA1 flip-flop is now cleared, in case it was set before, so we will not get an interrupt after the next instruction. The M6811 interrupt mask is then cleared to allow interrupts. The program is now free to execute the impressive routine it was born to do, rather than loop in a delay or gadfly loop, until the operation is complete. You will know that the buffer is full by testing the number in COUNT, which will become 0 at that time. Therefore, you can wait for the buffer to be output by a gadfly loop on the value of COUNT:

```
L    LDAA    COUNT   COUNT IS DEC. BY THE INTERRUPT HANDLER:
     BNE     L       LOOP HERE UNTIL HND. FINISHES LOADING BUFFER
```

After the gadfly loop, you know that the buffer is indeed full and ready to be used. However, such gadfly loops are just as wasteful as delay loops. If you don't get anything else done while interrupts are handling the input, you should consider using the cheaper real-time or gadfly synchronization mechanism.

The handler routine TPRDR for our example is shown next. The address HNDLR is put in locations $FFF2 and $FFF3 so that when the M6811 honors the interrupt, it will cause this handler to be executed.

```
        NAM   TPRDR
HNDLR   LDAA  $8000     GET PATTERN FROM PAPER TAPE
        LDX   POINT     GET POINTER TO BUFFER
        STAA  0,X       PUT IN BUFFER
        INX             MOVE POINTER
        STX   POINT     SAVE FOR NEXT INPUT
        DEC   COUNT     COUNT OUT INCOMING WORDS
        BNE   HNDLR1    IF BUFFER IS FULL, THEN
        CLR   $8001     PREVENT FURTHER INTERRUPTS
HNDLR1  RTI             RETURN TO GADFLY LOOP
        END
```

Table 5-1. Logic Analyzer Display for an Interrupt

-	-	R	0102	26	OP CODE BNE
-	-	R	0103	FB	DISPLACEMENT
-	-	R	FFFF	58	NULL CYCLE
-	-	R	0100	96	OP CODE LDAA - EXTERNAL REQUEST ASSERTED
R	I	R	0003	20	DATA - IRQ LINE DROPS LOW
R	I	R	0102	26	OP CODE BNE - CANT YET RECOGNIZE INTERRUPT
R	I	R	0103	FB	DISPLACEMENT - M6811 RECOGNIZES INTERRUPT
-	I	R	FFFF	58	NULL CYCLE - EXTERNAL REQUEST IS NEGATED
-	I	W	FFFF	58	NULL CYCLE - BEGIN HONORING INTERRUPT
-	I	W	03FB	00	PUSH LOW BYTE OF PC
-	I	W	03FA	01	PUSH HIGH BYTE OF PC
-	I	W	03F9	05	PUSH LOW BYTE OF Y
-	I	W	03F8	04	PUSH HIGH BYTE OF Y
-	I	W	03F7	07	PUSH LOW BYTE OF X
-	I	W	03F6	06	PUSH HIGH BYTE OF X
-	I	W	03F5	0B	PUSH ACCUMULATOR B
-	I	W	03F4	0A	PUSH ACCUMULATOR A
-	I	W	03F3	0C	PUSH CONDITION CODES
-	I	R	03F3	0C	IRRELEVENT STACK READ
-	I	R	FFF8	01	GET HIGH BYTE OF HANDLER ADDRESS
-	I	R	FFF9	80	GET LOW BYTE OF HANDLER ADDRESS
-	I	R	FFFF	58	NULL CYCLE
-	I	R	0180	B6	LDAA OP CODE - FIRST INSTRUCTION OF HANDLER
-	I	R	0181	80	HIGH BYTE OF DEVICE ADDRESS
-	I	R	0182	00	LOW BYTE OF DEVICE ADDRESS
-	I	R	2000	25	READ DATA FROM DEVICE, CLEAR INTERRUPT
-	I	R	0183	DE	LDX OP CODE - SECOND INSTRUCTION OF HANDLER

The handler looks very much like the INBUF program of section 4-2.1, except that we cannot assume that any registers can be used as local variables because, in principle, the handler can be "called" at any time. Therefore, we store our variables as global variables on page 0. However, we must expand upon some subtle points. The instruction LDAA $8000 not only performs the function of inputting the data from the input device, but also performs the critical function of clearing the interrupt request flip-flop by means of an address trigger. This negates the IRQ line high. The RTI instruction likewise restores the registers and clears the interrupt mask bit I. The instruction above the RTI returns the device to the idle state when all words have been moved.

A logic analyzer can be used to actually see what happens when an interrupt is requested and honored. Suppose the gadfly loop is at location $100, the handler is at $180, and the stack pointer is $3FC. Suppose the word input to the device is $24. Suppose locations $FFF2, $FFF3, and $FFFF have values $02, $00, and $58, and registers Y,X,B,A, and CC have values $405, $607, $B, $A, $C. This image could appear on the screen of a logic analyzer, where column 1 is the external request (R = request asserted), column 2 is the IRQ line (I = interrupt request asserted low), column 3 is the read/write signal (R = read, W = write), and the next two columns are the address and data in hexadecimal. (See table 5-1.)

This output from the logic analyzer shows an external interrupt being asserted on a CA1 pin in the middle of the second execution of the BNE instruction. In general, the machine may have been in this wait loop for a long time before the request was asserted. It takes 1 microsecond for the M6821 to set IRQA1 and assert the IRQ bus line low. The M6811 sees the interrupt request, but in general it will complete one extra instruction before it will honor it. The external request can be removed at any time after it has set the IRQA1 flip-flop but before it may need to request another interrupt, as the CA1 input is edge triggered. The interrupt is honored by pushing all the registers on the stack and getting the handler's address. Extra null cycles appear because the M6811 is doing some internal housekeeping before and after the words are pushed on the stack, and after the handler address is obtained. The first instruction of the handler is executed, and this clears IRQA1, which removes the source of the interrupt.

This example shows that interrupts are really not that complicated. A few more techniques are needed to handle more than one interrupt on a line, but these are also quite simple, as we now show.

5-2.4 Polled Interrupts

Since the IRQ line is a wire-OR bus line, any number of devices can be connected to it, so if any of these devices require service, they can assert this signal (low). The processor can recognize an IRQ interrupt when this line is low, but since it doesn't know which device asserted this IRQ line, it doesn't know what to do. However, by reading the status registers of all the devices connected to the IRQ line that could cause it to become low, the processor can determine a device that needs service, service it, and then clear the source of the interrupt in that device. Note that, since the 6821 IRQ outputs are wire-ORed, two or more devices could simultaneously request an interrupt, or one could request an interrupt while another is being serviced. Fortunately, it all works out. As the first interrupt is serviced, and the cause of that interrupt is cleared in that device, the other device still holds the IRQ line low. Thus, as soon as the handler for the first interrupt is left, the processor immediately recognizes an IRQ interrupt. It will then handle the second interrupt.

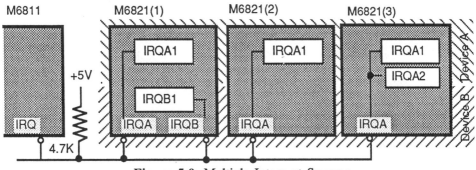

Figure 5-9. Multiple Interrupt Sources

The handlers become a bit more complicated for multiple interrupts. The *IRQ interrupt handler* just finds out which device needs service. Each device has its own *device handler* that actually services the interrupt. In the previous case where there is but one interrupt source on a line, these two handlers merge into one (or one can say the IRQ handler becomes trivial or disappears). In this case, when the IRQ line is low and the IRQ handler is executed, it *polls* the devices to see which one caused the interrupt. The polling program checks each device, one at a time, in *priority* order, highest priority device first. Each M6821 device can be checked for an IRQ1 interrupt, and the handler to service the interrupt can be executed. An example involving an assortment of four devices will be shown to demonstrate polling in an IRQ handler. The four devices are shown in figure 5-9.

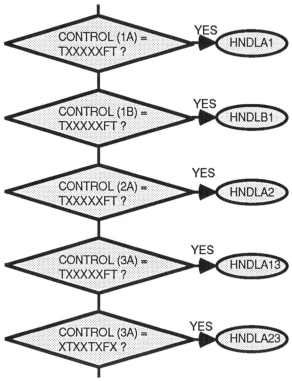

Figure 5-10. Flow Chart for Interrupt Polling

Suppose there are three M6821s such that device A of one is at locations $8000, $8001, device B is at $8002, $8003, device A of another is at $8004, $8005, and device A of a third is at $8008, and $8009, with the data/direction register having the lower address in each device. The IRQA and IRQB pins of the first M6821 and only the IRQA pins of the other two are connected to the IRQ bus line. (Note that we do not connect devices to the IRQ bus unless we intend to use them in an interrupt technique, nor do we poll devices that cannot cause an interrupt; if we did we might do something we don't need to and miss doing something else, because the polling routine will always go to this routine instead of the one that actually needs service.) Suppose, for simplicity, that the A and B devices of the first M6821 and the A device of the second M6821 have their control registers initialized to value 5, but the A device of the third is initialized to $D. Then the IRQA1 and IRQB1 flip-flops of the first device, the IRQA1 flip-flop of the second M6821, and both the IRQA1 and IRQA2 flip-flops of the third M6821 can cause an IRQ interrupt if asserted. The flow chart in figure 5-10 shows how simple the polling procedure is. A fragment of a C program can also express the simplicity of this polling procedure:

```
if((cntla1&0x83) == 0x81) /* goto hndlal */
else if((cntlb1&0x83) == 0x81) /* goto hndlbl */
else if((cntla2&0x83) == 0x81) /* goto hndla2 */
else if((cntla3&0x83) == 0x81) /* goto hndlal3 */
else if((cntla3&0x4a) == 0x48) /* goto hndla23 */
```

The program appears here:

```
        NAM    IRQHND
IRQHND  LDAA   $8001      GET STATE OF A DEVICE IN M6821(1)
        EORA   #$81       INVERT IRQA AND ENABLE
        BITA   #$83       TEST BITS 7,1,0 FOR F
        BEQ    HNDLA1     GO TO DEVICE A(1) HANDLER
        LDAA   $8003      GET STATE OF B DEVICE IN M6821(1)
        EORA   #$81       INVERT IRQB AND ENABLE
        BITA   #$83       TEST BITS 7,1,0 FOR F
        BEQ    HNDLB1     GO TO DEVICE B(1) HANDLER IF ALL F
        LDAA   $8005      GET STATE OF A DEVICE IN M6821(2)
        EORA   #$81       INVERT IRQA AND ENABLE
        BITA   #$83       TEST BITS 7,1,0 FOR F
        BEQ    HNDLA2     GO TO DEVICE A(2) HANDLER
        LDAA   $8009      GET STATE OF A DEVICE IN M6821(3)
        EORA   #$C9       INVERT IRQA1, IRQA2, AND BOTH ENABLES
        BITA   #$83       TEST BITS 7,1,0 FOR F
        BEQ    HNDA13     GO TO HANDLER FOR IRQA1 IN M6821(3)
        BITA   #$4A       TEST BITS 6,3 AND 1 FOR F
        BEQ    HNDA23     GO TO HANDLER FOR IRQA2 IN M6821(3)
        END
```

The first line reads the control register of an M6821 at location $8000, $8001. Bits 7 and 0 must both be true for an interrupt to be caused by this device. If bit 7 is true but bit 0 is false, the device interrupt did not cause the processor interrupt. Some other device must have caused it, so this one should be ignored. To test for two 1s in the M6811, the easiest way is to complement all the bits and use BIT to test for 0's. However, this simple test makes maintenance a bit more difficult than a slightly more complex test. If the first M6821 is burned out or is removed from the microprocessor, an attempt to read any word in the range $8000 to $8003 will probably read $FF. The IRQ device handler would read this word, so the test for T's in bits 0 and 7 would pass and the device handler HNDLA1 would be executed. Unfortunately, since there is no chip here, attempts to remove the source of the interrupt will be futile, so the IRQ interrupt will be recognized just as soon as the handler is executed, ad nauseam. To correct this troublesome problem, all that we have to do is also check for an F in the control word. Any F will do. Since we initialized the control register such that bit 1 is F, to execute the device handler, we check the word we read to verify that bits 7 and 0 are T, and bit 1 is F. Note that an exclusive-OR instruction with an immediate operand EORA #N inverts those bits in the accumulator in which the corresponding bit in the operand is T, and that a bit test instruction BITA #N sets condition code Z if all bits in accumulator A are F in those positions where the operand is T. Thus, the branch to the interrupt handler is taken if bits 7 and 0 are T, and bit 1 is F. HNDLA1 may be a handler routine like TPRDR, described earlier in this subsection. If this condition is not satisfied, the next device is tested, and, if it does not satisfy the test, the next is tested, then the next and the next, until all are tested. Note that the IRQA2 interrupt source from the M6821(3) requires a slightly different procedure. Reading the control word at location $8009, we invert bits 0 and 7 to prepare to check the IRQA1 interrupt source, and we simultaneously invert bits 3 and 6 to prepare to check the IRQA2 interrupt source. The IRQA1 source is checked as before. The IRQA2 source caused the interrupt if bits 3 and 6 are T and bit 1 is F.

The polling technique just described checks the devices in priority order. The program should first check the devices that need service fastest. The A device at location $8000, $8001 should be associated with the fastest or the most critical I/O system. Lower priority devices are handled after the higher priority device handlers clear the device interrupt that masks the lower priority interrupt, all of which happens only after the higher priority interrupt is fully handled. An alternative scheme is called a *round-robin* priority scheme. Here, the polling program is arranged as an infinite program loop. When the ith device in the priority order gets an interrupt and is serviced, the $i+1th$ device assumes the highest priority, and whenever an interrupt occurs the polling program starts checking the $i+1th$ device first. Polling in the same priority order is useful when some devices clearly need service faster than others; round-robin priority is more democratic and is especially useful if some device tends to hog the use of the computer by frequently requesting interrupts.

Some authors classify the polled interrupt and gadfly interrupt as similar techniques and use the name "polling" for both. However, each technique tests different bits and has different properties. Polling, in ordinary daily context, means sampling each respondent just once; if a poll is conducted by a newspaper, the same person is not asked the same question several times. Thus, the gadfly technique should not be called "polling," since in using it the same question is asked of a device until the device responds the way the program wants. However, for reading other books, you need to be aware that the term "polling" may be used for both polled interrupts and gadfly loops.

5-2.5 Vectored Interrupts

The previous example shows how multiple interrupts can be handled by connecting several devices to the IRQ line and polling them in the IRQ handler. The polling technique may take too much time for some devices that need service quickly. A *vectored interrupt* technique can be used to replace the interrupt handler software by a hardware device, so that the device handler is entered almost as soon as the device requests an interrupt. The basic idea is that each device puts its interrupt request signal on separate pins into a hardware module which does the same function as the polling routine. If the i*th* interrupt request line is asserted (low) and all interrupt requests on lines 0 to i-1 are not asserted, the hardware instantly supplies the address of the i*th* device handler just as it interrupts the processor, to start the processor at the specified location.

The M6811 is particularly rich in vectored interrupts, since it has many internal I/O devices with interrupts and these require so little hardware to be vectored. We consider an example using the two devices, the parallel port and the serial peripheral interface, which we have studied so far. In this example, a slave MC68HC11A8 will receive data from a master MC68HC11A8 via the serial interface, then punch that data on paper tape using the parallel port C, as in the gadfly example GADPNH of the punch interface in section 5-2.1. A queue will be used to store the data, if the serial interface provides data faster than it can be punched. (You may wish to review the discussion of queues in section 2-1.3.) As new data are received over the serial interface by means of an exchange operation discussed in section 4-4.3, this slave MC68HC11A8 will send back the length of the queue to the master so it can prevent an overrun of that queue. (You may also wish to review section 4-4.3 to see the master operation and the connections between master and slave.) The queue will be at address BUFFER and of size BUFSIZ. Pointers for input and output will be at INPTR and OUTPTR, and the current length of the queue will be at QUELEN.

The initialization ritual for both devices and for the queue is now shown. It ends in an infinite loop because, aside from the activities of the interrupt handlers, there is nothing else to do after the ritual.

```
        NAM  INTERS
* COMMON EQUATES FOR INITIALIZATION AND HANDLERS
SPE    EQU  $40       SERIAL PERIPHERAL INT. ENABLE (SLAVE MODE)
STAI   EQU  $40       STROBE A INTERRUPT ENABLE FOR PORT C
OHND   EQU  $18       CONFIGURATION BITS FOR OUTPUT HANDSHAKE
PIOC   EQU  2         PARALLEL IO CONTROL
PORTC  EQU  5         PARALLEL PORT C (ADDRESS OF STROBED REG.)
DDRC   EQU  7         PORT C DIRECTION
DDRD   EQU  9         PORT D DIRECTION
SPCR   EQU  $28       SERIAL PERIPHERAL CONTROL
SPD    EQU  $2A       SERIAL PERIPHERAL DATA
* INITIALIZE QUEUE
        LDX  #BUFFER BUFFER IS A GLOBAL VARIABLE
        STX  INPTR    INPUT POINTER IS A GLOBAL VARIABLE
        STX  OUTPTR OUTPUT POINTER IS A GLOBAL VARIABLE
        CLR  QUELEN NO WORDS IN QUEUE, SO MAKE LENGTH ZERO
* INITIALIZE SERIAL PORT
        LDD  #$400+SPE SET DIRECTION ON PORT D BITS 4,3, AND 2
        STAA DDRD,X  TO OUTPUT SO SERIAL PERIPHERAL WORKS
        STAB SPCR,X  ENABLE INTERRUPT ON SER. PER. INTERFACE
```

```
*INITIALIZE PARALLEL PORT
        LDD   #$FF00+OHND DISABLE INT., WR. HANDSHAKE ON PORT C
        STAB  PIOC,X   IN PARALLEL IO CONTROL REGISTER
        STAA  DDRC,X   MAKE ALL BITS OUTPUT ON C
        CLI            ENABLE INT. FROM SERIAL, PARALLEL PORTS
L       BRA   L        INFINITE LOOP: HANDLE INTERRUPTS
```

The serial peripheral interface interrupt vector is at $FFD8 and $FFD9. The address SHND is put there for the serial interrupt handler. Note that pushing a word from the serial input onto the queue is the main function of this handler. The queue length is put into the shift register, not only to keep the master informed so it won't overrun the queue, but also to negate the serial peripheral interrupt request. The last part of the handler, after the CMPA instruction, has to do with the parallel port handler, and will be discussed later. The serial handler is shown here:

```
SHND    LDAA  SPSR,X   CLEAR INTERRUPT
        LDAA  SPD,X    GET DATA
        LDY   INPTR    GET QUEUE POINTER
        STAA  0,Y      PUSH WORD IN QUEUE
        INY            MOVE POINTER
        CPY   #BUFFER+BUFSIZ
        BNE   SHND1    IF POINTER MOVES PAST END
        LDY   #BUFFER  RESET QUEUE POINTER
SHND1   STY   INPTR
        INC   QUELEN   THE QUEUE HAS INCREASED BY ONE WORD
        LDAA  QUELEN   GET CURRENT LENGTH OF THE QUEUE
        STAA  SPD,X    PUT IN SH. REG. , PICKED UP BY THE MASTER
        CMPA  #1       IF QUEUE SIZE HAS JUST BECOME 1, IT WAS 0
        BNE   SHND2    SO THE PAR. PORT INT. WOULD'VE BEEN OFF
        LDAA  #OHND+STAI SO ENABLE THE INTERRUPT
        STAA  PIOC,X   TO EMPTY THE QUEUE
SHND2   RTI            RETURN TO INFINITE LOOP
```

The address of the interrupt handler for the parallel port is put in the IRQ handler address $FFF2 and $FFF3 that we discussed earlier. The main part of this handler merely pulls a word from the queue and outputs it through the parallel port. The two lines before the RTI instruction will be considered shortly. The parallel handler is given here:

```
PHND    LDAA  PIOC,X   CLEAR STAF BIT
        LDY   OUTPTR   GET POINTER TO QUEUE
        LDAA  0,Y      GET DATA FROM QUEUE
        STAA  PORTC,X  PUT IN PORT C (ADDRESS OF BUFFER REGISTER)
        INY            MOVE POINTER
        CPY   #BUFFER+BUFSIZ
        BNE   PHND1    IF PAST THE END OF BUFFER
        LDY   #BUFFER  RETURN POINTER TO BEGINNING OF BUFFER
```

```
PHND1 STY    OUTPTR   SAVE POINTER
      DEC    QUELEN   NOTE: QUEUE LENGTH DECREASED BY ONE
      BNE    PHND2    IF QUEUE IS EMPTY
      LDAA   #OHND    RESET INTERRUPT ON PARALLEL PORT
      STAA   POIC,X   DISABLE INTERRUPT
PHND2 RTI            RETURN TO THE INFINITE LOOP
```

The last lines of the two handlers are responsible for starting and stopping interrupt requests from the parallel port. We do not want requests when there are no data to be sent. That condition arises immediately when the devices are initialized, so the initialization ritual sets up the parallel port with interrupts disabled. However, the serial port interrupt is always enabled, since we do not know when some data will be sent, and we must be vigilant for it. When some data are sent, we need to turn on the parallel port interrupt so the handler will begin pulling the data that were pushed on the queue. We do not want to keep enabling that interrupt but enable it only when it is previously disabled. We could test the interrupt enable flag on the serial peripheral control register, but that condition will occur exactly when the queue length changes from zero to one, as we confirm soon. As the queue is emptied in the parallel port handler, we need to stop parallel port interrupts when the queue length becomes zero. This is done in the two instructions before the RTI instruction. Thus, the parallel interrupt is disabled when the queue length is zero, after initialization and after it has been returned to zero by the parallel port handler. So the serial port handler should restart the parallel port interrupt exactly when the queue length changes from zero to one.

The main point of this example is that, because the addresses of both handlers are at different locations and there is no polling table to go through, the handler is executed without the delay of a polling routine. In effect, the polling routine is executed very quickly in hardware, and the winning handler is jumped to right after the registers are saved on the stack.

5-2.6 Vectored Interrupts in the M6811

The M6811 has three negative logic interrupt bus lines: the IRQ line, described in the last subsection, the RESET line that behaves like an interrupt line, and the extra interrupt request (XIRQ). This is what happens in hardware when these lines request some service.

If RESET becomes low, processing stops. The RESET line normally clears all I/O registers when the processor is stopped. When the signal rises again, memory words at location $FFFE and $FFFF are read and become the high and low bytes of the program counter. This starts the M6811 at the location specified by the contents of $FFFE and $FFFF. The program that is entered handles the initialization ritual after a reset, so we call it the *reset handler*. The reset handler configures many of the I/O devices not already configured as desired by the RESET signal and not to be configured later as part of the program that uses the device. In earlier discussions, we said that the rituals to be run just after power is applied are all put in the reset handler. The handler may also run diagnostic programs to check the microprocessor, memory, or I/O devices; clear all or part of memory; initialize some of the variables to be used in the following programs;

and set up the stack pointer register. The last part of this subsection discusses some special capabilities that can only be utilized in the reset handler. The reset handler then jumps to the applications program, if the microcomputer runs a dedicated application, or to a program called a *monitor* which allows the attendant to load and examine memory and registers, and execute or debug programs. The locations $FFFE, $FFFF, the reset handler, and the monitor or the applications program are normally in read-only memory, for if we didn't have these locations and programs in memory before executing the first instruction, we would have no way to start the machine. (You may laugh at this, but sometimes machines proposed even in learned papers have this problem – that they can't be started.)

A monitor is used to debug your program. The SWI instruction may be used as a *breakpoint* to stop your program at selected points, to examine memory or registers, or change their contents. The monitor replaces the opcode of an instruction in your program with the SWI instruction opcode, so when that instruction is executed, a software interrupt will occur. That interrupt handler is the monitor. A *trace* uses a timer to permit one instruction at a time to be executed. The monitor starts a timer, as discussed in chapter 7, and returns to the user program. The timer generates an interrupt a few memory cycles later, just long enough for one instruction to be run in your program. When the interrupt occurs, the monitor is entered, and it may display the registers so you can see the effect of the instruction that was executed in your program. A note about debugging a program that uses interrupts is worth stressing. You may have been reluctant to use a logic analyzer up to now. However, there is no way you can debug a program like this with simple monitor tools. Not only is timing critical in such programs – and timing would be grossly upset by a monitor – but interrupts must be turned off when in a handler, so interrupts used by a trace technique won't work in interrupt handlers. Logic analyzers are not intrusive and work independently of the system under test, so they work equally well whether interrupts are on or off.

Upon reset, the IRQ line and interrupt vector can be configured as a *non-maskable interrupt*, as will be described in section 5-4. If the non-maskable interrupt signal falls from high to low, we say *the processor recognizes a non-maskable interrupt,* and the following sequence of events occurs. Note that this interrupt occurs whenever there is a (falling) edge, rather than a (low) level, on the IRQ line. It is often called an *edge-sensitive* interrupt, while the normal IRQ is called *level-sensitive*. In the same way as the IRQ interrupt is honored, a non-maskable interrupt is honored, except that the I interrupt mask is not checked. It will service this interrupt. One very important thing it must do, moreover, is remove the cause of the low signal on the IRQ line, or the non-maskable interrupt signal will never fall again, and non-maskable interrupts will never be recognized again by the processor. The handler finally executes an RTI. It pulls all the values saved on the stack and returns them to their respective registers, which resumes the interrupted program so that it executes as if no interrupt occurred.

Other devices can be connected to the non-maskable interrupt line (IRQ) and can be polled in the non-maskable interrupt handler in a similar way. There are two additional considerations when the non-maskable interrupt line is used. First, it is possible to request a second interrupt at the same time or just after requesting another on the non-maskable interrupt line. The polling sequence will service one of them and then return via an RTI instruction. But the other device will still hold the non-maskable interrupt line down because it has not been serviced. The microcomputer does not recognize this interrupt because no falling edge of the non-maskable interrupt signal was noted, so it is not serviced. Moreover, no other non-maskable interrupts can be serviced because the line is being held low. To avoid this catastrophe, device handlers for devices attached to the non-maskable interrupt line must never terminate in an RTI instruction but must instead jump to the beginning of the non-maskable interrupt polling sequence. An RTI instruction should appear at the end of this polling sequence. This way, when a device is serviced and its interrupt request is removed, the other devices attached to the non-maskable interrupt line are checked to see if they have made a request. If none has, then the return from interrupt is completed at the end of the polling sequence. (Note that device handlers for devices connected to the IRQ line should end in an RTI instruction and need not be polled after an non-maskable interrupt is serviced.) The other consideration is that these interrupt requests cannot be disabled as a whole, because setting the I condition code disables all the IRQ interrupts. Each interrupt on a non-maskable interrupt line has to be individually disabled if we want to disable all interrupts. These two considerations indicate that the normal IRQ technique is easier to use for multiple interrupts, while the non-maskable interrupt line is better used for an omnipresent interrupt such as would be requested when an attendant presses an ABORT button. Nevertheless, the non-maskable interrupt line can be used to handle multiple interrupts, taking into account these two simple considerations.

The response to a signal on the XIRQ line is similar. Condition code bit 5, called the *X interrupt mask* X, is used to prevent unwanted interrupts from signals on the XIRQ line. Once the X bit is cleared by a TAP or RTI instruction, it cannot be set again easily. For that reason, the Motorola literature refers to this interrupt as pseudo-non-maskable. However, it must not be confused with the edge-sensitive non-maskable interrupt which can be initialized in the IRQ mechanism on power up. If the XIRQ signal is low and X is false, then we say *the processor recognizes an XIRQ interrupt*. As when it recognized an IRQ interrupt, the processor is probably executing an instruction, so it completes this and then saves the registers on the stack. The hardware sets X and I next and then reads the words at locations $FFF4 and $FFF5 into the program counter to start executing a handler program. During the execution of the handler, X is 1. We can return from such an interrupt by an RTI instruction which restores the registers, including the condition codes and the X and I bits in it, to their former values. (An IRQ interrupt, however, does not set the X bit, so an XIRQ interrupt can occur during the execution of an IRQ interrupt handler when I is set, but not vice versa.) This program is called the *XIRQ handler*. It services the interrupt that was requested. Like the IRQ handler, it must remove the source of the interrupt before it clears the X bit or it will promptly be interrupted again, ad nauseam. The X bit can be cleared by executing RTI at the end of an XIRQ interrupt handler or by executing TPA ANDA #$BF TAP and can be set by a processor reset or by altering the stacked condition code byte inside the XIRQ interrupt handler.

The rich set of interrupt vectors in the M6811 are shown in table 5-2. The rightmost column refers to sections in which the interrupt operation is more fully explained. Data sheets from Motorola on the MC68HC11A8 give further information on these interrupts, which is too detailed for this textbook.

We now rework our paper tape reader example, to illustrate the use of interrupt vectors and the reset handler. The request to put some data into the buffer will be handled by an IRQ interrupt, and the error condition will be recognized by an XIRQ interrupt. This requires that the M6821's IRQA output be connected to the IRQ pin (pin 41) and the IRQB output be connected to the XIRQ pin (pin 40). Both negative logic wire-OR bus lines need pull-up resistors. Continuing our example, the program shown next will read the paper tape pattern whenever a new pattern appears and will jump to the XIRQ handler whenever the reader runs out of paper.

Table 5-2. Interrupt Vectors in the M6811

Interrupt Vector	Name	Reference
$FFD6,D7	SCI SERIAL SYSTEM	4-4.3
$FFD8,D9	SPI SERIAL SYSTEM	8
$FFDA,DB	PULSE ACCUMULATOR INPUT EDGE	7-3.1
$FFDC,DD	PULSE ACCUMULATOR OVERFLOW	7-3.1
$FFDE,DF	TIMER OVERFLOW	7-1
$FFE0,E1	TIMER OUTPUT COMPARE 5	7-2
$FFE2,E3	TIMER OUTPUT COMPARE 4	7-2
$FFE4,E5	TIMER OUTPUT COMPARE 3	7-2
$FFE6,E7	TIMER OUTPUT COMPARE 2	7-2
$FFE8,E9	TIMER OUTPUT COMPARE 1	7-2
$FFEA,EB	TIMER INPUT CAPTURE 3	7-3.2
$FFEC,ED	TIMER INPUT CAPTURE 2	7-3.2
$FFEE,EF	TIMER INPUT CAPTURE 1	7-3.2
$FFF0,F1	REAL TIME INTERRUPT	7-2.3
$FFF2,F3	IRQ	5-3.1
$FFF4,F5	XIRQ	5-3.1
$FFF6,F7	SWI	1-2.1
$FFF8,F9	ILLEGAL OP CODE	5-3.3
$FFFA,FB	COP FAILURE	5-3.3
$FFFC,FD	CLOCK FAILURE	5-3.3
$FFFE,FF	RESET	5-3.1

The first few lines have assembler directives that make room for pointer and counter variables and for the buffer itself. They must be in read-write memory, and should be on page 0 because they are global variables. The remaining lines consist of the program stored in read-only memory. The reset handler begins at label RSTHND and has eleven instructions. It initializes the registers and the variables needed by the program, initializes the stack pointer, clears the interrupt mask, and jumps to a user program called PROGRM to do something useful. (To avoid having to show a useful program, we show an infinite wait loop, but if you have to use a wait loop, you are better off using the gadfly mechanism for synchronization.) When power is first applied, or after the user presses a panic button to assert the RESET line low, the processor picks up the 2 words at locations $FFFE and $FFFF, which happen to be the address of this routine, to start executing it.

```
              NAM    INTERS
              ORG    0              LOW MEMORY IS RAM
POINT   RMB    2              ALLOCATE TWO WORDS FOR POINTER
COUNT   RMB    1              ALLOCATE ONE WORD TO COUNT WORDS
BUFFR   RMB    $80            ALLOCATE 128 WORDS FOR THE BUFFER
              ORG    $FC00          TOP 1K MEMORY IS ROM OR PROM
RSTHND  LDAA   #$25           SET UP DEVICE A TO SET IRQA1 ON
              STAA   $8001          FALL OF CA1, ALLOW INTERRUPT TO IRQA
              LDAA   #$05           SET UP B DEVICE TO SET IRQB1 ON
              STAA   $8003          FALL OF CB1, ALLOW INTERRUPT TO IRQB
              LDAA   #$80           GET SIZE OF BUFFER
              STAA   COUNT          SAVE IN WORD TO COUNT INPUTS
              LDX    #BUFFER        GET ADDRESS OF FIRST WORD IN BUFFER
              STX    POINT          SAVE IN WORDS FOR BUFFER POINTER
              LDS    #$3FB          INITIALIZE STACK POINTER
              CLI                   CLEAR INTERRUPT MASK FOR IRQ
              JMP    PROGRM         GO TO USEFUL PROGRAM
PROGRM  BRA    PROGRM         WAIT LOOP TO REPLACE USEFUL PROGRAM

IRQHND  LDAA   $8000          GET DATA
              LDX    POINT          GET POINTER TO BUFFER
              STAA   0,X            PUT IN BUFFER
              INX                   MOVE POINTER
              STX    POINT          SAVE FOR NEXT INPUT
              DEC    COUNT          COUNT OUT INCOMING WORDS
              BNE    IRQHN1         IF BUFFER IS FULL, THEN
              CLR    $8001          PREVENT FURTHER INTERRUPTS
IRQHN1  RTI                   RETURN TO MAIN PROGRAM

XRQHND  LDAA   $8002          CLEAR SOURCE OF INTERRUPT (IRQB1)
* REPORT ERROR TO ATTENDANT
              RTI

              ORG    $FFF2
              FDB    IRQHND
              FDB    XRQHND
              FDB    0              (SWI HANDLER ADDRESS GOES HERE)
              FDB    0              (ILLEGAL OP CODE HAN. ADDR. GOES HERE)
              FDB    0              (COP FAILURE  HAND. ADDRESS GOES HERE)
              FDB    0              (CLOCK FAIL HANDLER ADD. GOES HERE)
              FDB    RSTHND
              END
```

Device A of the M6821 is initialized almost the same way as for the gadfly technique, but bit 0 is also set so that when IRQA1 is asserted, it will assert the IRQA pin (low), which will send the interrupt request to the processor. Also, device B is initialized almost as before, but bit 0 is set to allow assertion of IRQB1 to send an interrupt request. The buffer pointer is initialized to the address of the first word of the buffer, and the counter is initialized to N – the number of words to be input. The stack pointer must be initialized, or you may be trying to save return addresses, registers, and local variables in non-existent memory locations. Note that when power is turned on and RESET is asserted, the microcomputer sets the I condition code, inhibiting IRQ interrupts. At the end of the RESET handler after the I/O devices have been configured as required, the I bit has to be cleared. If this is not done, IRQ interrupts cannot be recognized. If this is done sooner, an interrupt could be generated while an I/O device is being configured. Incidentally, the main program can keep reading the value of COUNT; when it is 0 the buffer is full, and some routine that uses it could be started. The IRQ handler is "called up" in the same way as we showed the TPRDR handler in section 5-2.3 being "called up." If an error ever occurs, the IRQB1 flip-flop is asserted, which makes the XIRQ line drop, which then causes the processor to recognize an XIRQ interrupt, which in turn causes the XIRQ handler to be executed. This informs the attendant that an error has occurred. Note that the source of the XIRQ interrupt is cleared by the XIRQ interrupt handler. The LDAA $8002 instruction clears the IRQB1 flip-flop by means of an address trigger. If this is not done, then the XIRQ line will remain low, and the processor will not recognize any more XIRQ interrupts.

5-3 Fast Synchronization Mechanisms

In the previous section, we discussed the synchronization mechanisms used for slower I/O devices. There are four mechanisms used for faster devices. These are direct memory access, context switching, time-multiplexed memory, and isolated buffer memory. The first two are strongly related and require a processor like the M6809 to implement them. These are discussed in the first subsection. The last two again are strongly related and are described in the last subsection.

5-3.1 Direct Memory Access and Context Switching

This subsection discusses two techniques for I/O synchronization that are faster than interrupts. *Direct memory access* (DMA) is a well-known technique, whereby an I/O device gets access to memory directly without having the microprocessor in between. By this direct path, a word input through a device can be stored in memory, or a word from memory can be output through a device, on the device's request. The second technique, *context switching*, is actually a more general type of DMA. The *context* of a processor is its set of accumulators and other registers (as Texas Instruments uses the term) and the instruction set of the processor. To switch context means to logically disconnect the existing set of registers – bringing in a new set to be used in their place – or to use a different instruction set. In DMA, as we soon see, both the instruction set and the registers are switched. A primitive instruction is used to move the data from or to the I/O device, and a new pair of registers is used to keep track of the moved word's placement in a buffer. These two techniques are now studied. DMA and context switching use mechanisms that are not available on the M6811. The M6809, a close cousin to the M6811, has these mechanisms and will be used in the examples in this subsection.

The fastest way to input data to a buffer is direct memory access. Compared to other techniques, this technique requires considerably more hardware and is considerably faster. It is the best technique for fast I/O, like disks, that require the lowest latency. This technique can be used for input or output. It will be described soon for the input operation, which can be easily applied to the output operation. In DMA, a word is moved from the device to a memory in a *DMA transfer cycle*. Successive words moved this way are put into a buffer. Two DMA techniques are available for the M6800 microcomputer. If an I/O system wishes to input data, it *steals a memory cycle* to transfer 1 word or it *halts the microprocessor* to transfer one or more words. First, the cycle steal technique is described, then the halt technique will be discussed.

In the cycle steal technique, the device requests to transfer a newly read word into memory. The microprocessor may be in the middle of an operation; so it simply stops what it is doing for one memory cycle and *releases control* of the address and data bus to its memory by disabling the tristate drivers in it that drive these busses. The I/O system is then expected to use this memory cycle to transfer the word from its input register to a memory location. The cycle steal technique can transfer 1 word with latency time of around 3 microseconds (because of delays in handling the DMA request signals), but can transfer only 1 word before the processor resumes its operation. The processor is usually in the middle of an operation, with data stored in dynamic logic registers (as charges on capacitors), so if the processor doesn't keep moving, these temporary variables will become lost as the charges decay. In this mode, the device can only steal a cycle, then give the processor a cycle, and so on.

Another technique, the halt DMA, uses the same principle the interrupt technique uses. When a device wants to output a word to be stored in memory, it requests that the processor finish its current instruction – when all data are in user visible registers which are not dynamic – and then release control of the address and data bus so the I/O device can use them to store the word in memory. This technique permits the device to transmit as many words as it wants in successive memory cycles, because the microprocessor will not lose any data while the transfer is going on. It permits the greatest throughput, but the latency can be around 20 microseconds because the instruction that was being executed when the request was made must be completed.

Intended for transferring buffers of data, DMA requires an *address register* to supply the memory address where the data are to be written. This address is incremented after a word is moved so the next input word will be written in the next location. Also, as a number of words are to be moved, a *counter* is needed to keep track of how many words remain to be moved. As each word is moved, this counter is decremented. Finally, DMA requires a busy-done mechanism, which can be tested by an interrupt mechanism or a gadfly loop, to inform the computer when the entire block of words has been entered. An IDLE state indicates that no DMA activity is in progress, a BUSY state indicates that a word will be transferred whenever the device needs it, and a DONE state indicates that all words in the buffer have been transferred. To use DMA, the program must initialize the address register to the address where the first input word will be stored and must initialize the counter to the number of words that will be moved. The interrupt handler must be prepared to recognize the interrupt when all words are transferred and to jump to an appropriate device handler that will supply the operations needed when all words have been transferred; a gadfly loop could also be used to monitor the busy-done state of the DMA system. DMA requires extra hardware – an address register, a counter, and a busy-done mechanism – but permits data to be moved at a rate of one data word per memory cycle from an input device to memory.

Microcomputers implement direct memory access by means of a *direct memory access controller* (DMAC) chip. This, together with another I/O chip like the M6821, can implement a *DMA device.* Together the two chips can act like another microprocessor: the DMAC chip sending a read or write command on R/W and addresses on the address bus, and the other chip sending the data when the DMAC chip sends the address.

To show how DMA works, we will introduce a simplified M6844 direct memory access controller. The chip itself has four complete DMAC modules in it that can implement up to four separate DMA I/O systems, and each has a plethora of modes and features, which the reader is invited to study by reading the data sheet and the applications notes on the chip. Furthermore, to get all this flexibility, the designers used and reused the chip's 40 pins to such an extent that is a great example of why we are running out of pins to interconnect these large ICs. For our purposes, one of the simpler modes is just what we need to make our discussion of DMA concrete. This is all we will discuss.

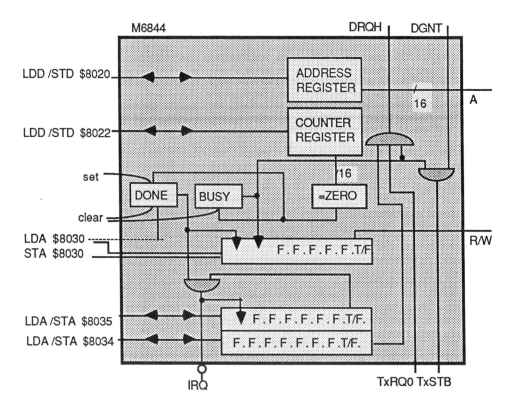

Figure 5-11. Simplified Block Diagram of the M6844

We will rework our good old paper tape reader example to show how DMA works. DMA should only be used when very low latency is required, such as for disk output or CRT input. However, to be consistent, we will illustrate its use with the slow paper tape reader. The computer for this example has some random access memory, an M6821 device A connected to a paper tape reader, with data/direction register at $8000 and control register at $8001, and an M6844 which is described soon. We introduce the M6844 first and discuss its registers and its signals to and from the I/O chip (M6821) and the microprocessor chip. Next we show all the chips and the interconnections needed to make a practical DMA system. Finally, we exhibit a simple program to read patterns from paper tape into a buffer – the same end our previous examples have accomplished.

On turning power on, the RESET signal clears all registers; this configures the M6844 for the mode we will use: with the halt mode, transferring each word, 1 word at a time, as it is input from the paper tape reader into a buffer, as in our previous examples, and incrementing the address each time a word is put in the buffer. (See figure 5-11.) (Other modes can be selected by making some of the bits true in the registers shown in figure 5-11. For one of the problems at the end of this chapter, we note that the DMAC will request a read command if the least significant bit of $8030 is false and will request a write command to memory if that bit is true.)

To transfer 128 words from the input device (the paper tape reader) to a buffer, the DMA controller is initialized in this way. The program loads the address of the first word of the buffer into the ADDRESS REGISTER and loads the number N of words to be moved into the COUNTER REGISTER. The DONE and BUSY flip-flops indicate the state of the DMA transfer; IDLE is FF, BUSY is FT, and DONE is TF. When reset, the M6844 is put into the IDLE state, of course. The program starts the DMA by setting the least significant bit of the register in location $8034, and the M6844 enters the BUSY state as transfers begin. After 128 words have been transferred, the controller enters the DONE state. This state indicates that the buffer is available to be used.

The DMA transfer takes place in the following manner. When in the busy state, if the I/O device asserts the TxRQ0 line, then the DRQH line is asserted by the DMAC. This line tells the microprocessor that it should halt to permit the DMA operation. When the processor finishes its instruction, it asserts the DGNT line. This in turn causes the M6844 to assert the TxSTB line which indicates that the device should read out a word on the data bus at that time. Meanwhile, the M6844 controls the address bus and the R/W line. It sends out the address and instructs memory to write the data at the address. It then decrements the COUNTER REGISTER and increments the ADDRESS REGISTER. If the counter reaches 0, BUSY is cleared and DONE is set, as the DMA operation is completed and the DONE state is entered. Register $8030 exhibits the busy-done state. It can be checked in a gadfly loop. The least significant bit of the register at location $8035 is ANDed with the DONE signal, and this result is available in the most significant bit of this same register, as well as being sent out the IRQ pin (in negative logic). This signal can be used to request an interrupt.

The M6844 can be connected to an M6809, an M6821 and some random access memory, as shown in figure 5-12. The M6844 has – just as any other I/O chip has – data bus connections and register select address lines, and an R/W and a chip enable so the processor can write or read the registers. It can also drive the R/W line and all the address bus lines when it commands a DMA transfer. An address decoder, labeled "A," asserts its output, when an address between $8000 and $8003 is presented, to enable the M6821, and an address decoder labeled "B" asserts its output when an address between $8020 and $803F is presented, to enable the M6844 to read or write in its registers. The M6809 has two lines to receive requests from the M6844 and issue grants. The (negative logic) HALT line is a request to halt the computer. When the computer is using the bus, the bus available (BA) signal is false, but when the processor is halted and the tristate drivers within it are disabled, the BA signal is asserted. These two lines are attached, the HALT line to the (negative logic) DRQH pin and the BA line to the DGNT pin, to the M6844.

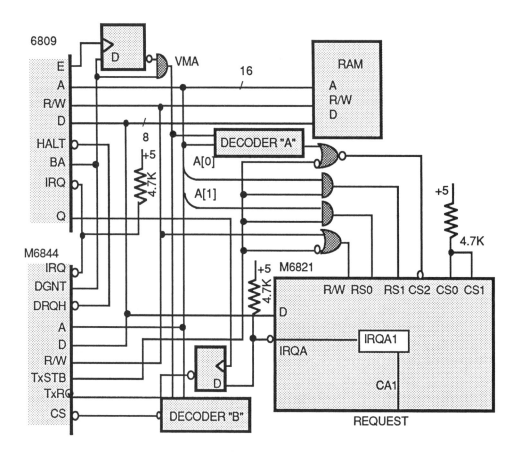

Figure 5-12. Interconnections for DMA

The interrupt mechanism in the M6821 can be used to generate DMA requests. A request will be made by a falling edge on the CA1 line, much as in the earlier examples. This sets IRQA1, which asserts IRQA (low), as if to request an interrupt. But the IRQA output of the M6821 is connected to the TxRQ input. (Some minor points are noted about the D flip-flop between them. The TxRQ input has an interval around the rising edge of the E clock where an indeterminate signal will actually cause it and the M6809 to freeze up completely. It is necessary to maintain a stable signal at this time.

Therefore a D edge-triggered flip-flop, clocked on the rising edge of the Q clock, is used. Moreover, an inversion of the logic levels is needed, and this can be obtained by taking the negative logic Q output from the flip-flop.) Asserting TxRQ will assert DRQH and HALT. When the processor completes its current instruction, it asserts BA which is DGNT, and this asserts TxSTB. TxSTB is asserted in the memory cycle when the M6844 puts the address on the address bus and sends a write command on the R/W line. A trick is played on the M6821. When TxSTB is asserted, it is forced to read out the data in the device A data register. Note that reading the data register also clears IRQA, which negates IRQ (TxRQ), which in turn negates DRQH (HALT), which then effectively cancels the request until another is made by a falling signal on the CA1 line.

We now study this trick that is played on the M6821. Since this chip also has to be written in and read from in the usual way so the processor can initialize its control registers, this trick is played by some gates, which normally let the address decoder respond to processor addresses, but when TxSTB is asserted, the register select, chip select, and R/W lines are switched to make the chip read the data register.

Finally, we look at a program to move words from the paper tape reader to a buffer. The M6809 instruction LDA is the same as the M6811 instruction LDAA, and STA is the same as STAA.

```
        NAM     DMASET
        LDA     #25             CONFIGURE M6821 TO ASSERT IRQA
        STA     $8001           ON FALL OF CA1, USE CA2 IN HANDSHAKE
        LDX     #BUFFER         GET ADDRESS OF FIRST WORD IN BUFFER
        STX     $8020           PUT IN M6844 ADDRESS REGISTER
        LDX     #$80            GET SIZE OF BUFFER
        STX     $8022           PUT IN COUNTER REGISTER
        INC     $8034           PUT M6844 INTO BUSY STATE
L       LDA     $8030           EXAMINE STATE
        BPL     L               LOOP UNTIL DONE
        END
```

The program is quite simple, because the hardware in the M6844 is doing most of the work. The first two lines configure the M6821 as usual, to let the device inform the M6821 when a new word is input by dropping CA1. The next four lines set up the address and count registers. Notice how similar this is to our previous examples. Then the least significant bit of the register at location $8034 is set by incrementing that word, thus starting the DMA operation. Then a gadfly loop is executed to wait for the DONE state. When this loop is left, the buffer is full and ready to be used.

This sequence of events happens when a DMA request is made:

1. As in an interrupt request, an external request is recognized by the IRQA1 flip-flop, which requests an "interrupt" by asserting IRQA low. This makes TxRQ high.
2. If TxRQ is high and the least significant bit of location $8034 is high and the DMA controller is in the busy state, then it asserts DRQH low. This asserts the M6809 HALT signal low.

3. If the HALT is asserted in the M6809, then, at the end of the current instruction, the M6809 disables its tristate drivers on the R/W line and address and data bus lines, and asserts the bus available signal BA. This asserts the M6844 grant signal DGNT.
4. If the DGNT signal is asserted and the M6844 is busy, it asserts TxSTB low. This signal in the M6821 address decoder causes the M6821 to receive the signals that would be appropriate for reading data register A onto the data bus.
5. When the M6821 reads the data register, an address trigger clears IRQA1. This negates TxRQ, which negates HALT, which permits the M6809 to resume execution of the next instruction.

An interrupt could be used to indicate that the buffer is full, if the processor can do some useful work while the buffer is being filled. The IRQ output of the M6844 is connected to the IRQ bus, and the least significant bit of location $8035 is set. When the M6844 is done, it will generate an interrupt. The IRQ handler should check word $8035 in exactly the same way it checked word $8001 in the example of a polling IRQ handler; it should branch to the M6844 handler if bits 0 and 7 are H and bit 1 is L.

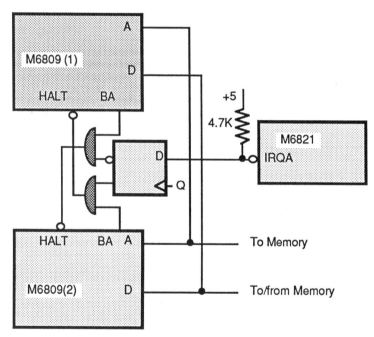

Figure 5-13. Connections for Context Switching

An interesting variation to DMA, uniquely attractive because it is inexpensive, is to use two or more microprocessors on the same address and data bus. One runs the main program. This one stops when a device requests service, as if a DMA request were being honored, and another microprocessor starts. When the first stops, it releases control over the address and data busses, which are common to all the microprocessors and to memory and I/O, so the second can use them. The second microprocessor, which then can execute the device handler is started more quickly because the registers in the first are saved merely by freezing them in place rather than saving them on a stack. The registers in the second could already contain the values needed by the device handler, so they would not need to be initialized. DMA using a DMA chip is restricted to just inputting a word into, or outputting a word from, a buffer, whereas the second microprocessor can execute any software routine after obtaining direct memory access from the first microprocessor.

In the following example, a processor can read the word, i, from the input register and then increment the ith word in memory, thus collecting statistics on the occurrence of the value i. This processor is turned on when a new number i is presented at an input port, $0 < i < 256$, and we will assume that, at most, 256 occurrences of any i will ever be counted.

Suppose that two M6809s are connected to the same address and data busses, and an M6821 is connected to be addressed at location $8000 to $8003, with its IRQA output connected as shown in figure 5-13. Note that when power is applied, IRQA is high. This causes the top processor to run, while the bottom one thinks a DMA is going on because its HALT line is low. (Note also the need for an edge-triggered flip-flop to prevent the HALT lines from changing around the time when the E clock rises. The same problem occurred in the DMA system and is handled in the same way here. If this is not done, the M6809s will stop running because they get an indeterminate signal on their HALT input when they sample it.)

We will first consider the response to an input i, and then we will study the technique used to initialize the second processor - M6809(2) - to respond in that way. Assume that the index register X of the M6809(2) points to the beginning of the buffer and that the M6821 is configured to work in the handshake mode. When the CA1 line drops, the bottom processor executes the following program. It reads i from the data register, and increments the ith word in the buffer. This collects statistics on the occurrence of different numbers that appear on the input register when an interrupt is requested. It is easy to do with context switching, while ordinary DMA cannot do this operation, and is quite a bit faster than ordinary interrupt synchronization because, not only are the registers not saved, but also they remain in the second M6809, so they usually don't have to be initialized.

```
      NAM   STATS
L     LDB   $8000        GET I FROM M6821
      LDX   #BUFFER
      ABX
      INC   0,X          INCREMENT BUFFER(I)
      BRA   L            LOOP
      END
```

Curiously, the second processor will read the data in the first line, which will clear IRQA1, which will then turn off the second processor and turn on the first one. When the next input is obtained, however, the second processor will resume its operation, incrementing the buffer word corresponding to the previous input, then reading the current input and halting. But this shows how the context is switched and how this permits a synchronization method almost as fast as DMA yet almost as flexible as the interrupt mode.

To get the second processor to act this way, it must be initialized when the power is applied. To initialize both processors, the following reset handler can be used:

```
LDX     #BUFFER     IN (2), SET X TO POINT TO BUFFER
TST     $8001       CHECK IF YOU ARE (2)
BMI     L           IF SO, GO TO PROGRAM STATS
LDA     #$05        OTHERWISE YOU ARE (1) SO PERFORM
STA     $8001       STANDARD RESET HANDLER FUNCTIONS
LDS     #STKP       SETTING UP STACK ETC.
...                 THEN GO TO MAIN PROGRAM
```

When power is applied, the main processor M6809(1) executes the routine first. Loading its X register does not hurt, since it will be loaded again before it will be used. Then the M6821 control register is tested. At this time, since the RESET line has just cleared it, it will be 0. Hence the branch is not taken, and the control register is initialized for handshaking so that IRQA becomes a high output. The main program is entered after the reset handler is executed. One thing done here is a copy is made of the program for processor M6809(2) in RAM so it will be there when some data arrive. When the first number i is presented, IRQA becomes low, which requests the M6809(1) to halt. After it has completed its current instruction, the M6809(2) is allowed to proceed. The M6809(2) has not yet gone through its reset sequence, so it must do that first. In executing the reset handler, it will load the X register as required. Testing the M6821 control register, it will then enter the program described earlier.

Finally, any set of microcomputers having DMA capability can be used in this manner; the one operating the main program need not be the same model as the one handling a device. This means you can put a new microprocessor in your old microcomputer. The old microprocessor is turned on to run programs left over from earlier days, and the new microprocessor is turned on to execute the new and better programs. This is an alternative to simulation or emulation in microprogramming. It is better because the best machine to emulate itself is usually itself. And putting two microprocessors in the same microcomputer hardly has an impact on the whole system's cost.

Though this technique is rarely used by designers because they are not familiar with it, it is useful for microcomputers because the added cost for a microprocessor is so small and the speed and flexibility gained are the equivalent of somewhere between those attained by true DMA and vectored interrupt, a quality that is often just what is required.

5-3.2 Isolated Buffer Memories and Time-Multiplexed Memories

The last techniques we will consider that synchronize fast I/O devices involve their use of memory, which is not restricted by conflicts with the microprocessor. One technique uses a completely separate and possibly faster memory, called an *isolated buffer memory.* The other uses the same memory as the microprocessor, but this memory is fast and can be *time multiplexed* which means that the processor gets one time slice, then the I/O device gets one time slice, in an endless cycle. (These are shown in figure 5-14.) In a sense, these techniques solve the synchronization problem by avoiding it, by decoupling the processor from the I/O with a memory.

Figure 5-14a shows an isolated memory buffer. The multiplexor takes the 16 address lines that go into the isolated buffer and the 8 data lines that go to or from the buffer and switches them between the microprocessor and the I/O device. The I/O device has total and unrestricted use of the isolated memory buffer when I/O operations take place, assuming the microprocessor does not use the isolated buffer memory then. The multiplexor switches are both in the lower position at that time. The microprocessor can access its primary memory and I/O at this time because they are separate from the isolated buffer memory used by the I/O device. Then when the microprocessor wishes to get the data in the isolated buffer memory, the multiplexor switches are in the upper position, and the microprocessor has access to the isolated memory just as it has to its own primary memory. It can load and store data with LDAA and STAA instructions. The synchronization problem is solved by avoiding it. Data is moved to and from the I/O device from and to the isolated memory, which requires synchronization, but the buffer memory is wholly controlled by the I/O device, so synchronization is not too difficult. The processor can move data to and from the isolated buffer memory at leisure. It can even tolerate the delays that result from handling an interrupt at any time.

A variation of an isolated buffer memory uses a parallel I/O device like an M6821 in place of the multiplexor. The processor writes an address to a parallel output port and then reads (or writes) the data to (or from) another port to access the memory. The isolated memory is separate from the microprocessor primary memory, and only the memory-mapped parallel I/O device takes up memory space in the primary memory. The technique described in the previous paragraph has the whole isolated buffer memory in the primary memory address space when the processor accesses it.

A very similar mechanism uses the same memory for the primary memory and the buffer memory, but that memory is twice as fast as is necessary for the processor. (See figure 5-14b.) In one processor cycle (E clock) the memory executes two memory cycles, one for the processor and one for the I/O device. The multiplexor is switched to the I/O device (when the E clock is low) and to the processor (when the E clock is high) to time-multiplex the memory. The I/O device always gets one memory cycle all to itself because the processor only uses the other memory cycle.

The time-multiplexed memory is obviously less costly than the isolated memory buffer because a single large memory is used rather than two smaller memories. Its operation is very similar to DMA. In fact, it is sometimes called *transparent DMA*. However, the memory must be twice as fast as the processor, and the I/O device must synchronize to the processor (E) clock in this technique. The isolated buffer memory is more costly, but a very fast (40-nanosecond cycle time) memory can be used in the buffer and run at full speed when the I/O device accesses it, but run at the speed of the E clock when the processor accesses it. Both techniques provide for faster synchronization to the I/O device than the techniques discussed in the previous subsection. They can transfer data on every memory cycle, without handshaking with the processor to acquire memory or to use the processor. They find considerable use in CRT, hard disk, and fast communication I/O devices.

Section 5-3   Fast Synchronization Mechanisms   243

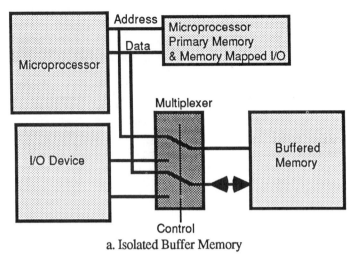

a. Isolated Buffer Memory

b. Time Multiplexed Memory

Figure 5-14. Fast Synchronization Mechanisms using Memory Organizations

5-4 M6811 Reset and Interrupt Features

The M6811 has some features that are generally related to interrupts or the reset handler. We did not want to interrupt our sequence of eight synchronization techniques, even though we are in fact discussing interrupts. But the notions in this section should be placed soon after the discussion of interrupts because they are so strongly related. We discuss the interrupt-related instructions in the first subsection. Then we examine the initialization configurations of the M6811 which are generally set up by a ritual in the reset handler.

5-4.1 The WAI, STOP, SWI, and Illegal Instructions Revisited

The 6811 has two instructions, WAI and STOP, that are used to manage interrupts. Though we introduced these in chapter 1, we postponed a serious discussion of them until now, because they are strongly related to interrupts. WAI is an improved kind of wait loop, and STOP can be a fast gadfly loop. We also have the SWI instruction and illegal instructions; these are considered again now that interrupts have been studied.

WAI waits for an interrupt, rather like the infinite wait loop in section 5-3.3. Once the WAI instruction is executed, the 6811 goes to "sleep," to be "awakened" by a reset or by an IRQ or XIRQ interrupt. This is like an infinite wait loop executed in microcode. However, WAI is optimized to reduce latency time. As soon as WAI is executed, it pushes all the registers on the stack as if honoring an interrupt. When an interrupt occurs, it does not have to save the registers. If you looked at a logic analyzer at the time an external interrupt was requested, as we did for the single interrupt example in section 5-3.3, you would see null cycles before the interrupt was recognized by the M6811, then you would see the address being read from locations $FFF2 and $FFF3, and then another null cycle, after which the first instruction in the handler would be executed. WAI can be used to reduce the latency to about five memory cycles. You could use WAI in place of infinite wait loops like L BRA L in the previous examples.

WAI stops everything except the crystal oscillator that runs the E clock. Although the MC68HC11A8 requires only 20 milliamperes of 5-volt supply current, WAI reduces this to 4 milliamperes (if the serial interfaces SCI, SPI and timer are not running). Another instruction, STOP, does stop the oscillator, as well as the entire microcomputer, reducing the supply current to a miserly 300 microamperes. Obviously, interrupts from the serial interfaces and timer cannot restart the processor because they too are turned off, but an external reset or IRQ or XIRQ signal can restart the processor. However, after STOP, about 2 milliseconds are needed for the oscillator to restart so the processor can resume the next operation. (A reset handler option, discussed in the next section, can reduce this to four E clock cycles, but only if an external stable clock source is used rather than a crystal powered by the MC68HC11A8.)

STOP can be used to synchronize to an external signal on the XIRQ bus lines when X is set. Setting the mask bit prevents the XIRQ interrupt from being recognized and honored by the M6811. When the XIRQ line is asserted low, the instruction following the STOP instruction is executed. The registers are not saved on the stack, and the XIRQ interrupt handler is not executed. If an external oscillator is used so the delay in restarting is only four memory cycles, STOP is, in effect, an optimized gadfly loop

The SWI instruction has been discussed in chapter 1. We note here that the interrupt mask bit I in the condition code register is set by the SWI instruction exactly as if a hardware interrupt occurred as a result of a signal on the IRQ or XIRQ lines.

A number of opcodes are not implemented in the 6811 instruction set. To catch bugs in programs, these unimplemented instructions result in an SWI-like operation, jumping to the location specified in $FFF8 and $FFF9.

5-4.2 M6811 System Control and EEPROM Programming

The M6811 has control registers like an I/O device. There are rituals to configure the M6811 in two stages: 1. There are variables that can be selected just after power-up and may be chosen in the reset handler. Using an I/O register lock, these variables must be set in the first 64 memory cycles after reset, or they become read-only bits. 2. There are variables in electrically erasable programmable read-only memory (EEPROM) that can be written to be used by hardware upon reset before the reset handler is executed. They involve the registers shown in figure 5-15. The CONFIG register at $3F in the I/O register area is an EEPROM word.

We digress for a moment to describe the programming of EEPROM words, including the CONFIG register. This register and the 512-byte memory from $B600 to $B7FF are in EEPROM. Though they can be read in one E cycle, they require 10 milliseconds to be written in. They can be written in or erased by writing bit patterns into the PPROG register at $3B in the I/O register area. Four modes of erasure or writing into these EEPROM words are 1. full EEPROM erase, 2. 32-byte erase, 3. 1-byte erase and 4. n-byte write. The CONFIG register may be written into in mode 1. For mode 2, the EEPROM memory is organized into *rows* of 32 bytes, where all the addresses of words in a row have the same high-order 11 bits. The bit patterns written into the PPROG register have meaning as follows (if the bit is T): ODD and EVEN are used in mode 2 to signify an odd-numbered or even-numbered row, BYTE indicates erasing or writing a word at a time, ROW indicates erasing a row at a time, ERASE indicates erasing, EELAT latches the next address and data that appear after this bit is set for programming or erasing, and EEPGM applies the programming voltage. For normal reading of EEPROM words, the pattern in the PPROG register must have the 2 least significant bits FF.

These modes of erasing or writing into the EEPROM are described as C programs, shown here:

```
full_erase(configuration) char configuration;
{
    char *config, *pprog; /* configuration register, prom programming register */
    char *eeprom; /* any word in EEPROM */
    int i,dummy;
    *pprog = 6; /* select "all" erasure, latch next address and data for program. */
    *eeprom = dummy; /* put anything into any word of the EEPROM */
    *config = configuration; /* optional step: to chng CONFIG, write its value */
    *pprog = 7; /* turn on erasure voltage */
    for(i=0; i<T10ms; i++); /* wait 10 milliseconds */
    *pprog = 6; /* turn off erasure voltage */
    *pprog = 0; /*return to normal read mode */
}

row_erase(eeprom) char *eeprom; /* *eprom is an add of a wd in rw to be erased */
{
    char *pprog; /* prom programming register */
```

```
      int i,dummy;
      *pprog = 0xe; /* specify "row" er., latch next add. and data for programming */
      *eeprom =dummy; /* put anything to any wd of rw of EEPROM to be er. */
      *pprog = oxf; /* turn on erasure voltage */
      for(i=0; i<T10ms; i++); /* wait 10 milliseconds */
      *pprog = 0xe; /* turn off erasure voltage */
      *pprog = 0; /*return to normal read mode */
}


word_erase(eeprom) char *eeprom; /*eeprom is an addr. of the word to be erased */
{
   char *pprog; /* prom programming register */
   int i,dummy;
   *pprog = 0x16; /* specify "word" erasure, latch next addr. and data for prog. */
   *eeprom = dummy; /* put anything into the wd of the EEPROM to be erased*/
   *pprog = ox17; /* turn on erasure voltage */
   for(i=0; i<T10ms; i++); /* wait 10 milliseconds */
   *pprog = 0x16; /* turn off erasure voltage */
   *pprog = 0; /*return to normal read mode */
}


word_write(eeprom,data) char *eeprom,data; /* write data into the address eeprom */
{
   char *pprog; /* prom programming register */
   int i,dummy;
   *pprog = 2; /* specify "word" erasure, latch next addr. and data for programming */
   *eeprom = data; /* put data into the word of the EEPROM to be programmed */
   *pprog = 3; /* turn on erasure voltage */
   for(i=0; i<T10ms; i++); /* wait 10 milliseconds */
   *pprog = 2; /* turn off erasure voltage */
   *pprog = 0; /*return to normal read mode */
}
```

These programs are all very similar: they specify the mode, latch the address and data, apply the programming voltage, wait 10 milliseconds, remove the programming voltage, and then clear the PPROG register to permit normal reads from the EEPROM words. The last program can write multiple bytes by repeating steps 2 (*eeprom = data;*) to 5 (*pprog = 2;*) for each word to be programmed.

The CONFIG register specifies options that are used upon reset. These options must be put in an EEPROM register to be defined before the first instruction is executed, and changing the bits in the CONFIG register affects subsequent reset configurations until CONFIG is written into again. The NSEC bit, if T, enables the use of expanded multiplexed mode and, if F, disables this mode so only the single-chip mode can be used; it can be used to provide security for a program written in ROM or EEPROM so a software thief cannot read the program in expanded multiplexed bus mode. (Trying to use the special bootstrap mode to get around this security mechanism results in erasing EEPROM and RAM, but ROM can be read this way.) A computer operating properly (COP) circuit, described in the next paragraph, can be used to check programs to see if they are not behaving as expected – perhaps because they "got lost." The NCOP bit, if T, disables the COP feature and if F, enables this feature. Finally, the ROM and EE bits, if T, enable the ROM memory and EEPROM memory to be read from, and if F, these memories disappear from the memory map and their addressed memory areas are availalable for external use in the expanded multiplexed bus mode.

The OPTION register can only be changed in the first 64 E clock cycles after reset. The IRQE bit determines whether the IRQ line will be treated as a level-sensitive IRQ signal (as discussed in 5-2.2) if F, or a non-maskable interrupt (discussed in 5-3.1) if T. DLY determines whether a 4064 E clock delay will be used after STOP, if T, or a 4 E clock delay will be used, if F. The longer delay is mandatory if the MC68HC11A8 powers a crystal oscillator on its XTAL and EXTAL pins, because time is needed for the oscillator to stabilize; but very little delay is needed if an external circuit provides a square wave to the EXTAL pin. CME enables, if T, the clock monitor. If the E clock rate drops below about 200 KHz and CME is T, a routine is executed whose interrupt vector is at $FFFC, $FFFD. This feature can be used to detect an imminent failure, if the clock rate is normally faster than 200 KHz and the handler can shut down the system in a reasonable way, possibly saving critical data in EEPROM.

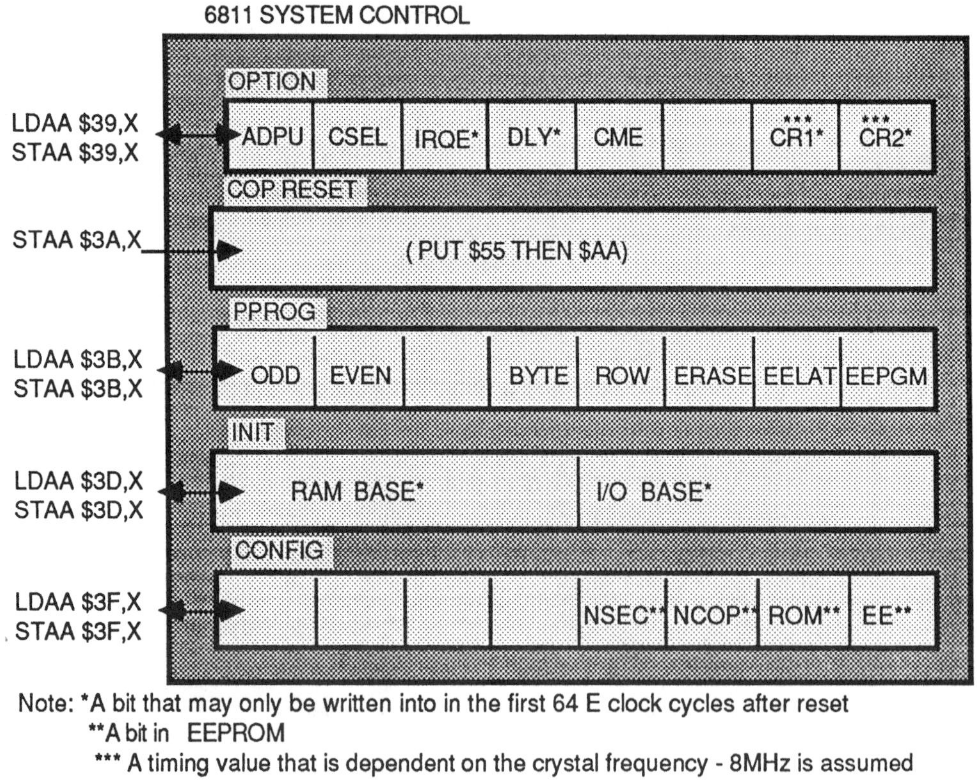

6811 SYSTEM CONTROL

Note: *A bit that may only be written into the first 64 E clock cycles after reset
**A bit in EEPROM
*** A timing value that is dependent on the crystal frequency - 8MHz is assumed

Figure 5-15. M6811 System Control Registers

The COP circuit is a timer that must be attended to periodically in properly running software, and if it is not attended to (because the program has gone astray), it causes an interrupt. CR1 and CR2 determine the rate at which the COP circuit must be attended to: if they are FF, then every 16,384 microseconds; if FT, then every 65.54 milliseconds; if TF, then every 262 milliseconds; and if TT, then every 1.05 seconds (for an 8 MHz crystal). The COP is attended to by writing $55, followed by $AA, to the COP RESET register. If the COP is not attended to in the specified time, then a handler at $FFFA, $FFFB is entered. The handler can attempt to restart the program that "got lost."

We finally discuss the INIT register. The two nibbles in it establish the high-order nibbles of the RAM and of the I/O registers. For example, if $01 is put in this register (as it is upon reset), then RAM is at addresses 0 to $00FF, and I/O and system configuration registers are at addresses $1000 to $103F. The reset handler can move the RAM and I/O to any location (on a 4-Kbyte boundary specified by the high-order nibble of the address) by writing any value in this register. For example, you may want more contiguous memory available externally if you have a 64Kbyte RAM memory on the external multiplexed bus; so, to move the I/O to $D000 but leave RAM at low memory, write $0D into INIT. If you wish to use page 0 addressing to access I/O, interchange the RAM and I/O areas in memory by writing $10 into INIT. The programming of this register in the reset handler permits you to alter the memory map to suit your needs.

5-5 Conclusions

We have discussed eight alternatives for solving the synchronization problem. Each has some advantages and some disadvantages.

Real-time synchronization uses the least hardware and is practical if an inexpensive microcomputer has nothing to do but time out an I/O operation. However, it can be difficult to program. Gadfly programs are easier to write, but require that the hardware provide an indication of the DONE state. Also, a computer cannot do anything else when it is in a gadfly loop, so this is as inefficient as real-time synchronization.

The interrupt-polling technique and the vectored interrupt technique require more hardware to request service from the processor. They are useful when the device needs service in a shorter time. However, the tendency to use them just because they are available should be avoided. Except when the processor has enough interrupt request lines to handle all interrupts, to provide the device handler's address, vectored interrupt may require an extra chip, which is a significant cost. Although interrupt-polling only requires a bus line from device to processor, if the gadfly approach is exclusively used, this line invites the mayhem of an unrecognizable interrupt if a software error rewrites the control register in the device. Also, the interrupt technique can be used together with the gadfly technique. With the gadfly technique, the interrupts are all disabled by setting the I condition code, as in the SEI instruction, or by clearing control bit 0 in the M6821 device. Then the program can loop as it tests the device, without fear of being pulled out by an interrupt. Commonly, gadfly is used for careful, individual stepping of an I/O system, and interrupt is useful for automatic and rapid feeding of the data.

The DMA technique is useful for fast devices that require low latency. This technique can only store data in a buffer or read data from a buffer. A variation of it, context switching, is almost as fast and flexible as the interrupt technique. Isolated memories and time-multiplexed memories can be used for the fastest devices.

With these various techniques, the designer has the opportunity to pick one that suits the application. This chapter has shown how simple and flexible these techniques are.

The option and configuration registers in the 68HC11 are critical features designed for the automotive industry, which requires very high reliability in drastically different and extreme environments. These features are attractive in many process control systems.

For more concrete information on the 68HC11, please consult the *MC68HC11A8 HCMOS Single-chip Microcomputer (ADI 1207)*. In particular, Section 3 describes interrupts, Section 2.4.4 discusses the procedures to program EEPROM, and sections 2.4.7, 4.2, 4.3, and 9 describe the OPTION and CONFIGURATION registers. As noted earlier, we have not attempted to duplicate the diagrams and discussions in that book because we assume you will refer to it while reading this book; we also present an alternative view of the subject, so you can use either or both views.

Problems

Problems 1, 9, 13, and 21 are paragraph correction problems; for guidelines, refer to the problems at the end of chapter 1. Guidelines for software problems are given at the end of chapter 2, and guidelines for hardware problems, at the end of chapter 3.

1.* Synchronization is used to coordinate a computer to an input-output device. The device has busy, completion, and done states. The busy state is when data can be given to it or taken from it. The device puts itself into the done state when it has completed the action requested by the computer. A paper tape punch, by analogy to the paper tape reader, is in the idle state when it is not in use; in the busy state when it is punching a pattern that corresponds to the word that was output just before the done state was entered; and in the done state when the pattern has been punched. The busy and idle states are indistinguishable in an output device like this one, unless error conditions are to be recognized (in the idle state). An address trigger will generate a pulse whenever an address is generated. Its output should never be asserted if valid memory address (VMA) is false, nor when the E clock is high. Address triggers are often used to start a device or to indicate completion by the device.

2. Design an address trigger that asserts its output (low) only when the location $3F0A is read from.
    a. Show the logic diagram.
    b. Indicate the timing of the output (as on an oscilloscope trace) if an instruction INC $3F0A is executed. Show the signal for the complete execution of the instruction, and show timing marks indicating the beginning of each memory cycle (which is 1 microsecond per memory cycle).

3. A 74HC74 dual D flip-flop is to store the busy-done states of a device. Show a logic diagram, including address triggers, that will start the device if address $5A31 is presented, stop it if address $4D21 is presented, and enter the done state if an input signal CMPLT rises from low to high. Assume that idle is FF, busy is TF, and done is coded as FT. (Hint: use CMPLT as a shift register clock to change the state from busy to done.)

4. Show the initialization ritual to configure an M6821 at locations $8000 (data/direction) and $8001 (control) so the data register is an input register for the following cases:
    a. IRQA1 is set when CA1 rises, CA2 outputs a low signal, and IRQA is never asserted.
    b. IRQA1 is set when CA1 rises, IRQA2 is set when CA2 falls, and IRQA is asserted only when IRQA1 is set.
    c. IRQA1 is set when CA1 falls, IRQA2 is set when CA2 rises, and IRQA is asserted when either IRQA1 or IRQA2 are set.

d. IRQA1 is set when CA1 rises, CA2 pulses low when location $8000 is read, and IRQA is asserted when IRQA1 is set.

e. IRQA1 is set when CA1 falls, CA2 falls when CA1 falls and rises when $8000 is read, and IRQA is never asserted.

5. Show the initialization ritual to configure MC68HC11A8 ports B and C, assuming the I/O registers are at $1000 to $103F, for the following cases:

a. Port B is strobed output (writing puts negative pulse on STRB); port C is strobed input (strobed register C loaded on rising edge of STRA) and has open drain outputs and no interrupts.

b. Port C is full handshake input (strobed port C loaded on falling edge of STRA, STRB is pulsed high when STROBED C is read), port C outputs are tristate, and there are no interrupts.

c. Port C is full handshake output (falling edge of STRA indicates the external device has taken data from port C, STRB is low after port C is written into, high after STRA is pulsed), port C outputs are tristate, and there are no interrupts.

6. Note that the M6821 sets its IRQA1 input on a rising or falling edge of the CA1 input, rather than a level. Design an input device, using the A device in an M6821, that will cause an interrupt on a high-level signal and another that will cause an interrupt on a low-level signal. For each case, show the logic diagram and an initialization ritual that will set IRQA1 if that high- or low-level signal appears.

7. Repeat problem 6 for the MC68HC11A8 in full handshake input. Replace CA1 with the STRA input, device A on the 6821 with port C, and IRQA1 with STAF.

8. Suppose IRQB is connected to a pull-up resistor and channel 1 of a dual-trace oscilloscope, while CB2 is connected to channel 2. Show an oscilloscope trace of the signals that will appear after CB1 causes IRQB1 to be set, assuming the B device is configured as an output device in the handshake mode, as the following program segment is executed (be accurate to within a memory cycle, and show each instruction execution interval next to your traces):

```
LDX     POINT
LDAA    0,X
STAA    $8002
INX             CB1 RISES RIGHT AFTER HERE
STX     POINT
LDAA    $8002
```

9.* The real-time synchronization technique times the duration of external actions using the microcomputer E clock as a timing reference and the program counter as a kind of frequency divider. This technique uses the least amount of hardware, because the program itself contains segments that keep account of the busy-done state of the device. It is easy to program and to change a program without upsetting the synchronization, because program segments execute in the same time regardless of the instructions in the segment. Computer scientists, for no good reason, abhor real-time synchronization, so it should never be used, even on a microcomputer dedicated to a single control function. Real-time synchronization cannot be used to synchronize error conditions, because we cannot predict the time until the next error. That's why the program REAL (section 5-2.1) didn't include an error handler. Gadfly synchronization requires the hardware to keep track of the state of a device, and the program watches the outputs from this hardware. It is therefore possible to use feedback from the device so that an I/O operation can be completed as soon as possible. Nevertheless, real-time synchronization is always faster than gadfly synchronization, because the former is always timed for the minimum time to complete an action in the device.

10. Write a single-chip MC68HC11A8 program to punch $80 words from the buffer at location OUTBUF onto paper tape, the first word (at lowest address) punched first on the tape. Assume port C, with tristate output, used in output handshake mode with level output on STRB, is connected to the hardware that punches a pattern of holes, and STRB is connected to a motor that advances the paper. Use real-time synchronization, assuming the E clock is 2 MHz, the hole punches must be pulsed high for 10 milliseconds to punch a hole, and STRA rises from low to high when the paper has been advanced.

11. Write a single-chip MC68HC11A8 program to output eight signals through port B, outputting an entire $80 word buffer each time a rising edge signal appears on a signal STRA (using the simple handshake mode). The buffer will be read out 1 word at a time, outputting the next word every 100 microseconds. Use real-time synchronization to output the steady stream of words after the gadfly loop finds the edge of STRA. Assume port B at location $1004 is used and the rising edge signal on the STRA input is sensed by the gadfly loop. (This routine could be used to turn on incandescent lamps controlled by a triac, as discussed in the next chapter.)

12. Write an SWI handler to input a word from port C or output a word to port C of a single-chip MC68HC11A8, depending on the argument in the argument list below the SWI instruction. Assume the I/O registers are at $1000 to $103F. The sequence

```
        SWI
        FCB     0
```

will input a word, putting it into accumulator A so it can be used by the calling routine after the "call," and

```
        SWI
        FCB     1
```

will output the word that was in accumulator A. Use a transfer vector, as described in section 2-3.3 in the discussion of SWI "subroutines," to execute the proper routine, and use a gadfly loop before inputting or outputting the word to check on whether the device is busy. (This type of SWI handler is commonly used to call all the I/O "subroutines" from a high-level language program.)

13.* Interrupts permit the computer to perform some useful function while waiting for a device to become busy or for an error condition to arise. Interrupts are always faster than a simple gadfly loop, because they save the state of the machine and restore it, while the gadfly technique has to loop a long time. When an external device requests an interrupt, if the device is enabled, the interrupt request flip-flop is set. Then, if the device is not disabled, the IRQ output is asserted (high). This signal could be used to light a lamp to signal an error, or it could be connected to the M6811 IRQ pin. When this signal is seen low by the M6811, it immediately honors the interrupt, saving the values in all output registers on the stack and jumping directly to a handler routine. The handler may have just an RTS instruction to return to the program that was originally running. Vectored interrupts use external hardware to eliminate the polling routine in the device handler, so the interrupt handler can be executed immediately. Interrupts, and vectored interrupts in particular, should be used whenever the latency time requirement is critically small or something useful can be done while waiting for an interrupt; otherwise, real-time or gadfly synchronization should be used.

14. Complete the remainder of a logic analyzer's output that would appear the first time the interrupt handler TPRDR is executed, as it was shown in table 5-1. Show what happens in each memory cycle until the main program is resumed and one BRA instruction is executed in it.

15. In problem 23 at the end of chapter 4, you may have designed an address comparator that checks for breakpoints. In this problem, you can design the rest of the system. The CA2 output will be compared against the R/W signal so you can distinguish between a write into a location and a read from it. The signal CMP is high when the address matches the two words in the data registers and R/W matches the CA2 output; this signal is put into the CA1 input. Write a program to interrupt when the machine writes a word to location $0025, and then jump to a monitor program (do not write the interrupt handler, which is the monitor program).

16. The interrupt handler IRQHND at the end of section 5-2.4 could use a general subroutine CHK21 to check for interrupts in one of the devices of an M6821. It would be called thus:

```
BSR     CHK21
FDB     LOC21
FDB     ADDR1
FDB     ADDR2
```

and it would jump to a device handler at location ADDR1, if IRQA1 (or IRQB1) of the device whose data/direction register is at location LOC21 requested an interrupt or it would jump to ADDR2, if IRQA2 (or IRQB2) requested an interrupt but IRQA1 (or IRQB1) did not. (Note that this subroutine checks only the A device or the B device, but must be executed twice to check both devices.) Write this subroutine, and then rewrite the handler IRQHND using this subroutine. Then compare the program length and execution time for both versions, assuming the lowest priority interrupt handler is to be executed, and the E clock is 1 MHz.

17. Write a round-robin IRQ handler that replaces the handler IRQHND at the end of section 5-2.4.

18. Assume that the IRQ handler in the IRQHND program (section 5-2.4) is now an edge-sensitive interrupt handler, because bit 5 of the OPTION register (in figure 5-15) was set right after initialization and the program at location HNDLA1 is to do the same thing for a paper tape reader as the program segment TPRDR. Write the edge-sensitive IRQ handler and the device handler HNDLA1.

19. Rewrite the program INTERS in section 5-2.5 so input words from the serial handler are handled using interrupts, but parallel words are output using gadfly synchronization. Use PortC tristate output interlocked handshake with the input handshake active on the rising edge of STRA and output handshake active on low STRB. Show the entire program, including the RESET handler.

20. Rewrite the program in section 5-2.6 so both the A and B devices of the 6821 cause an IRQ interrupt and neither causes an XIRQ interrupt. Show the entire program, including the RESET handler.

21.* Direct memory access is a synchronization technique that uses an extra processor that is able to move words from a device to memory, or vice versa. With an output device, when the device is able to output another word, it will assert a request to the DMA chip, which checks its busy-done state, and, if done, it requests that the M6809 stop and release control of R/W and address and data bus. The M6809 will send a signal to the DMA chip when it has released control, the DMA chip will output on the data bus and will send a signal to the I/O device to put a signal on the R/W line and an address on the address bus. The device must also negate the line to the DMA chip when it receives the word to be output. A DMA chip itself is an I/O device, whose busy state indicates that a buffer full of data has been moved. The busy state then is an interrupt request. Either gadfly or interrupt synchronization can be used to start a program when the buffer has been moved.

22. Show the block diagram (similar to figure 5-12, but ignoring negative logic) of a DMA system using an M6844 controller and an M6821 whose B device will be used to output words, punching them on paper tape. Show also the initialization ritual like DMASET in section 5-3.1 that will cause the words in the buffer BUFFER to be punched on tape.

23. Show the block diagram (similar to figure 5-13) and the reset handler that can set up an M6809 and an M6800 on the same data and address bus to implement context switching. Then show a program segment that will call a "subroutine" in the M6800 from the M6809 and a program segment that will call a "subroutine" in the M6809 from the M6800. In both cases, the calling routine simply turns on the other processor at an

address SUB (stored as a global variable) and turns itself off, so that when it is turned back on it merely executes the next instruction. The other processor will load the address of SUB into its program counter and execute the program there as a conventional subroutine. The subroutine will execute an RTS instruction, which is supposed to jump to a program segment to turn on the other processor. Finally, to maintain order, the value in the M6800 stack pointer when the M6800 is started or stopped should be 1 minus the value in the M6809 stack pointer when the M6809 is stopped or started. (Use a global variable STKPNT to transfer the stack pointer between processors.)

24. Show a logic diagram of an isolated buffer, using an expanded bus M68HC11A8, a 6116 memory, and 74HC parts for the multiplexor. The memory is read (never written) by the processor at $1000 to $17FF, and a 74HC4040 counter is used by the external device to provide an address to write data into the memory. Show all pin connections between these chips.

25. Write a program to copy the contents of locations 0 to $10 into EEPROM locations $B600 to $B610 in an MC68HC11A8 using a 2 MHz E clock, assuming EEPROM was erased.

26. Write a reset handler for an MC68HC11A8 that puts I/O at 0 to $3F, RAM at $1000 to $10FF, and initializes the option register to all 0's. What are the meanings of the option register bits?

6

Analog Interfacing

Analog circuits are commonly used to interconnect the I/O device and the "outside world." This chapter will focus on such circuits as are commonly used in microcomputer I/O systems. In this chapter, we will assume you have only a basic knowledge of physics, including mechanics and basic electrical properties. While many of you have far more, some, who have been working as programmers, may not. This chapter especially aims to provide an adequate background for studying I/O systems.

Before analog components are discussed, some basic notions of analog signals should be reviewed. In an *analog* signal, voltage or current levels convey information by real number values, like 3.1263 volts, rather than by H or L values. A *sinusoidal alternating current* (AC) signal voltage (or current) has the form $v = A \sin (P + 2\pi Ft)$ as a function of time t, where the *amplitude* A , the *phase* P, and the *frequency* F, can carry information. The *period* is 1/F. (See figure 6-1a.) One of the most useful techniques in analog system analysis is to decompose any *periodic* (that is, repetitive) waveform into a sum of sinusoidal signals, thus determining how the system transmits each component signal. The *bandwidth* of the system is the range of frequencies which it transmits faithfully (not decreasing the signal by a factor of .707 of what it should be). A square wave, shown in figure 6-1b, may also be used in analog signals. Amplitude, phase, and frequency have the same meaning as in sinusoidal waveforms.

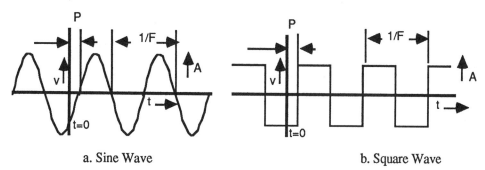

a. Sine Wave   b. Square Wave

Figure 6-1. Waveforms of Alternating Voltage Signals

257

Two kinds of analog signals are important. These correspond to AM and FM radio. In this chapter, we consider analog signals whose amplitude carries the value, whether the signal is a direct current or an alternating current signal, as AM radios carry the sound. In the next chapter, we consider analog signals whose frequency or phase carries the value of the signal, as FM radios carry the sound. Amplitude analog signals are more pervasive in interface design. It is hard to find examples of interface hardware that do not have some analog circuitry (we had to search long and hard to find some decent problems for chapter 3 that did not have analog circuits in them). It is even hard to discuss frequency analog circuits without first discussing amplitude analog circuits. So we study amplitude analog circuits in this chapter and frequency analog circuits in chapter 7.

Analog signals are converted to digital signals by *analog to digital converters* (A-to-D converters), and digital signals are converted to analog by *digital to analog converters* (D-to-A converters) such that the digital signal – usually a binary or binary coded decimal number – corresponds in numerical value to the analog signal level. Analog signals are also converted to a single digital bit (H or L) by a *comparator*, and digital signals control analog signals by means of *analog switches*. The frequency of an AC signal can be converted to or from a voltage by *voltage to frequency converters* (V-to-F converters) or by *frequency to voltage converters* (F-to-V converters). Finally, analog signals are generated by *transducers* that change other measurements into voltages or currents, such as temperature to voltage transducers, and are amplified and modified by *operational amplifiers* (OP AMPs).

A basic theme of this chapter is that many functions can be done using digital or analog hardware, or using software. The smart designer determines the best technique from among many alternatives to implement a particular function. Thus, the designer should know a little about analog circuitry. On the one hand, a basic understanding of analog circuits' operation and use is essential in making intelligent hardware-software tradeoffs and is quite useful even for programmers who write code to interface to such devices. So we want to include the required material in this chapter. On the other hand, to use them well, one can devote an entire year's study to these devices. We have to refrain from covering that much detail. Therefore, our aim is to give enough detail so readers can make good hardware-software tradeoffs in the design of microprocessor-analog systems and to encourage those who seek more detail to read some of the many excellent books devoted to the topic of analog signal processing.

In the following sections, we will discuss conversion of physical quantities to voltages and from voltages, the basics of operational amplifiers and their use in signal conditioning and keyboard/display systems, digital to analog conversion, analog to digital conversion, and data acquisition systems. Much of the material is hardware oriented and qualitative. However, to make the discussion concrete, we discuss in some detail the use of the popular CA3140 operational amplifier and the 4066 and 4051 analog switches. Some practical construction information will be introduced as well. The reader might wish to try out some of the examples to understand firmly these principles.

This chapter should provide enough background on the analog part of a typical microcomputer I/O system so the reader is aware of the capabilities and limitations of analog components used in I/O and can write programs that can accommodate them.

6-1 Input and Output Transducers

A *transducer* changes a physical quantity, like temperature, to or from another quantity, often a voltage. Such a transducer enables a microcomputer that can measure or produce a voltage or an AC wave to measure or control other physical quantities. Each physical property - position, radiant energy, temperature, and pressure - will be discussed in turn, and for each we will examine the transducers that change electrical signals into these properties and then those that change the properties into electrical signals.

6-1.1 Positional Transducers

About 90% of the physical quantities measured are positional. The position may be linear (distance) or angular (degrees of a circle or number of rotations of a shaft). Of course, linear position can be converted to angular position by a rack and pinion gear arrangement. Also, recall that position, speed, and acceleration are related by differential equations: if one can be measured at several precise times, the others can be determined.

A microcomputer controls position by means of *solenoids* or *motors*. A *solenoid* is an electromagnet with an iron plunger. As current through the electromagnet is increased, an increased force pulls the plunger into its middle. The solenoid usually acts against a spring. When current is not applied to the solenoid, the spring pulls the plunger from the middle of the solenoid; and when current is applied, the plunger is pulled into the solenoid. Solenoids are designed to be operated with either direct current or alternating current, and are usually specified for a maximum voltage (which implies a maximum current) that can be applied and for the pulling force that is produced when this maximum voltage (current) is applied. A *direct current motor* has a pair of input terminals and a rotating shaft. The (angular) speed of the shaft is proportional to the voltage applied to the terminals (when the motor is running without being loaded) and the (angular) force or torque is proportional to the current. A *stepping motor* looks like a motor, but actually works like a collection of solenoids. When one of the solenoids gets current, it pulls the shaft into a given (angular) position. When another solenoid gets current, it pulls the shaft into another position. By spacing these solenoids evenly around the stepping motor and by giving each solenoid its current in order, the shaft can be rotated a precise amount each time the next solenoid is given its current. Hence the term stepping motor. The *universal motor* can be given either direct current or alternating current power. Most home appliances use these inexpensive motors. Their speed, however, is very much dependent on the force required to turn the load. *Shaded pole motors* require alternating current, and the shaft speed is proportional to the frequency of the AC power rather than the voltage. The torque is proportional to the current. These inexpensive motors often appear in electric clocks, timers, and fans. *Induction motors* are usually larger power AC motors, and their speed is proportional to frequency like the shaded pole motor. Finally, the *hysteresis synchronous motor* is an AC motor whose speed is accurately synchronized to the frequency of the AC power. These are used to control the speed of Hi-Fi turntables and tape decks.

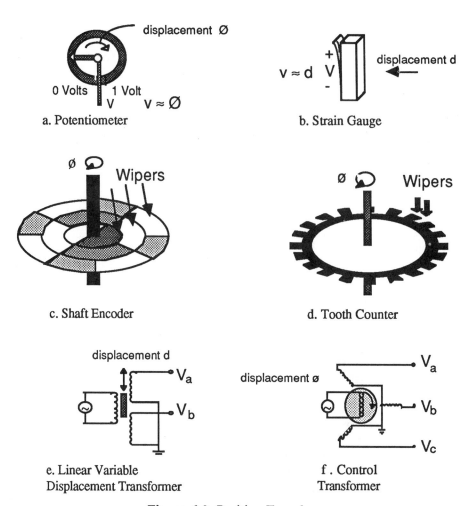

Figure 6-2. Position Transducers

In inexpensive systems, linear position or angular position is usually converted into a resistance, which determines a voltage level in a voltage divider circuit, or which determines a frequency of some kind of RC oscillator. A *potentiometer* converts angular position to resistance. (See figure 6-2a.) A *slide potentiometer* converts linear position to resistance. Both transducers are inexpensive but are prone to inaccuracy as the wiper arm in the potentiometer wears down the resistor or as a coat of dirt or oil builds upon the resistor. Also, these transducers are sensitive to vibration. Overall accuracy is limited to about 3%. Minute position displacements can be measured by piezo-electric crystal, such as in commercial *strain gauges*. A crystal phono cartridge uses the same mechanism. (See figure 6-2b.) Angular position of a disk can be converted directly into a digital signal by *shaft encoders*, which use mechanical wipers or photodetectors to read a track on the disk, the tracks being laid out so that the wipers or detectors read a digital word corresponding to the angle of rotation ø of the disk. (See figure 6-2c.) Also, a pair of wipers or detectors can sense the teeth of a gear or gear-like disk, so they can count the teeth as the gear turns. (See figure 6-2d.) Two wipers are needed to determine both the motion and the direction of motion of the teeth. Finally, the most accurate and reliable position transducer is the *linear variable displacement transformer*. (See figure 6-2e.) In this device, a transformer having a primary winding and two secondary windings has a movable slug. As the slug moves, the two secondary windings of the transformer producing V_1 and V_2 get more or less alternating current from the primary winding, and the relative phase of the sine waves output from the windings changes. Either the voltage level of the sine wave or the relative phase difference between the sine waves may be used to sense the position of the slug. The linear variable displacement transformer is the most accurate device for measuring linear distances because it is not affected by dirt, wear, or vibration as other devices; however, it is the most expensive. Angular position can be measured by a *control transformer* using the same kind of technique. (See figure 6-2f.) This device's rotor has a primary coil that can be turned by a shaft, and secondary windings in the housing, which is held stationary, that surrounds the rotor. The angular position of such a device's rotor of determines the amount and phase of a sine wave that is picked up by the secondaries of the transformer.

Velocity and acceleration can be determined by measuring position using one of the aforementioned transducers above, and then differentiating the values in software or using an electrical circuit that differentiates the voltage. Also, a *direct current tachometer* is a direct current generator. Being an inverse of a DC motor, its output voltage is proportional to the rotational speed of the shaft. An AC tachometer is an AC motor run as a generator; its output frequency is proportional to the (angular) speed of its shaft. Finally, acceleration can also be measured by producing a force F as a mass m is accelerated at rate a (F = m a), then letting the force act against a spring, and then measuring the displacement of the spring. This type of device, an *accelerometer*, can convert the acceleration into a position using mechanical techniques, thereby measuring acceleration at the output of the transducer. This is an alternative to measuring position, then using software to differentiate the values to determine acceleration. Conversely, an accelerometer can be used to measure acceleration, which can be integrated by a software program to derive velocity, or integrated twice to get position. This is the basis of an inertial guidance system. The examples in this paragraph show that functions can be done by means of mechanical, electrical hardware, or software methods, or a combination of all three.

6-1.2 Radiant Energy Transducers

Radiant energy – light and infrared – can be produced or controlled by a microprocessor using lamps, *light emitting diodes* (LEDs), and *liquid crystal displays* (LCDs). The terms used for light and infrared radiant energy are those used for radio waves. In a continuous wave (CW) or pulse coded mode (PCM), the radiant energy is either on (high) or off (low). In an amplitude modulated mode (AM), the amplitude of the radiation varies with a signal that carries analog information. In frequency modulated mode (FM), the frequency varies with an analog signal. The common incandescent lamp is lit by applying a voltage across its terminals. The radiant energy is mostly uniformly distributed over the light spectrum and includes infrared energy. Gas discharge lamps and fluorescent lamps work in a similar fashion but require current limiting resistors in series with the lamp and usually need higher voltages. Their radiant energy is confined to specific wavelengths which are determined by the material in the lamp. While these are sometimes used with microprocessors, their relatively high voltage and current requirements and the electrical noise generated by gas discharge lamps and fluorescent lamps, limit their usefulness. More popular are the LEDs and LCDs. An LED is basically a diode which will emit light if about 10 milliamperes are sent through it. The light is generated in specific wavelengths: red and infrared are the easiest to generate, but green, yellow, and orange are also widely available. Current passing through an LED drops about 1.7 to 2.3 volts, depending on the diode material. LEDs are often used in displays to indicate some output from a microcomputer and are also used in communications systems to carry information. Inexpensive LEDs can be pulse modulated at better than 10 kiloHertz, and special ones can work at around a gigaHertz. An LCD is electrically a capacitor which is clear if the (RMS) voltage across it is less than about a volt and is opaque if above about two volts; it consumes very little power. The voltage across an LCD must be AC, however, because DC will polarize and destroy the material in the LCD. Usually, one terminal has a square wave signal. If the other terminal has a square wave signal in phase with the first, the display is clear, and if it has a square wave signal out of phase with the first, the display is opaque.

Radiant energy is often measured in industrial control systems. A *photodetector* converts the amplitude to a voltage or resistance for a given bandwidth of the very high frequency sine wave carrier. Often this bandwidth covers part of the visible spectrum and/or part of the infrared spectrum. The *photomultiplier* can measure energy down to the photon – the smallest unit of radiation – and has an amplification of about one million. However, it requires a regulated high voltage power supply. The *photodiode* is a semiconductor photodetector able to handle signals carried on the amplitude of the radiant energy around 10 megaHertz. The current through the diode is linearly proportional to the radiation if the voltage drop across it is kept small. This is done by external circuitry. However, it is inefficient because a unit of radiant energy produces only 0.001 units of electrical energy. A photodiode might be used in a communication linkage to carry a signal on a light beam because of its high bandwidth and ease of use with integrated circuits. If the diode is built into a transistor, a *phototransistor* is made that relates about one unit of electrical energy to one unit of radiant energy, but the signal carried on the amplitude is reproduced up to about 100 kiloHertz. Finally, a *photoresistor* is a device whose resistance varies with the intensity of the light shone upon it. While this device is also temperature sensitive, has poor frequency response, and is quite nonlinear, it can be used to isolate a triac, as we discuss later.

Photodiodes, phototransitors, photoresistors, and other detectors are often used with LEDs or lamps to sense the position of objects, or to isolate an external system from the microcomputer. Photodetectors are commonly used with an LED light source to detect the presence or absence of an object between the light source and the photodetector. To sense the pattern on the disc under the contacts, a shaft encoder or tooth counter can use this kind of sensor in place of a mechanical contact. Similar techniques place an LED and a phototransistor inside an integrated circuit package, called an *opto-isolator*, to isolate the circuitry driving the LED from the circuitry connected to the detector so that they can be kilovolts apart and so that electrical noise in the driver circuitry is not transmitted to the detector circuitry.

Temperature is controlled by means of heaters or air conditioners. To control the temperature of a small component, such as a crystal, the component is put in an *oven*, which has a resistive heater and is fairly well insulated. As more current is passed through the heater, it produces more heat; as less current is passed, the natural loss of heat through the insulated walls brings down the temperature. The temperature of a large room or building is controlled by means of a furnace or air conditioner, of course. Since these usually require AC power at high currents and voltages, the microcomputer has to control a large AC current. An interesting problem in controlling air conditioners is due to the back pressure built up in them. If the air conditioner has just been running, is then turned off and is quickly turned on, the motor in it will stall because it cannot overcome the back pressure in it. So in controlling an air conditioner, if it is turned off, it must not be turned on for an interval of time, which is long enough for the back pressure to drop off.

Temperature is often sensed in a microprocessor system. Very high temperatures are measured indirectly, by measuring the infrared radiation they emit. Temperatures in the range -250 degrees centigrade to +1000 degrees centigrade can be measured by a *thermocouple*, which is a pair of dissimilar metals (iron and constantan, for instance), where the voltage developed between the metals is around 0.04 millivolts times the temperature. Note that such a low-level signal requires careful handling and amplification before it can be used in a microprocessor system. The most popular technique for measuring temperatures around room temperature is to put a constant current through a diode (or the diode in the emitter junction of a bipolar transistor) and measure the voltage across it. The output voltage is typically 2.2 millivolts times the temperature in Kelvin. This voltage level requires some amplification before conversion to digital values is possible. Provided the current through the diode is held constant (by a constant current source), the transducer is accurate to within 0.1 degrees Kelvin. While a common diode or transistor can be used, a number of integrated circuits have been developed that combine a transistor and constant current source and amplifier. One of these (AD590) has just two pins, and regulates the current through it to be 1 microampere times the temperature in Kelvin. Converting to and then transmitting a current has the following advantage: the voltage drops in wires whose sensor is a long distance from the microprocessor, or in switches that may have unknown resistance, and thus does not affect the current. The current is converted to a voltage simply by passing it through a resistor. Finally, temperature can be sensed by a temperature sensitive resistor called a *thermistor*. Thermistors are quite nonlinear and have poor frequency responses, but relatively large changes in resistance result from changes in temperature.

6-1.3 Other Transducers

Pressure can be produced as a by-product of an activity controlled by a microcomputer. For instance, if a microcomputer controls the position of a valve, it can also control the flow of liquid into a system, which changes the pressure in the system. Pressure is sometimes measured. Usually, variations in pressure produce changes in the position of a diaphragm, so the position of the diaphragm is measured. While this can be implemented with separate components, a complete system using a Sensym chip in the LX1800 series of chips (formerly a National Semiconductor series) can measure absolute or relative pressure to within 1% accuracy. These marvelous devices contain the diaphragm, strain gauge position sensor, compensation circuits for temperature, and output amplifier on a hybrid integrated circuit. Finally, weight is normally measured by the force that gravity generates. The weighing device, called a *load cell*, is essentially a piston. Objects are weighed by putting them on top of the piston, and the pressure of the fluid inside the piston is measured.

Other properties -including chemical composition and concentration, the Ph of liquids, and so on- are sometimes measured by transducers. However, a discussion of these transducers goes beyond the scope of this introductory survey.

6-2 Basic Analog Processing Components

Basic analog devices include power amplifiers, operational amplifiers, analog switches, and the timer module. These will be discussed in this section. The first subsection discusses transistors and SCRs, the next discusses OP AMPs and analog switches in general, and the last discusses practical OP AMPs and analog switches.

6-2.1 Transistors and Silicon Controlled Rectifiers

To convert a voltage or current to some other property like position or temperature, an amplifier is needed to provide enough power to run a motor or a heater. We briefly survey the common power amplifier devices often used with microcomputers. These include power transistors, darlington transistors, and VFETs for control of DC devices (motors, heaters, and so on) and SCRs and triacs for control of AC devices.

The *(bipolar) transistor* is a device which has terminals called the collector, base, and emitter. (See figure 6-3a.) The collector current I_c is a constant (called the *beta*) times the base current I_b. The *power transistor* can be obtained in various capacities: able to handle up to 100 amperes, and up to 1000 volts. These are most commonly used for control of DC devices. A *darlington transistor* has a pair of simple transistors connected internally so it appears to be a single transistor with very high beta. (See figure 6-3b.) Power darlington transistors require less base current I_b to drive a given load, so they are often used with microprocessor I/O chips that have limited current output. *Field effect transistors* (FETs) can be used in place of the more conventional (bipolar) transistor. In an FET, the current flowing from drain to source is proportional to the voltage from gate to source. Very little current flows into the gate, which is essentially a capacitor with a small leakage current. (See figure 6-3c.) However, a *vertical field effect transistor* (VFET) is faster than a standard FET and can withstand larger voltages (about 200 volts) between drain and source. The VFET is therefore a superb output amplifier that is most compatible with microcomputers. Suffice to say for this survey, a power transistor, a darlington, or a VFET is usually required to drive a DC device like a motor, heater or lamp.

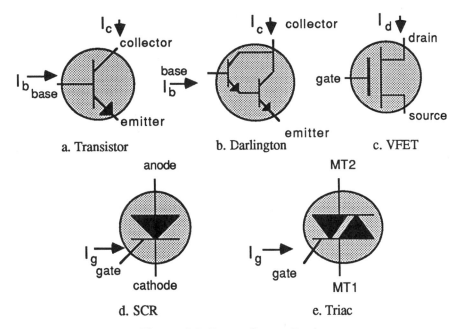

Figure 6-3. Power Output Devices

An AC device like an AC motor uses a *silicon controlled rectifier* (SCR) or a *triac* to amplify the voltage or control signal output from a microcomputer. The SCR has anode, cathode, and gate terminals, as in figure 6-3d. When sufficient current I_g (about 50 milliamperes) flows into the gate through the anode, the device looks like a diode, passing positive current from anode to cathode but inhibiting flow from cathode to anode. That is why it is called a controlled rectifier, since a rectifier is an older name for a diode. Moreover, the SCR has memory; once turned on, it remains on, regardless of the current through the gate, until the current through the anode tries to reverse itself and is thus turned off. The gate controls only half a cycle, since it is always turned off for the half cycle when current tries to but cannot go from cathode to anode; and it is turned on only when the gate is given enough current and the current will then flow from anode to cathode. To correct this deficiency, a pair of SCRs are effectively connected "back to back" to form a triac. (See figure 6-3e.) The power current flows through main terminal 1 (MT1) and main terminal 2 (MT2) under the control of the current I_g through the gate and MT1. If the gate current is higher than about 50 milliamperes either into or out of the gate, MT1 appears shorted to MT2 and continues appearing as such regardless of the current through the gate until the current through MT1 and MT2 passes through 0. Otherwise, MT1 and MT2 appear disconnected. SCRs and triacs handle currents from half an ampere up to 1000 amperes and can control voltages beyond 800 volts.

SCRs and triacs control motors, heaters, and so on by controlling the percentage of a cycle or the number of cycles in which full power is applied to them. The types of control are discussed next in terms of triacs, but they also apply to SCRs.

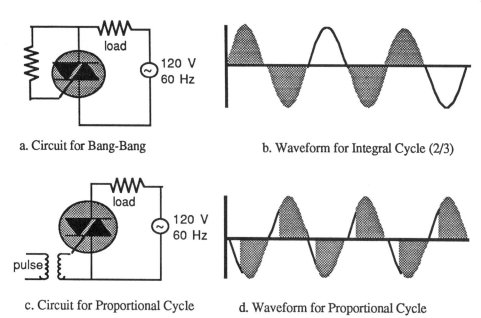

a. Circuit for Bang-Bang

b. Waveform for Integral Cycle (2/3)

c. Circuit for Proportional Cycle

d. Waveform for Proportional Cycle

Figure 6-4. Triac Control Techniques

In *on-off*, or "*bang-bang*," control, the triac applies either full power or no power to the motor. To do this, either full current or no current is applied to the gate. A simple variation of this technique applies gate current from MT2 through a resistor, so that if the resistance is low, when voltage on MT2 begins to build up, current flows through the resistor to turn on the triac. (See figure 6-4a.) As soon as it is turned on, however, the voltage on MT2 disappears. Thus, the current through the resistor stops as soon as it has done its work. This reduces the power dissipated in the resistor. If the resistance is large, no current flows through the gate, so the triac is off. The resistor can be a photoresistor, coupled to an incandescent lamp or an LED in an optocoupler. When the LED or lamp is lit, the photoresistor has a low resistance, which turns the triac on. Otherwise, the resistance is high and the triac is off. This configuration is particularly suited to on-off control of large AC loads by means of triacs.

A simple variation is called *integral cycle control*. Here, the triac is turned on for n out of every m half cycles. (See figure 6-4b.) The gate current has to be turned on at the beginning of each half-cycle when the triac is supposed to be on. A final variation is called *proportional cycle control*. A pulse generator of some kind is commonly used to send a current pulse through the gate at a precise time in each half-cycle. (See figure 6-4c.) For a fraction F of each half-cycle, the triac is turned on. (See figure 6-4d.) Full power is applied to the device for the last F*th* of the cycle. Roughly speaking, the device gets power proportional to the fraction F. A pulse transformer is often used to isolate the controller from the high voltages in the triac circuitry. (See figure 6-4c.) The controller provides a short (5-microsecond) voltage pulse across the primary winding (shown on the left) of the transformer, which provides a current pulse to the triac to turn it on. The controller has to provide this pulse at the same time in each half-cycle. If the pulse is earlier, more current flows through the triac and more power goes to the load.

On-off control is used where the microprocessor simply turns a device on or off. A traffic light would be controlled like this. Bang-bang control is commonly used in heating systems. You set your thermostat to 70 degrees. If the temperature is below 70 degrees, the heater is turned on fully, and, if above 70 degrees, the heater is completely off. Integral cycle control is useful in electric ranges, for instance, to provide some control over the amount of heating. Finally, variable duty cycle control is common in controlling lighting and power tools, since the other types of control would cause the light to flicker perceptibly or the tool to chatter. However, this type of control generates a lot of electrical noise whenever the triac is turned on fully in the middle of a half-cycle. This kind of noise interferes with the microcomputer and any communications linkages to and from it. So variable duty cycle control is normally used when the other forms generate too much flicker or chatter.

6-2.2 Basic Linear Integrated Circuits

The basic module used to process analog signals is the operational amplifier, or OP AMP. It is used in several important configurations, which we will discuss here. We will then discuss the analog switch, which allows convenient microprocessor control of analog signals, and consider several important applications of this switch.

The OP AMP has two inputs labled + and -, and an output. (See figure 6-5.) The output voltage signal Vout is related to the signals V+ on the + input and V- on the - input by the expression

$$Vout = A\ (\ V+\ -\ V-\ )$$

where A is a rather large number, such as 100,000. The OP AMP is in the *linear mode* if the output voltage is within the range of the positive and negative supply voltages, otherwise it is in the *saturated mode* of operation. Clearly, to be in the linear mode, V+ has to be quite near V-.

The first use of the OP AMP is the *inverting amplifier*. Here, the + input is essentially connected to ground, so V+ is 0, and *feedback* is used to force V- to 0 volts, so the OP AMP is in the linear mode. In figure 6-5a, if Vin increases by one volt, then V- will increase by a small amount, so the output Vout will decrease 100,000 times this amount, large enough to force V- back to 0. In fact, Vout will have to be

$$Vout = -\ (Rf/Rin)\ Vin$$

in order to force V- to 0. The *amplification* of this circuit, the ratio Vout/Vin is exactly Rf/Rin and can be selected by the designer as needed. In a slight modification of this circuit, one or more inputs having signals Vin1, Vin2,... can be connected by means of resistors Rin1, Rin2, ... (as in figure 6-5b) and the output voltage is then

$$Vout = -\ (\ (\ (\ Rf/Rin1\ )\ Vin1\ ) + (\ (\ Rf/Rin2\ )\ Vin2\ ) + ...)$$

in a circuit called a *summing amplifier*.

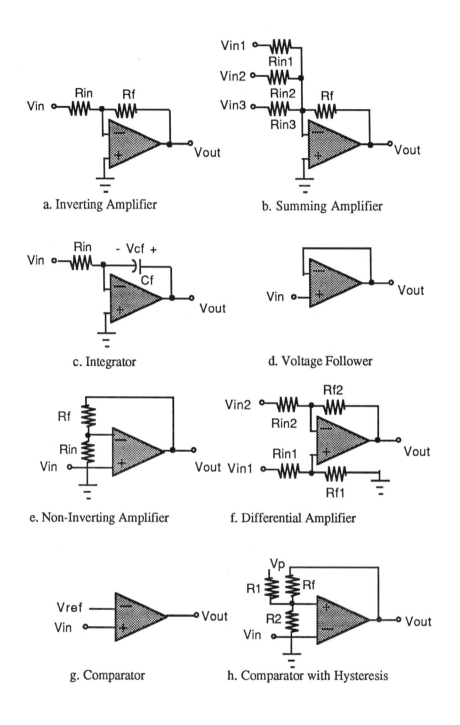

a. Inverting Amplifier

b. Summing Amplifier

c. Integrator

d. Voltage Follower

e. Non-Inverting Amplifier

f. Differential Amplifier

g. Comparator

h. Comparator with Hysteresis

Figure 6-5. Operational Amplifier Circuits

Another classical use of an OP AMP is integration of a signal. A capacitor has the relation of current through it, i, to voltage across it, v, as follows:

$$i = Cf \, dv/dt$$

where Cf is the capacitance. In figure 6-5c, if Vin increases by 1 volt, then Vout will have to change by 1 volt per second so the current through the capacitor can offset the current through Ri to force V- to 0. Generally, the relationship is

$$Vout = Vcfi - (1 / (Ri \; Cf)) \int_{t_0}^{t} Vi \; dt$$

where Vcfi is the voltage across the capacitor at the time we began integrating the input signal.

In these three techniques, the voltage V- is forced to 0. V- is called a *virtual ground*. Of course, it cannot really be connected to ground or no current would be available for the OP AMP V- input. However, complex circuits, such as amplifiers, integrators, differentiators, and active filters, are analyzed using circuit analysis techniques, assuming that V- is effectively grounded.

A different use of the OP AMP puts the incoming signal on the + input and uses feedback to try to force V- to the same voltage as V+. The *voltage follower* (shown in figure 6-5d) does this by connecting V- to Vout. The *non-inverting amplifier* uses the same principle (as shown in figure 6-5e) and satisfies the relationship

$$Vout = (1 + (Rf / Rin)) \; Vin$$

and the output voltage has the same polarity as the input voltage. Combining the ideas underlying the summing amplifier with those of the non-inverting amplifier, we have the *differential amplifier* (shown in figure 6-5f.) One or more inputs such as Vin1 are connected via resistors like Rin1 to the + input of the OP AMP, and one or more inputs such as Vin2 are connected via resistors such as Rin2 to the - input of the OP AMP. The output is then

$$Vout = K1 \; Vin1 - K2 \; Vin2$$

where
$$K1 = \frac{Rf1}{Rin1+Rf1} \left(1+ \frac{Rf2}{Rin2}\right) \quad \text{and} \quad K2 = \frac{Rf2}{Rin2}$$

In this circuit, if more than one input Vin is connected to the + OP AMP input via a resistor Rin, it appears like the term for Vin1 adding its contribution to Vout; and if connected to the - input, it subtracts its contribution to Vout like the term for Vin2.

A final technique used in the OP AMP is to depend on the finite output range it has using the saturation mode of operation. The comparator has the connections shown in figure 6-5g. Here, the output is a high logical signal, H, if Vin > Vref, else it is L. The comparator can be reversed, so that Vref is on the + input and Vin is on the - input.

Then Vout is high if Vin < Vref. Also, Vref can be derived from a voltage divider: Vref = Vp R2/(R1+R2), where Vp is an accurate voltage. Finally, feedback can be made to change the effective Vref a little. Using this variation, the comparator can be made insensitive to small changes in Vin due to noise. By connecting the output to V+ (as shown in figure 6-5h) the effective Vref can be changed so it is higher when the output is H than when the output is L, so that the output remains H or L even when the input varies a bit. Suppose, for instance, that the input is low and the output is high. The input must exceed the higher reference before the output goes low. The output remains low until the input drops below the lower reference. When the input finally drops below the lower reference and the output goes high, the input has to exceed the higher reference again before the output can go low, and so on. This stubborn-like mechanism is called *hysteresis* and is the basis of the *Schmitt trigger* gate used to ignore noise in digital systems.

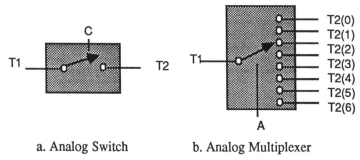

a. Analog Switch   b. Analog Multiplexer

Figure 6-6. Analog Switches

The analog switch is implemented with field-effect transistors and has a control C, and two terminals T1 and T2. (See figure 6-6a.) If C is high, T1 is connected to T2 and the switch is said to be *on*, else they are disconnected and the switch is *off*. Some number (eight) of such switches can be connected at the T1 terminal, and a decoder with (3-bit) address A can be on a chip. The A*th* switch can be turned on by the decoder, the others being turned off. This chip then behaves like an (eight) position rotary switch that is controlled by the address input. (See figure 6-6b.) This kind of chip is an *analog multiplexer*. Single analog switches and analog multiplexers are valuable as ways to control analog signals from a microcomputer.

The final important device is the *timer*. A timer outputs a periodic signal whose period is proportional to the value of a resistor and a capacitor connected to it. (Often, the period can be adjusted by a control voltage, but the voltage to frequency converter is generally better.) The timer allows resistor-based transducers to generate AC signals, where the information is carried by the frequency (period). Such signals are easy to handle and measure, as we will see in the next chapter.

6-2.3 Practical Linear Integrated Circuits

We now consider an operational amplifier, the CA3140, which is particularly suitable for microprocessors. This device has CMOS inputs, which use almost no current and has bipolar transistor outputs which can supply plenty of current. Its characteristics are listed in table 6-1 and will be discussed here.

In this book, Vs+ is the positive supply voltage and Vs- is the negative supply voltage. The first two table entries indicate that the total supply voltage may not be greater than 36 volts nor less than 4 volts. Two very common connections are the *dual supply*, where Vs+ is exactly the negative of Vs- (for example, Vs+ = +15 volts, Vs- = - 15 volts), and the *single supply*, where either Vs+ or Vs- is 0 (for example, Vs+ = 5 volts, Vs- = 0 volts). A ± 15-volt dual supply is useful when almost maximum output voltage range is needed, and a single +5-volt supply is useful when the only power supply is the one supplying 5 volts to the logic part of the system. A good OP AMP for microcomputer applications should be capable of operating in either of the preceding cases. Clearly, both connections are within the specifications listed in the first two rows of table 6-1 for the CA3140. To make the information in the table more concrete, we will consider its significance for a single-ended +5-volt supply application. The reader is invited to consider the significance of these parameters for a ±15-volt dual supply application.

Table 6-1. Characteristics for the CA3140

Characteristic	Value
Maximum (Vs+ - Vs-)	36 V
Minimum (Vs+ - Vs-)	4 V
Maximum (V+ or V-)	Vs+ + 8
Minimum (V+ or V-)	Vs- - .5
Max common mode input	Vs+ - 2.5
Min common mode input	Vs- -.5
Input resistance	1 TΩ
Input capacitance	4 pF
Input current	2 pA
Input offset voltage	5 mV
Input offset current	.1 pA
Output resistance	60Ω
Maximum output voltage	Vs+ - 3 v
Minimum output voltage	Vs- +.13 v
Maximum sourcing current	10 mA
Maximum sinking current	1 mA
Amplification	100,000
Slew rate	7 v/μs
Gain bandwidth product	3.7 MHz
Transient response	80 ns
Supply current	1.6 mA
Device dissipation	8 mW

The next four entries indicate the range of input voltages. The maximum and minimum values of V+ and V- should not be exceeded or the OP AMP may be destroyed. For example, if Vs+ is 5 volts and Vs- is 0 volts, then neither the + nor the - input should have a voltage higher than 13 volts, nor lower than -0.5 volts. The full range of voltages can be used in the saturated mode of operation. This OP AMP has adequate capabilities using a +5-volt single supply for comparator applications. However, if the linear mode of operation is used, the input voltages should be kept within the maximum and minimum *common mode* voltages. For our previous example, using the same supply voltages, the inputs should be kept within 2.5 volts and -0.5 volts for operation in the linear mode. Note that inputs above 2.5 volts will pull the OP AMP out of the linear mode, and this can be a problem for voltage follower, non-inverting amplifiers or for differential amplifiers. However, since the common mode voltage range includes both positive and negative voltages around 0 volts, inverting amplifiers, summers, and integrators can be built using a single +5-volt supply. This is a very attractive feature of a modern OP AMP like the CA3140.

The next five lines of the table show the input characteristics that cause errors. The + and - inputs appear to be a resistor, a capacitor, and a current source, all in parallel. The equivalent input resistance, 1 teraohm, is very high. This high input resistance means that a voltage follower or non-inverting amplifier can have such high input resistance, which is especially important for measuring the minute currents output from some transducers like pH probes and photodetectors. Moreover, it means that quite large resistors (100,000-ohm) and quite small capacitors (.01-microfarad) can be used in the circuits discussed earlier, without the OP AMP loading down the circuit. Especially when the rest of the system is so miniaturized, larger capacitors are ungainly and costly. The input capacitance, 4 picofarads, is very low, but can become significant at high frequencies. The current source can cause some error, but is quite high in this OP AMP, and the error can often be ignored. The + and - inputs have some current flowing from them, which is less than 2 picoamperes according to the table. If the + input is just grounded but the - input is connected by a 1 MΩ resistor to ground, this input current causes 2 microvolts extra, which is multiplied by the amplification (100,000) to produce an error of 0.2 millivolts in Vout. The error due to input current can be minimized by making equal the resistances that connect the + and - inputs to ground. In figure 6-5a, a resistance equal to Rin in parallel with Rf can be connected between the + input and ground, just to cancel the effect of the input current on the output voltage. However, this particular OP AMP has such low input current that the error is usually not significant, and the + input is connected directly to ground.

The offset voltage is the net voltage that might be effectively applied to either the + or the - inputs, even when they are grounded. The offset current is the current that can be effectively applied to either input, even when they are disconnected. These offsets have to be counterbalanced to get 0-output voltage when no input signal is applied. An *offset adjustment* is available on OP AMPs like the 3140 to cancel the offset voltage and current.

The next five entries describe the output of the OP AMP. The output resistance is the effective resistance in series with the output of the amplifier considered as a perfect voltage source. In this case, it is 60 ohms. A high output resistance limits the OP AMP's ability to apply full power to low resistance loads, such as speakers. However, the effective output resistance of an amplifier is substantially decreased by feedback. The output voltage can swing over a range of from 2 to 0.13 volts, if the power supply Vs+ is 5 volts and Vs- is 0 volts. This means that for linear operation the amplifier can support about a 1.8-volt peak-to-peak output signal, but this signal has to be centered around 1.07 volts. Note that the output range is a serious limitation for a comparator whose output drives a digital input, because a high signal is usually any voltage above 2.7 volts. An external (10,000-ohm) pull-up resistor, from the output to +5 volts, can be used such that whenever the OP AMP is not pulling the output low, the output is pulled up to nearly 5 volts. The output can source (supply) 10 milliamperes and can sink (absorb) 1 milliampere to the next stage. It can supply quite a bit of current to a transistor or a sensitive gate triac because these devices require current from the output of the OP AMP. However, this OP AMP's ability to sink only 1 milliampere restricts its use to low-power (CMOS, LSTTL, microprocessor NMOS) digital inputs; and it cannot sink 1.6 milliamperes reliably as is required to input signals to conventional TTL gates.

Recall that the bandwidth of an amplifier is the range of frequencies over which the gain is at least $(1/\sqrt{2})$ times the maximum gain. If the bandwidth of an amplifier is 100,000 Hertz, then any small signal sine wave whose frequency is between direct current and 100,000 Hertz will be correctly amplified. Moreover, any complex periodic waveform can be decomposed into a sum of sine waves. To correctly amplify the waveform, all the component sine waves must be amplified correctly. (The phase delays also must be matched for all components.) Generally, a square wave of frequency F will be reproduced fairly accurately if the amplifier bandwidth is at least 10 F.

For most OP AMPs, the bandwidth decreases as the gain increases, so the product is constant. In the 3140, this constant is 3.7 MHz. That means that if the circuit amplification is 1, the bandwidth is 3.7 MHz. For an OP AMP (shown in figure 6-5a) with an amplification of 10, the bandwidth is 370,000 Hertz. The bandwidth is an important limitation on the OP AMP's ability to amplify small high-frequency signals. The slew rate is the maximum rate at which the output can change (due to a sudden change on the input). The slew rate usually limits the effective bandwidth of large signals less than the available bandwidth of small signals, because the output cannot change fast enough. This OP AMP has a very good slew rate; the output can change at a rate of 7 volts in 1 microsecond. The transient response is the time delay between a sudden change in the input and the corresponding change in the output. A related parameter, the *settling time,* is the time it takes for the output to reach the desired voltage. It is not specified in the table because it depends on the external component configuration and on what we mean by reaching the desired voltage. The transient response and settling time can be of concern to a programmer who must compensate for such delays. In circuits where a digital device interfaces with an OP AMP, the slew rate and transient response may be the limiting factor on the use of an OP AMP.

Finally, the power requirements of the device are given. It dissipates about 8 milliwatts when operated using a single 5-volt supply, taking 1.6 milliamps from the power supply under normal conditions. It takes about 6 milliamperes and dissipates about 180 milliwatts when operated from dual $\pm$ 15-volt supplies. This parameter determines how big the power supply has to be to supply this device and can be significant when little power is available.

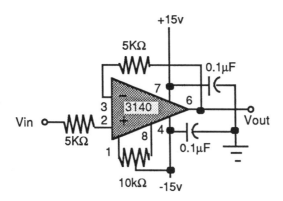

Figure 6-7. A Practical Voltage Follower

Figure 6-7 shows the pin connections for a CA3140 and some practical considerations in using it for a dual supply voltage follower. To avoid noise input and unwanted oscillation, 0.1-microfarad capacitors, called *bypass capacitors*, are connected between the Vs+ pin and ground and between the Vs- pin and ground. The connection should be made as close to the pin as possible. Wherever practical, every OP AMP should be bypassed in this manner. The 10,000-ohm potentiometer between pins 1 and 5 is used to counterbalance the voltage offset. The inputs (to the whole circuit, not the OP AMP) are connected momentarily to ground, and this potentiometer is adjusted to output 0 volts. Although the voltage follower needs no resistors (as in figure 6-5d), resistors are put in the feedback loop and the input to prevent excessive currents from flowing when the OP AMP is driven out of its linear mode of operation. Since the inputs have very high resistance in normal operation, these resistors have no effect in that mode. However, they should be put in if the OP AMP can enter a saturation mode of operation. Note that if the power to this OP AMP is off and a signal is applied to the input, excessive current can flow unless these resistances are put in because that operation will be in the saturated mode.

Some other considerations are offered. When handling devices with such high input resistances, tools, soldering irons, and hands should be connected via a large (15,000,000-ohm) resistance to ground. Such a device should never be inserted or removed from a socket when power is on, and signals should not be applied to inputs (unless a series resistor is used, as in the voltage follower recently described) when power is off. Especially if high (1-megohm) resistances are used, keep them clean, keep the leads short, and separate the components on the input of an OP AMP as far as possible from the output circuitry. A sheet of metal connected to ground provides some isolation from electrical noise, and all components and wires should be close to this *ground plane*. However, the ground reference points for such high gain OP AMPs should be connected at one single point, running separate wires from this point to each "ground" point, to avoid so-called *ground loops*. If this advice is ignored, the OP AMP may become an oscillator because the minute voltages developed across the small but finite resistance of a ground wire could be fed back into an input of the OP AMP.

We now turn to some practical aspects of using CMOS analog switches. The analog switch is almost perfect: its bandwidth is about 40 MHz, when closed it is almost a short circuit, and when open it is almost an open circuit. We now focus on the meaning of "almost." Look at figure 6-8, wherein the 4066 and the 4051 are shown.

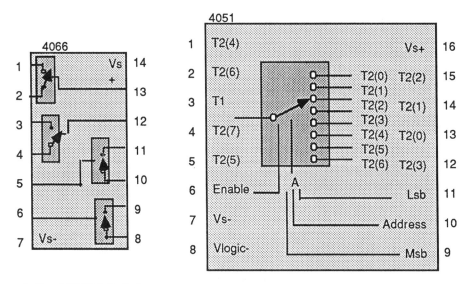

a. A Quad CMOS Switch   b. A CMOS Analog Multiplexer

Figure 6-8. Practical Analog Switches

We consider the problem of supplying control signals that are compatible with the voltage levels on the terminals of the switch. The maximum Vs+ - Vs- voltage across the 4066 is 15 volts. Sometimes, a dual ± 7.5-volt supply is used. If so, the control signals on pins 5,6,12 and 13 must be around -7.5 volts to be considered low enough to open the corresponding switch, and around +7.5 volts to be considered high enough to close the switch. Control signals from a microcomputer are normally in the range of 0 to 5 volts and must be translated to control the switch. However, the 4051 has some level translation ability. The logic signals to address and enable the switches are referenced to Vs+ and pin 8, so a high signal is close to Vs+ and a low signal is close to the voltage level on pin 8. However, the analog levels on the switch's terminals can be between Vs+ and Vs-, which is on pin 7. Commonly, Vs+ is +5 volts, pin 8 is grounded, and Vs- is -5 volts, to directly use control signals from a microcomputer, yet provide some range of analog voltages on the terminals.

When a switch is closed, it appears as a small resistance, about 80 ohms for the 4066 or about 120 ohms for the 4051. This resistance is not exactly linear, varying over a range of 2 to 1. The resistance is more linear if Vs+ - Vs- is as large as possible. However, if used with external resistances around 10,000 ohms in series with the switch, less than 0.5 percent distortion is introduced by the nonlinear resistance of the 4066, even for Vs+ - Vs- = 5 volts.

When the switch is off, each terminal appears to be a small current source, about 100 nanoamperes for the 4066 and about 500 nanoamperes per analog switch in the

4051. This small current increases substantially with temperature and can be a serious source of error if the associated circuitry has very high resistance. To minimize it, we sometimes see a *heat sink* (a metal attachment to a transistor or integrated circuit to dissipate the heat) on an analog switch, and it is sometimes placed away from heat-producing components. Finally, a substantial amount of unwanted current flows from the power supply to the terminals if the voltage from a terminal to Vs- is greater than 0.6 volts and positive current flows from pin 3 of the 4051, or from pins 2,3,9, or 10 in the 4066. One should insure that positive current flows into these pins or that the voltage drop across the switch is never more than .6 volts. In summary, the 4066 has a bit better performance, lower "on" resistance and lower "off" current, and may be used individually; but the 4051 incorporates eight switches into one chip and translates the control signal level from 0 to 5 volts to control signals between ± 5 volts.

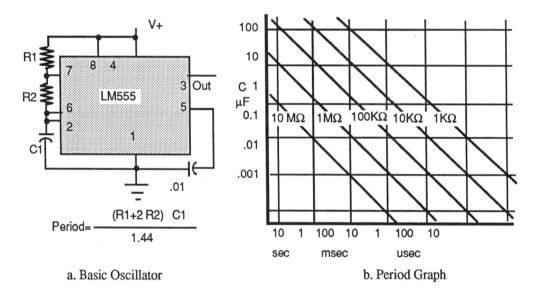

a. Basic Oscillator   b. Period Graph

Figure 6-9.   555 Timer

Finally, we discuss the timer module. The ubiquitous 555 is the most popular and least expensive timer. (See figure 6-9a for the circuit that generates repetitive signals.) In figure 6-9b we see a graph that gives the period of the signal as a function of the resistance, which is the value R1+2R2 in figure 6-9a, and the capacitance, which is the value of C1.

6-3 Signal Conditioning Using OP AMPs and Analog Switches

OP AMPs and analog switches are often used with microcomputers to condition analog signals before converting them to digital signals, to control analog signals used for other purposes, or to clean up or modify analog signals generated by D/A converters. The four main aspects of conditioning a signal are the filtering of frequency components, the selection of inputs, the amplification of or scaling of input levels, and the nonlinear modification of signal voltages. These are now considered in turn.

6-3.1 Filters

Recall that any periodic waveform can be considered a sum of sine waves. Frequency filtering is commonly done when the signal of interest is accompanied by unwanted noise, and most of the noise is at frequencies other than those of the signal's sine wave components. If the signal frequencies are low and the noise frequencies are high, a *low-pass filter* is used. (See the amplitude versus frequency characteristic of a low-pass filter in figure 6-10a and the circuit diagram in figure 6-10b.) Intuitively, we see that capacitor C1 tends to integrate the signal, smoothing out the high-frequency components, and capacitor C2 further shorts out the high-frequency components to ground. Some D/A conversion techniques generate high-frequency noise, so a low-pass filter is commonly used to remove the noise from the signal. If the signal frequencies are higher than the noise frequencies, a *high-pass filter* is used to reject the noise and pass the signal. (See figure 6-10c for the amplification characteristics and 6-10d for a high-pass filter circuit.) Intuitively, we see that the capacitors pass the high-frequency components, bypassing the low-frequency components through the resistors. A signal from a light pen on a CRT gets a short pulse every time the electron beam inside the CRT writes over the dot in front of the light pen. The signal has high-frequency components, while the noise – mostly a steady level due to ambient light – is lower in frequency. A high-pass filter passes the signal and rejects the noise. Finally, a *bandpass filter* can reject both higher- and lower-frequency components, passing only components whose frequencies are between the lower and upper limits of the band, and a *notch filter* can reject frequencies within the upper and lower limits of a band. (See figures 6-10e through 6-10h for the amplification characteristics and circuit diagrams of these filters.)

Compound filters can be used to reject various frequencies and emphasize other frequency components. Two techniques can be used: in one, the output from one filter feeds the input to the next filter to *cascade* them in a chain configuration; and in the other, the signal is fed to both filters and the outputs are added by a summing amplifier in a *parallel* configuration. For instance, a bandpass filter can be made from a low-pass filter that rejects components whose frequency is above the band, cascaded into a high-pass filter that rejects components whose frequency is below the band. A notch filter can be made by summing the outputs of a parallel high-pass and low-pass filter. Compound filters can be used to more sharply attenuate the signals whose frequencies are above the low-pass band or below the high pass band. The best way to cascade n low-pass filters to more sharply attenuate high-frequency components and thus get a *2 nth order filter* is a nice mathematical study and three types of filters have been shown mathematically optimal in one sense or another. The *butterworth* filter has the flattest amplification versus frequency curve in the low-frequency band where we pass the signal in a low-pass filter. However, the phase delays are quite different for different components. A square wave comes out with a few notches and humps. The *bessel* filter has the most linear

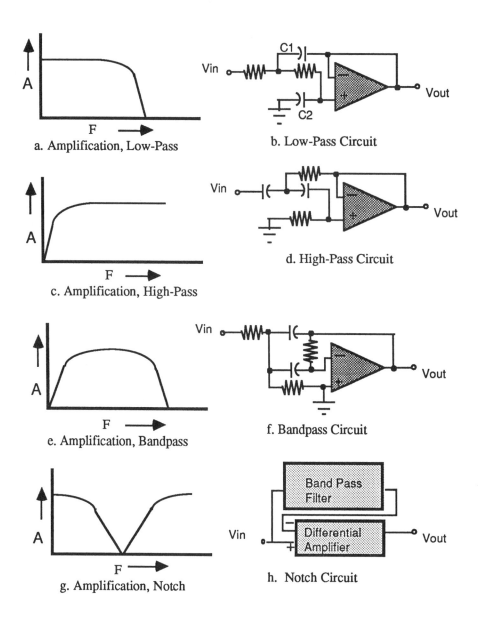

Figure 6-10. Some Filters

relationship between frequency and phase delay and is especially useful for processing signals whose information is carried, in part, by the phase of its components and its pulse edges and shapes. The *chebyshev* filter is characterized by a designer-specified irregularity in the amplification versus frequency curve in the low-frequency band and maximum rejection just outside this band in a low-pass filter. All these filters look alike, but differ in the precise values of the components. These precise values can be obtained from tables, using simple transformations on the values in the tables, or by means of commonly available computer programs. Finally, while the preceding discussion concentrated on low-pass filters, the same terms and concepts apply to high-pass filters. And high-pass filters can be cascaded with low-pass filters to get bandpass filters or paralleled to get notch filters.

6-3.2 Selection of Inputs and Control of Gain

The selection of inputs and distribution of outputs is normally accomplished by means of analog switches under the control of a microcomputer parallel output port. The individual analog switches of a 4066 can be controlled, each by a bit from an output port, to obtain maximum flexibility throughout the system being controlled. Alternatively, the 4051 can select from one of eight inputs, or distribute to one of eight outputs, using 3 bits from a parallel output port.

Microcomputers are appearing in almost every electronic product. They are useful in a stereo system, for example, because the listener can program a selection of music for a day or more. The microcomputer acts as a very flexible "alarm clock." Analog switches can be used to control the selection and conditioning of analog signals in the preamplifier. We now discuss an example of the use of 4051 switches for selection of inputs to a stereo preamplifier. (See figure 6-11.)

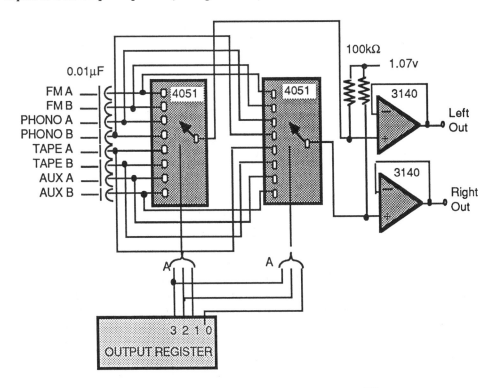

Figure 6-11. Selecting Inputs for a Stereo Preamplifier

This preamplifier has four sources (FM radio, phono, tape, and auxilliary) and each source has two channels (for example, phono A and phono B). All signals are no larger than 1.5 volts peak-to-peak and are as close to that range as possible. The 4 bits from the output port control the two switches such that the high-order 2 bits are the high-order bits of the addresses of both switches, but the lowest-order bit is the low bit of the address of one of the switches, and the next lowest-order bit is the low address bit of the other switch. The 2 high-order bits select the source: FF selects the tuner, FT selects the phono, TF selects the tape input, and TT selects the auxilliary input. The 2 low-order bits select the mode: FF puts the A channel into both speakers, FT puts the A input channel into the A speaker and B input channel into the B speaker (stereo), TF puts the A input into the B speaker and the B input into the A speaker (reverse stereo), and TT puts the B input into both speakers. To select the phono inputs in the stereo mode, the program would put the value $5 into the output register.

We note some fine points of the hardware circuit in figure 6-11. Using a single +5-volt supply both for the analog switches and the OP AMP makes level conversion of the control signals unnecessary. To achieve this, the direct current component of the analog signal must be *biased* by adding a constant to it. The OP AMP has its + input connected to a voltage midway between the limits of the input and output voltage of the CA3140 to keep it in its linear mode of operation. The inputs are connected through capacitors to shift the input signal so it is between 0.2 volts and 2.5 volts.

The analog signal often has to be conditioned either by amplifying or scaling down its magnitude. This is often required because to get maximum accuracy, A to D converters require a voltage range as wide as possible without exceeding the range of the converter; and D to A converters produce an output in a fixed range which may have to be amplified or reduced before it is sent out of the system. Two techniques for scaling down a signal are discussed first, then a technique for amplifying a weak signal at an amplification selected by the computer is discussed. The first technique for scaling down a signal is not unlike the selection of inputs discussed earlier; the scale factor is selected by a switch. The second technique uses a fast switch to sample the input at a given duty cycle. We will discuss examples of these techniques now. Then we explain how the amplification of a signal can be controlled by a computer.

We now consider a mechanism for reducing an analog signal by a factor controlled by an output port of a microcomputer. This mechanism might be used on a microcomputer-controlled digital meter to select the range of the voltmeter. Suppose an input voltage in the range of 0 to 500 volts is to be reduced to a voltage in the range 0 to 0.5 volts to be used in the next stage of the meter. (See figure 6-12a.)

The 4051 selects one of the resistors, connecting it to ground. That resistor becomes part of the voltage divider that reduces the input voltage to be within the range needed by the next stage. The other resistors not selected by the 4051 are effectively connected to very large resistors (turned-off analog switches), so they disappear from the circuit. The voltages across all the switches are kept within 0.6 volts because the computer will select the appropriate resistor to divide the input voltage so the next stage gets a voltage within its range. Thus, the analog switch is not corrupted by unwanted current flow, as we worried about in the last section. This technique can be used to reduce the magnitude of incoming analog signals under the control of a microcomputer.

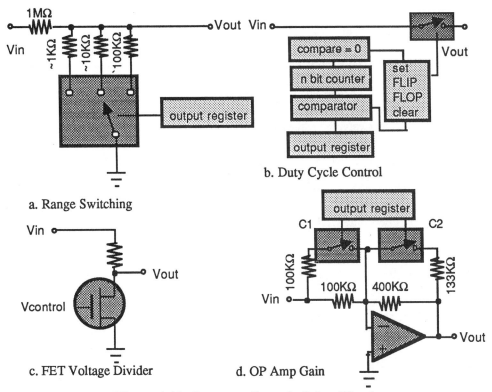

Figure 6-12. Computer Control of Amplification

Another very useful technique is to open and close a switch at a very fast rate, about ten times the maximum frequency of the analog signal being processed. (See figure 6-12b.) If the analog switch is closed, the amplification is unity. If open, the amplification is 0; if open 50% of the time, the amplification is one half. The microcomputer can control the duty cycle of the switch (the percentage of the time the switch is closed) to control the scaling of the analog signal. The output of this switch has a fair amount of high-frequency noise, which can be eliminated by passing it through a low-pass filter. Since an analog switch can operate well at 10 MHz, making the control signal frequency as high as possible eases the requirements on the low-pass filter. A simple way to control the duty cycle is to use an n bit binary counter, a comparator fed from an output port, and a set-clear flip-flop. The counter should be clocked fast enough so that it completes its 2**n count cycle in about ten times the maximum frequency of the analog signal, because that will determine the frequency of the switch control. When the counter passes 0, the flip-flop is set. When the value in the counter is equal to the value in the output register, as determined by the comparator, the flip-flop is cleared. Its output controls the switch, so the duty cycle of the switch is proportional to the number in the output register. A single counter can be used with a number of comparator /flip-flop/switches to control several analog signals. For instance, an octave filter used in sophisticated stereo systems has a band-pass amplifier for each octave so the listener can compensate for irregularities in the reproduction of each octave. Ten comparator/flip-flop/switches can control the amplification of each octave from a microcomputer. This would enable a microcomputer to automatically "calibrate" a stereo system by adjusting the amplification of each octave as tones are generated and responses are measured under its control.

Two other techniques useful for scaling an analog signal deserve mention. A field effect transistor (FET) behaves like a fairly linear resistor, provided the voltage across it, from drain to source, is not too high. The resistance is proportional to the voltage from gate to drain. Alternatively, the resistance of a light sensitive FET is proportional to the light shone on it. Used in an opto-isolator, a light sensitive FET can be used as any resistor in a voltage divider or an operational amplifier circuit. (See figure 6-12c.) Finally, some operational amplifiers (like the CA3180) have a pin whose voltage controls the amplification. These devices can be controlled by a microcomputer sending out a voltage to adjust the light of the opto-isolator FET or by the gain of a suitable operational amplifier. Finally, the level of a signal can be determined and used to adjust the amplification of these devices automatically, in an *automatic gain control* (AGC) circuit. An AGC circuit is sometimes useful to adjust the input voltage to a filter to prevent saturating it.

Amplification (greater than 1) must be done with an OP AMP, but can be controlled with analog switches. By effectively connecting or disconnecting a resistor R1 in parallel with another resistor R2, the resistance can be changed from R2 to (R1 R2)/(R1 + R2). The two resistors in an inverting amplifier can be switched by this method to alter the gain. (Consider figure 6-12d.) If control signals C1 and C2 are HL, the amplification is 1, if LL, the amplification is 2, if HH, 4, and if LH, 8. A second stage, cascaded onto this one, could be built to have amplification 1, 16, 256, or (a rather high) 4096, and so on; so the computer can select the amplification by setting these control signals to the analog switches. Amplification ratios lower than 2 provide closer control and can be obtained by appropriate resistors in the circuit.

6-3.3 Nonlinear Amplification

The final type of signal conditioning is the nonlinear modification of analog signals. A number of fascinating circuits have been advanced to multiply and divide one analog signal by another or to output the square root, log, or sine of an analog signal. Unless the signal is too fast, however, hardware/software tradeoffs usually favor doing this processing in the microcomputer. Three special cases often favor analog hardware signal conditioning; absolute value, logarithmic function, and sample-and-hold. (See figure 6-13.)

A diode is capable of extracting the absolute value of a waveform, and this is the basis of the AM radio detector. An accurate absolute value function is sometimes very useful if, for example, an input voltage whose range is over ± 1 volt is to be measured by an analog to digital converter that can only measure positive signals and perhaps has only a single-ended 5-volt supply. Figure 6-13a puts the diode into the feedback loop of an OP AMP to increase the linearity of the absolute value function. For positive inputs, the diode disconnects the OP AMP so the output is connected to the input via the feedback resistor R2. For negative inputs, the OP AMP simply inverts the input to get the output. Using a CA3140, this circuit can derive the absolute value of sine waves even beyond 100,000 Hertz.

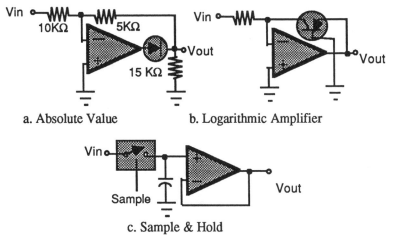

a. Absolute Value   b. Logarithmic Amplifier

c. Sample & Hold

Figure 6-13. Nonlinear Signal Conditioning

The logarithm of an input voltage is sometimes obtained using analog signal conditioners, because audio levels, light levels, and so on are logarithmically related to voltages measured by transducers. Conditioning the analog signal by a logarithmic function drastically compresses the range of signal that must be converted by an analog to digital converter. The transistor's emitter current I is related to its emitter voltage V by the exponential law

$$I = (e^{V/a} - 1)$$

where a is a constant. It can be put into a feedback circuit of an OP AMP to derive a logarithmic function signal conditioner. (See figure 6-13b.) The output Vout is related to the input Vin by

$$Vout = A \log (Vin/ B)$$

where A and B are constants that depend on the resistor in the circuit and on the transistor and its temperature.

The last of the nonlinear signal conditioners of particular use in microcomputer systems is the sample-and-hold circuit. Sometimes used by itself to sample an input signal at a precise time, it is also an important building block in digital to analog converters, covered in section 6-5, and in multiple output data acquisition systems. (See figure 6-13c.) The signal is input through an analog switch. When the switch is on, the voltage on the capacitor quickly approaches the input voltage. When off, the voltage across the capacitor remains steady. The voltage follower makes the output voltage equal to the voltage across the capacitor without changing its voltage by taking current from the capacitor, even though the output may have to supply considerable current to the device it feeds. Turning the switch on causes this circuit to *sample* the input. A microcomputer output register can control the switch to sample an incoming waveform at a precise time so the output voltage from the sample-and-hold circuit can be converted to a digital value.

6-4 A Keyboard and LED Display Module

We now consider the design of a typical keyboard and light emitting diode (LED) display module. This example illustrates some alternatives in analog and digital hardware and in software for solving the problem of contact bounce. This design is also important as a module you'll see on a lot of microcomputers.

This example could well have been introduced in chapter 4 as an application of parallel I/O, and indeed that in an early version of this book we did. However, parallel I/O is just a small part of the design; analog circuits or functions which can be performed by analog, digital, or software techniques are also part of the design. So we put this discussion here, after analog circuits have been introduced. Besides, it offers an opportunity to review parallel I/O, which we have been ignoring in introducing other concepts. It is a good opportunity to tie together the material of the previous three chapters.

6-4.1 Key Debouncing

A keyboard is a collection of switches. Switches have some imperfections, including electrical noise and *contact bounce*. The former is the false signal picked up by the wires due to motors, fluorescent lights, lamp dimmers, and so on; it is more likely a problem in a keyboard module mounted where the user wants to have it than in a microcomputer properly enclosed and isolated from noise. The latter is due to the dynamics of a closing contact. Though a contact appears to close firmly and quickly, at the fast running speeds of a computer, the motion is comparatively slow, and, as it closes, the contact bounces like a ball. This generates a ragged signal, as we soon observe.

A single switch is normally connected as in figure 6-14a. The resistor serves to pull the voltage V to high if the switch is open; the voltage drops to low if the switch is closed. Since we normally think of a variable associated with such a switch as true when the switch is closed, the signal V is in negative logic. This choice is due to the nature of TTL logic, which requires a low resistance connection to ground to reliably input a low signal. Therefore, the resistor is connected to +5 volts, and a switch is connected to ground. This configuration is not necesssary but is usually used for MOS integrated circuits so they can be compatible with TTL in case an existing design using TTL is converted to a microcomputer implementation. This signal can be attached to any input device, such as an M6821 configured as an input, or the 74HC244 discussed earlier. In the following example, we connect it to the most significant bit of the A device because that bit can be easily tested in the program, and because the A device has an internal pull-up resistor so the resistor in figure 6-14a is not needed outside the M6821. If the B device were used, or if a 74HC244 were used as an input device to read the signal from this switch, a separate pull-up resistor would be used.

The noise and contact bounce problem can be solved in analog or digital hardware or in software. The signal V resulting from closing the switch shown in figure 6-14a is shown in figure 6-14b. The signal falls and rises a few times within a period of about 5 milliseconds as the contact bounces. Since a human cannot press and release a switch faster than 20 milliseconds, a *debouncer* will recognize that the switch is closed, after the voltage is low for about 10 milliseconds and will recognize that the switch is open after the voltage is high for about 10 milliseconds.

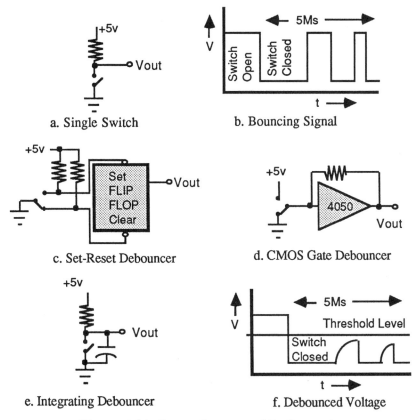

a. Single Switch   b. Bouncing Signal

c. Set-Reset Debouncer   d. CMOS Gate Debouncer

e. Integrating Debouncer   f. Debounced Voltage

Figure 6-14. Contact Bounce and Its Prevention

The bouncing problem can be reduced by using a good switch. A mercury switch is much faster, and an optical switch (whereby a beam of light from an LED to a photodetector is interrupted) or a hall effect switch (whereby the magnetic flux by a semiconductor is changed) are free of bounce. However, it is not difficult to eliminate bounce. Hardware solutions include an analog circuit using a resistor and capacitor to integrate the voltage and two digital solutions using set-reset flip-flops or CMOS buffers and double throw switches. These are discussed next.

In the commonly used set-reset debouncer (figure 6-14c), the switch wiper sets or clears a flip-flop when it contacts the top or bottom plate, respectively. When the switch wiper was up (the flip-flop output was therefore high) and the wiper is moved down, the output remains high because the (negative logic) set and clear signals are false. The first instant the wiper hits the bottom plate, it clears the flip-flop by asserting the clear input. As it bounces (it does not bounce up enough to make contact with the top plate) it continually clears the already cleared flip-flop, so the output remains low. A similar effect occurs when the wiper is moved to the top plate, and the flip-flop is repetitively set on each bounce. In either case, the output changes just once when the wiper is moved to the other plate, so the output is debounced.

A better way uses a non-inverting CMOS gate with a high-input impedance, as shown in figure 6-14d. The wiper normally holds the gate input, and, thus, the gate output, high or low when it is resting on the top or bottom plate. When the wiper is moving, the resistor tends to hold the input where it was. On the first bounce, the output changes, and remains at that level as the wiper leaves the plate, because of the resistor. Successive bounces do not change the output. Thus, the output is debounced.

Several analog debouncers are possible. We will look at the integrating debouncer because it leads to the software technique that we advocate. Figure 6-14e shows how easy an integrating debouncer can be implemented. The input circuit functions like an analog comparator; the input to the microcomputer is high if the voltage sensed by the comparator is above a threshold level. The waveform for the voltage across the capacitor and the threshold are shown in figure 6-14f. While a comparator can be used to precisely sense the voltage level, any gate and the input to the M6821 in particular can be used as a not-too-accurate comparator. Then an integrating comparator can be implemented by simply connecting the peripheral data input of the M6821 through a capacitor to ground.

Software solutions include the *wait-and-see* technique and the software simulation of the *integrating debouncer* just discussed. In the wait-and-see technique, when the input drops indicating the switch might be closed, the program waits 10 milliseconds and looks at the input again. If it is still low, the program decides that the key has indeed been pressed. If it is high, the program decides that the input signal was noise, or that the input is bouncing – which will later certainly show that the key has been pressed. In either case, the program returns to wait for the input to drop.

The integrating debouncer can be simulated by keeping in accumulator B a binary number that represents the voltage across the capacitor in the hardware approach. If the input is low, indicating the switch is closed, the count is incremented; otherwise the count is decremented. This count more or less simulates the voltage across the capacitor. A threshold is used to determine if the key is closed. Suppose accumulator B is initially set to 1 and the input is sampled every millisecond. Then the key is certainly pressed when the count is above 10. This technique is shown in the following program. The key signal is input to the most significant bit of the A device of an M6821 whose data register is at location $8000. (To use this routine in a few later examples, the 2 high-order bits are made input bits.) This device is configured in the reset handler routine by the following ritual:

```
        CLR     $8001
        LDD     #$3F04
        STD     $8000
```

The following program can test this input, remaining in a loop until the key is closed; then, when it is closed, jumping to location L2.

```
        NAM     DEBNCE
        LDAB    #1          INITIALIZE NUMBER OF "CLOSURES" TO 1
L0  LDX     #333        SET UP A DELAY LOOP FOR 2 MHZ CLOCK
LP  DEX                 TO WAIT ABOUT 1 MILLISECOND
        BNE     LP          LOOP UNTIL TIME OUT
        CMPB    #10         SWITCH CLOSED FOR 10 MILLISECONDS?
        BEQ     L2          IF SO, GO TO NEXT ROUTINE
        LDAA    $8000       GET INPUT FROM SWITCH IN MSB.
        BMI     L1          IF HIGH (NEGATIVE) THEN SWITCH NOT CLOSED
        INCB                OTHERWISE (CLOSED) WE INCR. THE COUNTER
        BNE     L0          IF COUNT CHANGES FROM $FF TO 0
        LDAB    #$FF        THEN RESET TO $FF (SATURATE COUNTER)
        BRA     L0          REPEAT CHECK OF KEY
L1  DECB                IF KEY WAS OPEN, DECREMENT COUNT
        BNE     L0          IF IT CHANGED FROM 1 TO 0
        LDAB    #1          THEN RESET IT TO 1 (SATURATE COUNT)
        BRA     L0          REPEAT CHECK OF KEY
L2  RMB     0
        END
```

The first line initializes the count to 1. The next three lines provide a 1-millisecond delay. The count is then tested for the threshold, 10. If the threshold is achieved, go to the next program. The next line inputs the switch signal in the leftmost bit, and this is tested in the next line. If high, the switch is not pressed, and the bottom four lines decrement the counter; otherwise the four lines above it increment the counter. Note that by incrementing and decrementing, we guard against the count cycling through the threshold value of 10; otherwise we would produce the same effect as that of a keyboard repeat key. We conveniently do this by testing the result of incrementing or decrementing the count for 0; if the result reaches 0, it is reset to its former value.

The preceding program can be improved by providing hysteresis, much as a schmitt trigger comparator in hardware improves the integrating debouncer. When the count reaches 10, and the key is sensed closed, the count is changed to $FF, so that if noise decrements it after it has been sensed it will not be affected. If the count is decremented and reaches $F4, which indicates the switch has been open for 10 milliseconds, the count is reset to 1. This simulated hysteresis makes the switch highly immune to noise and quite usable with cheap, bouncy, switches. Modifications to include this feature are simple and are left as an exercise for the reader.

6-4.2 Keyboard Scanning Techniques

A single key is sometimes all that is needed. The preceding hardware and software approaches are often used; the best one depends on cost analysis, as in any hardware-software tradeoff. But we are often in need of tens of switches, as in a typewriter keyboard. Again, there are both hardware and software approaches, and they are mutually analogous.

Keyboards are arranged in arrays for the sake of describing the connections, although physically they can be arranged for the user's convenience. Using terminology from core memory arrays, a *linear select* keyboard uses one decoding and selecting device and is useful for around 10 keys. A *coincident select* or matrix keyboard uses two decoding and selecting devices to determine which key was pressed by coincidental recognition of the row and column the key is in. A diagram of an 8-key linear select keyboard is shown in figure 6-15a, and a 64-key keyboard diagram is sketched in figure 6-15b. Though there are dozens of good keyboard designs, these two are used here because with them we can extend the preceding example to introduce the "key" ideas in a nice way. The selector is an *analog switch,* such as a CMOS 4051. For a given address A output from the low-order 3 bits of the M6821, the A*th* input on the left is connected to the output on the right through a small (200-ohm) resistance. In the coincident select keyboard, a decoder such as the 74LS138 is used to select a column. For a given address B output from the next 3 low-order bits of the M6821 to the decoder, the B*th* column is made low while the others are made high.

The keyboards have to be *scanned* to determine which key is pressed. For the moment, we assume no keys are pressed or only one key is pressed. A scanning program can search for the pressed key, then the debounce routine recently described can be used to verify that the key is closed.

The scanning program will be described for the linear select keyboard, using the hardware illustrated in figure 6-15a. The initialization of the M6821 is the same as that used earlier in this section, and the following routine can precede the recently described debounce program so that the key found by the scanner will be debounced.

```
          NAM    SCAN
    L     INC    $8000
          BMI    L
          DEC    $8000
          END
```

The routine uses several capabilities of the M6821 to advantage. The low-order 6 bits of the device have been configured by the initialization ritual as a readable output register, so an instruction like INC $8000 will increment them, but the high-order 2 bits are input and thus are not affected by this instruction. The most significant bit is the signal from the switch selected by the low-order 3 bits output from the device. The next low-order bit is always a false value. (This prevents the carry from the INC operation from propagating into the most significant bit.) Then the instruction INC $8000 will first read the device, including the scanning count in the low-order 3 bits and the input from the switch in the high-order bit, increment this number, set the condition code, and then store the result back in the device. Note that the N condition code is true if the signal S is low; this means that the switch selected by the low-order bits in the device output register was closed. Even though the number counts from 0 to 63, only the low-order 3 bits are used, so the count seen by the selector counts from 0 to 7 repetitively until a key is seen to be closed. The condition code senses the key selected by the count before it is incremented, so the scan count should be decremented before it is used to select the key sensed by the debounce routine.

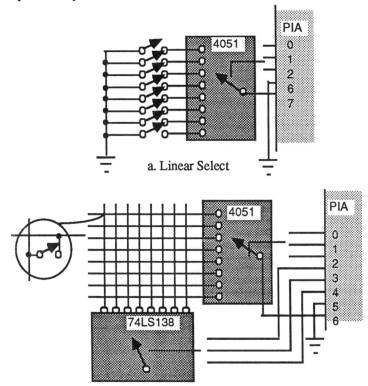

a. Linear Select

b. Coincident Select

Figure 6-15. Keyboard Structures

The program for the coincident select keyboard scan is actually identical to the one for the linear select keyboard. Suppose this program is executed using the hardware illustrated in figure 6-15b on the M6821's peripheral data lines. If the 3 bits sent to the decoder are held constant while the scan program samples keys, any key in the column selected by those 3 bits will be scanned, and the debounce program will be entered whenever any one of them appears to have been pressed. If a key in any other column were pressed, the scan program would not see any different signals (as long as the 3 bits to the decoder don't change). If the 3 bits to the decoder are allowed to change naturally by the INC instruction, all the columns will be sampled one after the other, and as each column is sampled, all keys in it will be sampled by the scan routine. The same scan routine used by the linear select keyboard also works with this keyboard.

The preceding scan and debounce routines have some limitations. It is possible to eliminate the hardware selector and decoder modules by using both devices in an M6821, one to shift a low bit to scan the columns and another to input all eight row signals to be studied by software. The principle uses singulary rather than binary number scanning, and the patterns are rotated instead of incremented. This is often desirable because it reduces the number of hardware components. However, it uses more lines to an M6821. If these lines are needed for some other function, like controlling an LED display, two small chips can be used in place of another M6821.

The preceding technique assumes that only one key is pressed at a time. If we allow two keys to be pressed simultaneously – as is often done by proficient keyboard users who press a new key before releasing the key being pressed – the program might keep picking up the first key, not seeing the new key while the first is in its scan. Any technique that can correctly recognize a new key even though n-1 keys are already pressed and are still down is said to exhibit *n-key roll-over*. Two-key roll-over is a common and useful feature that can be achieved with most keyboards, but for larger numbers one must guard against sneak paths through the keys. Sneak paths appear when three keys at three corners of a rectangle are pushed, and the fourth key seems to have been pushed because current can take a circuitous path through the pressed keys when the fourth key is being sensed. This can be prevented by putting diodes in series with each switch to block this sneak path current, but the solution is rather expensive and n-key rollover is not usually useful.

The hardware approach for keyboard scanning and debouncing actually uses the same principles as the software approach does. A special purpose integrated circuit connects to the keyboard and executes routines like those just described; the microprocessor connects to an output from them, from which the code for the key appears. Though this takes all the effort out of keyboard interfacing, it adds another large chip to the hardware; in addition, the microprocessor may anyhow be twiddling away in a delay loop while awaiting a command entered through the keyboard. The software approach to scanning and debouncing is therefore rather commonly used.

6-4.3 Displays

We now extend the example to include a display for the keyboard. The hardware and software to support the keyboard and display are quite similar and can be shared. These two modules are both used very often for user input/output. We'll study the LED, the LED display, and the scanned display, giving concrete examples, including those for the very convenient MC14499 LED display and 145000 LCD display chips.

Recall that an LED is a diode that emits light if about ten milliamperes of positive current flow from anode to cathode. These diodes can be arranged in the form of a block 8, a diode per bar in the figure 8. To save pins, either the cathodes or the anodes are tied together internally. The first is called a *common cathode* LED display, and the cathode is connected to ground. (See figure 6-16a.)

To display a digit, the LEDs are turned on or off in each segment. Using the lettering system shown in figure 6-16a, which is widely used in practice, a *seven-segment code* covers the values variables a through g. The seven-segment code for the number 2 is TTFTTFT. The representation of the number in the computer is hexadecimal (or binary-coded decimal). This representation must be recoded into its seven-segment form, and the seven-segment variables must be applied to the display to turn on the LEDs. This can be done in hardware or software. In the hardware approach, a *seven-segment decoder-driver* integrated circuit chip is used. The hexadecimal number from the computer output device is input to this chip, and its output is attached to the display LEDs. In the software approach, the hexadecimal number is converted by a routine -usually a table lookup routine- into the desired seven-segment code, which is then output to the LEDs. However, since the output device may be able to supply about 1 milliampere, a *segment driver* integrated circuit amplifies the signal. figure 6-16a diagrams a popular segment driver, the 75491, which was designed for the high-volume calculator market. To use it with a microcomputer, a pull-up resistor on its input is often needed. If the input to the 75491 is high, current flows through the transistor. This current, limited by the small (100-ohm) current limiting resistor, goes through the LED to light it.

A typical program to generate the seven-segment code for a display uses table lookup. Suppose a table TBL stores the seven-segment codes for the digits; the i*th* row is the code for the i*th* digit, and the hexadecimal number to be displayed is in accumulator B. This routine will output the code through an output device at location $8002:

```
NAM    LOOK
LDX    #TBL    GET ADDRESS OF TABLE IN X
ABX            ADD B TO X
LDAA   0,X     GET 7-SEGMENT CODE IN A
STAA   $8002   OUTPUT IT
END
```

A single display may be needed in some applications, but we are often in need of several displays. Just as the concepts used for the single switch can be easily expanded to a keyboard, the preceding technique can be easily expanded to handle multiple displays. One way to handle multiple displays is to have one output device for each display. Alternatively, the displays can be *multiplexed*. Multiplexing is usually used because it saves the cost of several output devices; but sometimes it generates noise which might be intolerable, for instance, if a sensitive radio is near the display. In that case, separate displays must be used.

In multiplexed displays, the cathode of a common cathode display is connected to ground through a transistor. If the transistor is turned off, no current can flow through any of the LEDs in the display, so it appears dark regardless of the signals applied to the anodes. Suppose n displays are connected, with corresponding anodes connected to a segment driver as in the previous example and the transistors connected to a second output device so that only one is turned on. If the first transistor is turned on and the preceding program is executed, the number in accumulator A is displayed on the first display. If another number is put in accumulator A and the second display is turned on, that number is displayed in the second display, and so on. The number can be read from a table, for instance. The displays are turned on one at a time as the numbers to be displayed are picked up from the table by a table interpreter and are entered through putting them in accumulator A and executing the preceding program. Each is turned on for the same amount of time. Note that each display is on for 1/*nth* of the time. The current limiting resistor is made smaller so that n times as much current is sent through the LED, thus ensuring it is as bright as if driven as a single display. (See figure 6-16b.)

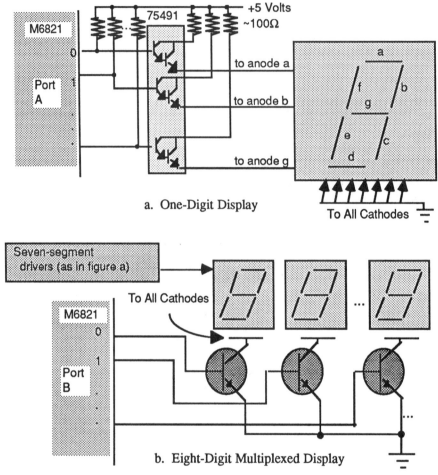

a. One-Digit Display

b. Eight-Digit Multiplexed Display

Figure 6-16. Seven-Segment Displays

Multiplexed displays are widely used in calculators. The *digit driver* 75492 integrated circuit has six transistors capable of being used in the cathode line of these displays; and *peripheral drivers* like the 75451 have two NAND gates, each connected to a transistor, that can be used in this application. Multiplexing is useful for up to about ten displays; beyond that, too much current must be put through the LEDs for the small percentage of the cycle in which they are scanned. Even with six displays, if something goes wrong while one display is being driven so it remains on for longer than one-sixth the scan time, it can be burned out by the rather large currents flowing through it.

Other types of displays are used. A liquid crystal display is configured like an LED display, except that the bars are capacitors. A digit is displayed by putting voltages across the appropriate bars, much as in the LED display. However, if an LCD display has direct current across the capacitor, it weakens due to polarization of the chemical in it. An alternating voltage must be imposed to darken it. If the root mean square (RMS) voltage is below about 1 volt, the display is clear, and if above about 2 volts, it is opaque. The control circuitry supplies a voltage of 0, 1, 2, or 3 volts to the plates of the capacitors. The common connection analogous to the cathode in the LED display is senta square wave of 1 volt alternating with 2 volts if the digit is not selected, and of 0 volts alternating with 3 volts if the digit is selected. The connection analogous to the anode in the LED display is also sent a square wave. If the segment square wave is 2 volts whenever the common connection of a selected segment is at 0 volts, and is 1 volt whenever it is at 3 volts, then the segment in the selected digit will have enough RMS voltage to darken. If the segment square wave is 1 volt when the common connection of a selected terminal is 0 volts, and 2 volts when it is 3 volts, the segment does not have quite enough voltage across it to darken. Note too that none of the segments of the non-selected digits have enough RMS voltage to darken. When one digit is selected, all the segments to be darkened in it are given a signal that will darken them. One digit is scanned at a time. This technique provides the required alternating voltage free of DC to protect the LCDs. However, if the number of digits scanned this way increases, the RMS voltage of the segments to be darkened decreases so the ratio of the clear to dark levels gets too small to work reliably. So LCDs can be multiplexed, but only about three or four can be multiplexed together. The technique is to multiplex half the seven-segment display, consisting of four segments, at the same time the other half is multiplexed, and do this for each segment. In effect, the multiplexing is done orthogonally to the way it is done in LED displays -by scanning down half a segment rather than across all the segments. Finally, incandescent, gas discharge, and fluorescent seven-segment displays are also used, and self-scanning PANAPLEX displays can be used for user messages.

One can see that there is a similarity between the keyboard scan and the display scan hardware and software. Indeed, the decoder that selects the column of the keyboard can also select the digit to be displayed, and, as the rows are read from the keyboard the segments can be driven to display the digit through another output device. One can feast the imagination on all the variations of this technique that can be implemented.

The MC14499 and MC145000 are two chips that use the serial interface technique introduced in section 4-4. Serial interfacing uses a small number of the 6811's pins, such as the data, clock, and enable pins, and is suitable for rather slow I/O devices, such as displays that cannot be read by the eye any faster than one pattern every few seconds. As discussed in section 4-4.1, series and parallel configurations of these chips are possible, so they very effectively solve the display problem for microcomputers like the 6811.

The MC14499 seven-segment LED display with serial interface is a very convenient package. (See figure 6-17a.) One chip can multiplex four digits (and chips can be serially cascaded to handle more digits). Data on the data pin is shifted on the falling edge of the clock input Ck into a 20-bit shift register when the enable input En is low, to specify four digits and four decimal points, as illustrated in figure 6-17b. The decimal points (1 = ON) are sent first, and that for digit 1 is sent first. Then the binary-coded digits are sent in, digit 1 first and most significant bit first. When all bits are sent in, the En input is made high, which causes the data in the shift register to be transferred to the register that drives the LED display. The chip multiplex timing frequency is set by a capacitor on pin 6.

The MC145000 is a multiplexed LCD driver with serial interface capable of driving up to 6 seven-segment digits, (and can be cascaded to handle more). LCD displays are not uniformly configured, but figure 6-17c shows one way (used on the General Electric LXD69D3F09KG LCD display). Data are shifted into a 48-bit shift

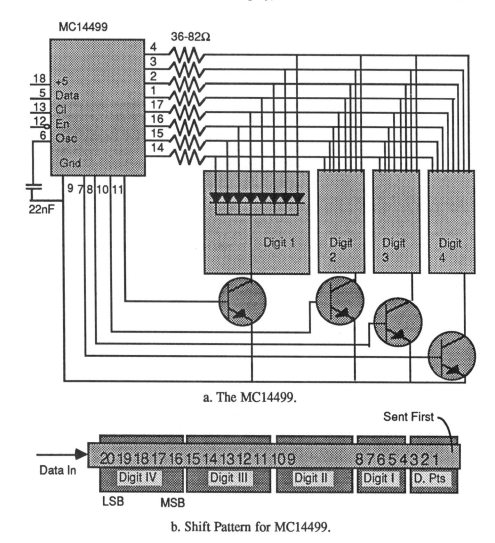

a. The MC14499.

b. Shift Pattern for MC14499.

Figure 6-17. Special Serial Interface Chips for LED and LCD Displays

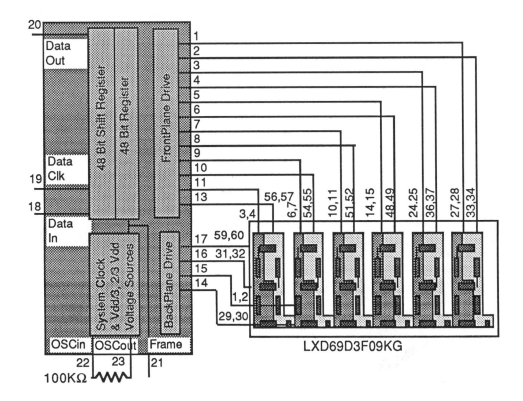

c. The MC145000

Figure 6-17. (continued)

register on the falling edge of the data clock. When the LCD display is fully updated, an output pulse appears on the frame pin (pin 21), and the contents of the shift register is transferred to the output register, which determines what will be displayed in the next display period. The first 8 bits shifted in will govern the least-significant digit location, 1 bit per segment (d first, then e, g, f, decimal point, c, b, and a). The next 8 bits govern the next digit in like manner, and so on. The chip multiplex timing frequency is set by a resistor between pins 22 and 23, whose value depends on the LCD display. Whereas the LED display gets the bcd data and decodes them in the chip, the actual segment pattern is sent to the MC145000, so a translation routine like LOOK is needed.

6-5 Converters

We often convert analog signals into digital signals and vice versa. Also, we convert analog amplitude signals into analog frequency signals and vice versa. The first subsection describes the digital-to-analog converters that are commonly available for microcomputer I/O systems. The next subsection describes analog-to-digital converters.

Though they seem to be more common than digital-to-analog converters, we discuss them later because some analog-to-digital converters use digital-to-analog converters inside them. Finally, the frequency-to-voltage and voltage-to-frequency converters are discussed.

The following are some important concepts that cover the various converters. In general, the analog input is either sampled, using a sample-and-hold circuit or its equivalent, or integrated, using an integrator circuit or its equivalent. Analog output is either produced in samples or is output from an integrator. Integration smooths out the signal, reducing noise, but limits the upper-frequency signal components. Sampling provides a "snapshot" of the data and also the noise. In sampling converters, another problem is caused by high frequencies. The *sampling rate* is obviously the rate at which the data samples are taken. The *Nyquist rate* is one-half the sampling rate. Components of the signal that have higher frequency than the Nyquist rate "beat against" the frequency of the sampling rate in the same manner as radio frequency signals are "beat against" the frequency of a local oscillator in a radio, generating *alias* frequency components. For example, if a component has a frequency equal to the sampling rate, it will appear as a direct current component. To eliminate the generation of these alias components, a low-pass filter is used to eliminate all frequencies above the Nyquist rate.

6-5.1 Digital-to-Analog Converters

Three basic digital to analog converters (D-to-A's) are introduced now: the summing amplifier, the ladder, and the exponential superposition D-to-A's. The summing amplifier converter most readily shows the basic principle behind all D-to-A converters, which is that each digital bit contributes a weighted portion of the output voltage if the bit is true, and the output is the sum of the portions. The ladder converters are easier to build because the resistors in a ladder network can be trimmed precisely without much effort. Ladder networks for these D-to-A converters are readily available, quite fast, and inexpensive. The exponential superposition converter is quite a bit slower and less accurate, but doesn't need precision components, so it would be very useful in microcomputer-based toys or appliance controllers. A convenient package of 6-bit D-to-A converters, the MC144110, will be considered at the subsection's end.

The summing amplifier can be used in an A-to-D converter, as in figure 6-18a. Keeping in mind that the output voltage is

$$V_{out} = - Rf (V1/R1 + V2/R2 + ...)$$

if $V1 = V2 = ... = 1$ volt, and Ri is either infinity (an open switch) or a power of 2 times Rf (if the corresponding switch is closed), then the output voltage is

$$V_{out} = C1 / 2 + C2 / 4 + C3 / 8 + ...$$

where C_i is 1 if the switch in series with the ith resistor is closed; otherwise it is 0. An output device can be used to control the switches, so the ith most significant bit controls the ith switch. Then the binary number in the output register, considered as a fraction, is converted into a voltage at the output of the summing amplifier. Moreover, if the reference input voltage is made v volts rather than 1 volt, the output is the fraction specified by the output register times v volts. V can be fixed at a convenient value, like 10 volts, to *scale* the converter. Usually, a D-to-A converter is scaled to a level, so for largest output value the summing amplifier is nearly, but not quite, saturated, to minimize errors due to noise and to offset voltages and currents. Alternatively, if V is itself an analog signal, it is multiplied by the digital value in the output register. This D-to-A converter is thus a *multiplying D-to-A converter*, and can be used as a digitally controlled voltage divider -an alternative to the range switch and duty cycle control techniques for amplification control.

Although conceptually neat, the above converter requires using from eight to twelve precision resistors of different values, which can be difficult to match in the 2-to-1 ratios needed. An alternative circuit, an *R-2R ladder* network, can be used in a D-to-A converter that uses precision resistors, all of which have values R or 2R ohms. This network can be used as a voltage divider or a current divider; the former is conceptually simpler but the latter is more commonly used. (See figure 6-18b for a diagram of a current ladder D-to-A converter.) A pair of analog switches for each "2R" resistor connect the resistor either into the negative input to the OP AMP or to ground, depending on whether the control variable is high or low, respectively. The current through these switches, from left to right, varies in proportion to 1/2, 1/4, 1/8, ..., as can be verified by simple circuit analysis. If the *ith* control variable is true, a current proportional to $2^{**}-1$ is introduced into the negative input of the OP AMP, which must be counterbalanced by a negative current through Rf to keep the negative input at virtual ground, so the output voltage proportional to $2^{**}-i$ is generated. The components for each input i are added, so the output is proportional to the value of the binary number whose bits control the switches. Like the previous A-to-D converter, this can be scaled by appropriately selecting the voltage Vin and can be used as a digitally controlled amplification device. It, too, is a multiplying A-to-D converter.

A program for outputting a voltage by means of either a summing or an R-2R D-to-A converter is very simple. One merely stores the number to be converted onto an output register that is connected to the converter.

A ladder network for a converter can be obtained as an integrated circuit for 6 to 12 bits of accuracy. The chip contains the switches and the resistors for the circuit. The output settles to the desired voltage level in less than a microsecond in a typical converter, so the programmer usually does not have to worry about settling time.

The last converter uses a sample-and-hold circuit to sample a voltage that is the sum of exponential voltages corresponding to bits of the digital word being converted. The circuit, in figure 6-18c, is simplicity itself. We first offer some observations on an exponential waveform and the superposition principle. Consider an exponential waveform as shown in figure 6-18d. Note that for such a signal there is a time T (not the time constant of the network, though) at which the signal is 1/2 the initial value of the signal. And at times 2 T, 3 T, 4 T, and so on, the signal level is 1/4, 1/8, 1/16 of the initial value, and so on. Furthermore, in a linear circuit, the actual voltage can be computed from the sum of the voltages of each waveform. This is called superposition. Now if a sample-and-hold circuit samples a voltage that is a sum of exponential voltages, an exponential waveform that was started T time units before will contribute

1/2 its initial value; one that was started 2 T time units before will contribute 1/4 its initial value; one started 3 T units before will contribute 1/8 its initial value; and so on. Thus, by generating or not generating each of the exponential waveforms from left to right in figure 6-18d, the voltage sampled will or will not have a component of 1/8, 1/4, 1/2, and so on. These waveforms are generated by asserting control variable P if the shifted bit is true, as the least significant bits are shifted out each T time units. This closes the switch if the bit shifted out is true, so that the current source pumps a charge into the capacitor to generate the exponential that contributes its component of the sampled voltage. The control variable S is asserted to sample the waveform after all bits have been shifted out. The sampled voltage is the desired output of the D-to-A converter. The output can be scaled by selecting an appropriate current source, but this A-to-D converter doesn't make a good multiplying converter because dynamically changing the input current level will destroy its accuracy.

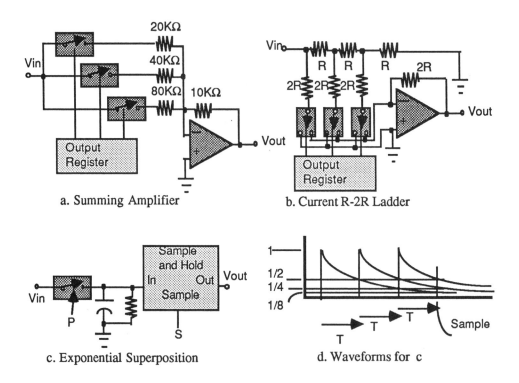

Figure 6-18. D-to-A Converters

The following program to convert an 8-bit number in ACCA to a voltage assumes that an M6821 output register at location $8000 is a readable output device, and bit 0 controls the switch via control variable P (see figure 6-18c.) It also assumes that an address decoder supplies an address trigger (as discussed in section 4-1.1) to assert the S control signal and thus sample the data, whenever the address $8004 is generated in a read or write operation.

```
NAM  EXSP
CLR   $8001   MAKE $800 THE DIRECTION REGISTER
LDX   #$FF04  PUT $FF IN DIRECTION, $04 IN CONTROL
STX   $8000   TO MAKE ALL BITS READABLE OUTPUT SO LSR WORKS
STAA  $8000   PUT NUMBER IN OUTPUT REG., OUTPUT LSB TO A/D
LSR   $8000   NEXT LSB TO A/D CONTROL
LSR   $8000   3RD BIT TO A/D CONTROL
LSR   $8000   4TH BIT TO A/D CONTROL
LSR   $8000   5TH BIT TO A/D CONTROL
LSR   $8000   6TH BIT TO A/D CONTROL
LSR   $8000   7TH BIT TO A/D CONTROL
LSR   $8000   MSB TO A/D CONTROL
LDAA  $8004   PULSE TO SAMPLE COMPOSITE EXPONENTIAL SIGNAL
END
```

The first three lines initialize the M6821 to output the least significant bit of the data register and make the other bits act like a read/write memory word (that is, also make them "output" bits). In the next line, the data to be converted are stored into the data register. Note that this will cause the least significant bit to be sent to the A-to-D converter to generate an exponential signal if the bit is true. Then the number to be converted is shifted seven times to generate the other seven exponential waveforms. Finally the address $8004 is generated, so the address decoder will output a pulse to the S line to cause the sample-and-hold module to sample the waveform. As explained earlier, this waveform contains components from each output bit if that bit was true, and the component generated by the most significant bit is twice as big as the component for the next, and so on.

Accuracy of this simple converter is limited to just a few bits. The sample-and-hold circuit loads the capacitor, and the current source doesn't supply a fixed current if its output is stopped and started. Nevertheless, this converter requires a minimum of adjustment. The resistor is adjusted so the exponential decay time T corresponds to the time to execute the LSR instruction in the preceding program. This simple converter would be most suitable, for instance, where a microcomputer runs a toy train by controlling a voltage supplied to the motor.

The last D-to-A converter we discuss is the MC144110, a serial interface chip that has six 6-bit converters. (See figure 6-19.) A serial interface requires fewer pins than a parallel interface and also is easier to isolate using opto-isolators if the analog voltage must be on a different ground system than the microcomputer. The data are shifted in from the data pin serially, left to right (msb first), on the falling edge of the bit clock Ck, when En is low. When 36 bits have been shifted in, En should rise and the data will be put in the register, where each 6 bits will govern the analog output of a D-to-A converter; the register bit switches the bottom of the 2R resistor to ground or to +5v. The outputs of the ladder networks (pins 3, 5, and so on) can be used as inputs to FET OP AMP voltage followers. The transistors in each D-to-A converter can be used as emitter follower current amplifiers for low-impedance bipolar OP AMPs.

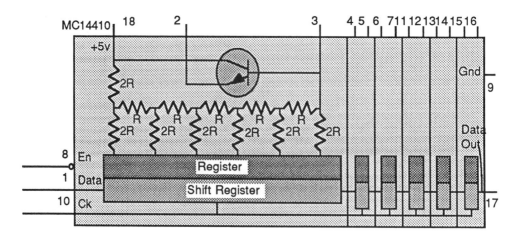

Figure 6-19. The MC144110

6-5.2 Analog to Digital Converters

In a manner like that of the previous subsection, six analog-to-digital converters (A-to-Ds) are introduced. These have different costs, accuracies, and speeds. We discuss them in approximate order of decreasing speed and cost. The parallel and pipeline converters are fastest, followed by the delta and successive approximation converters and the ramp converters.

The *parallel* A-to-D converter uses comparators to determine the input voltage and can be made to operate almost as fast as the comparators. One avoids using too many comparators because they are expensive, so this converter's accuracy is limited by the number of its comparators. Figure 6-20a illustrates a typical 3-bit converter that has, for ease of discussion, a range of 0 to 7 volts. The resistor divider network establishes reference voltages for each comparator, from top to bottom, of 0, 1, 2,...,7 volts. If the input voltage Vin is between i-1 and i volts, the i bottom comparators output a true value. A priority encoder module encodes this set of values to a binary number that is the most prior true input address, which is i.

A variation of the parallel converter, a *pipeline converter*, consists of n identical stages of a comparator and differential amplifier (see figure 6-20b and figure 6-20c) to achieve n bits of accuracy. In a typical stage illustrated in figure 6-20b, the signal Vin is sent to the input, and the output Vout of the differential amplifier on the right of the stage is then sent to the input of the next stage to the right. Suppose the voltage range is Vmax. The output of the comparator on the left of the stage is either Vmax if the V+ input is higher than the V- input of the comparator or it is 0 volts. If the input is above half Vmax, then half Vmax is subtracted from the input and then doubled – otherwise the input is just doubled – in the differential amplifier that feeds the output Vout. If a steady signal is fed into the input, Vin, then as the signal flows through the stages, bits from most significant bit are obtained from each stage, being true if half Vmax was subtracted, otherwise being false. Moreover, the conversion is actually done as the leading edge of the analog signal flows through each stage. It is possible, then, to begin the next conversion when the first stage has settled, even though later stages may yet be settling. Its rather like oil flowing through a pipeline. This kind of system is then called a pipeline. A few years ago, an experimental 6-bit converter was reported to have an incredible 8-gigaHertz conversion rate. Digital oscilloscopes, anyone?

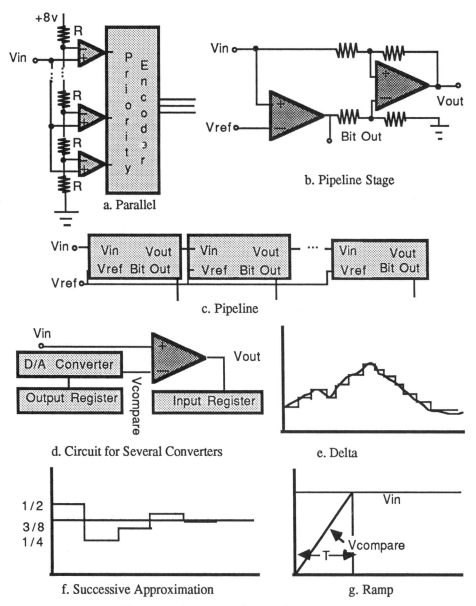

Figure 6-20. A-to-D Conversion Techniques

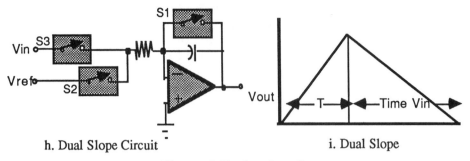

h. Dual Slope Circuit   i. Dual Slope

Figure 6-20. (continued)

Successive approximation, delta, and ramp converters can be implemented with the hardware illustrated in figure 6-20d. The programs differ for each method. For *delta* or *servo* conversion, a D-to-A converter outputs a voltage Vcomp which is compared to Vin. If Vcomp > Vin, then Vcomp is diminished; otherwise Vcomp is increased by a small amount. Assuming Vin changes slower than Vcomp can change, Vcomp should "track" Vin in the manner of a feedback control or servo system. By another analogy to communications systems, the digital output changes by delta increments, as in delta modulation systems. Figure 6-20e shows a varying Vin and a tracking Vcomp for a delta converter. The following program for an 8-bit delta converter assumes that location $8000 is an output register, whose output is converted by the 8-bit D-to-A converter to Vcomp, and location $8001 is an input register, whose sign bit is true if Vin > Vcomp.

```
L1 TST   $8001   INPUT BIT TO SIGN CONDITION CODE
   BMI   L2      IF 1 (NEGATIVE) THEN GO TO INCREMENT
   DEC   $8000   ELSE DECREASE OUTPUT VOLTAGE
   BRA   L1      REPEAT TEST AND ADJUSTMENT
L2 INC   $8000   INCREMENT OUTPUT, INCREASE OUTPUT VOLTAGE
   BRA   L1      REPEAT TEST AND ADJUSTMENT
```

The number in location $8000, which tracks the input voltage, can be read at any time. A servo converter can also be built using digital hardware, so a processor is not tied up in the loop, but the technique is identical. Servo converters are as fast as the comparator, D-to-A converter, and up-down counter that track the input. However, like OP AMPs, they have a slew rate limitation that may be unacceptable.

A *successive approximation* converter uses the same circuit but requires a program that embodies a different principle – the principle of divide-and-conquer. We observe the same technique in long division. Suppose the input is in the range 0 to Vmax. The D-to-A converter is so loaded as to output Vmax/2. If the comparator senses Vin > Vmax/2, then the D-to-A converter is set to output Vmax 3/4, otherwise it is set to output Vmax/4. Note that this is done by either adding or subtracting Vmax/4 from the current output, depending on the result of comparing this output with Vin. In successive trials, Vmax/8, then Vmax/16, Vmax/32,... are added or subtracted from the value output to the D-to-A converter. The comparison voltage Vref approaches Vin, as shown in figure 6-20f. The subroutine, shown below is written as a subroutine because we will call this subroutine in a program in section 6-6.

```
        NAM  SUCCESS
        LDAA #$80        START AT MID VALUE, AS FIRST GUESS
        PSHA             COPY, TOP STACK WORD HOLDS "ADJUSTMENT"
        TSY              GET REFERENCE TO TOP OF STACK FOR INDEX ADDR.
L1      LSR  0,Y         DIVIDE ADJUSTMENT VALUE BY 2 TO ADJUST NEXT BIT
        BEQ  L3          IF ZERO, ALL BITS HAVE BEEN ADJUSTED
        STAA $8000       OUTPUT TOTALIZED VALUE TO COMPARE TO INPUT
        TST  $8001       LOOK AT COMPARATOR, SIGN BIT IS COMP. OUTPUT
        BPL  L2          IF LOW (POSITIVE) THEN SUBTRACT ADJUSTMENT
        ADDA 0,Y         ELSE ADD ADJUSTMENT TO TOTALIZED VALUE
        BRA  L1          REPEAT TO ADJUST NEXT BIT
L2      SUBA 0,Y         SUBRTACT ADJUSTMENT TO TRY LOWER VOLTAGE
        BRA  L1          THEN REPEAT TO ADJUST NEXT LESS SIGNIFICANT BIT
L3      PULA             RESTORE STACK
        RTS  RETURN TO CALLER
        END
```

Accumulator A is generally output in line 5, and the word on the top of the stack is added to or subtracted from A. These are initialized to half the range so the D-to-A converter will initially try Vcomp = Vmax/2. In the loop, in line 3, the adjustment value is divided by 2, so that in the first execution of the loop, Vmax/4 will be added to or subtracted from the comparison voltage; in the second execution of the loop, Vmax/8 will be added or subtracted, and so on. Next, the adjustment value is examined; if it has become 0 the conversion must be complete. If so, a jump to L3 completes the program. Otherwise, that number in accumulator A is output to try the comparison voltage Vcomp, in line 4. The comparator output is tested in line 5. If Vin > Vcomp, then accumulator B is added to A to get the next comparison voltage; otherwise it is subtracted. (This program always leaves the least significant bit true, regardless of the input; this can be fixed by further processing.) Successive approximation converters are quite fast, because each execution of the loop determines one more digit of the result. Moreover, by implementing this technique in hardware (called a successive approximation register), the computer can concentrate on other things as the voltage is being converted.

A *ramp* analog to digital converter can use the same circuit as in figure 6-20d or a simpler circuit as in figure 6-20h. Simply, in figure 6-20d, the comparator voltage Vcomp is initialized to 0 by clearing location $8000, then is gradually increased by incrementing $8000 until Vcomp > Vin is sensed by the comparator. (See figure 6-20g.) The circuit illustrated in figure 6-20h uses a *dual slope* technique that is shown in figure 6-20i. The output voltage from the integrator, sensed by the comparator, is initially cleared by closing only switch S1. Then, by closing only S2 for a specific time T, the reference Voltage − Vref is integrated, charging the capacitor in the integrator. Lastly only S3 is closed, so that the voltage Vin is integrated to discharge the capacitor. The time to discharge the capacitor is proportional to Vin. Moreover, the time is proportional to the average value of Vin over the time it is integrated, which nicely reduces noise we don't want to measure; and the accuracy of the converter does not depend on the values of the components (except Vref), so this converter is inexpensive.

However, it is the slowest converter. It finds great use, nevertheless, in digital voltmeters, multimeters, and panel meters, because it can achieve about 12 bits (3-and-a-half digits) of accuracy at low cost, and it is faster than the eye watching the display.

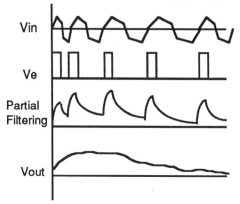

a. Frequency-to-Pulse-Train-to-Voltage-Conversion

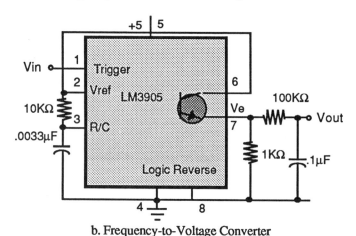

b. Frequency-to-Voltage Converter

Figure 6-21. Frequency-to-Voltage Conversion

Related to the digital to analog converter, a *frequency-to-voltage converter* (FVC) outputs a voltage that is proportional to the input frequency. For high frequencies, an FM detector serves this function. Several integrated circuits are available for detecting FM signals. For a broad range of frequencies, a phase-locked loop can be used. The error voltage used to lock the oscillator in it to the frequency of the incoming signal is proportional to the difference between the frequency to which the oscillator is tuned and the frequency of the incoming signal. For audio frequencies, a common technique is to trigger a one-shot with the leading edge of the input signal. The output is a pulse train, where the pulses are of constant width and height and occur with the same frequency as the input signal. (See figure 6-21a.) This signal is passed through a low-pass filter to output a signal that is proportional to the area under the pulses, which is in turn proportional to the frequency. The LM3905 is especially suited to this application, as it is a one-shot (monostable) with built-in voltage reference and an output transistor that is capable of producing output pulses of precise height. (See figure 6-21b.) Another way to convert frequency to voltage is to use an integrated circuit specially made for the vast automobile market to implement a tachometer, since a tachometer senses spark pulses whose frequency is proportional to engine speed, and it outputs an analog level to a meter to display the engine speed. This technique can be used with subaudio frequencies, since it is designed to measure low-rate spark pulse trains. Frequency to voltage converters have the advantage that information is carried by the frequency of a signal on a single wire, which can be easily opto-isolated, and is remarkably immune to noise and degradation due to losses in long wires from microcomputer to output. However, the signal they carry has to pass through a low-pass filter, so its maximum frequency must be much lower than that of the carrier which is being converted to the voltage.

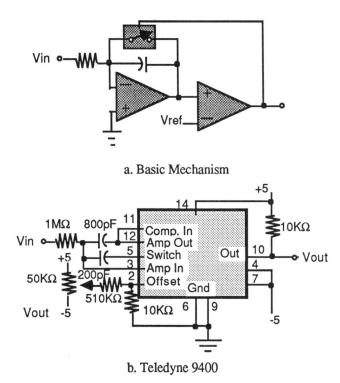

a. Basic Mechanism

b. Teledyne 9400

Figure 6-22. Voltage to Frequency Conversion

The final converter of interest is the voltage-to-frequency converter. It generates a square wave whose frequency or period is proportional to the input voltage Vin. (See figure 6-22a.) Internally, Vin is integrated, until the integrated voltage reaches a reference voltage Vref, when the integrated voltage is cleared. An output pulse, occurring as the integrator is cleared, has a frequency that is proportional to the input Vin. If desired, this can be fed to a toggle flip-flop to square the signal as its period is doubled. By reversing the role of the reference and input voltage so the reference voltage is integrated and compared to the input voltage, the period of the output is proportional to the voltage Vin. So this makes a voltage-to-period converter. But noise on Vin is not averaged out in this technique. Other circuits are used for VFCs, but the principles are similar to those discussed here. VFCs can be quite accurate and reasonably fast; the Teledyne 9400 (see figure 6-22b) accurately converts voltage to frequency to about 13 bits of accuracy and remains equally accurate after two cycles have occurred on the output wave. That means the converter is faster for higher voltages, since they result in higher frequencies, than for lower voltages. Used in an integrating mode, moreover, the VFC can reduce noise the way the dual ramp converter does. The VFC is of particular value where the microprocessor has a built-in counter to measure frequency, especially since the frequency carrying signal is easy to handle, being carried on only one wire.

6-6 Data Acquisition Systems

A *data acquisition system* (DAS) consists of switches, a D-to-A converter, and signal conditioning circuits so that several inputs can be measured and several outputs can be supplied under the control of a microcomputer. In the first subsection, we consider the basic idea of a data acquisition subsystem. Then we consider the MC145040 A-to-D converter that is the input part of a data acquisition system, and the A-to-D port on the 68HC11. The final subsection considers how these data acquisition systems can be used in control systems.

6-6.1 Basic Operation of a Data Acquisition System

A DAS can be purchased as a printed circuit board, or even as a (hybrid) integrated circuit module. Such a DAS would be better to use than the system we discuss, but we introduce it to show how such a system works and to bring together the various concepts from previous sections. Finally, in this section, we will show how a DAS can be used to implement a digital filter or feedback control system.

The DAS described in this section is diagramed in figure 6-23. From left to right, an analog switch selects from among eight inputs an input for the comparator. This is used to measure the input voltages. The D-to-A converter is used, with the comparator, for prompting the A-to-D converter to measure the inputs, and for supplying the output voltages. The analog switch and voltage followers on the right impel sample-and-hold circuits, which act like analog flip-flops, to store the output voltages after they have been set by the microcomputer. In the following discussion, location $8000 will be an output register to the D-to-A converter, and location $8001 will be an input whose sign bit is true if Vin (selected by the analog switch) is greater than Vcomp. Location $8002 will be a readable output port that addresses both the analog switches. If, for instance, 3 is put in this register, then input 3 is sent to the comparator (as Vin), and the output of the D-to-A converter is made available to the sample-and-hold circuit that supplies output 3. Finally, the analog switch is enabled by an address trigger. If the microcomputer addresses location $8003, as it does in two memory cycles when executing an instruction like INC $8003, then the address decoder will provide a one-microsecond pulse which will enable the analog switch for that time. Recall that, when enabled, the addressed input is connected to the output of the switch, but when not enabled, all inputs and the output are not connected.

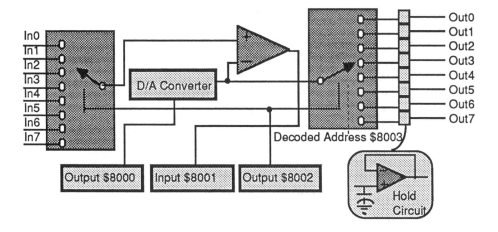

Figure 6-23. Data Acquisition System

The DAS is controlled by a program, shown soon, which will be called as a subroutine whenever the inputs are to be measured and the outputs are to be adjusted. Eight output values are stored in a table TBL, so that TBL[0] is converted to a voltage on output 0; TBL[1] on output 1; and so on. TBL is loaded with the desired values just before this subroutine is called. After returning from the subroutine, the eight inputs are, to keep things simple, converted and stored in the same table. TBL[0] will store the number equal to the voltage on input 0; TBL[1], that equal to the voltage on input 1; and so on.

The output register that selects inputs and outputs is initialized by the first three lines to select the last input or output, and the index register is initialized to access the last row of the table TBL. Thereafter, in the loop, a number is read from the table to the D-to-A converter via output register $8000, and then the output analog switch is enabled for two consecutive memory cycles by executing the instruction INC $8003. The address trigger technique discussed in section 4-1.1 is used here. This instruction should read the word at $8003, increment it, and write the result there. But no output register or RAM word is at this location, so nothing is actually done by the microprocessor. However, location $8003 is accessed twice. This enables the analog switch twice. At that time, the output of the D-to-A converter is sampled by the sample-and-hold circuit that feeds output 7, since the analog switch addresses the bottom position. The voltage output from the D-to-A converter is now sampled, and will remain on this output until it is changed when this subroutine is called again. Thus, the sample-and-hold behaves rather like an analog storage register. Next, a successive approximation subroutine like that discussed in the previous section is called. The subroutine converts the bottom input, since output register $8002 is 7, to a digital value that is left in accumulator A. This value is then stored in the bottom row of the table TBL. The index register and the contents of output register $8002 are decremented to output row 6 of TBL to the sixth output, and they put the value of the sixth input into row 6 of TBL in the next iteration of the loop. When all rows are output and input, this subroutine is left. The above routine can be made more useful by using two tables, one for outputs and one for inputs, but we do not show this here because more code would be needed in which no new important ideas would be demonstrated.

```
          NAM   DAS
          LDAB  #7       PUT 7 TO THE SELECTOR ADDRESS
          STAB  $8002    VIA OUTPUT PORT &8002
          LDX   #TBL+8   START AT BOTTOM OF TABLE
L1        DEX            MOVE POINTER
          LDAA  0,X      GET ENTRY FROM TABLE
          STAA  $8000    OUTPUT IT VIA D/A CONVERTER
          INC   $8003    SEND TWO ADDR. PULSES TO SAMPLE AND HOLD
          BSR   S        EXECUTE SUCCESSIVE APPR. ROUTINE "SUCCES"
          STAA  0,X      ROUTINE RETURNS DIGITAL VALUE IN ACCA
          DEC   $8002    SELECT NEXT LOWER ANALOG INPUT/OUTPUT
          BPL   L1       LOOP IF MORE TO INPUT AND OUTPUT
          RTS            RETURN TO CALLER
          END
```

6-6.2 The MC145040 Chip and the A-to-D Converter in the 68HC11

Two very convenient ways to measure analog voltages in the 6811 microcomputer are with the 145040 chip or with the A-to-D converter in the 6811 itself. Both of these are similar to a Data Acquisition System in that they use an analog multiplexor (mux) to select a number of inputs for the converter.

A serial interface is desirable for an A-to-D converter because it uses fewer pins than a parallel interface and thus can be easily isolated using opto-isolators. The MC145040 is one of the better serial interface A-to-D converters.

Data are shifted into and out of the 145040 at the same time, using the "exchange" technique discussed in section 4-4.3. During bit movement, CS must be low and should rise after all bits are moved because that edge transfers the data to the mux address register and begins the conversion. An input "address" is sent first (to select input i, $i=0$ to 11, send $i<<4$, msb first), and each bit is clocked in on the rising edge of SClk. Conversion is done with the A/D Clk using the successive approximation technique, with Vref as the maximum and VAG as the minimim reference voltage. If the "address" is $B, then a voltage (Vref+VAG)/2 is input, and should convert to a value of $80; this can be used for a check. Wait 32 A/D Clk pulse cycles, and then input the 8-bit digital value, msb first, that was converted from the ith analog input. Data is sent from the chip on the falling edge of SClk. The "address" for the next conversion can be sent out while the data from the previous conversion are being read in, in an exchange operation.

MC145040

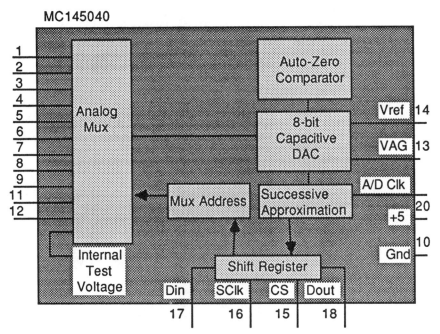

Figure 6-24. Serial Interfaced A-to-D Converter

The MC68CH11A8 48-pin chip has an A-to-D converter in the microcomputer chip. It is essentially free, unless the pins it uses are really needed by some other system; so we would prefer to use it when we have to measure analog voltage inputs. (Figure 6-25 shows the block diagram of this subsystem.) Using VRH as high- and VRL as low-reference voltages, the analog voltages on inputs PE0 to PE3 can be converted to 8-bit digital values and put into registers Result[0] to Result[3]. Initially, bit 7 of the OPTION register, the A-to-D power up bit ADPU, must be set to apply power to this subsystem (100 μsec are needed for the voltages to become stable), and bit 6, CSEL, selects the A-to-D clock and should be 0. The conversion is begun when the control register (at $30,X) is written into, and the mode of conversion is dictated by the value put into the control register, using the low-order four bits of this register, Address, to determine which input pin voltages are converted. If SCAN is 1, then the inputs are sampled continuously; otherwise they are sampled just once. For the Address i provided $i<4$, if MULT is 1, the voltage on PEi is put into Result[i]; otherwise the voltage on PEi is sampled four times and put in each Result[j] register, $j=1$ to 3. Similarly, when MULT is 0, if $i=$C$, VRH is converted; if $i=$D$, VRL is converted; and if $i=$E$ VRH/2 is converted; and each is put in a Result[j] register, $j=0$ to 3. If $i \geq C and MULT is 1, then all three are converted and put as follows: VRH into Result[0], VRL into Result[1], and VRH/2 into Result[2]. Each time a sample is converted (32 E clock cycles), CCF is set, and CCF is cleared when this register is read. The following ritual will convert the voltages on the inputs and put the results into Result[0 to 3], assuming X points to the block of I/O registers in memory:

```
        LDAA #$80    TURN ON THE A-TO-D SYSTEM
        STAA $39,X   BY SETTING BITS IN THE OPTION REGISTER
                     (wait 100 μsec)
        LDAA #$20    REQUEST SCAN=1 TO SAMPLE ALL INPUTS
        STAA $30,X   AND MULT=0 TO DO IT JUST ONCE
   L    TST  $30,X   WAIT FOR COMPLETION (CCF=1)
        BPL  L       NOW THE DIGITAL VALUES ARE IN RESULT[I]
```

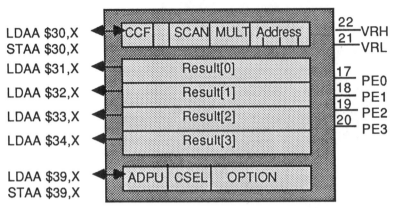

Figure 6-25. A-D Subsystem of the MC68CH11A8

6-6.3 Applications of Data Acquisition Systems in Control Systems

The DAS and subroutine in section 6-6.1 or the A-to-D converters in 6-6.2 and D-to-A MC144110 converter in 6-5.1 can be used in control systems. The three main applications are the collection and generation of analog data and feedback control.

The microcomputer is admirably suited for collecting analog data. The DAS and subroutine recently discussed can collect a sample of up to eight analog inputs. The collected data could be stored in a table, transmitted across a data link, or operated on. The programs for these operations should be simple enough, so that they are not spelled out here. However, it should be stressed that data collection using microcomputers has a unique advantage over simpler techniques: its software can execute functions on the incoming data. In particular, functions can, as we discuss, correct errors in the measurement apparatus.

Suppose the incoming data actually has value x, but the measurement apparatus reports the value as $y = F(x)$. The function F can be empirically obtained by inputting known values of x, then reading the values of y. Suppose F is an invertible function and the inverse fuction is G; then $x = G(y)$. The software can read y from the measurement apparatus, then compute $G(y)$ to get the accurate value of x.

A number of techniques can be used to evaluate some arbitrary function $G(y)$, such as might be obtained for correcting errors. The well-known Taylor series expansion is sometimes useful; but to evaluate such a polynomial may take a long time and accumulate a lot of rounding error. A better technique is to evaluate G(y) as a continued fraction G(y) = A / B + G'(y), where G'(y) is either y or a continued fraction. The most suitable for microcomputers, however, is the *spline* technique. Just as a complex curve is often drafted by drawing sections of it with a "French curve," the complex function G(y) is approximated by sections of simpler functions (called splines) like parabolas. (See figure 6-26.) Given a value y, we determine which section of G(y) it is in, to choose which spline to evaluate. We do this by comparing y against the values yi that separate the splines. A fast way is to test y against the middle yi, then if y < yi, check y against the yi a quarter of the way across the scale; otherwise, check against the yi three-quarters of the way; and so on in the same manner as the successive approximation technique for A-to-D conversion. Once the section is determined, evaluate the function by evaluating the spline. If the spline is a parabola, then X = A y**2 + B y + C for some constants A, B, and C. The values yi for the boundaries and the constants A,B, and C can be stored in a table. Software for searching this table to select the correct spline and for evaluating the spline is quite simple and fast on a microcomputer.

Analog signals can be converted to digital values, then filtered using digital techniques, rather than filtered using OP AMPs, as discussed earlier in this chapter. The following is a discussion of digital filtering as a feedback control technique.

In a manner similar to that just discussed, if analog values are to be output from a microcomputer, errors in the output apparatus may be corrected in software. If the true output value is y but x is sent to the output, the output is actually y = F(x); then if F is invertible and G is the inverse of x (x = G(y)), the microcomputer can evaluate G(y) and send this value to the output system. The program that evaluates G(y) compensates ahead of time for the error to be made in the output apparatus.

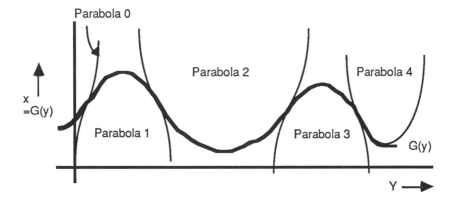

Figure 6-26. The Spline Technique

A test system might be designed using the preceding techniques to output some analog voltages to the object being tested, then to measure the voltages it returns. While these systems are important, the feedback control system is even more important and interesting. Figure 6-27 shows the classic model of the feedback control system. The entire system has a stimulus x (or a set of stimulae considered as a vector) as input, and an output z (or a set of outputs, a vector z). The system that outputs z is called the *plant*. The plant usually has some deficiencies. To correct these, a *feedback system* is implemented (as diagramed in figure 6-27), which may be built around a microcomputer and DAS. The output of this system, an error signal, is added to the stimulus signal x, and the sum of these signals is applied to the plant. Feedback control systems like this have been successfully used to correct for deficiencies in the plant, thus providing stable control over the output z.

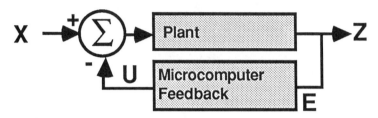

Figure 6-27. Feedback Control

Three techniques have been widely used for feedback control systems; the proportional integral differential, the linear filter, and the multi-input-output controllers.

The simplest and most popular controller is called the *proportional integral differential* controller (PID). Its form is easy to implement on a microcomputer. The output of the feedback system U is a weighted sum of the current input to the feedback E, the integrated value of E, and the differential value of E:

$$U = A\,E + B\,\int E(t)\,dt + C\,d(E(t))/dt$$

Integration is nicely approximated in a microcomputer by adding each input value to a number in memory each time the inputs are sampled. If the feedback control system is working correctly, the inputs will be positive and negative, so this running sum will tend to 0. The differential is simply approximated by subtracting the current value of the input from its last value.

A more general kind of controller can be implemented as a digital version of a filter. (As a filter, it can be used to correct errors in analog measurement and output systems, as we previously discussed.) A *digital filter* is defined by a *Z-transform*, which is an expression like this:

$$D(z) = \frac{U(z)}{E(z)} = \frac{A0 + A1\,Z^{**}-1 + A2\,Z^{**}-2 + \ldots + An\,Z^{**}-n}{1 + B1\,Z^{**}-1 + B2\,Z^{**}-2 + \ldots + Bn\,Z^{**}-n}$$

This expression is evaluated in a microcomputer as follows. Call the input at time k Ek and the output at time k Uk. Then the output Uk at any given time is just the weighted sum of the inputs and outputs of the n prior times:

$$Uk = A0\,Ek + A1\,Ek\text{-}1 + \ldots + An\,Ek\text{-}n$$
$$- B1\,Uk\text{-}1 - \ldots - Bn\,Uk\text{-}n$$

The program should keep the vectors A, B, E, and U. Each time it updates the most recent output value Uk, it can shift all values of E and U back one place to get the output Uk at the next time k.

A particularly suitable technique is the *multi-input multi-output controller*, which has a mathematical definition as follows. Let **E** be an (eight-variable) input and **U** be an (eight-variable) output, and **S** be an (n-variable) state vector, stored in a table in memory. **A, B, C,** and **D** are matrixes having suitable dimensions. Then the controller is defined by matrix multiplication equations that give the next value of the state vector S in terms of the current value of the state vector and the input E:

$$S = A \, S + B \, E$$

and that give the output values in terms of the current value of the state vector and the input:

$$U = C \, S + D \, E$$

These equations can be implemented by subroutines that perform matrix multiplication and vector addition, together with the subroutine that exercises the DAS to get the input vector **X** and to output the values of **Z**.

These techniques show how simply a microcomputer with a DAS can, with programs to correct for nonlinear errors or to digitally filter the data or with one of several feedback controllers, implement multiple input analog measurement systems or multiple sources of analog output voltages. All we have to do is determine the coefficients for the aforementioned formulas. That is a nontrivial problem, but it is treated in many excellent texts on control theory. Our only intent in this chapter was to show that, once a desired control system has been defined, it can be implemented easily in a microcomputer.

6-7 Conclusions

This chapter has covered a lot of ground. We studied transducers, analog devices and a keyboard and display system. The A-to-D, D-to-A converters and the data acquisition system were surveyed and software techniques for them were discussed.

In general, most I/O devices have some analog circuitry. On one extreme, some analog controllers use only OP AMPs without a microprocessor. This often is the best way if the frequencies of the signal are higher than the Nyquist rate of an economically acceptable microprocessor based system. On the other extreme, everything can be implemented in software, thus minimizing the analog hardware. This appears attractive where flexibility is valuable and the signal rates are not higher than the Nyquist rate of the system. In between, just about every design has some analog hardware, some software, and some digital hardware. A good designer must therefore be aware of the analog devices and circuits and must be aware of the advantages of the different ways to implement some functions in analog or digital hardware, or in software.

This chapter should provide sufficient background for understanding what the analog circuitry in an I/O device is supposed to be doing, and for sorting out many of the analog, digital, and software alternatives for implementing important I/O functions. If you want further information, we recommend Garrett's *Analog Systems for Microprocessors and Minicomputers*, Reston Publishing Company. Many of the concepts we've introduced in this chapter were inspired by that fine book. Applications notes from linear integrated circuits manufacturers, and even catalogues from some of them, have a wealth of useful information about how to use the chips they make. National Semiconductor's two books *Linear Applications Handbooks I and II* are very good, as is the catalogue for Analog Devices Incorporated. Further information on Motorola analog interface chips is available in Motorola data sheets such as the *CMOS/NMOS Special Functions Data*, (DL130). We think that Vanlandungham's *Introduction to Digital Control Systems*, Macmillan Publishing Co., 1985 is an excellent modern coverage of the theory of digital control. Finally, *Electronics* magazine provides design information on the use of these analog circuits, and other trade and hobby magazines often show interesting and useful circuits. For more concrete information on the 68HC11, please consult the *MC68HC11A8 HCMOS Single-Chip Microcomputer (ADI 1207)*. In particular, section 7 discusses the analog-to-digital converter in the 6811. As noted earlier, we have not attempted to duplicate the diagrams and discussions in that book because we assume you will refer to it while reading this book; in addition, we present an alternative view of the subject, so you can use either or both views.

You should now be ready to use analog circuits in microcomputers. We now turn our attention to frequency analog signals, and then to communication systems and storage and display systems that use frequency analog signals.

Problems

Problems 1, 5, 12, 13, and 28 are paragraph correction problems; for guidelines, see the problems at the end of chapter 1. Guidelines for software problems can be found at the end of chapter 2, and guidelines for hardware problems can be found at the end of chapter 3.

1.* A transducer changes physical properties – such as distance – to or from voltages or frequencies. The most accurate position measurements can be made using a potentiometer. Acceleration can be measured by measuring distance at several specific times and integrating the results in software. A light-emitting diode is clear when no voltage appears across it and is opaque when a voltage appears across it. The photoresistor is the fastest light-to-voltage transducer, but it is nonlinear. Very high temperatures are best measured with a diode, whose output voltage is 2.2 volts per degree kelvin. Pressure is generally measured by converting pressure to heat, and then measuring the temperature.

2. A stepping motor has three windings and the power signals for them are called A, B, and C. These are singulary (only one is asserted at a time) and the stepping motor is made to go clockwise by making A, B, and C run in the sequence TFF FTF FFT TFF ... and counterclockwise by making them run in the sequence FFT FTF TFF FFT .... Each time the next pattern is output in either sequence, the stepping motor rotates 7 1/2 degrees in the direction indicated by the sequence.

   a. Write an MC68HC11A8 single-chip mode system initialization routine and a subroutine with two entry points CW and CCW that will cause the stepping motor to rotate 7 1/2 degrees clockwise, and 7 1/2 degrees counterclockwise, respectively. Use port B, which will be output on the 3 least significant bits at location $1004.

   b. Write a routine to rotate the motor at one rotation per second. Use the subroutine in part a and use real-time synchronization.

   c. Assume the input at port E ($100A) has most significant bit true when the motor has moved an object to a terminal position, which is the most counterclockwise position; otherwise the bit is false. Write a routine to position the object *N* positions clockwise from the terminal position, where each position corresponds to 7 1/2 degrees rotation of the motor. Assume the object position is initially unknown and the number *N* is in accumulator A, so the object has to be positioned in the terminal position first, then stepped out to the *N*th position. Use real-time synchronization, and assume that the motor can be pulsed for 10 milliseconds with each pattern to cause it to rotate. (This is basically the mechanism used to position the head on a floppy disk.)

3. A gear has a tooth every 10 degrees of rotation, the teeth are 5 degrees wide, and two wiper contacts are 2 degrees apart. The contacts output a low signal when they touch a tooth.

    a. Write a (Mealy) sequential machine description of the state transitions, where the internal states are the signal pair on the contacts, LL, LH, HL, and HH, and the input states are CW for moving clockwise, CCW for moving counterclockwise and NULL for no movement. The leftmost contact value of the pair corresponds to the more counterclockwise of the two wiper contacts as they appear close together.

    b. Write an initialization routine and interrupt handler that will keep track of the position of the gear. The more counterclockwise of the two contacts is connected to the STRA input of an MC68HC11A8 and is to cause an IRQ interrupt each time the signal falls, and the other contact can be read as the most significant bit of port C. The position of the gear, in $36ths$ of a revolution, will be kept as a double precision signed number POSN, positive numbers indicating clockwise rotation. (When the machine is turned on, we will just assume that the position of the gear is defined as 0.)

4. A home temperature control will control a furnace and an air conditioner, based on the temperature measured in the home. The temperature in degrees centigrade can be read from an A/D input at $1031, the furnace and air conditioner are controlled by port B pins 0 and 1, such that writing 0 in bit 0 turns off the air conditioner, writing 1 there turns it on, writing 0 in bit 1 turns off the furnace, and writing 1 there turns it on. Suppose the desired temperature is stored at location SETTMP. Write a complete program to control the furnace and air conditioner to adjust the home temperature to this value. If the temperature is 3 degrees cooler than it, turn on the furnace (fully), but turn it off when the temperature is 1 degree lower than it (because residual heat will cause the temperature to rise after the furnace is off); if the temperature is 3 degrees higher, turn on the air conditioner (fully), but if the air conditioner was on within the last two minutes, do not turn it on (because the back-pressure in the compressor has to dissipate or the motor will stall when it is turned on). Turn off the air conditioner when the desired temperature is reached. Use real-time synchronization, assuming the E clock is 2 MHz.

5.* Bipolar transistors have very high input impedances and are commonly used to measure bipolar (AC) voltages. The VFET or darlington transistor is a good output for a microcomputer for controlling direct current. SCRs can be used to control AC. A single SCR alone can control both positive and negative cycles of an AC power signal. Proportional cycle control is most attractive for microcomputer systems because it provides the most precise control over the amount of power applied to the load. Proportional cycle control is commonly used to control the heat of an electric range. An operational amplifier has two inputs, and it outputs a voltage which is a large number times the difference between the voltages on the inputs, as long as the OP AMP is in the saturated mode. To sample the incoming voltage, an integrator uses a capacitor on the input to an OP AMP. A comparator is an OP AMP used in the saturated mode. A modern OP AMP such as the CA3140 has very high input impedance, which is useful in microcomputer I/O systems because it allows the use of small capacitors and permits the sensing of minute currents from transducers such as Ph measurement devices. The analog switch allows one to switch a digital signal after it has been compared to an analog signal. The timer is a useful device which is most commonly used to convert a voltage into a frequency.

6. Write a routine to control an incandescent lamp using proportional control. Assume that the most significant bit of port E at location $100A is true when the 60-Hertz power signal is positive and false otherwise, that the number in LGHT is the number of degrees of phase that the light should be on in every half-cycle (8.333 milliseconds) and that the most significant bit of port B at $1004 has to be pulsed high for exactly 5 microseconds to fire the Triac that controls the lamp. Use real-time synchronization and assume the E clock is 1 MHz.

7. For each of the circuits in figure 6-28, show the output voltage Vo as a function of V1, V2, ... (and the initial value of Vo for circuit c):

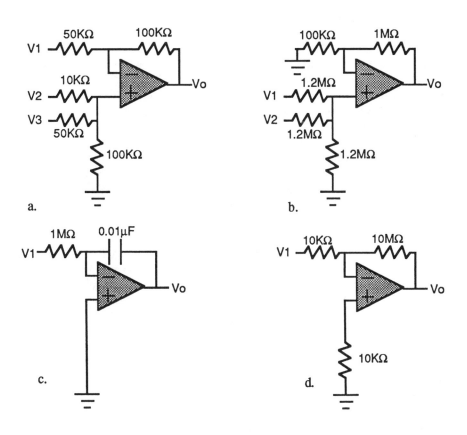

Figure 6-28. Some OP AMP Circuits

8. Section 6-2.3 discussed in detail the limits of input voltages and other parameters for +5-volt single-supply use of the CA3140. Discuss all the limits and parameters that are different and give their values for ±15-volt dual-supply use of this same OP AMP.

9. Show all connections in the logic diagram for a 555 timer and eight resistors that can be put into the timing resistor position (R2 in figure 6-9) using a 4051 analog multiplexor. The multiplexor will be controlled by an output register.

10. Show all connections and values of all components in a diagram of an amplifier whose gain is controlled by an output register. The (4-bit) unsigned binary number N in the register sets the gain to -N. Use a CA3140 OP AMP, 4066 analog switch, and resistors in the range of 100K to 10M.

11. Show all connections and values of all components in a diagram for a circuit that uses two CA3140 OP AMPs to output the absolute value on Vabs and the (logical) sign on SGN of an input voltage Vin.

12.* Filters are used to remove noise from the signal being measured or output. A high-pass filter has capacitors connected to ground and to the output to short out the low-frequency components and integrate them out of the signal. A light pen develops a signal that corresponds to the average brightness of the CRT screen, so a high-pass filter is commonly used to eliminate the noise, which is a higher-frequency "signal." A butterworth filter is often used in digital systems because it delays all frequency components about the same, so that square waves do not develop humps or grooves. Analog switches are useful for selecting inputs and for nonlinear signal conditioning. One of the ways a microcomputer can control the loss of a signal is to chop it at a fixed frequency so that it is chopped off for a proportion of each cycle that corresponds to the loss. Three nonlinear functions that are often performed in analog hardware are absolute value, logarithm, and sample-and-hold. The logarithm function is often used before an A-to-D converter because microcomputers have difficulty multiplying, and multiplication can be performed by adding the logarithm.

13.* Key bounce is a problem when the user bangs on a key repeatedly to get something done. It can be eliminated by a sample-and-hold circuit that takes a "snapshot" of the signal just once. Software debouncing is rather rarely done in microcomputers because it takes too much of the microcomputer's valuable time to monitor the key. Keyboards are often used on microcomputers because the user may want to enter different commands, and this is most easily done with a set of keys. Linear selection is often used for a keyboard that has a lot of keys, like a typewriter. N-key roll-over is a property of keyboards whereby the microcomputer can correctly determine what keys were pressed and in what order they were pressed, provided that no more than N keys are pressed at one time. Two-key rollover is commonly used in microcomputer systems but is rather inadequate for most adept users, who often hold several keys down at once. The LED seven-segment display is used on many inexpensive microcomputer systems because it uses very little power. LCDs have to be multiplexed carefully, because they require AC (square wave) signals, and the difference in RMS voltage between a clear and an opaque segment is rather small. Therefore we do not multiplex more than two or three LCDs on the same drive circuitry. A typical keyboard system is often integrated with a multiplexed display system because the hardware to scan the keyboard can also be used to scan the display.

14. Write a program that uses three counts of hysteresis to debounce a switch (as in DEBNCE in section 6-4.1). The count of the number of closures is initially 1 and is incremented each time the switch is closed, as in that program, but is set to $F8 (-8) when the closure is recognized after the count reaches $10 and is set to 8 when the count reaches $F0 (-16) because we recognize that the switch is indeed open. This program should exit to a routine DOIT when the key has been recognized pressed, but that routine will jump to label RETN in your program when it is finished. At that time, your program should assume the key is still pressed, so it won't repeat the program DOIT until the key is released and pressed again.

15. Show, for successive memory cycles, the output of a logic analyzer – left column being the R/W signal, the next two columns the address and data bus values in hexadecimal, and each row – for two complete executions of the loop in the program SCAN (section 6-4.2). Assume that, in the beginning of the first execution, the readable output register is 2 and the third key is the only one pressed.

16. Implement the coincident scanner of figure 6-15b with a 74HC595 to "short" a column to ground in place of the 74HC138, and a 74HC589 to sense the row inputs in place of the 4051. Use the SPI (section 4-5.3) to output a pattern via the 74HC595 while simultaneously inputting the previous pattern from the 74HC589.
   a. Show the logic diagram of this subsystem and all pins connecting these chips.
   b. Give a subroutine, as well as its initialization ritual, to read the keys so that 0 is returned by the subroutine in accumulator A if the top left key in your logic diagram is pressed, 1 if the next right key, and so on up to 7 if the top right key is pressed, ... , and $3F if the bottom right key is pressed. Assume only one key may be pressed at a time and use "wait-and-see" debouncing.

17. Write the table for the program LOOK (section 6-4.3) so that the hexadecimal number in accumulator A will be converted and output to light the correct LEDs to display the number. Your answer should be in hexadecimal, not binary, in a FCB assembler directive or two, and you should display the numbers 6 and 9 without their "tails," 1 should appear on the right of the display, and B, C, and D should be lower case letters.

18. Write a reentrant 6811 program equivalent to the program LOOK in section 6-4.3 for the LCD display in figure 6-17c. It should display ACCB bits 3 to 0 in the right digit and clear the others.

19. Section 6-4.3 explained a technique for multiplexing LCD displays. Assuming the voltages are 0, 1, 2, and 3 volts and each segment is displayed for 1 millisecond, draw an oscilloscope trace for the following waveforms, so that the top trace is the waveform on

one plate of a LCD display segment and the bottom trace is the waveform on the other plate. The single waveform will have four (1-msec.) sections:

a. for a segment that is off, in a digit that is off (clear segment)
b. for a segment that is on, in a digit that is off (clear segment)
c. for a segment that is off, in a digit that is on (clear segment)
d. for a segment that is on, in a digit that is on (dark segment)

20. Suppose the current source at Vin in figure 6-18c is 1 microampere. What is the largest value of resistor that will apply at most 4 volts to the input to the sample-and-hold circuit when the program EXSP in section 6-5.1 is executed, and what should the capacitor value be for this resistor, assuming a 2 MHz clock and that $FF in the output register will produce 1.99 volts.

21. Show a diagram of a summing D-to-A converter (like figure 6-18a) that outputs the value of a 4-bit 2's complement number in volts (for example, 1100 puts out -4 volts). Use a CA3140 OP AMP and 4066 analog switches and use resistors in the range 100K to 10M. Show all pins and component values, and show the bypass capacitors so the circuit can be built from your diagram.

22. Write a program to follow SUCCES (section 6-5.2) to determine the least significant bit of the result.

23. Write a reentrant 6811 program to read all 11 inputs of the MC145040 into locations $1000 to $100A. The serial interface has Din connected to port B bit 7, SClk to port B bit 6, CS to port B bit 5, and Dout to port E bit 2. (See section 6-6.2.)

24. Write a reentrant 6811 program to input the voltage on pin PE2 for four consecutive samples, putting the sampled values in $1031 to $1033 (assuming the I/O registers are at $1000 to $103F). Assume a 2 MHz E clock, and show the real-time timing loop.

25. Problem 4 of this chapter assumed the temperature was available at $1031 (assuming I/O is from $1000 to $103F). Write an initialization ritual to implement this in the MC68HC11A8.

26. Write a routine to evaluate a spline as specified by a table. The table has a row for each parabola, and a column for the larger limit yi on the interval where that parabola is to be used, and three columns for the constants A, B, and C, from left to right in the table, for the coefficients of the parabola ($G(y) = A y^2 + B y + C$). The parabolas are in successive rows of the table in order of increasing values of yi, so the ith parabola should be evaluated by your routine if the input y is between yi in that row and yi in the row above it, and the last row has $yi = 0$ as a marker of that row. Assume input y is in accumulator A, all $yi's$ are unsigned 8-bit numbers, and all A, B, and C values in the table are 2's complement numbers.

27. Write a digital filter program equivalent to the Z transform $(3 - 2 Z^{-1})/ (1 + 4 Z^{-1})$. Evaluate the filter function repetitively on the input, read at $8000, so that the filtered output is fed out the output at location $8001. Use 8-bit signed numbers throughout.

28.* Converters are based on integrators or sample-and-hold circuits. The sampling converters have a Nyquist rate, which is the rate at which they sample the analog signal. A high-pass filter is commonly used to remove frequencies below this Nyquist rate to prevent alias signals from appearing. D-to-A converters include the ladder networks, commonly available on integrated circuits, and exponential superposition converters, which are exceptionally accurate yet very cheap. D-to-A converters, like the successive approximation converter, are able to sample the input signal quite rapidly; but parallel and pipeline converters are the fastest, using more hardware to achieve the greater speed. A frequency to voltage converter is based on a very accurate one-shot that is triggered at the rate of the input frequency, and whose output is filtered through a low-pass filter to recover the voltage. A tachometer is a good voltage to frequency converter, but is limited to low frequencies. A data acquisition system uses sample-and-hold circuits to sample the input signals, and uses a D-to-A converter to develop the output voltages and a reference voltage for an A-to-D converter. The A-to-D converter can use delta, ramp, or successive approximation programs to measure input voltages.

7

Counters and Timers

The counter/timer is one of the most flexible parts of a single-chip microcomputer. It can generate a square wave. The square wave can be used to generate sine waves, or any periodic wave. Sine waves can be used in cassette tape recorders, telephone systems (touch-tone), and signals to the user (bleeps). The counter/timer can be used to generate single-shot pulses. These can control motors, solenoids, or lights to give precisely timed pulses that are independent of the timing errors to which the real-time programmed microprocessor is susceptible, such as dynamic memory and DMA cycle steals, and interrupts. The counter/timer can itself provide interrupts to coordinate a program; to effect an instruction step or a real-time clock. To effect an instruction step, the timer is set up as the monitor is left so that it allows one instruction to be executed in the user program before the interrupt returns control to the monitor. The monitor is used to examine or modify memory or registers, then the monitor is left and the next instruction in the user program is executed, and so on. Or a real-time clock can be effected if the timer interrupts every millisecond. The module can be used to count the number of events (falling edges of a signal input to the module), and thus the number of events in a fixed interval of time (the frequency). It is also capable of measuring pulse width and period. Several things can be converted to the period of a signal: voltage can be converted using the voltage to frequency converter integrated circuits, and resistance or capacitance can be converted to the period of a waveform using a linear timer integrated circuit like the ubiquitous 555. We also observe that a single signal can be easily isolated using optical isolators, so the voltage of the system being measured can be kept from the microcomputer and the user. Counter/timers in the MC68HC11 and the M6840 chips were designed for these purposes.

The counter/timer is the principal component, then, in interfacing to frequency analog signals. These signals, like FM radio signals, are easier to handle than amplitude analog signals and are comparatively free of noise. We observe that, at the time of writing, amplitude analog signals are pervasively used in interface circuits; but we believe that frequency (or phase) analog signals will become equally important.

The primary objective of this chapter is to explain the principles of using the counter/timer module. To make these principles concrete, the MC68HC11 counter/timer system is introduced first and the M6840 chip is described later. A further objective of this chapter is to emphasize a fundamental principle of top-down design. A counter/timer in a microcomputer is so fascinating that the designer may decide to use it before examining the alternative hardware and/or software techniques. This is an instance of bottom-up design: I've got this marvelous counter in my microcomputer, now where can I use it? As we pointed out in an earlier chapter, this is rather like the popular TV character, Carnack the Magnificent, who answers a question sealed in an envelope before he knows the question. Bottom-up design is especially evident whenever a new and powerful integrated circuit, like the MC68HC11 or M6840, appears on the market. This design approach generally leads to bad designs. So we emphasize the need to examine alternatives and discuss some of the alternatives to using this counter/timer subsystem.

This chapter should acquaint you with the hardware and software of the counter/timer in the MC68HC11 and M6840 and with alternative techniques using a simple parallel I/O port and more hardware, or a parallel I/O port and more software. Upon finishing the chapter, you should be able to connect a counter/timer in a microcomputer like the MC68HC11, and write software to generate square waves or pulses, or measure the frequency or period of a periodic wave or the pulse width of a pulse. With these techniques, you should be able to interface to I/O systems that generate or use periodic signals or pulses, or to interface through voltage-to-frequency or frequency-to-voltage converters to analog I/O systems.

7-1 The MC68HC11 Counter/Timer Subsystem

We introduce the block diagram of the entire counter/timer subsystem in the MC68HC11 in this section for further reference in this chapter. (See figure 7-1.) There are a lot of registers, as this subsystem constitutes almost half the registers in the MC68HC11. The subsystem has six components, shown by differently shaded boxes. These are the main counter for other components; the output compare, used for generating square waves and pulses; the input capture for measuring the period of square waves and the width of pulses; the real-time interrupt for processor timing; the pulse accumulator for event counting and frequency measurements; and the computer operating properly, for software and hardware checking.

The input capture and output compare subsystems use a main common counter. This makes possible the simultaneous use of different input and output timings; the presence of the common clock means they can be synchronized. (Figure 7-2 shows this main counter.)

This counter can be incremented each E clock cycle, or at that rate divided by 4, 8, or 16, by writing 00, 01, 10, or 11 into the low-order 2 bits of the mask 2 register. However, these 2 bits may only be changed shortly (before 64 clock cycles) after reset, so that a program does not accidentally mess up some applications that are using this master counter. The sign bit of the flag 2 register is set when the 16-bit counter has an overflow. This bit can be tested in a gadfly loop, or, if the sign bit of the mask 2 register is also set, it causes an interrupt vectored through $FFDE, DF. The gadfly loop exit routine or the interrupt handler can increment a software counter to extend the number of bits beyond the 16 bits of the hardware counter. The flag 2 register bit *must*

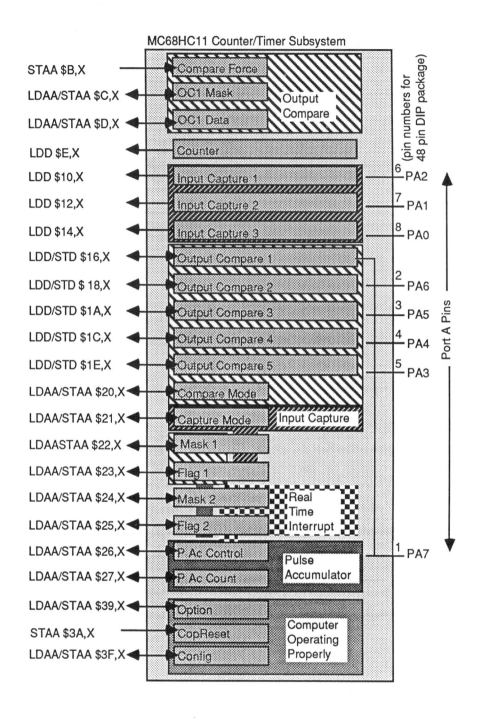

Figure 7-1. The Counter/Timer Subsystem

be cleared before it can be sensed again; it is cleared by just writing a T (true) into it. Do not use the BSET instruction to achieve this because the BSET instruction may do more than you want: other bits may be cleared because that instruction reads out the register value, sets a bit, and writes the updated value back. Any T that is read will be written and will clear the bit it is written to. Other flag register bits associated with the counter/timer system behave this way.

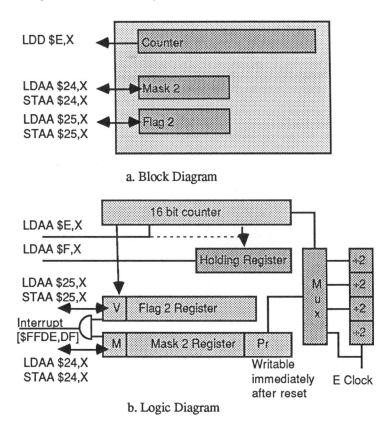

a. Block Diagram

b. Logic Diagram

Figure 7-2. The Basic Counter

As shown in figure 7-2a, the counter is a 16-bit read-only memory register. It can be read to determine the current "time." There could be a problem reading a moving counter when it takes two memory cycles to read 16 bits. However, the problem is solved: the counter is actually implemented, as shown in figure 7-2b, with an additional hidden register. When the high byte of the counter is read at I/O location $E, by means of an address trigger, the low byte is simultaneously copied into the hidden register, to be read later when the low byte of the counter is read at I/O location $F. That way, reading the counter with an instruction like LDD will give a consistent 16-bit count that is correct when the high byte was read.

7-2 Signal Generation

We want to cover the generation of square waves and pulses for external hardware first because you can implement these examples as experiments and see results on the output pins. Later, we look at frequency measurement techniques, which can be studied using a microcomputer to generate the signals using techniques introduced in this section. We can also generate interrupts for the microcomputer that can be used to time operations, which include the timing of output signals. This section covers the generation of signals with the MC68HC11 counter/timer system and with alternative hardware and software techniques. We begin by describing the hardware used in generating either square waves or pulses. The generation of square waves and subsequent generation of arbitrary repetitive waveforms will be considered in the first subsection. The next subsection covers the techniques for pulse generation. The last subsection shows how to generate interrupts, which are used to implement real-time clocks.

The signal generation subsystem uses four identical "output compare" modules and one modified "output compare" module. The term *output compare* comes from the notion that a fixed number in a register is compared to the running counter, and when a compare is sensed, an output operation is done. Figure 7-3a shows its block diagram; figure 7-3b shows a more detailed logical diagram of one of the four identical output

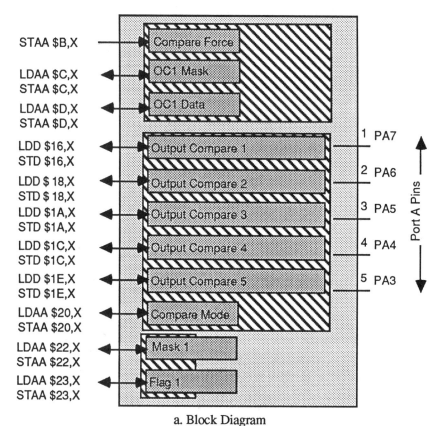

a. Block Diagram
Figure 7-3. Output Compare Logic

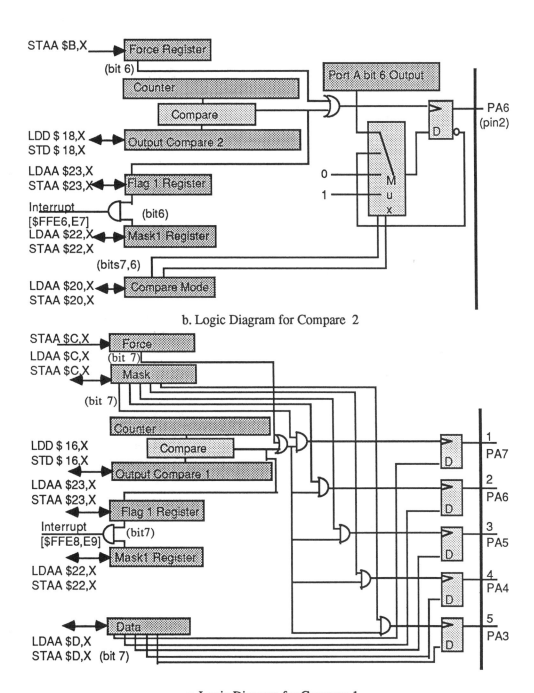

b. Logic Diagram for Compare 2

c. Logic Diagram for Compare 1
Figure 7-3. (Continued)

compare modules; table 7-1 shows the substitutions in figure 7-3b for the other three modules; figure 7-3c shows the special output compare 1 module. The output flip-flops in figures 7-3b and 7-3c, and the output pins, are the same. That is, the flip-flop in the right side of figure 7-3b is the same as the second from top flip-flop in the right side of figure 7-3c. Similarly, the other three modules like module 2 have flip-flops which are identical to those in figure 7-3c. The outputs on pins 2 through 5 are the PORT A register bits, readable and writable (at I/O relative location 00) if the compare mode bits are 00. If the compare mode is any other value, the outputs are the values of the flip-flops in figures 7-3b or 7-3c. If, in a single clock cycle, a flip-flop gets conflicting commands, the output compare 1 operation (figure 7-3c) overrides the other compare operation (figure 7-3b).

Table 7-1. Output Compare Substitutions

Module	2	3	4	5
Bit of Force, Mask 1 and Flag 1	6	5	4	3
Bits of Compare Mode Register	7,6	5,4	3,2	1,0
Pins	PA6 (2)	PA5 (3)	PA4 (4)	PA3 (5)
Interrupt Vector	FFE6,E7	FFE4,E5	FFE2,E3	FFE0,E1
Compare Register	$18,X	$1A,X	$1C,X	$1E,X

The basic operation of the output compare is to load the output compare register with a "time" at which an output operation is to occur. When the counter "time" equals the "time" in the output compare register, the output operation will take place. The operation is specified by 2 most significant bits in the compare mode register (timer control register 1). If 00 no change takes place, if 01 the output is toggled, if 10 the output is cleared, if 11 the output is set to 1. The comparison match also sets bit 6 of the flag 1 register, which can be tested by a gadfly loop, and if bit 6 of the mask 1 register is set, an interrupt is vectored through $FFE6, E7. The output operation takes place if bit 6 of the compare force register is written with a 1 but the Flag 1 register is not changed and an interrupt is not generated.

The special output compare 1 module can affect any or all the five output pins at the same time. Bit 7 of the compare force, Flag 1 and Mask 1 registers work the same as the other output compare modules, but when an output comparison match is detected, the bits of the data register are forced into the output flip-flops wherever the Mask register is 1 (bit 7 of data register to bit 7 of the PORT A register, under control of bit 7 of the mask register and so on). Also, the compare 1 output on PORT A bit 7 (pin 1) is an input/output bit also used by the pulse accumulator, discussed later in this chapter.

7-2.1 The Square Wave Generator

A very economical way to generate a square wave is by means of a software loop that outputs alternate ones and zeros to an output port. The only hardware needed is a single flip-flop with an address decoder suitable to load, say, bit 6 of the PORT A register at location $1000. The following program shows how simple this operation is:

```
            NAM    SQUREAL
            CLRA
    L1      STAA   $1000
            EORA   #$40
            LDAB   #N
    L2      DECB
            BNE    L2
            BRA    L1
            END
```

The outer loop complements bit 6 in accumulator A each time the loop is executed, and then outputs the word. A delay loop is executed N times (N is supplied by the programmer). The output will change every $(11 + 5\,N)/2$ microseconds (if the M6811 has a 2 MHz clock), so the output period will be $11 + 5\,N$ microseconds.

This simple approach is often indicated because of its low cost. However, it has some basic limitations. The minimum period (maximum frequency) is limited to the microcomputer clock period divided by two times the time to execute the outer loop. Without the inner delay loop, the minimum period is 9 microseconds. You can control the period by supplying the appropriate value of N. Other values can be selected by putting instructions with the appropriate execution time inside the loop to stretch it out. However, a different routine is needed for each desired value of the period. Alternatively, a routine to handle arbitrary period values would be rather hard to implement. Moreover, if the microcomputer handles an interrupt while in this loop, the timing will be upset. Direct memory access on other computers will cause similar timing problems, as will the use of cycles to refresh dynamic memories. Finally, the microcomputer is unable to do any other useful work while executing the routine to output a square wave. Nevertheless, this approach is recommended wherever a square wave with fixed or a small number of period times is needed and no interrupts, direct memory access, dynamic memory refresh, or running of other programs are done while generating the square wave.

Analog hardware techniques provide almost continuous control, without side effects due to interrupts, and can be operated at higher frequencies than the microcomputer clock. However, they are subject to noise and inaccuracies due to dependence of voltages on temperature, aging, and so on.

Two analog hardware solutions use a voltage-controlled oscillator or a timer like the 555. The microcomputer can output a voltage via an analog multiplexor that selects voltages from taps on a voltage divider chain, or via a D-to-A converter, which can control the frequency of a voltage-to-frequency converter. This approach permits several discrete voltages, or an almost continuous range of voltages, to select several fixed frequencies, or an almost continuous range of frequencies, from the oscillator. Alternatively, the resistor in a timer module like the 555 can be selected by an analog multiplexor. The microcomputer output register provides the address to the analog multiplexor, which then selects the resistor and thus the period of the output signal. Later in the chapter, we'll discuss a circuit like this, where the microcomputer selects different joysticks to control a 555 so the microcomputer can read the period of the signal and thus determine the position of the joysticks.

Three digital hardware solutions are to build a programmable counter, a multistage binary counter with taps at each stage or a phase-locked loop, using digital integrated circuits. A *programmable counter* is an integrated circuit able to count when clocked, and able to load a word into the counter when a load command is signaled. If this word is supplied by an output register, and is loaded each time the counter increments to its largest number and cycles to zero, then the period of the counter is determined by the word in the output register. A second technique uses a selector whose address is specified by an output port. The selector chooses an input from a stage i of the counter, to output a signal with period $p/(2^i)$. It allows scaling of the frequency by powers of 2.

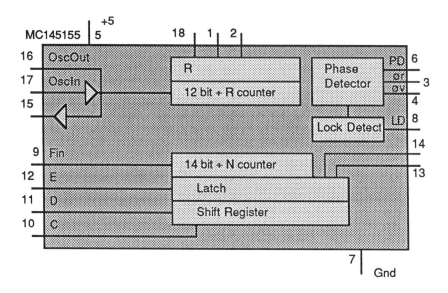

a. The MC145155 Serial Input PLL Frequency Synthesizer

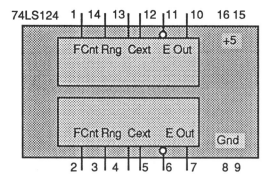

b. A Dual Voltage-Controlled Oscillator

Figure 7-4. Phase-Locked Loop

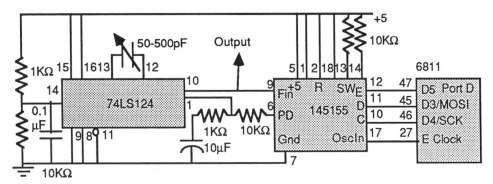

c. A Simple Circuit
Figure 7-4. (Continued)

The phase-locked loop (PLL) is used to generate higher frequencies than can be achieved by a microcomputer using a counter/timer. (See figure 7-4.) Figure 7-4a shows the digital part and figure 7-4b shows the analog part of a PLL that can generate almost any frequency within a wide range. Figure 7-4a diagrams one of several chips that use a serial input and that can handle the digital logic for a PLL. Serial input is desirable to save pins because the frequency of the oscillator is not changed that often and changes do not have to be prompt. The chip contains two down-counters: one divides the variable frequency of a signal Fin on pin 9 by N, where N is a 14 bit number sent from the computer, while the other divides a reference frequency of a signal generated by an oscillator on pin 17 by R, where R is chosen by the levels on pins 2, 1, and 18. The number N is shifted in, using the techniques discussed in section 4-4. Actually, the low-order 14 bits of the 16 bits shifted in (most significant bit first) are N; the high-order 2 bits are output as signals on pins 13 and 14, which are "open collector" outputs that can be used in any way the designer needs to use 2 control bits. The average voltage on the phase detector output PD (pin 6) is raised if the variable frequency divided by N is less than the reference frequency divided by R, and it is lowered if the variable frequency divided by N is greater than the reference frequency divided by R. Other outputs ør, øv, and lock detect LD can be used in more advanced PLLs.

Figure 7-4b is the analog part of the PLL. The chip contains two variable-frequency oscillators (VCOs). We describe the upper one here. The capacitor Cext between pins 12 and 13 sets the nominal frequency of the oscillator – about (500/Cext) MHz, where Cext is in picoFarads. The frequency of the output on pin 10 is proportional to the voltage on pin 1. The range control Rng on pin 14 sets the sensitivity; the larger Rng voltage makes oscillator frequency changes more sensitive to input voltage changes. The enable E must be low for the output to oscillate.

Figure 7-4c shows a simple application. Some new chips require unusual clock frequencies. For example, the author found a very interesting voice-output chip needing a 3.123 MHz crystal, but could not find the crystal. The PLL just mentioned could be used to generate frequencies in the range of 1 to 8 MHz in place of a crystal. It is a feedback control system of the kind described in section 6-6.3 that uses voltage analog and frequency analog signals. The 145155 compares a frequency on input Fin to one generated by the OscIn input, and outputs a voltage on PD that is proportional to the difference. This voltage, passed through a low-pass filter, is put into FCnt of the 74LS124 VCO to generate a frequency Fin. When stable, the voltage PD is just the right voltage to generate the frequency Fin that is (R/N) times the frequency of the signal OscIn. In this example, OscIn is generated from the 2 MHz E clock of the MC68HC11A8, and R is set to 8192 = 2^{13}. To set up the oscillator at frequency F, the connection from pin 6 of the 145155 to pin 1 of the 74LS124 is broken, a voltage of 2.5 volts is put on pin 1, the VCO capacitor Cext is set to cause oscillations at about the desired frequency F, and then a number N = (F/ 2MHz) * 8192 is shifted into the 145155 so that the output PD is about 2.5 volts. Then the broken connection is put back. The output signal should have frequency F. The design of the low-pass filter is quite involved: whole books are available on this topic. In the preceding circuit, the resistor connected to output PD determines the frequency of oscillation of the locking error, and the resistor connected to the 10 µF capacitor determines its damping; these can be twiddled to get acceptable results. This technique is useful in generating high frequencies up to about 15MHz. Note that the frequency can be changed (over a 2:1 range) by changing the number in the shift register, so the pitch of the voice-output chip can be altered to get a more natural speech. A similar technique is used with FM and TV tuners and a divide-by-16 prescaler to control the frequencies of oscillators up to the 300-MHz range used by FM radios and television sets.

Digital hardware techniques provide frequencies as accurate as that used to clock the counter and can easily run at 300-MHz input frequency. They also are immune to the effects of interrupts and so on. The M6840 chip can generate square waves too, as we will discuss in section 7-4.2. However, they require more integrated circuits, which can increase the size and cost of the final product.

The other techniques having been discussed, we return to the MC68HC11 counter/timer system to generate a square wave. We will use output compare 2 module, shown in figure 7-3b. Other output compare modules could be substituted for it, of course. (See the problems at the end of the chapter.) The square wave is to start immediately with an edge, rather than at a random time. If this starting requirement is missing, the programs simplify quite a bit (see problems at the end of the chapter). The period P (divided by 2 because there are 2 half cycles in a period, then multiplied by 2 because the clock is 2 MHz) is the number N in the program. Either gadfly, used in our program, or interrupt synchronization may be used. The minimum period is 30 µseconds using this approach. It is longer than the approach using a single parallel output port discussed earlier. We do not recommend it, but it leads to the interrupt approach discussed next.

```
          NAM    SQUGAD
          LDX    #$1000 SET UP POINTER TO I/O REGISTERS
          LDAA   #$40   GENERATE A 1 IN BIT 6
          STAA   $20,X  SET MODULE TO TOGGLE ON EACH COMPARE
          STAA   $B,X   FORCE COMPARE TO GENERATE AN EDGE
          LDD    $E,X   GET CURRENT "TIME"
   L1     ADDD   #N     ADD DESIRED DELAY TO IT
          STD    $18,X  PUT IT IN OUTPUT COMPARE 2 REGISTER
```

```
            STAA   $23,X  CLEAR THE FLAG BEFORE THE LOOP
L2          BRCLR  $23,X $40 L2   WAIT FOR COMPARE DONE
            LDAA   #$40   GENERATE A 1 IN BIT 6
            LDD    $18,X  GET LAST CHANGE VALUE
            BRA    L1
```

The interrupt-based routine uses the following initialization ritual. Its minimum period is about 45 μseconds. While this minimum time is longer than the previous approaches, the microcomputer is free to do other work when it uses this approach.

```
            NAM    SQUINT
            LDD    $100E  GET CURRENT "TIME"
            ADDD   #N     ADD DESIRED DELAY TO IT
            STD    $1018  PUT IT IN OUTPUT COMPARE 2 REGISTER
            LDAA   #$40   GENERATE A 1 IN BIT 6
            STAA   $1020  TOGGLE OUTPUT COMPARE 2 EACH TIMEOUT
            STAA   $1022  PUT IN MASK TO PERMIT INTERRUPTS
            STAA   $1023  CLEAR INTERRUPT IF THERE BEFORE
            CLI           ALLOW INTERRUPTS
L           BRA    L      WAIT FOR INT. (OR DO SOMETHING USEFUL)
```

The interrupt handler, where the address of label HNDLR is in $FFE6-7, is:

```
HNDLR  LDAA   #$40   GENERATE A 1 IN BIT 6
       STAA   $1023  CLEAR THE FLAG
       LDD    $1018  GET LAST CHANGE VALUE
       ADDD   #N     ADD DESIRED DELAY TO IT
       STD    $1018  PUT IT IN OUTPUT COMPARE 2 REGISTER
       RTI           RETURN TO MAIN PROGRAM
```

The analysis of these methods shows that the MC68HC11 counter/timer system using interrupts may be best for generating square waves with periods above 45 μseconds, since the processor is free to do other things while waiting for an interrupt. A simple parallel output register may be used for square waves (periods ≥ 9 μsecs) if the processor is doing nothing else, but phase-locked loops or digital hardware oscillators and counters may be needed for square waves with shorter periods.

We now consider an application of this oscillator to the production of touch-tone signals. A *touch-tone* signal is a pair of sine waves having frequencies that represent the digits used in dialing a telephone. A touch-tone generator can generate these signals so that the microcomputer can dial up on the telephone, and it can generate such tones to be sent via radio remote control or to be stored on cassette tape, and so on. In a top-down design, one must consider all the relevant alternatives. One possibility is integrated circuits that output touch-tone signals in response to keyboard contact closings, but these would require the microcomputer to act like the keyboard to such a chip. Another is analog switches in place of the keys that can be controlled by an output port. (A few other alternatives are also possible.) However, the number of chips needed in any alternative would be at least two, if not more. So we next consider generating a square wave with 2 N times the frequency of the sine waves that make up the touch-tone signal, using an N-stage Johnson counter to generate the sine wave.

A touch-tone signal consists of two sine waves transmitted simultaneously over the phone. The following table shows the tones required for each digit that can be sent. Table 7-2a shows the mapping of digits to frequencies shown in table 7-2b, and table 7-2b shows the frequencies in Hertz and the corresponding values of n to be added to the output compare module to generate the desired frequencies, as they will be used later in the example. Thus, to send the digit 5, send two superimposed sine waves with frequencies 770 Hertz and 1336 Hertz.

Table 7-2. Touch-Tone Codes

Digit	Coding
0	R4,C2
1	R1,C1
2	R1,C2
3	R1,C3
4	R2,C1
5	R2,C2
6	R2,C3
7	R3,C1
8	R3,C2
9	R3,C3

Code	Hertz	Counter
R1	697	$B4
R2	770	$A2
R3	852	$92
R4	941	$84
C1	1209	$68
C2	1336	$5E
C3	1477	$54
C4	1633	$4C

a. Codes for Digits   b. Frequencies for Codes

To send a sine wave, a Johnson counter is almost ideal. This counter is actually just a shift register whose output is inverted, then shifted back into it. (See figure 7-5.) A 4-bit Johnson counter would have the following sequence of values in the flip-flops:

```
L L L L
H L L L
H H L L
H H H L
H H H H
L H H H
L L H H
L L L H
```

As described in Don Lancaster's marvelous little book, *The CMOS Cookbook*, Howard Sams Inc., these counters can be used to generate sine waves simply by connecting resistors of value 33 KΩ to the first and third stages and 22 KΩ to the second stage of the shift register. (See figure 7-5.) Although the wave will look like a stair-step approximation to a sine, it is free of the lower harmonics and can be filtered if necessary. Moreover, using more accurate values of resistors and a longer shift register, it is possible to eliminate as much of the low-order harmonics as desired before filtering. In this case, if we want a sine wave with frequency F, we clock the shift register with a square wave whose period should be $1/(8 \times F)$.

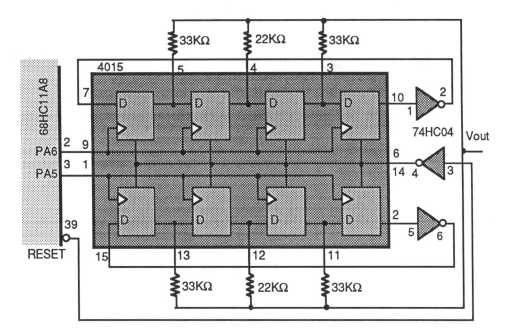

Figure 7-5. A Touch-Tone Generator

Now we consider ways to implement two square-wave generators whose frequencies are each one of four values. A software solution would require two microcomputers since a whole microcomputer is dedicated to outputting just one square wave; instead, a rather complex program just might be possible; or a table could be read out to supply the right sequences, but a different table is needed for each frequency, so each table would be quite long. The digital and analog hardware solutions require more than two chips, so we consider the counter/timer subsystem of the MC68HC11, using interrupts. The maximum required frequency has a shortest period of 612 μseconds, well within the range of the interrupt technique. Note that the MC68HC11 has five independent output compare modules, so two square waves can be implemented using two of the modules. This design, using a MC68HC11 to control a pair of Johnson counters, needs only one-and-a-half chips, so we will select it. (Be warned, however, that it is not always the most suitable way.)

Consider now the approach to generating a sine wave with frequency F using the MC68HC11 counter/timer system to drive a four-stage Johnson counter. Note that the number n added to the output compare register should be 2,000,000/(16xF). The values, stored in global memory to be added to the compare registers each time there is an interrupt, are shown in the right half of table 7-2b for the touch-tone codes. For instance, to send the digit 8, we add the numbers $92 and $5E into the two compare registers upon each interrupt, which will each generate a sine wave to comprise the signal.

Two devices are used to generate the two sine waves required by the touch-tone signal. The external connections are shown in figure 7-5. Note that the CLEAR control on the shift register is connected to the microcomputer RESET bus line to ensure that the shift register does not have some unusual pattern in it after power is applied. The desired signal is simply the sum of the sine waves produced by two shift registers and is obtained by merely connecting to the common points of the resistors. The initialization ritual, termination routine, and two interrupt handlers to send a touch-tone code are shown soon. The initialization ritual is used to begin generating a pattern for a number in ACCA, the termination routine is used to stop the waveform, and the two handlers are used to respond to interrupts for the two square wave generators. Here, ACCB has the digit number we wish to transmit. Output compare modules 2 and 3 are used. Module 2 is set up exactly as in the previous example and module 3 is set up as is module 2.

```
        NAM  TTONE
*
*    GLOBAL MEMORY
*
P1      RMB   2
P2      RMB   2
TBL1    FCB   $6A,8,$A,$C,$28,$2A,$2C,$48,$4A,$4C
TBL2    FDB   $B4,$A2,$92,$84,$68,$5E,$54,$4C
*
START   ANDB  #$F    EXTRACT LOW 4 BITS
        LDX   #TBL1  GET TABLE FOR DIGIT (TABLE 7-2A)
        ABX          ADD OFFSET TO GET ADD. OF TABLE ENTRY
        LDAB  0,X    GET CODES FOR DIGIT
        TBA          SAVE TO GET COLUMN PERIOD
        LDX   #TBL2  TABLE FOR CODE TO PERIOD (TABLE 7-2B)
        ANDB  #$F    GET COLUMN FREQUENCY ENTRY
        ABX          COMBINE TO GET ADDRESS OF ENTRY
        LDX   0,X    GET ENTRY
        STX   P1     SAVE IN GLOBAL
        TAB          GET FOR SECOND PERIOD
        LSRB         GET ROW NUMBER (HIGH NIBBLE)
        LSRB         TO LOW NIBBLE FOR COMBINING WITH INDEX
        LSRB
        LSRB
        ANDB  #$F    TO GET ROW PERIOD
        LDX   #TBL2  TABLE FOR CODE TO PERIOD (TABLE 7-2B)
        ABX          ADD OFFSET TO GET ADDR. OF TABLE ENTRY
        LDX   0,X    GET 16-BIT VALUE
        STX   P2     SAVE IN GLOBAL
        LDD   $1018  GET CURRENT "TIME"
        ADDD  P1     ADD DESIRED DELAY TO IT
        STD   $1018  PUT IT IN OUTPUT COMPARE 2 REGISTER
        LDD   $100A  GET CURRENT "TIME"
        ADDD  P2     ADD DESIRED DELAY TO IT
        STD   $101A  PUT IT IN OUTPUT COMPARE 3 REGISTER
        LDAA  #$60   GENERATE A 1 IN BITS 6 AND 5
```

```
        STAA    $1022  PUT IN MASK TO PERMIT INTERRUPTS
        CLI            ENABLE INTERRUPTS
L       BRA     L      WAIT FOR INT. (OR DO SOMETHING USEFUL)
```

The interrupt handler, whose address (of label HNDLR1) is in $FFE6 and $FFE7, is as follows:

```
HNDLR1  LDAA    #$40   GENERATE A 1 IN BIT 6
        STAA    $1023  CLEAR THE FLAG
        LDD     $1018  GET LAST CHANGE VALUE
        ADDD    P1     ADD DESIRED DELAY TO IT
        STD     $1018  PUT IT IN OUTPUT COMPARE 2 REGISTER
        RTI            RETURN TO MAIN PROGRAM
```

The interrupt handler, whose address (of label HNDLR2) is in $FFE4 and $FFE5, is as follows:

```
HNDLR2  LDAA    #$20   GENERATE A 1 IN BIT 5
        STAA    $1023  CLEAR THE FLAG
        LDD     $101A  GET LAST CHANGE VALUE
        ADDD    P2     ADD DESIRED DELAY TO IT
        STD     $101A  PUT IT IN OUTPUT COMPARE 3 REGISTER
        RTI            RETURN TO MAIN PROGRAM
```

The termination routine merely stops interrupts: if X points to the I/O registers, use BCLR $22,X $60.

A slight variation of this technique can be used to generate any periodic waveform. The square wave can be used to increment a counter which supplies an address to a read-only memory. It can output words to a D-to-A converter and can store the desired pattern to be developed. Thus, generating a square wave can generate other periodic waves. Finally, as discussed in the previous chapter, a square wave can be integrated to get a ramp signal, and this can be shaped by nonlinear analog techniques. Also, as in music generation, a periodic signal can be shaped by attenuating it under control of an output port to apply attack and decay characteristics in a music synthesizer.

The MC68HC11 counter/timer system is seen as a valuable tool in generating square waves, which can be used to generate other periodic waves using Johnson counters or read-only memories and D-to-A converters. However, the designer must not assume that this chip, or any counter/timer chip, is so much better than any other generator. He must consider the software approach as well as the hardware approaches and pick the best one for his application.

7-2.2 The Pulse Generator

Like the square-wave generator, a pulse generator has many uses. The device normally outputs a false value, but outputs a true value for a specified time after it actually is triggered. It can be triggered by software or by an external signal. And, like the square-wave generator, there are software and hardware techniques to implement it. The software technique to supply a pulse triggered by software merely outputs a true, waits the required time, and then outputs a false value. To react to an external signal, the external signal can be sensed in a gadfly loop or can generate an interrupt so that the pulse is generated when the signal arrives. But, like the software square wave generator, the software pulse generator is susceptible to timing errors due to interrupts, direct memory access, and dynamic memory refresh cycles. A 555 timer can act like a pulse generator, triggered by a microcomputer or an external signal; and the length of the pulse, determined by the value of a resistor and a capacitor, can be controlled by selecting of the resistor by means of an analog switch controlled from an output port. One-shot integrated circuits can be controlled in like manner. Finally, the MC68HC11 counter/timer system or M6840 chip (see section 7-4.2) can be used to generate pulses when the computer starts them (or started by an external signal and then sensed by the computer, as discussed later), and the pulse length can be computer controlled, as we now discuss.

A pulse can be generated entirely under software control, using real-time programming and a bit of a parallel output register to output the pulse. However, the MC68HC11 counter/timer system provides significant advantages. The pulse width is precisely timed to within a memory cycle time, which is usually one-half microsecond, and this time is not affected by processor interrupts, dynamic memory refresh requests, or other subtle problems that affect the timing of real-time programs. Moreover, the program has to put a compare value into the output compare register sometime after the last time the output changed and before the time the next output changes, rather than precisely at the time the output must change. This is quite useful in automobile engine control, where the pulse width controls the amount of gasoline injected into the engine, the spark timing, and other key factors in running the engine. A counter/timer system, with five output compare modules, is sufficient to control an engine so the microcomputer can measure input signals and compute the values of the pulse widths for the timers. In fact, the MC68HC11 was developed for the vast automobile industry.

We now have a need that is very nicely handled by the MC68HC11 counter/timer system: we wish to generate three waveforms (see figure 7-6) to control something.

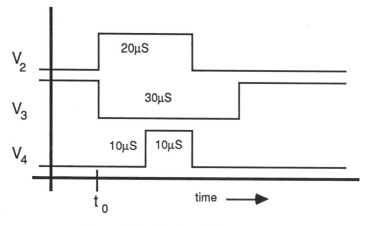

Figure 7-6. Timing of Some Pulses

The program that achieves this uses gadfly synchronization. Output V_i is to be generated by output compare module i. We assume we have initialized the outputs of the modules by storing $20 in the force compare register. (This can be done in a program using LDAA #$20 STAA $100B or by using a change memory command in the BUFFALO monitor.) We first set up the data register of the output compare 1 module to give the signals levels at time t_0. Time t_0 occurs when the FORCE register is written into. The numbers in the compare registers are set up to output the signals at the time the changes are required.

```
     NAM    PULSE
     LDX    #$1000 SET UP POINTER TO I/O REGISTERS
     LDD    #$7040 MASK   AND   DATA   FOR   MODS   2,3,4
     STD    $C,X   PUT A IN OC1 MASK AND B IN OC1 DATA
     LDAA   #%10111100    MOD. 2 RDY-CLR, MODS 3 AND 4 SET.
     STAA   $20,X  COMPARE MODE
     LDD    $E,X   GET CURRENT "TIME"
     ADDD   #20+39 ADD DESIRED DLY ADJ. FOR DLY OF PROG.
     STD    $1C,X  PUT IT IN OUTPUT COMPARE 4 REGISTER
     ADDD   #40    ADD DESIRED DELAY TO IT
     STD    $1A,X  PUT IT IN OUTPUT COMPARE 3 REGISTER
     SUBD   #20    ADD DESIRED DELAY TO IT
     STD    $18,X  PUT IT IN OUTPUT COMPARE 2 REGISTER
     PSHA          SAVE "TIME"
     LDAA   #$80   GENERATE A 1 IN BIT 7
     STAA   $B,X   FORCE COMP.E TO GEN. AN EDGE (THIS IS T0)
L    BRCLR  $23,X $10 L    WAIT FL-4 TO GO T SHOW COMP DONE
     LDAA   #8     PREPARE ONLY MODULE 4 TO CLEAR
     STAA   $20,X  COMPARE MODE
     PULA          RESTORE "TIME"
     STD    $1C,X  PUT IT IN OUTPUT COMPARE 4 REGISTER
```

Pulses are used for many things, such as a telephone that uses a rotary dialer. A relay connected in series with the dialer contacts will be pulsed to dial the number. The telephone standards require the relay to be closed for at least 40 milliseconds and then opened for at least 60 milliseconds for each pulse, and the number of pulses corresponds to the number being dialed. 600 milliseconds is needed between each number being dialed. We consider a software approach using a single-bit output device to control the relay, using the counter/timer system as a pulse generator, and using additional digital or analog hardware. Each designer has individual preferences. In fact, we really wanted to use the counter/timer system. But unless the pulse generation and timing are done by the counter/timer system so the microcomputer can do something else, the program is actually less efficient than a simpler approach using real-time synchronization. Therefore, we swallow our pride and implement the dialer using real-time programming.

```
          NAM   DIAL
DIAL      PSHA              SAVE DIAL NUMBER AS LOCAL VARIABLE
          TSY               USE Y AS STACK POINTER
L1        LDD   #$4002 OUTPUT HIGH FOR 2 x 20 MILLISECONDS
          BSR   DEL
          LDD   #3     OUTPUT LOW FOR 3 x 20 MILLISECONDS
          BSR   DEL
          DEC   0,Y    COUNT DOWN NUMBER OF PULSES
          BNE   L1
          LDD   #30     OUTPUT LOW FOR 30 x 20 MILLISECONDS
          BSR   DEL
          PULA          DELETE LOCAL VARIABLE, RET. FROM SUB
          RTS
DEL       STAA  $1000  OUTPUT BIT 6 IN PORTA TO RELAY
L2        LDX   #5000  SET DELAY FOR 5000 x 8 / 2 =20000 µSECONDS
L3        NOP          PAD LOOP TO 8 CYCLES
          DEX          COUNT DOWN
          BNE   L3     TO DELAY 20 MILLISECONDS
          DECB         COUNT OUT NUMBER OF 20 mSEC. LOOPS
          BNE   L2
          RTS
```

The routine uses a simple subroutine DEL that outputs the value in bit 6 of accumulator A to the relay and then waits N times 20 milliseconds, where N is in accumulator B. The main routine dials a number by outputting a true value to PORT A bit 6 for N = 2 to the subroutine, then a false value for N = 3 to it, and so on for each pulse. The subroutine is then called with a false value and N = 30 to provide the spacing between digits as required by the telephone company.

This example gives me an opportunity to relate one of the truly great stories in electronics – the invention of the dial telephone. It seems that in the 1880s Almond B. Strowger, one of two undertakers in a very small town, couldn't get much business. His competitor's wife was the telephone operator for the town. When someone suffered a death in the family, they called up to get an undertaker. The wife naturally recommended her husband, diverting callers from our poor friend, Almond. Necessity is the mother of invention. With a celluloid shirt collar and some pins, he contrived a mechanism that could be operated by the caller, using a stepping relay mechanism that would connect the caller to the desired telephone, so that calls for his business would not go through his competitor's wife. It worked so well that it became the standard mechanism for making calls all over the world. Even today, about a quarter of all telephones use this "step-by-step" or Strowger system.

7-2.3 Real-Time Clock

Using a configuration almost identical to that used for a pulse generator, a device can be used either as a real-time clock or a trace mode interrupt. In this section we'll cover these applications, as well as an example using a real-time alarm clock that illustrates how precise timing can be achieved.

Look back at the last subsection and note that the flag 1 register is set when an output compare occurs. This can be used to set an interrupt if the corresponding mask 1 register bit is also set. Finally, this activity is done even if there is no effect on the output port bit because the Compare mode bits are 00. Thus, the "pulse" output could be a "software pulse" that affects the program rather than the outside world.

An instruction trace can be built from this mechanism. In chapter 1 we explained that a monitor is a program used to help you debug programs. The monitor behaves like an SWI handler, since it may be "called up" by a breakpoint, which is an SWI instruction, so it is left by an RTI instruction. To "trace" a user program, we can leave the monitor to execute just one instruction, then reenter the monitor to see what happened. Just before we leave the monitor, we read the counter, then a number N and write the result in the output compare register, after which we execute RTI. The user program will be given enough time to execute just one instruction, and N will be chosen to permit that to happen. Then an interrupt will occur and the monitor will be reentered to display the changes wrought by the executed instruction.

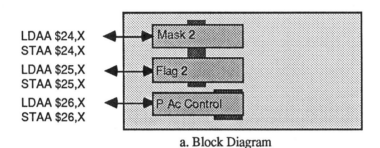

a. Block Diagram

b. Logic Diagram

Figure 7-7. Real-Time Interrupt

This interrupt can be used to cause parts of a routine to occur at precise times, even though the parts take varying times to execute (provided they do not take longer than the time between these precise times). The output compare register is loaded with an "alarm clock" value, which is the time we wish to execute the next operation, and, after we complete the current operation, we can gadfly loop on the flag bit of the output compare module. Alternatively, the interrupt handler can execute the next step, using a state machine technique, an example of which is included at the end of this section.

Before we proceed to the example, we look at two related parts of the counter/timer system, the real-time interrupt module (figure 7-7) and the computer operating properly module (figure 7-8). The purpose of the former is to provide, at millisecond intervals, interrupts which can be used to check a keyboard or build a rudimentary multitasking operating system; and the purpose of the latter is to reset the computer if the software does not pay homage to this module within the required time periods, to be sure the software does not run off out of control.

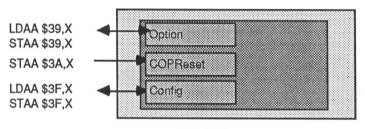

a. Block Diagram

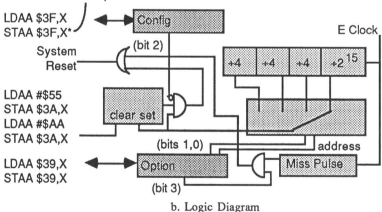

b. Logic Diagram

Figure 7-8. Computer Operating Properly Mechanism

The real-time interrupt module (figure 7-7) uses parts of the mask 2 and flag 2 registers, and part of the pulse accumulator control register. The 2 low-order bits of the latter register determine the time between real-time timeouts. If they are 00, then the time is 4.1 milliseconds; if 01, then 8.19 milliseconds; if 10, then 16.38 milliseconds; and if 11, then 32.77 milliseconds (for an 8-MHz crystal). When a timeout occurs, flag 2 bit 6 is set, and this may be tested by a gadfly loop. If the corresponding mask 2 bit is set, an interrupt occurs, which is vectored through locations $FFF0,1. The flag 2 bit must be cleared by writing a 1 into it. The interrupt handler may check something, like a keyboard, to see if any new activity has occurred. This permits the main software the freedom of not checking this thing, so it can be simpler to write.

The computer operating properly module (figure 7-8) uses the option, COPreset and config registers. Bit 2 of the config register must be 0 for this feature to be used. Bits 1, 0 of the option register set the rate at which this module must be attended to: if 00, then every 16.38 milliseconds; if 01, then every 65.5; if 10, then every 262.14 milliseconds; and if 11, then every 1.049 seconds (for an 8 MHz crystal). The software must write $55, then $AA into the COPreset register, within the selected time period. If it fails to do this, the microcomputer is reset (and the RESET pin is dragged low to also reset all the I/O chips). A similar control is used to check the clock rate. If bit 3 of the option register is 1 and the clock rate drops below about 200 kHz, the microcomputer will be reset in like manner.

The M6840 can also be used to generate real-time interrupts, as will be covered in section 7-4.2.

Consider an "alarm clock" in a battery-powered microcomputer. We need to keep track of the time, in minutes, up to a day and compare that time to a given number. When a match is detected, we will execute a routine, whose address is given.

To keep track of time, we can use an external hardware pulse generator, such as an opto-isolator connected to 60-Hz power, an extra time-of-day chip (see section 4-4), real-time software in the MC68HC11 or one of the parts of the 6811's counter/timer system. As a solution, the counting of 60-Hz pulses from the power line has best long-term stability, but, because we want to illustrate certain concepts, we arbitrarily eliminate this solution. The extra chip is more costly than the 6811 alone. A real-time software solution means nothing else can be done at the same time, so that is not acceptable. So we'll use one of the counter/timer subsystems. The real-time interrupt could be used, but we desire to keep track of whole numbers of minutes, and the periods for the real-time interrupt are in awkward fractions of seconds. So we use an output compare module, module 2, to generate interrupts every $1/32th$ second (which is the largest time that can be accurately measured using the 16-bit timer that is clocked at 2 MHz). The interrupt handler will count down by $32 * 60 = 1920$ to get a one-per-minute base period. Each minute, the global memory time in HOURS and MINUTES is updated, and if the time matches a compare value ALARM, a subroutine whose address is in ROUTINE is executed.

```
            NAM     ALARM
    *
    * GLOBAL VARIABLES
    HOURS   RMB     1       CURRENT TIME IN HOURS
    MINUTESRMB      1       CURRENT TIME IN MINUTES
```

```
TICKS    RMB    2       NUMBER OF ELAPSED TICKS
ALARM    RMB    2       WHEN WE WANT TO DO SOMETHING
ROUTINE RMB    2       WHAT WE WANT TO DO
*
* INITIALIZATION RITUAL
*
START    CLRA           (WE ASSUME THAT THE INIT. TIMING ERR. IS
         CLRB           NEGLIGIBLE, AND OTHER GLOBAL VARS ARE
         STD    TICKS CORRECTLY INIT.) SET TICK COUNT TO 0
         LDAA   #$40    GENERATE A 1 IN BIT 6
         STAA   $1022 PUT IN MASK TO PERMIT INTERRUPTS
         STAA   $1023 CLEAR INTERRUPTS THAT WERE SET BEFORE
         CLI            ALLOW INTERRUPTS
L        BRA    L       WAIT FOR INT. (OR DO SOMETHING USEFUL)
```

The interrupt handler, whose address (of label HNDLR) is in $FFE6 and $FFE7, is as follows:

```
HNDLR    LDAA   #$40    GENERATE A 1 IN BIT 6
         STAA   $1023   CLEAR THE FLAG
         LDD    $1018   GET LAST CHANGE VALUE
         ADDD   #62500  ADD 1/32 SEC. DEL. (FOR +1 PRESCALE)
         STD    $1018   PUT IT IN OUTPUT COMPARE 2 REGISTER
         DEC    TICKS+1 COUNT DOWN 2400 TICKS = 1 MINUTE
         BNE    HNDLR2 IN DBLE PRECISION GLOBAL MEMORY
         DEC    TICKS   (NOTE THAT DEC REQUIRES ADDING $100
         BNE    HNDLR2 SO IT BECOMES 0 AFTER 2400 TICKS)
         LDD    #1920+$100    WE GET HERE ONCE EACH MINUTE
         STD    TICKS   RESET FOR NEXT MINUTE
         LDD    HOURS   GET MINUTES, HOURS
         INCB           INCREMENT MINUTES
         CMPB   #60     IF AT END OF HOUR
         BNE    HNDLR1
         CLRB           PUT MINUTES BACK TO 0
         INCA           BUMP HOURS
         CMPA   #24     IF AT END OF DAY
         BNE    HNDLR1
         CLRA           CLEAR HOURS TOO
HNDLR1 STD    HOURS
         CPD    ALARM   COMPARE TO ALARM
         BNE    HNDLR2 IF MATCH
         LDX    ROUTINE GET ADD. OF ROUTINE TO BE EXECUTED
         CLI            PERMIT INT. (DISABLED IN THE HANDLER)
         JSR    0,X     GO TO ROUTINE (ENDS IN RTS)
HNDLR2 RTI             RETURN TO MAIN PROGRAM
```

This real-time interrupt, or any interrupt that causes things to happen when an interrupt occurs, can be viewed as a Mealy model sequential machine. The state transition occurs when there is an interrupt. The internal state of the sequential machine is kept in one or more global variables, like HOURS and TICKS in the preceding example, and the input states are determined from reading input registers or the program's global variables. Output states may be put in output registers or the program's global variables or may be programs that are executed, like the subroutine whose address is in ROUTINE in the preceding example. This type of *real-time interrupt programming* is quite useful in process control applications.

The counter/timer chip is seen to be a valuable component for generation of pulses. But don't forget to consider the alternatives to this chip. Another could be better.

7-3 Frequency Analog Measurement

Converse to generating square waves or pulses, one may need to measure the frequency or period of a square wave or repetitive signal, or the width of a pulse. Many important outputs carry information by their frequency: tachometers, photodetectors, piezo-electric pressure transducers. The voltage-to-frequency converter integrated circuit can change voltages to frequencies economically and with high accuracy. The frequency of output from a timer chip like the 555 timer is inversely proportional to the resistance and capacitance used in its timing circuit. Therefore, a by-product of measuring frequency is that one can easily obtain measurements of resistance or capacitance. Better yet, the period of the signal is linearly proportional to resistance and capacitance. Period can be measured directly. Moreover, for high frequencies, frequency is easier and faster to measure, while for low frequencies, period is easier and faster. The 6811 is quite capable, if necessary, of inverting the value using its IDIV and FDIV instructions. For nonrepetitive waveforms, pulse width measurement is very useful. This can be measured too. Also, the time between two events can be measured by using the events to set, then clear, a flip-flop. The pulse width of the output of this flip-flop can be measured. Sometimes the microcomputer has to keep track of the total number of events of some kind. The event is translated into the rising or falling edge of a signal, and the number of edges is then recorded. Note that the number of events per second is the frequency. Thus, events are counted in the same way as frequency is measured, but the time is not restricted to any specific value.

In this section, we first study the measurement of frequency. The counting of events is similar to this, and even though it won't be discussed explicitly, it can be done in the same way as the measurement of frequency. We next describe the period measurement, after which we include a short example that shows how period measurement can be used to read the positions of several potentiometers. Finally, we describe pulse width measurement.

7-3.1 Frequency Measurement

As with the square wave generator and pulse generator, frequency and period measurement can be done in the M6811 by software using a simple input port, by digital hardware read by a parallel input port, by an analog technique, and by using a counter/timer system. The designer should consider all techniques – those based on software, digital or analog hardware, and counter/timer – for frequency and period measurement. We'll mainly discuss how the counter/timer module is used to measure frequency or period, before which we'll consider the other approaches.

The software technique for measuring frequency uses a parallel port. It is quite tricky, and, although it can be done, there is no need to study it because the MC68HC11's I/O devices are so easy to use and available that they make this awkward approach merely an academic exercise.

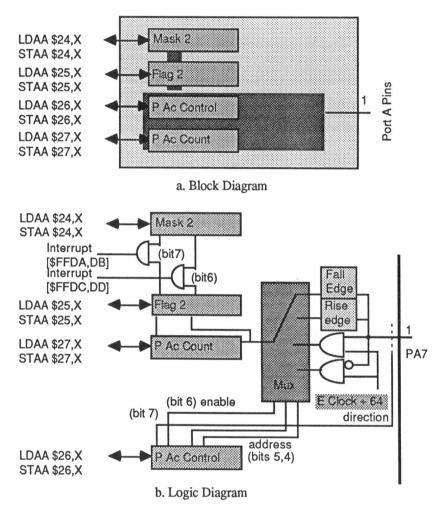

a. Block Diagram

b. Logic Diagram

Figure 7-9. The Pulse Accumulator

A digital hardware approach would use one or more counter ICs that can be cascaded to make up a counter of sufficient width. A parallel I/O register can be used to clear the counter and then read the counter output word, say, one second later. The counter can count input transitions from low to high between these two times. A note of caution: if the width is greater than 8 bits, then two or more 8-bit bytes will be read at different times and the counter could be incremented between successive reads. The counter should be examined with this in mind. For instance, a 16-bit counter should be read most significant byte first, then least significant byte, and then most significant byte again. If the readings of the most significant byte differ, the reading should be considered erroneous and should be tried again.

An analog approach would be to convert the frequency to a voltage, then measure the voltage by an analog-to-digital converter. An FM demodulator, a frequency-to-voltage converter, or a tachometer can convert high frequencies, audio frequencies, or subaudio frequencies to a voltage.

Finally, we focus on the use of a counter/timer system for frequency measurement or event counting. One counter can count the number of an input signal's high to low transitions. The fixed interval of time can be measured out by another counter in the chip or by real-time programming. The latter technique, which we discuss soon, is easier to explain. The counting is done by the pulse accumulator in the M6811 (see figure 7-9.) This subsystem uses an 8-bit pulse accumulator counter PAcCount, bits 5 and 4 of the mask 2 and flag 2 registers, and the 4 most significant bits of the pulse accumulator control register PAcControl. For the pulse counter to change, bit 6 of the control register must be set. Bits 5 and 4 of that register determine what is counted. If they are 00, then falling edges on the signal on the input PA7 cause the counter to increment; if 01, then rising edges of that input cause the counter to increment. If those control bits are 10, then as long as the PA7 input is high, the counter is incremented each 32 μseconds; and if those bits are 11, then as long as the PA7 input is low, the counter is incremented each 32 μseconds (assuming a 2-MHz E clock). Bits 5 and 4 of the flag 2 register indicate (bit 5) that the counter has overflowed, and (bit 4) that the counter has incremented; they are cleared by writing a 1 into them; and if the corresponding bits are set in the mask 2 register, interrupts will occur via $FFDC,DD (for overflow) and $FFDA,DB (for incrementing). This subsystem is very flexible and can be used to count events and measure frequency or pulse width, as we will see in the following sections. Here we concentrate on event counting and frequency measurement.

To count events that correspond to falling edges, set bits 5, 4 of the control register to 00. Then, each time an event occurs, the pulse counter is incremented. When it overflows, an interrupt can be used to count overflows, thus extending the range of the counter to 16 or 24 bits. To measure frequency, we count events in a fixed time interval, such as one second. Alternatively, we can count the number of events in 1/2 second and double the number. Further, we can accurately measure an interval of 1/32 second using a real-time interrupt – as we did in the program ALARM – and count pulses. The resulting number times 32 is the frequency. The upcoming program shows how this can be done.

```
                NAM    FREQ
      * GLOBAL VARIABLES
      HIPCNT  RMB    1      COUNT HIGH-ORDER BYTE,
      LOPCNT  RMB    1      LOW-ORDER BYTE, WILL BE FREQUENCY
      STATE   RMB    1      INTERNAL STATE OF SEQUENTIAL MACHINE
```

```
START   LDX     #$1000 SHORTEN CODE: USE INDEX ADDRESSING
        LDAA    #1      SET STATE TO SENSE 2 CONSECUTIVE EDGES
        STAA    STATE FOR INTERRUPT HANDLER
        BCLR    $26,X $F0      CLEAR HIGH NBL OF PULSE CONTROL
        LDD     $E,X    GET CURRENT TIME
        ADDD    #100    ADD SMALL DLY TO GET AN INT. SOON
        STD     $18,X   PUT IT IN OUTPUT COMPARE 2 REGISTER
        LDD     #$4020 GEN. A 1 IN BIT 6 OF A, AND A 1 IN BIT 5 OF B
        STAA    $22,X   PUT IN MASK 1 FOR OUTPUT COMP. INT.
        STAA    $23,X   CLEAR PREVIOUS INTERRUPTS
        STAB    $24,X   PUT IN MASK 2 FOR PULSE ACC. INTERRUPTS
        CLI             MAKE SURE INTERRUPTS ARE ENABLED
L       TST     STATE WAIT FOR INT. HANDLER TO SET FLAG TO 0
        BNE     L       WHEN IT IS DONE
        LDD     HIPCNT          GET THE SAVED COUNT
        ASLD            MULTIPLY BY 32
        ASLD
        ASLD
        ASLD
        ASLD
```

The output compare interrupt handler used to measure 1/32th of a second, whose address (of label HNDLR1) is in $FFE6 and $FFE7, is as follows:

```
HNDLR1   LDX  #$1000     BCLR, BSET NEED INDEX ADDRESSING
         LDAA #$40       GENERATE A 1 IN BIT 6
         STAA $23,X      CLEAR THE FLAG
         LDAA STATE      GET SEQUENTIAL MACHINE STATE
         BEQ  HNDLR1B IF ALREADY 0, EXTRANEOUS INT.
         DEC  STATE      COUNT DOWN
         BEQ  HNDLR1A THE FIRST TIME, SET UP PULSE ACC.
         LDD  $18,X      GET LAST TIME
         ADDD #62500     ADD 1/32 SECOND DELAY TO IT
         STD  $18,X      PUT IT IN OUTPUT COMPARE 2 REGISTER
         CLR  $27,X      SET LOW BYTE OF COUNT TO 0
         CLR  HIPCNT     CLEAR HIGH BYTE OF COUNT
         BSET $26,X $40 ENABLE PULSE ACC. INPUT (BIT 5 IS 0)
         RTI
HNDLR1A LDAA $27,X       THE SECOND INT., GET LOW COUNT
         STAA LOPCNT     SAVE FOR USER
HNDLR1B BCLR $26,X $40  DISABLE PULSE ACCUMULATOR INPUT
         BCLR $24,X $20  DISABLE PULSE ACC. INTERRUPTS
         BCLR $22,X $40  DISABLE OUTPUT COMPARE INTERRUPTS
         RTI
```

With HNDLR2 in $FFDC and $FFDD, the pulse accumulator interrupt handler is:

```
HNDLR2  LDAA   #$20    GENERATE A 1 IN BIT 5
        STAA   $1025   CLEAR THE FLAG
        INC    HIPCNT       INC HIGH PART OF PULSE COUNT
        RTI
```

Each of the techniques just described has some advantages and disadvantages. Although the software approach (which was not shown) is least expensive – requiring just a 1-bit parallel I/O port – interrupts, direct memory access operations, or dynamic memory refresh cycles can interfere with the timing, the processor can do nothing but this one activity, and the maximum frequency is limited by the long time taken in the loop to sample the inputs. To time out a fixed fraction of one second, the counter/timer subsystem can use a real-time interrupt, which uses the counter/timer to count events. The measurement can thus be independent of interrupts, DMA, and dynamic memory refresh operations. The digital hardware technique, using an external counter, can directly measure much higher frequencies. The analog hardware method can be used with A-to-D converters and is attractive if a data acquisition system is already needed and has some free inputs to be used with this approach; but this method is susceptible to noise and errors in the analog signal. The best approach for any specific application requires some consideration of each of the above methods.

7-3.2 Period Measurement

We now turn to the direct measurement of the period of a waveform. Period can be measured in about the same way as frequency, but the role of the reference signal that establishes the sampling time and the role of the signal being measured are interchanged. Then by analogy, period can be measured by software, digital or analog hardware, or a counter/timer system. As in the last subsection, we'll mainly concentrate on the counter/timer approach, using the MC68HC11 for a concrete example – leaving the M6840 to be discussed in section 7-4.4 – and discussing the other approaches first.

The software approach to period measurement is simpler than the software approach to frequency measurement. A counter is cleared, then the input signal is sensed in a gadfly loop until a falling edge occurs. Then the main loop is entered. Each time the loop is executed, the counter is incremented and the input value is saved. The loop is left when the input value from the last execution of the loop is true and the input value in this execution of the loop is false – that is, on the next falling edge. The counter then contains a number N, and the period is N times the time taken to execute the loop. The analog hardware approach uses a voltage-to-frequency converter, in which the input voltage and the reference voltage are interchanged (see section 6-5.3 for details). The digital hardware approach uses a reference clock to increment a counter. The counter is cleared on the falling edge of the input signal and stops counting (or is examined) on the next falling edge of the input signal. Some reflection on these techniques shows that in each case the frequency measurement technique is used, but the roles of the reference frequency and the input frequency are interchanged.

Recall that the popular 555 timer integrated circuit can generate a digital signal with period $P = A + B (R_a + 2 R_b) C$, where A and B are constants, R_a and R_b are the resistors and C is the capacitor (as diagramed in figure 6-9.) The resistor R_b can be a "volume control" or "joystick" with which the computer may want to sense the wiper's position, or it may be a photoresistor or thermistor. In fact, under the control of a parallel output port and an analog multiplexor, the computer can insert any of a number of resistors in place of Rb, so that the selected resistor's value can determine the signal's period and the period can be measured by a counter/timer. This is a good way to "read" into the microcomputer the potentiometers on a stereo console, a game, or a toy.

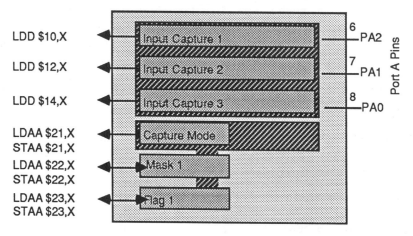

a. Block Diagram

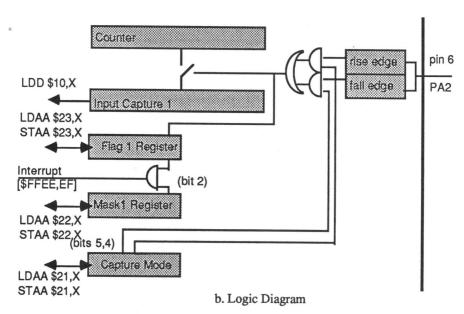

b. Logic Diagram

Figure 7-10. Input Capture Mechanism

The best way to measure the period of a waveform is with an input capture module of the 6811's counter/timer subsystem. (See figure 7-10.) Three input capture modules are provided (see figure 7-10a), so three waveforms can be measured at the same time. Input capture module 1 is diagramed in figure 7-10b. Table 7-3 shows the conversion for the other modules. An edge is selected by bits 5 and 4 of the capture mode register; if bit 5 is 1, then a transfer will occur when the signal on PA2 sees a falling edge; and if bit 4 is 1, then a transfer will occur when there is a leading edge on PA2; if both bits are 1, then a transfer occurs on either edge. A transfer causes the current value of the timer register to be copied into the input capture 1 register, and bit 2 of the flag 1 register is set. This bit can be sampled in a gadfly loop, or if mask 1 bit 2 is set, an interrupt is vectored through $FFEE and $FFEF.

Table 7-3. Input Capture Module Substitutions

Module	1	2	3
Bit of Mask 1 and Flag 1	2	1	0
Bits of Capture Mode	5,4	3,2	1,0
Pins	PA2 (6)	PA1 (7)	PA0 (8)
Interrupt Vector	FFEE,EF	FFEC,ED	FFEA,EB
Capture Register	$10,X	$12,X	$14,X

The period of a waveform can very simply be measured by reading the input capture register after two consecutive transfers. The following program PERIOD shows a gadfly technique for doing this (assuming the time count register does not overflow). A temporary location TEMP is needed to subtract the first reading from the second.

```
        NAM    PERIOD
        LDX    #$1000
        BSET   $21,X $20      TO SENSE FALL EDGE, SET BIT 5
        BCLR   $21,X $10      CLR CAPT. MD. BIT 4 FOR INP.CAPT 1
        LDA    #4      BIT 2 IS NEEDED FOR INPUT CAPTURE 1 FLAG
        STAA   $23,X  CLEAR FLAG
L1      BRCLR  $23,X 4 L1     WAIT FOR EDGE
        LDY    $10,X  GET READING
        STAA   $23,X  CLEAR FLAG
L2 BRCLR $23,X 4 L2  WAIT FOR EDGE
        LDD    $10,X  GET SECOND READING
        STY    TEMP  PUT WHERE SUBD CAN GET IT
        SUBD   TEMP  DIFFERENCE IS PERIOD
```

7-3.3 Pulse Width Measurement

The *pulse width* of a signal is the time from a rising edge to the next falling edge (that is, as the width of a positive pulse). If a negative pulse is to be measured, in hardware it is inverted and measured as a positive pulse; in software, such as the upcoming program PULSE, the sensing of rising and falling edges are interchanged. You may question why we might want to measure pulse width when we can already measure period, or vice versa. Usually the signal being measured is an analog signal, and this is converted to a digital signal by a comparator. Normally, the period is independent of the comparator's threshold, so it should be measured. The pulse width can depend on the comparator's threshold because the comparator outputs a high signal when the input is above the threshold; so the pulse width depends on the shape of the input and the threshold. It is naturally better to measure the pulse width if the waveform is not repetitive; in such a case, period could not be measured.

As usual, there are software, analog and digital hardware, and counter/timer techniques for pulse width measurement. Except for the analog hardware approach, they are all similar to the techniques for period measurement. Generally, in the software approach the main loop is entered when the input signal falls and is left when that signal rises. The hardware counter is cleared when the input falls and counts until the input rises. But the analog technique uses an integrator rather than a voltage-to-frequency converter. The input signal is conditioned so that it is normally zero and is a precise voltage when the input is low. This conditioned signal is merely integrated. After the pulse is over, the output voltage of the integrator is proportional to the pulse width.

Pulse width is measured by a counter/timer in a manner similar to period measurement. (Again we assume the counter doesn't overflow.) The only difference is that we must change the edge of the second reading of the input capture register to determine the time from a leading edge to the next falling edge.

```
        NAM   PULSE
        LDX   #$1000
        BCLR  $21,X $10   TO SENSE LD EDGE, CLR BIT 4
        BSET  $21,X $20   SET CAPT. MD BIT 5 FOR INP CAPT 1
        LDA   #4    BIT 2 IS NEEDED FOR INPUT CAPTURE 1 FLAG
        STAA  $23,X  CLEAR FLAG
L1      BRCLR $23,X 4 L1   WAIT FOR EDGE
        LDY   $10,X  GET READING
        BCLR  $21,X $20   TO SENSE FALL EDGE, CLEAR BIT 5
        BSET  $21,X $10   SET CAPT. MD BIT 4 FOR INP CAPT 1
        STAA  $23,X  CLEAR FLAG
L2      BRCLR $23,X 4 L2   WAIT FOR EDGE
        LDD   $10,X  GET SECOND READING
        STY   TEMP  PUT WHERE SUBD CAN GET IT
        SUBD  TEMP  DIFFERENCE IS PERIOD
```

The UART is an illustration of the use of pulse width measurement. In chapter 8, we will study the UART, which is used to communicate over a serial link. The UART requires a clock signal that is 16 times faster than the rate at which bits arrive on the serial link. An output compare module of a counter/timer system, configured as a square wave generator, is well suited to this task (although special chips are also available for it). An input capture module is also suited to automatic determination of the bit rate and setting of the clock rate, using pulse width measurement. The sender should send the capital U character – ASCII code $55 – repetitively. Each time it is sent, it generates five pulses (or six pulses if the parity is set even). The pulse rate can be measured using the counter/timer, then multiplied by 16 to establish the UART clock, which can be used in the interrupt handler of the output compare module that is configured to generate a square wave.

7-4 The M6840 Counter/Timer Chip

An external counter/timer system is available as an integrated circuit. It may be used with any computer, such as a microprocessor that, unlike the 6811, is without a counter/timer system. We'll discuss the use of such a counter/timer system chip in the expanded rather than the single-chip mode. We did not introduce it earlier because we wished to avoid any confusion between it and the MC68HC11 counter/timer system. It is an important alternative to the MC68HC11 counter/timer, especially if an application requires more modules than are available in the MC68HC11 system. An additional benefit is that this chip, the M6840, is rather complex, like the CRT generator and floppy disk controller chips discussed in chapter 9, and serves to introduce the reader to more complex I/O chips.

7-4.1 Overview of the M6840

A M6840 chip has three independent counter/timer devices. Each device has a 16-bit read-only *counter register*, a corresponding 16-bit write-only *latch* to reinitialize the counter each time it counts to 0, and an 8-bit write-only *control register*. The three counters have a common read-only *status register* to identify device interrupts. Each device has three connections to the outside world: negative logic *clock* C, negative logic *gate* G, and positive logic *output* O. The designers chose to make the counters 16 bits because this corresponds to about four-and-a-half decimal digits of accuracy, thus providing enough accuracy for control systems. Eight bits would be too small and more than 16 bits would be inconvenient to handle in a microcomputer. Three devices were put in this chip because relatively few pins are needed, and three could be put on a contemporary large-scale integrated circuit. Although we often need only one, the counter/timer's flexibility inspires many new applications which we can experiment with for only the small extra cost for the spare devices. Figure 7-11a shows the block diagram of the module, and figure 7-11b shows the pin connections.

Due to the use of a 2-MHz clock, a B realization of the M6840 must be used. The MC68B40 has 9 pins to connect to the outside world (three for each device), and 19 to connect to the MC68HC11 in extended multiplexed bus mode. (See figure 7-11b.) Eight data pins are connected to the corresponding lines of the data bus. The five-volt power supply, ground, the reset bus line, and the R/W line are connected to the appropriate pins. The E clock must be connected to the enable pin, and this signal may not be gated or otherwise modified. Register select pins RS0, RS1, and RS2 are normally connected to address bus lines 0, 1, and 2, respectively, to get the relative placement of registers shown in this chapter; and chip select pins CS0 (negative logic) and CS1 (positive logic) are connected to the address decoder that decodes some or all of the address lines A[15 to 3] to select the device. Finally, the IRQ pin is connected to the IRQ or XIRQ bus line if a device interrupt in this chip is to be handled by the IRQ handler or the XIRQ handler routines.

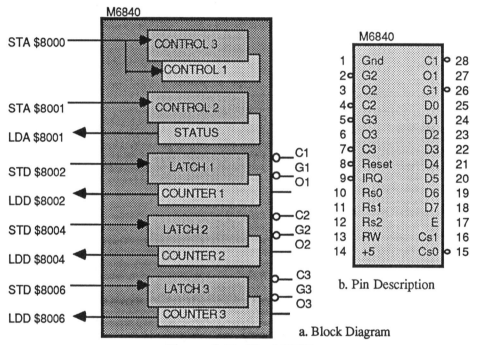

Figure 7-11. The M6840

Suppose, for concreteness, the module is addressed at locations $8000 through $8007. The control registers and status register are at locations $8000 and $8001, and each latch-counter register is at a pair of locations with addresses higher than $8002. Using two locations for each latch-counter allows them to be accessed by the LDD and STD instructions for convenient handling. LDD $8002 will read the current contents of the counter register of the first device and STD $8002 will write into the corresponding latch. Similarly, LDD $8004 and LDD $8006 will read the counter register of the second and third devices, respectively, while STD $8004 and STD $8006 will write into the latches of the second and third devices. LDAA $8001 will read the common status register, while STAA $8001 will write into the control register for the second device. Using the same technique we encountered with the M6821, bit 0 of the second device's control register is like a seventeenth address bit used to select the other control registers; if that bit is 0, STAA $8000 will store into the third device control register, and if 1, into the first device control register. Note that the control registers are write-only and the status register is read-only. Don't try to increment a control register in an INC $8000 instruction, since arithmetic operations on memory require readable output registers.

For most of the following examples, we need only one device, which is the first device. To store a word in accumulator A into the control register, we execute this ritual:

```
        LDAB    #1
        STAB    $8001
        STAA    $8000
```

The first two lines merely put a T in bit 0 of the control register for device 2, so that the third line can store the desired word in the control register for device 1. Using the gadfly approach, the following ritual will loop until the device interrupt for device 1 is set:

```
L       LDAA    $8001
        LSRA
        BCC     L
        LDD     $8002
```

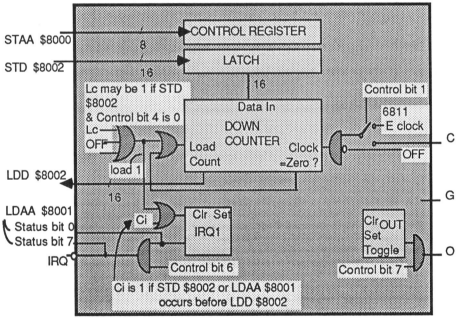

Figure 7-12. The Basic Counter Device

Here, status register bit 0 is put into the carry bit, and the branch instruction will loop in these instructions until the status bit is T. The LDD instruction reads the counter, thereby clearing the interrupt. On polling after an interrupt, the following ritual will jump to DEVHND if device 1 has a device interrupt:

```
LDAA    $8001
EORA    #$81
BITA    #$C1
BEQ     DEVHND
```

The first line reads the status register common to all the devices. A device 1 interrupt is indicated if bit 0 is T and the variable on the IRQ bus pin, read from bit 7, is also T. Bit 6 is always 0. Recall that we should test for one 0 when reading a control word, so we simplify troubleshooting by ensuring that the interrupt is not erroneously indicated when the chip is burned out or not in the socket. To test this, status bits 7 and 1 are inverted and BIT checks the resulting bits 0, 6 and 7 for F. In the interrupt handler, the device interrupt is cleared by reading the counter, as in the LDD $8002 instruction.

Here we discuss the several counter and interrupt request signals for device 1. (See figure 7-12.) The counter register has control variables LOAD and CLOCK and a 1-bit output =ZERO and a 16-bit output COUNT. The IRQ1 flip-flop has SET and CLR inputs. A flip-flop OUT drives the output pin O. Control bit 0, called OFF, turns the timer off if asserted. When the device is off, words in the latch are also put into the counter. When on, the counter can be decremented each time its CLOCK signal falls. If control bit 1 is T, the M6811 E clock is used; if F, the signal on the clock pin for this device is used to decrement the counter. Each time the counter reaches 0, the output =ZERO is true, and the 16-bit number in the latch is loaded into the counter register on the next falling CLOCK edge. If the number were n, the counter counts modulo $n + 1$. The IRQ1 interrupt request flip-flop is set as a function of the mode, but is always cleared when LOAD is asserted to load the counter or when the counter is read just after the status register is read. IRQ1 can be read as status register bit 0. IRQ2 ANDed with control bit 6 can be read as status bit 7; it outputs on the IRQ pin in negative logic to connect to a wire-OR bus line. Finally, OUT is ANDed with control bit 7 to drive the output pin O.

Table 7-4 illustrates the different configuration options available for the generation of square waves, interrupts, and measurement of frequency. When bit 0 (in device 1) is F, all devices decrement their counters. When T, all counters load their values from their latches continuously. Note that this bit in device 1 controls all devices. This feature permits easy synchronization of the devices in an M6840 chip. However, it also makes the independent use of the other devices of device 1 difficult. Bit 1 selects either the M6811 E clock or the signal on the C pin to decrement the counter. The signal on the C pin is actually sampled by the E clock as it passes through some buffer flip-flops. To be recognized as a falling edge on the C pin, a signal must be high on one and low on the next falling edge of the E clock. The maximum frequency of the C signal is then half the frequency of the E clock, about 1 megaHerz. This is the Nyquist rate of the sampling circuit. Also, the signal on this pin and on the G pin affects the counter three memory cycles later, due to delays in the buffering flip-flops, but this does not affect most uses of the counter.

Bit 2 has been carefully disregarded up to now. If T, it converts the 16-bit counter into a tandem pair of 8-bit counters. Suppose that the accumulator D has high byte H and low byte L and is stored in the latch of device 1 by the STD $8002 instruction. Then the first 8-bit counter counts modulo L+1. That is, when this counter becomes 0, the low byte L is loaded from the latch. Each time the first counter counts L + 1 falling edges of the clock, the second counter is decremented. If the second counter reaches 0, the high byte H is loaded into it from the latch. Thus, it counts modulo H. The device as a whole completes a count cycle in (L + 1) (H + 1) clock cycles. Note that if the latch has the value $0102 and if bit 2 is false, the counter counts modulo $0103, but if bit 2 were true, it the first counter counts modulo 3 and the second counts modulo 2, so the device as a whole counts modulo 6. In generating square waves (bit 5 low), the OUT signal is low throughout the cycle except for the last L clock cycles. In generating one-shot pulses, the OUT signal is low from the time the device is triggered, for ((L + 1) H) + 1 cycles, then high for L cycles, and then low until triggered again. This feature allows generation of a short pulse after the trigger was applied and a fairly long delay has elapsed. The tandem 8-bit counter mode is useful in generating the spark timing in an engine. However, it does not appear to be that useful, as some of the more recent timer chips from Motorola (timer-ROM, timer-CPU, and so on) have discarded this option.

Table 7-4. Signal Generation Modes

	Value	Meaning
	0 F	All counters count, load from latch when zero
	T	All devices OFF, no counting, latch loads counter
	1 F	Counter clocked on falling edge of C pin signal
	T	Counter clocked on falling edge of 6811 E clock
	2 F	Counters behave as a combined 16-bit counter
	T	Counters behave as two separate 8-bit counters
	3 F	Must be false for this set of modes
	4 F	Loading latch also loads counter, clears interrupt
	T	Loading latch only loads the latch
Control Bits	5 F	Output OUT is square wave, G must be low to count
	T	Output OUT is a pulse, counting independent of G
	6 F	IRQ pin not affected by IRQ1 flip-flop
	T	IRQ1 asserted causes IRQ pin to be low
	7 F	Output O is low
	T	Output O is OUT flip-flop

Control bit 3 identifies the class of operation and is F for the operations discussed here. It is T for the period and pulse measurement modes to be discussed shortly. If bit 4 is false, writing a value into the latch simultaneously writes it into the counter and also clears the interrupt flip-flop. If T, the latch can be changed without causing these other effects. It is usually F in the one-shot mode to let the software trigger the device by executing the STD $8002 instruction. It can be made T if one wishes to change the latch without affecting the current state of the counter. Note that the counter is always loaded from the latch when it is 0 and is clocked, when OFF (bit 0) is T, or when the G pin signal falls; and note that IRQ1 is always cleared when OFF is T, when the G pin signal falls, or when the counter is read after the status register is read.

If bit 5 is F, the device is configured as a square wave generator (or asymmetrical "square wave" generator if bit 2 is T). If bit 5 is T, the device becomes a one-shot. When configured as a one-shot, the counter can be clocked regardless of the level of the G pin signal, so we use this configuration for the real-time clock and for measuring frequency. Note, however, that falling edges of the G signal retrigger the device, so this input should not be allowed to float.

Bits 6 and 7 control the IRQ and O outputs. If bit 6 is T and IRQ1 is T, the IRQ pin signal is low; otherwise it is the wire-OR of other outputs. And if bit 7 is T and the OUT flip-flop has a T, the O pin signal will be high; otherwise it is low.

A few examples will illustrate the flexibility of this chip. We show square wave generation first, then pulse generation, real-time interrupt, and frequency and pulse width measurement.

7-4.2 Generation of Frequencies, Pulses, and Interrupts

The M6840 counter/timer can be used to output square waves. We will consider the configuration of the device, the ritual needed to configure it, and the software to use it as a square-wave generator.

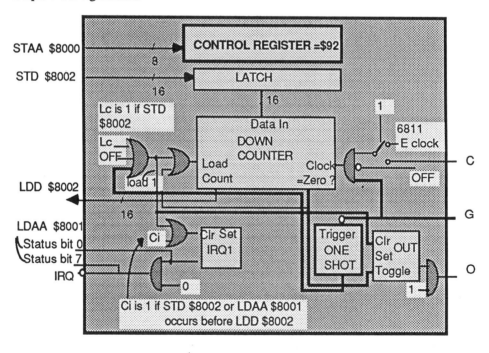

Figure 7-13. A Gated Square Wave Generator

To configure a simple square-wave generator, we put $92 in the control register and a number n in the latch. The gate input G is grounded (this is easy to forget). Then if the M6811 clock is 2 MHz, a square wave with period (n + 1) microseconds will appear on the output pin O. (See figure 7-13.)

To set up this simple generator, the following ritual is executed. Assume that the desired waveform has period p and p-1 is in the D accumulator.

```
STD     $8002
LDAB    #1
STAB    $8001
LDAB    #$92
STAB    $8000
```

The STD instruction puts the number p-1 into the latch. The next two instructions expose the control register for device 1; and the next two set it to $92, which configures device 1 to be a square wave generator.

This generator is gated. The gate input G must be low or the counter will not count - an option you may want for some applications. Note that the counter is loaded from the latch at the moment the G input falls, because the one-shot triggers at that moment, causing the LOAD control to be asserted. This means that, when gating is used, clean square waves will be generated that are low for n+1 memory cycles after the gate signal falls, then alternately high and low for each n+1 cycles after that. However, if you only want a square wave generator, you must remember to ground the G input.

We now show how a counter device in the M6840 can be used as a pulse generator. The configuration for a pulse generator is set up by putting the control code $A2 into the control register and the pulse width in the latch. Then the device appears as diagrammed in figure 7-14.

To set up a one-shot that produces pulses of length n clock cycles, the number n is put into the latch and the control word $A2 is put in the control register. Suppose the number n is in accumulator D. Initialization can be done as follows:

```
STD     $8002
LDAA    #1
STAA    $8001
LDAA    #$A2
STAA    $8000
```

The one-shot can be triggered in hardware by means of a falling signal on the gate input or, in software, by execution of a STD $8002 instruction. When triggered, if n is the number in the latch, the output will go high for n clock cycles. Due to a delay in setting the OUT flip-flop, the output goes high in the cycle after either the STD instruction or the falling edge of the gate input triggers the one-shot, and goes low in the cycle the counter reaches 0. The output is high for n clock periods (not n+1, as in the square-wave generator). After a pulse is generated, the output remains low until the device is triggered again.

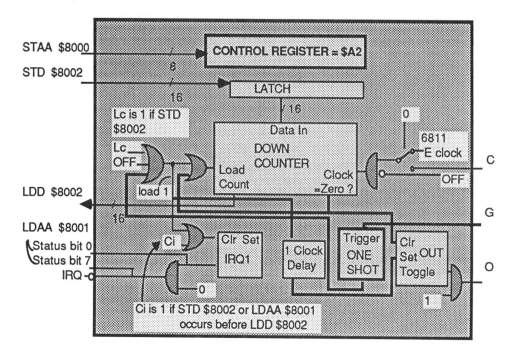

Figure 7-14. A Single-Shot Pulse Generator

Among the peculiarities of the M6840 chip, the best way for using interrupts to time a program is to configure the device as a pulse generator. The other configurations of the device also produce predictable and useful interrupt signals, but in this configuration, the counter is essentially independent of the gate input (as long as it is steady).

To get an interrupt in n memory cycles, the number n-1 is put into the latch and the control code $62 is put into the control register. The interrupt request flip-flop IRQ1 will be set every n+1 memory cycles. If the user promptly honors the interrupt and resets the IRQ1 flip-flop right after it is set, an interrupt will be generated every n+1 memory cycles. (The device appears as diagramed in figure 7-15.)

The device can be triggered by either turning the OFF control F, or by executing the STD $8002 instruction to load the latch. To set up the device to interrupt n+1 memory cycles after OFF goes F, or after STD $8002 is executed, n is put into accumulator D and the following ritual is executed:

```
STD    $8002
LDAA   #1
STAA   $8001
LDAA   #$62
STAA   $8000
```

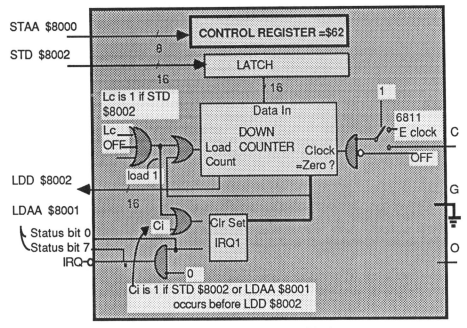

Figure 7-15. A Real-Time Clock

The processor will get an interrupt on the IRQ pin of the M6840 n+1 memory cycles after STAA $8000 causes the OFF bit to become F. The interrupt handler polling routine described in section 5-2.4 can test for the interrupt in device 1, and the interrupt can be cleared in the device handler as described in that section and as is shown again here:

```
        LDAA    $8001
        COMA
        BITA    #$81
        BEQ     L
        . . .
L       LDD     $8002
        . . .
        RTI
```

The interrupt is actually cleared in any of three ways. One way is to make the control variable OFF T. This turns off the device and is useful when the user does not want another interrupt from the device. Another is to read the control register first, then immediately read the counter register before any other register or latch in the chip is read or written. This permits you to examine the counter without inadvertently clearing an interrupt when you examine it. One important feature of this method of clearing the interrupt flip-flop is that it does not reload the counter from the latch. Then the next interrupt will occur exactly n+1 memory cycles after the last interrupt occurred. The last way is to store another number in the latch by means of an STD $8002 instruction. This last technique not only clears the interrupt but loads the latch with a new value n and causes an interrupt to occur in another n+1 memory cycles.

Some useful alternatives to the preceding example are considered in the next subsection. As shown in figure 7-15, the value in the counter can be read at any time by executing the LDD $8002 instruction. This value indicates how long the device will wait until it generates an interrupt. This can be used to decide whether to start a program that should not be interrupted by the real-time clock.

7-4.3. Event Counting, Frequency Measurement, and Variations

As shown in figure 7-15, control bit 1 determines whether the clock used by the counter is the M6811 E clock or the signal on the C pin for this device, and control bit 6 determines whether setting the IRQ1 flip-flop causes a processor interrupt. In the preceding example, both were T. If both are F – if $20 were put in the control register – the signal on the C pin would be used to clock the counter and setting the IRQ1 flip-flop would not cause an interrupt. This configuration will be used to implement the measurement of frequency. In this section, we employ it as a real-time clock using the gadfly technique.

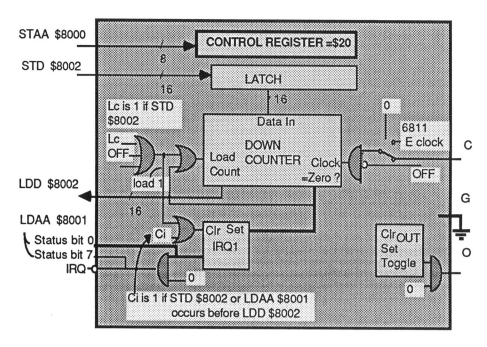

Figure 7-16. An Event Counter or a Frequency Counter

The following is a real-time program to measure the frequency of the C input:

```
        NAM     FREQ40
        LDD     #$FFFF          INITIALIZE LATCH,
        STD     $8002   AND THUS, COUNTER, TO LARGEST NUMBER
        LDX     #50000  SET UP LOOP TO TIME OUT 1 SECOND
        LDAA    #1      TO ACCESS COUNTER 1 CONTROL
        STAA    $8001   REGISTER, MAKE LSB OF $8001 TRUE
        LDAA    #$20    COMMAND WORD TO COUNT INPUT EVENTS
        STAA    $8000   TO COUNTER 1 CONTROL REGISTER
L1      MUL             EXPAND LOOP SO IT EXECUTES
        MUL             IN EXACTLY ONE SECOND
        MUL             MUL IS 10 CYCLES, NOP IS 2 CYCLES, NEED
        NOP             20 µSECONDS = 40 CYCLES IN THIS LOOP
        NOP             DEX AND BNE TAKE 6 CYCLES
        DEX             COUNT DOWN X REGISTER
        BNE     L1      TO WAIT 1 SECOND
        LDD     $8002   GET COUNT
        COMA            GET $FFFF-COUNT
        COMB            BY COMPLEMENTING EACH BIT
```

The usual initialization ritual puts $FFFF into the latch and $20 into the control register. Then the delay loop waits for 1 second. Since the loop is padded with NOP instructions so it will execute in 20 microseconds, the loop counter − index register X − is loaded with 50,000. The device counter register is read. If i events occurred on the C input during the second the program was in the wait loop, the counter would have the value $FFFF - i. Then to derive the value of i, merely subtract from $FFFF the value read from the counter. An easy way to subtract $FFFF - i is to complement all bits in the word i. The frequency in Hertz is left in accumulators A and B as a 16-bit binary number.

It is possible that the counter can overflow in one second, because it is only 16 bits long and can be incremented every microsecond. Let us suppose that, in reading the counter, an erroneous number is returned indicating a low frequency. To alert the user, the IRQ1 flip-flop is set if the counter passes 0. If set, it indicates an overflow and the number in the counter register is invalid. This bit can be read as bit 0 of the status register, by a LDAA $8001 instruction.

It would be a good exercise to review the examples in this section and determine for yourself the setting of the control codes for each configuration. We will look at another example here to show how easily the control code can be established. Suppose one wants a time-of-day clock. In this example, hours are to be counted in military 24-hour time, and days are to be counted in calendar 365 day time from January 1. The clock timing is to be derived from the 60-Hertz power line signal, as in the last chapter. A chain of counters C1 through C5 should operate as follows: C1 should divide the 60-Hertz signal so it delivers a 1-Hertz signal. C2 should count in seconds, C3 should count in minutes, C4 in hours, C5 in days. C1, C2, C3, and C4 all count modulo 60, 60, 60, and 24, respectively. They can be handled by an 8-bit counter. However, C5 must be handled by a 16-bit counter. One M6840 can be configured for this application; the 60-Hertz signal is input to C1 − the clock for device 1 − which is configured as a pair of tandem 8-bit counters to divide by 60 and to count in seconds. Output O1 is connected to clock C2 of device 2. Device 2 is also a pair of tandem 8-bit counters to count in minutes and hours. Output O2 is connected to clock C3. Device 3 is a 16-bit counter to count days since January 1. The gate inputs should all be grounded. The control code for devices 1 and 2 are identical. To derive them, circle the T or F options in table 7-4 (or a copy of it), then tilt the table and read the code word. From top to bottom, we want the devices on (F), we want them externally clocked (F), we want separate 8-bit counters (T), and bit 3 must be (F). It doesn't matter what we assign to bit 4 because we don't expect to rewrite the latches after initialization, so we make it (F). Bit 5 determines the output, which we don't use, so it too is a "don't care." However, the pulse mode is a slightly better choice, since the count input is independent of the G signal. Thus, for bit 5 we select pulse mode (T). We don't want a processor interrupt, and we don't want an output, so bits 6 and 7 are (FF). The control code is therefore FFTFFTFF or $24. The control word for device 3 differs only in bit 2, since we want a 16-bit counter. It is therefore FFTFFFFF or $20. Incidentally, to complete this example, latch 1 is loaded with $3B3B, latch 2 with $3B17, and latch 3 with 364. To read the time, read all three counters twice, looking for carry propagation while you read them, and if both readings agree, subtract each of the first three bytes from $3B, the fourth byte from $17, and the last two bytes from 364, and then convert to decimal if desired. (If the two readings disagree, reread the counters.) But the main point of this discussion is to show how easy it is to get the control code word that you need for any configuration you want.

7-4.4. Pulse and Period Measurement

Table 7-5 shows the settings of the control bits in a device to select various period and pulse measurement options. Control bits 0, 1, and 2 operate as in the signal generation modes. When set, bit 0 forces all counters into the READY state (see figure 7-17). When cleared, the device stays READY until the G pin signal falls (PG is true), which puts the device in the BUSY state to count out the period or pulse width. Bit 1 selects the M6811 clock if T, or the signal on the C pin if F. The internal M6811 clock is especially useful if it is generated by an accurate crystal-controlled oscillator. The C pin signal is useful if a slower rate of counting is desired. Note that one device, acting as a square wave generator, can clock another device, measuring period or pulse width. Note, however, that the signal on the C pin is buffered by flip-flops and cannot be faster than half the M6811 clock frequency. Bit 2 is normally set F, as period and pulse width are usually measured in binary. It is possible, but awkward, to measure them in decimal by putting $99 into the latches if bit 2 is T, but it is easier to measure in binary and convert to decimal in software.

   Bit 3 is T for this set of modes. Bit 4 determines when the state can change from BUSY to DONE1. If F, the change occurs when the G pin signal falls. Note that BUSY was entered when that signal fell the last time. So the device is BUSY for one complete cycle of the sine wave. If bit 4 is T, the change from BUSY to DONE1 occurs when the G signal rises. Since BUSY was entered when that signal last fell, the device is BUSY for the time the G input is low. Thus the counter measures the width of the (negative logic) pulse. Bits 4 and 5 change the sequential machine that sets the IRQ1 flip-flop. (See figure 7-17.)

Table 7-5. Pulse and Period Measurement Modes

Value	Meaning
0 F	All counters count, load from latch when zero
T	All devices OFF, no counting, latch loads counter
1 F	Counter clocked on falling edge of C pin signal
T	Counter clocked on falling edge of 6811 E clock
2 F	Counters behave as two separate 8-bit counters
T	Counters behave as a single 16-bit counter
3 F	Must be true for this set of modes
4 F	Enter DONE1 on falling edge of G (period)
T	Enter DONE1 when G is high (pulse width)
5 F	IRQ1 is true if in DONE1 state (measure overflow)
T	IRQ1 is true if in DONE2 state (alarm)
6 F	IRQ pin not affected by IRQ1 flip-flop
T	IRQ1 asserted causes IRQ pin to be low
7 F	Output O is low
T	Output O is garbage

Column at left labeled: Control Bits

The first two modes can be used to measure period or pulse width, as recently described. For frequency measurement (bits 5,4 = FF) IRQ1 is true if the device is in the DONE1 state. This indicates the counter has a valid measure of the frequency. A minor peculiarity of this mode is that if the counter passes 0 exactly when the G pin signal drops (PG is asserted), the device stays in the BUSY state. For pulse width measurement (bits 5,4 = FT) the state changes to DONE1 when G is high (which is the time when G rises). In both these cases, IRQ1 is T if the device is in the DONE1 state. The last two modes can be used to monitor a signal for too long a period or too long a pulse width. Both these modes merge the DONE1 state into the BUSY state, and IRQ1 is T if the device is in the DONE2 state. The frequency alarm (bits 5,4 = TF) reloads the counter each time the G pin signal drops, and stays in the BUSY state. If the counter passes 0, the DONE2 state is entered and IRQ1 is set. This can be used to monitor a frequency; if an interrupt is to occur if the period is ever longer than n+1 clock cycles, the number n is put in the latch in this mode. The period alarm (bits 5,4 = TT) returns to the READY state whenever G is T. When G falls again, the counter is loaded from the latch and begins to be decremented. If it passes 0, the state changes to DONE2 and IRQ is set. This can be used to monitor pulse widths; if an interrupt is to occur if ever the G signal is low for longer than n clock cycles, n+1 is put in the latch of a device in this mode.

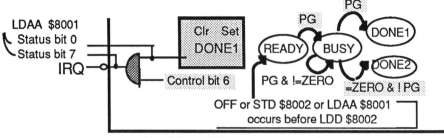

a. bits 5,4 = FF (frequency measure)

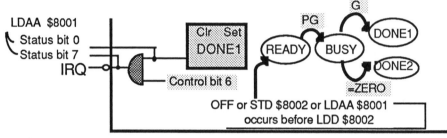

b. bits 5,4 = FT (pulse width measurement)

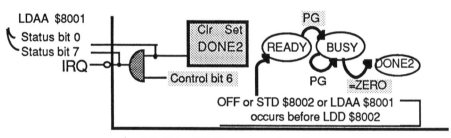

c. bits 5,4 = TF (frequency alarm)

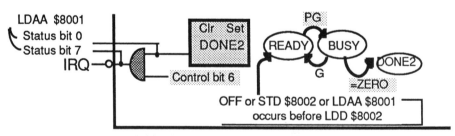

d. bits 5,4 = TT (pulse width alarm)

Figure 7-17. State Diagrams for Period and Pulse Width Measurements

If control bit 6 is T, and IRQ1 is T, the IRQ bus line is made low, otherwise this device has no effect. Bit 6 can be T for the alarm configurations so that a processor interrupt occurs whenever the period or pulse width of the signal being monitored is too long. Bit 6 should be F when the gadfly technique is used while waiting for a device interrupt due to too long a pulse or period, or when the IRQ1 value indicates an error in measuring period or pulse width, as it is usually explicitly tested in these cases. Finally, control bit 7 is normally F in these modes, as the output signal OUT is not defined.

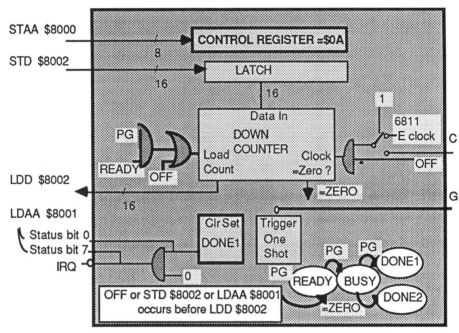

Figure 7-18. A Period or Pulse Width Timer

Finally, we discuss differences among the three devices, and the connection of pins on this chip. Each device has its own clock, gate, and output pins, and its own device interrupt flip-flop. For instance, these pins and the flip-flop in device 1 are C1,G1,O1, and IRQ1, but those of device 2 are C2,G2,O2, and IRQ2. Also each device has its own counter and latch, but they share some hidden temporary registers. They should be read and written as a complete 16-bit number, rather than reading 8 bits of one device, then 8 bits of another, because some shortcuts were taken in the chip's design so that such mixed reading produces the wrong results. We note that the three devices in the M6840 are not exactly alike. The use of control bit 0 differs. In device 1, control bit 0 is the OFF control for all the devices. In device 2, control bit 0 is an extra address bit that is used to select control register 1 or control register 3 at location $8000. The last device has an extra 3-bit counter. If control bit 0 is T, the signal input on the C pin or the M6811 clock (as selected by bit 1) clocks this extra counter, and the output of the counter is used within the device to clock the counter. In the previous discussion, we always set bit 0 to F. This disconnects the extra 3-bit counter in device 3 so it is identical to the other stages.

The M6840 can be used to measure period, as we might expect. To measure period, the control word $0A is put in the control register. Then the device is configured as shown in figure 7-18.

The following program can be used to measure the period of a waveform. The first six lines initialize the control register and latch, as in the previous program. The gadfly loop checks for entry into the DONE1 state while timing its waiting period. Under worst case conditions, the device may be put in the READY state just after the falling edge of the G signal, which can have a period of 32,000 microseconds, so it can be in the READY and the BUSY state that long. If the loop takes 7.5 microseconds and the counter is decremented twice each microsecond, then the device should enter the DONE1 state before 4266 executions of the loop; otherwise an error should be reported.

```
            NAM     PERIOD
            LDD     #$FFFF       INITIALIZE COUNTER 1
            STD     $8002   TO A LARGE (UNSIGNED) NUMBER
            LDAA    #1      PUT A T IN BIT 0 OF CONTROL REGISTER 2
            STAA    $8001   TO ACCESS CONTROL REGISTER 1
            LDAA    #$0A    CONTROL WORD FOR PERIOD MEASUREMENT
            STAA    $8000   PUT IN CONTROL REGISTER 1
            LDX     #4266   DO GADFLY LOOP FOR 32 MILLISECONDS
L1          LDAA    $8001   CHECK STATUS REGISTER
            BITA    #1      TO  SEE IF COUNTER 1 IS DONE
            BNE     L2      IF SO, THEN LEAVE LOOP
            DEX             ELSE LOOP (UP TO 14,000 TIMES)
            BNE     L1      IF NOT DONE BY THEN, IT IS IN DONE2 STATE
     ( GO TO ERROR ROUTINE - PERIOD IS TOO LONG )
      ...
L2          LDD     $8002   GET COUNT
            COMB            SUBTRACT FROM $FFFF BY COMPLEMENTING
            COMA            EACH BIT. THE RESULT IS IN ACC. D
```

7-5 Conclusions

Frequency or phase analog signals are often generated naturally, by an AC tachometer, for instance, and may be used directly, in firing a triac, for instance. Even when the signal is first an amplitude analog signal, conversion to frequency analog or phase analog signal simplifies the noise isolation and voltage level isolation between transducer and microcomputer. Moreover, several hardware and software techniques, including those that use a counter/timer like the MC68HC11 counter/timer system or M6840 chip, can be used to measure or generate frequency analog signals.

The counter/timer is a very useful and attractive I/O device for measuring or generating frequency or phase analog signals. It is useful in generating square waves, pulses, and timing interrupts; it can measure events, frequency, period, and pulse width; and it can monitor period or pulse width to interrupt the computer if too long a value is noticed. It is very attractive because a single wire sends the signal to or from the counter/timer. To the chip designer, it means that an I/O device can be put on a chip or inside a microcomputer chip without using a lot of pins. While counters take up a nontrivial amount of area on the chip, that area is comparatively cheap, while pins are in much shorter supply. Moreover, to the system designer, a single wire is easy to isolate with an optical isolator, to prevent the voltages of the system under test from getting to the microcomputer and the user, as well as to isolate noise generated in that system, to prevent it from getting into the microcomputer.

The MC68HC11 counter/timer system and M6840 were introduced to illustrate the discussion of the counter/timer module. The M6840 also illustrated how a single chip can be made more flexible when the devices in it are configured by setting the control word. This chapter prepares us for similar techniques in communication modules covered in chapter 8 and display and secondary storage chips, covered in chapter 9.

For further reading on phase-locked loops, we recommend *Digital PLL Frequency Synthesis Theory and Design*, by U. L. Rohde, Prentice-Hall 1983, and Motorola data sheets such as the *CMOS/NMOS Special Functions Data* (DL130) and applications notes such as the *Electronic Tuning Address System* (SG-72). For more concrete information on the 68HC11, please consult the *MC68HC11A8 HCMOS Single-Chip Microcomputer (ADI 1207)*. In particular, section 8 describes the programmable timer, real-time interrupt, and pulse accumulator. As noted earlier, we have not attempted to duplicate the diagrams and discussions in that book because we assume you will refer to it while reading this book; and, since we present an alternative view of the subject, you can use either or both views.

You should now be familiar with the counter/timer in general and with the MC68HC11 counter/timer system and M6840 in particular. Connecting the pins of the MC68HC11 counter/timer system, connecting the M6840 to an M6811, and writing software to initialize and use them should be well within your grasp. Moreover, you now have enough information to consider alternatives to this system and chip and to recognize whenever they are superior to the counter/timer.

Problems

Problem 1 is a paragraph correction problem; for guidelines, see the problems at the end of chapter 1. The guidelines for programming problems are at the end of chapter 2, and the guidelines for hardware design problems are at the end of chapter 3.

Problems involving the MC68HC11A8 counter/timer will all assume that I/O registers are at $1000 to $103F, and problems involving the 6840 will assume it is addressed as in figure 7-11, using a 2 MHz E clock unless otherwise indicated. All subroutines should assume the I/O control registers are unknown (as if the subroutine is called inside an arbitrary program) and must intialize them before using them. Results should be returned as unsigned binary numbers in accumulator D unless otherwise indicated. All handlers should be accompanied with a separate initialization routine that initializes the MC68HC11A8 counter/timer registers or registers in the MC68B40 and all global variables needed for the proper execution of the handler; and if the counter/timer (output or interrupts) should be turned off during or after the routine, the ritual to turn off the MC68HC11A8 counter/timer registers or MC68B40 should be included at the appropriate place in the handler.

1.* Communication using the frequency or phase is attractive because it can be accomplished using lower bandwidth channels than amplitude analog communication, and such signals can be generated or measured by microcomputers with counter/timer modules in them or counter/timer integrated circuits. These combination chips appear because the counter/timer does not require much surface area on a chip and the transistors needed to build counter/timers need not be as good as those needed for A-to-D converters, so the inclusion of such a function on another chip does not raise the cost. Moreover, many functions require counting and timing. Pulses from a pulse generator can generate tones, and Johnson counters can generate a stair-case approximation of a sine wave that is useful for touch-tone dialing. Pulses can be used to control automobiles, and interrupts from the timer can be used to implement real-time clocks. Frequency measurements can be used with a voltage-to-frequency converter to measure amplitude analog signals, and they can be used to measure intervals of time between two events. Period measurements are an alternative to frequency measurements, and one can always be obtained from the other by division; frequency measurement is preferable if the frequency is low because this will give more accuracy than period measurement. The 6811 counter/timer should be used for these different generation and measurement functions if the software approach is susceptible to errors due to interrupt handling, DMA, or dynamic memory refresh; and the MC68B40 can be used for slightly higher frequencies or when more timer functions are needed than are available on the 6811. But digital hardware or analog hardware approaches, such as the phase-locked loop, may be needed if the microcomputer software or 6811/6840 counter/timer approach is too slow.

2. Write 6811 program for a gadfly square wave generator
   a. that uses the output compare 3 module to generate the square wave on pin 3. The desired frequency F is given in accumulator D. Converted to a period, it is less than 2^{16} (16 Hz $\leq$ F $\leq$ 50KHz), accurate $\pm$19 μsec.

b. that uses a compare 3 module interrupt to generate the square wave on pin 3. The 24-bit period is in accumulator A (high byte) and register X. (The high byte is counted in software.)

3. A 555 timer and a binary counter are to be used to generate a square wave as determined by 6811 port B. The low-order three bits L of FRQ generate a square wave from the 555 with period $P = 2^{**}$ ($L / 8$) by selecting different capacitors, and the next more significant 3 bits N select a tap from the binary counter so the output period is 2^N x P. Show a logic diagram using some 74HC161, 4051, and 555 chips, showing pin numbers and values of resistors and capacitors.

4. Write a routine to generate a touch-tone dial sequence, calling up the subroutine TTONE in section 7-2.1. The number to be called is in a vector, such as

NUM FCB 5,5,5,1,2,1,2

Each tone is on for 50 milliseconds, and there is a mute period of 45 milliseconds between tones. Use output compare module 4 to time the delays. (These are the minimum times specified by the telephone industry.)

5. A music synthesizer has 16 voices and is to be built with 6811 output compare module 2 and port B, a (256,4) PROM, a 74LS161, and a 4-bit D-to-A converter. The output compare 2 (pin 2) clocks the 74LS161, which provides the low-order 4 bits of the PROM's address so that each voice is generated by 16 samples of the repetitive waveform. The low-order 4 bits of port B provide the PROM's high-order address to select the voice. The output from the PROM is a 4-bit 2's complement number, which is converted to a voltage between -8 and +7 volts by the D-to-A converter.
   a. Show a block diagram of the system.
   b. Write a routine to generate a tone that is specified by the value in accumulators A and B. The 4 most significant bits of A are the octave and the 4 least significant bits are the note in the octave, such that A is represented by zero, B♭ is 1, B is 2, ..., A♭ is $B and the lowest octave is represented by zero. Low A is 27.5 Hertz and is represented by 0,0. The frequency of each note is $^{12}\sqrt{2}$ times the frequency of the next lower note. The least significant 4 bits of accumulator B are the voice, which will be used by the PROM, and the most significant bits are the length of the note, in 1/16*ths*, where 1/16*th* note is played for 1/4 second. (Do not show the program that selects the next note. Hint: use table lookup to generate the basic frequency in the lowest octave, then shift it right to derive the required counter values.)
   c. Show the table, using FDB assembler directives and values in decimal, for the program in part b.

6. A widely available home remote control uses a high-frequency signal that is superimposed on the 60-Hertz power line to transmit commands from a single command module to up to 16 remote stations, which can turn appliances on or off or turn lamp dimmers up or down. The command module has a provision for a remote keyboard that

communicates to it using ultrasonic signals. To avoid connecting to the power line, we would like to control the remote stations by sending to the command module the ultrasonic signals that would have been sent by the remote keyboard. Write a subroutine that generates ultrasonic signals used for sending commands via the output of 6811 output compare module 4 to an ultrasonic transmitter which then transmits to the receiver in the control module. A true bit is sent for 8 milliseconds: 4 milliseconds of 40-kiloHertz square wave followed by 4 milliseconds mute output, and a false is 1.2 millisecond of a 40-kiloHertz square wave followed by 2.8 milliseconds mute output. A command to send data bit D to remote station N is sent as follows: A true bit is sent; then a 4-bit remote station number N is sent, most significant bit first; data bit D is sent; then the complement of the module number and data bits N and D are sent in the same order; and then 16 milliseconds of a 40-kiloHertz square wave are sent. The data bit D is in least significant bit of accumulator A, and the remote station number is in accumulator B. Use real-time synchronization to time out the sending of bits of the command.

7. Write a 6811 gadfly synchronized program to sequence pulses using the output compare modules. Outputs on port A bits 7, 6, and 5 are initially 0, 1, 0, respectively. When port A bit 0 falls, bits 5 rises, and 20 μsec later, bit 7 rises. After another 30 μsec, bits 5 and 7 fall together, and after yet another 40 μsec, bit 6 falls.

8. The program DIAL in section 7-2.2 will dial a number on a conventional "step-and-repeat" telephone, but will tie up the computer while it is dialing the number. Write an interrupt handler for the 6811 output compare 2 module that will cause an interrupt every 20 milliseconds. On each interrupt, the most significant bit of port B should be given a value to control the relay in series with the dial contacts for the next 20 milliseconds. Use global variables to keep track of what part of the sequence of numbers, what part of the number, and what part of the pulse has been output.
    a. Write the handler to output just one number, which is in global variable N.
    b. Write the handler to output the seven numbers in the vector NUM, as in problem 4.

9. Port A bit 0 is connected to a signal that pulses low at the moment that the 60-Hertz power line signal passes through 0. The three port A outputs for output compare modules 2, 3, and 4 are connected to pulse transformers that fire three triacs to implement proportional phase control of three lamps. Show a subroutine and interrupt handlers that set up and maintain output compare modules 2, 3, and 4 so that they output a waveform whose falling edge fires triac $N = 2$, 3, or 4 at time D degrees $0 \leq D < 180$ in each half-cycle. When this subroutine is called, N is in accumulator A, and D is an unsigned binary number in accumulator B.

10. An "alarm clock" can interrupt the computer at a given time in seconds, within an hour, if an output compare (such as 2) and software are used, the compare module counting the low-order bytes and interrupting the software which counts the high-order bytes. Write a routine ALARM that interprets a table of times that the "alarm" is supposed to "go off," so that when this happens a program corresponding to the "alarm"

will be executed. Suppose that a table of "alarms" is such that a row is stored thus:

FDB TH,TL,GO

where TH is the 2 high-order bytes, TL is the 2 low-order bytes of a time interval T, and GO is the address of a routine to be started when that interval is over. The time T in row $i+1$ is the interval in microseconds between the time the "alarm" went off for row i and the time it will go off for row $i+1$. Each routine such as that beginning at location GO ends with an instruction BRA ALARM or JMP ALARM, and your routine, beginning at address ALARM, starts with a WAI instruction to wait for the interrupt request from output compare 2. Note that a trivial interrupt handler must be included.

11. Frequency can be determined by the pulse accumulator, or by measuring pulse width using an input capture module and getting the inverse using the 6811 divide instruction. The former gives better accuracy for high frequencies, and the latter for low frequencies. Suppose a square wave is simultaneously input to the pulse accumulator (on port A bit 7) and to input capture register 1 (port A bit 2). Write interrupt handlers for the pulse accumulator overflow and input capture 1 and an initialization subroutine to wait for the measurement from both the period and frequency handlers, waiting exactly 0.1 seconds using a gadfly loop on output compare 2; then decide which gives the most accurate frequency reading and return that reading in accumulator D from the subroutine.

12. Period can be determined using an input capture module, or by measuring frequency using the pulse accumulator and getting the inverse using the 6811 divide instruction. The former gives better accuracy for low frequencies, and the latter for high frequencies. Suppose a square wave is simultaneously input to the pulse accumulator (on port A bit 7) and to input capture register 1 (port A bit 2). Write interrupt handlers for the pulse accumulator overflow and input capture 1 and an initialization subroutine to wait for the measurement from both the period and frequency handlers, waiting exactly 0.1 seconds using a gadfly loop on output compare 2; then decide which gives the most accurate period reading and return that reading in accumulator D from the subroutine.

13. Write a 6811 gadfly program to measure pulse width using the pulse accumulator module. Set up the mode to inhibit counting on '0' input and to watch it count. If the pulse accumulator is counting initially, restart the pulse accumulator when the counting stops, and count clock cycles until the pulse accumulator stops counting. Return the 16-bit count in ACCD.

14. Design a voltmeter using an isolated voltage-to-frequency converter.
   a. Show a diagram of the complete system, giving enough detail that they system could be built from it. Use the Teledyne 9400 (figure 6-22b), a 4N33 opto-isolator to isolate the voltage sensor from the microcomputer, and the 6811 pulse accumulator to measure the frequency.
   b. Write the subroutine VOLT to measure the frequency so that the voltage at the input of the hardware in part a, in millivolts, is returned in accumulator D when the subroutine is executed.

15. Rewrite the program ALARM (section 7-2.3) using the pulse accumulator module to get a suitable time delay to update the time of day and test for an alarm value match. Use interrupt synchronization and be accurate to 1 memory cycle.

16. An AM tuner has a local oscillator which is tuned to a frequency that is 455 kiloHertz higher than the frequency of a station that is tuned in, so that the "beat frequency" is the intermediate frequency amplified by the radio. Write a program to measure the frequency so that if the pulse accumulator input has the local oscillator frequency, divided by four, the program will output the frequency of the station being received, divided by four, in accumulator D.

17. Design a capacitance meter. A capacitor of unknown value C is put in the timing circuit of a 555 timer, C being lower than .01 microfarads.
    a. Show the hardware, pin numbers, and component values to build such a meter, using the pulse accumulator module.
    b. Write a subroutine CAPAC that evaluates the capacitance – using interrupt synchronization to detect pulse accumulator overflow – and returns the capacitance in picofarads in accumulator D.

18. Design a frequency and phase meter for audio frequencies, using an M6840.
    a. Show a diagram for the system so that device 1 will measure the period of input V1 and device 2 will measure the time from rising edge of V1 to the next rising edge of a second input V2.
    b. Write a subroutine to initialize an M6840 so that the hardware in a. can be used to output the frequency in index register X and the phase in accumulator D. Use IDIV.

19. Design a 32-bit square wave generator. Show the connections between the MC68HC11A8 and M6840 – especially to the O, G, and C pins for devices 1 and 2. Write a subroutine that generates a square wave from output O1, with period specified by the 32-bit number in accumulator D (high-order 16 bits) and index register X (low-order 16 bits).

20. The G1, G2, and G3 inputs of an M6840 are connected to a signal that pulses low at the moment that the 60-Hertz power line signal passes through 0. The three outputs O1, O2, and O3, are connected to pulse transformers that fire three triacs to implement proportional phase control of three lamps. Show a subroutine that sets up device N of the M6840 so that it outputs a waveform whose falling edge fires triac N at time D degrees in each half-cycle. When this subroutine is called, N is in accumulator A, N = 1, 2, or 3, and D is an unsigned binary number in accumulator B.

21. Design a TV sync signal generator using devices 1 and 2 of an M6840. O1 of device 1 is to output the horizontal sync pulse, which is 4 microseconds high, 60 microseconds low, repetitively. O2 of device 2 is to output the vertical sync pulse, which is clocked by the vertical sync pulse. The horizontal sync is high for 26 vertical pulses and low for 244 vertical pulses. Show a routine to configure the M6840 to generate these signals.

22. Parts of a logic analyzer have been designed in problems 4-23 and 5-15. A logic analyzer also has counters to permit the data it stores and displays to be the data on the bus before or after the comparator recognizes the pattern. The counters can allow N occurrences of the pattern C recognized by the comparator to occur and then can allow M clock cycles before the time Tf occurs. The (256) patterns, which appeared on the busses before time Tf, are displayed. The user can select N to be 0 and M to be 0, if Tf is to be the time the pattern occurred first; but the user can use another number N if the first N occurrences are to be ignored, as when the pattern appears inside a DO-LOOP, or another number M if the M words after the comparator detects a match and (256 - M) words before M are to be stored in memory and displayed by the logic analyzer. The 6840 can be used to count occurrences and delays. Show a block diagram of such a logic analyzer. It should be complete with M6821 output registers holding the comparator pattern C, a 16-bit address and 1-bit R/W comparator, an MC68B40 counter/timer, a (32,256) memory for the patterns stored, and a 74HC4040 counter needed to address the memory. The M6821 is addressed at locations $8008 to $800B in the normal way. Show clearly all the connections to C1, C2, O1, O2, G1, G2, and the logic needed to write the patterns into the memory. Finally, write a subroutine that sets up the logic analyzer by having the comparator address C in accumulator D, the number N in index register X, and the number M in index register Y. (Some other mechanism reads out the data later).

8

Communication Systems

The microcomputer has many uses in communication systems, and a communication system is often a significant part of a microcomputer. This chapter examines techniques for digital communications of computer data.

Attention is focused on a microcomputer's communication subsystem – the part that interfaces slower I/O devices like typewriters and printers to the microcomputer. This is often a universal asynchronous receiver transmitter (UART). Because of their popularity in this application, UARTs have been used for a variety of communications functions, including remote control and multiple computer intercommunications. However, their use is limited to communicating short (1-byte) messages at slow rates (less than 1000 bytes per second). The synchronous data link control (SDLC) is suitable for sending longer messages (about 1000 bytes) at faster rates (about 1,000,000 bits per second) – for sending data between computers or between computers and fast I/O devices. The IEEE-488 bus, for microcomputer control of instruments like digital voltmeters and frequency generators, and the SCSI bus, for communication to and from intelligent peripherals, send a byte at a time rather than a bit at a time.

The overall principles of communication systems, including the ideas of levels and protocols, are introduced in the first section. The signal transmission medium is discussed next, covering some typical problems and techniques communications engineers encountered in moving data.The UART and related devices that use the same communications mechanisms are fundamental to I/O interface design. So, we spend quite a bit of time on these devices, imparting basic information about their hardware and software. They will probably find use in most of your designs for communicating with teletypes or teletype-like terminals, keyboards, and CRTs, as well as for simple remote control. Finally, we look at the more complex communications interfaces used between large mainframe computers to control test and measurement equipment in the laboratory and to connect intelligent I/O.

Communications terminology is rather involved with roots in the (comparatively) ancient) telephone industry and in the computer industry, and some stemming uniquely from digital communications. Communications design is almost a completely different discipline from microcomputer design. Moreover, one kind of system, such as one using UARTs, uses quite different terminology than that used to describe another, similar system, such as one using SDLC links. While it is important to be able to talk to communication system designers and learn their terminology, we are limited in what we can do in one short chapter. We will as much as possible use terminology associated with the so-called X.25 protocol, even for discussing UARTs, because we want to economize on the number of terms that we must introduce, and the X.25 protocol appears to be the most promising protocol likely to be used with minicomputers and microprocessors. However, you should be prepared to do some translating when you converse with a communications engineer.

On completing this chapter, you should have a working knowledge of UART communications links. You should be able to use the 6811 SCI module, connect a UART or an M6850 to a microcomputer, and connect a UART or an M14469 to a remote control station so it can be controlled through the 6811 SCI module, M6850, or UART. You should understand the basic general strategies of communication systems, and the UART, SDLC, IEEE-488, and SCSI bus protocols in particular, knowing when and where they should be used.

8-1 Communications Principles

In looking at the overall picture, we will first consider the ideas of peer-to-peer interfaces, progressing from the lowest level to the higher level interfaces, examining the kinds of problems faced at each level.

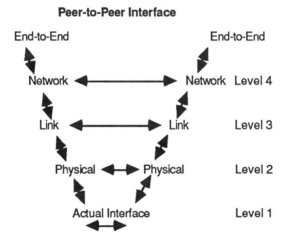

Figure 8-1. Peer-to-Peer Communication in Different Levels

Data movement is *coordinated* in different senses at different *levels* of abstraction, and by different kinds of mechanisms. At each level, the communication appears to take place between *peers* which are identifiable entities at that level; even though the communication is defined between these peers as if they did indeed communicate to each other, they actually communicate indirectly through peers at the next lower level. (See figure 8-1.)

Consider this analogy. The president of company X wants to talk to the president of company Y. This is called *end-to-end* communication. The job is delegated to the president's secretary, who calls up the secretary of the other president. This is referred to as *network control*. The secretary doesn't try to holler to the other secretary but dials the other secretary on the telephone. The telephone is analogous to the *link control* level. But even the telephone "delegates" the communication process to the electronics and the electrical circuits that make the connection at the telephone exchange. This is the *physical control* level. End-to-end communication is done between user (high-level) programs. User programs send information to each other like the presidents in the analogy. Network control is done at the operating system level. Like the secretary, this software must know where the communications object is and how to reach this object. Link control is done by I/O interface software and is responsible for setting up and disconnecting the link so the message can be sent. Physical control actually moves the data. In the design of I/O systems, we are primarily concerned with link control and secondarily with physical control.

The peer-to-peer interfaces are defined without specifying the interface to the next lower level. This is done for the same reasons that computer architecture is separated from computer organization and realization, as we explained in chapter 1. It permits the next lower level to be replaced by another version at that level without affecting the higher level. This is like one of the presidents getting a new secretary: the presidents can still talk to each other in the same way, even though communication at the next lower level may be substantially changed.

We now discuss some of the issues at each of the levels. At the lowest level, the main issue is the medium, and a secondary issue is the multiplexing of several channels on one link. The technique used to synchronize the transmission of bits may be partly in the physical interface level and partly in the link control level.

The *medium* that carries a bit of information is of great concern to the communications engineer. Most systems would probably use voltage level to distinguish between true and false signals. In other systems, mechanical motion carries information, or radio or light beams in free space or in optical fibers carry information. Even when the carrier is electric, the signal can be carried by current rather than voltage, or by presence or absence of a particular frequency component. The signal can be conveyed on two frequencies: a true is sent as one frequency while a false is sent as another frequency (*frequency shift keying*). More than one signal can be sent over the same medium. In *frequency multiplexing*, n messages are sent, each by the presence or absence of one of n different frequency components (or keying between n different pairs of frequencies). In *time multiplexing*, n messages can be sent, each one in a time slot every nth time slot. A frequency band or a time slot that carries a complete signal, enabling communication between two entities at the link control level, is called a *channel*. Each channel, considered by itself, may be *simplex* if data can move in one direction only, *half-duplex* if data can move in either direction but only one direction at a time, or *full duplex* if data can move in both directions simultaneously.

Usually, a bit of information is sent on a channel over a time period, the *bit time period*, and this is the same time for each bit. The *baud rate* is the inverse of this bit time period (or the shortest period if different periods are used). The *bit rate*, in contrast, is the rate of transfer of information, as defined in information theory. For simplicity in this discussion, the bit rate is the number of user information bits sent per time unit, while the baud rate is the total number of bits – including user information, synchronization, and error-checking bits – per time unit.

In general, a clock is a regular occurrence of a pulse, or even of a code word, used to control the movement of bits. If such a (regular) clock appears in the channel in some direct way, the system is *synchronous*, otherwise it is *asynchronous*. In a synchronous system, the clock can be sent on a separate line, as the clock is sent inside a computer to synchronize the transmission of data. The clock can also be sent on the same wire as the data – every other bit being a clock pulse and the other bits being data – in the so-called *Manchester code*. Circuitry such as a phase-locked loop detects the clock and further circuitry uses this reconstructed clock to extract the data. Finally, in an asynchronous link, the clock can be generated by the receiver, in hopes that it matches the clock used by the sender.

Link control is concerned with how data is moved as bits, as groups of bits, and as complete messages that are sent by the next higher level peer-to-peer interface.

At the *bit level*, individual bits are transmitted; at the *frame level*, a group of bits called a frame or packet is transmitted; and at the *message level*, sequences of frames, called messages, are exchanged. Generally, at the frame level, means are provided for detection and correction of errors in the data being sent, since the communication channel is often noisy. Also, because the frame is sent as a single entity, it can have means for synchronization. A frame, then, is some data packaged or framed and sent as a unit under control of a communications hardware/software system. The end-to-end user often wishes to send more data – a sequence of frames – as a single unit of data. The user's unit of data is known as the message.

At each level, a coordination mechanism is used, which is called a *protocol*. A protocol is a set of conventions that coordinate the transmission and receipt of bits, frames, and messages. Its primary functions in the link control level are the synchronization of messages and the detection or correction of errors. This term protocol suggests a strict code of etiquette and precedence countries agree to follow in diplomatic exchange, so the term aptly describes a communication mechanism whereby sender and receiver operate under some mutually acceptable assumptions but do not need to be managed by some greater authority like a central program. Extra bits are needed to maintain the protocol. Since these bits must be sent for a given data rate in bits per second, the baud rate must increase as more extra bits are sent. The protocol should keep efficiency high by using as few as possible of these extra bits. Note that a clock is a particularly simple protocol: a regularly occurring pulse or code word. An important special case, the *handshake protocol*, is an agreement whereby when information is sent to the receiver, it sends back an acknowledgment that the data is received either in good condition or has some error. Note, however, that a clock or a protocol applies to a level, so a given system can have a bit clock and two different protocols – a frame protocol and a message protocol.

The third level of peer-to-peer interface is the network level. It is concerned about relationships between a large community of computers and the requirements necessary so that they can communicate to each other without getting into trouble.

The *structure* of a communication system includes the physical interconnections among stations, as well as the flow of information. Usually modeled as a graph whose nodes are stations and whose links are communications paths, the structure may be a loop, tree graph, or a rectangular grid (or sophisticated graph like a banyan network or its homomorphic reduction).

A path taken by some data through several nodes is called *store and forward* if each node stores the data for a brief time, then transmits it to the next node as new data may be coming into that node; otherwise if data pass through intermediate nodes instantaneously (being delayed only by gate and line propagation), the path is called a *circuit* from telephone terminology. If such a path is half duplex, it is sometimes called a bus because it looks like a bus in a computer system.

Finally, the communication system is *governed* by different techniques. This aspect relates to the operating system of the system of computers, which indirectly controls the generation and transmission of data much as a government establishes policies that regulate trade between countries. A simple aspect of governance is whether the decision to transmit data is centralized or distributed. A system is *centralized* if a special station makes all decisions about which stations may transmit data; it is decentralized or *distributed* if each station determines whether to send data, based on information in its locale. A centralized system is often called a *master slave* system, with the special station the master and the other stations its "slaves." Other aspects of governance concern the degree to which one station knows what another station is doing, or whether and how one station can share the computational load of another. These aspects of a system are very important, but are still the subject of considerable research and debate.

8-2 Signal Transmission

The signal is transmitted through wires or light pipes at the physical level. This section discusses the characteristics of three of the most important linkages. Voltage or current amplitude logical signals, discussed first, are used to interconnect terminals and computers that are close to each other. The digital signal can be sent by transmitting it at different frequencies for a true and for a false signal (frequency shift keying). This is discussed in the next subsection. Finally, the optical link provides an unprecedented capability to send data at very high rates. It will likely radically change our approach to communication systems, although, at the time of writing, it is still new and expensive. Some observations are offered on the optical link in the last subsection.

8-2.1 Voltage and Current Linkages

In this section, we discuss the line driver and line receiver pair, the 20-milliampere current loop, and the RS232 standard.

Standard high current TTL or LSTTL drivers can be used over relatively short distances, as the IEEE-488 standard uses them for a bus to instruments located in a laboratory. However, slight changes in the ground voltage reference or a volt or so of noise on the link can cause a lot of noise in such links. A *differential line* is a pair of

Single- and Multiple-Chip Microcomputer Interfacing   Chapter 8

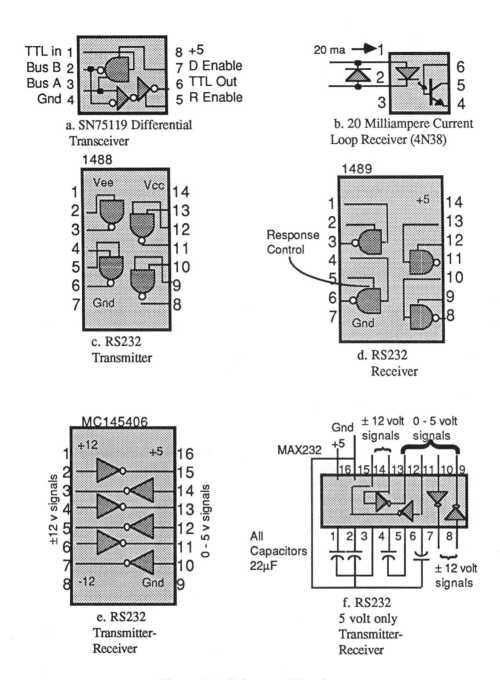

a. SN75119 Differential
Transceiver

b. 20 Milliampere Current
Loop Receiver (4N38)

c. RS232
Transmitter

d. RS232
Receiver

e. RS232
Transmitter-
Receiver

f. RS232
5 volt only
Transmitter-
Receiver

Figure 8-2. Drivers and Receivers

wires, in which the variable in positive logic is on one wire and in negative logic on the
other wire. If one is high, the other is low. The receiver uses an analog comparator to
determine which of the two wires has the higher voltage, and outputs a standard TTL

signal appropriately. If a noise voltage is induced, both wires should pick up the same noise so the differential is not affected and the receiver gets the correct signal. Similarly, imperfect grounding and signal ringing affect the signal on both wires and their effect is cancelled by the voltage comparator. A number of driver and receiver integrated circuits are designed for differential lines, but some require voltages other than +5, which may not be used elsewhere in the system. An integrated circuit suitable for driving and receiving signals on a half duplex line, using a single 5-volt supply, is the SN75119, shown in figure 8-2a. If driver enable DE (pin 7) is high, then the signal on IN (pin 1) is put on line LA (pin 3) and its complement is put on line LB (pin 2); otherwise the pins LA and LB appear to be (essentially) open circuits. If receiver enable RE (pin 5) is high, then the output OUT (pin 6) is low if the voltage on LA is less than that on LB, or high if the voltage on LA is greater than that on LB; if RE is low, OUT is (essentially) an open circuit. The *RS442 standard* (RS means recommended standard) uses basically this differential line, but a driver such as the Am26LS30 has means to control the slew rate of the output signal.

The 20-milliampere current loop is often used to interface to teletypes or teletype-like terminals. A pair of wires connect driver and receiver so as to implement an electrical loop through both. A true corresponds to about 20 milliamperes flowing through the loop, and a false corresponds to no current or to negative 20 milliamperes in the loop (for "neutral working" or "polar working" loops, respectively). A current, rather than a voltage, is used because it can be interrupted by a switch in a keyboard and can be sensed anywhere in the loop. A current is also used in older equipment because the 20-milliampere current loop was used to drive a solenoid, and a solenoid is better controlled by a current than a voltage to get faster rise times. The current is set at 20 milliamperes because the arc caused by this current will keep the switch contacts clean.

A 20-milliampere current loop has some problems. A loop consists of a current source in series with a switch to break the circuit, which in turn is in series with a sensor to sense the current. Whereas the switch and sensor are obviously in two different stations in the circuit, the current source can be in either station. A station with a current source is called *active*, while one without is *passive*. If two passive stations, one with a switch and the other with a sensor, are connected, nothing will be communicated. If two active stations are connected, the current sources might cancel each other or destroy each other. Therefore, one station must be active while the other is passive, and one must be a switch and the other must be a sensor. While this is all very straightforward, it is an invitation to trouble. Also, note that the voltage levels are undefined. Most 20-milliampere current loops work with voltages like +5 or -12 or both, which are available in most communication systems; but some, designed for long distance communication, utilize "telegraph hardware" with voltages upwards of 80 volts. Therefore, one does not connect two 20-milliampere current loop stations together without checking the voltage levels and capabilities. Finally, these circuits generate a fair amount of electrical noise which gets into other signals, especially lower level signals, and the switch in such a circuit generates noise that is often filtered by the sensor. This noise is at frequencies used by 1200-baud lines, so this filter can't be used in other places in a communication subsystem. The circuitry for a 20-milliampere current loop can be built with an opto-isolator, as shown in figure 8-2b. If the current through the LED is about 20 milliamperes, the phototransistor appears to be a short circuit; if the current is about 0 milliamperes, it is an open circuit and the output is high. The diode across the LED is there to prevent an incorrect current from destroying the LED.

Table 8-1. RS232 Pin Connections for D25P and D25S Connectors

Pin	Name	Function
1	Protective Ground	Connects machine or equipment frames together and to "earth"
2	Transmitted Data	Data sent from microcomputer to terminal
3	Receive Data	Data sent from terminal to microcomputer
4	Request to Send	(Full Duplex) enables transmission circuits (Half Duplex) puts link in transmit mode and disables receive circuitry
5	Clear to Send	Responds to Request to Send; when high, it indicates the transmission circuitry is working
6	Data Set Ready	(telephone links) The circuitry is not in test, talk, or dial modes of operation so it can be used to transmit and receive
7	Signal Ground	Common reference potential for all lines. Should be connected to "earth" at just one point, to be disconnected for testing
8	Data Carrier Detect	A good signal is being received
9	+P	+12 volts (for testing only)
10	-P	-12 volts (for testing only)
11		
25		Used for more elaborate options

An interface standard developed by the Electronic Industries Association (EIA) and other interested parties has evolved into the RS232-C (recommended standard 232 version C). A similar standard is available in Europe, developed by the Comite Consultatif Internationale de Telegraphie et Telephonie (CCITT), and is called the CCITT V.24 standard. These standards are supposed to be simple and effective, so that any driver conforming to it can be connected to any receiver conforming to it, covering the voltage levels used for the signals as well as the pin assignments and dimensions of the plugs. Basically, a false variable is represented by any voltage from +15 to +5 volts, and a true by any voltage from -5 to -15 volts (negative logic is used.) A number of specifications concerning driver and receiver currents and impedances can be met by simply using integrated circuit drivers and receivers that are designed for this interface – RS232 drivers and RS232 receivers. The MC1488 is a popular quad RS232 line driver, and the MC1489 is a popular receiver. (See figure 8-2c.) The driver requires +12 volts on pin 14 and -12 volts on pin 1. Otherwise, it looks like a standard quad TTL NAND gate whose outputs are RS232 levels. The four receiver gates have a pin called response control (pins 2, 5, 9, and 12). Consider one of the gates, where pin 1 is the input and pin 3 is the output. Pin 2 can be left unconnected. It can be connected through a (33K) resistor to the negative supply voltage (pin 1) to raise the threshold voltage a bit. Or it can be connected through a capacitor to ground, thus filtering the incoming signal. This controls the behavior of that gate. The other gates can be similarly controlled. The MC145406 is a chip that combines three transmitter and three receiver gates in one chip (figure 8-2e); and the MAX232 (figure 8-2f), made by a new company, MAXIM, has two transmitters and two receivers, and a charge pump circuit that generates ±10 volts needed for the transmitter, from the 5-volt supply used by the microcomputer. (This marvelous circuit is just what is needed in many applications, but the currently available chips have a small problem: if the 5-volt supply turns on too fast, the charge pump fails to start; put a small – 10Ω – resistor in series with the 5-volt pin and put a large – 100μF – capacitor from that pin to ground.)

The RS232 interface standard also specifies the sockets and pin assignments. The DB25P is a 25-pin subminiature plug, and the DB25S is the corresponding socket – both of which conform to the standard. The pin assignments are shown in table 8-1. For simple applications, only pins 2 (transmit data), 3 (receive data), and 7 (signal ground) need be connected; but a remote station may need to make pins 5 (clear to send), 6 (data set ready), and 8 (data carrier detect) 12 volts to indicate that the link is in working order, if these signals are tested by the microcomputer. These can be wired to -12 volts in a terminal when they are not carrying status signals back to the microcomputer.

8-2.2 Frequency Shift Keyed Links Using Modems

To send data over the telephone, a *modem* converts the signals to frequencies that can be transmitted in the audio frequency range. The most common modem, the Bell 103, permits full duplex transmission at 300 baud. Transmission is originated by one of the modems, referred to as the *originate modem*, and is sent to the other modem, referred to as the *answer modem*. The originate modem sends true (mark) signals as a 1270-Hertz sine wave and false (space) signals as a 1070-Hertz sine wave. Of course, the answer modem receives a true as a 1270-Hertz sine wave and a false as a 1070-Hertz sine wave. The answer modem sends a true (mark) as a 2225-Hertz sine wave and a false (space) as a 2025-Hertz sine wave. Note that the true signal is higher in frequency than the false signal, and the answer modem sends the higher pair of frequencies.

Some modems are originate only. They can only originate a call and can only send 1070- or 1270-Hertz signals and receive only 2025- or 2225-Hertz signals. Most inexpensive modems intended for use in terminals are originate only. The computer may have an answer-only modem, having the opposite characteristics. If you want to be able to send data between two computers, one of them has to be an originate modem. So an answer/originate modem might be used on a computer if it is expected to receive and also send calls. Whether the modem is originate-only, answer-only, or answer/originate, it is fully capable of sending and receiving data simultaneously in full duplex mode. The originate and answer modes determine only which pair of frequencies can be sent and received, and therefore whether the modem is capable of actually initiating the call.

Modems have filters to reject the signal they are sending and pass the signals they are receiving. Usually, bessel filters are used because the phase shift must be kept uniform for all components or the wave will become distorted. Sixth order and higher filters are common to pass the received and reject the transmitted signal and the noise, because the transmitted signal is usually quite a bit stronger than the received signal, and because reliability of the channel is greatly enhanced by filtering out most of the noise. The need for two filters substantially increases the cost of answer/originate modems.

The module that connects the telephone line to the computer is called a *data coupler*, and there is one that connects to the originator of a call and another that connects to the answerer. The data coupler isolates the modem from the telephone line to prevent lightning from going to the modem,and to control the signal level, using an automatic gain control; but the data coupler does not convert the signal or filter it. The data coupler has three control/status signals. *Answer Phone* ANS is a control command that has the same effect on the telephone line as when a person picks up the handset to start a call or answer the phone. *Switch hook* SH is a status signal that indicates that the telephone handset is on a hook, if you will, so it will receive and transmit signals to the modem. Switch hook may also be controlled by the microcomputer. Finally, *ring indicator* RI is a status signal that indicates the phone is ringing.

Aside from the fact that data are sent using frequency analog signals over a telephone, there is not much to say about the channel. However, the way an originate modem establishes a channel to an answer modem and the way the call is terminated is interesting. We now discuss how the Motorola M6860 modem originates a call and answers a call. Calling a modem from another, maintaining the connection, and terminating the connection involve handshaking signals *data terminal ready* DTR and *clear to send* CTS in both originate and answer modems. (See figure 8-3a for a diagram showing these handshaking signals.) If a modem is connected to an RS232C line, as it often is, data terminal ready can be connected to request to send (pin 4) and clear to send can be connected to the clear to send (pin 5) or the data set ready (pin 6), whichever is used by the computer. Figure 8-3b shows the sequence of operations in the modems and on the telephone line, showing how a call is originated and answered by the Motorola M6860 modem chip.

The top line of figure 8-3b shows the handshaking signals seen by the originator, the next line shows signals seen by the originator modem, the center line shows the telephone line signals, the next line shows signals seen by the answer modem, and the bottom line shows the handshaking signals seen by the answerer. As indicated, the originator asserts the switch hook signal. This might be asserted by putting the telephone handset on the modem hook or by an output device that asserts this signal. This causes the command ANS (answer phone) to become asserted, which normally enables the data coupler electronics to transmit signals. The telephone is now used to dial up the answerer. (17 seconds is allowed for dialing up the answerer.) The answering modem receives a command RI (ring indicator) from the telephone, indicating the phone is ringing. It then asserts the ANS signal to answer the phone, enabling the data coupler to amplify the signal. The answerer puts a true signal, 2225 Hertz, on the line. The originator watches for that signal. When it is present for 450 milliseconds, the originator will send its true signal, a 1270-Hertz sine wave. The answerer is watching for this signal. When it is present for 450 milliseconds, the answerer asserts the CTS command and is able to begin sending data. The originator meanwhile asserts CTS after the 2225-Hertz signal has been present for 750 milliseconds. When both modems have asserted CTS, full duplex communication can be carried out.

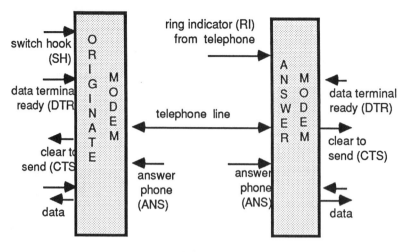

a. Block Diagram

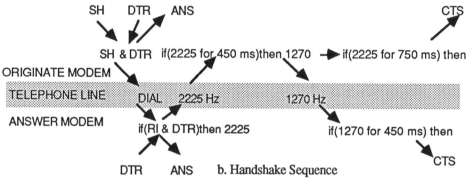

b. Handshake Sequence

Figure 8-3. Originating a Call on a Modem

Some answer modems will automatically terminate the call. To terminate the call, send more than 300 milliseconds of false (space) 1070 Hertz. This is called a *break* and is done by your terminal when you press the "break" key. The answer modem will then hang up the phone (negate ANS) and wait for another call. Other modems do not have this automatic space disconnect; they terminate the call whenever neither a high nor a low frequency is received in 17 seconds. This occurs when the telephone line goes dead or the other modem stops sending any signal. In such systems, the "break" key and low frequency sent when it is pressed can be used as an "attention" signal rather than a disconnect signal.

8-2.3 Optical Data Transmission

Transmission of data using light is no longer science fiction. A light transmitter, such as a LED or LASER, modulates the signal on the light. This is usually sent on a *light fiber* to a receiver, commonly a photodiode. Data can be sent at 20 megabaud or even higher – a gigabaud is feasible. The product of the data rate and the distance traveled is a constant for any given light fiber, however, so that data sent over long distances must be received and retransmitted every couple of miles.

Optical transmission will replace telephone lines in cities because one fiber can replace a few hundred pairs of copper wires. Bell Telephone can recover enough copper from under New York City to make that the largest copper mine in the world. Profits from the recovered copper may make installation of optical links quite attractive.

You may have noticed that some of the problems with I/O LSI chips are due to the fact that we are always short of pins. These problems will get worse as more and more logic can be put on the chip but the number of pins is not increased proportionally. Optical links between integrated circuits may someday replace most of an integrated circuit's pins and most of the printed circuit board's traces. Without the high capacity of optical links, we cannot satisfactorily get data into and out of those chips. We are currently studying this problem.

Optical links in communication systems are a bit of an embarrassment because of their unprecedented capacity. What can you do with a gigabaud line? (This is bottom-up design.) They clearly have use for communication between large computers and might be useful in microcomputer systems that are used to handling large amounts of data traffic in communication systems. The extraordinary capacity can be used to further distribute the components of a computer. The primary memory may be in another room. The organization of computing systems may be revolutionized.

While the technology is in its infancy, it is so important that we would like to mention a few of the exciting possibilities. One of these is called *ether-net*. The high-capacity electonic (or possibly optical) line is treated like a radio ether, and different transmitters send to different receivers at frequencies or time-slices rather as ham radio operators do. We are studying the *general propagating communication* (GPC) link. (See figure 8-4.) Each computer – or module or integrated circuit – has a generate (G) input for data, a propagate (P) for control, and an output named C. The P control is normally asserted to cause the data to propagate through the module, but can be negated to inhibit the data. By inhibiting the data at different modules, we cut the communication link into segments that act independently of each other. In each segment, the OR of the G inputs is sent leftward, or clockwise. The rightmost module can broadcast data to all modules to its left on the same segment, if all the other modules do not assert their G inputs. The leftmost module can collect the data from each of the G inputs in the same manner as a wire-OR bus collects data. Moreover, and this is very important, the segment can be made into a priority circuit, so that modules to the right in a segment, have higher priority. If a module wants to compete for priority, it asserts the G signal. If the C signal is asserted, it means that some other module of higher priority is requesting a grant, so the module that receives such a signal should not be granted its request. The module that asserts G and receives a negated C is granted the request. Finally, perhaps you have recognized it, this is the carry circuit of a ripple adder. The optical link can be used to link parts of an adder together. (We refer to the connections as G, P, and C, and to this link as GPC, because these are the names of the signals on a carry-lookahead generator, which is a faster implementation of the ripple carry logic of figure 8-4.)

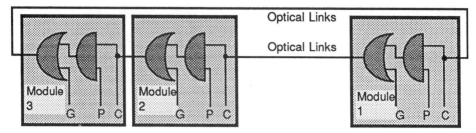

Figure 8-4. A GPC Linkage for Optical Communication

The GPC is intuitively a good communication linkage because the P signal ANDed into the link can be used to cut the link at any desired point, while the G signal can be used to insert data just as is done on a wire-OR bus. Moreover, the ability to implement priority logic right on the communication linkage has profound effects. It is possible to establish the right to use a resource, including some time on the communication link, using a simple and efficient protocol, because the priority link does most of the work in hardware. By comparison, protocols to use the ether-net require more effort. The ability to break up the GPC into separate segments to get more data moved, and especially the ability to establish priorities, makes the GPC link attractive for optical communication systems.

8-3 UART Link Protocol

By far the most common technique for transmitting data is that used by the *Universal Asynchronous Receiver Transmitter* (UART). This simple protocol is discussed in this section. Software generation of UART signals, discussed first, is quite simple and helps to show how they are sent. The UART-like chip – the M6850 – designed for the 6811 family is covered in the next subsection. A special remote control chip that uses the UART protocol is discussed in the next subsection. The UART chip is then discussed. A system inside the 6811 that is capable of UART signal generation and reception, the Serial Communications Interface (SCI), is discussed last, because it has several useful but non-standard extensions to the UART protocol.

8-3.1 UART Transmission and Reception by Software

As noted earlier, the Universal Asynchronous Receiver-Transmitter (UART) is a module (integrated circuit) that supports a frame protocol to send up to eight bit frames (characters). We call this the *UART protocol*. However, the UART protocol can be supported entirely under software control, without the use of a UART chip or its equivalent. A study of this software is not only a good exercise in hardware-software tradeoffs, but is also an easy way to teach the protocol; the software approach also is a practical way to implement communication in a minimum cost microcomputer. However, we do warn the reader that most communication is done with UART chips or their equivalent, and low-cost microprocessors such as the 6811 already have a built-in UART on the microprocessor chip itself.

The UART frame format is shown in figure 8-5. (The UART protocol is contained within the UART frame format.) When a frame is not being sent, the signal is high. When a signal is to be sent, a *start bit*, a low, is sent for one bit time. The frame, from 5 to 8 bits long, is then sent 1 bit per bit time, least significant bit first. A parity bit may then be sent and may be generated so that the parity of the whole frame is always even (or always odd). To generate even parity, if the frame itself had an even number of ones already, a low parity bit is sent, otherwise a high bit is sent. Finally, one or more *stop bits* are sent. A stop bit is high, and is indistinguishable from the high signal that is sent when no frame is being transmitted. In other words, if the frame has n stop bits (n = 1, 1 1/2 or 2) this means the next frame must wait that long after the last frame bit or parity bit of the previous message has been sent before it can begin sending its start bit. However, it can wait longer than that.

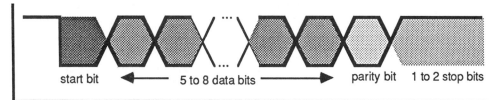

start bit ◄——— 5 to 8 data bits ———► parity bit 1 to 2 stop bits

Figure 8-5. Frame Format for UART Signals

In addition to the format above, the protocol has some rules for sampling data and for error correction. A clock, used in the receiver, is 16 times the bit rate, and a counter, incremented each clock time, is used to sample the incoming data. (The same clock is used in the transmitter to generate the outgoing data.) The counter is started when the input signal falls, at the beginning of a frame. After 8 clock periods, presumably in the middle of the start bit, the input is sampled. It should be low. If it is high, the falling edge that started the counter must be due to some noise pulse, so the receiver returns to examine the input for the leading edge of a start bit. If this test passes, the input is sampled after every 16 clock periods, presumably in the middle of each bit time. The data bits sampled are reassembled in parallel. The parity bit, if one is used, is then sampled and checked. Then the stop bit(s) are checked.

The following are definitions of error conditions. If the parity bit is supposed to be even, but a frame with odd parity is received, a *parity error* is indicated. This indicates that one of the frame bits or the parity bit was changed due to noise. Note that two errors will make the parity appear correct – but two wrongs don't make a right. Parity detection can't detect all errors. Even so, most errors are single-bit errors, so most errors are detetected. If a stop bit is expected, but a low signal is received, the frame has a *framing error*. This usually indicates that the receiver is using the wrong clock rate, either because the user selected the wrong rate or because the receiver oscillator is out of calibration. However, this condition can arise if the transmitter is faulty, sending frames before the stop bits have been timed out, or if more than one transmitter are on a link and one sends before the other's stop bits are completely sent. Finally, most UART devices use a buffer to store the incoming word, so the computer can pick up this word at leisure rather than at the precise time that it has been shifted in. This technique is called *double buffering*. But if the buffer is not read before another frame arrives needing to fill the same buffer, the first frame is destroyed. This error condition is called an *overrun error*. It usually indicates that the computer is not paying attention to the UART receiver, since if it were, it would empty the buffer before the next message arrives.

The UART communication technique is based on the following principle. If the frame is short enough, a receiver clock can be quite a bit out of synchronization with the transmitter clock and still sample the data somewhere within the bit time when the data are correct. For example, if a frame has 10 bits and the counter is reset at the leading edge of the frame's start bit, the receiver clock could be five percent faster or five percent slower than the transmitter clock and still, without error, pick up all the bits up to the last bit of the frame. It will sample the first bit five percent early or five percent late, the second ten percent, the third fifteen percent, and the last fifty percent. This means the clock does not have to be sent with the data. The receiver can generate a clock to within five percent of the transmitter clock without much difficulty. However, this technique would not work for long frames, because the accumulated error due to incorrectly matching the clocks of the transmitter and receiver would eventually cause a bit to be mis-sampled. To prevent this, the clocks would have to be matched too precisely. Other techniques become more economical for longer frames.

A subroutine SUART to generate a signal compatible with the UART protocol is quite simple. Assume an 8-bit word in accumulator B is to be sent in a frame with even parity and 2 stop bits. An output register at location $8000 outputs the least significant bit into the communication link. The following program uses a subroutine DELAY whose execution time is set to the time to send 1 bit. If the baud rate were 10, this subroutine would delay 100,000 microseconds. The program assumes that the output was high for some time, since the protocol requires a high signal when no frame is being sent. A low signal, the start pulse, is sent for one bit time. Then the data in accumulator B are output, then shifted, eight times, so each bit is sent out the output port in its least significant bit position. Meanwhile, the parity is determined by exclusive ORing B into A, which makes the least significant bit of A the parity of the bits shifted out. The parity bit is then output. Finally, 2 stop bits are sent out. The whole purpose of "sending" these stop bits is to make sure that this routine is not called up too soon to send another frame. If this were done, the receiver would detect a framing error.

```
            NAM    SUART
    SUART   CLR    $8000      SEND START BIT
            BSR    DELAY
            LDAA   #8         SET COUNTER FOR 8 BITS OF DATA
            STAA   TEMP1      SAVE ON STACK AS LOCAL VARIABLE
            CLRA              CLEAR PARITY BIT
    L       STAB   $8000      OUTPUT BIT
            BSR    DELAY
            STAB   TEMP2      PUT IN GLOBAL TEMP
```

```
          EORA    TEMP2     IN ORDER TO EXCLUSIVE-OR IT WITH A
          LSRB              NEXT BIT
          DEC     TEMP1     COUNT DOWN NUMBER OF BITS SENT
          BNE     L         LOOP UNTIL ALL SENT
          STAA    $8000     OUTPUT PARITY
          BSR     DELAY
          LDAA    #1        STOP BIT IS HIGH
          STAA    $8000
          BSR     DELAY     SEND STOP BIT
          BSR     DELAY     SEND SECOND STOP BIT
          RTS               RETURN FROM SUBROUTINE
          END
```

A subroutine RUART to receive a UART frame is also quite simple. Assume the protocol is the same as the preceding frame and the data are to be received from the most significant bit of an input register at location $8001, the low-order 7 bits of that register being 0. These data are assembled into accumulator B in the following subroutine. In addition to the DELAY subroutine, a subroutine HDELAY delays for one half of a bit time so it can begin sampling the inputs in the middle of the bit times. The first part of the program waits for the input signal's falling edge, which is the beginning of the start bit. HDELAY waits for the middle of the bit. If the input is not low, control returns to check again for the beginning of the start bit. Otherwise, after each full bit time, another bit is put into accumulator B (by ORing it in) and parity is updated in accumulator A. When the parity bit arrives, it is checked against the parity bit assembled in accumulator A. If they disagree, control goes to an error exit PARERR. Then 2 stop bits are sought. If either bit is low, a framing error is reported by branching to FRMERR.

```
          NAM     RUART
RUART     TST     $8001
          BMI     RUART     WAIT FOR FALLING EDGE
          BSR     HDELAY
          TST     $8001     SEE IF INPUT STILL LOW
          BMI     RUART     IF NOT LOW, GO BACK AND WAIT
          CLRA              READY TO COMPUTE PARITY BIT
          LDAB    #8        INPUT 8 BITS OF DATA
          STAB    TEMP      SAVE AS GLOBAL VARIABLE
L2        BSR     DELAY
          LSRB              MOVE FOR NEXT BIT
          ORAB    $8001     INPUT NEXT BIT
          EORA    $8001     UPDATE PARITY
          DEC     TEMP      ALL BITS INPUT?
          BNE     L2        IF NOT GO BACK
          BSR     DELAY
          CMPA    $8001     CHECK PARITY
          BNE     PARERR
          BSR     DELAY
```

```
TST      $8001      CHECK FOR FIRST STOP BIT
BPL      FRMERR
BSR      DELAY
TST      $8001      CHECK FOR SECOND STOP BIT
BPL      FRMERR
RTS                 RETURN FROM SUBROUTINE
END
```

Both the preceding programs are simple enough to follow. They can be done in software without much penalty, because the microprocessor is usually doing nothing while frames are being input or output. In an equivalent hardware alternative, essentially the same algorithms are executed inside the UART chip or an equivalent chip like the M6850. The hardware alternative is especially valuable where the microcomputer can do something else as the hardware tends to transmitting and receiving the frames, or when it might be sending a frame at the same time it might be receiving another frame (in a full duplex link or in a ring of simplex rings). In other cases, the advantages of the hardware and software approaches are about equal: the availability of cheap, simple UART chips favors the hardware approach, while the simplicity of the program favors the software approach. The best design must be picked with care and depends very much on the application's characteristics.

8-3.2 The UART

The UART chip is designed to transmit and/or receive signals that comply with the UART protocol (by definition). This protocol allows several variations (in baud rate, parity bit, and stop bit selection). The particular variation is selected by strapping different pins on the chip to high or to low. The UART can be used inside a microcomputer to communicate with a teletype or a typewriter, which was its original use, or with the typewriter's electronic equivalent, such as a CRT display. It can also be used in other remote stations in security systems, stereo systems controlled from a microcomputer, and so on. Several integrated circuit companies make UARTs, which are all very similar. We will study one that has a single-supply voltage and a self-contained oscillator to generate the clock for the UART, the Intersil IM6403.

The UART contains a transmitter and a receiver that run independently, for the most part, but share a common control that selects the baud rate and other variations for both transmitter and receiver. We discuss the common control first, then the transmitter, and then the receiver. The baud rate is selected by the crystal connected to pins 17 and 40 and by the divide control DIV on pin 2. If DIV is high, the oscillator frequency is divided by 16; if low, by 2^{11}. If the crystal is a cheap TV crystal (3.5795 MHz) and DIV is low, the baud rate is close to 110, which is commonly used for teletypes. When master reset MR, on pin 21, is high, it resets the chip; it is normally grounded. The other control bits are input on pins 39 to 35 and are stored in a latch inside the chip. The latch stores the inputs when pin 24 is high. This pin can be held high to defeat the storage mechanism, so the pin levels control the chip directly. Pin 36 selects the number of stop bits: low selects 1 stop bit, high selects 2 (except for an anomaly of little interest). If pin 35 is high, no parity bit is generated or checked otherwise pin 39 selects even parity if high, odd if low. Pins 37 and 38 select the number of data bits per frame; the number is five plus the binary number on these pins. The user generally determines the values needed on these pins from the protocol he or she is using, and connects them to high or low. However, these inputs can be tied to the data bus of a computer, and pin 34 can be asserted to load the control latch to effect an output register. When the computer executes the reset handler, it can then set the control values under software control.

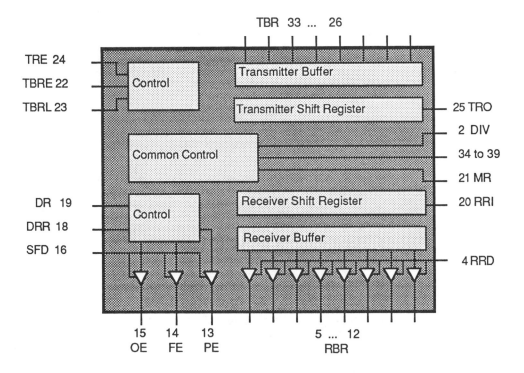

Figure 8-6. Block Diagram of a UART (IM6403)

The operation of the transmitter and receiver is compactly and simply explained in the data sheets of the 6403 and are paraphrased here. The transmitter has a buffer register, which is loaded from the signals on pins 33 (msb) to 26 (lsb) when transmitter buffer register load TBRL (pin 23) rises. If n < 8 bits are sent, the rightmost n bits on these pins are sent. Normally, these pins are tied to the data bus to make the buffer look like an output register, and TBRL is asserted when the register is to be loaded. When this buffer is empty and can be loaded, transmitter buffer register empty TBRE (pin 22) is high; when full it is low. (SFD, pin 16, must be low to read out TBRE.) The computer may check this pin to determine if it is safe to load the buffer register. It behaves as a BUSY bit in the classical I/O mechanism. The data in the buffer are automatically loaded into the transmitter shift register to be sent out as transmitter register output TRO (pin 25) with associated start, parity, and stop bits as selected by the control inputs. As long as the shift register is shifting out part of a frame, transmitter register empty TRE (pin

24) is low. Figure 8-7 shows a typical transmission, in which two frames are sent out. The second word is put into the buffer even as the first frame is being shifted out in this double buffered system. It is automatically loaded into the shift register as soon as the first frame has been sent.

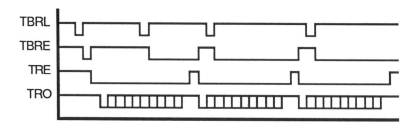

Figure 8-7. Transmitter Signals

The receiver shifts data into a receiver shift register. When a frame has been shifted in, the data are put in the receiver buffer. If fewer than 8 bits are transmitted in a frame, the data are right justified. This data can be read from pins 5 to 12, when receive register disable RRD (pin 4) is asserted low. Normally these pins are attached to a data bus, and RRD is used to enable the tristate drivers when the read buffer register is to be read as an input register. If RRD is strapped low, then the data in the read buffer are continuously available on pins 5 to 12. When the read buffer contains valid data, the data ready DR signal (pin 19) is high, and the error indicators are set. (DR can only be read when SFD on pin 16 is high.) The DR signal is an indication that the receiver is DONE, in the classical I/O mechanism, and requests the program to read the data from the receive buffer and read the error indicators if appropriate. The error indicators are reloaded after each frame is received, so they always indicate the status of the last frame that was received. The error indicators, TBRE, and DR can be read from pins 15 to 13 and 22 and 19 when SFD (pin 16) is asserted low, and indicate an overrun error, a framing error, and a parity error, and that the transmit buffer is empty and that the receive buffer is full respectively, if high. The error indicators and buffer status indicators can be read as another input register by connecting pins 22 and 19, and 15 to 13 to the data bus, and asserting SFD when this register is selected; or, if SFD is strapped low, the error and buffer status indicators can be read directly from those pins. When the data are read, the user is expected to reset the DR indicator by asserting data ready reset DRR (pin 18) high. If this is not done, when the next frame arrives and is loaded into the buffer register, an overrun error is indicated.

The UART can be used in a microcomputer system as follows. The control bits (pins 35 to 39) and the transmit buffer inputs (pins 26 to 33) can be inputs, and the buffer status and error indicators (pins 22 and 19, and 15 to 13) and receive data buffer outputs (pins 5 to 12) can be outputs. All the inputs and outputs can be attached to the data bus. TBRL, SBS, SFD, and RRD (pins 23, 36, 16, and 4) are connected to an address decoder so that the program can write in the control register or transmit buffer register, or read from the error indicators or the read buffer register. The TBRE signal (pin 22) is used as a BUSY bit for the transmitter; and the DR signal (pin 19) is used as a DONE bit for the receiver. When the UART is used in a gadfly technique, which can be extended to interrupt or even DMA techniques, the program initializes the UART by writing the appropriate control bits into the control register. To send data using the gadfly approach, the program checks to see if TBRE is high and waits for it to go high if it is not. When it is high, the program can load data into the transmitter buffer. Loading data into the buffer will automatically cause the data to be sent out. If the program is expecting data from the receiver in the gadfly technique, it waits for DR to become high. When it is, the program reads data from the receive buffer register and asserts DRR to tell the UART that the buffer is now empty. This makes DR low until the next frame arrives.

The UART can be used without a computer in a remote station that is implemented with hardware. Control bits can be strapped high or low, and CRL (pin 34) can be strapped high to constantly load these values into the control register. Data to be collected can be put on pins 33 to 27. Whenever the hardware wants to send the data, it asserts TBRL (pin 23) low for a short time, and the data get sent. The hardware can examine TBRE (pin 22) to be sure that the transmitter buffer is empty before loading it, but if the timing works out so that the buffer will always be empty there is no need to check this value. It is pretty easy to send data in that case. Data, input serially, are made available and are stable on pins 5 to 12. Each time a new frame is completely shifted in, the data are transferred in parallel into the buffer. RRD (pin 4) would be strapped low to constantly output this data in a hardware system. When DR becomes high, new data have arrived, which might signal the hardware to do something with the data. The hardware should then assert DRR high to clear DR. (DR can feed a delay into DRR to reset itself.) The buffer status and error indicators can be constantly output if SFD (pin 16) is strapped low, and the outputs can feed LEDs, for instance, to indicate an error. However, in a simple system when the hardware does not have to do anything special with the data except output them, it can ignore DR and ignore resetting it via asserting DRR. In this case, the receiver is very simple to use in a remote station.

8-3.3 The M6850

The M6850 is a "UART" that has been specially tailored to be used as an external chip for the 6811 microcomputer in extended bus multiplexed mode. It is called an *asynchronous communications interface adapter* (ACIA) by Motorola. As noted before, we don't use terms like PIA and ACIA because they are less specific than part numbers like M6821 or M6850, but we don't object to your using these terms. This section covers the M6850's highlights. A complete description is available as a Motorola data sheet in appendix G. The M6850 is designed for the Motorola microcomputer. It can also be used in other microcomputers, and other microcomputer manufacturers have special chips like the M6850 for their systems. The M6850 is different from a UART like the IM6403 in the following ways. To save pins, a bit of the transmitter buffer input, a bit of the receive buffer output, a bit of the control register, and a bit of the buffer/error status register output are internally connected and then connected to a single pin on this chip. Thus, only 8 pins are used to connect to the data bus. An external clock is needed to set the baud rate, and the transmitter can have a different clock than the receiver. Also, because this chip is designed to connect to a modem, discussed in the next section, it has three pins to control the modem so that the program can control it. Finally, it has a status register with interrupt request logic so that the 6811 can easily examine it in its interrupt handler. (A diagram of the M6850 is shown in figure 8-8; for simplicity, the system is configured so that this chip is addressed at locations $8000 and $8001.)

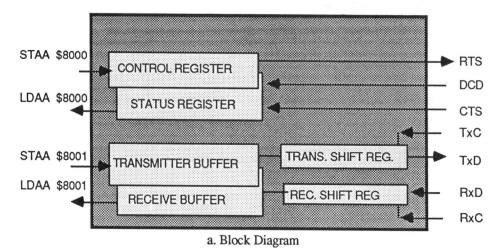

a. Block Diagram

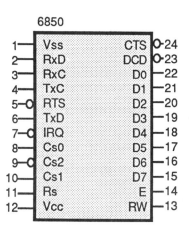

b. Pinouts

Figure 8-8. The M6850

The transmitter, with its buffer and shift register, and the receiver and its shift register operate just as in the UART. They are addressed in the same location because the transmit buffer is write-only, while the receive buffer is read-only. Once the control register is set up, a word is transmitted simply by writing it in location $8001, and an incoming word is picked up by reading it from location $8001.

The control register, written into at location $8000, sets up the baud rate (it is also set by the frequency of the external clocks), the frame format, and the interrupt mechanism. The transmitter interrupt control also controls a signal called request to sent RTS on an output pin, which can be used to control a modem. (These control values are shown in table 8-2a.) The user determines the bit pattern from the protocol and sets this register up in a ritual. An example will be given shortly that uses this table.

Table 8-2. M6850 Control and Status Bits

Bits	Function
1,0	Clock frequency
0 0	divide by 1
0 1	divide by 16
1 0	divide by 64
1 1	master reset

Bits	Function	
6,5	Trans. int	RTS
0 0	disable	low
0 1	enable	low
1 0	disable	high
1 1	disable	low *

* Transmit data output is low

Bits	Function
4,3,2	Frame format
0 0 0	7 bits, even parity, 2 stop bits
0 0 1	7 data, odd parity, 2 stop bits
0 1 0	7 data, even parity, 1 stop bit
0 1 1	7 data, odd parity, 1 stop bit
1 0 0	8 data, 2 stop bits
1 0 1	8 data, 1 stop bit
1 1 0	8 data, even parity, 1 stop bit
1 1 1	8 data, odd parity, 1 stop bit

Bits	Function
7	receiver interrupt
0	disable
1	enable

a. Control Register

b. Status Register

The frame format is controlled by bits 4 to 2 in an obvious way. Note that the UART has more combinations, but the most popular combinations of data, parity, and stop bits are available in the M6850. The clock frequency is divided to get the baud rate under control of bits 1 and 0. If division is by 1, the baud rate is the same as the frequency of the clock input, which is set by an external oscillator. Each clock cycle shifts out 1 bit of data. This is useful for high baud rates, such as would be used to communicate between two microcomputers that are a short distance apart. Normally, division is by 16, as discussed in earlier sections. However, division by 64 is useful if a slow baud rate is desired and if the external clock would have to be divided by 4 in another (counter) chip to get the desired frequency. The last code for this field is the master reset. Unfortunately, this chip does not have a reset pin, unlike most of the other I/O chips in the 6811 family. Before it can be used, the M6850 must be reset by putting 11 into bits 1 and 0. The other bits can be 0. So the first thing to do with this chip is store $03 into the control register. This is usually done just before the control register is set up with the bits that determine the modes of operation. Be warned, moreover, that if this is not done, the chip will appear to be bad. The author spent a frustrating week and several chips finding this out. The transmitter is controlled by bits 6 and 5. If interrupts are enabled, each time the transmit buffer is empty an interrupt will be generated so the software can refill it. Interrupts should be enabled and an appropriate device handler should be used when a sequence of words are to be output as to a typewriter, if the microcomputer can do some useful work while the M6850 tends to transmitting the message. Interrupts should be disabled when the microcomputer uses the gadfly technique. The RTS signal is often used to control a modem. This (negative logic) signal is set by bits 6 and 5. If these control bits are 11, the transmitter outputs a low signal. This is used to test and to control a modem. Finally, bit 7 controls the receiver interrupt. If true, an interrupt is requested whenever the receive buffer is full (data are available) – so the software can move the word – or whenever there is an error in the receiver such as parity, framing, overrun, or a problem with the modem indicated by a low signal on the data carrier detect DCD pin. Bit 7 should be true if interrupts are used to service the reader and false if the gadfly technique is used.

Suppose that a simple program is to be written to test the M6850's transmitter, using an oscilloscope to view the output. The word $C5 has an instructive pattern, so it will be continuously transmitted. The transmitter clock input is 1600 Hz, and the data are to be sent at 100 baud, with 8 data bits, even parity, and 1 stop bit. Neither the transmitter nor the receiver should generate interrupts, and RTS should be low. Consulting table 1, the control bits should be as follows: bit 7 should be 0 to disable the receiver interrupt; bits 6 and 5 should be 00 to disable the transmitter interrupt and set RTS low; bits 4, 3, and 2 should be 110 to select 8 data, bits, even parity, and 1 stop bit; bits 1 and 0 should be 01 to divide the clock rate, 1600 Hz, by 16, so they can deliver bits at 100 baud. The control word should be $19. The following program initializes the M6850 by first resetting it, then putting in the control word. Then a constant, $C5, is put into accumulator A in a program loop so that every time the buffer is empty it is immediately refilled with the constant. (If the buffer is already full, writing another word into it does not cause an error but does cause it to lose the word that was in it. Normally the program checks a status bit to be sure this buffer is empty before filling it. But in this case, there is no harm in constantly writing the same word into it.) The output of the shift register would appear on an oscilloscope, as shown in figure 8-9.

```
        LDAA    #$03
        STAA    $8000
        LDAA    #$19
        STAA    $8000
        LDAA    #$C5
   L    STAA    $8001
        BRA     L
```

The M6850's status bits can be read from location $8000. (See table 8-2b.) RDRF (bit 0) is true if the receive buffer is full. TDRE (bit 1) is true if the transmit buffer is empty. Bits 2 and 3 indicate the signals from a modem, DCD and CTS, that normally indicate the data carrier is present and the channel is clear to send. FE, OVRN, and PE, (bits 4, 5 and 6) are the framing overrun and parity error indicators. IRQ (bit 7) is a composite interrupt request bit, which is true if the interrupt enable, control bit 7, is true and any one or several of the status bits 0, 2, 4, 5, or 6 are true, or if control bits 6 and 5 are 01 and status bit 1 is true.

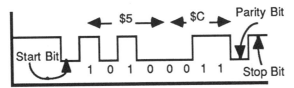

Figure 8-9. Output of a Test Program

To show the use of the M6850 status bits, a portion of an interrupt handler will be written to check this device. It will branch to NEXT if the M6850 does not request an interrupt; NEXT is some routine to check other I/O devices. If the chip is not in its socket, we also want to jump to NEXT. We test for all 1s to see if the chip is not in its socket. We would like to check for a 0 bit to ensure that the chip is in its socket, but none of the status bits can be insured to be 0. So we check for all 1s. While this pattern could conceivably show up, it would require so many coincidences far less likely than the chip not being in its socket that we use this test. If the receiver buffer is full, it will branch to a routine STORE that will store the word in the receive buffer in some table or character string. If an error is made upon reception, however, it will branch to a routine ERROR to correct or report the error. Lastly, if the transmitter buffer is empty, it will branch to LOAD which will read another word from some character string or file into the buffer register.

```
LDAA    $8000
BPL     NEXT
CMPA    #$FF
BEQ     NEXT
BITA    #$74
BNE     ERROR
LSRA
BCS     STORE
LSRA
BCS     LOAD
```

The M6850 is connected to the 6811 system in the standard way. (See figure 8-8 for the pin connections.) Pins 15 to 22 are connected to the data bus, pin 7 to the IRQ bus line if interrupts are used, pin 14 to the E clock, and pin 13 to the R/W line. To select the chip, pins 8, 9, and 10 must be high, low, and high, respectively. These are normally connected to an address decoder, and, if it is used, VMA must be true to select the chip, because reading or writing in the data buffer registers clears the associated interrupts. VMA can be connected directly to pin 8 or 10 for convenience. Pin 11 is normally connected to address bit 0, so it can select control/status if this bit is false or a data buffer if true. An external clock is connected to pins 3 and 4 to set the baud rate for the receiver and transmitter, respectively. While the two clocks can be different, they are usually the same. Finally, pins 5, 23, and 24 are available to connect to a modem, as discussed in section 8-2.2. If not used, pins 23 and 24 should be grounded to prevent false interrupts.

8-3.4 The M14469

The M14469 is a "UART" specially designed for a remote station. We give a short description here and a full description in the Motorola data sheet for the chip. A CMOS chip, it can use an unregulated supply whose voltage can vary between 4.5 and 18 volts, and it uses very little current. It features a self-contained oscillator and an address comparator that permits the selection of a station when multiple stations are on the same link. A UART protocol is supported, in which the frame has even parity and 1 stop bit. The baud rate is determined by the crystal (or ceramic resonator) connected between pins 1 and 2, or by an external oscillator that can drive pin 1. The crystal (oscillator) frequency is divided by 64 to set the baud rate. A diagram of the M14469 is shown in figure 8-10.

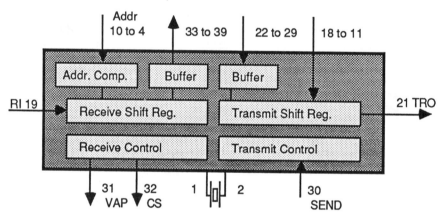

Figure 8-10. The M14469

The receiver is a standard UART receiver with an address comparator. A 7-bit address is sent as the low-order 7 bits of an 8-bit word, the most significant bit being true. The station has a 7-bit address, which is selected by strapping pins 10 to 4 low if a 0 bit is needed, or leaving them open if a 1 bit is needed in the address (these pins have an internal pull-up resistor to make them high if they are not connected). If the incoming address is equal to the station address, the valid address pulse VAP (pin 31) is made high momentarily, and the station is said to be *selected*. A 7-bit data word is sent as the low-order 7 bits of a word, the most significant bit being false. A station that has been selected will put any data word into its receive buffer when the word is completely shifted in, and make a command strobe CS (pin 32) high momentarily just after this happens. Error status is not available on a pin, but if a parity or framing error is detected, an address will not select a station, data will not be transferred to the receive buffer, and VAP or CS will not be pulsed.

Note that a typical message will consist of a frame with an address (most significant bit true) followed by zero or more frames with data (most significant bit false). A single address frame can be used to trigger a remote station to do something, by asserting VAP in it when the address is recognized; or a message with an address frame followed by a number of data frames will cause the data to be stored in the receive buffer each time a data frame arrives, and will pulse CS to command something to be done with the data.

The transmitter is a conventional UART transmitter modified to send out 16 bits of data in two consecutive frames if SEND is made high when VAL or CS is asserted (or within 8 data bit time units after that) and if it is not currently transmitting a pair of frames. Sixteen bits are sent from the signals on pins 11 to 18 and 29 to 22 by transferring the data on pins 11 to 18 directly into the transmitter shift register, and simultaneously transferring the data on pins 29 to 22 into the transmitter buffer. The data in the shift register are sent out (pin 11 data first) in the first UART frame, and the data in the buffer (pin 29 data first) are sent out immediately after that in the next frame. The data appear on the transmitter output TRO (pin 21) in negative logic. This output is in negative logic so that it can drive a transistor, which inverts the signal to power the link out of the station.

The chip is designed for full and half duplex, with some special provisions for the latter application. In full duplex applications, a master (likely an M6850 in a microcomputer) sends to all the slave stations (several M14469s) on one line (M6850 TxD output to RI input of each slave), while all the slave stations send to the master on another line (slave TRO output into transistor base, transistor collectors in each slave tied together, in a wire AND bus line, to RxD input of M6850), so that the master can be sending to a slave at the same time that a slave is sending to the master. In this case, VAP can be connected to SEND to send back the two frames as quickly as possible after a station is selected. The master should take care it does not send two address frames, one right after another, so that two slaves will send overlapping frames back. In the half duplex mode, a single bus line is used between master and all slaves so that the master can send data to the slaves or the slaves can send data to the master, but not at the same time. TxD and RxD in the master, and RI and the transistor collector in each slave, would be connected to this single line. In this application, SEND should be connected to CS so the slave that was selected will wait for an address frame and a data frame to be sent over the line from the master, before the slave returns its two frames. The master should wait for both frames to be returned before it sends more data on the same line.

To ensure the data have been received, handshaking is often used; and to permit handshaking, the M14469 is designed to prevent difficulties in the half duplex mode. The slave can be implemented so that the first frame it returns has its own station address. When the master sends a message, it can wait for the slave to respond with a frame having the address of the slave. If that frame is returned, the message must have been received without error and the slave must be active (as opposed to being shut off). This is a simple handshake protocol. However, if it is used in the half duplex mode, we don't want the return frame to be received by the same slave and for it to recognize its own address again to trigger itself nor do we want the return message stored in the receive buffer. Therefore, this chip is designed so that it deselects the receiver as soon as it begins transmitting a frame. And the frame being transmitted should be a data frame (most significant bit false) to prevent the address decoder from matching it, even though the frame really contains an address. This provision makes handshaking in a half duplex mode possible. However, the chip is designed that way, and these peculiarities are also apparent in the full duplex mode.

Before the end of this section, we present a short program that shows how the M6850 can communicate to several M14469s over a full duplex line. The object of the program is to select station 3, send a word of data to it, and receive a word of data from it. An M14469 is configured as station 3 by wiring pins 10 to 4 and pins 17 to 11 to represent the number 3. The data to be sent back from this station is connected to pins 23 to 29. Handshaking is used, so the transmission on the link will look as follows: The master will send the slave's address, then 7 bits of data to the slave on the line from master to slave then the slave will return its address and 7 bits of data on the other line.

The following program sets up an M6850 to send 8 bits of data, even parity, and one stop bit per frame, and to divide the clock by 64. The gadfly technique uses a subroutine WTBRE, shown at the bottom of the program, to wait until the transmitter buffer is empty, and then outputs the word in accumulator A to it. Initially, accumulator A has $5A, which is some data for station 3. The address is sent first, then the data. Then the receiver is checked for an incoming frame. While checking for the returned frame, the index register is used to keep track of elapsed time. The contents of this frame are compared with the address that was sent out. If too much time elapses before the frame returns, or if it contains the wrong address, the program exits to report the error. Otherwise, the data in the next frame are left in accumulator B, and this routine is left.

```
          NAM   REMOT
REMOT     STAA  TEMP      SAVE WORD TO BE OUTPUT
          LDAA  #$03      RESET THE M6850
          STAA  $8000     BY PUTTING 3 IN CONTROL REGISTER
          LDAA  #$1A      8 DATA, EVEN PARITY, 1 STOP
          STAA  $8000     DIVIDE BY 64, DISABLE INTERRUPTS
          LDAA  #$83      OUTPUT ADDRESS OF STATION 3 ($80 + $03)
          BSR   WTRBE     CHECK AND OUTPUT WORD IN ACC A
          LDAA  TEMP      GET SUBROUTINE ARGUMENT BROUGHT IN
          BSR   WTRBE     CHECK AND OUTPUT WORD IN ACC A
          LDX   #0        PUT LARGEST COUNT IN INDEX REGISTER X
L1        LDAB  $8000     CHECK STATUS
          LSRB            RDRF IS LEAST SIGNIFICANT BIT
          BCS   L2        WHEN TRUE, READ REG IS FULL, GO ON
          DEX   DECREMENT X
          BNE   L1        LOOP TIL WORD READ OR WAIT TOO LONG
          BRA   ERROR     LOOP HAS TIMED OUT
L2        CMPA  $8001     CHECK TO SEE IF THE ADDR IS OK
          BNE   ERROR     IF NOT, ERROR
L3        LDAB  $8000     CHECK STATUS BIT RDRF AGAIN
          LSRB
          BCC   L3        WAIT FOR IT TO BE TRUE
```

```
           LDAA  $8001    GET DATA WORD
           RTS
    *
    WTBRE  LDAB  $8000    CHECK STATUS OF TRANSMIT BUFFER
           BITB  #$02     TDRE IS BIT 1, TRUE WHEN CAN TRANS
           BEQ   WTBRF    IF FALSE, LOOP
           STAA  $8001    SEND WORD TO TRANS BUFFER REGISTER
           RTS
           END
```

8-3.5 The Serial Communication Interface System in the 6811

The 6811 has a UART-like system in it called the Serial Communication Interface (SCI). (See figure 8-11.) We describe the data registers, the baud rate generator, the control 1 register, the status register, and the control 2 register in turn, but we defer describing the wakeup feature until all these parts are described. Then we will show how the SCI can be used in a gadfly synchronization interface and discuss the features of this SCI system. For the following discussion, assume X points to the I/O registers.

As with the M6850, the SCI has, at the same address, a pair of data registers that are connected to shift registers. Eight bits of the data written at $2F,X are put into the shift register and shifted out as in the M6850, and 8 bits of the data shifted into the receive shift register can be read at address $2F,X.

The clock rate is established by the BAUD register at $2B,X. Bits 5 and 4 should be 11; then the baud rate is $(9600 / 2^n)$ baud, where n is the number in bits 2 to 0. For example, to get 1200 baud, put $33 into the BAUD register.

The control 1 register (CR1) at $2C,X is used for an extension of the data registers and for wakeup and word length control. The data length may be 8 or 9 bits with 1 stop bit, as determined by bit 4 of CR1 (bit=1 means 9 bits are sent/received). The extra bit sent (T8) is bit 6 of CR1, and the extra bit received (R8) is bit 7 of CR1. The extra ($9th$) bit (bit 8) may be used for parity generation/detection in software, because that bit is sent where the parity bit is normally sent; it may also be used to distinguish between ordinary data and an address in the network level of the protocol; or it may be used to signal the beginning of a new sequence of characters. The latter two uses are related to the wakeup mechanism discussed soon.

The status register at $2E,X indicates what is happening in the transmitter and receiver. The leftmost 2 bits indicate the status of the transmitter. Bit 7 (Tdre) is 1 if the transmit data register is empty. Tdre is set when data are moved from the data register to the shift register. Bit 6 (Tc) is 1 if the transmit is complete; it is set at the end of sending a frame. Tdre and Tc are cleared by a read of the status register followed by a write into the data register. The remaining status bits are for the receiver. Bit 5 (Rdrf) is 1 if the receive data register is full because a frame has been received. Bit 4 (Idle) is set when the receive input line remains high (1) for longer than a full frame (10 or 11 bit times) unless the SCI system is asleep, as described soon. Receive error conditions are indicated by bits 3 to 1. Bit 3 (Or) is set when the receiver overruns; that is, a word has to be moved from the input shift register before the previously input word is read from the data register. Bit 2 (Nf) is set if the receiver detects a short positive or negative pulse, longer than 1/16 of a bit time but shorter than a bit time, on the receiver input. Bit 1(Fe) is 1 if there is a framing error; that is, a stop bit is expected but the line is low. The receiver status and error condition bits are cleared by reading the status and then the data registers. Bit 0 always reads as a 0.

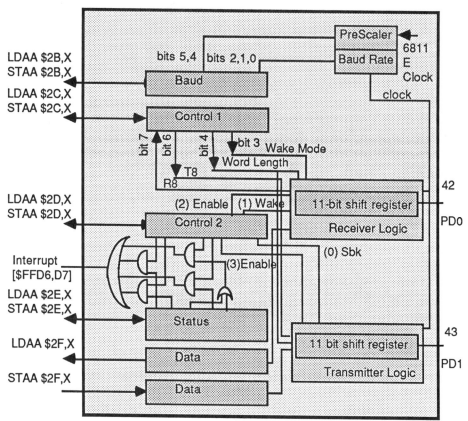

Figure 8-11. 6811 Serial Communication Interface

The leftmost 4 bits of the control 2 register at $2D,X contain interrupt enables for the first 5 status bits just described. Generally, each bit of the control 2 register is ANDed with the corresponding bit of the status register, except that the overrun indicator (Or) is ORed into the Rdrf indicator before being ANDed with bit 5 of the control 2 register. Bit 3 enables the transmitter and bit 2 enables the receiver, if they are 1. Writing a 1 into bit 0 sends a break (low) continuously, and writing 0 into bit 0 stops sending the break, but the break will last at least one frame time.

The SCI system in the 6811 has a wakeup feature. The receiver is put to sleep by setting bit 1 of the control 2 register to 1. The SCI ignores all incoming frames until it is wakened up, as if the receive enable, control 2 register bit 2, is cleared even though it is not. If bit 3 of the control 1 register is 0 and the receive input line remains high (1) for longer than a full frame (10 or 11 bit times), then the receiver is wakened up. Or if bit 3 of the control 1 register is 1 and a 1 is received in the ninth data bit, then the receiver is wakened up. Waking up permits interrupts, and if they are enabled, the interrupt handler will be able, if control 1 register bit 3 is 1, to read the data word with the ninth bit set.

The following initialization ritual will set the SCI for gadfly synchronization of 9600 baud and 8 data bits. As usual, we assume X points to the I/O register area.

```
INIT    LDD    #$300C    SET UP BOTH CONSTANTS FOR EFFICIENCY
        STAA   $2B,X     SET BAUD FOR 9600
        CLR    $2C,X     CLEAR WORD LENGTH BIT
        STAB   $2D,X     ENABLE TRANSMITTER AND RECEIVER
```

The routine to transmit a byte in ACCA is given here:

```
SEND    TST    $2E,X     WAIT FOR SIGN BIT OF STATUS REGISTER
        BPL    SEND      =1, TO INDICATE TRANS BUF IS AVAILABLE
        STAA   $2F,X     SEND THE DATA
```

The routine to receive a word into ACCA is equally simple:

```
GET     BRCLR  $2F,X $20 GET   WAIT FOR RDRF STATUS TO =1
        LDAA   $2F,X           GET DATA
```

The overwhelming advantage of the SCI system is that it is contained entirely within the 6811 chip. It is therefore free with the computer. The 9-bit data frame is not standard with other UART interfaces, but is very useful because the extra bit permits 8 bits of data to be sent with a separate flag bit that indicates, when it is 1, that there is something special about the other 8 bits. This can be used in the network and link levels of the protocol to indicate a network address or the beginning of a series of frames that belong together in a message. The break, being at least one frame length long, can also indicate a separation between frames. The wakeup feature permits a microcomputer to ignore messages on a line if it finds the first few frames after a break, or a frame with the ninth bit set to 1, are not for it. This can be used to cut down on the overhead due to interrupts on every received frame.

8-4 Other Protocols

Besides the UART protocol, the two most important protocols are the synchronous bit-oriented protocols that include the SDLC, HDLC and ADCCP, X-25, the IEEE-488 bus protocol, and the Smart Computer System Interface (SCSI) protocol.

These are important protocols. We fully expect that many if not most of your interfaces will be designed around these protocols. If you are designing an I/O device to be used with a large mainframe computer, you will probably have to interface to it using a synchronous bit-oriented protocol. If you are designing a laboratory instrument, you will probably interface to a minicomputer using the IEEE-488 protocol, so the minicomputer can remotely control your instrument. Motorola has two integrated circuits, the M6854 for the synchronous bit-oriented protocol and the M68488 for the IEEE-488 bus protocol.

These are complex protocols. The chips are correspondingly complex. The M6854 has four control registers - 32 control bits - to be initialized in a ritual to configure the device. It has two status registers - 16 bits - to be analyzed in an interrupt handler. The M68488 has six command/address/polling registers with a lot of rituals to control the bus, and seven status/address/polling registers to analyze. While a full discussion of these chips and the communications protocols is not in the scope of this book on I/O interfaces, this book gives you thorough basic information on the UART protocol and on the fairly challenging initialization rituals needed to configure the M6840, which should prepare you to handle more complex chips and protocols. We will survey the key ideas of these protocols in this section. The first subsection describes the bit-oriented protocols. The second subsection will discuss the 488 bus. The final subsection covers the SCSI interface.

8-4.1 Synchronous Bit-Oriented Protocols

Synchronous protocols are able to move a lot of data at a high rate. They are primarily used to communicate between *remote job entry* terminals (which have facilities to handle line printers, card readers, and plotters) and computers, and between computers and computers. The basic idea of a synchronous protocol is that a clock is sent either on a separate wire or along with the data in the Manchester coding scheme. Since a clock is sent with the data, there is little cause to fear that the receiver clock will eventually get out of sync after a lot of bits have been sent, so we are not restricted to short frames as we are in the UART. Once the receiver is synchronized, we will try to keep it in synchronism with the transmitter, and we can send long frames without sending extra control pulses, which are needed to resynchronize the receiver and which reduce the efficiency of the channel.

Asynchronous protocols, like the UART protocol discussed in the last section, are more useful if small amounts of data are generated at random times, such as by a computer terminal. Synchronous protocols would anyway have to get all receivers into synchronism with the transmitter when a new transmitter gets control of the channel, so their efficiency would be poor for short random messages. Synchronous protocols are more useful when a lot of data is sent at once because they do not require the overhead every few bits, such as start and stop bits, that asynchronous protocols need. Bit-oriented synchronous protocols were developed as a result of weaknesses in byte- or character-oriented synchronous protocols when they were used in sending a lot of data at once.

The precurser to the bit-oriented protocol is the binary synchronous *Bisync* protocol, which is primarily character-oriented and is extended to handle arbitrary binary data. This protocol can be used with the ASCII character set. The 32 non-printing ASCII characters include some that are used with the Bisync protocol to send sequences of characters. SYN - ASCII $16 is sent whenever nothing else is to be sent. It is a null character used to keep the receiver(s) synchronized to the transmitter. This character can be used to establish which bit in a stream of bits is the beginning of a character. Two Bisync protocols are used, one for sending character text and the other for sending binary data, such as machine code programs, binary numbers, and bit data.

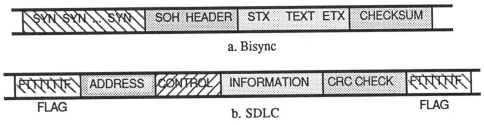

a. Bisync

b. SDLC

Figure 8-12. Synchronous Formats

Character text is sent as follows: A header can be sent; its purpose and format are user defined. It begins with the character SOH – ASCII $01. An arbitrary number of characters of text is sent after the character STX – ASCII $02, and is terminated by the character ETX – ASCII $03. After the ETX character, a kind of checksum is sent. (See figure 8-12a.)

To allow any data – such as a machine code program – including characters that happen to be identical to the character ETX, to be sent, a character DLE - ASCII $10 is sent before the characters STX and ETX. A byte count is established in some fashion. It may be fixed, so that all frames contain the same number of words, it may be sent in the header, or it may be sent in the first word or two words of the text itself. Whatever scheme is used to establish this byte count, it is used to disable the recognition of DLE-ETX characters that terminate the frame, so such patterns can be sent without confusing the receiver. This is called the *transparent mode* because the bits sent as text are transparent to the receiver controller and can be any pattern.

Bisync uses error correction or error detection and retry. The end of text is followed by a kind of checksum, which differs in differing Bisync protocols. One good error detection technique is to exclusive-OR the bytes that were sent, byte by byte. If characters have a parity bit, that bit can identify which byte is incorrect. The checksum is a parity byte that is computed "at 90 degrees" from the parity bits and can identify the column that has an error. If you know the column and the row, you know which bit is wrong, so you can correct it. Another Bisync protocol uses a *cyclic redundancy check* (CRC) that is based on the mathematical theory of error correcting codes. The error detecting "polynomial" $X^{**}16 + x^{**}15 + X^{**}2 + 1$, called the CRC-16 polynomial, is one of several good polynomials for detecting errors. The CRC check feeds the data sent out of the transmitter through a shift register that shifts bits from the $15th$ stage towards the $0th$ stage. The shift register is cleared, and the data bits to be transmitted are exclusive-ORed with the bit being shifted out of the $0th$ stage, and then is exclusive-ORed this bit into some of the bits being shifted in the register at the inputs to the $15th$, $13th$, and $0th$ stages. The original data and the contents of the shift register (called the CRC check bits) are transmitted to the receiver. The receiver puts the received data, including the CRC check bits, through the same hardware at its end. When done, the hardware should produce a 0 in the shift register. If it doesn't, an error (CRC error) has occurred. The Bisync protocol has means to request that the frame be sent over again if a CRC error is detected. If the frame is good, an ACK - ASCII $06 is sent, but if an error is detected a NAK - ASCII $15 is sent from the receiver back to the sender. If the sender gets an ACK, it can send the next frame, but if it gets a NAK, it should resend the current frame.

Though developed for communication between a computer and a single RJE station, Bisync has been expanded to include *multi-drop*. Several RJE stations are connected to a host computer on a half-duplex line (bus). The host is a master. It controls all transfers between it and the RJE stations. The master *polls* the stations periodically, just as we polled I/O devices after an interrupt, to see if any of them want service. In polling, the master sends a short packet to each station, so that each station can send back a short message as the master waits for the returned messages.

Bisync protocols have some serious shortcomings. It is set up for and is therefore limited to half-duplex transmission. After each frame is sent, you have to wait for the receiver to send back an acknowledge or a negative acknowledge. This causes the computer to stutter, as it waits for a message to be acknowledged. These shortcomings are improved in bit-oriented protocols. Features used for polling and multi-drop connections are improved. And the information is bit-oriented to efficiently handle characters, machine code programs, or variable width data.

The first significant synchronous bit-oriented protocol was the *Synchronous Data Link Control* (SDLC) protocol developed by IBM. The American National Standards Institute, ANSI, developed a similar protocol, ADCCP, and the CCITT developed another protocol, HDLC. They are all quite similar at the link control and physical levels, which we are studying. We will take a look at the SDLC link, the oldest and simplest of the bit-oriented protocols.

The basic SDLC frame is shown in figure 8-12b. If no data are sent, either a true bit is continually sent (idle condition) or a *flag* pattern, $7E (FTTTTTTF), is sent. The frame itself begins with a flag pattern and ends with a flag pattern, with no flag patterns inside. The flag pattern that ends one frame can be the same flag pattern that starts the next frame.

The frame can be guaranteed free of flag patterns by a five T's detector and F inserter. If the transmitter sees that five T's have been sent, it sends a F regardless of whether the next bit is going to be a T or a F. That way, the data FFTFFTTTTTTTF is sent as FFTFFTTTTTFTTF, and the data FFTFFTTTTTFTF is sent as FFTFFTTTTTFFTF, free of a flag pattern. The receiver looks for 5 T's. If the next bit is F, it is simply discarded. If the received bit pattern were FFTFFTTTTTFTTF, the F after the five T's is discarded to give FFTFFTTTTTTTF, and if FFTFFTTTTTFFTF is received, we get FFTFFTTTTTFTF. But if the received bit pattern were FTTTTTTF the receiver would recognize the flag pattern and end the frame.

The frame consists of an 8-bit station number address, for which the frame is sent, followed by 8 control bits. Any number of information bits are sent next, from 0 to as many as can be expected to be received comparatively free of errors or as many as can fit in the buffers in the transmitter and receiver. The CRC check bits are sent next. The address, control, information, and CRC check bits are free of flag patterns as a result of five T's detection and F insertion discussed above.

The control bits identify the frame as an *information frame*, or *supervisory* or *nonsequenced* frame. The information frame is the normal frame for sending a lot of data in the information field. The control field of an information frame has a 3-bit number N. The transmitter can send up to 8 frames, with different values of N, before handshaking is necessary to verify that the frames have arrived in the receiver. Like the ACK and NAK characters in Bisync, supervisory frames are used for retry after error. The receiver can send back the number N of a frame that has an error, requesting that it be resent, or it can send another kind of supervisory frame with N to indicate that all frames up to N have been received correctly. If the receiver happens to be sending other data back to the transmitter, it can send this number N in another field in the information frame it sends back to the transmitter of the original message to confirm receipt of all frames up to the N*th* frame, rather than sending an acknowledge supervisory frame. This feature improves efficiency, since most frames will be correctly received.

The SDLC link can be used with multi-drop (bus) networks, as well as with a ring network of the same structure as the GPC optical link (figure 8-4). The ring network permits a single main, *primary*, station to communicate with up to 255 other *secondary* stations. Communication is full duplex, since the primary can send to the secondary over part of the loop, while the secondary sends other data to the primary on the remainder of the loop. The SDLC has features for the primary to poll the secondary stations and for the transmitting station to abort a frame if something goes wrong.

The SDLC link and the other bit-oriented protocols provide significant improvements over the character-oriented Bisync protocols. Full-duplex communication, allowing up to 8 frames to be sent before they are acknowledged, permits more efficient communication. The communication is inherently transparent, because of the five T's detection feature, and can handle variable length bit data efficiently. It is an excellent protocol for moving large frames of data at a high rate of speed.

The *X.25* protocol is a three-level protocol established by the CCITT for high-volume data transmission. The physical and link levels are set up for the HDLC protocol, a variation of the SDLC bit-oriented protocol; but synchronous character-oriented protocols can be used so that the industry can grow into the X.25 protocol without scrapping everything. This protocol, moreover, specifies the network level as well. It is oriented to packet switching. Packet switching permits frames of a message to wander through a network on different paths. This dynamic allocation of links to messages permits more efficient use of the links, increases security (since a thief would have to watch the whole network to get the entire message) and enhances reliability. It looks like the communication protocol of the future. While we do not cover it in our discussion of I/O device design, we have been using its terminology throughout this chapter as much as possible.

8-4.2 IEEE-488 Bus Standard

The need to control instruments like voltmeters and signal generators in the laboratory or factory from a computer has led to another kind of protocol, an asynchronous byte-oriented protocol. One of the earliest such protocol was the CAMAC protocol developed by French nuclear scientists for their instruments. Hewlett-Packard, a major instrument manufacturer, developed a similar standard which was adopted by the IEEE and called the IEEE-488 standard. Although Hewlett-Packard owns patents on the handshake methods of this protocol, it has made the rights available on request to most instrument manufacturers, and the IEEE-488 is becoming available on most sophisticated instruments and minicomputers and microcomputers.

Communications to test equipment has some challenging problems. The communications link may be strung out in a different way each time a different experiment is run or a different test is performed. The lengths of the lines can vary. The instruments themselves do not have as much computational power as a large mainframe machine, or even a terminal, so the communications link has to do some work for them such as waiting to be sure that they have picked up the data. A number of instruments may have to be told to do something together, such as simultaneously generating and measuring signals, so they can't be told one at a time when to execute their operation. These characteristics lead to a different protocol for instrumentation busses.

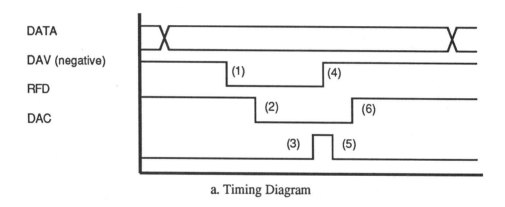

a. Timing Diagram

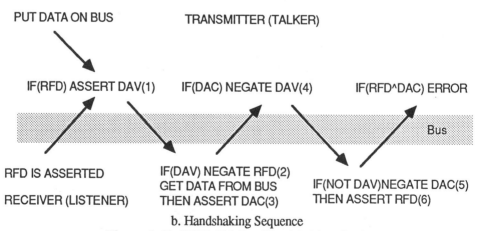

b. Handshaking Sequence

Figure 8-13. IEEE-488 Bus Handshaking Cycle

The IEEE-488 bus is fully specified at the physical and link levels. A 16-pin connector, somewhat like the RS232 connector, is prescribed by the standard, as are the functions of the 16 signals and 8 ground pins. The sixteen signal lines include an 8-bit parallel data bus, three handshaking lines, and five control lines. The control lines include one that behaves like the system reset line in the 6811 microcomputer. Others are used to get attention and perform other bus management functions. But the heart of the bus standard is the asynchronous protocol used to transmit data on the bus.

An asynchronous bus protocol uses a kind of expandable clock signal, which can be automatically stretched when the bus is longer or shortened if the bus is shorter. The way this happens is the "clock" is sent from the station transmitting the data to the station that receives the data on one line, then back to the transmitter on another line. The transmitter waits for the return signal before it begins another transmission. If the bus is lengthened, so are the delays of this "clock" signal. The IEEE-488 bus uses this principle a couple of times to reliably move a word on an 8-bit bus from a transmitter to a receiver. (See figure 8-13.)

The handshake cycle is like a clock cycle. Each time a word is to be moved, the bus goes through a handshake cycle to move the word, as shown in figure 8-13. The cycle involves (negative logic) *data available* (DAV), sent by the transmitter of the data, and (positive logic) *ready for data* (RFD) and (positive logic) *data accepted* (DAC), sent by the receiver of the data.

If the receiver is able to take data, it has already asserted RFD (high). When the transmitter wants to send a data word, it first puts the word on the bus, and then begins the handshake cycle. It checks for the RFD signal. If it is asserted at the transmitter, the transmitter asserts DAV (low) to indicate the data are available. This is step 1 in figures 8-13a and 8-13b. When the receiver sees DAV asserted, it negates RFD (low) in step 2 because it is no longer ready for data. When the processor picks up the data from the interface, the receiver asserts DAC (high) to indicate data are accepted. This is step 3. When the transmitter sees DAC asserted, it negates DAV (high) in step 4 because it will soon stop sending data on the data bus. When the receiver sees DAV negated, it negates DAC in step 5. The data are removed sometime after the DAV has become negated. When it is ready to accept new data, it asserts RFD (high) in step 6 to begin a new handshake cycle.

The IEEE-488 bus is designed for some special problems in bussing data to and from instruments. First, the bus is asynchronous. If the receiver is far away and the data will take a long time to get to it, the DAV signal will also take a long time, and the other handshake signals will be similarly delayed. So, long cables are automatically accounted for by the handshake mechanism. Second, the instrument at the receiver may be slow or just busy when the data arrive. DAC is asserted as soon as the data get into the interface, to inform the transmitter that they got there; but RFD is asserted as soon as the instrument gets the data from the interface, so the interface won't get an overrun error that a UART can get. Third, although only one station transmits a word in any handshake cycle, a number of stations can be transmitters at one time or another. Fourth, the same word can be sent to more than one receiver, and the handshaking should be able to make sure all receivers get the word. These last two problems are solved using open collector bus lines for DAV, RFD, and DAC. DAC, sent by the transmitter, is negative logic so the line is wire-OR. That way , if any transmitter wants to send data, it can short the line low to assert DAV. RFD and DAC, on the other hand, are positive logic signals so the line is a wire-AND bus. RFD is high only if all receivers are ready for data, and DAC is high only when all receivers have accepted data.

The IEEE-488 bus is well suited to remote control of instrumentation and is becoming available on much of the instruments being designed at this time. You will probably see a lot of the IEEE-488 bus in your design experiences.

8-4.3 The Smart Computer System Interface (SCSI)

The microcomputer has made the intelligent I/O device economical. In a lot of systems today, a personal computer communicates with a printer that has a microcomputer to control it, or a disk that has its own microcomputer. Communications between a personal computer and the intelligent I/O device can be improved with an interface protocol specially designed for this application. The *Smart Computer System Interface (SCSI)* is designed for communications between personal computers and intelligent I/O devices.

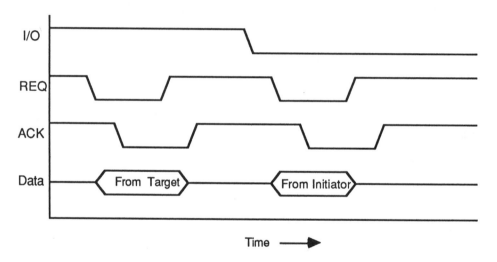

Figure 8-14. SCSI Timing

The asynchronous protocol is quite similar to the IEEE-488 bus, having a 9-bit (8 data plus parity) parallel bus, a handshake protocol involving a direction signal (I/O), a request (REQ), and an acknowledge (ACK). (See figure 8-14.) (There are also six other control signals, and the interface uses a 50-pin connector.) Up to eight bus controllers can be on an SCSI bus, and they may be *initiators* (processors) or *targets* (disk drives). A priority circuit assures that two initiators will not try to use the SCSI bus at the same time. After an initiator acquires the bus, a command stage is entered. The 10-byte command packet selects a target controller and is capable of specifying the reading or writing of up to 256 bytes of data on up to a 1024-gigabyte disk. After the command packet is sent, data are transferred between the initiator and target.

Each command or data byte is transferred using the direction, request, and acknowledge signals. The direction (I/O) signal is low when the requestor wishes to write a command or data into the target, and high when it wants data. Whether the requestor is sending data or a command, or receiving data, it drops the request line (REQ) low; and puts the data or command on the nine-bit parallel bus if sending them. If the target is to receive the data, it picks up the data and drops the acknowledge signal (ACK) low. If the target is to send the data, it puts the data on the bus and drops the acknowledge signal (ACK) low. When the initiator sees the ACK line low, it raises REQ, and if it is receiving data, it picks up the data from the data bus. When the target sees REQ high, it raises ACK high so the next transfer can take place. Up to 1.5 megabytes per second can be transferred on an SCSI bus this way.

The SCSI bus is specially designed for communication between a small but powerful computer like a personal computer, and an intelligent I/O device. Many systems that you build may fit this specification and thus may use an SCSI interface.

8-5 Conclusions

Communication systems are among the most important I/O systems in a microcomputer. The microcomputer communicates with keyboards, displays, and typewriters, as well as with remote control stations and other microcomputers, using the UART protocol. The microcomputer can be in a large computer system and have to communicate with other parts of the system using the SDLC protocol. It may be in a laboratory and have to communicate with instrumentation on an IEEE-488 bus. It may have to talk with other systems in a different protocol.

If you would like additional reading, we recommend the excellent *Technical Aspects of Data Communication,* by John McNamara, Digital Equipment Corporation (DEC). It embodies an exceptional amount of practical information, especially at the physical level, and also covers many of the widely used protocols. Motorola offers some fine applications notes on the SDLC protocol and its 6854 chip, such as *MC6854 ADLC, An Introduction to Data Communication,* by M. Neumann. For the IEEE-488 protocol using the 68488 chip, the applications note *Getting Aboard the 488-1975 Bus,* is very informative. These applications notes are well written and take you from where this book leaves off to where you can design systems using these protocols.

For more concrete information on the 68HC11, please consult the *MC68HC11A8 HCMOS Single-Chip Microcomputer (ADI 1207).* In particular, section 5 describes the serial communication interface. As noted earlier, we have not attempted to duplicate the diagrams and discussions in that book because we assume you will refer to it while reading this book, and since we present an alternative view of the subject, you can use either or both views.

This chapter covered the main concepts of communication systems at the physical and link control levels. You should be aware of these concepts so you can understand the problems and capabilities of specialists in this field. You should be able to handle the UART protocol – the simplest and most widely used protocol – and its variations, and you should be able to use the SCI system in the 6811 and the M6850 chip, as well as the UART, in hardware designs. You should be able to write initialization rituals, interrupt handlers, and gadfly routines to input or output data using such hardware. Hardware and software tools like these should serve most of your design needs and prepare you for designing with the SDLC, IEEE-488, or SCSI interface protocol systems.

Problems

Problem 1 is a paragraph correction problem; for guidelines, see the problems at the end of chapter 1. The guidelines for software problems are given at the end of chapter 2, and those for hardware problems are at the end of chapter 3. Special guidelines for problems using the 6811 counter/timer modules and M6840 counter/timer chip are presented at the end of chapter 7.

1.* To avoid any ambiguity, the peer-to-peer interfaces in communications systems are specified in terms of all lower level interfaces. The physical level, which is at the lowest level, is concerned with the transmission of signals such as voltage levels, with multiplexing schemes, and with the clocking of data if the clock must be sent with the data or on a separate line. The baud rate is the number of bytes of user data that can be sent per second. A channel is a data path between entities at the link control level. It is half duplex if every other bit is a data bit and the remainder are clock bits. Protocols are conventions used to manage the transmission and reception of data at the link control level and to negotiate for and direct communications at the network level. A handshake protocol is one in which congratulations are extended whenever a frame is correctly sent, but the receiver is silent if the data don't look correct. A store-and-forward network is one that sends frames, called packets, from node to node and stores a frame in a node before negotiating to send it to the next node closer to its destination. The bus is a particularly common half-duplex store-and-foreward network.

2. Design a 1-bit input/output port using the SN75119 differential transceiver that is connected to a full-duplex differential line. Reading port C bit 7 will read the input data, and writing bit 6 will output that signal for 2 cycles (1 μsec) after the MC68HC11A8 writes in the output register.

3. Design a differential line transmitter using two CA3140s. Both lines should be driven with the low impedance outputs of the OP AMPs. Design a differential line receiver using a CA3140. In both designs, show all pin numbers and component values.

4. Design an RS232-C level translator to drive an RS232-C line from a TTL level using a CA3140. Design a level translator to provide a TTL level output from an RS232-C line using a CA3140. In both designs, show all pin numbers and component values.

5. A "null modem" is a simple module permitting an RS232-C plug from one computer to connect to an RS232-C plug from another computer that has the same connections. Suppose the computer uses only transmitted and received data, request to send, data set ready, and signal ground. Show connections between the two sockets in the "null modem" that can correctly interconnect the two computers so that each looks like a terminal to the other.

6. The 6811 output compare module 2 and Johnson counter of figure 7-5 can generate the frequencies, and the 6811 input capture 1 module, after appropriate filtering, can

detect the frequencies for frequency shift keyed data transmission on the telephone. A signal will be recognized if its period is within five percent of the period the receiver should be getting for at least 10 cycles. Show a gadfly program (including initialization ritual) that will implement the handshaking sequence of figure 8-3, supplying the data and ANS commands and monitoring the RI status of the data coupler:

a. in the originate modem, assuming that ANS is the MSB of port C.

b. in the answer modem, assuming RI is able to be read as the second most significant bit of port C and ANS is the third most significant bit of port C.

7. Give the logic diagram of a round-robin priority circuit (section 4-2.2) using the GPC link (figure 8-4). Use gates in the 74HC series. Each module has a request input R and a grant flip-flop G, and all are clocked with a common clock. The modules have no other connections between them. In each clock cycle, the request is determinate for the whole clock cycle, and at the end of the cycle the grant is determined to be put in the G flip-flop for the next cycle. The module that gets a grant, setting G, becomes the lowest priority module. (Hint: use negative logic to inhibit the signal on the output of the module in figure 8-4.)

8. Design a modified Pierce loop using a GPC link and the 6811 SPI module. A Pierce loop is a big shift register, with, say, 8 bits of the shift register in each module (computer). Data circulate in the register synchronously. A frame consists of a 3-bit source address, a 3-bit destination address, and a 2-bit data field. One module sends data to another by putting the address of the destination first, then the address of the module sending the data, and then the data, in a frame. When a frame is entirely in a shift register in a module, all modules will have a frame in them, and we say the data is framed. When the frame shifts by the destination module, the data are taken from the frame. In a modification of this protocol, the 8-bit segments of the shift register are initially bypassed so the loop appears to be a short-circuited wire. A module desiring to transmit a frame inserts its part of the shift register – with the frame in it – into the loop and lets this be shifted out when the data are framed. As the frame passes the destination, the destination copies it, but lets it go around the loop. When the frame gets back into the sender and the data are framed, the sender takes the shift register out of the loop. In the 6811, the SPI module requires one microcomputer to supply the clock for the Pierce loop, and that microcomputer is the "master"; the others are all "slaves."

a. Design a module using the SPI module to shift the data and using port C bit 7 to control the P signal of a GPC link, so the GPC can insert the frame. Assume the SPI data and SPI clock are sent on identical nets, and show the logic for one net. Use standard 74HC chips, and show all pin connections between the MC68HC11A8 and GPC gates.

b. Write a gadfly program (including initialization ritual) to output the word in accummualtor A, assuming it is already formatted as a frame. Show the entire program, including initialization rituals, for both the master and slave 6811s.

9. Write a program to input and output UART signals using the 6811 output compare 1 module to time the samples. The most significant bit of port C is an input bit from and bit 6 of that port is an output bit to the serial communications link.

a. Initialize the output compare 1 module for 110 baud rate, to request an interrupt each 1/110 second, and initialize the output compare 2 module to request an interrupt every 1/1760 second for part of this problem.

b. Write a device handler to send the word in global variable URTOUT. Use a global variable TCKOUT to count the occurrences of interrupts and thus keep track of the timing. On each interrupt from output compare 1, send one bit through port C, but when the word is sent, send stop bits on each interrupt.

c. Write a device handler to receive a word from the input register into global variable UARTIN. On each interrupt from output compare 2 module, check the input. First check for a start bit; 8 interrupts later, check the start bit; and every 16 interrupts thereafter, get another bit from the input port. Use a global variable TICKIN to count the number of interrupts and sequence the sampling of the input signal.

10. Show a logic diagram of an I/O device using an IM6403 connected to an MC68HC11A8. Use completely specified decoding, so the transmit buffer is at location $8000, the receive buffer at $8001, the control register at $8002 and the OE, FE, PE, DR, and TBRE status bits can be read at location $8003. Connect control and status so that the lower-numbered pins on the IM6403 are connected to lower-numbered data bits for each I/O word, and use the lower-number data bits if fewer than 8 bits are to be connected. Show all pin connections to the MC68HC11A8 and the IM6403, and show the address decoder using standard 74HC gates.

11. Show the logic diagram of a remote station that uses an IM6403 UART and a 74HC259 addressable latch so that when the number $I + 2N$ is sent, latch N is loaded with the bit I. Be careful about the timing of DR and DRR signals, and the G clock for the 74HC259.

12. Show initialization rituals to initialize the M6850 for the following:
   a. 8 data, 2 stop bits, divide clock by 1, all interrupts disabled, RTS high.
   b. 7 data, even parity, 2 stop bits, divide clock by 16, enable only receiver interrupt, RTS low.
   c. 8 data, 1 stop bit, divide clock by 16, only transmitter interrupt enabled.
   d. 7 data, even parity, 1 stop bit, divide clock by 64, all interrupts enabled.
   e. 7 data, even parity, 2 stop bits, clock divide by 1, interrupts disabled, RTS low.

13. Write a simple M6850 word-oriented teletype handler, using the gadfly synchronization technique. The M6850 is at locations $8000 and $8001.
   a. Write the initialization routine for parts b and c. Use 7 data, odd parity, and 2 stop bits, and divide the clock by 16.
   b. Write a subroutine OUTCH to output the character in accumulator A. If the device is busy, wait in OUTCH until the word can be output.
   c. Write a subroutine INCH to input a character into accumulator A. If no character has arrived yet, wait in INCH until it comes.

14. Write an M6850 background teletype handler. The purpose of this handler is to feed characters to the slow teletype using the interrupt synchronization technique so you can continue working with the computer as the printing is being done. A $100 word queue contains characters yet to be printed. Part b will fill this queue when your program is ready to print something, but the interrupt handler in part c will pull words from the queue as they are sent through the M6850.

   •   a. Write the initialization routine to configure the M6850 for 7 data, even parity, and 1 stop bit, dividing the clock by 16, and to initialize in global memory the pointers and counter for the queue.

        b. Write a subroutine OUTFL that will, starting at address ADDR, output N words by first pushing them on the queue (if the queue is not full) so they can be output by the handler in part c. If the queue is full, wait in OUTFL until it has room for all words.

        c. Write a device handler that will pull a word from the queue and output it, but if the queue is empty it will output a SYNC character ($16).

15. A stereo can be remotely controlled using an M14469. Show the logic diagrams, including pin numbers, HCMOS circuits, and component values, for the following:

        a. A single volume control, whose volume is set by sending a 7-bit unsigned binary number to the M14469 with address $01, using the duty cycle control technique (figure 6-12b).

        b. A source and mode selector, whose source and mode are set by sending a 4-bit code to the M14469 with address $02. Use the select hardware in figure 6-11.

16. Consult the *MC68HC11A8 HCMOS Single-Chip Microcomputer*, section 5, and show initialization rituals to initialize the 6811 SCI module (using an 8-MHz clock crystal) for

        a. 8 data, 1 stop bit, 9600 baud, all interrupts disabled, enable receiver and transmitter.

        b. 9 data, 1 stop bit, 300 baud, enable only receiver interrupt, enable receiver and transmitter.

        c. 8 data, 1 stop bit, 9600 baud, all interrupts disabled, enable transmitter only, send break.

        d. As in part a, but interrupt (wake up) when the line is idle.

        e. As in part a, using a 4.9152-MHz clock crystal.

17. Write a simple 6811 SCI word-oriented teletype handler, using the gadfly synchronization technique as in problem 8-13. Write the initialization routine, OUTCH, and INCH.

18. Write a 6811 SCI background teletype handler, as in problem 8-14.

        a. Write the initialization routine, as in problem 8-14a.

        b. Write a subroutine OUTFL, as in problem 8-14b.

        c. Write a device handler, as in problem 8-14c.

19. Write a Newhall loop routine, using gadfly synchronization and a 6811 SCI. A Newhall loop is a ring of modules (microcomputers) in which messages are sent from one module to the next in the loop. The message contains a 1-word address to which the message is to be sent, a 1-byte word count of the number of words left in the message, and the data words in the message. The number of words is less than $100. Each module will input all the words of a message to a buffer first, then check the address, and if the address is not the address of this module, the message is sent to the next module in the ring. Show the routine that will move a message through the loop but, if the address is $05, will jump to a routine MYMSG to do something with the message.

20. Write a routine, using a gadfly loop to find the SYNC character and real-time synchronization to pick up the first word of the text that is sent in Bisync after the STX character. Assume the data are sent at 100 baud and the clock is not sent with the data. Data arrive in the least significant bit, and are output in the second LSB, of port C.

21. Write a gadfly routine to receive bits and compute the CRC check value for the polynomial $X**16 + X**15 + X**2 + 1$. Data arrive in the LSB, and the clock arrives in the MSB, of port C. Data are determinate when the clock rises from F to T.

22. Write a real-time routine to output the stream of data bits in buffer OUTBUF, most significant bit of lowest-addressed word first, checking for five T's and inserting F, as in the SDLC protocol. Send the data at 100 baud using the output compare 2 module to time the bits. Data are sent in the least significant bit, and the clock is sent in the second least significant bit, of port C.

23. Write a gadfly routine to handshake on the IEEE-488 bus. Data can be read or written in port C, and DAV, RFD, and DAC are the 3 least significant bits of port D.
   a. Show a routine to initialize the ports, send a word in accumulator A, and perform the handshake for a transmitter (talker)
   b. Show a routine to initialize the ports, perform the handshake, and get the received word into accumulator A for a receiver (listener).

24. Write a gadfly routine to handshake on the SCSI bus. Data can be read or written in port C and I/O, REQ, and ACK are the 3 least significant bits of port D. Show a routine to initialize the ports and:
   a. send a word in accumulator A, and perform the handshake for an initiator.
   b. perform the handshake, and get the received word into ACCA for a target.
   c. send a word in accumulator A, and perform the handshake for a target.
   d. perform the handshake, and get the received word into accumulator A for an initiator.

9

Storage and Display Systems

The previous chapter discussed the techniques by which microcomputers can communicate with other computers. They may also have to communicate with humans, using LED or LCD displays covered in chapter 6 or using more complex CRT displays. We now cover CRT display technology. Also, a microcomputer may have to store data on a magnetic tape or disk. This stored data can be used by the microcomputer later, or it may be moved to another computer. Thus, on an abstract level, a magnetic storage medium can be an alternative to an electronic communication link.

This chapter covers both the CRT display and the magnetic storage device. We discuss the storage systems first and then the display systems. In each case, we will use a single-chip 6811 alone to implement a primitive device and then use special chips to implement a more realistic device. First using the surprisingly powerful 6811 alone lets us show the principles of these devices and allows you the opportunity to experiment with them without much expense. However, the special purpose chips are quite easy to use and are likely to be designed into real systems.

In this chapter, we spend quite a bit of time on the details of video and disk formats. We also present some rather larger system designs and refer to earlier discussions for many concepts. We have somewhat less space for the important notion of top-down design than in previous chapters because the design alternatives for CRT and disk systems are a bit too unwieldly to include in this short chapter. They are important, nevertheless, and are covered in problems at the end of the chapter.

Upon completing this final chapter, you should be able to implement an audio cassette interface. The audio cassette interface can be used to record and play back data for a microcomputer, or use it to move data to or form it from or to another computer. You should have gained enough information to understand the 5 1/4" double density floppy disk and you should be able to use a floppy disk controller chip to record and play back data for a microcomputer, or use it to move data to or form it from or to another computer. You should have gained enough information to understand the format of the black-and-white NTSC television signal and implement a primitive CRT display with the 6811 alone. You should be able to use a more realistic CRT controller chip set with the 6811 to implement a system capable of being a "dumb" terminal. Moreover, you will see a number of fairly complete complete designs similar to those you will build.

9-1 Storage Systems

Most microcomputers require either a communications system to move data into and out of them or a storage system to get data from or to save data in. The latter, called secondary storage, generally uses some form of magnetic medium. There are four useful alternatives for secondary storage. Audio cassette tape is the least costly storage system. It might be usable in storing some data in low cost systems, such as a weather monitor. Paper tape, discussed in chapter 5, is generally more suitable for industrial monitoring and control systems, especially in environments hostile to computers; and floppy disk systems have become so cheap that they are more likely to be used in most small systems and inexpensive personal computers. Finally, hard disks provide larger and better storage for professional personal computers and word processors.

This section describes techniques for data storage on cassette tapes and floppy disks. Using a single-chip 6811 with very little external logic, we illustrate the concepts with a simple audio cassette tape interface because it is easiest to implement. Then we discuss a floppy disk format. Finally, we will use a Western Digital 1772 chip, which is particularly easy to interface to the 6811, to show a floppy disk interface.

9-1.1 Cassette Storage

The personal computer market engendered the need to share software using inexpensive, readily available hardware for storage and transportation of data. The audio cassette tape recorder provided the best means for doing this. The main problem with this secondary storage device is its limited bandwidth. It is capable of storing data at a transmission rate of up to 2500 Baud. The higher rates require more care in processing because a small noise pulse in the tape might cause loss of data. A lower Baud rate is easier to handle. An audio cassette might be suitable for the collection of data at remote locations, from which the data are manually transported to where they are read and analyzed.

Table 9-1. Kansas City Standard Cassette Tape Format

Bit Transmission
A true T (mark) is eight cycles of a 2400-Hertz sine wave. A false F (space) is four cycles of a 1200-Hertz sine wave.
Character Format
A character is sent (left to right) FDDDDDDDDTT where D is a data bit (T or F), sent least significant bit first.
Record Format
A record is five seconds of T, followed by any number of characters. Characters can be separated by any number of T's

To exchange information, a standard format was defined by a convention, brought about by *Byte* magazine, that was held at Kansas City and thus was called the "Kansas

City Standard." The standard was set up so that even the slowest microcomputers, like the Intel 8008, could keep up with the data rate and even the cheapest cassette recorders could be used. (However, one has to use good cassette tapes to record data reliably.) Its essential features are listed in table 9-1.

The standard is clearly a refinement of a 300-baud UART protocol introduced in the last chapter, with further specification of the frequency shift keying at the physical level of the protocol. Magnetic storage formats are very strongly related to communication protocols.

The hardware of an interface to an audio cassette recorder that records information and reads it back is very simple. (See figure 9-1.) We present the output routine first because it uses a simple gadfly synchronization mechanism and because you can experiment with it to verify that it is working. After you get it working, you can prepare a tape to be read by the input routine. That routine uses interrupts and is a bit more difficult to understand. However, it uses concepts you are already familiar with and, once you get the output routine working, you'll also enjoy getting the input routine to work.

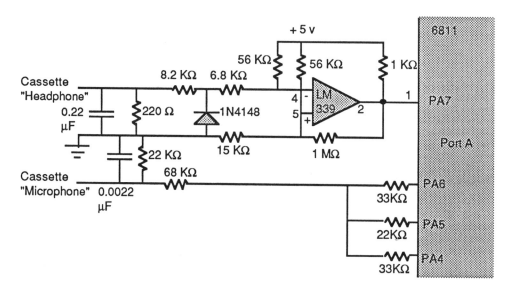

Figure 9-1. Cassette Interface Circuit

In developing an effective output routine, the main problem is generating eight cycles of a 2400-Hertz sine wave or four cycles of a 1200-Hertz sine wave. The exact frequency is not critical since the tape recorder will introduce up to ten percent frequency variation, but the shape of the waveform should be sinusoidal, with low harmonic and net DC component content. From section 7-2.1, we saw how easily the counter/timer system with one compare output module and Johnson counter can generate a sine wave. We will be able to emulate the Johnson counter in software, using a 3-parallel-bit output register. The output compare module is used with gadfly synchronization to time the changes in the output pattern, but the hardware output of the compare module is not used to generate pulses. This is quite a bit easier than real-time programming, since we do not have to count memory cycles and maintain a logically correct program while at the same time maintaining an accurate time delay. It is easier than interrupts because we are not as exposed to random events.

The main routine shown soon, beginning at label START, outputs the "leader" format of 5 seconds of 2400-Hz tone as required by the format, and outputs all 10 bytes in the buffer LIST. The subroutine WORDOUT is basically the same as the UART output routine SUART of section 8-3.1, with no parity and 1 stop bit. The subroutines OUT0 and OUT1 (which are entry points into the same routine that initializes BSIZE and index register X differently) send a 0 bit and a 1 bit respectively. The output part of this routine, beginning with LSL PATTERN and ending with STAA $1000, simulates a Johnson counter in software. The latter part of this subroutine sets up the output compare 2 register to set the "done" flag bit for it after a number of cycles specified by BSIZE, and the first part of this subroutine waits for this "done" flag bit to become set. This loop is repeated a number of times specified by index register X.

```
            NAM   KCOUT
            ORG   0
WORD        RMB   1          HOLDS WORD BEING OUTPUT
COUNT       RMB   1          COUNTS BITS BEING OUTPUT
BSIZE       RMB   2          LENGTH OF BIT CYCLE
PATTERN     RMB   1          SOFTWARE JOHNSON COUNTER
LIST        RMB   10         OUTPUT BUFFER
LISTEND     RMB   0          END OF BUFFER
LENGTH      EQU   LISTEND-LIST
*
            ORG   $C000
START       CLR   PATTERN    SOFTWARE JOHNSON COUNTER
LOOP        LDY   #300*5     5 SECONDS OF T
LOOP1       BSR   OUT1       OUTPUT ONES
            DEY
            BNE   LOOP1
            LDX   #LIST      NOW SEND LIST
            LDY   #LENGTH    OF GIVEN LENGTH
LOOP2       LDAA  0,X        GET A CHARACTER
            INX
            PSHX             SAVE POINTER
            BSR   WORDOUT    SEND A WORD
            PULX             RESTORE POINTER
            DEY              COUNT DOWN NUMBER OF WORDS
            BNE   LOOP2      UNTIL ALL ARE OUT
            . . .            TO NEXT ACTIVITY
*
WORDOUT     STAA  WORD
            BSR   OUT0       SEND START
            LDAA  #8         8 DATA
            STAA  COUNT      TEMPORARY BIT COUNTER
```

```
WORD1    ROR    WORD        GET A BIT
         BCC    WORD2       IF ONE
         BSR    OUT1        SEND ONE
         BRA    WORD3
WORD2    BSR    OUT0        ELSE SEND ZERO
WORD3    DEC    COUNT
         BNE    WORD1
         BSR    OUT1        SEND STOP
         BSR    OUT1        SEND STOP
         RTS
*
OUT0     LDX    #207        DELAY FOR 1200 HZ
         STX    BSIZE
         LDX    #8*4        SET UP FOR 4 CYCLES
         BRA    OUT11
*
OUT1     LDX    #104        DELAY FOR 2400 HZ
         STX    BSIZE
         LDX    #8*8        SET UP FOR 8 CYCLES
OUT11    LDAA   #$40        GENERATE A 1 IN BIT 6
OUT12    BITA   $1023       CHECK FOR COMPLETE DELAY
         BEQ    OUT12       IF ZERO, NOT DONE
         STAA   $1023       ELSE DONE: CLEAR "DONE" FLAG
         LSL    PATTERN     GET MSB BIT OUT INTO CARRY
         ADCA   #$FF        INVERT CARRY BIT, FILL ACCA
         ANDA   #$10        JUST KEEP BIT 4
         ADDA   PATTERN     COMBINE WITH PATTERN
         STAA   PATTERN     AND SAVE
         STAA   $1000       PUT IN PORT A OUTPUT
         LDD    $1018       GET CURRENT "TIME"
         ADDD   BSIZE       ADD DELAY
         STD    $1018       PUT IT IN OUTPUT COMPARE 2
         DEX                COUNT DOWN 8 CYCLES
         BNE    OUT11
         RTS
```

The input interface is a bit more involved, but it uses concepts that we have covered. (See figure 9-2.) There is a hierarchy of hardware and software components that process the incoming signal and generate the data, where each higher (outer) module "calls up" the next lower module multiple times. At the lowest level, signal conditioning and threshold detection are done using an analog comparator with hysteresis, following the techniques discussed in section 6-2.2. The input capture hardware in the 6811 is used to determine the period of each cycle, and a bit is stored if the cycle is that for a T or an F in the format that follows the period measurement techniques in section 7-3.2. This is synchronized by means of interrupts so that the period of each cycle is converted to a bit in real time while other processing is done.

Meanwhile, an output compare module of the 6811 is used to generate real-time interrupts (as discussed in section 7-2.3) that sample this bit stored in memory in the middle of the bit period of the UART frame, somewhat as in the RUART program in section 8-3.1. The first occurrence of an F (1200-Hz cycle) is detected in the input capture interrupt handler that initiates the sampling of the bit periods by the output compare interrupt handler. The latter handler counts bits and assembles the received word. It also puts the word into the buffer LIST. The main program waits in a gadfly loop for this buffer to become full, before going on.

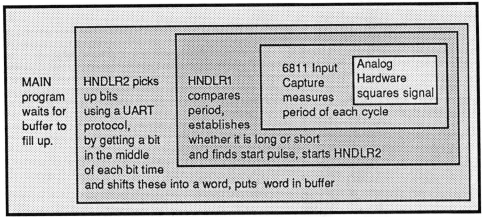

Figure 9.2 The Hierarchy of Hardware and Interrupt Software

The input routine is shown next. The input capture interrupt is enabled to look for the start pulse. Then the buffer variables are initialized and it gadflies on the buffer pointer POINT. When the buffer is full, the input capture interrupt is disabled and the next activity is begun. The input capture interrupt handler HNDLR1 resets the hardware for the next interrupt, then gets the input capture value and determines the elapsed time from the last edge to get the period. It compares this with a number that is midway between the period for a 2400- and a 1200-Hz cycle and stores the bit result in BITS. Also, BCOUNT is used for counting bits received by the output compare handler.

```
             NAM    KCIN
THRES        EQU    8*152       A THRESHOLD FOR COMPARISON
             ORG    0
POINT        RMB    2           POINTER FOR INPUT BUFFER
TEMP         RMB    2           LOCAL VARIABLE FOR HANDLER
BCOUNT       RMB    1           NUMBER OF BITS PROCESSED
BITS         RMB    1           COLLECTOR OF BITS
WORD         RMB    1           COLLECTOR OF A WORD
ERRCT        RM     1           ERROR COUNT
LIST         RMB    10          BUFFER
LISTEND      RMB    0
             ORG    $C000
```

```
            LDAA   #$10
            STAA   $1021      SET TO CAPTURE ON RISING EDGE
            LDAA   #4
            STAA   $1022      ENABLE INTERRUPTS
            STAA   $1023      CLEAR FLAG
            CLR    BCOUNT     INDICATE NO BITS RECEIVED
            LDX    #LIST
            STX    POINT      SET UP POINTER
            LDX    #LISTEND   SET UP FOR COMPARE
            CLI
L3          CPX    POINT      CHECK IF MOVED
            BNE    L3
            CLR    $1022      STOP INPUT CAPTURE INTERRUPTS
            . . .             TO NEXT ACTIVITY
*
HNDLR1      LDAA   #4         ASSUME ADDRESS HNDLR1 IN $FFEE,EF
            STAA   $1023      CLEAR FLAG
            LDD    $1010
            PSHB              COPY TO
            PSHA              STACK
            SUBD   TEMP       SET DIFFERENCE
            PULX              RECOVER
            STX    TEMP       SAVE FOR NEXT COMPARE
            CMPD   #THRES     SEE IF HIGH FREQUENCY (C=1)
            TPA               SAVE CARRY
            ROL    BITS       IN LSB OF BITS
            TAP               RECOVER CARRY
            BCS    HNDLRX     IF HIGH, EXIT
            LDAB   BCOUNT     IF NO DATA BITS SO FAR
            BNE    HNDLRX
            INC    BCOUNT     SET COUNTER TO COLLECT BITS
            LDAA   #$44       ENABLE INTERRUPTS
            STAA   $1022      FOR OUT COMPARE 2 AND IN CAPTURE 1
            LDD    $100E      GET CURRENT "TIME"
            ADDD   #1666      ADD (1/300) / 2 SEC DELAY TO
            STD    $1018      PUT IT IN OUTPUT COMPARE 2 REG
HNDLRX      RTI
*
HNDLR2      LDAA   #$40       ASSUME ADDRESS HNDLR2 IN $FFE6, E7
            STAA   $1023      CLEAR FLAG
            LDD    $1018      GET TIME OF LAST EDGE
            ADDD   #3333      ADD (1/300) SEC DELAY TO IT
            STD    $1018      PUT IT IN OUTPUT COMPARE 2 REG
            LDAA   BCOUNT     GET COUNT OF # OF BITS PROCESSED
            BEQ    BAD        IF ZERO, THIS IS AN ERROR: STOP
            CMPA   #1         IF 1, THIS IS IN THE MIDDLE OF START
```

```
          BEQ    STARTB
          CMPA   #9          IF HIGHER THAN 9
          BCC    STOPB       THIS IS A STOP BIT: CONFIRM IT IS HIGH
          LSR    BITS        ELSE THIS IS DATA: GET CURRENT BIT
          ROR    WORD        SHIFT INTO WORD
NXT       INC    BCOUNT      COUNT UP RECEIVED BITS
          RTI
STARTB    BRSET  BITS 1      GOOD CONFIRM THIS IS A START
          BRA    NXT         IF IT IS, JUST EXIT; ELSE RESTART
STOPB     BRCLR  BITS 1 BAD CONFM IT IS A STOP
          LDAA   WORD        IT IS; COLLECT WORD
          LDX    POINT       PUT IT IN A BUFFER
          STAA   0,X
          INX
          STX    POINT
          BRA    GOOD
BAD       INC    ERRCT       BUMP ERROR COUNT
GOOD      CLR    BCOUNT      THIS RESETS TO LOOK FOR START BIT
          LDAA   #4          ENABLE ONLY INPUT CAPTURE 1
          STAA   $1022       INTERRUPT
          RTI
```

If BCOUNT is 0, then we are waiting for a start bit, and if a 1200-Hz period is then detected, the output compare hardware is initialized. The output compare handler will be entered next when the signal is expected to be in the middle of a start pulse. If so, we continue; otherwise we reset the input interface to begin looking for a start pulse again. When successive output compare interrupts are handled, data bits from BITS are shifted into WORD; and when the stop bit is received, WORD is put into the buffer LIST. This is the hierarchy of hardware and software components that process the incoming signal and generate the data.

9-1.2 Floppy Disk Format

We now describe the 5 1/4" double density floppy disk format. Data can be stored on the disk using either of two popular formats. Figure 9-3 shows how a bit and a byte of data can be stored on a disk, using FM (single density) and MFM (double density) formats. The FM format is just Manchester coding, as introduced in section 8-1. Figure 9-3a shows a bit cell, and figure 9-3c shows a byte of data, in the FM format. Every 8 μseconds there is a clock pulse. If a 1 is sent, a pulse is put in between the clock pulses, and if a 0 is sent, no pulse is put between the clock pulses. MFM format provides half the bit cell size as FM format; it does this by using minimal spacing between pulses in the disk medium: MFM format has at most one pulse per bit cell. It is thus called "double density" storage. The idea is that a 1 cell, which has a pulse in it, doesn't need a clock pulse, and a 0 cell only needs a clock pulse if the previous cell is also a 0 cell. Figure 9-3b shows a byte of data in the MFM format. Every 4 μseconds there is a data bit. If a 1 is sent, a pulse is put near the end of the bit time; if a 0 is sent after a 1, no pulse is put between the clock pulses; and if a 0 is sent after a 0, a pulse appears early in the bit time. Note that data must be read or written at the rate of 1 byte per 32 μseconds, which is 64 memory cycles for the MC68HC11. For the remainder of this section, we discuss the "double density" MFM format. The FM format is basically identical to the MFM format.

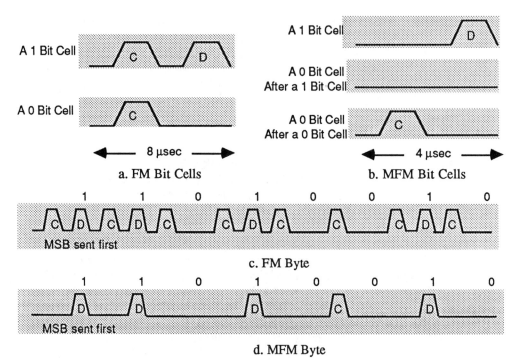

Figure 9-3. Bit and Byte Storage for FM and MFM Encoding of 5 1/4" Floppy Disks

Data read from the disk are separated by a phase-locked loop (PLL) of the kind described in section 7-2.1. The PLL synchronizes to the bit cell like a fly-wheel. Once the bit cell is locked on to, the data bits can be extracted from the input analog signal. The PLL must be designed to lock into the bit cells within 48 bit cell times.

A disk drive may have one or more disks, stacked pancake-style, and each disk may have one or two *surfaces*. Figure 9-4a shows a surface of a disk; a *track* is shown, and tracks are numbered – track 0 on the extreme outside, and track i+1 next towards the center to track i. The track spacing density is the number of tracks per inch and is generally 48 or 96 tracks per inch. Floppy disks have diameters of 8", 5 1/4", or 3 1/2", and these typically have at least 77, 35, and 35 tracks, respectively. Although disks exist which have a head on each track, generally disks have a single head per surface – used to both read and write the data on that surface – which is moved by a stepper motor to a track that is to be read or written. In a multiple surface disk, the same tracks are accessed on each surface by a comb-like mechanism holding the read-write head for each surface; the collection of tracks accessed at the same time is called a *cylinder*. We soon describe an example of a single-sided 5 1/4" disk's track format. The formats for other types of disks are similar.

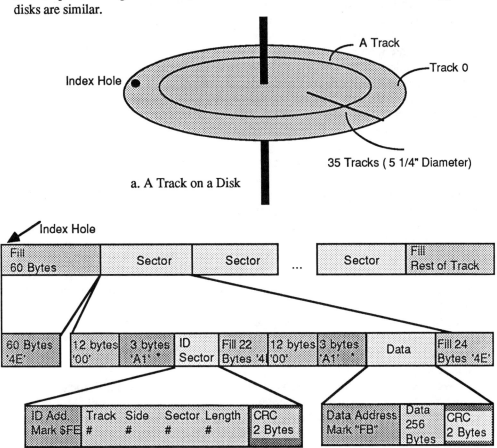

a. A Track on a Disk

b. Sectors In a Track

Figure 9-4. Organization of Sectors and Tracks on a Disk Surface

Relative to later discussions of the operation of the floppy disk controller, timing of head movements significantly affects the disk system's performance. The *step rate* is the rate at which the stepping motor can be pulsed to move the head from track i to track i+1 (step in) or to track i-1 (step out). There is also a *settling time*, which is the time needed to allow the mechanical parts to stop bouncing (see contact bounce in chapter 6). Floppy disk drives have stepping rates from 2 to 30 milliseconds and settling times of about 30 milliseconds. If a drive has a 3-millisecond stepping rate and a 30-millisecond settling time, the time to move from track i to track j is 3*li-jl +30 milliseconds. The average time to position from track 0 to a random track is the time to move over half of the (35) tracks of the disk. There is some additional time needed to get to the data on the track, as discussed soon. Thus, on the average, about 80 milliseconds would be used to move the head, and no data is transferred during that time.

The problem with a disk is that, to record data, a head must be energized, and the process of energizing or de-energizing a head erases the data below the head. The track is thus organized with *fill* areas where data are not stored and where the head may be energized to begin, or de-energized to end, writing, and the data between these fill areas, called *sectors*, are written in their entirety if they are written at all. A disk's indivisible storage objects thus are sectors. Figure 9-4b shows the breakdown of a typical track in terms of sectors and the breakdown of a sector in terms of its ID pattern and data. There is an *index hole* on the disk (figure 9-4a) that defines a track's beginning; it is sensed by an optical switch that provides an *index pulse* when the hole passes by the switch. The track first contains a 60 byte fill pattern. (Each fill pattern is $4E.) There are then 18 sectors, as described soon. The remaining part of the track is filled with the fill pattern.

Regarding the timing of disk accesses, after the head moves to the right track, it may have to wait 1/2 revolution of the disk, on the average, before it finds a track it would like to read or write. Since a floppy disk rotates at 10 revolutions per second, the average wait would be 50 milliseconds. If several sectors are to be read together, the time needed to move from one track to another can be eliminated if the data are on the same track, and the time needed to get to the right sector can be eliminated if the sectors are located one after another. We will think of sectors as if they were consecutively numbered from 0 (the *logical sector number*), and we will position consecutively numbered sectors on the same track, so consecutively numbered sectors can be read as fast as possible. (Actually, two consecutively read sectors should have some other sectors between them because the computer has to process the data read and determine what to do next before it is ready to read another sector. The number of sectors actually physically between two "consecutively numbered" sectors is called the *interleave factor*, and is generally about four.)

We need to know which sector is passing under the head as the disk rotates, since sectors may be put in some different order, as just described, and we would also like to be able to verify that we are on the right track after the head has been moved. When the read head begins to read data (it may begin reading anywhere on a track), it will examine this address in an ID pattern to find out where it is.

There is a small problem identifying the beginning of an ID pattern or a data field when the head makes contact with the surface and begins to read the data on a track. To solve this, there is a special pattern whose presence is indicated by the deletion of some of the clock pulses that would have been there when data are recorded in MFM format, and there are identifying patterns called the ID address mark and data address mark. The special pattern, shown in figure 9-5, is said to have a data pattern of $A1 and a missing clock pulse between bits 4 and 5. The ID address mark $FE is used to locate the beginning of an ID pattern on a track. The data address mark similarly identifies the beginning of data in the sector, but is $FB rather than $FE.

The ID pattern consists of a 1-byte ID address mark ($FE), a track number, side number, sector number and sector length (each is 1 byte and is coded in binary), and a 2-byte CRC check. The track number, beginning with track 0 (outermost), and the sector number, beginning with either sector 0 (zero-origin indexing) or 1 (one-origin indexing), is stored in 2 of the bytes. A simple method of mapping the logical sector number into a track and zero-origin indexing sector number is to divide the logical sector number by the number of sectors per track: the quotient is the track number, and the remainder is the sector number. The side number for a single-surface drive is 0, and the sector length for a 256-byte sector is 1.

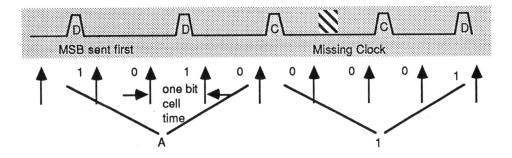

Figure 9-5. A Special Byte (Data=$A1, Clock Pulse Missing Between Bits 4,5)

A sector is composed of a pattern of 12 0's followed by 3 bytes of $A1 (in which a clock pulse is missing). There is then an ID pattern as just described, a 22-byte fill, and another pattern of 12 0's, followed by 3 bytes of $A1 (in which a clock pulse is missing). The 256 bytes of data are then stored. The ID pattern and the data in a sector have some error detection information called a CRC, discussed in section 8-4.1, to ensure reliable reading of the data. The track may have a total capacity of about 6500 bytes, called the *unformatted capacity* of the track, but because so much of the disk is needed for fill, ID, and CRC, the *formatted capacity* of a track (the available data) may be reduced to 4600 bytes.

The *format* of a disk is the structure just described, disregarding the content of the data field. To *format* a disk is to write this structure. When data are written, only the data part of the sector, together with its data address mark and CRC check, are written. The ID pattern is not rewritten. If it is altered, you will be unable to read or write the data in the sectors because the controller will be unable to find the sector, and you will have to reformat the disk, destroying all the data in it.

9-1.3. The Western Digital 1772 Floppy Disk Controller

We now examine a hardware-software system for reading a single-sided double density 5 1/4" (or 3 1/2") floppy disk using the Western digital WD1771 chip. There are two ways to build the hardware using the convenient WD1772 controller chip. Figure 9-6a shows how the chip is attached to a 6811 expanded multiplexed bus system. This kind of system may be required to access external memory if the memory must be expanded beyond that available in the chip, and permits a simpler software interface. The single-chip mode may access a floppy controller using indirect I/O (section 4-4), as shown in figure 9-6b. It uses only one extra chip, the 74HC240, so it is easier to connect up. It might be useful in a single-chip application for collecting data and storing it on a floppy disk, and it is easier to experiment with. We concentrate on the single-chip mode in the following text and leave the expanded multiplexed mode for problems at the end of the chapter.

The user may wish to read one or more bytes from the disk. Since it is only possible to read whole sectors, the sector or sectors that the data are at are read, and the data are extracted once the sectors are read. To read a sector, the user must *seek* the track first, then *read* the desired *sector*. The two commands, seek and read sector, are given to the floppy disk controller. The seek command puts the read/write head in the disk drive over the desired track, and the read sector command causes the data from a sector on that track to be read into primary memory. If the read/write head is definitely over the right track, the seek command may be omitted. Also, in some floppy disk controllers having intelligence in them, the user only gives a read command regardless of where the read/write head is and an *implied seek* may be automatically generated as a result, without the user giving it, if the head is in the wrong place. The user may wish to write one or more bytes into the disk. The commands to seek and *write sector* are given as for the read operations above. Good programs often read a sector each time right after it is written to be sure there are no errors in writing the sector. Finally, when the system is started up, it is necessary to establish the position of the read/write head to determine how to move it to a desired track. This operation is called *restoring* the drive.

The following floppy disk controller interface program is quite substantial, so we'll introduce it in sections, with some discussion between sections. First, we will give the equates needed to improve the documentation. As figure 9-6b shows, the bidirectional port C is used to send a byte of data to the 1772 or take data from it. The output port B is used to provide addresses and control signals (such as reset) to the 1772. An input part of port A, which is bit 0 and bit 7 (assuming that port A bit 7 is configured as an input, bit 7 of $10xx = 0), is used to sense the Drq (data request) line, which in turn is used to signal the arrival of a byte of input data or the need for a byte of output data, and to sense the (interrupt request) Irq line, which is used to signal the end of an operation. (Note that the Irq line is in positive logic in this chip.) Although this information is available by reading the status register of the 1772, described soon, there is a tight timing loop in which Irq and Drq must be read as direct inputs in port A, rather than read indirectly by reading the 1772's status register of the 1772.

The begining of the program lists constants used for the indirect I/O technique, for further reference. These constants match the implementation shown in figure 9-6b.

```
        NAM   FLOPPY
PORTA   EQU   $1000          BIT 7 IS DRQ
IRQ     EQU   1              BIT 0 IS IRQ
*
PORTB   EQU   $1004
RADDR   EQU   3              REGISTER ADDRESS
RW      EQU   4              WRITE LINE
RESET   EQU   8              INTERRUPT
ECLK    EQU   $10
*
PORTC   EQU   $1003          DATA I/O
DIRC    EQU   $1007          DIRECTION
```

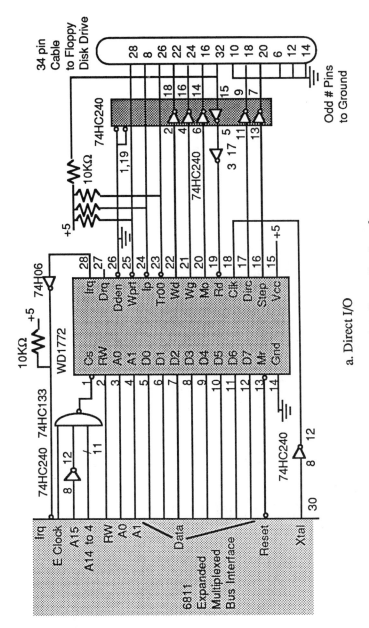

Figure 9-6. Floppy Disk Controller Interface

a. Direct I/O

433

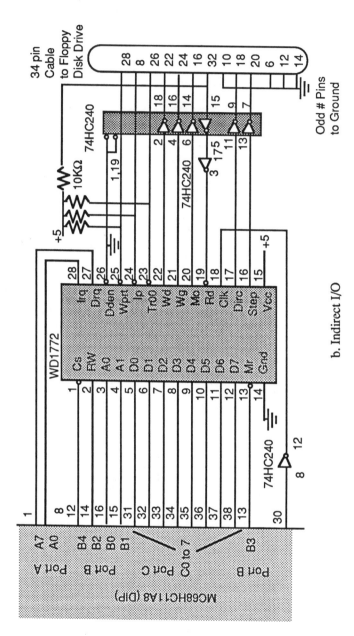

Figure 9-6. (Continued)

b. Indirect I/O

434

WD1772

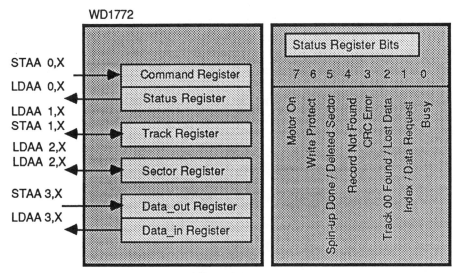

a. Block Diagram

Command	Bit Pattern (bits 7 to 0)							
Restore	0	0	0	0	h	V	r1	r0
Seek	0	0	0	1	h	V	r1	r0
Step	0	0	1	u	h	V	r1	r0
Step-in	0	1	0	u	h	V	r1	r0
Step-out	0	1	1	u	h	V	r1	r0
Read Sector	1	0	0	m	h	E	0	0
Write Sector	1	0	1	m	h	E	P	a0
Read Address	1	1	0	0	h	E	0	0
Read Track	1	1	1	0	h	E	0	0
Write Track	1	1	1	1	h	E	P	0
Force Interrupt	1	1	0	1	i3	i2	i1	i0

h=0 - Enable h=1 Disable Spin-up Sequence
V=0 - Disable V=1 Enable Verify on Destination Track
u=0 - Disable u=1 Enable Update Track Register
m=0 - Disable m=1 Enable Multiple Sector
E=0 - Disable E=1 Enable 30-msecond Delay for Settling Time
P=0 - Enable P=1 Disable Write Precompensation
a0 = 0 write normal data mark a0 = 1 write deleted data mark
r1 r0 = 00 2-msecond step rate
r1 r0 = 01 3-msecond step rate
r1 r0 = 10 5-msecond step rate
r1 r0 = 11 6-msecond step rate

b. Command Summary

Figure 9-7. Programmer's View of the WD1772

The registers of the WD1772 are shown in figure 9-7a as they would appear in an expanded multiplexed bus mode, diagramed in figure 9-6a, if index register X pointed to the first register on the chip. The read-write registers, TRACK and SECTOR, are used to specify the track the drive head is on and the sector that is to be read or written. The read-only registers status and data_in give the status of the chip and data being input, and the write-only registers command and data_out are used to give commands to the 1772 and put data out to the disk. As we discuss each command, the use of each of these registers will be explained in detail. The I/O's indirect mode requires a sequence of instructions to "emulate" the control signals on the expanded multiplexed bus so it can read or write in these registers; these instructions are best put into subroutines like those below:

```
OUTCMD  PSHB              OUTPUT A CMD TO THE CMD REGISTER
        LDAB  #RESET+ECLK WRITE IS LOW, NO INTERRUPT
        BRA   OUTA
OUTTRK  PSHB              PUT ACCA INTO TRACK REGISTER
        LDAB  #RESET+ECLK+1 WRITE IS LOW, NO INTERRUPT
        BRA   OUTA
OUTSEC  PSHB              PUT ACCA INTO SECTOR REGISTER
        LDAB  #RESET+ECLK+2 WRITE IS LOW, NO INTERRUPT
        BRA   OUTA
OUTDATA PSHB              PUT ACCA INTO DATA REGISTER
        LDAB  #RESET+ECLK+3 WRITE IS LOW, NO INTERRUPT
OUTA    PSHB              PUT ACCA INTO REG SPECIFIED BY ACCB
        LDAB  #$FF        MAKE PORT C
        STAB  DIRC        AN OUTPUT PORT
        STAA  PORTC       DATA TO PORT C
        PULB
        STAB  PORTB       ADDRESS TO PORT B
        ANDB  #$FF-ECLK
        STAB  PORTB       ASSERT CLOCK LOW
        ORAB  #ECLK       REMOVE CLOCK
        STAB  PORTB
        CLR   DIRC        MAKE PORT B INPUT AGAIN
        PULB
        RTS
*
INSTAT  PSHB              GET STATUS REGISTER TO ACCA
        LDAB  #RESET+ECLK+RW WRITE IS LOW, NO INTERRUPT
        BRA   INA
INTRK   PSHB              GET TRACK REGISTER TO ACCA
        LDAB  #RESET+ECLK+RW+1 WR. IS LOW, NO INTERRUPT
        BRA   INA
INSEC   PSHB              GET SECTOR REGISTER TO ACCA
        LDAB  #RESET+ECLK+RW+2 WR IS LOW, NO INTERRUPT
        BRA   INA
INDATA  PSHB              GET DATA REGISTER TO ACCA
```

```
          LDAB  #RESET+ECLK+RW+3 WR. IS LOW, NO INTERRUPT
INA       STAB  PORTB       ADDRESS TO PORT B, STROBE TO CE
          ANDB  #$FF-ECLK
          STAB  PORTB       ASSERT CLOCK LOW
          LDAA  PORTC       GET DATA
          ORAB  #ECLK       REMOVE CLOCK
          STAB  PORTB
          PULB
          RTS
```

Observe the emulation of control signals in the port B register output bits. The basic signal in ACCB is modified to cause the emulated E clock sent to the chip select pin to fall and rise so the data transfer is executed. For the output subroutines, ACCA is used to hold the output data, and ACCB is used to hold the basic pattern of control signals which are sent via port B but are modified to clock the data out. For the input subroutines, ACCB is used as in the output routines, and the data read from the chip appear in ACCA. In an expanded multiplexed mode system, these subroutines would be replaced by single instructions. It is fortunate that this state-of-the-art microcomputer, the 6811, is fast enough to meet the timing requirements of the WD1772 using indirect I/O and subroutines just shown, and that the WD1772 has no maximum time limits on pulse widths, so we can wire up the simpler indirect I/O system.

We now examine the commands executed by the WD1772. (See figure 9-7b.) Basically, the most significant bits of the word written into the command register identify the command, and the rest of the bits, depending on the command, specify the parameters or arguments needed by the command. The first five commands merely position the head to a desired track, without reading or writing the data on the track. The next five commands read or write data on the track, and the last one is used mainly to abort a command in progress (setting bits i3 to i0 to 0).

The first five commands have parameters h, V, and r1r0. The value of "r1r0" is used to specify the *step rate* – the rate at which pulses cause the stepping motor to move the head. This number has to be set to the stepping rate given by the drive manufacturer: if you set it too fast, the drive will not respond to step commands, and if too slow, the drive stepping motor will "chatter" and work harder than if you set it correctly. "V" specifies whether the ID pattern will be read to verify that the track moved to is correct. To prevent wear, the WD1772 automatically turns off the motor turning the disk if you don't use it for about a second. It can be turned on in a "spin-up sequence" if "h" is 1.

In the restore command, the head is in an unknown state and must be moved to a known state (track 00) so it can determine which way and how far to move the head to get to a desired track. There is a sensor on the drive that sends a signal (Tr00) when the head is at the outermost track, and the restore instruction steps the head outward until this signal is received. The step-in command causes the stepping motor to move the head in one track (and similarly, step-out steps outward and step steps in the same direction the last step took). It is generally desirable to step in about three times before restoring, since otherwise the head could have been moved further out than track 00, and the restore command would be unable to get it to track 00 by stepping outward.

The seek command is used before any of the five read/write commands to get the head to the correct track. The track and data_out registers should have the (presumed) present track and the desired track, respectively, just before the command is given. Upon a successful seek, the track register will get the destination track number. Note that the track register generally contains the track the head is on and (in single-drive systems) need never be rewritten after it has been initialized after a restore command. You put the track number into the data_out register and then execute the seek command. This command generally takes a long time, as we noted in previous comments. A gadfly loop can wait for it to be completed if there is nothing else to do.

Subroutines for three of the the first five commands used in our example are shown next. After each of them, the status register (figure 9-7a) is read in a gadfly loop until the busy bit is cleared. A realistic program should examine the error flags returned in the status register and retry the operation in a finite number of times if errors are detected; but the details needed for such a program are beyond the scope of this book. They can be obtained, however, from the WD1772 data sheet and from examining a well-written disk handling program.

```
SEEK     JSR   OUTDATA PUT DESIRED TRACK INTO DATA REG.
         LDAA  #$14        SEEK, NO UPDT BUT SPIN-UP AND VER.
         BRA   ISSCMD
STEPIN   LDAA  #$50        STEP IN, NO UPDT OR VER, BUT SPIN-UP
         BRA   ISSCMD
RESTORE  CLRA              RESTR, NO UPDT OR VER, BUT SPIN-UP
         BSR   ISSCMD
         CLRA              SET TRACK TO 0
         JMP   OUTTRK
ISSCMD   BSR   OUTCMD  ISSUE A CMD, WAIT FOR IT TO BE DONE
ISSCMD1  BSR   INSTAT  GET STATUS REGISTER
         BITA  #1      CHECK BUSY BIT
         BNE   ISSCMD1 LOOP WHILE BUSY
         RTS
```

Once the desired track is moved to, we can read or write a sector. The subroutine to read a sector, INBUF, is shown next. Index register X is set to the address of a buffer, and ACCA has the desired sector number before the subroutine is begun.We have to put the desired sector number into the SECTOR register. The desired track number will be in the TRACK register because a seek will be done just before this subroutine. Then we issue a command to the WD1772 to read a sector. The parameters m, h, and E are 0 in this command because we are not reading multiple sectors; and immediately after a seek command, the motor is on and the head is stable so no spin-up sequence or settling delay is called for. If you execute a sector read without a seek (because you know you are on the correct track), you may need to set the h bit if the motor is off; WD1772 status bit 7 tells you if the motor is on. The following subroutine below checks the Drq line from the WD1772 chip, in port A bit 7. When that input becomes 1, data are read from data_in and put in a buffer. It also checks the Irq line – input in port A bit 0 – for Irq to become 1. That occurs when the command is completed and the buffer is filled with

256 bytes of data. The Drq and Irq signals are also available as bits 0 and 1 of the WD1772 status register, but the extra time needed to read the status register using indirect I/O is just too long for the 32 μseconds available to move a word from the WD1772 to the buffer. Thus, these connections must be put in the hardware.

```
INBUF    BSR    OUTSEC
         LDAA   #$88        READ TO BUF, NO SPIN-UP, STLG DELAY
INBUF0   JSR    OUTCMD
         LDAB   #RESET+RW+ECLK+3
INBUF1   LDAA   PORTA       GET DRQ, IRQ
         BPL    INBUF2
         STAB   PORTB       ADDRESS TO PORT B
         LDAB   #RESET+RW+3
         STAB   PORTB       ASSERT CLOCK LOW
         LDAA   PORTC       GET DATA
         LDAB   #RESET+RW+ECLK+3
         STAB   PORTB
         STAA   0,X         STORE IN BUFFER
         INX                MOVE POINTER
         BRA    INBUF1
INBUF2   BITA   #1          CHECK IRQ
         BEQ    INBUF1      IF LOW, MORE TO GET
         JMP    INSTAT
```

The subroutine to write a sector is shown next. It is analogous to INBUF .

```
OUTBUF   BSR    OUTSEC
         LDAA   #$A8        COMMAND TO WRITE SECTOR
         JSR    OUTCMD
         LDAB   #$FF        MAKE PORT C
         STAB   DIRC        AN OUTPUT PORT
         LDAB   #RESET+ECLK+3 WRITE IS LOW
OUTBUF1  LDAA   0,X         GET DATA
         INX                MOVE POINTER
         STAA   PORTC       DATA TO PORT C
         STAB   PORTB       ADDRESS TO PORT B
         LDAB   #RESET+3
         STAB   PORTB       ASSERT CLOCK LOW
         LDAB   #RESET+ECLK+3 REMOVE CLOCK
         STAB   PORTB
OUTBUF2  LDAA   PORTA       GET DRQ, IRQ
         BMI    OUTBUF1     GET MORE DATA
         BITA   #1          CHECK IRQ
         BEQ    OUTBUF2     NO END, CONTINUE
         CLR    DIRC        MAKE PORT B INPUT AGAIN
         BRA    INSTAT
```

Tying all the subroutines together, we next present a sample program for an MVB board that emulates a single-chip 6811 with extra memory at $C000 - $DFFF. The initialization sequence uses the STEPIN and RESTORE subroutines to establish the location of the head. All your disk programs should start this way. We then fill a buffer, at location $D800, with numbers. We write this buffer to the disk. Then we clear this buffer and read the data from the disk back into it. After we stop, we can examine ACCA, which gives the error flags, and dump and verify the buffer.

```
INIT    CLR   DIRC        DIRECTION IS IN
        LDAA #RW+ECLK
        STAA PORTB        RESET BIT LOW, READ-WRITE HIGH
        LDAA #RESET+RW+ECLK REL. RESET, READ-WRITE HIGH
        STAA PORTB
*
        BSR   STEPIN      MOVE IN A TRACK
        BSR   STEPIN      MOVE IN A TRACK
        BSR   STEPIN      MOVE IN A TRACK
        BSR   RESTORE     RESTORE TO TRACK 0
        LDX   #$D800
        CLRA
INLP1   STAA 0,X          FILL BUFFER AT $D800
        INX               WITH 0 - $FF
        INCA
        BNE   INLP1
*
        LDAA #33           TRACK 33 NEAR CENTER
        BSR   SEEK         SEEK A TRACK
        LDAA #1            SECTOR 1
        LDX   #$D800       FROM BUFFER AT $D800
        JSR   OUTBUF       WRITE A SECTOR TO DISK
*
        LDX   #$D800
        CLRA
INLP2   CLR   0,X          FILL BUFFER AT$D800
        INX   WITH 0
        INCA
        BNE   INLP2
*
        LDAA #33           TRACK 33 NEAR CENTER
        BSR   SEEK         SEEK A TRACK
        LDAA #1            SECTOR 1
        LDX   #$D800       TO BUFFER AT$D800
        JSR   INBUF        READ A SECTOR FROM DISK
        SWI
```

Each operating system has its way of organizing the data on the disk. We briefly describe the technique used in OS9, sold by Microware and used in the 6809 and 68000 systems. Data are organized in *files,* where a file is a collection of one or more segments, a *segment* is a sequence of consecutive logical sectors on the disk. For instance, a file named MYDATA might be $903 bytes long, and the first $800 bytes might be stored in 8 sectors in the first segment starting at logical sector $503, while the last $103 bytes would be stored in 2 sectors in the second segment starting at logical sector $7F3. This could occur if there is room on the disk at logical sector $503 for just 8 sectors, and the first segment can be fit there, and there is room starting at logical sector $7F3 for the remaining sectors. A file is described by a sector called a file descriptor. The *file descriptor* lists the logical sector Pi of the beginning and length Li of each of the segments of the file, where the first L0 sectors of the whole file are in the first segment (P0,L0) and the next L1 sectors are in the second segment (P1,L1), and so on. For our example, (P0,L0) would be ($503,8) and (P1,L1) would be ($7F3,2). These data in the file descriptor might be in logical sector $12E. A *directory* is used to find the files: in it, an ASCII string file name and the logical sector of its file descriptor are stored for each file. To find a file with a given name, the operating system searches the directory for a matching name, and gets the logical sector of its file descriptor. For our example, the string "MYDATA" and the logical sector number $12E are in the directory file. By matching the name of the file in the directory, the operating system can locate the file descriptor, and from there, it can find any sector in the file.

Sectors are perceived by the end user as if they were consecutively numbered, even though they may be in different segments. To read a given sector of the file, the operating system reads the file descriptor, and measures out the sizes of each segment to find the one containing the desired sector, and then gets the logical sector the given sector is in. For instance, to read sector 9 of the file MYDATA, the operating system goes to the directory with the string "MYDATA", finding the logical sector $12E. It then determines the desired sector is in the second segment and is the second sector in that segment. So it determines that logical sector $7F4 is to be read. The operating system does not have to go through all this each time a sector is read, but it keeps the computed locations used in the last access and tries to use them in the next access where possible.

To write a new file, care must be taken to avoid writing over sectors used by existing files. Unused sectors are known by a *bit map,* which is stored in one or more sectors on the disk. Unused sectors are represented by 0's and used sectors by 1's. Unused sectors are chosen from this bit map, and marked as being used, when a new file is created or an old file is expanded.

Finally, we have not discussed strategies that are used to recognize errors and recover from those errors that can be automatically corrected. A disk driver for a good operating system has to use extensive techniques to recover from errors so the end user is not bothered by recoverable errors, but is alerted when irrecoverable errors prevent the data on the disk from being correctly read or written.

This rather long example shows almost all the key routines needed to handle a WD1772 floppy controller chip, to read and write data on a 5 1/4 or 3 1/2 inch floppy disk. We do not show how to format the disk since that requires a lot of information but can be done on another computer. We also do not discuss an interrupt version of the software. That is available in the problems at the end of the chapter. With this example, you now have enough information to build a practical disk interface.

9-2 Display Systems

A microcomputer may be used in an intelligent terminal or in a personal computer. Such systems require a display. Any microcomputer, requiring the display of more than the few digits an LED or LCD display can handle, may have to use a CRT display.

This section describes the concepts of CRT display systems. We present the format of the NTSC black-and-white signal and then show a program which enables the 6811 to display a black block on a white screen. This program is so simple that you can implement it quickly to get some hands-on experience with television signals. Then we present a chip set, using the Signetics 2670, 2672, and 2673 chips, that implements a realistic CRT display system. It is more involved but is more satisfying because it can be used as the display part of a useful terminal.

9-2.1 A 6811 SPI Display

A *National Television System Committee (NTSC)* signal is used in the United States and Canada for all commercial television. A computer display system consists of the CRT and its drive electronics – essentially a specialized TV set – and hardware and software able to send pulses to time the electron beam, which is a stream of bits to make the TV screen black or white at different points. Figure 9-8 diagrams the front of a TV screen. An electron beam, generated by a hot cathode and controlled by a grid, is deflected by electromagnets in the back of the CRT and made to move from left side to right side and from top to bottom across the face of the CRT. More electrons produce a whiter spot. The traversal of the beam across the face is called a *raster line*. The set of raster lines that "paint" the screen from top to bottom is a field. NTSC signals use two fields, one slightly offset from the other, as shown in figure 9-8a, to completely paint a picture *frame*.

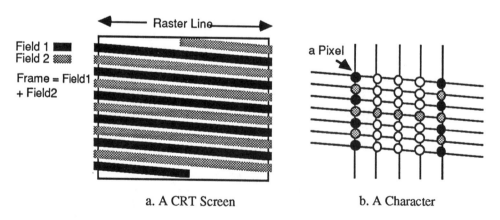

a. A CRT Screen   b. A Character

Figure 9-8. The Raster Scan Display Used in Television

In NTSC signals, a frame takes 1/30th second and a field takes 1/60th second. The raster line takes 1/15,750th second, a field has 262 1/2 raster lines and a frame has 525 raster lines. As the beam moves from side to side and from top to bottom, the electron beam is controlled to light up the screen in a pattern. Figure 9-8b shows how a letter H is written in both fields of a frame. A *pixel* is the (smallest controllable) dot on the screen; a clear circle represents a pixel having no light, and a dark circle (black for field 1 and gray for field 2) shows a pixel where there is light on the screen.

The *NTSC composite video signal* is an analog signal, diagramed in figure 9-9. The displayed signal is an analog signal where a maximum voltage (about 1/2 volt) produces a white dot, a lower voltage (3/8 volt) produces gray, and a lower voltage (1/4 volt) produces a black dot. The part of the signal corresponding to the time when the electron beam is moved to the left side (*horizontal retrace*) or to the top (*vertical retrace*) occurs between the displayed parts. At these times, *horizontal sync* and *vertical sync* pulses appear as lower voltage (0 volts) or "blacker-than-black" pulses. The CRT system uses a *sync separator* circuit to extract these pulses so it can derive the horizontal and vertical sync pulses, which are used to time the beam deflections on the screen. This signal is called the composite video signal because it has the video signal and the sync signals composed onto one signal. If this signal is to be sent over the air, it is modulated onto a radio frequency (r.f.) carrier (such as channel 2). Alternatively, the separate video, horizontal, and vertical sync signals can be sent over different wires to the CRT system, so they do not need to be separated; this gives the best resolution, such as is needed in 1024 by 1024 pixel CRT displays in "engineering workstations." The composite video is used in character displays that have 80 characters per line. The r.f. modulated signals are used in games and home computers intended to be connected to unmodified home TV sets, but are capable of only about 51 characters per line.

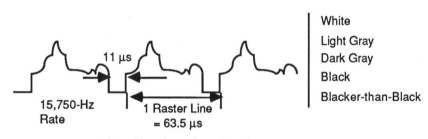

a. Video Signal and Sync Levels

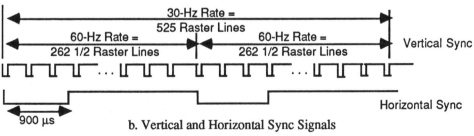

b. Vertical and Horizontal Sync Signals

Figure 9-9. The Composite Video Signal

The frequency of the vertical sync pulses, which corresponds to the time of a field, is generally fixed to 60 Hz, to prevent AC hum from making the screen image have bars run across it, as in cheap TVs. It is also about the lowest frequency at which the human eye does not detect flicker. American computer CRTs almost universally use this vertical sync frequency. The horizontal sync frequency in computer CRTs is usually about 15,750 Hz, as specified by the NTSC standard, but may be a bit faster to permit more lines on the screen yet keep the vertical sync frequency at 60 Hz. The magnetic beam deflection on the CRT is tuned to a specific frequency, and the electronics must provide horizontal sync pulses at this frequency, or the picture will be nonlinear. The pulse widths of these horizontal and vertical pulses are specified by the electronics that drive the CRT. Thus, the CRT controller must be set up to give a specific horizontal and vertical frequency and pulse width, as specified by the CRT electronics.

We are fortunate that the 6811 has a built-in counter and shift register able to generate the synchronization pulses and the bit stream to implement a primitive CRT display. The 6811 output compare timers, described in chapter 7, are capable of generating the vertical and horizontal sync pulses and the Serial Peripheral Interface (SPI), introduced in chapter 4, has the capability of generating a CRT display having poor, but useful, resolution. The upcoming program SPITV should produce a picture as shown in figure 9-10, using the simple hardware diagramed in figure 9-11 with a single-chip 6811. It might be useful for multicomputer systems as a diagnostic display on each microcomputer. It is quite useful for explaining the principles of CRT display systems, since it uses the familiar 6811 instruction set and peripherals. We have found it useful in testing some "bargain basement" CRTs when we did not have specifications on the permissible range of horizontal and vertical sync pulse widths and frequencies. This little program lets us easily test these systems to generate the specifications. We now describe how that "built-in" CRT generator in the 6811 can produce a CRT display.

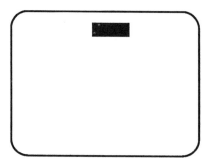

Figure 9-10. Screen Produced by the Program SPITV

Figure 9-11 shows a simple circuit for the generation of composite video. If your CRT requires separated video, horizontal, and vertical sync signals, these can be taken directly from pins 45, 2, and 3, respectively, and the circuit diagramed in figure 9-11 is not needed. We soon show the program. It is just a pair of interrupt-based pulse generator programs, as described in section 7-2.2. The vertical sync pulse, generated by output compare 3, is controlled by HNDLR2. An output compare 3 interrupt occurs each time the output is supposed to switch – to output a low pulse for 900 microseconds and to output a high pulse for the rest of the 16 milliseconds (60 Hz). Bit 0 in FLAGS keeps track of whether the next pulse should be high or low. It is toggled each interrupt, and determines which value to put in the output compare register. The horizontal sync pulse, generated by output compare 2, is controlled by HNDLR1. An output compare 2 interrupt occurs at the beginning of each raster scan line; the interrupt itself toggles the output low. The pulse width being very short, software toggles the output back to high by putting a bit in the force compare register. Then, using a primitive "character generator" based on a 24-bit shift register, either a 0 or $FF byte is put into the SPI register, which is shifted out as the video signal. The 24-bit shift register pattern in memory locations LINE to LINE+2 is initialized by HNDLR2 each vertical retrace time. For the first 8 raster lines of a field shifting LINE to LINE+2, 0 is shifted out, and for the next 16 lines, $FF is shifted out. This produces the black box in the center top of the screen, as shown in figure 9-10.

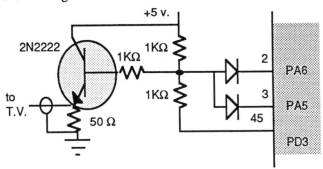

Figure 9-11. Circuit Used for TV Generation

```
            NAM  SPITV
FLAGS       RMB  1
HSTATE      EQU  1              HORIZONTAL RETRACE STATE
LINE        RMB  3
*
            CLRA
            CLRB
            STAA FLAGS          INITIALIZE STATE
            STD  LINE           AND LINE NUMBER
            LDX  #$1000         BASE FOR ALL I/O
            LDD  #$3F50         SPI INTERFACE CONSTANTS
            STAA 9,X            PORT D IS OUTPUT FOR MOSI, BIT 5
            STAB $28,X          MAKE SPI MASTER, NORMALLY LOW
            LDD  #$5060         INITIALIZATION CONSTANTS
            STAA $20,X          MODULES TO TOGGLE OUTPUT
            STAB $22,X          PERMIT INTERRUPTS
            CLI                 ALLOW ALL INTERRUPTS
L1          WAI                 WAIT FOR INTERRUPT
            BRA  L1             TO ALLOW ACCURATE TIMING
*
```

```
HNDLR1   EQU   *           HOR SYNC: ASSUME ADD IS IN $FFE6,E7
         LDAA  #$40         COMPARE 2 "DONE" FLAG
         STAA  $23,X        CLEAR FLAG IN INTERRUPT REGISTER
         BRN *              HAVE TO WASTE 6 CYCLES
         BRN *              TO GET 11 MICROSEC PULSE
         STAA  $B,X         FORCE COMPARE TO ASSERT OUTPUT
         LDD   $18,X        GET LAST COMPARE "TIME"
         ADDD  #127         ADD DELAY FOR 15,750 HZ
         STD   $18,X        PUT IT IN OUTPUT COMPARE 2
         LDAA  $2A,X        CLEAR SPI
         LDAA  $29,X        CLEAR SPI
         LSL   LINE+2       WE WANT 16 ROWS DARK
         ROL   LINE+1       GET BIT:
         ROL   LINE         IF 0,
         LDAB  #$FF         MAKE ALL 1'S
         ADCB  #0           ELSE ALL 0'S
         STAB  $2A,X        PUT ROW PATTERN INTO SPI
HNDLR11  RTI
*
HNDLR2   EQU   *           VTL SYNC: ASSUME ADD IS IN $FFE4,E5
         LDAA  #$20         COMPARE 3 "DONE" FLAG
         STAA  $23,X        CLEAR FLAG IN INTERRUPT REGISTER
         BRSET FLAGS HSTATE HNDLR21 CHECK IF OUTPUT LOW
         BSET  FLAGS HSTATE CHANGE STATE: REMEMBER LOW
         LDD   #1800        900 MICROSECONDS LOW
         BRA   HNDLR22
HNDLR21  BCLR  FLAGS HSTATE CHANGE STATE: REMEMBER HIGH
         LDD   #$FFFF       START HORIZONTAL LINE COUNT
         STD   LINE+1       TO IDENTIFY LINE NUMBER
         LDD   #33401-1800 REST OF 16 MILLISEC HIGH
HNDLR22  ADDD  $1A,X        ADD LAST COMPARE "TIME"
         STD   $1A,X        PUT IT IN OUTPUT COMPARE 3
         RTI
```

This basic program has been expanded by Kevin Williams in a Master's thesis to produce a rather acceptable display having six characters per row, and 5 rows of characters per screen. Some very tricky real-time programming had to be used, rather than interrupts, because of the short time available to generate the characters and shift them out, and the even number characters in a character row were output during one frame, then the odd number characters in the character row were output in the next frame. This thesis implemented a debug monitor that would work with a keyboard, an r.f. modulator and a standard TV, and use only three additional chips (two shift registers to scan the keyboard and one exclusive-NOR gate chip to generate the composite video). Would you like to debug your projects at home? What is mildly surprising is that the 6811, with very little external hardware, has the ability to generate CRT signals. Motorola can therefore claim that the 6811 has a built-in CRT controller.

9-2.2 The Signetics 2670-73 CRT Controller Chip Set

A more realistic CRT controller uses a few extra chips to generate a character display. The chips in this set – the 2670, 2672, and 2673 – were designed by Signetics and are described in the Signetics *MOS Microprocessor Data Manual 1982*. They are second-sourced by Motorola and are described in the Motorola *8-Bit Computer and Peripheral Data* book. Although they are available from Motorola, these chips are designed for the Intel bus timing and illustrate the mixing of bus timings that is not only possible but also even implicitly recommended by Motorola. In this section, we enumerate the general techniques used to produce useful displays, and then give a detailed example of a useful display system.

There are two modes of display, called *bit-mapped* and *character displays*, and a CRT system may be capable of only one or of both modes.

In the bit-mapped mode, a RAM holds an image of the display exactly as it appears; each pixel on the display is a bit in RAM. The display controller just dumps memory out, word by word, and each word is then shifted out serially to get the video signal.

In the character display mode, generally an ASCII character code is stored in memory and is read into the controller when needed. A *character generator* – a ROM with character patterns in it – translates this ASCII code into the bit pattern that corresponds to the pixels. Basically, at the address that is the ASCII character code concatenated to the line number, the bit pattern for that row of that character is stored as a word. Reading in the ASCII code and the line number, you get the bit pattern to put on the screen. Suppose there are 80 characters in a row, and each character is 7 raster scan lines high, as in figure 9-8b. The character H is stored in RAM in ASCII code. For the 7 raster line scan times that this character is to be displayed, the character is read from RAM into the character generator; the line number is also put into the character generator; and the output of the character generator is shifted out to get the video signal. The ASCII character H, like the other 79 characters in the row that H is on, must be cycled out of memory seven times so that each character like H is sent to the character generator when each line in it is displayed. Some time back, the ASCII character codes for a row were actually stored in a shift register, called a row buffer, which circulated the characters; but now RAMs are cheaper and the shift register is simulated by supplying the addresses of the buffer area cyclically.

The character display mode is suited to simple terminals, whether they are "intelligent," having programmable features, or "dumb," emulating a teletypewriter. If you have an 80-character-per-row by 24-character row per screen display, the RAM needs only 1920 bytes, and an inexpensive 2K by 8 static RAM such as the 6116 is ideal. The bit-mapped mode requires much more memory. If each character is represented by a matrix of 10 pixels horizontally by 12 pixels vertically, the memory needs to be 120 times larger, or 230,400 bits, or 28,800 bytes. That's about half of the primary memory the 6811 is capable of addressing. The character generator really saves a lot of memory. However, bit-mapped displays are able to display different fonts and font sizes for a more pleasing display, as well as graphics and text mixed with graphics. As memory prices have dropped, bit-mapped displays have become much more popular. The Macintosh personal computer, upon which this book was written, the Atari 520, and the Amiga use bit-mapped displays. The main disadvantage remaining with bit-mapped displays is the rather large amount of software, including the patterns of the characters and the programs to generate different font sizes. The character generator supplies the basic features you need in one chip, so your program is much simpler. Further, the 2670 character generator used in the 2670-73 chip set is designed so that all you need to do is put it into a circuit as instructed and you have all the display functions you need for a character display. The main disadvantage of using such a character generator is you are given all the display functions for a character display – they are fixed by the manufacturer. You cannot easily add a special feature.

As listed in the Signetics or Motorola data sheets, there are four ways to build a character mode CRT controller using the 2670-73 chip set. These ways, and one additional way often used for bit-mapped displays, are shown in figure 9-12.

The easiest circuit to build is for the *independent mode*, shown in figure 9-12a. The 6811 processor is able to read and write the registers in the 2672 controller, and write a byte in a buffer register. The 2672 will be given a command; then, when it can, it generates an address for the 6116 memory, and the byte in the buffer register is put on the data bus to be written into the 6116. Otherwise the 6116 continually dumps its contents through the character generator to the video chip (which is basically a shift register) to get the video signal. We will use this mode in our example.

Second and third methods use the *shared mode* and the *transparent mode* of the chip set. Both use the same hardware, diagramed in figure 9-12b. The 6116 display memory appears to be part of the addressable primary memory of the computer, and display memory can be read from or write in just like any other word in primary memory. An address decoder decodes the processor memory address to determine if the address is in the range of words in the 6116; if so, it forces the 6116 to be part of the processor memory. The hardware requires an address multiplexor, or mux, to select the memory address from the 2672 when the 6116 supplies characters for display, or from the processor address bus when the processor reads or writes into the 6116. A bidirectional bus driver separates the 6116 data bus from the processor data bus so the 6116 can send characters to the character generator while the processor is doing something totally different in its primary memory; but the driver joins the busses when the processor reads or writes in the 6116. The mode is called transparent if processor accesses do not affect the image on the CRT; this is done by limiting the processor accesses to the time when horizontal or vertical retrace occurs. If the processor has unrestricted access to the 6116, the mode is called shared, and a blip can occur on the screen if the processor accesses the 6116 at the time a character is being read to the character generator.

A fourth way uses the *row buffer* mode. It is similar to the independent mode, diagramed in figure 9-12a, but has a bus driver rather than a register between the 6116 data bus and the processor data bus. Basically, the 6116 simulates a shift register. It is loaded when a new row of characters is about to be displayed, and it is cyclically read out to provide the character generator with the character codes as each raster scan line of the row is displayed. Once one row of characters is read from the primary memory, it is used over and over again in the CRT system until another row is needed. The processor can be synchronized to provide the characters from its own primary memory by means of DMA or by interrupts at the beginning of each character row. The processor must provide a byte at the time the 6116 is writing the byte, since the bus driver between the CRT and processor has no memory. The Intel 8275 CRT controller uses such a row buffer mode and works well with DMA.

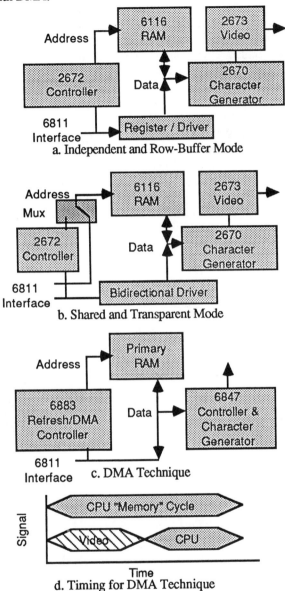

a. Independent and Row-Buffer Mode

b. Shared and Transparent Mode

c. DMA Technique

d. Timing for DMA Technique

Figure 9-12. Five Approaches to CRT System Design

A fifth way, ideally suited to bit-mapped displays and to the 6883 and 6847 chips, uses a time-multiplexed primary memory. The technique takes advantage of the fact that most memories are twice as fast as most processors. (See figure 9-12d.) If a 2-MHz cycle time memory is used with a 1-MHz memory cycle time processor, the memory can execute two cycles in the time the processor executes one cycle. The top trace in figure 9-12d represents the processor cycle. The latter of the two memory cycles, shown as the right part of the bottom trace, is used by the processor. The first of the two memory cycles is available for the CRT display and can be used to dump words out to the display in a bit-mapped display, or read characters to a character generator in a character display. The 6883 and 6847 chips are designed to work with the 6809 to do this very simply. (See figure 9-12c.) The 6883 passes the addresses from the processor to the memory in the latter half of each processor "memory" cycle and generates an address to read bits or characters to the 6847 in the first half of each cycle. It also provides addresses to refresh a dynamic memory. The 6847 can just shift the bits out to get a bit-mapped display, or, using a character generator in it, it can generate the image from "ASCII"-coded characters read from primary memory. (They are somewhat different codes, but are easily translated to or from ASCII.)

The independent mode, using the 2670-73 chip set, is the easiest to use with the 6811. The shared mode permits the processor to fill the 6116 much faster, and should be considered for higher performance character displays. The DMA mode is especially suited to bit-mapped displays.

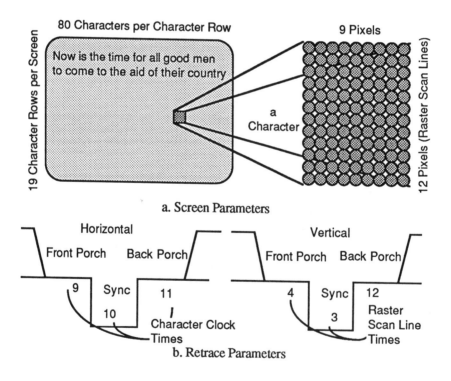

a. Screen Parameters

b. Retrace Parameters

Figure 9-13. Characteristics of a CRT Display

We now show an implementation of the "independent" technique. This rather lengthy program is divided into parts. The first part shows the settings of the various parameters needed to implement the display. These are derived from the characteristics of the CRT we will use; and these determine parameters used in the program and values of a table that will be forced into the CRT controller to direct its operation. We then show the hardware, which uses the indirect I/O technique for simplicity, and the subroutines needed to use this technique to read and write the registers in the CRT controller. We then show the subroutine to insert characters into the screen. Finally, we show the initialization routine and the table used to initialize the CRT control registers. The program and hardware are selected to make it fairly easy to implement and experiment with. In particular, some powerful instructions in the 2672, such as "fill from cursor to pointer" are not used, but software is used to repeatedly change the pointer and write there. We also derived the clock from the 8-MHz 6811 clock to avoid the need to build an oscillator. This discussion is aimed at getting you started so that, if you wish, you can expand upon it and build your own customized terminal.

First, based on the availability of a suitable CRT, we find we can build a 12-raster-line-per-character, 80-character-per-row, 19-row-per-screen, display. (See figure 9-13.) Each pixel is written at 16 MHz, so a *character clock*, the time to write one raster line of one character, is 16/9 = 1.78 MHz. We determine from the specifications that the horizontal pulse width and front and back porches (which shall always be at the black level because they correspond to the perimeter of the CRT screen which is too nonlinear to display characters) are as follows: front porch 9-character clocks, horizontal sync width 10-character clocks, and horizontal back porch width 11-character clocks. The sync width and back porch parameters are put in the 2672 in the upcoming program; they are limited to certain values that can be coded in a table. The sum of horizontal front porch, horizontal sync pulse width, and back porch times gives the horizontal blanking interval which is encoded into a parameter EQUC that is put into the 2672; it has a limited range that implies the range of the front porch. This gives a raster scan line of 1.78 MHz/(80 displayed characters + 30 character clock times) = 14,814 Hz, a little slower than that used by the NTSC standard. The vertical front porch was determined to be 4 raster lines, vertical sync width 3 raster lines (this is fixed by the 2672, and we must use it), vertical back porch width 12 raster lines. The vertical front and back porch widths are encoded in the table that is loaded into the 2672 upon initialization. The sum of vertical front porch, vertical sync pulse width, and back porch times gives the vertical blanking interval. Other parameters were chosen and put in the equates shown, to fully specify the operation of the system. Their meaning can be found by reading the data sheets for the 2672. Your CRT will likely have different values, but you can use these as a start and get the correct values by experiment.

```
        NAM  CRTC
*
* PARAMETERS FOR TABLE AND PROGRAM CONSTANTS
*
* PARAMETERS OTHER THAN HORIZ, VERT, SCREEN, CURSOR
*
```

```
INTERL    EQU    0              0 - NO INTERLACE 1 INTERLACE
BUFMD     EQU    0              BUF MD 0 - IND, 1 - TRNS, 2 - SHD, 3 - RW
SYNC      EQU    0              0 - VSYNC, 1 - CSYNC
CHBR      EQU    0              0 - CHR BLK @ 1/16 , 1 - @ 1/32 VSYNC
DBLHT     EQU    0              1 - DOUBLE HEIGHT, 0 - SINGLE HEIGHT
LPL       EQU    5              LIGHT PEN LINE 3, 5, 7, 9
ULP       EQU    11             UNDERLINE POSITION 0 - 15
SCR       EQU    0              SPLIT SCREEN INTERRUPT ROW 0 - 127
*
* VISIBLE SCREEN
*
SPCR      EQU    12             SCANS PER CHARACTER ROW
* FOR SPCR, IF NON-INTLCD SPCR MAY BE 1 - 16, ELSE 5, 7,..., 31
ACS       EQU    19             ACTIVE CHR ROWS PER SCREEN 1 - 128
ACR       EQU    80             ACTIVE CHARACTERS PER ROW 3 - 256
DBLA      EQU    $7FF           DISPY BUF LAST ADDR 1023, 2047, .16383
DBS       EQU    ACR*ACS        DISPLAY BUFFER SIZE
DBFA      EQU    DBLA-DBS+1 DISPLAY BUFFER FIRST ADR 0 - 4095
*
* HORIZONTAL SYNC PARAMETERS
*
HFP       EQU    9              HOR FRNT PORCH - CHECK EQUC BELOW
HSW       EQU    10             HORIZONTAL SYNC WIDTH 2, 4, ... 32
HBP       EQU    9              HORIZONTAL BACK PORCH 1, 5, ... 29
EQUC      EQU    ACR+HFP+HSW+HBP/2-HSW-HSW 35 EQ CNST 1 - 128
*
* VERTICAL SYNC PARAMETERS (VERT SYNC WIDTH IS FIXED AT 3)
*
VFP       EQU    4              VERTICAL FRONT PORCH 4, 8, ... 32
VBP       EQU    12             VERTICAL BACK PORCH 4, 6, ... 66
*
* CURSOR
*
FLC       EQU    0              FIRST LINE OF CURSOR 0 - 15
LLC       EQU    11             LAST LINE OF CURSOR 0 - 15
CBK       EQU    1              1 - CURSOR BLINK, 0 - NO BLINK
CUBR      EQU    0              0 CSR BLINK 1/16 VSYNC 1 - 1/32 VSYNC
```

The hardware in figure 9-14 uses a rather standard connection among the chips in the 2670-72-73 chip set for the "independent" mode. We use indirect I/O so that mis-wiring the CRT controller system does not debilitate the 6811 and the BUFFALO monitor. This makes debugging relatively easy. Pin names are different from those given in the data sheets because we give the same name to a signal at each pin it is connected to, where it helps to facilitate following the wires. The 2670-72-73 chip set provides the sync timing and control (2672), the character generation (2670) and the assembly of the video signal (2673), and the 6116 2K x 8 static RAM holds the text being displayed.

The 2673 produces the video output signal on pin 28. The circuit generating this signal is a current source that requires a 75Ω resistor to ground. That resistor, ideally, should be inside the CRT itself to terminate the 75Ω coax cable properly. If it is not there, then it must be added, as shown following the 2673 in figure 9-14. The 74HC266 quad exclusive-NOR with open drain outputs provides all the extra functions. The 8-MHz 6811 oscillator signal is frequency-doubled by two gates in the 266. This circuit exclusive-NORs a square-wave with itself delayed a quarter of a cycle. It avoids the need for an extra crystal and produces a dot-clock of 16 MHz. (However, in one system we built, this circuit produced eratic pulses. You should verify that it gives a stable 16-MHz square wave with 25 to 75% duty cycle.) Another gate in the 266 works as an inverter to get the output enable of the 6116 from the write enable of that chip, and the 266 generates a combined horizontal and vertical sync to "short out" the video signal when sync pulses are sent and to generate the composite video signal. One can build this circuit on a small (6" x 6") card, with a 16-pin "dip" header connection to the 6811. Some pins (pins 9, 11, 20, 27, 31, 34, and 35 of the 2673 and pins 13 and 14 of the 2670) are wired to ground while other pins (pins 10, 12, and 33 of the 2673) should be tied together and connected to +5 volts through a 1kΩ "pull-up" resistor to configure some of the chips, particularly the 2673. These should be triple-checked, as the symptoms of mis-wiring these pins are hard to trace. A similar system, using direct I/O, should be used in a real CRT controller. The connections for such a system and the changes in the program are left for exercises at the end of this chapter. This system is useful as an intermediate step in designing the direct I/O system, because wiring errors do not completely bring down the debugger.

Consistent with the pin connections in figure 9-14, the following declarations are used:

```
*
PORTB    EQU    $1004
RADDR    EQU    7          REGISTER ADDRESS
RD       EQU    8          READ ENABLE
WR       EQU    $10        INTERRUPT
CE       EQU    $20        CHIP ENABLE FOR 2672
EN       EQU    $40        ENABLE FOR 374
ALL      EQU    RD+WR+CE+EN
*
PORTC    EQU    $1003      DATA I/O
DIRC     EQU    $1007      DIRECTION
*
```

A simple subroutine puts an ASCII-coded character or an attribute byte in ACCA into the 74HC374. Bidirectional port C is made an output. Then the character is put into port C. The control bits are sequenced by storing constants into port B so that the 74HC374 chip enable EN is toggled. This copies the byte in port C into the 374. The 2672 will eventually cause it to be written into the 6116 display memory at the appropriate time.

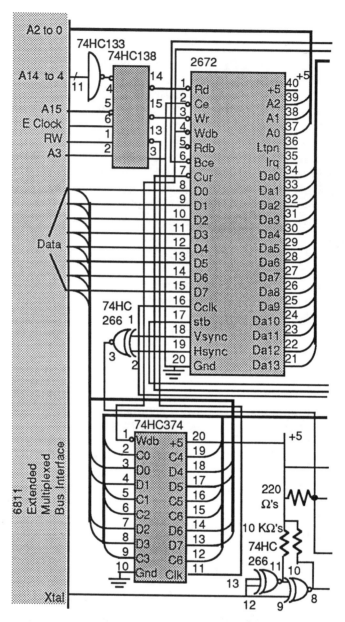

Figure 9-14. A CRT Display System

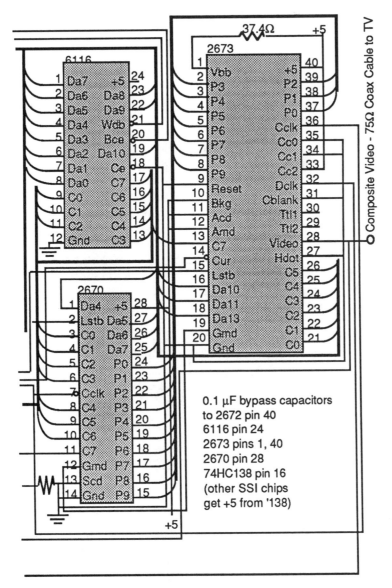

Figure 9-14. (Continued)

```
OUTREG    LDAB  #$FF
          STAB  DIRC
          STAA  PORTC
          LDAB  #ALL
          STAB  PORTB
          LDAB  #ALL-EN ENABLE 374
          STAB  PORTB
          LDAB  #ALL
          STAB  PORTB
          CLR   DIRC
          RTS
```

To put control data into the 2672, a set of subroutines similar to the preceding can be used. OUTCMD puts ACCA into the command register, OUTSTRT puts ACCD into the screen start register, and OUTCURS puts ACCD into the cursor. They use subroutine OUTA, which puts data in ACCA to the register selected by ACCB. WAITRDY inputs the status register to ACCA and gadflies until the "ready" bit in the status register of the 2672 signals it is done; it is shown last.

```
OUTCMD  PSHA            SAVE COMMAND BYTE (ACCA)
        JSR    WAITRDY  MAKE SURE NO OTHER CMD IS EXING
OUTCMD2 PULA            O.K., GET DATA TO BE WRITTEN
OUTCMD3 LDAB  #1        WRITE REG 1
        BRA   OUTA
*
OUTSTRT PSHB            REG DTA IN ACCD; SAVE LOW PART
        LDAB  #3        WRITE HIGH TO REG 3
        BSR   OUTA
        PULA            RECOVER LOW PART
        LDAB  #2        WRITE LOW TO REG 2
        BRA   OUTA
*
OUTCURS PSHB            REG DATA IN ACCD; SAVE LOW PART
        LDAB  #5        WRITE HIGH TO REG 5
        BSR   OUTA
        PULA            RECOVER LOW PART
        LDAB  #4        WRT LOW TO REG 4 - FL THRU TO OUTA
*
OUTA    PSHB            SAVE
        LDAB  #$FF      MAKE PORT C
        STAB  DIRC      AN OUTPUT PORT
        STAA  PORTC     PUT DATA, TO GO INTO REG, INTO PT C
        PULB
        ORAB  #ALL
        ANDB  #$FF-CE   ASSERT REG ADDRESS, CHIP ENABLE
        STAB  PORTB     ADDRESS TO PORT B
```

```
        ANDB  #$FF-WR
        STAB  PORTB      ASSERT WRITE LOW
        ORAB  #WR        REMOVE WRITE
        STAB  PORTB
        ORAB  #CE        REMOVE CE
        STAB  PORTB
        CLR   DIRC       MAKE PORT B INPUT AGAIN
        RTS
*
WAITRDY LDAB  #ALL+1
        ANDB  #$FF-CE    ASSERT REG ADDRESS, CHIP ENABLE
        STAB  PORTB      ADDRESS TO PORT B, STROBE TO CE
        ANDB  #$FF-RD
        STAB  PORTB      ASSERT READ LINE LOW
        LDAA  PORTC      GET DATA
        ORAB  #RD        REMOVE READ
        STAB  PORTB
        ORAB  #CE        REMOVE CHIP ENABLE
        STAB  PORTB
        BITA  #$20       SEE IF READY
        BEQ   WAITRDY    IF FALSE, WAIT
        RTS
```

The next subroutine, used in character insertion described next, calculates the cursor position from the row and column numbers, and inserts the cursor position into the 2672. It permits the rest of the program to make decisions based on the row and column of the character being inserted, and translates the row-column number into an address in the 6116 memory, to be used by the 2672. This subroutine is just a two-dimensional vector address calculation, discussed in chapter 2.

```
        ORG   0          GLOBAL VARIABLES IN LOW MEMORY
ROWN    RMB   1
COLN    RMB   1
        ORG   $C000      PUT IN WITH REST OF THE PROGRAM
SETCUR  JSR   WAITRDY    WAIT UNTIL READY
        LDAA  ROWN       GET ROW NUMBER
        LDAB  #ACR       MULTIPLY BY CHARACTERS PER ROW
        MUL
        ADDB  COLN       ADD COLUMN NUMBER
        ADCA  #0         PROPAGATE CARRY
        ADDD  #DBFA      ADD DISPLAY BUFFER FIRST ADDRESS
        BRA   OUTCURS    SET CURSOR THERE
```

We now examine the main subroutine needed to insert characters into the display memory (6116). It is described in two parts. The first part handles the carriage return. We show both parts, then explain them, the second part first.

```
OUTDATA  CMPA  #$0D      CARRIAGE RETURN
         BNE   OUTDATA3
         LDAA  ROWN      GET ROW NUMBER
         INCA            NEXT ROW
         CMPA  #ACS      ACTIVE CHARACTERS PER SCREEN
         BCS   OUTDATA1 IF PAST
         CLRA            START AT BEGINNING
OUTDATA1 STAA  ROWN      REESTABLISH ROW
         CLR   COLN      START AT LEFT COLUMN
         BSR   SETCUR    SET UP CURSOR
OUTDATA2 LDAA  #$80      ATTRIBUTE FILLED SPACE
         BSR   OUTDATA   INTO ROW
         LDAA  COLN      UNTIL COLUMN
         CMPA  #ACR      IS AT END
         BNE   OUTDATA2 TO CLEAR ALL OF THE ROW
         LDAA  ROWN      GET ROW NUMBER
         INCA
         CMPA  #ACS
         BNE   OUTDATA9
         CLRA
OUTDATA9 LDAB  #ACR      MULTIPLY BY CHARACTERS PER ROW
         MUL
         ADDD  #DBFA     ADD DISPLAY BUFFER FIRST ADDRESS
         BSR   OUTSTRT   SET CURSOR THERE
         CLR   COLN      RETURN TO LEFT COLUMN
         BRA   SETCUR    MOVE CURSOR
```

The second part of the subroutine handles the backspace and normal character insertion.

```
OUTDATA3 CMPA  #$08      BACKSPACE
         BNE   OUTDATA4
         TST   COLN      IF AT LEFT
         BEQ   OUTDATA5 IGNORE
         DEC   COLN      ELSE MOVE LEFT
         BSR   SETCUR    MOVE CURSOR
         LDAA  #$20
         JSR   OUTREG    PUT SPACE IN OUTPUT REGISTER
         BSR   OUTDATA7
         BRA   SETCUR    MOVE CURSOR
OUTDATA4 PSHA            SAVE VALUE
         LDAA  COLN      GET COLUMN NUMBER
         CMPA  #ACR      COMP TO ACTIVE CHAR PER ROW
         BCS   OUTDATA6 IF BEYOND SCREEN
         PULA            BALANCE STACK
OUTDATA5 RTS             EXIT
```

```
OUTDATA6 PULA                    OK, GET DATA TO BE WRITTEN
        JSR    OUTREG            PUT DATA IN REGISTER
        INC    COLN
OUTDATA7 LDAA  #$AB              WRITE AT CURSOR AND INC CURSOR
        BRA    OUTCMD3
```

If any character other than carriage return ($0D) or backspace ($08) is in ACCA when OUTDATA is called, we jump to OUTDATA4 to put it in the display memory. We first check that we have not run off the end of the line, for if we have we shall just ignore the character. If it is on the screen, we use the subroutine OUTREG to put the byte into the 74HC374, and then we give a command to the 2672 to write the byte in the 347 into the 6116 display memory where the cursor is and move the cursor to the next column in the same row. We also keep track of the cursor column in COLN. Backspace is handled, in code after label OUTDATA3, by decrementing the column number COLN. However, this should not be done if the cursor is on column 0. To erase it, we should put a space character over the character that was backspaced over; but using the existing subroutine OUTDATA to output a space character, we have to juggle the cursor using the subroutine SETCUR.

Carriage return, handled in the first half of the subroutine OUTDATA, causes the next character to be put on a new line. We choose to implement our display such that data are always written on the bottom line of the screen and data formerly there are moved up a line. The 2672 has a feature that makes this easy to do. Basically, the characters displayed on the screen are selected by an address counter in the 2672 from the data stored in the 6116 memory. The characters come from a buffer area (which must end in an address, called DBLA, whose low-order 9 bits are all 1s). This address DBLA and the address of the first byte of this buffer (called DBFA) are in the registers in the 2672 that are loaded when it is initialized, as the initialization table is dumped into the 2672. As the 2672 address counter generates addresses to read data from the 6116 to the 2673, if an address equals the address DBLA, the next address in the counter will be DBFA. This makes the character buffer circular. So, the value in the START register, loaded by subroutine OUTSTRT, is used to initialize the 6116 address counter when a new frame is about to be displayed, during the vertical retrace time. Thus, it is the address of the character to be displayed at the top left of the screen. Because the buffer is circular, about all that a carriage return needs to do is load the START register with the address just beyond the end of that new row where succeeding characters will be put. Well, that row needs to be cleared before any characters are put into it. The row is cleared, rather as in the backspace routine, by writing "spaces" in the loop below label OUTDATA2, and the START address is set up in the code around label OUTDATA9.

An annoying problem with this system is that the 6116 memory may have attribute characters (with bit 7 set to 1) when power is applied, and an attribute called BLANK can make the display invisible. We do not further discuss attributes in this section, except to note that they need to be forced off. Problems at the end of the chapter show how they can be used. Fortunately, attribute characters are displayed as spaces. Therefore, we use an attribute character $80, rather than the ASCII space, $20, as a "space" character to fill after a carriage return, to repeatedly force the attributes off.

Upon initialization, the memory should be filled with "spaces" as just explained. A subroutine to fill the display memory with attribute bytes $80 (to initialize the display to no attributes) is shown next and is used shortly in the initialization routine.

```
FILLDATA  BSR    WAITRDY  GET STATUS
          LDD    #0       DBFA DATA BUFFER FIRST ADDRESS
FILLDATA1 PSHA
          PSHB
          JSR    OUTCURS
          LDAA   #$80     ATTRIBUTE FILLED SPACE
          BSR    OUTREG   PUT DATA IN REGISTER
          BSR    OUTDATA7
          PULB
          PULA
          ADDD   #1
          CMPD   #$7FF    DBLA DATA BUFFER LAST ADDRESS
          BNE    FILLDATA1
          LDAA   #ACS-1   LAST ROW
          STAA   ROWN
          CLR    COLN
          BRA    SETCUR   SET CURSOR
```

We now present the initialization routine. The table for it is shown at the end. The routine sets up the ports and resets the 2672 twice, as required by that chip. Then a command is given to turn off the display. The 11 bytes of the table TBL are then written into the "initialization registers" IR0 through IR10 by writing these bytes into the same location in the 2672 chip. Successively written bytes are put in successive initialization registers. Although these registers can be changed after initialization for special effects, they are normally left alone after they are initialized. The routine ends in a loop that uses a BUFFALO monitor subroutine to get a character from the RS232 input and feeds the byte to the preceding OUTDATA subroutine. (The address of this RS232 input subroutine is different in different 68HC11A8s and different boards.)

```
INCH EQU  $FFCD
*
INIT      LDAA   #$FF
          STAA   PORTB
          CLR    DIRC
          STAA   PORTC
          CLR    FLAGS
          CLRA            NEED TO RESET TWICE
          JSR    OUTCMD
          CLRA
          JSR    OUTCMD
          LDAA   #$3E     DISPLAY OFF
```

```
            JSR     OUTCMD
            LDAA    #$9F        DISABLE ALL INTERRUPTS
            JSR     OUTCMD
            LDAA    #$10        LOAD IR 0
            JSR     OUTCMD
            LDX     #TBL
OUTBUF1 LDAA 0,X
            CLRB                WRITE TO REGISTER 0
            JSR OUTA
            INX
            CPX     #ENDTBL
            BNE     OUTBUF1
            LDD     #DBFA
            JSR     OUTSTRT     SET START TO 0
            LDAA    #$39        TURN ON CURSOR, SCREEN
            JSR     OUTCMD
            BSR     FILLDATA FILL SCREEN WITH SPACES
OUTLOOP JSR     INCH
            BSR OUTDATA         AT BEGINNING OF BUFFER
            BRA OUTLOOP
```

The table needed in the initialization routine is shown next. Parameters from the beginning of this program are combined into fields in 11 bytes, which are fed into the initialization registers IR0 to IR10 in the 2672. The details of which bytes are loaded with which parameters can be found in the 2672 data sheets. EQU directives are used to create these bytes because the assembler does not permit parentheses in its expressions.

```
TBL EQU *
* CALCULATIONS (BECAUSE WE DO NOT HAVE PAREN IN EXPRES.)
TEMP1       EQU     SPCR-1-INTERL-INTERL IF INTERLEAVE, THEN
TEMP2       EQU     INTERL+1        PUT IN (SPCR-3)/2
TEMP3       EQU     TEMP1/TEMP2 ELSE SPCR-1
TEMP4       EQU     HSW/2-1
TEMP5       EQU     HBP-1
TEMP6       EQU     TEMP5/4
TEMP7       EQU     VFP/4-1
TEMP8       EQU     VBP/2-2
TEMP9       EQU     LPL-3
TEMP10      EQU     DBFA/256
TEMP11      EQU     TEMP10*256
TEMP12      EQU     DBLA+1
TEMP13      EQU     TEMP12/1024-1
* THE TABLE
            FCB     TEMP3*2+SYNC*4+BUFMD         IR0
            FCB     INTERL*128+EQUC-1            IR1
            FCB     TEMP4*8+TEMP6                IR2
```

```
          FCB      TEMP7*32+TEMP8                    IR3
          FCB      CHBR*128+ACS-1                    IR4
          FCB      ACR-1                             IR5
          FCB      FLC*16+LLC                        IR6
          FCB      TEMP9+CBK*2+DBLHT*16+ULP          IR7
          FCB      DBFA-TEMP11                       IR8
          FCB      TEMP13*16+TEMP10                  IR9
          FCB      CUBR*128+SCR                      IR10
ENDTBL    EQU *
```

This section introduced a realistic character display for a dumb terminal. The system shown in figure 9-14 is suitably flexible so you further experiment with it to get a comprehensive understanding of character display. We encourage you to study it.

9.3 Conclusions

This chapter introduced two common interfaces: the secondary storage and CRT display. These rather complete case studies give a reasonably full example of common interface designs. They also embody the techniques you have studied in earlier chapters. Besides presenting these important interfaces, this chapter serves to complete the book by showing how the techniques in the other chapters will find extensive application in almost any interface design.

For further reading on floppy disks, we strongly recommend the data sheets for the 1772 from Western Digital. Harold Stone's "Microcomputer Interfacing" has additional general information on the analog aspects of storage devices. The 2670-73 chip set is described in the Signetics application note 401, "Using the 2670/71/72/73 Chip Set," available at the end of their MOS Microprocessor Data Manual, and in an excellent Motorola application note AN895, "Using the MC267X CRT Set with the MC6809E," by Arnaldo Cruz. These can be consulted for further examples and inspiration.

This text has been fun for us. Microcomputers like the 6811 are such powerful tools that it challenges the mind to dream up ways to use them well. We sincerely hope you have enjoyed reading about and experimenting with the 6811 microcomputer.

Problems

Problems 7 and 22 are paragraph correction problems; see guidelines at the end of chapter 1. Programming guidelines are given at the end of chapter 2, and hardware design guidelines are at the end of chapter 3.

1. The Radio Shack TRS-80 Color Computer uses a tape format similar to the Kansas City Standard, as shown in table 9-2. An output mechanism uses an address trigger at location $8000, that will put a short positive and a short negative pulse on the tape.

Table 9-2. TRS80 Cassette Tape Format

A word is 8 bits, sent most significant bit first.
A False bit is a short positive, then negative pulse followed by 2 msec. mute (with no pulses).   A True bit is a short positive, then negative pulse, a msec. mute, a short positive, then negative pulse, and a msec. mute

A record is a leader, a name, one or more data blocks,
      and an entry point address, where the following apply:
 The leader is 255 bytes of zero words and the sync code $A5.
 The name is the word $55 and the 6 letter ASCII name of the record
      padded on the right with blanks (ASCII code $20).
 The data block is described next
 The entry point is the word $78 and the least significant and then
      the most significant bytes of the starting address.

The data block is the block size, the data, and the checksum, where the following apply:
 The block size is the word $3C, the number of bytes in the block
      (00 represents 256), and the low byte and then the high byte
      of the address of the first data word in the block.
 The data are up to 256 words to be stored in ascending addresses.
 The checksum is the 8-bit sum of the bytes in the address and data words.

    a. Write a 6811 subroutine WOUT to output a word in accumulator A by means of the address trigger onto a cassette, using real-time synchronization.

    b. Write a 6811 handler CASWD that is entered every millisecond, which will output the word stored in global variable WD, using the address trigger. Use a global variable TICK that tells how many milliseconds are left in the time to output the word. Use output compare 1 to request an interrupt each millisecond.

    c. Write a program to output the buffer at location BUFFR of length LEN onto the cassette. The buffer is already completely formatted as described in table 9-2 and contains all the words from the 255 0's through to the high byte of the starting address.

d. Write an interrupt handler which outputs the contents of the buffer BUFFR of part c. Use global variables to keep track of how many words are yet to be output (LEN), how many bits are to be output in that word, and where we are in the current word (TICK).

2. Rewrite the Kansas City Standard Routine KCIN of section 9-1.1 to use gadfly synchronization. Use the capture 1 timer module for measuring pulse width and the compare 2 timer module to measure $1/300th$ second. Use the same I/O hardware diagramed in figure 9.1.

3. Rewrite the Kansas City Standard Routines to use real-time synchronization. Use the same I/O hardware diagramed in figure 9.1.
    a. The tape output KCOUT of section 9-1.1. (See SUART of section 8-3.1).
    b. The tape input KCIN of section 9-1.1. (See RUART of section 8-3.1).

4. The input routine in KCIN in section 9-1.1 compares the pulse width against a constant THRES to determine whether a long or short pulse is sent. Rewrite HNDLR1 of KCIN to have an adaptive threshold, determined as follows: There are two fixed-length (8-element) queues (software shift registers) QUEUL and QUEUS that store the (8) most recent long pulse widths and the (8) most recent long pulse widths (as 2-byte elements initialized to $8*152$). Using the current threshold, which is the sum of the elements of both queues divided by 16, determine if the pulse is long or short; if long, push it into QUEUL, and if short, push it into QUEUS. Then use the long/short bit as in KCIN.

5. The Kansas City Standard tape interface can be handled by the Serial Communication Interface (SCI) of the 6811, using analog hardware to shape the "sine wave" output and to measure the input pulse width. Show the logic diagram (excluding pin numbers) for the following circuits:
    a. Use a $2400*16$-Hz oscillator, 74HC4040 counter, logic to clear that counter, a (256,8) ROM, and 8-bit D-to-A converter that generates 8 cycles of a sine wave of 2400-Hz or 4 cycles of a sine wave of 1200-Hz, depending on whether the MSB if the ROM address is 0 or 1. The MSB comes from the SCI TX output signal, and the 74HC4040 is cleared each time there is a change of that signal.
    b. Assume the cassette tape output is input to the shaping circuit in figure 9-1. Using a 555 and 74HC74, clock the latter to sample the input such that its output can connect to the SCI Rx input.

6. Write the following routines for the 6811:
    a. KCOUT for the circuit in problem 9-5a.
    b. KCIN for the circuit in problem 9-5b.
    c. An initialization ritual for the SCI module for parts a and b.

7.* A surface of a typical floppy disk is divided into concentric rings called sectors, and each sector is divided into segments. A sector may be read or written as a whole, but individual bytes in it may not be read or written. The format of a sector has only some 0's, a $A1 flag pattern, data address mark, the data, and a CRC check; counters are used to keep track of the track and sector. To read (write) a sector, it is necessary to first give a command to seek the track, then give a command to read (write) the sector.

8. Explain why 9 512-byte sectors must be able to be put on the same track of the floppy disk as is described in figure 9-4, which currently has 18 256-byte sectors. Draw figure 9-4 for such a format. (This format is used on the IBM PC.)

9. Exhaustively prove that the special pattern in figure 9-5 cannot occur in the normal coding of MFM data shown in figure 9-3. (This pattern also has the property that a phase-locked loop will not lose synchronization.)

10. Show a logic diagram of the address decoder in figure 9-6a (connected to Cs of the WD1772). Show all pin numbers of the MC68HC11A8, 74HC374 that demultiplexes the address, and the 74HC240 and 74HC133 that decode the address $7FFx.

11. Show the hexadecimal values of the WD1772 commands to
   a. Restore, enable spin-up, disable verify, using a 5-ms step rate.
   b. Seek, disable spin-up, disable verify, using a 2-ms step rate.
   c. Step in, disable spin-up, enable verify, using a 3-ms step rate.
   d. Read a single sector, enable spin-up.
   e. Write normal multiple sectors, disable spin-up, enable write precompensation.

12. Rewrite the SEEK subroutine of section 9-1.2 (and add appropriate handlers and initialization rituals) for direct I/O as shown in figure 9-6a.
   a. Use gadfly synchronization.
   a. Use interrupt synchronization.
Enable the IRQ interrupt, where the IRQ pin is connected as in figure 9-6a, so the handler is entered when the track is found. The interrupt handler should jump to a subroutine whose address is in the double-byte variable GOTO, and then return to the interrupted routine.

13. Rewrite the SEEK subroutine of section 9-1.2 (which uses indirect I/O) so it is given a logical sector in ACCD rather than a track number. It should seek the track for an 18-sector track, 35-track single-sided zero-origin indexed disk and put the sector number in the WD1772 sector register.

14. Rewrite the SEEK subroutine of section 9-1.2 (which uses indirect I/O shown in figure 9-6b) to check for errors after the track is supposedly found. If SEEK executes correctly, return Carry=0, otherwise return Carry=1 and an error code in ACCA. Consult the WD1772 data sheet and explain exactly what the bits in the error code mean.

15. Rewrite the INBUF subroutine of section 9-1.2 for direct I/O as shown in figure 9-6a. Use gadfly synchronization.

16. Rewrite the INBUF subroutine of section 9-1.2 (which uses indirect I/O) to check for errors after the sector is supposedly read. If the subroutine executes correctly, return

Carry=0, otherwise, return Carry=1 and an error code in ACCA. Consult the WD1772 data sheet and explain exactly what the bits in the error code in ACCA mean.

17. Rewrite the OUTBUF subroutine of Section 9-1.2 for direct I/O as shown in figure 9-6a. Use gadfly synchronization.

18. Rewrite the OUTBUF subroutine of section 9-1.2 (which uses indirect I/O shown in figure 9-6b) to check for write permission first, check for errors after the sector is supposedly written, and then read the sector using the subroutine INBUF and check for errors there. If the subroutine executes correctly, return Carry=0, otherwise, return Carry=1 and an error code in ACCA. Consult the WD1772 data sheet and explain exactly what the bits in the error code in ACCA mean.

19. Write subroutines to seek and read/write a sector, given a logical sector in ACCD, using the following retry strategy: (1) SEEK, if error go to step 6, (2) READ/WRITE the sector, (3) if no errors, exit (Carry (C)=0), (4) READ/WRITE the sector, (5) if no errors, exit (C=0), (6) STEP-IN and STEP-OUT, if error go to step 9, (7) READ/WRITE the sector, (8) if no errors, exit (C=0), (9) RESTORE, (10) repeat steps 1-8 twice, (11) quit and return error number (C=1).
    a. For the read routine, using the subroutine INBUF in problem 9-16.
    b. For the write routine, using the subroutine OUTBUF in problem 9-18.

20. Write a fixed bootstrap routine for indirect I/O (figure 9-6b). Sectors 0 to 17 of track 34 are read into locations $8000 to $91FF, and $8000 is jumped to. Do not use subroutines. Will this routine fit into the 512-byte EEPROM of an MC68HC11A8?

21. Write a flexible bootstrap routine for indirect I/O (figure 9-6b). Logical sector 0, bytes $10,$11 contain the first logical sector, and bytes $12,$13 contain the number of bytes to be read into locations $8000 and above, and $8000 is jumped to. Do not use subroutines. Will this routine fit into the 512-byte EEPROM of an MC68HC11A8?

22.* A TV screen is a series of fields; and in the NTCS format, a field takes 1/30 second. There are about 500 raster lines in a field, each line scanning from top to bottom of the screen, and each raster line takes about 60 µseconds. Sync pulses are incorporated into the composite video signal as gray level signals, and these are used to synchronize the horizontal and vertical oscillators that cause the electron beam to scan the screen. CRT controllers use either character or graphics display modes at any time. The former can use an independent mode, where the CRT gets characters from the primary memory of the processor using DMA; or the shared mode, where the processor writes into a separate display memory only during the horizontal retrace periods.

23. Rewrite the program in section 9-2.1 that outputs the same picture to a TV as in figure 9-10:
    a. Using gadfly synchronization, and the same counter and SPI modules.
    b. Using real-time synchronization, without counter modules, but with the SPI module.

24. Suppose port B of an MC68HC11A8 is connected to a 74HC165, shifting MSB out first, and clocked at 1 MHz. Rewrite the SPITV program to generate the following:
   a. The picture of figure 9-10.
   b. A letter A, where a pixel corresponds to 1 μsec. from the shift register, and is 4 lines high, and the letter is in the upper left 5 by 7 area of an 8 by 8 pixel format.

25. The 2670 (figure 9-14) is a ROM that inputs an ASCII code for a character in pins C7 to C0 and a raster line number of a character line in pins Da4 to Da7 and outputs the dot pattern that is to go on the screen on pins P9 to P0 (which go to a shift register and then the CRT). Suppose the 2670 is connected such that its C7 to C0 pins are connected to port B (which specifies the ASCII code) and its Da4-Da7 pins are connected to port C pins 3 to 0 (which specifies the raster line number of a character line). Write a subroutine that displays the ASCII-coded text, in buffer CRTBUF, on the TV screen, where a pixel corresponds to 1 μsec. from the shift register and is 3 lines high and the letter is in the upper left 7 by 9 area of a 10 by 12 pixel format.

26. Design a direct I/O CRT display system using the 2670, 2672, and 2673, comparable to figure 9-14, where the 2672 parameter register is at location $7FF0 and 74HC374 is at $7FF8 (see the decoder in figure 9-6a). Show only the different connections between the expanded multiplexed bus 6811 and the 2672 and 74HC374, rather than all the connections in figure 9-14.

27. Write an OUTDATA subroutine (section 9-2.2) for the direct I/O system in problem 9-26.

28. Write a FILLDATA subroutine (section 9-2.2) for the direct I/O system in problem 9-26.
   a. Use the "write at cursor, increment cursor" command, but do not use subroutines.
   b. Consult the 2672 data sheet. Use "write from cursor address to pointer address."

29. Assuming no control characters, page-mode writes consecutive characters from the top left to bottom right of the screen and repeats this after the screen is full, and scroll-mode writes consecutive characters only on the last line of the screen, moving the screen up when the bottom line is filled up. The OUTDATA program in section 9-2.2 operates in scroll-mode only.
   a. Rewrite OUTDATA to work in page-mode only.
   b. Rewrite OUTDATA to initially work in page-mode until the screen is full, and then work in scroll-mode.

30. Show the hexadecimal values of the 11 rows of the table TBL at the end of section 9-2.2, which are loaded into the 2672 parameter registers.

31. The parameters of the program CRTC are set up for a 14,814-Hz horizontal rate. Show the different parameters needed to get as near as possible to the NTSC 15,750-Hz

rate (smallest absolute value error), by contracting the horizontal front porch. Show the different parameters needed to get the vertical rate as close as possible to 60 Hz for this horizontal rate, by adjusting the number of character lines to get the maximim number with no less a front and back porch than in the current program and then contracting or expanding the vertical back porch.

Index

Bug, 6
Busy state, 204
Bus (or buss), 107
Bus available, 238
Bus driver, 107
Butterworth filter, 277
Bypass capacitor, 106, 274
Byte, 4

C

C language, 62
Call by name, 78
Call by reference, 78
Call by value and result, 77
Carriage return, 52
Carry bit C, 22
Cascade filter, 277
Case, 66
CCITT V.24, 383
Centralized communication system, 380
Channel, 378
Char, 63
Character clock, 451
Character display, 447
Character generator, 447
Character string, 56
Chebyshev filter, 278
Chip, 11
Chip enable (CE), 111
Circuit (communication system), 380
Clear to send, 385
Clock, 104, 109
Clocked flip-flop, 109
Coat hanger diagram, 80
Code, microprogram, 115
Coincident select keyboard, 288
Column major order, 55
Common cathode (LED), 290
Common-mode voltage, 272
Comparator (analog), 258
Compare instruction, 25
Complementary metal oxide (CMOS), 105
Complement (16's), 32

Complement a variable, 104
Completing an I/O action, 205
Composite video signal (NTSC), 443
Conditional jump instruction, 7
Condition code register, 22
Configure an I/O device, 167
Contact bounce, 284
Context of a processor, 234
Context switching, 234
Control instructions, 28
Controller, 4, 115
Control memory, 8, 116
Control register, 167, 168
Control transformer, 261
Control variables, 115
Coordinated data movement, 377
Copy name, 105
Counter, 110, 235, 322
Current loop, 382
Cycle, programmed logic, 159
Cycle steal DMA, 235
Cyclic redundancy check (CRC), 407
Cylinder, disk, 428

D

D flip-flop, 109
Darlington transistor, 264
Data-acquisition system (DAS), 306
Data-carrier-detect, 398
Data coupler, 385
Data operator, 4
Data structure, 49
Data terminal ready (DTR), 385
Data transfer, 8, 114
Debouncer, 285
Decision tree, 32
Declaration, 63
Decode, 8, 115
Del (delete), 52
Delay loop, 159
Delta A-to-D converter, 302
Deque, 58
Determinate signal, 104
Device is enabled, 219

Device handler, 7, 224
Die, 11
Differential amplifier, 269
Differential line, 380
Digital filter, 312
Digital-to-analog (D-to-A) converter, 258
Digit driver, 292
Direct addressing, 15
Direct current motor, 259
Direct current tachometer, 261
Direct I/O, 174
Direction register, 168
Direct memory access (DMA), 234
Direct memory access device, 236
Direct memory access controller (DMAC), 236
Directory, disk, 441
Displacement, 16
Distributed communication system, 380
DMA device, 236
DMA transfer cycle, 235
Do-loops, 31
Do while, 68
Done state, 204
Double buffer, 390
Double density disk format, 427
Driver, bus, 107
Dual in-line package, 11, 105
Dual power supply, 271
Dual-rank flip-flop, 109
Dual slope A-to-D, 303
Duty cycle, 281
Dyadic operation, 90
Dynamic efficiency, 10
Dynamic local variables, 73
Dynamic logic, 108

E

E clock (E), 128
Edge-sensitive interrupt, 230
Edge-triggered flip-flop, 109
Edit instructions, 27
Effective address, 5, 6

Electrically erasable programmable read-only memory (EEPROM), 37, 112
Enable clock, 128
Enabled, device, 219
Enabled, interrupt device is, 219
Enabled, microprocessor, 219
Enable, gate, 107
Encode, 115
End-of-text EOT, 52
End-to-end communication, 378
Entry point, 70
Equate assembler directive (EQU), 51
Equivalent signal, 104
Erasable programmable read-only memory (EPROM), 112
Ether-net, 387
Execute cycle, 9
Exit point, 70
Expanded multiplexed bus, 38
External interrupt is requested, 219
Extra 1-bit output mode (M6821), 207

F

False variable, 104
Family of integrated circuits, 105
Fan-in, 107
Fan-out, 106
Feedback, 267
Feedback system, 312
Fetch-execute cycle, 8
Fetching an instruction, 4
Fetch cycle, 8
Field, display, 442
Field effect transistor (FET), 264
Fields of a linked-list structure, 165
File, disk, 441
File descriptor, disk, 441
Fill area, disk, 430
Filter, 2 n th order, 277
Flag pattern, 408
Flip-flop, 109
Flow chart, 32
FM disk format, 427
For, 68, 75

Formal parameter, 77, 105
Format, disk, 431
Formatted capacity, disk, 431
Form constant byte (FCB), 51
Form constant character (FCC), 52
Form double byte (FDB), 51
Form feed, 52
Formula tree, 91
Frame, display, 442
Frame-level protocol, 379
Framing error (UART), 389
Frequency, 257
Frequency multiplexing, 378
Frequency shift keying, 378
Frequency-to-voltage converter (F-to-V), 258, 304
Full, buffer, 204
Full duplex channel, 378

Handshake protocol, 379
Handshaking mode (M6821), 207
Hardware interrupt, 7
Hash coding, 86
Hat-trick register, 167
Heat sink, 276
Hexadecimal notation, 4
High-pass filter, 277
High signal, 103
High speed CMOS (HCMOS), 105
Hold time, 110
Honor an interrupt, 219
Horizontal microprograms, 115
Horizontal retrace, 443
Horizontal sync, 443
Huffmann code, 57
Hysteresis, 270
Hysteresis-synchronous motor, 259

G

Gadfly loop, 214
Gadfly synchronization, 214
Gate, 106
General propagating communication link (GPC), 387
Generator, gated square wave, 358
Generator, pulse, 339, 360
Global data, 17
Global variables, 71
Govern (communication system), 380
Ground, 106
Ground loop, 274
Ground plane, 274

I

Idle state, 204
IEEE-488 bus standard, 410
If-then-else, 66
Immediate addressing, 17
Implementation of a computer, 3
Implied addressing, 16
Implied seek, 432
Incompletely specified decoding, 134
Independent mode, display, 448
Indeterminate signal, 104
Indexable deque, 60
Indexable stack, 60
Index addressing, 18
Index hole, 430
Index pulse, 430
Index register, 18
Indirect I/O, 174
Induction motor, 259
Information frame (SDLC), 409
Information structure, 49
Initialize a word, 51, 73
Initialized I/O register, 167
Initiator (SCSI), 412

H

Half-carry bit H, 22
Half-duplex channel, 378
Halt DMA, 235
Halt the microprocessor, 235
Handler, interrupt, 7, 219
Handling interrupts, 7

Single- and Multiple-Chip Microcomputer Interfacing

Input capture module, 323, 350
Input buffer, 158
Input/Output (I/O), 4
Input/Output instructions, 148
Input/Output interrupt, 7
Input port, 104
Input state, 163
Input instruction, 148
Instruction, 4
Int, 63
Integral-cycle control, 266
Integrated circuit, 11
Integrating debouncer, 286
Interleave factor, disk, 430
Internal state, 163
Interpreter, 161
Interrupt, 7, 218
Interrupt handler, 7, 224
Interrupt inhibit bits I and X, 21, 219
Interrupt mask, 22
Interrupt-request flip-flop, 219
Interval arithmetic, 138
Inverting amplifiers, 267
IRQA1 recognizes an interrupt, 206
IRQA1 requests an interrupt, 219
IRQ interrupt handler, 224, 231
Isolated buffer, 242
Isolated I/O, 148

J

Johnson counter, 334
Jump instruction, 6
Jump to subroutine instruction, 6

K

Kansas City Standard, 421

L

Large-scale integrated circuit (LSI), 105
Latch, 110

Latency time, 9
Level-sensitive interrupt, 230
Levels of a protocol, 377
Light emitting, diode (LED), 261
Light fiber, 387
Light pattern, 159
Line feed, 52
Linear mode, op-amp, 267
Linear-select keyboard, 288
Linear-variable-displacement transformer, 261
Link control, communications, 378
Linked list data structure, 54, 164
Link variable (wire), 104
Liquid crystal display (LCD), 261
List data structure, 54
Load cell, 264
Load instruction, 5
Local data, 17
Local variables, 71
Location counter, 50
Lock for I/O, 149
Logarithmic amplifier, 283
Logical sector, 430
Logic analyzer, 123
Logic diagram, 105
Logic instructions, 26
Logic-timer control, 159
Loop control, 31
Loop initialization, 31
Low-pass filter, 277
Low-power schottky TTL (LSTTL), 105
Low signal, 104

M

Machine coded instruction, 4
Machine state, 7
Macro, 9
Manchester code, 379, 427
Master slave communication system, 187, 380
Master-slave flip-flop, 109
Mealy sequential machine, 162

Single- and Multiple-Chip Microcomputer Interfacing